Inside Terrorism

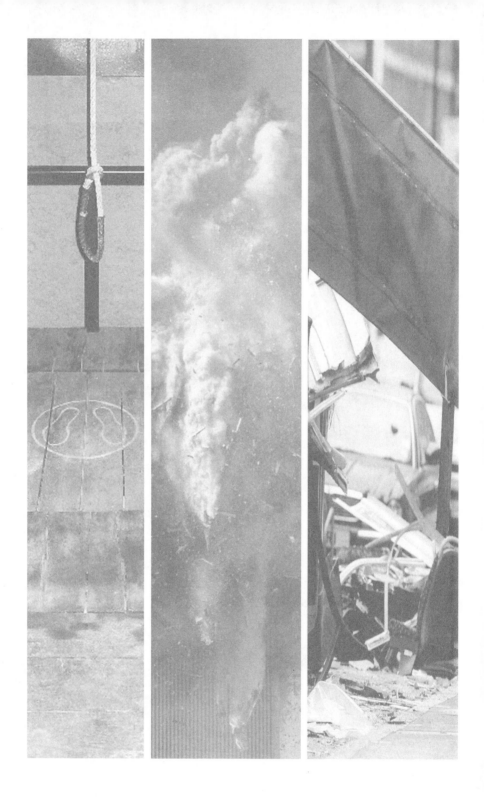

Inside Terrorism

REVISED AND EXPANDED EDITION

Bruce Hoffman

 Columbia University Press   New York

Columbia University Press
Publishers Since 1893
New York, Chichester, West Sussex
Copyright © 2006 Bruce Hoffman
All rights Reserved

Library of Congress Cataloging-in-Publication Data

Hoffman, Bruce, 1954–
　Inside terrorism / Bruce Hoffman—Rev. and expanded ed.
　p. cm.
　Includes bibliographical references and index.
　ISBN 978-0–231–12698–4 (cloth : alk. paper)
　ISBN 978–0–231–12699–1 (pbk. : alk. paper)
　ISBN 978-0–231–51046–2 (electronic)
　1. Terrorism. I. Title.
　HV6431.H626 2006
　363.325—dc22　　　　　　　　　　　2005033841

∞

Columbia University Press books are printed on permanent
and durable acid-free paper

Printed in the United States of America
Designed by Audrey Smith

c 10 9 8 7 6 5
p 20 19 18 17 16 15 14 13 12 11

For my parents

Contents

photographs appear as a group after page   80

Preface to the Revised and Expanded Edition

This sequel to *Inside Terrorism* was written between March and July 2005. My original intention was simply to update and refresh a work that had retained both its relevance and its acuity despite having first been published in 1998. Once I became engrossed in these revisions, however, it soon became clear to me that a more extensive treatment of the trends and developments in terrorism that had unfolded since September 11, 2001, was needed. Before I knew it, my initially modest intentions had produced some seventy thousand new words—an amount nearly equal to the first edition's total word length.

That I was able to write so quickly and effortlessly is perhaps a reflection of the solid analytical foundation that the first edition of *Inside Terrorism* provided. Readers will recall its central theme that the nature and character of terrorism was changing because new adversaries with very different rationales and motivations had emerged to challenge the conventional wisdom on terrorists and terrorism. We were therefore at the dawn of a new era of terrorist violence, the first edition had concluded, even bloodier and more destructive than before. The attacks on 9/11 clearly validated that conclusion. Indeed, on that day long-standing suppositions that terrorists were more interested in publicity than in killing and that terrorists who justified violence with theological imperatives were no more bloody-minded than their secular counterparts were swept aside in a deafening crescendo of death and destruction. Since then, the connection between terrorism motivated by religion and higher levels of lethality has been demonstrated repeatedly by the succession of suicide terrorist attacks that have occurred in places as diverse as Israel and Indonesia and Moscow and Mombasa. A new chapter of this expanded work accordingly analyzes this phenomenon in detail, assessing the reasons for suicide terrorism's increased popularity as a terrorist strategy and tactic and exploring the means and policies required to counter it.

The other completely new chapter in the book focuses on terrorist use of the Internet and other contemporary, cutting-edge communications technologies. It describes how terrorists are now able to bypass traditional print and broadcast media via the Internet, through inexpensive but professionally produced and edited videotapes, and even with their own dedicated 24/7 television and radio news stations. The consequences of these developments, the chapter argues, are as far-reaching as they are still poorly understood, having already transformed the ability of terrorists to communicate without censorship or other hindrance and thereby attract new sources of recruits, funding, and support that governments have found difficult, if not impossible, to counter.

New material, in fact, can be found in every chapter of the book, ranging from a discussion of the lethally indiscriminate bombing campaign mounted by Irish terrorists on the London Underground more than a century ago to the likely repercussions of the ongoing Iraqi insurgency on future terrorist targeting and tactics. Particular attention in the new edition has been paid to such critical issues as the differences and similarities between terrorists and insurgents; the growing threat of terrorist use of chemical, biological, radiological, and nuclear weapons; and the likely future trajectory of al Qaeda—including a detailed assessment of the reasons for its continued resilience, resonance, and longevity.

It is no coincidence that I should have begun thinking about and then writing a new edition of *Inside Terrorism*, for I have recently returned (albeit part-time) to teaching both undergraduates and graduate students. I should therefore like to thank all the students whom I have had the privilege to teach over the past three years at three unique and world-class institutions devoted either to the study of terrorism specifically or to defense and security studies in general.

The Combating Terrorism Center at the U.S. Military Academy in West Point, New York, helps ensure that new generations of U.S. Army officers are well schooled in the theory and practice of terrorism and counterterrorism and insurgency and counterinsurgency. I am continually humbled and honored by the opportunity to teach and also learn from these outstanding young men and women who often within months of our class literally are in the front lines of the war on terrorism, commanding troops fighting in Iraq and Afghanistan, among other places.

No less important to the intellectual vitality that I hope informs this book are the graduate students I have had the pleasure of teaching in the

Security Studies Program (SSP) at Georgetown University in Washington, D.C. The diversity of their views, backgrounds, and professional experiences has appreciably enriched my understanding of, and knowledge about, terrorism. The research assistance provided by one of those students, Mr. Weimeng Yeo, was immensely helpful to me in completing this work. No less critical were the translations of original Japanese-language sources concerning Aum Shinrikyo and the 1995 nerve gas attack on the Tokyo subway provided by another SSP student, Ms. Mayuka Yamazaki.

Finally, I am indebted to Ambassador Barry Desker, director of the Institute of Defence and Strategic Studies at Nanyang Technological University in Singapore, and to Professor Rohan Gunaratna, of that institute's International Centre for Political Violence and Terrorism Research, for providing me with an extraordinarily convivial setting in which both to finish this book and to teach part of a novel course on counterterrorism and counterinsurgency. The students in that class, hailing from at least a dozen different countries, opened my eyes to a range of issues and concerns specific to Asian security and stability.

Perhaps my greatest debt, however, is to James A. Thomson and Michael D. Rich, respectively president and CEO and executive vice president of the RAND Corporation. Just a week before the August 1998 bombings of the U.S. embassies in Kenya and Tanzania, they offered me the opportunity to return to RAND. The timing could not have been better or more prescient. RAND, an independent, objective, nonpartisan research institution, and especially its Washington, D.C. office, have provided an ideal base from which both to study terrorism and to observe the formulation and implementation of counterterrorism policy. Both Jim and Michael were enthusiastic supporters of both the first edition of *Inside Terrorism* and the revisions and expansion undertaken in this work.

Two other RAND colleagues, Ambassador David Aaron and Brent Bradley, not only supported this effort but arranged for the corporate funds that enabled me to take some time away from my other research and managerial responsibilities to complete this work. I would be remiss not to cite the help, advice, and guidance variously provided by other valued colleagues and friends at RAND, including Peter Chalk, Kim Cragin, Sara Daly, David Egner, Anna-Britt Kasupski, John Parachini, Hilary Peck, Jim Quinlivan, Bill Rosenau, Shirley Ruhe, Karen Treverton, and Mike Wermuth. Suzanne Jones provided critical support as my executive administrative assistant and helped me to carve out the time to concentrate on this effort. That I could do so while still fulfilling my managerial responsibilities as director of the RAND Washington, D.C., office, was made possible by the other members of the office management team—Casey Kane, Kathy Mills, Kathi Webb, David Johnson, and Tammy Pritt—to whom I am also grateful.

Friends and colleagues outside RAND were no less instrumental in the help that they provided to facilitate the completion of this new edition. Foremost among them are current or former police officers like David Brannan, Lindsay Clutterbuck, Roger Kelly, Bob Mathiessen, Keith Weston, and Mark Tuley. Their insights, and especially their friendship, have made more of a difference to me than they know. Equally critical have been some of my closest friends and most valued colleagues in academe, government, and private security, including Peter Bergen, Daniel Byman, Martha Crenshaw, Joe Felter, Eric Herren, Russ Howard, Cindi Jebb, Rob Litwak, Michael Meese, Kip McCormick, Ami Pedahzur, Dennis Pluchinsky, Magnus Ranstorp, Fernando Reinares, Reid Sawyer, Michael Scheuer, Michael Smith, Anders Strindberg, and David Veness. Rohan Gunaratna, Carol Ann Bernheim, Ruti Lande, Arie Perliger, and Dan Schueftan played particularly instrumental roles in facilitating my research on suicide terrorism over the years, for which I remain deeply appreciative. Some eight years ago, Walter Laqueur was kind enough to endorse the first edition of *Inside Terrorism*. This in turn has led to a deep and immensely rewarding friendship that similarly informs and has greatly influenced this work.

There are many other friends and colleagues who, because of their jobs and responsibilities, must remain unidentified. My intellectual debt to them is as profound and important as is the need for them to remain anonymous. I must, however, acknowledge an entirely different set of people without whom this work genuinely would not have been possible. Sincere thanks are thus due to Andrew Umhau, Stuart Danovitch, Samuel Potolicchio, Dan Hanfling, and Peter Shields.

The editors and publisher of the *Atlantic Monthly*—Benjamin Schwarz, the late Michael Kelly, Cullen Murphy, Toby Lester, Corby Kummer, and David Bradley, respectively—have consistently encouraged and helped shape my research and writing on terrorism and related security issues since 9/11. Three of that magazine's superb fact-checkers—Sue Parilla, Elizabeth Shelburne, and Hilary McClellen—indirectly contributed to this book through their previous meticulous work on some material contained herein that was first published in the *Atlantic Monthly*. I am grateful to the *Atlantic Monthly* too for permission to include that material in this work and for the many opportunities I have been given to write for the magazine.

I also have benefited from a long professional association with Taylor and Francis Publishers in my role as editor in chief of the premier scholarly journal in the field, *Studies in Conflict and Terrorism*. I should like to thank Jill

Millard and Lily Palladino and also Taylor and Francis, not least, of course, for permission to adapt some material for this book from articles I had previously written that first appeared in *Studies in Conflict and Terrorism*.

From the start, Anne Routon, my editor at Columbia University Press, was an enthusiastic proponent of the idea of a new edition of *Inside Terrorism*. Her tireless, and indeed Herculean, support is gratefully acknowledged. A similar debt of gratitude is owed to Peter Sillem, my editor at Fischer Verlag, one of Germany's oldest and most distinguished publishing houses. Peter has long been the driving force behind the success and popularity of *Inside Terrorism*'s German-language edition, *Terrorismus: Der unerklärte Krieg*, for which I am extremely grateful. As always, my old friend and longtime editor, Sean Magee, who commissioned the first edition of *Inside Terrorism* nearly a decade ago, has been there to provide support, wise advice, and encouragement. I was very fortunate to have Jan McInroy copyedit the manuscript. Her sharp eye and stylistic adjustments appreciably improved this edition. Thanks, too, are due Paula C. Durbin-Westby for her splendid and exact index and Leslie Bialler for his patience and attention to detail in overseeing the manuscript through publication. And, lastly, thanks to my brother, Lance Hoffman, for his help with some of the photographs used in this edition of Inside Terrorism.

Although I have been studying terrorists and terrorism for nearly thirty years, until September 11 I personally had never known anyone who had been killed by terrorists. Since that time, the number of friends or professional acquaintances who have perished as result of terrorist acts has tragically multiplied. Although each died either serving his or her nation or helping his or her community, some were deliberately marked for assassination and then stalked and murdered. This edition of *Inside Terrorism* was written with their memory, sacrifice, and inspiration firmly in my thoughts.

It remains for me to express my profound gratitude and love to my wife and children for their patience, understanding, and unmitigated support and enthusiasm for all that I do. Without them, life wouldn't be worth living. My parents in particular deserve special mention. For as long as I can remember, they have inculcated in me a love of books and learning that is manifestly reflected in this work. It is to them, with love and appreciation, that this revised and expanded edition of *Inside Terrorism* is dedicated.

Bruce Hoffman
Washington, D.C.
February 2006

Preface to the First Edition

I have been studying terrorists and terrorism for more than twenty years. Yet I am still always struck by how disturbingly "normal" most terrorists seem when one actually sits down and talks to them. Rather than the wild-eyed fanatics or crazed killers that we have been conditioned to expect, many are in fact highly articulate and extremely thoughtful individuals for whom terrorism is (or was) an entirely rational choice, often reluctantly embraced and then only after considerable reflection and debate. It is precisely this paradox, whereby otherwise apparently "normal" people have nonetheless deliberately chosen a path of bloodshed and destruction, that has long intrigued me and indeed prompted me to write this book.

My aim, however, is not to offer some new theoretical treatise or conceptual reinterpretation of the subject. Instead, I have focused on what I believe to be the most salient and important trends in terrorism—both past and present—as a means to explain why terrorists "do what they do" as well as to shed light on likely future patterns and potentialities. This somewhat selective—and thus perhaps idiosyncratic—approach deliberately emphasizes key historical themes over abstract theory and relies on empirical evidence rather than explanatory models to illustrate and support its main arguments. As such, this book is also intended to address a conspicuous gap in the literature by providing a work that is as accessible to students as it is relevant to scholars and that may therefore appeal equally to general as well as more specialized audiences.

The extensive bibliography of published and unpublished sources I consulted in the course of this project is alone evidence of my indebtedness to the many other people who have thought and written about terrorism. Their efforts have long shaped and influenced my own thinking, and I would be remiss not to acknowledge the seminal contributions to this field of study made by Martha Crenshaw, Brian Jenkins, Walter Laqueur, David Rapoport, Grant Wardlaw, and Paul Wilkinson. I have also benefited greatly from the work of—and not infrequently the helpful advice and trenchant criticism offered by—Konrad Kellen, Ariel Merari, and Dennis Pluchinsky. I am of course solely responsible for any errors, solecisms or deficiencies that follow.

Over the years various people in various places who would prefer not to be identified have enhanced immeasurably my understanding of both terrorists and terrorism by granting me access to facilities not usually open to the public, introducing me to or arranging meetings with important personages or themselves by agreeing to discuss with me any number of sensitive matters. Even while I have respected their wish for anonymity, their impact is reflected—however obliquely—throughout this work, and I remain eternally grateful for their assistance.

This book was researched and written during a period of time when I was afforded no respite from my teaching or administrative and fund-raising responsibilities at the University of St. Andrews. That I was able to find the time and mental space to complete the work is in no small way due to the assistance, support, and friendship offered by my colleagues there. I should especially like to thank John Anderson, Rick Fawn, Ali Watson, and particularly Gina Wilson in the Department of International Relations; David Claridge, Donna Hoffman, Suzanne Neilson, Magnus Ranstorp, and Paul Wilkinson at the Centre for the Study of Terrorism and Political Violence; and Colin Vincent and John Beath. The many students I have had the privilege to teach or supervise since coming to St. Andrews nearly four years ago have also contributed in often less perceptible ways to this book. In particular, I would also like to thank Gavin Cameron, Rohan Gunaratna, Melissa McPherson, and the successive classes of IR 3008—more colloquially known as Honours International Terrorism.

I am grateful to the Center for Nonproliferation Studies, Frank Cass and Co., Jane's Information Group Ltd., and Taylor and Francis, the publishers, respectively, of the *Nonproliferation Review, Terrorism and Political Violence, Jane's Intelligence Review,* and *Studies in Conflict and Terrorism,* for permission to use some material from articles I had previously written for those journals.

This undertaking could not have been realized without my family's unstinting love and encouragement. My gratitude to my parents and brother and most especially to my wife and children is as incalculable as it is immutable. No less critical have been the support and friendship provided by Karen Gardela, Ben and Tina Schwarz, Anders Stephanson, and Jennifer Taw.

It remains for me to thank the people at Gollancz, who made publication of this book possible. Kate Hordern said the right things at a critical time that, unbeknownst to her, propelled the book to completion. Hugo Cox and Viv Redman were unfailingly helpful, and Gillian Bromley's superlative editorial skills rescued yet another author from solecistic ignominy. My greatest debt, though, is to Sean Magee, who commissioned and helped develop this project—and never lost faith.

Bruce Hoffman
St. Andrews
January 1998

Inside Terrorism

Chapter 1

Defining Terrorism

What is terrorism? Few words have so insidiously worked their way into our everyday vocabulary. Like "Internet"—another grossly overused term that has similarly become an indispensable part of the argot of the early twenty-first century—most people have a vague idea or impression of what terrorism is but lack a more precise, concrete, and truly explanatory definition of the word. This imprecision has been abetted partly by the modern media, whose efforts to communicate an often complex and convoluted message in the briefest amount of airtime or print space possible have led to the promiscuous labeling of a range of violent acts as "terrorism." Pick up a newspaper or turn on the television and—even within the same broadcast or on the same page—one can find such disparate acts as the bombing of a building, the assassination of a head of state, the massacre of civilians by a military unit, the poisoning of produce on supermarket shelves, or the deliberate contamination of over-the-counter medication in a drugstore, all described as incidents of terrorism. Indeed, virtually any especially abhorrent act of violence perceived as directed against society—whether it involves the activities of antigovernment dissidents or governments themselves, organized-crime syndicates, common criminals, rioting mobs, people engaged in militant protest, individual psychotics, or lone extortionists—is often labeled "terrorism."

Dictionary definitions are of little help. The preeminent authority on the English language, the much-venerated *Oxford English Dictionary*, is disappointingly unobliging when it comes to providing edification on this subject, its interpretation at once too literal and too historical to be of much contemporary use:

> Terrorism: A system of terror. 1. Government by intimidation as directed and carried out by the party in power in France during the revolution of 1789–94; the system of "Terror." 2. *gen.* A policy intended to strike with terror those against whom it is adopted; the employment of methods of intimidation; the fact of terrorizing or condition of being terrorized.[1]

These definitions are wholly unsatisfying. Rather than learning what terrorism is, one instead finds, in the first instance, a somewhat pedestrian historical—and, in respect of the modern accepted usage of the term, a uselessly anachronistic—description. The second definition offered is only slightly more helpful. While accurately communicating the fear-inducing quality of terrorism, the definition is still so broad as to apply to almost any action that scares ("terrorizes") us. Though an integral part of "terrorism," this definition is still insufficient for the purpose of accurately defining the phenomenon that is today called "terrorism."

A slightly more satisfying elucidation may be found in the *OED*'s definition of the perpetrator of the act than in its efforts to come to grips with the act itself. In this respect, a "terrorist" is defined thus:

> 1. As a political term: a. Applied to the Jacobins and their agents and partisans in the French Revolution, esp. to those connected with the Revolutionary tribunals during the "Reign of Terror." b. Any one who attempts to further his views by a system of coercive intimidation; *spec*, applied to members of one of the extreme revolutionary societies in Russia.[2]

This is appreciably more helpful. First, it immediately introduces the reader to the notion of terrorism as a *political* concept. As will be seen, this key characteristic of terrorism is absolutely paramount to understanding its aims, motivations, and purposes and is critical in distinguishing it from other types of violence.

Terrorism, in the most widely accepted contemporary usage of the term, is fundamentally and inherently political. It is also ineluctably about power: the pursuit of power, the acquisition of power, and the use of power to achieve political change. Terrorism is thus violence—or, equally important, the threat of violence—used and directed in pursuit of, or in service of, a political aim. With this vital point clearly illuminated, one can appreciate the significance of the additional definition of "terrorist" provided by the *OED*: "Any one who attempts to further his views by a system of coercive intimidation." This definition underscores clearly the other fundamental characteristic of terrorism: that it is a planned, calculated, and indeed systematic act.

Given this relatively straightforward elucidation, why, then, is terrorism so difficult to define? The most compelling reason perhaps is because the meaning of the term has changed so frequently over the past two hundred years.[3]

The Changing Meaning of Terrorism

The word "terrorism" was first popularized during the French Revolution. In contrast to its contemporary usage, at that time terrorism had a decidedly *positive* connotation. The system or *régime de la terreur* of 1793–94—from which the English word came—was adopted as a means to establish order during the transient anarchical period of turmoil and upheaval that followed the uprisings of 1789, and indeed many other revolutions. Hence, unlike terrorism as it is commonly understood today, to mean a *revolutionary* or antigovernment activity undertaken by nonstate or subnational entities, the *régime de la terreur* was an instrument of governance wielded by the recently established revolutionary *state*. It was designed to consolidate the new government's power by intimidating counterrevolutionaries, subversives, and all other dissidents whom the new regime regarded as "enemies of the people." The Committee of General Security and the Revolutionary Tribunal ("People's Court" in the modern vernacular) were thus accorded wide powers of arrest and judgment, publicly putting to death by guillotine those convicted of treasonous (i.e., reactionary) crimes. In this manner, a powerful lesson was conveyed to any and all who might oppose the revolution or grow nostalgic for the ancien régime.

Ironically, perhaps, terrorism in its original context was also closely associated with the ideals of virtue and democracy. The revolutionary leader Maximilien Robespierre firmly believed that virtue was the mainspring of a popular government at peace, but that during the time of revolution virtue must be allied with terror in order for democracy to triumph. He appealed famously to "virtue, without which terror is evil; terror, without which virtue is helpless" and proclaimed: "Terror is nothing but justice, prompt, severe and inflexible; it is therefore an emanation of virtue."[4]

Despite this divergence from its subsequent meaning, the French Revolution's "terrorism" still shared at least two key characteristics with its modern-day variant. First, the *régime de la terreur* was neither random nor indiscriminate, as terrorism is often portrayed today, but was organized, deliberate, and systematic. Second, its goal and its very justification—like that of contemporary terrorism—was the creation of a "new and better society" in place of a fundamentally corrupt and undemocratic political system. Indeed, Robespierre's vague and Utopian exegeses of the revolution's central goals are remarkably similar in tone and content to the equally turgid, millenarian manifestos issued by many contemporary revolutionary—primarily left-wing, Marxist-oriented—terrorist organizations. For example, in 1794 Robespierre declared, in language eerily presaging the communiqués issued by groups such as Germany's Red Army Faction and Italy's Red Brigades nearly two centuries later:

> We want an order of things . . . in which the arts are an adornment to the liberty that ennobles them, and commerce the source of wealth for the public and not of monstrous opulence for a few families. . . . In our country we desire morality instead of selfishness, honesty and not mere "honor," principle and not mere custom, duty and not mere propriety, the sway of reason rather than the tyranny of fashion, a scorn for vice and not a contempt for the unfortunate.[5]

Like many other revolutions, the French Revolution eventually began to consume itself. On 8 Thermidor, year two of the new calendar adopted by the revolutionaries (July 26, 1794), Robespierre announced to the National Convention that he had in his possession a new list of traitors. Fearing that their own names might be on that list, extremists joined forces with moderates to repudiate both Robespierre and his *régime de la terreur*. Robespierre and his closest followers themselves met the same fate that had befallen some forty thousand others: execution by guillotine. The Terror was at an end; thereafter "terrorism" became a term associated with the abuse of office and power—with overt "criminal" implications.[6] Within a year of Robespierre's demise, the word had been popularized in English by Edmund Burke, who, in his famous polemic against the French Revolution, described the "Thousands of those Hell hounds called Terrorists . . . let loose on the people."[7]

One of the French Revolution's more enduring repercussions was the impetus it gave to antimonarchical sentiment elsewhere in Europe. Popular subservience to rulers who derived their authority from God through "divine right of rule," rather than from their subjects, was increasingly

questioned by a politically awakened Continent. The advent of nationalism, and with it notions of statehood and citizenship based on the common
identity of a people rather than the lineage of a royal family, were resulting
in the unification and creation of new nation-states such as Germany and
Italy. Meanwhile, the massive socioeconomic changes engendered by the
Industrial Revolution were creating new "universalist" ideologies (such as
communism/Marxism), born of the alienation and exploitative conditions
of nineteenth-century capitalism. From this milieu a new era of terrorism
emerged, in which the concept had gained many of the familiar revolutionary, antistate connotations of today. Its chief progenitor was arguably the
Italian republican extremist Carlo Pisacane, who had forsaken his birthright
as duke of San Giovanni only to perish in 1857 during an ill-fated revolt
against Bourbon rule. A passionate advocate of federalism and mutualism,
Pisacane is remembered less on this account than for the theory of "propaganda by deed,"[8] which he is credited with defining—an idea that has
exerted a compelling influence on rebels and terrorists alike ever since. "The
propaganda of the idea is a chimera," Pisacane wrote. "Ideas result from
deeds, not the latter from the former, and the people will not be free when
they are educated, but educated when they are free."[9] Violence, he argued,
was necessary not only to draw attention to, or generate publicity for, a
cause, but also to inform, educate, and ultimately rally the masses behind
the revolution. The didactic purpose of violence, Pisacane argued, could
never be effectively replaced by pamphlets, wall posters, or assemblies.

Perhaps the first organization to put into practice Pisacane's dictum
was the Narodnaya Volya, or People's Will (sometimes translated as "People's Freedom"), a small group of Russian constitutionalists that had been
founded in 1878 to challenge czarist rule. For the Narodnaya Volya, the apathy and alienation of the Russian masses afforded few alternatives besides
resorting to daring and dramatic acts of violence designed to attract attention to the group and its cause. However, unlike the many late-twentieth-
century terrorist organizations that have cited the principle of "propaganda
by deed" to justify the wanton targeting of civilians in order to assure them
publicity through the shock and horror produced by wholesale bloodshed,
the Narodnaya Volya displayed an almost quixotic attitude toward the violence it wrought. To this group, "propaganda by deed" meant the selective
targeting of specific individuals whom the group considered the embodiment of the autocratic, oppressive state.[10] Hence the victims—the czar,
leading members of the royal family, senior government officials—were
deliberately chosen for their "symbolic" value as the dynastic heads and
subservient agents of a corrupt and tyrannical regime. An intrinsic element

in the group's collective beliefs was that "not one drop of superfluous blood" should be shed in pursuit of aims, however noble or utilitarian they might be.[11] Even having selected their targets with great care and the utmost deliberation, group members still harbored profound regrets about taking the life of a fellow human being. Their unswerving adherence to this principle is perhaps best illustrated by the failed attempt on the life of Grand Duke Serge Alexandrovich made by a successor organization to the Narodnaya Volya in 1905. As the royal carriage came into view, the terrorist tasked with the assassination saw that the duke was unexpectedly accompanied by his children and therefore aborted his mission rather than risk harming the intended victim's family (the duke was killed in a subsequent attack). By comparison, the midair explosion caused by a terrorist bomb on Pan Am Flight 103 over Lockerbie, Scotland, in December 1988 indiscriminately claimed the lives of all 259 people on board—innocent men, women, and children alike—plus eleven inhabitants of the village where the plane crashed.

Ironically, the Narodnaya Volya's most dramatic accomplishment also led directly to its demise. On March 1, 1881, the group assassinated Czar Alexander II.[12] The failure of eight previous plots had led the conspirators to take extraordinary measures to ensure the success of this attempt. Four volunteers were given four bombs each and deployed along the alternative routes followed by the czar's cortege. As two of the bomber-assassins stood in wait on the same street, the sleighs carrying the czar and his Cossack escort approached the first terrorist, who hurled his bomb at the passing sleigh, missing it by inches. The whole entourage came to a halt as soldiers seized the hapless culprit and the czar descended from his sleigh to check on a bystander wounded by the explosion. "Thank God, I am safe," the czar reportedly declared—just as the second bomber emerged from the crowd and detonated his weapon, killing both himself and his target. The full weight of the czarist state now fell on the heads of the Narodnaya Volya. Acting on information provided by the arrested member, the secret police swept down on the group's safe houses and hideouts, rounding up most of the plotters, who were quickly tried, convicted, and hanged. Further information from this group led to subsequent arrests, so that within a year of the assassination only one member of the original executive committee was still at large. She too was finally apprehended in 1883, at which point the first generation of Narodnaya Volya terrorists ceased to exist, although various successor organizations subsequently emerged to carry on the struggle.[13]

At the time, the repercussions of the czar's assassination could not have been known or appreciated by either the condemned or their comrades languishing in prison or exiled to Siberia. But in addition to precipitating the beginning of the end of czarist rule, the group also deeply influenced individual revolutionaries and subversive organizations elsewhere. To the nascent anarchist movement, the "propaganda by deed" strategy championed by the Narodnaya Volya provided a model to be emulated.[14] Within four months of the czar's murder, a group of radicals in London convened an "anarchist conference," which publicly applauded the assassination and extolled tyrannicide as a means to achieve revolutionary change. In hopes of encouraging and coordinating worldwide anarchist activities, the conferees decided to establish the "Anarchist International" (or "Black International"). Although this idea, like most of their ambitious plans, came to naught, the publicity generated by even a putative "Anarchist International" was sufficient to create a myth of global revolutionary pretensions and thereby stimulate fears and suspicions disproportionate to its actual impact or political achievements. Disparate and uncoordinated though the anarchists' violence was, the movement's emphasis on individual action or operations carried out by small cells of like-minded radicals made detection and prevention by the police particularly difficult, thus further heightening public fears. For example, following the assassination of U.S. president William McKinley in 1901 (by a young Hungarian refugee, Leon Czolgosz, who, while not a regular member of any anarchist organization, was nonetheless influenced by the philosophy), Congress swiftly enacted legislation barring known anarchists or anyone "who disbelieves in or is opposed to all organized government" from entering the United States. However, while anarchists were responsible for an impressive string of assassinations of heads of state and a number of particularly notorious bombings from about 1878 until the second decade of the twentieth century,[15] in the final analysis, other than stimulating often exaggerated fears, anarchism made little tangible impact on either the domestic or the international politics of the countries affected. It does, however, offer an interesting historical footnote: much as the "information revolution" of the late-twentieth and early-twenty-first centuries is alleged to have made the means and methods of bomb-making and other types of terrorist activity more readily available via the Internet, on CD-ROM, and through ordinary libraries and bookstores, one of anarchism's flourishing "cottage industries" more than a century earlier was the widespread distribution of similar "how-to"- or "do-it-yourself"-type manuals and publications of violence and mayhem.[16]

Meanwhile, another series of developments was unfolding on the other side of Europe that would exert a similarly profound influence on future terrorist strategy and tactics. In this instance, the motivation was neither anti-monarchical nor anarchist, but nationalist and separatist. Although Britain's rule of Ireland already had a centuries-long history of restiveness and rebellion, in the mid-nineteenth century the locus of revolutionary activities had expanded from Ireland to include the United States as well. Among the mass of Irish emigrants who had fled the failure of successive potato crops and the resultant famine was a group of radical nationalists who in 1858 founded a secret society called the Fenian Brotherhood. The Fenians—and their Ireland-based offshoot, the Irish Revolutionary Brotherhood (IRB)—were at once as daring and determined as they were impatient and incompetent. Their motto of "revolution sooner or never"[17] accurately describes a string of half-baked plots that purported to kidnap the Prince of Wales,[18] invade Canada, and orchestrate a popular uprising in Ireland. So successful were British efforts to penetrate the organization, and so abject were the Fenians' failed grand schemes, that the movement fell into desuetude within a decade of its founding.[19] But the Fenians' unswerving commitment to both Irish republicanism and the use of violence to attain it[20] created a legacy that subsequently inspired a new generation of U.S.-based Irish revolutionaries.

Thus by 1873 a new organization, calling itself the Clan na Gael (United Irishmen), had taken up the Fenians' mantle. Its driving force was a firebrand named Jeremiah O'Donovan Rossa. Sentenced to life imprisonment for sedition in 1865, O'Donovan Rossa was released only six years later after a commission of inquiry substantiated his claims of mistreatment. The abuse inflicted on imprisoned terrorists like O'Donovan Rossa in the nineteenth century actually bears a disquieting resemblance to the treatment reportedly meted out to some detainees in the war on terrorism today.[21] Not only was O'Donovan Rossa held for more than a month with his hands handcuffed behind his back, but he was also "kept naked day and night" in a darkened cell and fed a meager ration of bread and water.[22] Exiled to the United States, O'Donovan Rossa quickly resumed his subversive activities. He was assisted in these endeavors by Patrick Ford, the editor of the *Irish World*, a newspaper that became the main platform for Clan na Gael propaganda and incitement. Together, they developed a new strategy for the republican movement. "We are not now advising a general insurrection," Ford explained in a December 4, 1875, column.

> On the contrary, we should oppose a general insurrection in Ireland as untimely and ill advised. But we believe in action nonetheless. The Irish cause requires Skirmishers. It requires a little band of heroes who will initiate and keep up without intermission a guerrilla warfare.

In words that accurately presaged the advent of a form of transnational terrorism that has become a permanent fixture of our time, Ford also described how these "Skirmishers" would "fly over land and sea like invisible beings—now striking the enemy in Ireland, now in India, now in England itself as occasion may present."[23]

O'Donovan Rossa and Ford displayed an uncommon understanding of the terrorist dynamic that went beyond even this early recognition of the media's power to communicate and amplify a violent message. Remarkably, both men grasped that just as money lubricates commerce, a solid financial base is required to sustain an effective terrorism campaign. It was thus not long before advertisements began to appear in the *Irish World* soliciting contributions on behalf of a "skirmisher fund."[24] By March 1877 $23,350 had been collected—a sum equivalent to nearly half a million dollars in 2005.[25] O'Donovan Rossa appears to have also fully appreciated terrorism's asymmetric virtues with regard to the disproportionate economic losses and damage that could be inflicted on the enemy state and the flood of contributions that a series of successful attacks might engender. "England," he explained in the *Irish World*, "will not know how or where she is to be struck. A successful strike that will do her half a million dollars' worth of damage will bring us enough funds to carry on the work."[26]

Four years later, the Skirmishers commenced operations. On January 14, 1881, they bombed the Salford Infantry Barracks in Manchester. Their choice of target reflected yet another now-familiar pattern of contemporary terrorism: attacks on buildings or other inanimate objects designed to commemorate, and thereby draw attention to, some event of historic significance to the perpetrators. In this instance, the Salford Barracks was where three Fenians—the so-called Manchester Martyrs—had been hanged in 1867. Up until this point, the Irish terrorists seem to have differed only slightly from their Russian counterparts. Both attacked targets symbolizing their enemy (inanimate objects in the case of the Skirmishers and representatives of the czar by the Narodnaya Volya). Both also believed fervently in terrorism's didactic potential—whether directed toward the landless Irish or the Russian peasant.[27] But two years later, the Irish campaign diverged significantly from the highly discriminate terrorism practiced by the Narodnaya Volya to something both more sinister and consequential. The principal weapons in the Russians' campaign, as we have seen, were the handgun and the nineteenth-century equivalent of the hand grenade; employed in acts of individual assassination deliberately calculated to avoid death or injury to all but their intended target. By comparison, the Skirmishers had already spilled innocent blood: a seven-year-old boy had been killed and three other people injured in the Salford Barracks blast.[28] Still more innocent blood, however, was soon to be shed.

In 1883 the Clan na Gael and a rebranded IRB, now known as the Irish Republican Brotherhood, formed a tactical alliance and together embarked on a bombing campaign directed against the London Underground and mainline railway stations in both the United Kingdom's capital and other cities.[29] Although the bombers' intention was not to wantonly or deliberately kill or harm innocent persons, but instead to throttle Britain's economy and dramatically call attention to themselves and their cause,[30] their choice of both weapon (homemade bombs consisting of gunpowder detonated by primitive time-delay fuses) and target (locations in congested urban areas and public transportation) ensured that the effects of their operations could be neither constrained nor controlled. And, while it is true that these bombings claimed the lives of fewer than a dozen passersby or rail passengers, given that some of the explosive devices contained more than twenty pounds of commercial dynamite, this was more likely the result of luck and happenstance than any effort on the part of the bombers to limit by timing or placement the effect of their attacks.[31]

The "dynamite campaign," as this spasm of Victorian-era urban terrorism came to be known, lasted until 1887.[32] It spread beyond London to Liverpool and Glasgow before collapsing under the weight of intensified police surveillance, heightened border and port control, the effective use of informants, and unprecedented national and even international cooperation and liaison among hitherto entirely parochial law enforcement agencies. Indeed, the advances in police investigative, intelligence, and preemptive operations necessitated by the bombings led that same year to the formal establishment of Scotland Yard's famed Special Branch—the first such police unit dedicated specifically to political crime and counterterrorism.[33] More significant for our purposes, however, is the impact that nineteenth-century Irish political violence had on terrorism's evolution and development. In retrospect, we can see that it was at this time that patterns and modi operandi first appeared that would become standard terrorist operating procedures decades later. The Irish groups, for example, were among the first to recognize the importance of establishing a foreign base beyond the reach of their enemy in order to better sustain and promote a protracted terrorist campaign. They were also ahead of their time in understanding the value of such a sanctuary not only for planning and logistical purposes but also for the effective dissemination of propaganda and the critical solicitation of operational funds. Their use of time-delayed explosive devices so that the perpetrator could easily effect escape, and thereby ensure the terrorist campaign's sustainment, was another important innovation that became a standard feature of twentieth-century terrorism. Finally, terrorist targeting of mass transport—and especially subway systems—along with an almost callous, if not even casual, disregard of innocent life have now become commonplace. The July 2005 suicide attacks on London's transit system, which killed 52 people and wounded 700 others, and the ten near-simultaneous bombings of commuter trains arriving at Madrid's Atocha rail station in March 2004, which killed 191 people and wounded hundreds more, are especially apposite, and tragic, examples. "At the grand strategic level," Lindsay Clutterbuck cogently notes, the Clan na Gael and IRB's

> ideas enabled terrorism to move away from being a phenomenon consisting of a single event, or at best a loosely connected series of events, and to evolve into sustained campaigns underpinned by their own well developed sense of timing and tempo. There was a quantum leap beyond the limited aim of assassinating an individual to achieve their objectives and into operational scenarios where terrorism could persist for years and encompass the deaths of thousands of people.[34]

On the eve of the First World War, terrorism still retained its revolutionary connotations. By this time, growing unrest and irredentist ferment had already welled up within the decaying Ottoman and Hapsburg empires. In the 1880s and 1890s, for example, militant Armenian nationalist movements in eastern Turkey pursued a terrorist strategy against continued Ottoman rule of a kind that would later be adopted by most of the post–Second World War ethno-nationalist/separatist movements. The Armenians' objective was simultaneously to strike a blow against the despotic "alien" regime through repeated attacks on its colonial administration and security forces, in order to rally indigenous support, and to attract international attention, sympathy, and support.[35] Around the same time, the Inner Macedonian Revolutionary Organization (IMRO) was active in the region overlapping present-day Greece, Bulgaria, and Serbia.[36] Although the Macedonians did not go on to suffer the catastrophic fate that befell the Armenians during the First World War (when an estimated one million people perished in what is considered to be the first officially implemented genocide of the twentieth century),[37] IMRO never came close to achieving its aim of an independent Macedonia and thereafter degenerated into a mostly criminal organization of hired thugs and political assassins.

The events immediately preceding the First World War in Bosnia are of course more familiar because of their subsequent cataclysmic impact on world affairs. There, similar groups of disaffected nationalists—Bosnian Serb intellectuals, university students, and even schoolchildren, collectively known as Mlada Bosna, or Young Bosnians—arose against continued Hapsburg suzerainty. While it is perhaps easy to dismiss the movement, as some historians have, as comprising "frustrated, poor, dreary and maladjusted"[38] adolescents—much as many contemporary observers similarly denigrate modern-day terrorists as mindless, obsessive, and maladjusted—it was a member of Young Bosnia, Gavrilo Princip, who is widely credited with having set in motion the chain of events that began on June 28, 1914, when he assassinated the Hapsburg archduke Franz Ferdinand in Sarajevo, and culminated in the First World War. Whatever its superficially juvenile characteristics, the group was nonetheless passionately dedicated to the attainment of a federal South Slav political entity—uniting Slovenes, Croats, and Serbs—and resolutely committed to assassination as the vehicle with which to achieve that aim. In this respect, the Young Bosnians perhaps had more in common with the radical republicanism of Giuseppe Mazzini, one of the most ardent exponents of Italian unification in the nineteenth century, than with groups such as the Narodnaya Volya—despite a shared conviction in the efficacy of tyrannicide. An even more significant difference, however, was the degree of involvement in, and external support provided to, Young Bosnian activities by various shadowy Serbian nationalist groups. Principal among these was the pan-Serbian secret society, the Narodna Obrana (the People's Defense, or National Defense).

The Narodna Obrana had been established in 1908, originally to promote Serbian cultural and national activities. It subsequently assumed a more subversive orientation as the movement became increasingly involved with anti-Austrian activities—including terrorism—mostly in neighboring Bosnia and Herzegovina. Although the Narodna Obrana's exclusionist pan-Serbian aims clashed with the Young Bosnians' less parochial South Slav ideals, its leadership was quite happy to manipulate and exploit the Bosnians' emotive nationalism and youthful zeal for its own purposes. To this end, the Narodna Obrana actively recruited, trained, and armed young Bosnians and Herzegovinians from movements, such as the Young Bosnians, who were then deployed in various seditious activities against the Hapsburgs. As early as four years before the archduke's assassination, a Herzegovinian youth, trained by a Serbian army officer with close ties to the Narodna Obrana, had attempted to kill the governor of Bosnia. But while the Narodna Obrana included among its members senior Serbian government officials, it was not an explicitly government-controlled or directly state-supported entity. Whatever hazy government links it maintained were further and deliberately obscured when a radical faction left the Narodna Obrana in 1911 and established the Ujedinjenje ili Smrt (the Union of Death, or Death or Unification)—more popularly known as the Crna Ruka, the Black Hand. This more militant and appreciably more clandestine splinter group has been described by one historian as combining

> the more unattractive features of the anarchist cells of earlier years— which had been responsible for quite a number of assassinations in Europe and whose methods had a good deal of influence via the writings of Russian anarchists upon Serbian youth—and of the [American] Ku Klux Klan. There were gory rituals and oaths of loyalty, there were murders of backsliding members, there was identification of members by number, there were distributions of guns and bombs. And there was a steady traffic between Bosnia and Serbia.[39]

This group, which continued to maintain close links with its parent body, was largely composed of Serbian military officers. It was led by Lieutenant Colonel Dragutin Dmitrievich (known by his pseudonym, Apis), himself the chief of the Intelligence Department of the Serbian general staff. With this key additional advantage of direct access to military armaments, intelligence, and training facilities, the Black Hand effectively took charge of all Serb-backed clandestine operations in Bosnia.[40]

Although there were obviously close links between the Serbian military, the Black Hand, and the Young Bosnians, it would be a mistake to regard the relationship as one of direct control, much less outright manipulation. Clearly, the Serbian government was well aware of the Black Hand's objectives and the violent means the group employed in pursuit of them; indeed, the Serbian crown prince Alexander was one of the group's benefactors. But this does not mean that the Serbian government was necessarily as committed to war with Austria as the Black Hand's leaders were, or that it was prepared to countenance the group's more extreme plans for fomenting cross-border, anti-Hapsburg terrorism. There is some evidence to suggest that the Black Hand may have been trying to force Austria's hand against Serbia and thereby plunge both countries into war by actively abetting the Young Bosnians' plot to assassinate the archduke. Indeed, according to one revisionist account of the events leading up to the murder,[41] even though the pistol used by Princip had been supplied by the Black Hand from a Serbian military armory in Kragujevac, and even though Princip had been trained by the Black Hand in Serbia before being smuggled back across the border for the assassination, at the eleventh hour Dmitrievich had apparently bowed to intense government pressure and tried to stop the assassination. According to this version, Princip and his fellow conspirators would hear nothing of it and stubbornly went ahead with their plans. Contrary to popular assumption, therefore, the archduke's assassination may not have been specifically ordered or even directly sanctioned by the Serbian government.[42] However, the obscure links between high government officials and their senior military commanders and ostensibly independent, transnational terrorist movements, and the tangled web of intrigue, plots, clandestine arms provision and training, intelligence agents, and cross-border sanctuary that these relationships inevitably involved provide a pertinent historical parallel to the contemporary phenomenon known as "state-sponsored" terrorism (that is, the active and often clandestine support, encouragement, and assistance provided by a foreign government to a terrorist group).

By the 1930s, the meaning of "terrorism" had changed again. It was now used less to refer to revolutionary movements and violence directed against governments and their leaders and more to describe the practices of mass repression employed by totalitarian states and their dictatorial leaders against their own citizens. Thus the term regained its former connotations of abuse of power by government, and it was applied specifically to the authoritarian regimes that had come to power in Fascist Italy, Nazi Germany, and Stalinist Russia. In Germany and Italy, respectively, the accession to office of Hitler and Mussolini had depended in large measure on the "street"—the mobilization and deployment of gangs of brown- or black-shirted thugs to harass and intimidate political opponents and root out other scapegoats for public vilification and further victimization. "Terror? Never," Mussolini insisted, demurely dismissing such intimidation as "simply . . . social hygiene, taking those individuals out of circulation like a doctor would take out a bacillus."[43] The most sinister dimension of this form of "terror" was that it became an intrinsic component of Fascist and Nazi governance, executed at the behest of, and in complete subservience to, the ruling political party of the land—which had arrogated to itself complete, total control of the country and its people. A system of government-sanctioned fear and coercion was thus created whereby political brawls, street fights, and widespread persecution of Jews, communists, and other declared "enemies of the state" became the means through which complete and submissive compliance was ensured. The totality of party control over, and perversion of, government was perhaps most clearly evinced by a speech given by Hermann Göring, the newly appointed Prussian minister of the interior, in 1933. "Fellow Germans," he declared,

> my measures will not be crippled by any judicial thinking. My measures will not be crippled by any bureaucracy. Here I don't have to worry about Justice; my mission is only to destroy and exterminate, nothing more. This

struggle will be a struggle against chaos, and such a struggle I shall not conduct with the power of the police. A bourgeois State might have done that. Certainly, I shall use the power of the State and the police to the utmost, my dear Communists, so don't draw any false conclusions; but the struggle to the death, in which my fist will grasp your necks, I shall lead with those there—the Brown Shirts.[44]

The "Great Terror" that Stalin was shortly to unleash in Russia both resembled and differed from that of the Nazis. On the one hand, drawing inspiration from Hitler's ruthless elimination of his own political opponents, the Russian dictator similarly transformed the political party he led into a servile instrument responsive directly to his personal will, and the state's police and security apparatus into slavish organs of coercion, enforcement, and repression. But conditions in the Soviet Union of the 1930s bore little resemblance to the turbulent political, social, and economic upheaval afflicting Germany and Italy during that decade and the previous one. On the other hand, therefore, unlike either the Nazis or the Fascists, who had emerged from the political free-for-alls in their own countries to seize power and then had to struggle to consolidate their rule and retain their unchallenged authority, the Russian Communist Party had by the mid-1930s been firmly entrenched in power for more than a decade. Stalin's purges, in contrast to those of the French Revolution, and even to Russia's own recent experience, were not "launched in time of crisis, or revolution and war . . . [but] in the coldest of cold blood, when Russia had at last reached a comparatively calm and even moderately prosperous condition."[45] Thus the political purges ordered by Stalin became, in the words of one of his biographers, a "conspiracy to seize total power by terrorist action,"[46] resulting in the death, exile, imprisonment, or forcible impressment of millions.

Certainly, similar forms of state-imposed or state-directed violence and terror against a government's own citizens continue today. The use of so-called death squads (often off-duty or plainclothes security or police officers) in conjunction with blatant intimidation of political opponents, human rights and aid workers, student groups, labor organizers, journalists, and others has been a prominent feature of the right-wing military dictatorships that took power in Argentina, Chile, and Greece during the 1970s and even of elected governments in El Salvador, Guatemala, Colombia, and Peru during the upheavals that afflicted those countries, particularly in the 1980s. But these state-sanctioned or explicitly ordered acts of *internal* political violence directed mostly against domestic populations—that is, rule by violence and intimidation by those *already* in power against their own citizenry—are generally termed "terror" in order to distinguish that phenomenon from "terrorism," which is understood to be violence committed by nonstate entities.

Following the Second World War, in another swing of the pendulum of meaning, "terrorism" regained the revolutionary connotations with which it is most commonly associated today. At that time the term was used primarily in reference to the violent revolts then being prosecuted by the various indigenous nationalist/anticolonialist groups that emerged in Asia, Africa, and the Middle East during the late 1940s and 1950s to oppose continued European rule. Countries as diverse as Israel, Kenya, Cyprus, and Algeria, for example, owe their independence at least in part to nationalist political movements that employed terrorism against colonial powers. It was also during this period that the "politically correct" appellation of "freedom fighters" came into fashion as a result of the political legitimacy that the international community (whose sympathy and support were actively courted by many of these movements) accorded to struggles for national liberation and self-determination. Sympathy and support for the rebels extended to segments of the colonial state's own population as well, creating a need for less judgmental and more politically neutral language than "terrorist" and "terrorism" to describe these revolutionaries and the violence they committed in what were considered justified "wars of liberation."[47] Many newly independent Third World countries and communist-bloc states in particular also adopted this vernacular, arguing that anyone or any movement that fought against "colonial" oppression and/or Western domination should not be described as "terrorists" but were properly deemed to be "freedom fighters." This position was perhaps most famously explained by Palestine Liberation Organization (PLO) chairman Yasir Arafat, when he addressed the United Nations General Assembly in November 1974. "The difference between the revolutionary and the terrorist," Arafat stated, "lies in the reason for which each fights. For whoever stands by a just cause and fights for the freedom and liberation of his land from the invaders, the settlers and the colonialists, cannot possibly be called terrorist."[48]

During the late 1960s and 1970s, terrorism continued to be viewed within a revolutionary context. However, this usage now expanded to include nationalist and ethnic separatist groups outside a colonial or neocolonial framework as well as radical, entirely ideologically motivated organizations. Disenfranchised or exiled nationalist minorities—such as the PLO, the Quebecois separatist group FLQ (Front de Liberation du Quebec), the Basque ETA (Euskadita Askatasuna, or Freedom for the Basque Homeland), and even a hitherto unknown South Moluccan irredentist group seeking independence from Indonesia—adopted terrorism as a means to draw attention to themselves and their respective causes, in many instances with the specific aim, like their anticolonial predecessors, of attracting international sympathy and support. Around the same time, various left-wing political extremists—drawn mostly from the radical student organizations and Marxist/Leninist/Maoist movements in Western Europe, Latin America, and the United States—began to form terrorist groups opposing American intervention in Vietnam and what they claimed were the irredeemable social and economic inequities of the modern capitalist liberal-democratic state.

Although the revolutionary cum ethno-nationalist/separatist and ideological exemplars continue to shape our most basic understanding of the term, it was not long before "terrorism" was being used to denote broader, less distinct phenomena. In the early 1980s, for example, terrorism came to be regarded as a calculated means to destabilize the West as part of a vast global conspiracy. Books like *The Terror Network* by Claire Sterling propagated the notion to a receptive American presidential administration and similarly susceptible governments elsewhere that the seemingly isolated terrorist incidents perpetrated by disparate groups scattered across the globe were in fact linked elements of a massive clandestine plot, orchestrated by the Kremlin and implemented by its Warsaw Pact client states, to destroy the Free World.[49] By the middle of the decade, however, a series of suicide bombings directed mostly against American diplomatic and military targets in the Middle East was focusing attention on the rising threat of state-sponsored terrorism. Consequently, this phenomenon—whereby various renegade foreign governments such as the regimes in Iran, Iraq, Libya, and Syria became actively involved in sponsoring or commissioning terrorist acts—replaced communist conspiracy theories as the main context within which terrorism was viewed. Terrorism thus became associated with a type of covert or surrogate warfare whereby weaker states could confront larger, more powerful rivals without the risk of retribution.[50]

In the early 1990s the meaning and usage of the term "terrorism" were further blurred by the emergence of two new buzzwords: "narco-terrorism" and the so-called gray area phenomenon.[51] The former term revived the Moscow-orchestrated terrorism conspiracy theories of previous years while introducing the critical new dimension of narcotics trafficking. Thus "narco-terrorism" was defined by one of the concept's foremost propagators as the "use of drug trafficking to advance the objectives of certain governments and terrorist organizations"—identified as the "Marxist-Leninist regimes" of the Soviet Union, Cuba, Bulgaria, and Nicaragua, among others.[52] The emphasis on "narco-terrorism" as the latest manifestation of the communist plot to undermine Western society,[53] however, had the unfortunate effect of diverting official attention away from a bona fide emerging trend. To a greater extent than ever in the past, entirely criminal (that is, violent, *economically* motivated) organizations were now forging strategic alliances with terrorist and guerrilla organizations or were themselves employing violence for specifically political ends. The growing power of the Colombian cocaine cartels, their close ties with left-wing terrorist groups in Colombia and Peru, and their repeated attempts to subvert Colombia's electoral process and undermine successive governments constitute perhaps the best-known example of this continuing trend.[54]

Those who drew attention to this "gray area phenomenon" were concerned less with grand conspiracies than with highlighting the increasingly fluid and variable nature of subnational conflict in the post–cold war era. Accordingly, in the 1990s "terrorism" began to be subsumed by some analysts within the "gray area phenomenon." Thus the latter term came to be used to denote "threats to the stability of nation states by non-state actors and non-governmental processes and organizations";[55] to describe violence affecting "immense regions or urban areas where control has shifted from legitimate governments to new half-political, half-criminal powers";[56] or simply to group together in one category the range of conflicts across the world that no longer conformed to traditionally accepted notions of war as fighting between the armed forces of two or more established states, but instead involved irregular forces as one or more of the combatants.[57] Terrorism had shifted its meaning again from an individual phenomenon of subnational violence to one of several elements, or part of a wider pattern, of nonstate conflict.

The terrorist attacks on September 11, 2001, inevitably, redefined "terrorism" yet again. On that day, nineteen terrorists belonging to a group calling itself al Qaeda (or al-Qa'ida) hijacked four passenger aircraft soon after they took off from airports in Boston, Newark, New Jersey, and Washington, D.C. Two of the planes were then deliberately flown into the twin towers of New York City's World Trade Center. Both structures collapsed shortly afterward. A third aircraft similarly smashed into the Pentagon, where the U.S. Department of Defense is located, severely damaging the southwest portion of that building. Meanwhile, passengers on board the fourth aircraft learned of the other attacks and struggled to subdue the hijackers. In the ensuing melee, the plane spun out of control and crashed into a field in rural Pennsylvania. A total of nearly three thousand people were killed in the attacks.[58] To put that death toll in perspective, in the entirety of the twentieth century no more than fourteen terrorist incidents had killed more than one hundred people.[59] And until 9/11 no terrorist operation had ever killed more than five hundred people.[60] Among the dead were citizens of some eighty different countries,[61] although the largest number of fatalities by far were U.S. citizens. Indeed, more than twice as many Americans perished on 9/11 than had been killed by terrorists since 1968[62]—the year acknowledged as marking the advent of modern, international terrorism.

So massive and consequential a terrorist onslaught required nothing less than an equally comprehensive and far-reaching response. "This is a new kind of evil . . . [and we] will rid the world of the evildoers," President George W. Bush promised just days later. "Our nation was horrified," he continued, "but it's not going to be terrorized."[63] Yet when the president addressed a special joint session of the U.S. Congress on September 20, 2001, he repeatedly invoked the word "terror"—that is, the "state of being terrified or greatly frightened," according to the *OED*'s definition[64]—rather than the specifically political phenomenon "terror*ism*." "Our war on terror," the president famously declared, "begins with al-Qaida, but it does not end there."[65] The consequences of his semantic choice, whether deliberate or not, nonetheless proved as portentous as they were significant: heralding a virtually open-ended struggle against anyone and anything that arguably scared or threatened Americans. The range of potential adversaries thus expanded beyond Osama bin Laden, al Qaeda's leader, and his minions, who, the president explained, "hate us . . . [and] our freedoms,"[66] now to include "rogue" states arrayed in an "axis of evil" (e.g., Iraq, Iran, and North Korea)[67] and especially heinous Middle East dictators thought to possess weapons of mass destruction (WMD). As Professor Sir Michael Howard, the world's leading authority on strategy and military history, later reflected,

> President Bush's declaration of a "war on terror" was generally seen abroad as a rhetorical device to alert the American people to the dangers facing them, rather than as a statement to be taken seriously or literally in terms of international law. But further statements and actions by the Bush Administration have made it clear that the President's words were intended to be taken literally.[68]

The implications of this policy were clearly demonstrated by the relationship that the president and his advisers believed existed between al Qaeda and Saddam Hussein. Although White House suspicions that Iraq was somehow behind 9/11 never completely faded,[69] they were eventually eclipsed by growing concerns about terrorists acquiring WMD from Iraqi stockpiles.[70] Indeed, it was precisely this fear that President Bush cited to justify the March 2003 invasion. The Bush administration's conflation of terrorism and WMD was specifically cited by Richard Dearlove, then head of MI-6, Britain's Secret Intelligence Service, in his report to Prime Minister Tony Blair of high-level U.S.-U.K. consultations held in Washington, D.C., seven months before the invasion. "Military action was now seen as inevitable," notes of Dearlove's meeting with the prime minister stated. "Bush wanted to remove Saddam, through military action, justified by the conjunction of terrorism and WMD."[71] The chain of events that began on 9/11 and the declaration of a "war on terror" that thereafter set America on the path to war with Iraq thus prompted Michael Howard again to note how it was evidently "not enough" for Americans

> to be at war with an abstract entity described by their president as "Terror." They need a specific adversary who embodies the spirit of evil against whom national sentiment can be mobilised, as it was mobilised against Hitler in 1941. Osama bin Laden proved too evasive and evanescent a figure to provide the necessary catharsis, but prominent among the usual suspects was Saddam Hussein. There was little evidence to link him with this particular crime, but he was a bad guy, with whom many members of the Bush administration had unfinished business. . . . He was, in short, the most powerful and dangerous figure among the declared enemies of the US, which in itself gave them the right indeed the duty—to destroy him.[72]

The "war on terror" thus became, in President Bush's infelicitous choice of words, as much a "crusade"[73] against evil as it was an unwavering reaction to the multiplicity of new security threats confronting the nation—and therefore accounts for the way terrorism was redefined in the early twenty-first century, according to Stanford University linguist Geoffrey Nunberg, in order to "encompass both the dark forces that threaten 'civilization' and the fears they arouse."[74]

Why Is Terrorism So Difficult to Define?

Not surprisingly, as the meaning and usage of the word have changed over time to accommodate the political vernacular and discourse of each successive era, terrorism has proved increasingly elusive in the face of attempts to construct one consistent definition. At one time, the terrorists themselves were far more cooperative in this endeavor than they are today. The early practitioners didn't mince their words or hide behind the semantic camouflage of more anodyne labels such as "freedom fighter" or "urban guerrilla." The nineteenth-century anarchists, for example, unabashedly proclaimed themselves to be terrorists and frankly proclaimed their tactics to be terrorism.[75] The members of Narodnaya Volya similarly displayed no qualms in using these same words to describe themselves and their deeds.[76] Such frankness did not last, however. Although the Jewish terrorist group of the 1940s known as Lehi (the Hebrew acronym for Lohamei Herut Yisrael, the Freedom Fighters for Israel), but more popularly called the Stern Gang after its founder and first leader, Abraham Stern, would admit to its effective use of terrorist tactics, its members never considered themselves to be terrorists.[77] It is significant, however, that even Lehi, while it may have been far more candid than its latter-day counterparts, chose as the name of the organization not Terrorist Fighters for Israel but the far less pejorative Freedom Fighters for Israel. Similarly, although more than twenty years later the Brazilian revolutionary Carlos Marighela displayed little compunction about openly advocating the use of "terrorist" tactics,[78] he still insisted on depicting himself and his disciples as "urban guerrillas" rather than "urban terrorists." Indeed, it is clear from Marighela's writings that he was well aware of the word's undesirable connotations and strove to displace them with positive resonances. "The words 'aggressor' and 'terrorist,'" Marighela wrote in his famous *Handbook of Urban Guerrilla War* (also known as the "Mini-Manual"), "no longer mean what they did. Instead of arousing fear or censure, they are a call to action. To be called an aggressor or a terrorist in Brazil is now an honour to any citizen, for it means that he is fighting, with a gun in his hand, against the monstrosity of the present dictatorship and the suffering it causes."[79]

This trend toward ever more convoluted semantic obfuscations to sidestep terrorism's pejorative overtones has, if anything, become more entrenched in recent decades. Terrorist organizations almost without exception now regularly select names for themselves that consciously eschew the word "terrorism" in any of its forms. Instead these groups actively seek to evoke images of

- freedom and liberation (e.g., the National Liberation Front, the Popular Front for the Liberation of Palestine, Freedom for the Basque Homeland);
- armies or other military organizational structures (e.g., the National Military Organization, the Popular Liberation Army, the Fifth Battalion of the Liberation Army);
- actual self-defense movements (e.g., the Afrikaner Resistance Movement, the Shankhill Defence Association, the Organization for the Defence of the Free People, the Jewish Defense Organization);

- righteous vengeance (the Organization for the Oppressed on Earth, the Justice Commandos of the Armenian Genocide, the Palestinian Revenge Organization)

—or else deliberately choose names that are decidedly neutral and therefore bereft of all but the most innocuous suggestions or associations (e.g., the Shining Path, Front Line, al-Dawa (the Call), Alfaro Lives—Damn It!, Kach (Thus), al-Gamat al-Islamiya (the Islamic Organization), the Lantaro Youth Movement, and *especially* al Qaeda (the Arabic word for the "base of operation"[80] or "foundation"—meaning the base or foundation from which worldwide Islamic revolution can be waged—or, as other translations have it, the "precept" or "method").[81]

What all these examples suggest is that terrorists clearly do not see or regard themselves as others do. "Above all I am a family man," the archterrorist Carlos, the Jackal, described himself to a French newspaper following his capture in 1994.[82] Similarly, when the infamous KSM—Khalid Sheikh Mohammed, mastermind of the 9/11 attacks whom bin Laden called simply "al Mukhtar" (Arabic for "the brain")—was apprehended in March 2003, a photograph of him with his arms around his two young sons was found next to the bed in which he had been sleeping.[83] Cast perpetually on the defensive and forced to take up arms to protect themselves and their real or imagined constituents only, terrorists perceive themselves as reluctant warriors, driven by desperation—and lacking any viable alternative—to violence against a repressive state, a predatory rival ethnic or nationalist group, or an unresponsive international order. This perceived characteristic of self-denial also distinguishes the terrorist from other types of political extremists as well as from people similarly involved in illegal, violent avocations. A communist or a revolutionary, for example, would likely readily accept and admit that he is in fact a communist or a revolutionary. Indeed, many would doubtless take particular pride in claiming either of those appellations for themselves. Similarly, even a person engaged in illegal, wholly disreputable, or entirely selfish violent activities, such as robbing banks or carrying out contract killings, would probably admit to being a bank robber or a murderer for hire. The terrorist, by contrast, will *never* acknowledge that he is a terrorist and moreover will go to great lengths to evade and obscure any such inference or connection. Terry Anderson, the American journalist who was held hostage for almost seven years by the Lebanese terrorist organization Hezbollah, relates a telling conversation he had with one of his guards. The guard had objected to a newspaper article that referred to Hezbollah as terrorists. "We are not terrorists," he indignantly stated, "we are fighters." Anderson replied,

"Hajj, you are a terrorist, look it up in the dictionary. You are a terrorist, you may not like the word and if you do not like the word, do not do it."[84] The terrorist will always argue that it is society or the government or the socioeconomic "system" and its laws that are the *real* "terrorists," and moreover that if it were not for this oppression, he would not have felt the need to defend either himself or the population he claims to represent.[85] Another revealing example of this process of obfuscation-projection may be found in the book *Invisible Armies*, written by Sheikh Muhammad Hussein Fadlallah, the spiritual leader of the Lebanese terrorist group responsible for Anderson's kidnapping. "We don't see ourselves as terrorists," Fadlallah explains, "because we don't believe in terrorism. We don't see resisting the occupier as a terrorist action. We see ourselves as *mujihadeen* [holy warriors] who fight a Holy War for the people."[86] Indeed, Hezbollah's efforts to distance itself entirely from any terrorist associations and appellations have only intensified in the years since it first entered mainstream Lebanese politics.[87] Perhaps because it now has thirteen elected members of the Lebanese Parliament, Hezbollah spokespersons persistently argue that it is a bona fide political party, cum "resistance movement."[88]

On one point, at least, everyone agrees: "Terrorism" is a pejorative term.[89] It is a word with intrinsically negative connotations that is generally applied to one's enemies and opponents, or to those with whom one disagrees and would otherwise prefer to ignore. "What is called terrorism," Brian Jenkins has written, "thus seems to depend on one's point of view. Use of the term implies a moral judgement; and if one party can successfully attach the label *terrorist* to its opponent, then it has indirectly persuaded others to adopt its moral viewpoint."[90] Hence the decision to call someone or label some organization "terrorist" becomes almost unavoidably subjective, depending largely on whether one sympathizes with or opposes the person/group/cause concerned. If one identifies with the victim of the violence, for example, then the act is terrorism. If, however, one identifies with the perpetrator, the violent act is regarded in a more sympathetic, if not positive (or, at the worst, ambivalent) light, and it is not terrorism.

The implications of this associational logic were perhaps most clearly demonstrated in the exchanges between Western and non-Western member states of the United Nations following the 1972 Munich Olympics massacre, in which eleven Israeli athletes were killed. The debate began with the proposal by the UN secretary general, Kurt Waldheim, that the UN should not remain a "mute spectator" to the acts of terrorist violence then occurring throughout the world but should take practical steps that might prevent further bloodshed.[91] While a majority of the UN member states supported the secretary general, a disputatious minority—including many Arab states and various African and Asian countries—derailed the discussion, arguing (much as Arafat would do two years later in his own address to the General Assembly) that "people who struggle to liberate themselves from foreign oppression and exploitation have the right to use all methods at their disposal, including force."[92]

The Third World delegates justified their position with two arguments. First, they claimed that all bona fide liberation movements are invariably decried as "terrorists" by the regimes against which their struggles for freedom are directed. The Nazis, for example, labeled as terrorists the resistance groups opposing Germany's occupation of their lands, Moulaye el-Hassen, the Mauritanian ambassador, pointed out, just as "all liberation movements are described as terrorists by those who have reduced them to slavery." Therefore, by condemning "terrorism" the UN was endorsing the power of the strong over the weak and of the established entity over its nonestablished challenger—in effect, acting as the defender of the status quo. According to Chen Chu, the deputy representative of the People's Republic of China, the UN thus was proposing to deprive "oppressed nations and peoples" of the only effective weapon they had with which to oppose "imperialism, colonialism, neo-colonialism, racism and Israeli Zionism."[93] Second, the Third World delegates argued forcefully that it is not the violence itself that is germane but its "underlying causes"—that is, the "misery, frustration, grievance and despair"—that produce the violent acts.[94] As the Mauritanian representative again explained, the term "terrorist" could "hardly be held to apply to persons who were denied the most elementary human rights, dignity, freedom and independence, and whose countries objected to foreign occupation."[95] When the issue was again raised the following year, Syria objected on the grounds that "the international community is under legal and moral obligation to promote the struggle for liberation and to resist any attempt to depict this struggle as synonymous with terrorism and illegitimate violence."[96] The resultant definitional paralysis subsequently throttled UN efforts to make any substantive progress on international cooperation against terrorism beyond very specific agreements on individual aspects of the problem (concerning, for example, diplomats and civil aviation).

The opposite approach, in which identification with the victim determines the classification of a violent act as terrorism, is evident in the conclusions of a parliamentary working group of NATO (an organization comprising long-established, status quo Western states). The final report of the 1989 North Atlantic Assembly's Subcommittee on Terrorism states: "Murder, kidnapping, arson and other felonious acts constitute criminal behavior, but many non-Western nations have proved reluctant to condemn as terrorist acts what they consider to be struggles of national liberation."[97] In this reasoning, the defining characteristic of terrorism is the act of violence itself, not the motivations or justification for or reasons behind it. After decades of debate and resistance, the UN itself finally embraced this rationale by adopting the International Convention for the Suppression of Terrorist Bombings. The convention outlawed the unlawful delivery, placement, discharge, or detonation of an

> explosive or other lethal device in, into or against a place of public use, a State or government facility, a public transportation system or an infrastructure facility with the intent to cause death or serious bodily injury; or with the intent to cause extensive destruction of such a place, facility or system, where such destruction results in or is likely to result in major economic loss.[98]

It came into force just four months before the 9/11 attacks.[99]

Indeed, this approach has long been espoused by analysts such as Jenkins who argue that terrorism should be defined "by the nature of the act, not by the identity of the perpetrators or the nature of their cause."[100] But this is not an entirely satisfactory solution either, since it fails to differentiate clearly between violence perpetrated by states and by nonstate entities, such as terrorists. Accordingly, it plays into the hands of terrorists and their apologists who would argue that there is no difference between the "low-tech" terrorist pipe bomb placed in the rubbish bin at a crowded market that wantonly and indiscriminately kills or maims everyone within a radius measured in tens of feet and the "high-tech" precision-guided ordnance dropped by air force fighter-bombers from a height of twenty thousand feet or more that achieves the same wanton and indiscriminate effects on the crowded marketplace far below. This rationale thus equates the random violence inflicted on enemy population centers by military forces—such as the Luftwaffe's raids on Warsaw and Coventry, the Allied firebombings of Dresden and Tokyo, and the atomic bombs dropped by the United States on Hiroshima and Nagasaki during the Second World War, and indeed the countervalue strategy of the postwar superpowers' strategic nuclear policy, which deliberately targeted the enemy's civilian population—with the violence committed by substate entities labeled "terrorists," since both involve the infliction of death and injury on noncombatants.[101] Indeed, this was precisely the point made during the above-mentioned UN debates following the 1972 Munich Olympics massacre by the Cuban representative, who argued that "the methods of combat used by national liberation movements could not be declared illegal while the policy of terrorism unleashed against certain peoples [by the armed forces of established states] was declared legitimate."[102]

It is a familiar argument. Terrorists, as we have seen, deliberately cloak themselves in the terminology of military jargon. They consciously portray themselves as bona fide (freedom) fighters, if not soldiers, who—though they wear no identifying uniform or insignia—are entitled to treatment as prisoners of war (POWs) if captured and therefore should not be prosecuted as common criminals in ordinary courts of law. Terrorists further argue that, because of their numerical inferiority, far more limited firepower, and paucity of resources compared with an established nation-state's massive defense and national security apparatus, they have no choice but to operate clandestinely, emerging from the shadows to carry out dramatic (in other words, bloody and destructive) acts of hit-and-run violence in order to attract attention to, and ensure publicity for, themselves and their cause. The bomb in the rubbish bin, in their view, is merely a circumstantially imposed "poor man's air force":[103] the only means with which the terrorist can challenge—and get the attention of—the more powerful state. "How else can we bring pressure to bear on the world?" one of Arafat's political aides once inquired. "The deaths are regrettable, but they are a fact of war in which innocents have become involved. They are no more innocent than the Palestinian women and children killed by the Israelis and we are ready to carry the war all over the world."[104]

But rationalizations such as these ignore the fact that, even while national armed forces have been responsible for far more death and destruction than terrorists might ever aspire to bring about, there nonetheless is a fundamental qualitative difference between the two types of violence. Even in war there are rules and accepted norms of behavior that prohibit the use of certain types of weapons (for example, hollow-point or "dum-dum" bullets, CS "tear" gas, chemical and biological warfare agents) and proscribe various tactics and outlaw attacks on specific categories of targets. Accordingly, in theory, if not always in practice, the rules of war—as observed from the early seventeenth century when they were first proposed by the Dutch jurist Hugo Grotius and subsequently codified in the famous Geneva and Hague Conventions on Warfare of the 1860s, 1899, 1907, and 1949—not only grant civilian noncombatants immunity from attack but also

- prohibit taking civilians as hostages;
- impose regulations governing the treatment of captured or surrendered soldiers (POWs);

- outlaw reprisals against either civilians or POWs;
- recognize neutral territory and the rights of citizens of neutral states; and
- uphold the inviolability of diplomats and other accredited representatives.

Even the most cursory review of terrorist tactics and targets over the past quarter century reveals that terrorists have violated all these rules. They not infrequently have

- taken civilians as hostages, and in some instances then brutally executed them (e.g., the former Italian prime minister Aldo Moro and the German industrialist Hans Martin Schleyer, who, respectively, were taken captive and later murdered by the Red Brigades and the Red Army Faction in the 1970s and, more recently, Daniel Pearl, a *Wall Street Journal* reporter, and Nicholas Berg, an American businessmen, who were kidnapped by radical Islamic terrorists in Pakistan and Iraq, respectively, and grotesquely beheaded);
- similarly abused and murdered kidnapped military officers—even when they were serving on UN-sponsored peacekeeping or truce supervisory missions (e.g., the American Marine Lieutenant Colonel William Higgins, the commander of a UN truce-monitoring detachment, who was abducted by Lebanese Shi'a terrorists in 1989 and subsequently hanged);
- undertaken reprisals against wholly innocent civilians, often in countries far removed from the terrorists' ostensible "theater of operation," thus disdaining any concept of neutral states or the rights of citizens of neutral countries (e.g., the brutal 1986 machine-gun and hand-grenade attack on Turkish Jewish worshipers at an Istanbul synagogue carried out by the Palestinian Abu Nidal Organization (ANO) in retaliation for a recent Israeli raid on a guerrilla base in southern Lebanon); and
- repeatedly attacked embassies and other diplomatic installations (e.g., the bombings of the U.S. embassies in Nairobi and Dar es Salaam in 1998 and in Beirut and Kuwait City in 1983 and 1984, and the mass hostage-taking at the Japanese ambassador's residence in Lima, Peru, in 1996–97), as well as deliberately targeting diplomats and other accredited representatives (e.g., the British ambassador to Uruguay, Sir Geoffrey Jackson, who was kidnapped by leftist terrorists in that country in 1971, and the fifty-two American diplomats taken hostage at the Tehran legation in 1979).

Admittedly, the armed forces of established states have also been guilty of violating some of the same rules of war. However, when these transgressions do occur—when civilians are deliberately and wantonly attacked in war or taken hostage and killed by military forces—the term "war crime" is used to describe such acts and, as imperfect and flawed as both international and national judicial remedies may be, steps nonetheless are often taken to hold the perpetrators accountable for the crimes. By comparison, one of the fundamental raisons d'être of international terrorism is a refusal to be bound by such rules of warfare and codes of conduct. International terrorism disdains any concept of delimited areas of combat or demarcated battlefields, much less respect for neutral territory. Accordingly, terrorists have repeatedly taken their often parochial struggles to other, sometimes geographically distant, third-party countries and there deliberately enmeshed people completely unconnected with the terrorists' cause or grievances in violent incidents designed to generate attention and publicity.

The reporting of terrorism by the news media, which have been drawn into the semantic debates that divided the UN in the 1970s and continue to influence all discourse on terrorism, has further contributed to the obfuscation of the terrorist/"freedom fighter" debate, enshrining imprecision and implication as the lingua franca of political violence in the name of objectivity and neutrality. In striving to avoid appearing either partisan or judgmental, the American media, for example, resorted to describing terrorists—often in the same report—as variously "guerrillas," "gunmen," "raiders," "commandos," and even "soldiers." A random sample of American newspaper reports of Palestinian terrorist activities between June and December 1973, found in the terrorism archives and database maintained by the RAND Corporation,[105] provides striking illustrations of this practice. Out of eight headlines of articles reporting the same incident, six used the word "guerrillas" and only two used "terrorists" to describe the perpetrators. An interesting pattern was also observed: those accounts that immediately followed a particularly horrific or tragic incident—that is, involving the death and injury of innocent people (in this instance, a 1973 attack on a Pan Am airliner at the Rome airport, in which thirty-two passengers were killed)—tended to describe the perpetrators as "terrorists" and their act as "terrorism" (albeit in the headline in one case only, before reverting to the more neutral terminology of "commando," "militants," and "guerrilla attack" in the text) more frequently than did reports of less serious or nonlethal incidents.[106] One *New York Times* editorial, however, was far less restrained than the stories describing the actual incident, describing it as "bloody" and "mindless" and using the words "terrorists" and "terrorism" interchangeably with "guerrillas" and "extremists."[107] Only six months previously, however, the same newspaper had run a story about another terrorist attack that completely eschewed the terms "terrorism" and "terrorist," preferring "guerrillas" and "resistance" (as in "resistance movement") instead.[108] The *Christian Science Monitor*'s reports of the Rome Pan Am attack similarly avoided "terrorist" and "terrorism" in favor of "guerrillas" and "extremists";[109] an Associated Press story in the next day's *Los Angeles Times* also stuck with "guerrillas,"[110] while the two *Washington Post* articles on the same incident opted for the terms "commandos" and "guerrillas."[111]

This slavish devotion to terminological neutrality, which David Rapoport first observed nearly thirty years ago,[112] is still in evidence today. A telling illustration of the semantics of terrorism reportage can be found in some of the press coverage of the terrorist violence that afflicted Algeria during the 1990s and claimed the lives of an estimated hundred thousand people. An article appearing in the *International Herald Tribune* (a Paris-based newspaper then published in conjunction with the *New York Times* and the *Washington Post)* reported a 1997 incident in Algeria in which thirty people had been killed by perpetrators who were variously described as "terrorists" in the article's headline, less judgmentally as "extremists" in the lead paragraph, and as the still more ambiguous "Islamic fundamentalists" in the article's third paragraph.[113] In a country where terrorist-inflicted bloodshed was endemic, one might think that the distinctions between "terrorists," mere "extremists," and ordinary "fundamentalists" would be clearer. Equally interesting was the article that appeared on the opposite side of the same page of the newspaper that described the "decades of sporadic *guerrilla* [my emphasis] warfare by the IRA" in Northern Ireland.[114] Yet sixty years ago this newspaper apparently had fewer qualms about using the word "terrorists" to describe the two young Jewish men in pre-independence Israel who, while awaiting execution after having been convicted of attacking British military targets, committed suicide.[115] Other press accounts of the same period in *The Times* of London and the *Palestine Post* similarly had no difficulties, for example, in describing the 1946 bombing by Jewish terrorists of the British military headquarters and government secretariat located in Jerusalem's King David Hotel as a "terrorist" act perpetrated by "terrorists."[116] And, in perhaps the most specific application of the term, the communist terrorists against whom the British fought in Malaya throughout the late 1940s and 1950s were routinely referred to as "CTs"—for "Communist terrorists." As Rapoport warned in the 1970s, "In attempting to correct the abuse of language for political purposes, our journalists may succeed in making language altogether worthless."[117]

More recently, the coverage given by the *Washington Post* and the *New York Times* to the barricade-and-hostage situation that unfolded at a Beslan, North Ossetia, school in early September 2004 underscored these continuing semantic ambiguities. Even in the post-9/11 era, few terrorist attacks have evoked quite the horror and revulsion that the fifty-two-hour ordeal and its deliberate targeting of children produced. According to official Russian figures, at least 331 hostages—including more than 172 children—were killed, although many believe the actual numbers to be much higher. Yet the perpetrators, an indisputably cruel and ruthless group of Chechen terrorists, were repeatedly described in far more neutral and anodyne terms by both of America's national newspapers of record. The *Washington Post*'s initial report of the seizure and its account of the rescue operations, for example, did not use the words "terrorism" and "terrorists" at all, except in the context of direct quotations or statements made by an aide to Russian president Vladimir Putin, various other Russian official spokespersons, or President Bush himself. Instead, a variety of other adjectives were employed in the two articles sampled, including "guerrillas" (seventeen references), "hostage takers" (eleven), "rebels" (six), "fighters" (three), and "separatists" (two).[118] The *New York Times*'s reporting and rhetorical choices were little different. Admittedly, its first article detailing the incident used the word "terrorist" twice, in both instances independently of quotes or statements made by Russian officials. But more inoffensive terms such as "guerrillas" (seventeen references), "fighters" (nine), "insurgents" (six), "rebels" (six), and "hostage takers" (two) predominated in both this story and the report of the siege's grisly denouement.[119] The word "terrorist" again appeared twice in the second piece, but only when quoting Russian president Vladimir Putin and his spokesman.[120] Indeed, the "unrelenting use of such euphemistic language" in the *Washington Post*'s reporting of the Beslan incident prompted one reader to ask in a letter to the editor, "Why can't your editors just identify these people for what they are . . . terrorists?"[121] The *New York Times*'s first public editor, Daniel Okrent, devoted a column to the subject after readers similarly complained about the paper's reluctance to use the words "terrorist," "terrorism," and "terror." His explanation was that the *Times* in fact has no policy governing the use of such words—except to eschew them as much possible.[122]

The cumulative effect of this proclivity toward equivocation is that today there is no one widely accepted or agreed-upon definition for terrorism. Different departments or agencies of even the same government will themselves often have very different definitions for it. The U.S. State Department, for example, uses the definition of terrorism contained in Title 22 of the United States Code, Section 2656f(d):

premeditated, politically motivated violence perpetrated against non-combatant targets by subnational groups or clandestine agents, usually intended to influence an audience.

In an accompanying footnote is the explanation that:

For purposes of this definition, the term "noncombatant" is interpreted to include, in addition to civilians, military personnel who at the time of the incident are unarmed and/or not on duty. . . . We also consider as acts of terrorism attacks on military installations or on armed military personnel when a state of military hostilities does not exist at the site, such as bombings against US bases in Europe, the Philippines, or elsewhere.[123]

The U.S. Federal Bureau of Investigation (FBI) defines terrorism as

the unlawful use of force or violence against persons or property to intimidate or coerce a Government, the civilian population, or any segment thereof, in furtherance of political or social objectives,[124]

while the Department of Homeland Security (DHS) states that terrorism is

any activity that involves an act that:
     is dangerous to human life or potentially destructive of critical infrastructure or key resources; and . . . must also appear to be intended
     (i) to intimidate or coerce a civilian population; (ii) to influence the policy of a government by intimidation or coercion; or (iii) to affect the conduct of a government by mass destruction, assassination, or kidnapping.[125]

And the U.S. Department of Defense defines it as

the calculated use of unlawful violence or threat of unlawful violence to inculcate fear; intended to coerce or to intimidate governments or societies in the pursuit of goals that are generally political, religious, or ideological objectives.[126]

Not surprisingly, each of the above definitions reflects the priorities and particular interests of the specific agency involved. The State Department's emphasis is on the premeditated and planned or calculated

nature of terrorism in contrast to more spontaneous acts of political violence. Its definition is also the only one of the four to emphasize both the
ineluctably political nature of terrorism and the perpetrators' fundamental "subnational" characteristic. The State Department's approach is also
noteworthy in that it expands the definition of a terrorist act beyond the
usual, exclusive focus on civilians to include "noncombatant targets." This
broad category encompasses not only assassinations of military attachés
and military forces deployed on peacekeeping missions, but also attacks
on cafes, discotheques, and other facilities frequented by off-duty service
personnel, as well as on military installations and armed personnel—provided that a "state of military hostilities does not exist at the site." Under
this rubric, incidents such as the 1983 suicide truck bombing of the U.S.
Marine barracks at Beirut International Airport; the similar attack thirteen years later against a U.S. Air Force housing complex in Khobar, Saudi
Arabia; and the October 2000 seaborne suicide assault on a U.S. Navy
destroyer, the USS *Cole* while it was at anchor in Aden, Yemen, are defined
as terrorist acts.[127] The State Department definition is deficient, however,
in failing to consider the psychological dimension of terrorism. Terrorism is as much about the threat of violence as the violent act itself and,
accordingly, is deliberately conceived to have far-reaching psychological
repercussions beyond the actual target of the act among a wider, watching, "target" audience. "Terrorism," as Jenkins succinctly observed two
decades ago, "is theatre."[128]

Given the FBI's mission of investigating and solving crimes—both political (e.g., terrorism) and other—it is not surprising that its definition focuses
on different elements. Unlike the State Department's, this definition does
address the psychological dimensions of the terrorist act described above,
laying stress on terrorism's intimidatory and coercive aspects. The FBI definition also identifies a much broader category of terrorist targets than only
"noncombatants," specifying not only governments and their citizens but
also inanimate objects, such as private and public property. Accordingly,
politically motivated acts of vandalism and sabotage are included, such as
attacks on:

- abortion clinics by militant opponents of legalized abortion in the
  United States;
- retail businesses and stores by anti-globalists and/or anarchists;
- medical research facilities by groups opposing experimentation on
  animals, such as the Animal Liberation Front (ALF); and

- ski resorts, condominium vacation developments, commercial logging operations, or automobile dealerships by radical environmentalists associated with the Earth Liberation Front (ELF).[129]

Although the FBI definition recognizes social alongside political objectives as fundamental terrorist aims, it offers no clear elucidation of the differences between them to explain this distinction. The Department of Homeland Security (DHS) definition clearly reflects its mission: concentrating on attacks to critical infrastructure and key national resources that could have grave societal consequences. In this respect, the DHS cites specifically in its definition the threat of "mass destruction," the better to differentiate and distinguish its responsibilities from those of other agencies.

The Department of Defense definition of terrorism is arguably the most complete of the four. It highlights the terrorist threat as much as the actual act of violence and focuses on terrorism's targeting of whole societies as well as governments. Curiously, unlike the State Department definition, it does not include the deliberate targeting of individuals for assassination and makes no attempt to distinguish between attacks on combatant and noncombatant military personnel. The Defense Department definition, significantly, also cites the religious and ideological aims of terrorism alongside its fundamental political objectives—but omits the social dimension found in the FBI's definition.

It is not only individual agencies within the same governmental apparatus that cannot agree on a single definition of terrorism. Experts and other long-established scholars in the field are equally incapable of reaching a consensus. In the first edition of his magisterial survey, *Political Terrorism: A Research Guide*,[130] Alex Schmid devoted more than a hundred pages to examining more than a hundred different definitions of terrorism in an effort to discover a broadly acceptable, reasonably comprehensive explication of the word. Four years and a second edition later, Schmid was no closer to the goal of his quest, conceding in the first sentence of the revised volume that the "search for an adequate definition is still on."[131] Walter Laqueur despaired of defining terrorism in both editions of his monumental work on the subject, maintaining that it is neither possible to do so nor worthwhile to make the attempt.[132] "Ten years of debates on typologies and definitions," he responded to a survey on definitions conducted by Schmid, "have not enhanced our knowledge of the subject to a significant degree."[133] Laqueur's contention is supported by the twenty-two different word categories occurring in the 109 different definitions that Schmid identified in his survey (see table 1). At the end of this exhaustive exercise, Schmid asks "whether the above list contains all the elements necessary for a good definition. The answer," he suggests, "is probably 'no.'"[134]

If it is impossible to define terrorism, as Laqueur argues, and fruitless to attempt to cobble together a truly comprehensive definition, as Schmid admits, are we to conclude that terrorism is impervious to precise, much less accurate definition? Not entirely. If we cannot define terrorism, then we can at least usefully distinguish it from other types of violence and identify the characteristics that make terrorism the distinct phenomenon of political violence that it is.

TABLE 1 Frequencies of definitional elements in 109 definitions of "terrorism"

Element	Frequency (%)
1 Violence, force	83.5
2 Political	65
3 Fear, terror emphasized	51
4 Threat	47
5 (Psychological) effects and (anticipated) reactions	41.5
6 Victim-target differentiation	37.5
7 Purposive, planned, systematic, organized action	32
8 Method of combat, strategy, tactic	30.5
9 Extranormality, in breach of accepted rules, without humanitarian constraints	30
10 Coercion, extortion, induction of compliance	28
11 Publicity aspect	21.5
12 Arbitrariness; impersonal, random character; indiscrimination	21
13 Civilians, noncombatants, neutrals, outsiders as victims	17.5
14 Intimidation	17
15 Innocence of victims emphasized	15.5
16 Group, movement, organization as perpetrator	14
17 Symbolic aspect, demonstration to others	13.5
18 Incalculability, unpredictability, unexpectedness of occurrence of violence	9
19 Clandestine, covert nature	9
20 Repetitiveness; serial or campaign character of violence	7
21 Criminal	6
22 Demands made on third parties	4

Source: Alex P. Schmid, Albert J. Jongman, et al., Political Terrorism: A New Guide to Actors, Authors, Concepts, Data Bases, Theories, and Literature (New Brunswick, N.J.: Transaction Books, 1988), pp. 5–6.

Distinctions as a Path to Definition

Guerrilla warfare and insurgency are good places to start. Terrorism is often confused or equated with, or treated as synonymous with, guerrilla warfare and insurgency. This is not entirely surprising, since guerrillas and insurgents often employ the same tactics (assassination, kidnapping, hit-and-run attack, bombings of public gathering places, hostage-taking, etc.) for the same purposes (to intimidate or coerce, thereby affecting behavior through the arousal of fear) as terrorists. In addition, terrorists as well as guerrillas and insurgents wear neither uniform nor identifying insignia and thus are often indistinguishable from noncombatants. However, despite the inclination to lump terrorists, guerrillas, and insurgents into the same catchall category of "irregulars," there are nonetheless fundamental differences among the three. "Guerrilla," for example, in its most widely accepted usage, is taken to refer to a numerically larger group of armed individuals,[135] who operate as a military unit, attack enemy military forces, and seize and hold territory (even if only ephemerally during daylight hours), while also exercising some form of sovereignty or control over a defined geographical area and its population. "Insurgents" share these same characteristics; however, their strategy and operations transcend hit-and-run attacks to embrace what in the past has variously been called "revolutionary guerrilla warfare,"[136] "modern revolutionary warfare," or "people's war"[137] but is today commonly termed "insurgency." Thus, in addition to the irregular military tactics that characterize guerrilla operations, insurgencies typically involve coordinated informational (e.g., propaganda) and psychological warfare efforts designed to mobilize popular support in a struggle against an established national government, imperialist power, or foreign occupying force.[138] Terrorists, however, do not function in the open as armed units, generally do not attempt to seize or hold territory, deliberately avoid engaging enemy military forces in combat, are constrained both numerically and logistically from undertaking concerted mass political mobilization efforts, and exercise no direct control or governance over a populace at either the local or the national level.[139]

It should be emphasized that none of these are pure categories and considerable overlap exists. Established terrorist groups like Hezbollah, FARC (Revolutionary Armed Forces of Colombia), and the LTTE (Liberation Tigers of Tamil Eelam, or Tamil Tigers), for example, are also often described as guerrilla movements because of their size, tactics, and control over territory and populace. Indeed, nearly a third of the thirty-seven groups on the U.S. State Department's "Designated Foreign Terrorist Organizations" list could just as easily be categorized as guerrillas.[140] The ongoing insurgency in Iraq has further contributed to this semantic confusion. The 2003 edition of the State Department's *Global Patterns of Terrorism* specifically cited the challenge of making meaningful distinctions between these categories, lamenting how the "line between insurgency and terrorism has become increasingly blurred as attacks on civilian targets have become more common."[141] Generally, the State Department considers attacks against U.S. and coalition military forces as insurgent operations and incidents such as the August 2003 suicide vehicle-borne bombings of the UN headquarters in Baghdad and the Jordanian embassy in that city, the assassinations of Japanese diplomats, and kidnapping and murder of aid workers and civilian contractors as terrorist attacks.[142] The definitional rule of thumb therefore is that secular Ba'athist Party loyalists and other former regime elements who stage guerrilla-like hit-and-run assaults or carry out attacks using roadside IEDs (improvised explosive devices) are deemed "insurgents," while foreign jihadists and domestic Islamic extremists who belong to groups like al Qaeda in Mesopotamia,[143] led by Abu Musab Zarqawi, and who are responsible for most of the suicide attacks and the videotaped beheading of hostages, are labeled terrorists.

It is also useful to distinguish terrorists from ordinary criminals. Like terrorists, criminals use violence as a means to attain a specific end. However, while the violent act itself may be similar—kidnapping, shooting, and arson, for example—the purpose or motivation clearly is different. Whether the criminal employs violence as a means to obtain money, to acquire material goods, or to kill or injure a specific victim for pay, he is acting primarily for selfish, personal motivations (usually material gain). Moreover, unlike terrorism, the ordinary criminal's violent act is not designed or intended to have consequences or create psychological repercussions beyond the act itself. The criminal may of course use some short-term act of violence to "terrorize" his victim, such as waving a gun in the face of a bank clerk during a robbery in order to ensure the clerk's expeditious compliance. In these instances, however, the bank robber is conveying no "message" (political or otherwise) through his act of violence beyond facilitating the rapid handing over of his "loot." The criminal's act therefore is not meant to have any effect reaching beyond either the incident itself or the immediate victim. Further, the violence is neither conceived nor intended to convey any message to anyone other than the bank clerk himself, whose rapid cooperation is the robber's only objective. Perhaps most fundamentally, the criminal is not concerned with influencing or affecting public opinion; he simply wants to abscond with his money or accomplish his mercenary task in the quickest and easiest way possible so that he may reap his reward and enjoy the fruits of his labors. By contrast, the fundamental aim of the terrorist's violence is ultimately to change "the system"—about which the ordinary criminal, of course, couldn't care less.[144]

The terrorist is also very different from the lunatic assassin, who may use identical tactics (e.g., shooting, bombing) and perhaps even seeks the same objective (e.g., the death of a political figure). However, while the tactics and targets of terrorists and lone assassins are often identical, their purpose is different. Whereas the terrorist's goal is again ineluctably *political* (to change or fundamentally alter a political system through his violent act), the lunatic assassin's goal is more often intrinsically idiosyncratic, completely egocentric and deeply personal. John Hinckley, who tried to kill President Reagan in 1981 to impress the actress Jodie Foster, is a case in point. He acted not from political motivation or ideological conviction but to fulfill some profound personal quest (killing the president to impress his screen idol). Such entirely *apolitical* motivations can in no way be compared to the rationalizations used by the Narodnaya Volya to justify its campaign of tyrannicide against the czar and his minions, nor even to the Irish Republican Army's efforts to assassinate Prime Minister Margaret Thatcher or her successor, John Major, in hopes of dramatically changing British policy toward Northern Ireland. Further, just as one person cannot credibly claim to be a political party, so a lone individual cannot be considered to constitute a terrorist group. In this respect, even though Sirhan Sirhan's assassination of presidential candidate and U.S. senator Robert Kennedy in 1968 had a political motive (to protest against U.S. support for Israel), it is debatable whether the murder should be defined as a terrorist act since Sirhan belonged to no organized political group and there is no evidence that he was directly influenced or inspired by an identifiable political or terrorist movement. Rather, Sirhan acted entirely on his own, out of deep personal frustration and a profound animus.[145]

Finally, the point should be emphasized that, unlike the ordinary criminal or the lunatic assassin, the terrorist is not pursuing purely egocentric goals; he is not driven by the wish to line his own pocket or satisfy some personal need or grievance. The terrorist is fundamentally an *altruist*: he believes that he is serving a "good" cause designed to achieve a greater good for a wider constituency—whether real or imagined—that the terrorist and his organization purport to represent. The criminal, by comparison, serves no cause at all, just his own personal aggrandizement and material satiation. Indeed, a "terrorist without a cause (at least in his own mind)," Konrad Kellen has argued, "is not a terrorist."[146] Yet the possession or identification of a cause is not a sufficient criterion for labeling someone a terrorist. In this key respect, the difference between terrorists and political extremists is clear. Many people, of course, harbor all sorts of radical and extreme beliefs and opinions, and many of them belong to radical or even illegal or proscribed political organizations. However, if they do not use violence in the pursuit of their beliefs, they cannot be considered terrorists. The terrorist is fundamentally a *violent intellectual*, prepared to use and, indeed, committed to using force in the attainment of his goals.

In the past, terrorism was arguably easier to define than it is today. To qualify as terrorism, violence had to be perpetrated by an individual acting at the behest of or on the behalf of some existent organizational entity or movement with at least some conspiratorial structure and identifiable chain of command. This criterion, however, is no longer sufficient. In recent years, a variety of terrorist movements have increasingly adopted a strategy of "leaderless networks" in order to thwart law enforcement and intelligence agency efforts to penetrate them.[147] Craig Rosebraugh, the publicist for a radical environmentalist group calling itself the Earth Liberation Front (ELF), described the movement in a 2001 interview as a deliberately conceived "series of cells across the country with no chain of command and no membership roll . . . only a shared philosophy." It is designed this way, he continued, so that "there's no central leadership where [the authorities] can go and knock off the top guy and [the movement then] will be defunct."[148] Indeed, an ELF recruitment video narrated by Rosebraugh advises "individuals interested in becoming active in the Earth Liberation Front to . . . form your own close-knit autonomous cells made of trustworthy and sincere people. Remember, the ELF and each cell within it are anonymous not only to one another but to the general public."[149] As a senior FBI official conceded, the ELF is "not a group you can put your fingers on" and thus is extremely difficult to infiltrate.[150]

This type of networked adversary is a new and different breed of terrorist entity to which traditional organizational constructs and definitions do not neatly apply. It is populated by individuals who are ideologically motivated, inspired, and animated by a movement or a leader, but who neither formally belong to a specific, identifiable terrorist group nor directly follow orders issued by its leadership and are therefore outside any established chain of command. It is a structure and approach that al Qaeda has also sought to implement. Ayman al-Zawahiri, bin Laden's deputy and al Qaeda's chief theoretician, extolled this strategy in his seminal clarion call to jihad (Arabic for "striving," but also "holy war"), *Knights Under the Prophet's Banner:*

Meditations on the Jihadist Movement. The chapter titled "Small Groups Could Frighten the Americans" explains:

Tracking down Americans and the Jews is not impossible. Killing them with a single bullet, a stab, or a device made up of a popular mix of explosives or hitting them with an iron rod is not impossible. Burning down their property with Molotov cocktails is not difficult. With the available means, small groups could prove to be a frightening horror for the Americans and the Jews.[151]

Whether termed "leaderless resistance," "phantom cell networks," "autonomous leadership units,"[152] "autonomous cells," a "network of networks,"[153] or "lone wolves," this new conflict paradigm conforms to what John Arquilla and David Ronfeldt call "netwar":

an emerging mode of conflict (and crime) at societal levels, short of traditional military warfare, in which the protagonists use network forms of organization and related doctrines, strategies, and technologies attuned to the information age. These protagonists are likely to consist of dispersed organizations, small groups, and individuals who communicate, coordinate, and conduct their campaigns in an internetted manner, often without precise central command.[154]

Unlike the hierarchical, pyramidal structure that typified terrorist groups of the past, this new type of organization is looser, flatter, more linear. Although there is a leadership of sorts, its role may be more titular than actual, with less a direct command and control relationship than a mostly inspirational and motivational one. "The organizational structure," Arquilla and Ronfeldt explain,

is quite flat. There is no single central leader or commander; the network as a whole (but not necessarily each node) has little to no hierarchy. There may be multiple leaders. Decisionmaking and operations are decentralized and depend on consultative consensus-building that allows for local initiative and autonomy. The design is both acephalous (headless) and polycephalous (Hydra-headed)—it has not precise heart or head, although not all nodes may be "created equal."[155]

As part of this "leaderless" strategy, autonomous local terrorist cells plan and execute attacks independently of one another or of any central command authority, but through their individual terrorist efforts seek the eventual attainment of a terrorist organization or movement's wider goals. Although these ad hoc terrorist cells and lone individuals may be less sophisticated and therefore less capable than their more professional, trained counterparts who are members of actual established terrorist groups, these "amateur" terrorists can be just as bloody-minded. A recent FBI strategic planning document, for instance, describes lone wolves as the "most significant domestic terrorism threat" that the United States faces. "They typically draw ideological inspiration from formal terrorist organizations," the 2004–09 plan states, "but operate on the fringes of those movements. Despite their ad hoc nature and generally limited resources, they can mount high-profile, extremely destructive attacks, and their operational planning is often difficult to detect."[156]

Conclusion

By distinguishing terrorists from other types of criminals and irregular fighters and terrorism from other forms of crime and irregular warfare, we come to appreciate that terrorism is

- ineluctably political in aims and motives;
- violent—or, equally important, threatens violence;
- designed to have far-reaching psychological repercussions beyond the immediate victim or target;
- conducted *either* by an organization with an identifiable chain of command or conspiratorial cell structure (whose members wear no uniform or identifying insignia) or by individuals or a small collection of individuals directly influenced, motivated, or inspired by the ideological aims or example of some existent terrorist movement and/or its leaders; and
- perpetrated by a subnational group or nonstate entity.

We may therefore now attempt to define terrorism as the deliberate creation and exploitation of fear through violence or the threat of violence in the pursuit of political change. All terrorist acts involve violence or the threat of violence. Terrorism is specifically designed to have far-reaching psychological effects beyond the immediate victim(s) or object of the terrorist attack. It is meant to instill fear within, and thereby intimidate, a wider "target audience" that might include a rival ethnic or religious group, an entire country, a national government or political party, or public opinion in general. Terrorism is designed to create power where there is none or to consolidate power where there is very little. Through the publicity generated by their violence, terrorists seek to obtain the leverage, influence, and power they otherwise lack to effect political change on either a local or an international scale.

Chapter 2

The End of Empire and the Origins of Contemporary Terrorism

Although terrorism motivated by ethno-nationalist/separatist aspirations had emerged from within the moribund Ottoman and Hapsburg empires during the three decades immediately preceding the First World War, it was only after 1945 that this phenomenon became a more pervasive global force. Two separate, highly symbolic events that had occurred early in the Second World War abetted its subsequent development. At the time, the repercussions for postwar anticolonial struggles of the fall of Singapore and the proclamation of the Atlantic Charter could not possibly have been anticipated. Yet both, in different ways, exerted a strong influence on indigenous nationalist movements, demonstrating as they did the vulnerability of once-mighty empires and the hypocrisy of wartime pledges of support for self-determination.

On February 15, 1942, the British Empire suffered the worst defeat in its history when Singapore fell to the invading Japanese forces. Whatever Singapore's strategic value, its real significance—according to the foremost military strategist of his day, Basil Liddell Hart—was as the

> outstanding symbol of Western power in the Far East. . . . Its easy capture in February 1942 was shattering to British, and European, prestige

in Asia. No belated re-entry could efface the impression. The white man had lost his ascendancy with the disproof of his magic. The realisation of his vulnerability fostered and encouraged the post-war spread of Asiatic revolt against European domination or intrusion.[1]

Indeed, within weeks Japan had also conquered the Dutch East Indies (Indonesia) and Burma. Hong Kong had already capitulated the previous Christmas, and more than a year earlier Japan had imposed its rule over French Indochina. Thus, when the American garrison holding out on Corregidor in the Philippines finally surrendered in May 1942, Japan's conquest of South-East Asia—and the destruction of the British, French, Dutch, and American empires there—was complete.

The long-term impact of these events was profound. Native peoples who had previously believed in the invincibility of their European colonial overlords hereafter saw their former masters in a starkly different light. Not only had the vast British Empire been dealt a crushing blow, but American pledges of peace and security to its Pacific possessions had been similarly shattered. France's complete impotence in the face of Japanese bullying over Indochina had greatly undermined its imperial stature among the Vietnamese, and in Indonesia, Japanese promises of independence effectively negated any lingering feelings of loyalty to the Dutch. In the blink of an eye, the European powers' prewar arguments that their variegated Asian subjects were incapable of governing themselves were swept aside by Japan's policy of devolving self-government to local administrations and nominal independence to the countries they now occupied. Paradoxically, in many places it was the natives who now ruled the interned Europeans—many of whom found themselves forced to perform the most menial and backbreaking tasks. It is not surprising, therefore, that even as the tide of war shifted in the Allies' favor over the following years, almost all these peoples resolved never again to come under European imperial rule.

It was not only the Asian subjects of these declining colonial powers who clamored for independence and self-determination. The litany of humiliating defeats had struck responsive chords in other places also, everywhere challenging the myth of European—indeed, Western—power and military superiority, if not omnipotence. In the Middle East as well as in Africa, India, the Mediterranean, and North Africa, indigenous peoples chafed at the prospect of returning to their prewar colonial status quo. They were encouraged, however unintentionally, by promises of independence and self-determination made by the Allies early in the Second World War.[2] Even before the United States had entered the war in 1941, President Franklin D.

Roosevelt had met with Britain's prime minister, Winston Churchill, on a warship off the coast of Newfoundland to formulate both countries' postwar aims. The result was an eight-point document known as the Atlantic Charter, whose main purpose, one historian has observed, was to "impress enemy opinion with the justice of the western cause."[3] Its effects, however, went far beyond that lofty aim.

The charter's first point innocuously affirmed that both countries sought no "aggrandisement, territorial or other," from the war; it was the next two points that would be the source of future difficulties for the European powers. The second point declared unequivocally that neither Britain nor the United States desired to "see . . . territorial changes that do not accord with the freely expressed wishes of the peoples concerned," while the third point further pledged both countries to "respect the right of all peoples to choose the form of government under which they will live."[4] These principles were embodied in the "Declaration of the United Nations," agreed to by Britain and the United States on January 1, 1942, and subsequently signed by all the governments at war with Germany, thus committing their countries to respect promises that in some instances they had no intention of keeping. Although on the first anniversary of the charter's signing Churchill attempted to qualify and restrict the terms of the original agreement—arguing that it was not intended that these principles should apply to either Asia or Africa, and especially not to India and Palestine, but only to those peoples in hitherto sovereign countries conquered by Germany, Italy, and Japan[5]—the damage had already been done. Indeed, all subsequent efforts by the European colonial powers to redefine or reinterpret the charter in ways favorable to the prolongation of their imperial rule fell for the most part on deaf ears.

The situation in postwar Algeria was perhaps typical of the bitterness, engendered by broken promises and misplaced hopes, that nurtured intractable conflict. In 1943, shortly after the Allied landings had liberated North Africa from Vichy rule, a delegation of Algerian Muslims sought an audience with the newly installed Free French commander, General Henri Giraud. Their request amounted to nothing more than recognition of the rights and freedoms that had been so loftily proclaimed in the Atlantic Charter, of which, of course, the French government-in-exile was a signatory. Giraud's reply was dismissively brusque. "I don't care about reforms," he thundered. "I want soldiers first."[6] The ever-compliant Algerians obligingly provided these volunteers—much as they had some thirty years before, but they did so now in the expectation, shared by other European powers' colonial subjects elsewhere, that their loyalty would be rewarded appropriately at the war's end. As was the case in at least a dozen other colonial settings, however, their anticipation was to be disappointed. Indeed, by 1947 the future leader of the anti-British guerrilla campaign in Cyprus, General George Grivas (a Greek Cypriot who had fought beside the Allies), had already despaired in the face of repeated prevarications concerning Britain's own wartime promises of self-determination. "More and more," he recalled, "it seemed to me that only a revolution would liberate my homeland."[7] The Algerians were rapidly coming to the same conclusion. They were further encouraged by the catastrophic defeat inflicted on the French at Dien Bien Phu in 1954 and by France's subsequent ignominious withdrawal from Indochina. Meanwhile, a revolt against British rule had broken out in Palestine, waged by two small Jewish terrorist organizations—the Irgun Zvai Le'umi (National Military Organization, or Irgun) and the Lohamei Herut Yisrael (Freedom Fighters for Israel, known to Jews by its Hebrew acronym, Lehi, and to the British as the Stern Gang). The Irgun's campaign was the more significant of the two, in that it established a revolutionary model that thereafter was emulated and embraced by both anticolonial- and postcolonial-era terrorist groups around the world.

Postwar Palestine

Palestine had, of course, long been the scene of numerous riots and other manifestations of intercommunal violence that between 1936 and 1939 had culminated in a full-scale rebellion by its Arab inhabitants. In 1937, a new element was added to the country's incendiary landscape when the Irgun commenced retaliatory terrorist attacks on the Arabs. The group expanded its operations to include British targets in 1939 following the government's promulgation of a White Paper in May that imposed severe restrictions on Jewish immigration to Palestine, thereby closing one of the few remaining avenues of escape available to European Jews fleeing Hitler. But the Irgun's inchoate revolt against British rule was short-lived. Less than three months after it began, Britain was at war with Germany. Confronted by the prospect of the greater menace of a victorious Nazi Germany, the Irgun declared a truce and announced the suspension of all anti-British operations for the war's duration. Like the rest of the Jewish community in Palestine, who had also pledged to support the British war effort, the Irgun hoped that this loyalty would later result in the recognition of Zionist claims to statehood.

In May 1942 a young private attached to General Wladyslaw Anders's Polish army-in-exile arrived in Palestine. Menachem Begin's journey had been a circuitous one. Born in 1913 in Brest Litovsk, Poland, the future prime minister of Israel (1977–83) had first become involved in Zionist politics as a teenager when he joined Betar, a right-wing nationalist Jewish youth group. By the time he had received his law degree from Warsaw University in 1935, Begin was head of the group's Organization Department for Poland. Three years later he was appointed its national commander. However, when Germany invaded Poland in September 1939, Begin was forced to flee to Lithuania. A year later, Russian secret police arrested him on the ironic charge of being "an agent of British imperialism." After spending nine months in a local jail, Begin was sentenced to eight years of "correctional labor." In June 1941, when Germany invaded Russia, he was on a Russian ship carrying political prisoners to a Stalinist labor camp in Siberia. A reprieve came in the form of an offer to join the Polish army or continue his journey. Begin chose the former and found himself in a unit ordered to Palestine. Shortly after his arrival, he established contact with the Irgun high command.

Since the suspension of its revolt, the Irgun had fallen into disarray. The deaths of its ideological mentor, Vladimir Jabotinsky, in August 1940 and its military commander, David Raziel, nine months later had deprived the group of leadership and direction at a time when its self-imposed dormancy required someone at the top with the vision and organizational skills necessary to hold it together. Throughout 1943, Begin met with the Irgun's surviving senior commanders to discuss the group's future. As the war against Germany moved decisively in the Allies' favor, they became convinced that the Irgun should resume its revolt. Four dominant considerations influenced this decision. First and foremost was news of the terrible fate that had befallen European Jewry under Nazi domination. Second, the expiration in March 1944 of the White Paper's rigidly enforced five-year immigration quota would likely choke off all future Jewish immigration to Palestine. Third, the Irgun's leaders agreed that the reasoning behind the self-imposed truce they had declared four years before—that harming Britain might help Germany—was no longer tenable since the course of the Second World War had now virtually assured an Allied victory. Finally, by renewing the revolt, the Irgun's revamped high command sought to position themselves and their organization at the vanguard of the active realization of the Jews' political and nationalist aspirations.

On December 1, 1943, Begin formally assumed command of the group and finalized plans for the resumption of anti-British operations. As a lowly enlisted man in an exile army with only the bare minimum of formal military training, Begin was an unlikely strategist. But he possessed an uncanny analytical ability to cut right to the heart of an issue and an intuitive sense about the interplay of violence, politics, and propaganda that ideally qualified him to lead a terrorist organization. Begin's strategy was simple. The handful of men and the few weapons that in 1943 constituted the Irgun could never hope to challenge the British Army on the battlefield and win. Instead, the group would function in the setting and operate in the manner that best afforded the terrorist with means of concealment and escape. Based in the city, its members would bury themselves within the surrounding community, indistinguishable from ordinary, law-abiding citizens. At the appropriate moment, they would emerge from the shadows to strike, then disappear back into the anonymity of Palestine's urban neighborhoods, remaining safely beyond the reach of the authorities. The Irgun's plan, therefore, was not to defeat Britain militarily but to use terrorist violence to undermine the government's prestige and control of Palestine by striking at symbols of British rule. "History and our observation," Begin later recalled, "persuaded us that if we could succeed in destroying the government's prestige in Eretz Israel [Hebrew: literally "the Land of Israel"], the removal of its rule would follow automatically. Thenceforward, we gave no peace to this weak spot. Throughout all the years of our uprising, we hit at the British Government's prestige, deliberately, tirelessly, unceasingly."[8]

In contrast to other colonial rebellions that either had sought decisive military victories in actual battle or had relied on a prolonged strategy of attrition, the Irgun adopted a strategy that involved the relentless targeting of those institutions of government that unmistakably represented Britain's oppressive rule of Palestine. Thus the Irgun recommenced operations in February 1944 with the simultaneous bombings of immigration department offices in Palestine's three major cities—Jerusalem, Tel Aviv, and Haifa. Subsequent attacks were mounted against the government land registry offices, from which the White Paper's provisions restricting Jewish land purchase were administered; the department of taxation and finance, responsible for collecting the revenue used to fund the government's repressive policies; and of course the security forces—the police and army—that were charged with enforcement of the White Paper.

The Irgun's most spectacular operation was without doubt its bombing in July 1946 of Jerusalem's King David Hotel. Although much has been written about this controversial incident, it is worth recalling that the King David was no ordinary hotel. On two floors of its southern wing (beneath which the explosives were placed), the hotel housed the nerve center of British rule in Palestine: the government secretariat and headquarters of British military forces in Palestine and Transjordan. The attack's target, therefore, was neither the hotel itself nor the people working or staying in it, but the government and military offices located there. Nor was its purpose random, indiscriminate carnage. Unlike many terrorist groups today, the Irgun's strategy was not deliberately to target or wantonly harm civilians. At the same time, though, the claim of Begin and other apologists that warnings were issued to evacuate the hotel before the blast cannot absolve either the group or its commander from responsibility for the ninety-one people killed and forty-five others injured—men and women, Arabs, Jews, and Britons alike. Indeed, whatever nonlethal intentions the Irgun may or may not have had, the fact remains that a tragedy of almost unparalleled magnitude was inflicted at the King David Hotel, so that to this day the bombing remains one of the world's single most lethal terrorist incidents of the twentieth century.

Despite—or perhaps because of—the tragic loss of life, so far as the Irgun was concerned the bombing achieved its objective: attracting worldwide attention to the group's struggle and the worsening situation in Palestine. Editorials in all the British newspapers focused on the nugatory results of recent military operations against the terrorists that had been previously trumpeted as great successes. Typical of these was the *Manchester Guardian*'s observation that the bombing "will be a shock to those who imagined that the Government's firmness had put a stop to Jewish terrorism and had brought about an easier situation in Palestine. In fact, the opposite is the truth."[9] These reactions accorded perfectly with Begin's plan to foster a climate of fear and alarm in Palestine so pervasive as to undermine confidence both there and in Britain in the government's ability to maintain order. Indeed, in these circumstances, the government could respond only by imposing on Palestine a harsh regimen of security measures encompassing a daily routine of curfews, roadblocks, snap checks, cordon-and-search operations and, for a time, even martial law. The failure of these measures to stop the Irgun's unrelenting terrorist campaign would, Begin hoped, have the effect of further underscoring the government's weakness. He also banked on the fact that the massive disruptions caused to daily life and commerce by the harsh and repressive countermeasures that the British were forced to take would further alienate the community from the government, thwart British efforts to obtain the community's cooperation against the terrorists, and create in the minds of the Jews an image of the army and the police as oppressors rather than protectors. Moreover, the more conspicuous the security forces seemed, the stronger the terrorists appeared.

At the foundation of this strategy was Begin's belief that the British, unlike the Germans who during the war had carried out wholesale reprisals against civilians, were incapable of such barbarity.[10] "We knew," he explained, "that Eretz Israel, in consequence of the revolt, resembled a glass house. The world was looking into it with ever-increasing interest and could see most of what was happening inside. . . . Arms were our weapons of attack; the transparency of the 'glass' was our shield of defence."[11] By compelling a liberal democracy like Britain to take increasingly repressive measures against the public, the terrorists sought to push Britain to the limit of its endurance. In this respect, the Irgun did not have to defeat Britain militarily; it had only to avoid losing. Accordingly, British tactical "successes" did nothing to change the balance of forces or bring the security forces any closer to victory. Rather, measures such as massive cordon-and-search operations and the imposition of martial law proved to bring only ephemeral benefits, bought at the cost of estranging the population from the government. Nearly a quarter of a century later, the Brazilian revolutionary theorist Carlos Marighela would advocate the same strategy in his famous "Mini-Manual," the *Handbook of Urban Guerrilla War*.[12]

In sum, this was not a war of numbers. Success was measured not in terms of casualties inflicted (between 1945 and 1947, the worst years of the conflict, just under one hundred fifty British soldiers were killed) or assets destroyed, but—precisely as Begin had wanted—by psychological impact. In place of a conventional military strategy of confrontation in battle, Begin and his lieutenants conceived operations that were designed less to kill than to tarnish the government's prestige, demoralize its security forces, and undermine Britain's resolve to remain in Palestine. Explaining his strategy, Begin argued, "The very existence of an underground must, in the end, undermine the prestige of a colonial regime that lives by the legend of its omnipotence. Every attack which it fails to prevent is a blow at its standing. Even if the attack does not succeed, it makes a dent in that prestige, and that dent widens into a crack which is extended with every succeeding attack."[13] Thus, even though the British forces outnumbered the terrorists by twenty to one—so that there was, according to one account, "one armed soldier to each adult male Jew in Palestine"[14]—even with this overwhelming numerical superiority, the British were still unable to destroy the Irgun and maintain order in Palestine.

Finally, an integral and innovative part of the Irgun's strategy was Begin's use of daring and dramatic acts of violence to attract international attention to Palestine and thereby publicize simultaneously the Zionists' grievances against Britain and their claims for statehood. In an era long before the advent of CNN and instantaneous satellite-transmitted news broadcasts, the Irgun deliberately attempted to appeal to a worldwide audience far beyond the immediate confines of the local struggle, beyond even the ruling regime's own homeland. In particular, the Irgun—like its nonviolent and less violent Zionist counterparts—sought to generate sympathy and marshal support among powerful allies such as the Jewish community in the United States and its elected representatives in Congress and the White House, as well as among the delegates to the fledgling United Nations, to bring pressure to bear on Britain to grant Jewish statehood. The success of this strategy, Begin claims, may be seen in the paucity of global coverage afforded to the civil war that had erupted in Greece after the Second World War, compared to that devoted to events in Palestine. Palestine, he wrote, had undeniably become a "centre of world interest. The revolt had made it so. It is a fact," Begin maintains,

> that no partisan struggle had been so publicized throughout the world as was ours. . . . The reports on our operations, under screaming head-lines, covered the front pages of newspapers everywhere, particularly in the United States. . . . The interest of the newspapers is the measure of the interest of the public. And the public—not only Jews but non-Jews too—were manifestly interested in the blows we were striking in Eretz Israel.[15]

In this respect, pro-Irgun Jewish American lobbyists were noticeably successful in obtaining the passage of resolutions by the U.S. Congress condemning "British oppression" and reaffirming American support for the establishment of a Jewish state in Palestine.[16] These activities, which presaged the efforts undertaken more recently by Irish American activists on behalf of Sinn Fein and the IRA, had similarly corrosive effects on Anglo-American relations more than half a century ago.

By 1947 the Irgun had in fact achieved its objectives. Reporting on the situation to Washington, the American consul general in Jerusalem observed that

> with [British] officials attempting to administrate from behind masses of barbed wire, in heavily defended buildings, and with the same officials (minus wives and children evacuated some time ago) living in pathetic seclusion in "security zones," one cannot escape the conclusion that the Government of Palestine is a hunted organization with little hope of ever being able to cope with conditions in this country as they exist today.[17]

Indeed, each successive terrorist outrage illuminated the government's inability to curb, much less defeat the terrorists. Already sapped by the Second World War, Britain's limited economic resources were further strained by the cost of deploying so large a military force to Palestine to cope with the tide of violence submerging the country. Public opinion in Britain, already ill disposed to the continued loss of life and expenditure of effort in an unwinnable situation, was further inflamed by incidents such as the King David Hotel bombing and the Irgun's hanging in July 1947 of two sergeants in retaliation for the government's execution of three convicted Irgun terrorists. As the renowned British historian of the Middle East Elizabeth Monroe has noted with respect to the hangings: "The British public had taken Palestine in its stride . . . and had looked upon 'disturbances' and 'violence' there much as it viewed 'the troubles' in Ireland—as an unpleasant experience that was part of the white man's burden." All this changed, however, with the cold-blooded murder of the sergeants. Photographs of the grim death scene—depicting the two corpses just inches above the ground, the sergeants' hooded faces and bloodied shirts—were emblazoned across the front pages of British newspapers under headlines decrying their execution as an act of "medieval barbarity." As inured to the almost daily reports of the death and deprivation suffered by the army in Palestine as the British public was, the brutal execution of the two sergeants made a deep and unalterable impression on the national psyche. "All home comment on that deed," Monroe continued, was "different in tone from that on earlier terrorist acts, many of which caused greater loss of life—for instance, the blowing up of the officers' club or of the King David Hotel."[18] For both the British public and the press, the murders seemed to demonstrate the futility of the situation in Palestine and the pointlessness of remaining there any longer than was absolutely necessary.

At the time, Britain was also, of course, coming under intense pressure from the United States and other quarters regarding the admission to Palestine of tens of thousands of Jewish displaced persons still languishing throughout liberated Europe and was itself trying to stem the flood of illegal Jewish immigrants attempting to enter Palestine. In addition, throughout the summer of 1947 the Special Committee on Palestine (UNSCOP) appointed by the UN General Assembly was completing its investigations regarding the country's future.[19] It is a measure of the Irgun's success that Begin was twice granted audiences with the committee to explain the group's aims, motivations, and vision for a Jewish state in Palestine. The committee's unanimous recommendation calling for the immediate termination of British rule and granting of independence to Palestine finally forced the government's hand.[20] In September the colonial secretary, Arthur Creech-Jones, announced that Britain would no longer be responsible for governing Palestine and that all civilian and military personnel would be evacuated as soon as was practicable.

A decade and a half after the event, Creech-Jones cited four pivotal considerations that influenced the government's decision. First, there were the irreconcilable differences between Palestine's Arab and Jewish communities; second, the drain on Britain's shrinking financial resources imposed by the country's heavy military commitment in Palestine; third, the force of international, American, and parliamentary opinion; and finally—and, he believed, most significant—the public outcry in Britain that followed the Irgun's hanging of the two sergeants. Describing the confluence of events that compelled the government to surrender the mandate, the former colonial secretary recalled specifically, "Terrorism was at its worst and the British public seemed unable to stand much more." Hence, with "accelerating speed," Creech-Jones explained, "the Cabinet was pushed to the conclusion that they could [no] longer support the Mandate."[21] On May 15, 1948, Britain's rule over Palestine formally ended and the establishment of the State of Israel was proclaimed. In a communiqué issued that same day by the Irgun, Begin declared:

After many years of underground warfare, years of persecution and suffering . . . [the] Hebrew revolt of 1944–48 has been crowned with success. . . . The rule of enslavement of Britain in our country has been beaten, uprooted, has crumbled and been dispersed. . . . The State of Israel has arisen. And it has arisen "Only Thus": through blood, fire, a strong hand and a mighty arm, with suffering and sacrifices.[22]

The Anticolonial Struggles of the 1950s: Cyprus and Algeria

The Irgun's revolt provided a template for subsequent anticolonial uprisings elsewhere. Indeed, the most effective irredentist struggles of the immediate postwar era were those that emulated Begin's strategy and deliberately sought to appeal to—and thereby attract the attention and sympathy of—an international audience. "Our intention," explained General George Grivas, the founder and commander of EOKA (Ethniki Organosis Kyprion Agoniston, or National Organization of Cypriot Fighters), in his memoirs, "was to focus the eyes of the world on Cyprus and force the British to fulfil their promises."[23] Similarly, the 1954 proclamation of revolt against French rule of Algeria by the FLN (Front de Liberation Nationale, or National Liberation Front) prominently cited the "internationalism of the Algerian problem" as among its principal goals.[24]

In pursuit of this end, both groups also made a conscious effort to appeal directly to the United Nations for help. EOKA's own proclamation of revolt, for example, was specifically addressed to "Diplomats of the World." It called upon them to "Look to your duty. It is shameful that, in the twentieth century, people should have to shed blood for freedom, that divine gift for which we too fought at your side and for which you, at least, claim that you fought against Nazism."[25] In Algeria, FLN offensives, general strikes, and other demonstrations were timed to occur when the UN General Assembly reconvened or was already scheduled to discuss the conflict. In January 1957 the fabled Battle of Algiers, immortalized by the 1966 Gillo Pontecorvo film of the same name, when the FLN unleashed its campaign of mass urban terrorism, was deliberately choreographed to coincide with the General Assembly's annual opening session. The FLN communiqué announcing the strike that accompanied the new terrorist offensive candidly admitted to this timing, announcing its desire to "bestow an incontestable authority upon our delegates at the United Nations in order to convince those rare diplomats still hesitant or possessing illusions about France's liberal policy."[26] To a large extent, therefore, the success of both EOKA and the FLN in ending foreign rule of their respective countries was predicated upon their ability to attract external attention to their respective struggles, much as the Irgun had a decade before.

In Cyprus, from the very start, Grivas appreciated the necessity of reaching out to an audience beyond the immediate geographical boundaries of his group's struggle. "The enlightenment of international public opinion," he recognized, "was bound to play an important part in bringing home to all concerned the Cypriot people's demand for self-determination. It is a fact that there were many foreigners and even United Nations representatives who were completely ignorant of why we were demanding our freedom."[27] Accordingly, Grivas enshrined this principle in the "Preparatory General Plan" that he had formulated in 1953—two years before the campaign actually began—whose opening paragraph clearly states the fundamental objective "to arouse international public opinion . . . by deeds of heroism and self-sacrifice which will focus attention on Cyprus until our aims are achieved."[28] Although there is no evidence that Grivas ever read Begin's book (an English-language translation of *The Revolt* had been published in London and New York in 1951) or studied the Irgun's campaign, the parallels between the two struggles are unmistakable. Grivas's strategy, like Begin's, was not to win an outright military victory against the numerically superior British forces but to rely on dramatic, well-orchestrated, and appropriately timed acts of violence to focus international attention on the situation in Cyprus and the Greek Cypriots' demand for *enosis*—unification with Greece.

"My small force was outnumbered by more than a hundred to one," Grivas later recalled, "but, as I have said, this made no difference to the type of subversive warfare I was planning."[29] His plan was to deploy the majority of EOKA forces in the island's urban centers, where they were organized into individual terrorist cells numbering no more than eight to ten men each. Their mission was to tie up as many British troops as possible on static guard duties in the cities, thereby allowing EOKA to consolidate its control over the rest of the island. In words reminiscent of Begin's, Grivas explained in his treatise on guerrilla warfare that

> our strategy consisted in turning the whole island into a single field of bat-
> tle in which there was no distinction between front and rear, so that the
> enemy should at no time and in no place feel himself secure. The enemy
> never knew where and when we might strike. . . . This strategy achieved
> the dispersal, intimidation and wearing down of the enemy's forces and
> especially serious consequences resulting from our use of surprise.[30]

By concentrating on urban operations, as the Irgun had in Palestine, EOKA also gained immediate access to the news media dispatched to the island to cover the escalating violence. Had EOKA, like traditional guer-rilla forces, confined its operations to the island's rugged and isolated rural areas and mountain ranges, it would arguably have lost this access and for-feited the exposure so critical to Grivas's strategy. The urban terrorist cam-paign was thus pivotal in securing the propaganda platform required by the group to broadcast its cause to the world. In this respect, Grivas was able to derive great satisfaction from the fact that within five months of the revolt's proclamation, EOKA had succeeded in attaining what a decade of patient diplomacy and insistent lobbying had failed to achieve: UN consideration of the Greek Cypriots' nationalist claims. Hitherto, the General Assembly had upheld British arguments that the situation in Cyprus was an entirely *inter-nal* matter and therefore outside the organization's purview. Now, for the first time, Cyprus had been placed on the UN's agenda. "This proved," Grivas later recalled, "that inside this international body the idea was beginning to penetrate that something must be done about the Cyprus question."[31]

Indeed, by the end of 1955, Grivas had succeeded in plunging the island into complete disorder. An average of two British soldiers or policemen were being killed each week. The security forces had been thrown on the defen-sive, kept off balance by repeated EOKA hit-and-run attacks and unable to mount any effective offensive operations. Like Begin, Grivas also calculated that the unrelenting terrorist onslaught would sap the morale of British forces and compel them to overreact with counterproductive, self-defeat-ing measures directed against the law-abiding Greek-Cypriot community.

"The 'security forces' set about their work in a manner which might have been deliberately designed to drive the population into our arms," Grivas recalled. "These attempts to frighten the people away from EOKA always had exactly the opposite effect to that intended: the population were merely bound more closely to the Organisation."[32] Once again, the fundamental asymmetry between the terrorists' apparent ability to strike anywhere, at any time, and the security forces' inability to protect all conceivable targets, all the time, was glaringly demonstrated. As in Palestine, the more visible and pervasive the security forces in Cyprus became, the greater the public frustration caused by disruption to daily life, and the more powerful and omnipresent the terrorists appeared. At the height of the conflict, British security forces on Cyprus totaled nearly 40,000 men, arrayed against a hard core of fewer than 400 active terrorists, backed by some 750 "auxiliaries."[33] Again, as in Palestine, this was not a war of "numbers." The massive deployment of British troops had little overall impact on the situation. As Grivas later reflected about his opponent commanding the British forces, Field Marshal Sir John Harding: "He underrated his enemy on the one hand, and overweighted his forces on the other. But one does not use a tank to catch field mice—a cat will do the job better."[34]

Throughout the campaign, Grivas coordinated his underground campaign with the aboveground diplomatic efforts of Archbishop Makarios III (Michael Christodoros Mouskos). As the appointed head of the Ethnarchy (Church Council) of Cyprus, Makarios was also the Greek-Cypriot community's de facto political leader. He and Grivas had met as early as 1950 to plan the general outline of the revolt, and prelate and soldier worked closely together throughout the struggle to achieve their shared goal of *enosis*. Thus the symbiotic relationship that today exists between Sinn Fein ("We Ourselves," an Irish nationalist political party) and the IRA has a historical parallel in that between the Ethnarchy and EOKA forty years ago, with Makarios playing the role allegedly performed today by Gerry Adams, Sinn Fein's president. Like Adams, Makarios was interned, and in 1956 he was exiled to the Seychelles, being allowed to return to Cyprus two years later as a condition for Greek-Cypriot participation in British-sponsored multiparty talks on the island's future. It was not until February 1959 that agreement was reached.

Under intense pressure from Greece, Makarios reluctantly accepted the proposal for the creation of an independent republic of Cyprus, with Britain being allowed to retain two strategic bases on the island. Fears that Turkey would otherwise forcibly impose partition (as in fact occurred fifteen years later) led Makarios to acquiesce in the arrangement despite Grivas's vehement opposition. The revolt officially ended a month later, when EOKA surrendered a large enough quantity of arms to satisfy the government that the peace agreement could be implemented. Although *enosis* was never achieved, British rule was forcibly ended and Cyprus was granted its independence. The fruits of the terrorists' labors were also apparent in the new republic's general election: Makarios was elected the country's first president, polling 67 percent of the popular vote.[35]

At the other end of the Mediterranean, the revolt against French rule over Algeria between 1954 and 1962 was the last of the immediate postwar anticolonial struggles. For that reason, perhaps, it had the most direct and discernible impact on many later ethno-nationalist terrorist campaigns. Yasir Arafat, for example, in his authorized biography, cites the pivotal influence that the FLN had on the PLO's struggle and the critical material assistance that Algeria later provided to the Palestinians. "I started my contacts with the Algerian revolutionaries in the early 1950s," he recalled. "I stayed in touch with them and they promised they would help us when they had achieved their independence. I never doubted for one moment that they would win, and that their victory would be very important for us."[36] In his own candid memoir, Nelson Mandela similarly identifies the seminal influence that the FLN's struggle had on the decades-long effort of the African National Congress (ANC) to end minority white rule of South Africa. "The situation in Algeria," Mandela wrote, "was the closest model to our own in that the rebels faced a large white settler community that ruled the indigenous majority." Accordingly, the ANC studied the Algerian conflict closely, deriving the main lesson that a pure military victory was impossible to achieve in such circumstances. Instead, Mandela assiduously applied the advice given to him by an Algerian revolutionary that "international opinion . . . is sometimes worth more than a fleet of jet fighters."[37] It was a lesson that the FLN itself had learned only belatedly. By the middle of 1956, the rebellion against French rule had been raging for nearly two years; the FLN, however, had precious few tangible achievements to show for its efforts, and recent advances by the security forces in the countryside had seriously undermined the group's rural insurgent strategy. Accordingly, the FLN embarked on a new strategy that would, for the first time, focus on the country's capital, Algiers, and thereby apply pressure to France by appealing directly to international opinion. The architect of this new strategy, first unveiled during the August 1956 summit convened at Soummam, Morocco, in hopes of reversing the FLN's declining fortunes, was Ramdane Abane, a leading figure in the movement until his execution the following year during an internecine power struggle. As the group's chief theoretician, he was also its most potent intellect. From an impoverished background and entirely self-educated, he was as completely unsentimental as he was ruthless, maintaining an unalterable faith in the efficacy of violence. This was clearly evident in his famous directive number nine, wherein he succinctly explained not just the purpose of the FLN's new strategy but the elementary logic behind urban terrorism. "Is it preferable for our cause to kill ten enemies in an oued [dry riverbed] of Telergma when no one will talk of it," he rhetorically asked, "or a single man in Algiers which will be noted the next day by the American press?"[38]

The chain of events that led to the FLN's full-scale urban terrorist campaign, however, had actually begun two months earlier, in June, with the execution by guillotine of two convicted FLN fighters. As had occurred countless times elsewhere (Palestine and Cyprus included), such attempts by the ruling regime to deter further violence with a particularly harsh exemplary punishment backfired catastrophically. The recipients of this lesson, rather than serving as abject examples, as often as not become martyrs: emblematic rallying points for the revolutionary cause around which still greater sacrifice and still further bloodshed and destruction are demanded and justified. Thus it was in Algeria, where the FLN announced that for every FLN fighter executed, a hundred Frenchmen would meet a similar fate. Hitherto, the group could boast that its campaign in the capital had been deliberately nonlethal, its bombs directed against inanimate "symbols" of French rule—government offices and buildings, military cantonments and police stations—but not deliberately against people. This now changed with Abane's instructions to the FLN's urban cadres to unleash a reign of unprecedented bombings and terror. Within seventy-two hours, forty-nine French civilians had been gunned down. Then, in August, as a result of the new strategic direction approved that same month at Soummam, the bombings began.

The campaign was spearheaded not by the group's hardened male fighters but by its attractive young female operatives—whose comely bearing and European looks, as Saadi Yacef, the group's operations officer in Algiers (who later reprised his real-life role in the Pontecorvo film), correctly guessed, would arouse far less suspicion than their male counterparts. Their targets, moreover, were neither military nor even governmental, but the crowded seaside milk bar frequented by *pied noir* (French colonist) families after a day at the beach; a cafeteria particularly favored by European university students; and the downtown Air France passenger terminal. The coordinated operations killed three people and injured some fifty others—including several children, some of them among the dozen or so victims requiring surgical amputation of mangled limbs. Throughout it all, Abane was unmoved. Drawing the same analogy between the terrorist bomb in the dustbin and the "poor man's air force" cited in chapter 1, Abane is said to have dismissively observed, "I see hardly any difference between the girl who places a bomb in the Milk-Bar and the French aviator who bombards a *mechta* [village] or who drops napalm on a *zone interdite* [interdiction, or free-fire, zone]."[39]

The urban campaign continued throughout the remainder of the year, climaxing on December 28, 1956, with the assassination of the mayor of Algiers. Widespread anti-Muslim rioting broke out, only to be followed by a new round of FLN assassinations. This was the last straw. In despair over the deteriorating situation, the governor-general called out the army. On January 7, 1957, General Jacques Massu, commander of the elite Tenth Parachute Division, assumed complete responsibility for maintaining order in the city. The FLN responded by declaring a general strike for January 28, to coincide, as noted above, with the UN's annual opening session. Its purpose—and that of the terrorist attacks that accompanied it: to focus international attention on Algeria. Once again, Yacef's bombers set about their work with startling efficiency. The FLN's target set now expanded to include popular bars and bistros, crowded city streets and sports stadiums packed with spectators. Within two weeks 15 people had been killed and 105 others wounded.

Massu went on the offensive. Having fought in Indochina, he and his senior commanders prided themselves on having acquired a thorough understanding of revolutionary warfare and how to counter it. Victory, they were convinced, would be entirely dependent on the acquisition of intelligence. "The man who places the bomb," declared Colonel Yves Godard, one of Massu's sector commanders, "is but an arm that tomorrow will be replaced by another arm"; the key was to find the individual commanding the arm. Accordingly, Godard and his men set out to uproot and destroy the FLN's urban infrastructure. Their method was to build up a meticulously detailed picture of the FLN's apparatus in Algiers that would home in relentlessly on the terrorist campaign's mastermind. Godard's approach, dramatically depicted onscreen by Pontecorvo, was described by the British historian Alistair Home as a "complex *organigramme* [that] began to take shape on a large blackboard, a kind of skeleton pyramid in which, as each fresh piece of information came from the interrogation centres, another name (and not always necessarily the right name) would be entered."[40] That this system proved effective, there is no doubt. The problem was that it also depended on, and therefore encouraged, widespread abuses, including torture, for Massu and his men were not particularly concerned about *how* they obtained this information. Torture of both terrorists and *suspected* terrorists became routine. The French army in Algeria found it easy to justify such extraordinary measures, given the extraordinary conditions. The prevailing exculpatory philosophy among the Tenth Parachute Division can be summed up by Massu's terse response to complaints, that "the innocent [that is, the next victims of terrorist attacks] deserve more protection than the guilty."[41]

The brutality of the army's campaign, however, completely alienated the native Algerian Muslim community. Hitherto mostly passive or apathetic, it was now driven into the arms of the FLN, swelling the organization's ranks and increasing its popular support. Domestic public opinion in France was similarly outraged, undercutting popular backing for continuing the struggle and creating deep fissures in French civil-military relations. Massu and his men stubbornly consoled themselves that they had achieved their mission and defeated the rebels' attempt to seize control of Algiers, but this military victory was bought at the cost of eventual political defeat. Five years later the French withdrew from Algeria and granted the country its independence.

For decades, Massu remained unrepentant, maintaining that the ends justified the means used to destroy the FLN's urban insurrection. In recent years, however, he has had second thoughts. In 2000, for instance, he told an interviewer that France should acknowledge that torture was routinely employed in Algeria and officially condemn it.[42] The officer under Massu's command at the time, retired general Paul Aussaresses, who was directly responsible for implementing this policy, however, has never softened. "For my part, I do not repent," Aussaresses told the same interviewer. "Torture never pleased me but I was resolute when I arrived in Algiers. At the time it was already widespread. If it were done again, it would piss me off, but I would do the same thing because I do not believe that one can do it differently."[43] Respect for the rule of law and the niceties of legal procedure, much less international conventions governing the rights of combatants, he contends, were totally irrelevant given the crisis situation enveloping Algeria in 1957. "Only rarely were the prisoners we had questioned during the night still alive the next morning," Aussaresses explained in his memoir, *The Battle of the Casbah*:

> Whether they had talked or not they generally had been neutralized. It was impossible to send them back to the court system, there were too many of them and the machine of justice would have become clogged with

cases and stopped working altogether. Furthermore, many of the prisoners would probably have managed to avoid any kind of punishment.[44]

Thus the battle was won and the terrorists' indiscriminate bombing campaign ended. Extraordinary measures were legitimated by extraordinary circumstances—all of which Aussaresses maintains is besides the point. As torturers before and since have claimed, he too contends, "I don't think I ever tortured or executed people who were innocent. I was mainly dealing with terrorists who had been involved in attacks."[45]

At the same time, there is no doubt that this "success" cut both ways. The FLN's tactical defeat in the city resulted in yet another complete reassessment of its strategy. Large-scale urban terrorism was now abandoned alongside the FLN's belief that France could be defeated militarily. The group's high command also concluded that the struggle could not be won inside Algeria alone; accordingly, the rebels relocated their operational bases to Tunisia, from which they pursued a rural hit-and-run strategy, making cross-border raids from their newly established sanctuaries. But the Battle of Algiers remains perhaps the most significant episode in bringing about the FLN's subsequent triumph, in that it succeeded in focusing world attention on the situation in Algeria, just as Abane had calculated. By provoking the government to overreact with torture, summary executions, and other repressive tactics, the FLN also revealed the bankruptcy of French rule, thereby hastening the complete destruction of Algérie Française.

Conclusion

The ethno-nationalist insurrections that followed the Second World War had a lasting influence on subsequent terrorist campaigns. Although governments throughout history and all over the world always claim that terrorism is ineffective as an instrument of political change, the examples of Israel, Cyprus, and Algeria, and of Begin, Makarios, and Ahmed Ben Bella (the FLN's leader, who became Algeria's first president), provide convincing evidence to the contrary. Admittedly the establishment of these independent countries was confined to a distinct period of time and was the product, in some cases, of powerful forces other than terrorism. At the same time, however, it is indisputable that, at the very least, the tactical "successes" and political victories won through violence by groups like the Irgun, EOKA, and the FLN clearly demonstrated that—notwithstanding the repeated denials of the governments they confronted—terrorism does "work." Even if this "success" did not always manifest itself in terms of the actual acquisition of power in government, the respectability accorded to terrorist organizations hitherto branded as "criminals" in forums like the United Nations and their success in attracting attention to themselves and their causes, in publicizing grievances that might otherwise have gone overlooked, and perhaps even in compelling governments to address issues that, if not for the terrorists' violence, would have largely been ignored, cannot be disregarded.

In sum, the anticolonial terrorism campaigns are critical to understanding the evolution and development of modern, contemporary terrorism. They were the first to recognize the publicity value inherent in terrorism and to choreograph their violence for an audience far beyond the immediate geographical loci of their respective struggles. The Irgun directed its message to New York and Washington, D.C., as much as to London and Jerusalem. EOKA similarly appealed to opinion in New York and London as well as in Athens and Nicosia. And the FLN was especially concerned with influencing policy not only in Algiers but in New York and Paris as well. The ability of these groups to mobilize sympathy and support outside the narrow confines of their actual "theaters of operation" thus taught a powerful lesson to similarly aggrieved peoples elsewhere, who now saw in terrorism an effective means of transforming hitherto local conflicts into international issues. Thus the foundations were laid for the transformation of terrorism in the late 1960s from a primarily localized phenomenon into a security problem of global proportions.

Chapter 3

The Internationalization of Terrorism

The advent of what is considered modern, international terrorism occurred on July 22, 1968. On that day three armed Palestinian terrorists, belonging to the Popular Front for the Liberation of Palestine (PFLP), one of the six groups that then constituted the Palestine Liberation Organization (PLO), hijacked an Israeli El Al commercial flight en route from Rome to Tel Aviv. Although commercial aircraft had been hijacked before (this was the twelfth such incident in 1968 alone), the El Al hijacking differed significantly from all previous ones. First, its purpose was not simply the diversion of a scheduled flight from one destination to another, as had been happening since 1959 with a seemingly endless succession of homesick Cubans or sympathetic revolutionaries from other countries commandeering domestic American passenger aircraft simply as a means to travel to Cuba. This hijacking was a bold political statement. The terrorists who seized the El Al flight had done so with the express purpose of trading the passengers they held hostage for Palestinian terrorists imprisoned in Israel. Second, unlike previous hijackings, in which the origin or nationality of the aircraft that was being seized did not matter so long as the plane itself was capable of transporting the hijacker(s) to a desired destination, El Al—as Israel's national airline and by extension, therefore, a readily evident national "symbol" of the Israeli state—had been specifically and deliberately targeted by the terrorists. Third, by engineering a crisis in which the consequences of a government's ignoring or rejecting the terrorists' demands could prove catastrophic, leading to the destruction of the aircraft and the deaths of all people on board, the terrorists succeeded in forcing their avowed enemy, Israel, to communicate directly with them and therefore with the organization to which they belonged, despite the Israeli government's previous declarations and policy pronouncements to the contrary. Finally, through the combination of dramatic political statement, "symbolic" targeting, and crisis-induced de facto recognition, the terrorists discovered that they had the power to create major media events—especially when innocent civilians were involved. As Zehdi Labib Terzi, the PLO's chief observer at the United Nations, reflected in a 1976 interview, "The first several hijackings aroused the consciousness of the world and awakened the media and world opinion much more—and more effectively—than 20 years of pleading at the United Nations."[1]

Many of the postwar anticolonial terrorist campaigns, as noted above, also had a prominent international orientation. With the El Al hijacking, however, the nature and character of terrorism demonstrably changed. For the first time, terrorists began to travel regularly from one country to another to carry out attacks. In addition, they also began to target innocent civilians from other countries who often had little if anything to do with the terrorists' cause or grievance, simply in order to endow their acts with the power to attract attention and publicity that attacks against their declared or avowed enemies often lacked. Their intent was to shock and, by shocking, to stimulate worldwide fear and alarm. These dramatic tactical changes in terrorism were facilitated by the technological advances of the time that had transformed the speed and ease of international commercial air travel and vastly improved both the quality of television news footage and the promptness with which that footage could be broadcast around the globe. Accordingly, terrorists rapidly came to appreciate that operations perpetrated in countries other than their own and directly involving or affecting foreign nationals were a reliable means of attracting attention to themselves and their cause.

At the forefront of this transformation were the constituent groups of the PLO. Between 1968 and 1980, Palestinian terrorist groups were indisputably the world's most active, accounting for more *international* terrorist incidents than any other movement.[2] The success achieved by the PLO in publicizing the Palestinians' plight through the "internationalization" of its struggle with Israel has since served as a model for similarly aggrieved ethnic and nationalist minority groups everywhere, demonstrating how long-standing but hitherto ignored or forgotten causes can be resurrected and dramatically thrust onto the world's agenda through a series of well-orchestrated, attention-grabbing acts. In order to understand how revolutionary a development this was, it is necessary to briefly review the Palestinians' modern history and to appreciate the depths of obscurity and international neglect from which the PLO emerged.

The PLO and the Internationalization of Terrorism

The end of the First Arab-Israeli War in 1949 introduced two new factors into Middle Eastern politics: the Jewish State of Israel and the Palestinian refugees exiled from it. During the war, many of Palestine's Arab inhabitants had fled their homes for the safety of neighboring countries. Some had left voluntarily; others had been forcibly expelled by the advancing Israeli forces. The exodus of Palestinian Arabs, however, did not end with the cessation of fighting. Fears of Israeli reprisals, coupled with the hope that the defeated Arab armies would shortly regroup and renew the fight against Israel, had convinced many Palestinians that they were better off becoming temporary exiles in the countries of their Arab brethren than remaining in the new Jewish state. The number of these displaced people soon climbed beyond 700,000 (some estimates put the figure as high as 950,000).

Crowded into decrepit refugee camps in Jordan, Syria, Lebanon, and Egypt, the Palestinians dreamed of the day when the Arab armies would arise to destroy Israel and return them to their homes. The Arab states, however, disheartened by the crushing defeat inflicted on them by the inferior Israeli forces, had no desire to launch another war. Furthermore, in the wretched conditions of the Palestinians' exile the region's Arab leaders seized upon an issue that could be exploited for their own ends. On the one hand, the Palestinian cause was a useful means by which to marshal international opprobrium against Israel and also to generate support among Arab states for greater regional unity against the common Zionist enemy; on the other, the refugee issue offered a convenient way to deflect attention from domestic problems by focusing popular discontent outward, against Israel, for the injustice done to the Palestinians. In any event, what the Palestinian refugees had once hoped would be a brief absence from their land evolved into indefinite displacement.

Meanwhile, inside the refugee camps, groups of desperate and disgruntled Palestinians were slowly banding together and establishing new political movements and associations. Out of these groups emerged new leaders, men who were untainted by the humiliation of the 1948–49 defeat and had not been party to the broken promises of their Arab hosts. These leaders argued that the Palestinians must henceforth rely on no one but themselves if they were ever to reclaim their homeland. Small groups of fedayeen (Arabic for "commandos") began to sneak out of the refugee camps to carry out cross-border hit-and-run attacks inside Israel. At a time when Egypt, like all other "front-line" Arab states, was militarily unprepared for another major war, its president, Gamal Abdel Nasser, saw in the raids a means by which he could both harass Israel and simultaneously advance his claim to leadership of the Arab world. Accordingly, Egypt began actively to train and arm the fedayeen. By 1953 Palestinian marauding had become both sufficiently frequent and sufficiently lethal to attract Israeli military reprisals. Thereafter a deadly cycle of raid and retaliation followed, culminating in the 1956 Suez crisis and providing Israel with the excuse it sought to invade the Sinai peninsula and eliminate the Egyptian bases supporting the fedayeen operations. Nearly a decade later, an almost identical tit-for-tat pattern of terrorist attack and Israeli reprisal set in motion a similar chain of events that resulted in the 1967 Six Day War.[3]

Yet although Palestinian terrorist activities precipitated a significant international crisis (Suez) and eleven years later led to a major regional war—notwithstanding the plight of hundreds of thousands of Palestinian refugees, many of whom were still living in the abject poverty of squalid refugee camps nearly two decades after their exile had begun—few outside the region took any notice of, much less cared about, the Palestinians. In fact, it was not until after 1968, when the fedayeen took their struggle against Israel outside the Middle East and began deliberately to enmesh citizens from more distant countries in their effort, that the Palestinians discovered an effective means of broadcasting their cause to the world and attracting its attention and sympathy. "When we hijack a plane it has more effect than if we killed a hundred Israelis in battle," PFLP founder and leader George Habash explained in a 1970 interview—echoing the same point made a decade earlier by the FLN's Ramdane Abane. "For decades world opinion has been neither for nor against the Palestinians," Habash noted. "It simply ignored us. At least the world is talking about us now."[4]

The premier example of terrorism's power to rocket a cause from obscurity to renown, however, was without doubt the murder of eleven Israeli athletes seized by Palestinian terrorists at the 1972 Munich Olympic Games. The purpose of the operation, according to Fuad al-Shamali, one of its architects, was to capture the world's attention by striking at a target of inestimable value (a country's star athletes), in a setting calculated to provide the terrorists with unparalleled exposure and publicity (the top global sporting event). "Bombing attacks on El Al offices do not serve our cause," al-Shamali had argued. "We have to kill their most important and most famous people. Since we cannot come close to their statesmen, we have to kill artists and sportsmen."[5]

The incident began on September 5, 1972, shortly before 5:00 a.m., when eight terrorists belonging to the PLO's Black September Organization (BSO) burst into the Israelis' dormitory, killing two athletes immediately and taking nine others hostage. As news of the attack spread and police rushed to the scene, the site was cordoned off and the terrorists issued their demands. They offered to exchange the hostages for 236 Palestinians imprisoned in Israeli jails and 5 other terrorists being held in Germany (including Andreas Baader and Ulrike Meinhof, the founders of the radical left-wing West German terrorist group the Red Army Faction), and they wanted a guarantee of safe passage to any Arab country (except Lebanon or Jordan). They also threatened to begin killing one hostage every two hours if their demands were not met. Fifteen hours of negotiations followed until a deal, brokered by the West Germans, was struck. The terrorists and their hostages, it was agreed, would be transported in two helicopters to the airbase at Fürstenfeldbruck, where they would then board a Lufthansa 727 aircraft and depart for Cairo. Once in Egypt, the exchange of prisoners would be effected and the terrorists allowed to proceed wherever they wished. The Egyptians, however, later changed their minds and decided to refuse the aircraft landing rights.

At 10:35 p.m. the two helicopters touched down at the German air base. Two terrorists emerged and went to inspect the airliner parked nearby. Two others took up positions outside the helicopters. The remaining four terrorists stayed inside, guarding the nine Israelis. Suddenly shots rang out. As part of a prearranged rescue plan, five West German police sharpshooters had opened fire. Three of the four terrorists outside the helicopters were cut down: the survivor, Mohammad Masalhah, the group's commander, took cover. The other terrorists immediately began to return fire and, according to some accounts, started to kill the hostages. A tense standoff now ensued as appeals were broadcast over loudspeakers in Arabic, German, and English to the remaining five terrorists to release their hostages and surrender. The terrorists again responded with gunfire. Finally, just after midnight, as German police prepared to mount a rescue assault, a terrorist leaped from one of the helicopters and tossed a hand grenade back into the cabin behind him. Pandemonium broke out when the grenade exploded. In the firefight that erupted, two more terrorists, including Masalhah, were killed. The three remaining terrorists, however, kept police at bay until roughly 12:30 a.m., when they finally surrendered and were taken into custody. All nine hostages lay dead, along with a West German policeman.[6]

Both operations—the hostage seizure and the rescue attempt—were colossal failures. The Palestinians had not only failed to obtain their principal stated demand—the release of terrorists imprisoned in Israel and West Germany—but, to many observers, had irredeemably tarnished the righteousness of their cause in the eyes of the world. Indeed, international opinion was virtually unanimous in its condemnation of the terrorists' operation. The grisly denouement on the airfield tarmac, broadcast via television and radio throughout the world, was initially regarded as disastrous to the Palestinian cause: a stunning failure and a grave miscalculation, generating revulsion rather than sympathy and condemnation instead of support.

As for the failure to save the hostages, for many other countries as well as for West Germany the botched rescue attempt provided stark evidence of how serious a threat international terrorism had become and how woefully inadequate their own counterterrorist capabilities were. The embarrassed West Germans lost little time in establishing a special antiterrorist detachment of their border police, known as GSG-9 (Grenzschutzgruppe Neun). Five years later, it acquitted itself brilliantly in Mogadishu, Somalia, rescuing all eighty-six hostages on board a Lufthansa flight hijacked en route from Mallorca by a mixed team of Palestinian and West German terrorists. In this incident, in marked contrast to the debacle at Fürstenfeldbruck, the GSG-9 commandos killed three of the hijackers and captured the fourth before they could harm any of the hostages (one GSG-9 officer was wounded in the rescue assault, as well as four hostages). In France, the Groupe d'Intervention de la Gendarmerie Nationale (GIGN) was created within the Gendarmerie Nationale as that country's dedicated counterterrorist unit; in Britain, the elite Special Air Services Regiment (SAS) was given permission to establish the Counter-Revolutionary Warfare detachment with a specific counterterrorism mission. In 1980 these SAS units successfully resolved the six-day siege at the Iranian embassy in Princes Gate, London, rescuing nineteen of the twenty-one hostages (two died during the rescue operation) and killing five of the six terrorists. Curiously, at the time the United States decided *not* to follow the example of its European allies and established no special, elite counterterrorist unit of its own—thus courting the disaster that came eight years later in the failed attempt to rescue the fifty-two Americans held hostage at the U.S. embassy in Tehran. Instead, President Richard Nixon ordered the formation of the special Inter-Departmental Working Group on Terrorism (chaired by Secretary of State Henry Kissinger) and elected to concentrate on diplomatic initiatives in the UN and elsewhere, focusing on the adoption of international conventions against terrorism.

The real lesson of Munich, however, was a somewhat counterintuitive one. The Olympic tragedy provided the first clear evidence that even terrorist attacks that fail to achieve their ostensible objectives can nonetheless still be counted successful provided that the operation is sufficiently dramatic to capture the attention of the media. In terms of the publicity and exposure accorded the Palestinian cause, Munich was an unequivocal success—a point conceded by even the most senior PLO officials. According to Abu Iyad, the organization's intelligence chief at the time, long-time confidant of Arafat and cofounder with him of al-Fatah, the Black September terrorists admittedly "didn't bring about the liberation of any of their comrades imprisoned in Israel as they had hoped, but they did attain the operation's other two objectives: World opinion was forced to take note of the Palestinian drama, and the Palestinian people imposed their presence on an international gathering that had sought to exclude them."[7]

Indeed, despite the worldwide condemnation of the terrorists' actions at the time, it soon became apparent that, for the Palestinians, Munich was in fact a spectacular publicity coup. The undivided attention of some four thousand print and radio journalists and two thousand television reporters and crew already in place to cover the Olympiad was suddenly refocused on Palestine and the Palestinian cause.[8] An estimated 900 million people in at least a hundred different countries saw the crisis unfold on their television screens.[9] According to one observer, "If one includes other forms of media it is safe to say that over a quarter of the world's population was at least aware of Black September's attack."[10] It seems fair to suppose that few viewers who tuned in to watch the games would forget the image emblazoned on their television screens of a terrorist, his face concealed by a balaclava, standing on the balcony of the Israeli suite at the Olympic village, preening in front of the cameras. Henceforth, those people throughout the world who before the games had neither known of the Palestinians nor been familiar with their cause were no longer as ignorant or dismissive. As an elderly Palestinian refugee remarked to a British reporter shortly after the attack, "From Munich onwards nobody could ignore the Palestinians or their cause."[11]

Further, the brutal dimensions of the operation, and its perpetrators' desperate plea for attention and recognition, convinced many across the world that the Palestinians were now a force to be reckoned with and possessed a cause that could no longer justifiably be denied. Black September was jubilant. In a communiqué published in a Beirut newspaper a week after the attack, the group proudly announced:

> In our assessment, and in light of the result, we have made one of the best achievements of Palestinian commando action. A bomb in the White House, a mine in the Vatican, the death of Mao Tse-Tung, an earthquake in Paris could not have echoed through the consciousness of every man in the world like the operation at Munich. The Olympiad arouses the people's interest and attention more than anything else in the world. The choice of the Olympics, from the purely propagandistic view-point, was 100 percent successful. It was like painting the name of Palestine on a mountain that can be seen from the four corners of the earth.[12]

During the weeks that followed the incident, thousands of Palestinians rushed to join the terrorist organizations.[13] It is perhaps not entirely coincidental, then, that eighteen months after Munich the PLO's leader, Yasir Arafat, was invited to address the UN General Assembly and shortly afterward the PLO was granted special observer status in that international body. Indeed, by the end of the 1970s the PLO, a nonstate actor, had formal diplomatic relations with more countries (eighty-six) than the actual established nation-state of Israel (seventy-two). It is doubtful whether the PLO could ever have achieved this success had it not resorted to international terrorism. Within four years, a handful of Palestinian terrorists had overcome a quarter century of neglect and obscurity. They had achieved what diplomats and statesmen, lobbyists and humanitarian workers had persistently tried and failed to do: focusing world attention on the Palestinian people and their plight. They had also provided a powerful example to similarly frustrated ethnic and nationalist groups elsewhere, and within the decade, the number of terrorist groups either operating internationally or committing attacks against foreign targets in their own country in order to attract international attention had more than quadrupled. According to the RAND Terrorism Incident Database,[14] the number of organizations engaged in *international* terrorism grew from only eleven in 1968 (of which just three were ethno-nationalist/separatist organizations, the remainder radical Marxist-Leninist or left-wing groups) to an astonishing fifty-five in 1978. Of this total, more than half (thirty, or 54 percent) were ethno-nationalist/separatist movements, all seeking to copy or capitalize on the PLO's success. They ranged from large international communities of displaced persons with profound historical grievances, such as the Armenian diaspora, to minuscule self-contained entities like the obscure expatriate South

Moluccan community in the Netherlands. What they all had in common, however, was a burning sense of injustice and dispossession and a belief that through *international* terrorism they too could finally attract world-wide attention to themselves and their causes.

The Palestinians as Model: The Rise of Ethno-Nationalist Terrorism

The Armenians, as noted in chapter 1, had waged an inchoate armed struggle against Ottoman rule during the 1880s and 1890s in hopes of eliciting Western sympathy and intervention. Their revolt had culminated in 1896 with the daring but ill-fated seizure of the Ottoman Bank in Constantinople. This event was followed by three days of intense anti-Armenian rioting and bloodshed during which untold numbers of Armenians lost their lives. Thereafter, most overt manifestations of Armenian nationalism lapsed into temporary abeyance, and those that did surface were forcibly suppressed. Nationalist activity was rekindled, however, during the First World War, mostly as a result of Russian efforts to foment Armenian unrest and thereby undermine the common enemy, Turkey. Ottoman suspicions of their Armenian subjects' loyalty, already aggravated by these Russian interventions, were further inflamed by the Armenians' refusal to support the Turkish war effort. Accordingly, in 1915, Taalat Pasha, the Ottoman interior minister, ordered the Armenians' expulsion from their traditional homelands in eastern Turkey to Syria and Iraq. Although the exact number of Armenians who perished at this time of widespread war and upheaval remains a matter of considerable debate, the figure most commonly cited is 1.5 million people—roughly 60 percent of Turkey's Armenian population. The events of 1915, therefore, are often cited as the first state "genocide" of the twentieth century.

Despite the magnitude of this catastrophe, for sixty years thereafter the Armenians' tragic history remained either ignored or forgotten. This began to change in 1975 when two Armenian terrorist groups—known as ASALA (the Armenian Army for the Secret Liberation of Armenia) and the JCAG (Justice Commandos of the Armenian Genocide)—emerged from the civil war then engulfing Lebanon. When asked to account for the sudden reemergence of Armenian terrorism, Hagop Hagopian, ASALA's founder and leader, unhesitatingly cited the Palestinian example. "There are substantially two factors to be taken into consideration," he stated in a 1975 interview, namely, the "general discovery as to the failure of the policy of the traditional Armenian parties [to publicize the Armenians' cause and grievances] . . . and the fact that many Armenians since 1966 participated in the Palestinian Arab struggle from which they learned many things."[15] Indeed, so important was the Palestinians' influence, and so close were their relations with the Armenian community in Lebanon, that ASALA can claim direct descent from both George Habash's PFLP and an even more radical splinter group of that organization, the PFLP Special Operations Group, led by Dr. Wadi Haddad.[16]

The similarities and circumstances of these two dispossessed peoples' respective plights had an almost hypnotic effect on young Armenians living in Beirut. Indeed, nearly twenty years later the Palestinian influence still burned bright for a new generation of young Armenians fighting for control over the Caucasus enclave of Nagorno Karabakh. As one observer noted in 1994 after meeting with these men while on a visit to Yerevan, most of them "viewed the 'Palestinian cause' as a model that had attracted world wide attention. Palestinians were seen as people like themselves—persecuted without a homeland."[17] In ASALA's case, the relationship between the two peoples was solidified through the PFLP's generous provision of arms, training, and other forms of assistance.

It was ASALA's early success in reinvigorating the Armenian cause that prompted the formation of a rival group, the JCAG. Although the two differed in their ideology—ASALA was avowedly Marxist-Leninist, adhering to the PFLP's global revolutionary orientation, while the JCAG tended to represent more mainstream Armenian nationalist views—both had the same three goals: to exact revenge for the events of 1915, to force the present Turkish republic to recognize the genocide committed by its Ottoman predecessors and thereby accept responsibility for it, and to compel the Turkish government to make reparations payments to the survivors and their descendants. In pursuit of these ends, between 1975 and 1985 more than forty Turkish diplomats and members of their families were murdered by Armenian terrorists. Whereas the JCAG (and its splinter group, the Armenian Revolutionary Army) preferred individual assassinations of Turkish diplomats or nonlethal, "symbolic" bombings of Turkish diplomatic and airline facilities, ASALA tended to employ more indiscriminate tactics and weapons, evincing little concern about who was killed or injured, Turk and non-Turk alike, so long as the operation succeeded in attracting attention. In July 1983, for example, ASALA bombed the Turkish airline's ticket counter at Orly Airport in Paris, killing seven people and wounding fifty-six others. A month later an ASALA attack at Ankara's Esenboga Airport killed nine people and injured seventy-eight, while an assault mounted in Istanbul's Grand Bazaar killed two and wounded twenty-seven. Indeed,

ASALA's brutal tactics and desperate bids for attention drew comparisons with the ruthlessness of the Palestinian Black September Organization in general and the Olympics massacre in particular.[18] It was even reported that Hagopian himself had participated in the Munich operation.[19]

By the early 1980s, the Armenians' use of terrorism had apparently paid off. "Thus it is true that the re-emergence of the Armenian question in the news—and especially of the Armenian genocide—is largely owing to Armenian terrorists," wrote Gerard Chaliand, a French Armenian scholar and one of the world's foremost authorities on terrorism and guerrilla warfare, in 1983.[20] A year earlier, in a study of the Armenian terrorist movements, Andrew Corsun, one of the U.S. State Department's leading analysts of terrorism, similarly argued that "by resorting to terrorism, Armenian extremists were able to accomplish in 5 years what legitimate Armenian organizations have been trying to do for almost 70 years—internationalize the Armenian cause."[21] However, while publicity and exposure proved to be easily gained through terrorism, the Armenian groups also found that attention does not necessarily translate into more tangible gains. For example, a detailed empirical study of American network news coverage of Armenian terrorism between 1968 and 1983 concluded that while the terrorist campaign had certainly increased public name recognition of the Armenians, it had not engendered any meaningful awareness or sensitivity about the Armenians' cause, their historical condition, or their political aims.[22] More critical, perhaps, was the fact that, unlike the Palestinians, the vast majority of the worldwide Armenian diaspora did not rally to, much less actively support, the terrorists. Despite expressions of understanding of the terrorists' goals and motivations, the Armenian community offered them little overt assistance and became increasingly alienated by the violent acts committed in its name. What minimal actual support did exist began to dry up following the 1983 Orly Airport attack, to the point that, by the end of the decade, none of the Armenian terrorist groups was still actively engaged in international terrorism.

The tiny South Moluccan expatriate community in the Netherlands is yet another example of an ethno-nationalist group that sought to duplicate the Palestinians' success during the period following the Munich Olympics attack. Some 15,000 South Moluccans had emigrated to the Netherlands in 1951 from their native Indonesia, following the incorporation of their Republic of the South Moluccas into the Indonesian state of Negara Indonesia Timur. For more than twenty years they nursed increasingly futile hopes of returning to their homeland and reestablishing their independent nation. In 1977, militant elements within the mainstream Free South Moluccan Organization lost patience and prepared to embark on a campaign of terrorism designed to "internationalize" their cause and realize their nationalist goals. In June of that year, two groups of terrorists, respectively, hijacked a Dutch passenger train and seized a nearby schoolhouse, taking hostages in both cases. They had in fact gotten their idea of seizing the train from press coverage of a similar operation attempted by Palestinian terrorists.[23] Both hostage seizures were successfully resolved by Royal Dutch Marine commandos who stormed both the train (killing six of the nine terrorists and two of the fifty-one hostages) and the schoolhouse, where all four terrorists were apprehended without bloodshed. Like the Armenians, the South Moluccans discovered the difficulties of converting publicity into actual political achievement. While the train and schoolhouse seizures brought the Moluccans more attention and publicity than they could otherwise ever have hoped to obtain, in the end this exposure did nothing to advance their cause or bring them any closer to obtaining their nationalist goals.

As a universally applicable model, therefore, the Palestinian archetype seems wanting. Nonetheless, nearly twenty years later, the Palestinian example continued to loom large for ethno-nationalist/separatist groups seeking international recognition and self-determination. During the 1990s, for example, Kurds fighting for autonomy in southeastern Turkey reportedly debated whether to adopt the Palestinian model for their own struggle. To date, the Kurdish Workers Party (PKK)—which renamed itself Kongra-Gel (KGK) in 2003—has largely eschewed *international* terrorism as a means to advance its nationalist claims, concentrating instead on an internal campaign of rural guerrilla warfare coupled with occasional acts of urban terrorism inside Turkey only. But its failure to win the international attention and stature that other, similar movements such as the PLO enjoy had reportedly led to increasing discontent among younger Kurdish militants. "Proponents of terrorism," one account from that time noted, argue that "the Palestinians have embassies in more than 100 countries while the Kurds, a far larger minority, have none."[24] Accordingly, they press for the adoption of an aggressive campaign of international terrorism—against the advice of their more moderate elders, who argue that such a strategy would ultimately deprive their cause of both credibility and international sympathy. The debate has yet to be resolved.

The Palestinians as Mentors: The Rise of Revolutionary Left-Wing Terrorism

The "internationalization" of terrorism that occurred in the late 1960s and early 1970s was not solely a product of Palestinian influence and success. Outside the Middle East, a combination of societal malaise and youthful idealism, rebelliousness and anti-militarism/anti-imperialism was rapidly transforming the collective political consciousness among the more affluent countries of Western Europe and North America. Perhaps the unprecedented economic prosperity of these years allowed the luxury of introspection and self-criticism that, in more radical political circles, generated a revulsion against the socioeconomic inequities endemic to the modern, industrialized capitalist state. "All they can think about," Ulrike Meinhof, the political activist and radical newspaper columnist turned Red Army Faction (RAF) terrorist, once dismissively remarked of her fellow Germans, "is some hairspray, a vacation in Spain, and a tiled bathroom."[25]

The sharp contrast between the highest and the lowest domestic levels of wealth and consumer consumption was further accentuated by the growing economic disparity between the developed world and the undeveloped world—as it came to be called, the "Third World." This was attributed by radicals as much to the "neocolonialist" ethos and economic exploitation inherent in capitalism as to the interventionist foreign policy championed by the United States under the banner of fighting the spread of communism. Thus, by the late 1960s, opposition to America's involvement in Indochina had emerged as the principal rallying cry for politically engaged, disaffected youth everywhere. "Anti-imperialism meant first of all the protest against the Viet-nam war, but also [against] the American predominance over most countries of the Third World," the former RAF terrorist Christoph Wackerngel explained in a 1995 speech recounting his own experience.[26]

Indeed, to a great extent, the Red Army Faction (in German, Rote Armee Fraktion, more popularly known as the Baader-Meinhof Group) and its sister terrorist organization, the Second of June Movement, encapsulated the revolutionary spirit and antiestablishment attitudes typical of left-wing terrorists in other Western countries at the time. Both groups emerged from the communes and student associations that were part of the "counterculture" in late-1960s West Germany, and it was consequently impossible to separate their radical politics from their "alternative" lifestyles. Revolution and armed struggle went hand in hand with sexual promiscuity and drug use. "You must understand," Astrid Proll, a member of the RAF's "first generation," later explained, "that then the most fantastic thing in the world was not to be a rock star, but a revolutionary."[27] Michael "Bommi" (the nickname given to him because of his penchant for bombing) Baumann, a leading member of the Second of June Movement, similarly describes in his memoir how

with me it all began with rock music and long hair. . . . It was like this: if
you had long hair, things were suddenly like they are for the Blacks. Do
you understand? They threw us out of joints, they cursed at us and ran
after us—all you had was trouble. . . . So you start building contact with
a few people like yourself, other dropouts, or whatever you want to call
them. You begin to orient yourself differently.[28]

Yet it would be a mistake to dismiss Proll and Baumann simply as apolitical narcissists or mere "dropouts" from society. Like many of their generation, they too were animated by a profound sense of social injustice coupled
with an intense enmity toward what they perceived as worldwide American
militarism and domination. "To my mind, it wasn't simply an international
question," the German terrorist Hans Joachim Klein recalled in a 1978 interview,[29] "but also an internal problem. The B-52s stopped over at Wiesbaden
on their way from Vietnam."[30] The pervasive influence of the Vietnam War
on German terrorism can be seen in several of the contemporary Second
of June statements reproduced in Baumann's autobiography,[31] as well as in
RAF communiqués issued long after the war and American involvement in
Indochina ended. The RAF's first *actual* terrorist operation (that is, other
than bank robberies) was in retaliation for the U.S. Air Force's mining of
North Vietnam's Haiphong harbor. The target was the U.S. Fifth Army
Corps officers' mess at Frankfurt: one person was killed and thirteen others
were injured in the bomb attack. As Brigitte Monhaupt, who later emerged
as one of the group's key leaders, explained to a German court in 1976, "The
strategic concept as developed by the RAF . . . was directed against the U.S.
military presence in the Federal Republic. . . . The concept was enveloped
by us all in the collective discussion process."[32]

With the end of the Vietnam War, the German terrorists in both the RAF
and other groups needed to find a new cause. Their choice again reflected the
international orientation of West German radical politics: common cause
was now to be made with the Palestinians. In his book Baumann described
the logic behind this decision. "Since Vietnam is finished," the argument
ran, "people should get involved with Palestine. It is actually much closer to
us, which is apparent today with the oil business, and has more to do with
us here in the European cities than does Vietnam. This was to become the
new framework to carry on the struggle here."[33]

The Palestinians were in fact the obvious candidates. As far back as 1968
the PLO—and Habash's PFLP especially—had welcomed terrorists from
around the world to its guerrilla camps in Jordan for training, indoctrination, and the general building of transnational revolutionary bridges.

In this respect, the Palestinians pioneered the "networking" dimension of international terrorism still in evidence among many groups today. In 1969 the Palestinians had welcomed the first delegation of West German terrorists—Baumann's comrades in the "Blues" group, an early precursor of the Second of June Movement—to their guerrilla training camps in Jordan. "They got some training there: how to shoot; how to make bombs; how to fight," Baumann recalled. "But the Palestinians told them to go back to Germany and make propaganda for them. That was all they were hot for—they offered no weapons."[34] The following year another party of German terrorists—including Andreas Baader, Gudrun Ensslin, Ulrike Meinhof, and six of their colleagues—secretly made their way to Beirut and then to Palestinian terrorist camps in Jordan, as much to escape the police dragnet closing in on them at home as to receive training as "urban guerrillas." Although relations between the Germans and their Palestinian hosts were strained to the point that, after two months, the group was asked to leave, Baader and company had by this time learned enough to enable them formally to establish their own terrorist group—the RAF. According to Rapoport, this development marked a significant milestone in the history of terrorism, since it was probably the first time that one terrorist group had trained another.[35]

Thereafter, the relationship between the German and Palestinian groups flourished. Combined teams of German and Palestinian terrorists were involved in the 1975 seizure of the OPEC (Organization of Petroleum Exporting Countries) oil ministers' conference in Vienna, the 1976 hijacking of an Air France flight to Entebbe, Uganda, and the hijacking (mentioned previously) of a Lufthansa flight to Somalia in 1977. The Germans also reportedly provided critical logistical assistance to the Palestinian Black September terrorists responsible for the Munich massacre. Although the closest ties were forged with the PFLP, Arafat's comparatively more moderate al-Fatah organization played a particularly important role in supplying the RAF with weapons. Its political agents in Germany, assigned primarily to fund-raising activities, operated a profitable business on the side selling handguns to the RAF. Indeed, according to leading German-Israeli counterterrorism analyst David Schiller, without the assistance provided by the Palestinian terrorists to their German counterparts the latter could not have survived.[36]

The profound influence exercised by the Palestinians over the Germans was perhaps never more clear than in 1985, when the RAF joined forces with the French left-wing terrorist organization Direct Action (in French, Action Directe, thus AD), in hopes of creating a PLO-like umbrella "anti-imperialist front of Western European guerrillas" that would include Italy's Red Brigades (RB) and the Belgian Communist Combatant Cells (CCC) as well. But, just as the Armenians' and South Moluccans' attempts to replicate the PLO's success had foundered, so did the efforts of German and French organizations. Within two years, the promised campaign of "Euroterrorism" against NATO's politico-military structure had fizzled out. The global conditions that had produced and nurtured these organizations, that indeed had endowed them with their fundamental raison d'être, were changing more rapidly than they could adapt, thus threatening to turn them into hopeless anachronisms. Crippled by the arrests of the leading members of the French and Belgian groups, the "anti-imperialist front" fell into disarray. Not surprisingly, perhaps, the Red Brigades shortly afterward drifted into complete lassitude. The forty-year revolutionary struggle it had so proudly proclaimed for the Italian people less than a decade earlier had run out of steam before even a generation had passed. In Germany, meanwhile, the RAF disconsolately carried on, despite the political revolutions then transforming the Soviet Union and Eastern Europe. The fall of the Berlin Wall in 1989 and the national reunification that followed deprived the group of its ideological resilience as well as a convenient cross-border sanctuary. Politically marginalized and bereft of either patron or safe haven, the RAF finally collapsed in 1992 under the weight of its own exhaustion and the indifference of those in the newly united Germany whom the group still purported to represent.

Thus, of the four radical movements that only two decades ago attempted collectively to realize the revolution that they believed was inevitable, none remains. Yet, more than forty years after its founding, the PLO—though still short of its ultimate goal of true sovereignty over a bona fide Palestinian state—has nonetheless survived expulsions and dislocations, internal rivalry and external enmity, to continue the struggle begun long ago in an equally transformed political environment.

Conclusion

The PLO, as a terrorist movement, is arguably unique in history. Not only was it the first truly "international" terrorist organization, it also consistently embraced a far more internationalist orientation than most other terrorist groups. Some accounts suggest that by the early 1980s at least forty different terrorist groups—from Asia, Africa, North America, Europe, and the Middle East—had been trained by the PLO at its camps in Jordan, Lebanon, and Yemen, among other places. The Palestinians' purpose in this tutelary role was not entirely philanthropic. The foreign participants in these courses were reportedly charged between five thousand and ten thousand dollars each for a six-week program of instruction. In addition, many of them were later recruited to participate in joint operations alongside Palestinian terrorists. Thus, according to Israeli defense sources, the PLO in 1981 had active cooperative arrangements with some twenty-two different terrorist organizations that had previously benefited from Palestinian training, weapons supply, and other logistical support.[37]

The PLO was also one of the first terrorist groups actively to pursue the accumulation of capital and wealth as an organizational priority. By the mid-1980s, it was estimated to have established an annual income flow of some $600 million, of which some $500 million was derived from investments.[38] The amassing of so vast a fortune is all the more astonishing given the fact that when the PLO was established in 1964, it had no funds, no infrastructure, and no real direction. It was not until Arafat's election as chairman in 1968 that the PLO started to become the major force in international politics that it is today. As renowned former *Sunday Times* journalist and authority on terrorism James Adams has observed,

as the PLO has grown in complexity and its income has risen accordingly, the organisation has had to adapt to a changing role and an altered image of itself. While the world still viewed the PLO as a bunch of terrorist fanatics robbing banks and blowing up aircraft to boost their cause, the secret side of the organisation was being rapidly transformed.[39]

Thus the attention that the PLO has received, the financial and political influence and power that it has amassed, and the stature that it has been accorded in the international community continues to send a powerful message to aggrieved peoples throughout the world. Ironically, this "success" has also had a profound effect on the PLO's commitment to terrorism. It can be argued that, despite the fiery rhetoric, even an international terrorist organization like the PLO does not necessarily have an overriding interest in upsetting the international order of which it yearns to become an accepted part. This is not entirely surprising, given the PLO's unique international orientation. But what makes this process especially noteworthy is that the PLO's "internationalist" efforts have long since expanded beyond the narrow goal of forging tactical alliances with other terrorist groups. Indeed, since the mid-1970s, al-Fatah in particular—but also the mainstream PLO in general—has actively sought to establish relations with as many countries as possible, regardless of their form of government or concern with the Palestinian cause. In pursuit of this policy, the PLO has often abjured committing certain types of operations against non-Israeli targets, has attempted to impose restrictions on the geographical range of terrorist acts committed by its constituent groups (as, for example, in Arafat's 1988 prohibition of Palestinian terrorist activities outside of Israel and the occupied territories and his previous 1974 edict banning terrorist operations in Europe), and has frequently tried to cover up its involvement in or sponsorship of terrorist incidents that have violated these declared self-imposed restraints. Over time, therefore, the most radical of its aims have been forsaken in favor of what the moderate leadership has defined as the organization's "national interest." Or, as Abu Iyad more dourly described this process, "What we feared most of all . . . has happened. Our movement has become bureaucratized. What it gained in respectability it lost in militancy. We have acquired a taste for dealing with governments and men of power."[40] Indeed, the PLO, as the ruling party in the Palestine Authority on the West Bank and Gaza until the January 2006 elections, had to deal with the same daily complaints of incompetence, lethargy, inefficiency, and corruption faced by governments the world over.[41]

Four faces of terrorism (clockwise from top left): Carlos, the Jackal; Yasir Arafat, George Habash; Leila Khaled (all from author's collection).

Osama bin Laden (Reuters/CORBIS).

Symbols of terrorism (top to bottom):
Red Army Faction; Red Brigades; Popular
Front for the Liberation of Palestine; Justice Commandos of the Armenian Genocide (all from author's collection).

Gallows at Central Prison facility, Russian Compound, Jerusalem, used by British to hang Jewish terrorists, 1947 (author's collection).

Popular Front for the Liberation of Palestine hijacking of BOAC airliner, Dawson's Field, Jordan, September 1970 (author's collection).

Americans held hostage in Iran, 1979–80 (author's collection).

Wanted poster for Red Army Faction terrorists, West Germany (author's collection).

(Top): The IRA targets London: Hyde Park, July 1982 (author's collection).

(Bottom): The IRA targets London: Aldwych, February 1996 (Popperfoto/Reuters/ Andrew Shaw).

(Top): Gate separating Catholic and Protestant communities, Woodvale, West Belfast, Northern Ireland, 1991 (author's collection).

(Left): IRA "Free Ireland" with Fist in Chains wall mural, Beechmount, West Belfast, Northern Ireland, 1991 (author's collection).

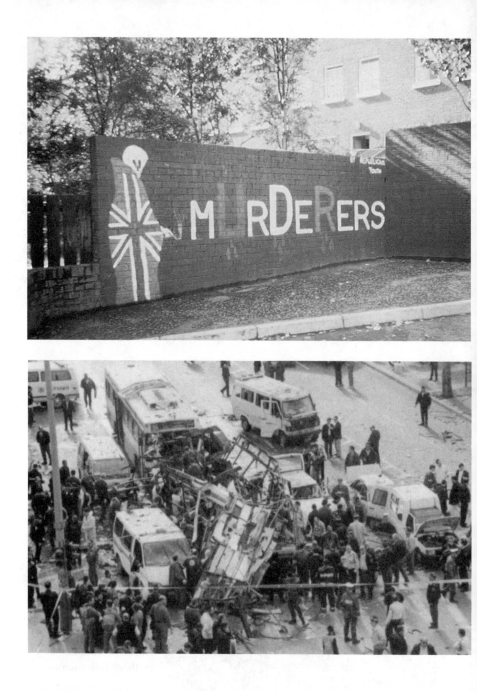

(Top): IRA "British Murderers" wall mural, New Lodge, North Belfast, Northern Ireland, 1990 (author's collection).

(Bottom): Jerusalem, February 1996: the wreckage of the bombed bus in which twenty-two Israelis were killed by Hamas (Popperfoto/Reuters/David Silverman).

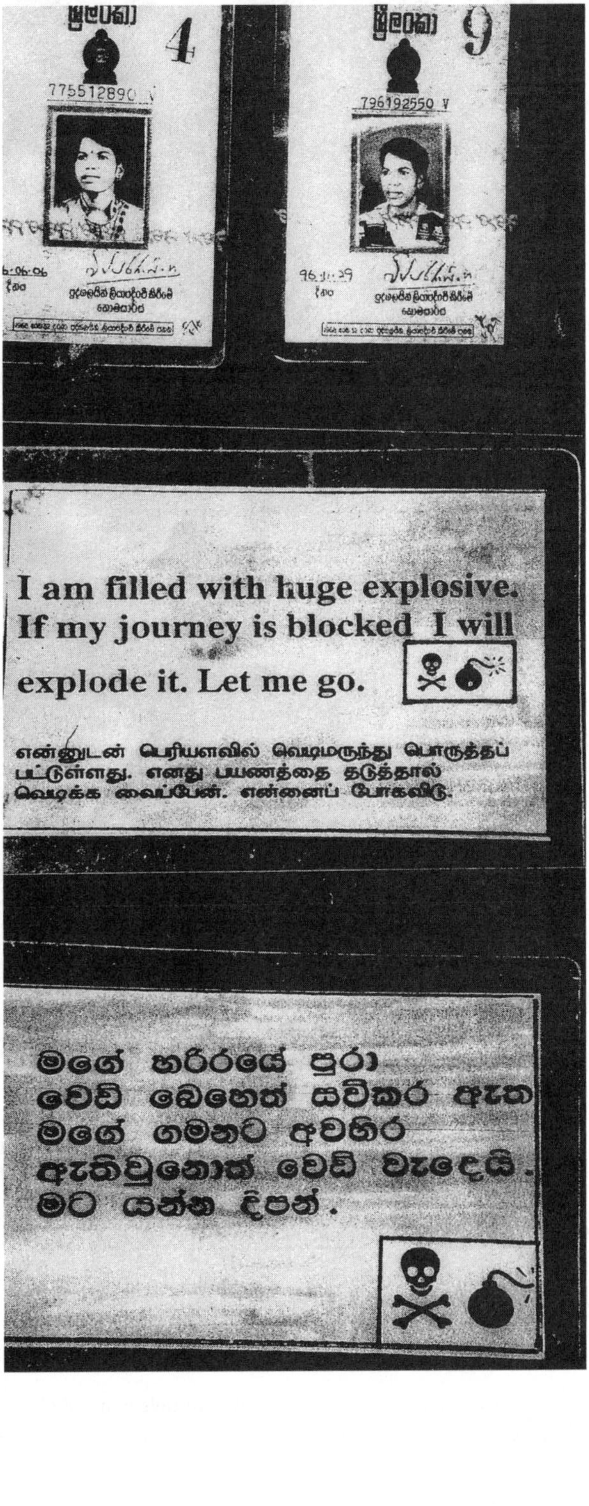

LTTE suicide terrorist ID card (author's collection).

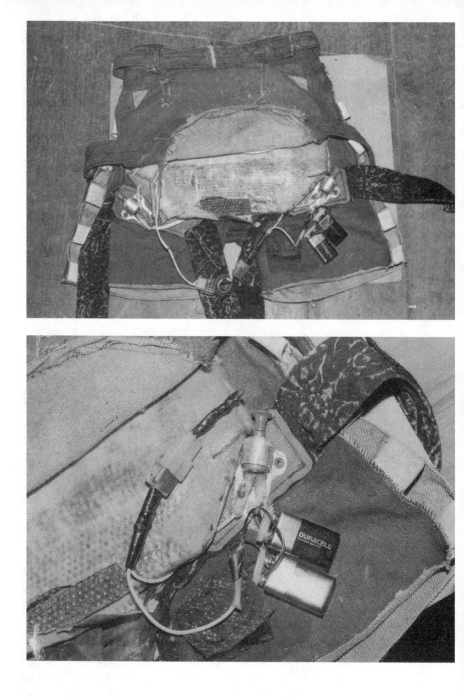

Terrorist suicide kit: plastic explosive belt concealed in trousers, triggered by battery-powered detonator with plunger activator (author's collection).

Destruction caused by massive truck bomb detonated by the LTTE outside the newly opened World Trade Center building, Colombo, Sri Lanka, October 1997. Eighteen people were killed and more than a hundred injured (author's collection).

(Above): Lockerbie, December 1988 (Popperfoto/Reuters).

(Opposite): Oklahoma City, April 1995 (Popperfoto/Reuters/Win McNamee).

الكيان الصهيوني حتما إلى زوال

החברה היהודית בטח תתקלקל

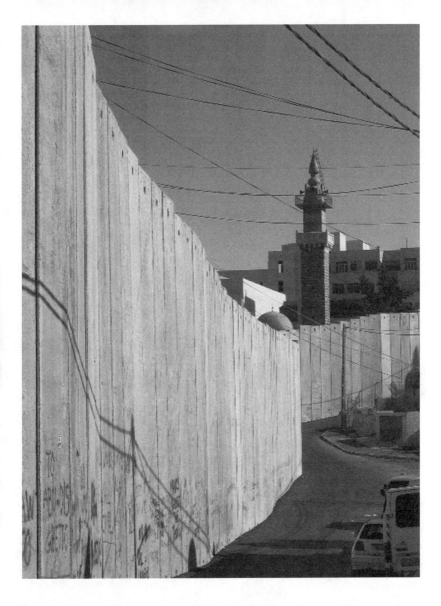

(Opposite top): Tokyo nerve gas attack, March 1995: troops decontaminating train (Popperfoto/Reuter/Japan's Ground Self-Defense Force).

(Opposite bottom): "The Zionist entity surely will disintegrate." Hamas poster in Arabic and Hebrew, 2004 (author's collection).

(Above): Section of separation barrier cutting through Abu Dis, East Jerusalem (author's collection).

(Opposite): 9/11, World Trade Center collapses, New York City (Reuters/CORBIS).

(Above): The Madrid train attack on March 11, 2004 (Kai Pfaffenbach/Reuters/CORBIS).

July 7, 2005, suicide bombing of a London bus (Dylan Martinez/Reuters/CORBIS).

Chapter 4

Religion and Terrorism

A few hours after the first American air strikes against Afghanistan began on October 7, 2001, a pre-recorded videotape was broadcast around the world. A tall, skinny man with a long, scraggly beard, wearing a camouflage fatigue jacket and the headdress of a desert tribesman, with an AK-47 assault rifle at his side, stood before a rocky backdrop. In measured yet defiant language, Osama bin Laden again declared war on the United States. Like all his previous statements, bin Laden's message that day was unmistakably religious in tone and content. "Praise be to God and we beseech him for help and forgiveness," it began.

> We seek refuge with the Lord of our bad and evildoing. He whom God guides is rightly guided but he whom God leaves to stray, for him wilt thou find no protector to lead him to the right way.
> I witness that there is no God but God and Muhammad is his slave and prophet.
> God Almighty hit the United States at its most vulnerable spot. He destroyed its greatest buildings. Praise be to God.
> Here is the United States. It was filled with terror from its north to its south and from its east to its west. Praise be to God.

In thanking his god for the death and destruction that al Qaeda wrought on 9/11, bin Laden clearly had cast his struggle in incontrovertibly theological terms. "As for the United States," he concluded, "I tell it and its people these few words: I swear by Almighty God, who raised the heavens without pillars, that neither the United States nor he who lives in the United States will enjoy security before we can see it as a reality in Palestine and before all the infidel armies leave the land of Muhammad, may God's peace and blessing be upon him."[1] Of course, many historical and contemporary terrorist groups also evidence a strong religious component, mostly by dint of their membership. Anticolonial, nationalist movements such as the Jewish terrorist organizations active in pre-independence Israel and the Muslim-dominated FLN in Algeria come readily to mind, as do more recent examples such as the overwhelmingly Catholic IRA; its Protestant counterparts, arrayed in various loyalist paramilitary groups like the Ulster Freedom Fighters, the Ulster Volunteer Force and the Red Hand Commandos; and the predominantly Muslim PLO. However, in all these groups it is the political, not the religious aspect of their motivation that is dominant; the preeminence of their ethno-nationalist and/or irredentist aims is incontestable.

For others like al Qaeda, however, the religious motive is overriding; and indeed, the religious imperative for terrorism is the most important defining characteristic of terrorist activity today. The consequences of the revolution that transformed Iran into an Islamic republic in 1979 have included its crucial role in the resurgence of this strand of terrorism; but, as I will show, the modern advent of religious terrorism has not been confined exclusively to Iran, much less to the Middle East or to Islam or to al Qaeda alone: since the 1980s it has involved elements of all the world's major religions and, in some instances, smaller sects or cults as well. "I have no regrets," said Yigal Amir, the young Jewish extremist who in 1995 assassinated Israeli prime minister Yitzhak Rabin, to the police. "I acted alone and on orders from God."[2] Today, Amir's words could just as easily have come from the mouths of the Islamic Hamas and Palestine Islamic Jihad (PIJ) terrorists responsible for the wave of suicide bombings of civilian buses and public gathering places that have convulsed Israel; the young Dutch-Moroccan Muslim who brutally murdered controversial filmmaker Theo van Gogh in November 2004;[3] the Japanese followers of Shoko Asahara in the Aum Shinrikyo sect who perpetrated the March 1995 nerve gas attack on the Tokyo subway in hopes of hastening a new millennium; or the American Christian white supremacist Patriot movement, which, acting on an even more complex and less comprehensible mixture of seditious, millenarian, paranoiac, and antigovernment beliefs has waged an inchoate campaign of bombing and assassination in the United States. As will become apparent, terrorism motivated either in whole or in part by a religious imperative, where violence is regarded by its practitioners as a divine duty or sacramental act, embraces markedly different means of legitimation and justification than that committed by secular terrorists, and these distinguishing features lead, in turn, to yet greater bloodshed and destruction.

The connection between religion and terrorism is not new. More than two thousand years ago the first acts of what we now describe as "terrorism" were perpetrated by religious fanatics. Indeed, some of the words we use in the English language to describe terrorists and their actions are derived from the names of Jewish, Hindi, and Muslim terrorist groups active long ago. The etymology of the word "zealot,"[4] for example, which to us means an "immoderate partisan" or a "fanatical enthusiast," can be traced back to a millenarian Jewish sect of the same name that fought in A.D. 66–73 against the Roman Empire's occupation of what is now Israel. The Zealots waged a ruthless campaign of assassination, mostly of individuals, relying on the *sica*, a primitive dagger. The Zealot would emerge from the anonymous obscurity of a crowded marketplace, draw the *sica* that had been concealed beneath his robes, and in plain view of those present, dramatically slit the throat of a Roman legionnaire or a Jewish citizen who had been judged by the group guilty of betrayal, apostasy, or both. Thus, in an era long before CNN television news and the transmission of instantaneous live satellite images, the Zealots' dramatic public acts of violence—precisely like those of terrorists today—were designed to have psychological repercussions far beyond the immediate victim(s) of the terrorist attack and thereby to send a powerful message to a wider, watching target audience—namely, the Roman occupation administration and Jews who collaborated with the invaders. The Zealots are also reputed to have employed a primitive form of chemical warfare, poisoning wells and granaries used by the Romans and even sabotaging Jerusalem's water supply.[5]

Similarly, the word "thug," now used to describe "a vicious or brutal ruffian,"[6] is derived from a seventh-century religious cult that terrorized India until its suppression in the mid-nineteenth century. The Thugs engaged in acts of ritual murder designed to serve the Hindu goddess of terror and destruction, Kali. On specified holy days throughout the year, group members would forsake their daily occupations and lie in wait for innocent travelers, who would be ritually strangled as sacrificial offerings to Kali. According to some accounts, the Thugs killed as many as a million people during their twelve-hundred-year existence, or more than eight hundred individuals every year, a murder rate rarely achieved by their modern-day counterparts armed with far more efficient and destructively lethal weaponry.[7]

Finally, the word "assassin"—"one who undertakes to put another to death by treacherous violence"[8]—was the name of a radical offshoot of the Muslim Shi'a Ismaili sect, which between A.D. 1090 and 1272 fought to repel the Christian crusaders attempting to conquer present-day Syria and Iran. Literally translated, "assassin" means "hashish eater," a reference to the ritual intoxication that, as legend has it, the Assassins undertook before embarking on their missions of murder. Violence for the Assassins was a sacramental act, a divine duty, commanded by religious text and communicated by clerical authorities. Accordingly, the Assassins' violence was meant not only to vanquish the sect's Christian enemies but also to hasten the dawn of a new millennium as well. An important additional motivation for an Assassin was the promise that, should he himself perish in the course of carrying out his attack, he would ascend immediately to a glorious heaven. This same ethos of self-sacrifice and suicidal martyrdom can be seen in many Islamic—and indeed other religious—terrorist organizations today.

Until the nineteenth century, in fact, as Rapoport points out in his seminal study of what he terms "holy terror," religion provided the only justification for terrorism.[9] Many of the political developments of this era discussed in chapter 1—including the end of divine, monarchical rule in Europe at the beginning of the nineteenth century, followed by the emergence of new concepts redefining the role of both citizen and state, alongside emergent notions of nationalism and self-determination—account for the shift in motivation and emphasis that then took place, and the growing popularity of various schools of radical political thought, embracing Marxist ideology (or its subsequent Leninist and Maoist interpretations), anarchism, and nihilism, completed the transformation of terrorism from a mostly religious to a predominantly secular phenomenon. This process of "secularization" was given fresh impetus by the anticolonialist/national liberation movements that arose after the Second World War to challenge continued Western rule in Asia, the Middle East, and Africa and subsequently exerted so profound an influence on ethno-nationalist/separatist and ideological terrorist organizations in the late 1960s and early 1970s.

While terrorism and religion share a long history, then, for the past century this particular manifestation has mostly tended to be overshadowed by ethno-nationalist/separatist and ideologically motivated terrorism. For example, none of the eleven *identifiable* international terrorist groups active in 1968—the year, as previously noted, credited with marking the advent of modern, international terrorism—could be classified as religious: that

is, having aims and motivations reflecting a predominant religious character or influence.[10] This, perhaps, is only to be expected at the height of
the cold war, when the majority of terrorist groups (eight) were left-wing,
revolutionary Marxist-Leninist ideological organizations, and the remaining three—including the various constituent groups of the PLO—reflected
the emergence of the first postcolonial ethno-nationalist/separatist organizations. Not until 1980—as a result of the repercussions of the revolution
in Iran the previous year—did the first "modern" religious terrorist groups
appear. Even so, despite the large increase in the total number of identifiable
international terrorist groups from eleven to sixty-four and the concomitant
tenfold increase (from three to thirty-two) of ethno-nationalist/separatist
organizations (for reasons described in chapter 3), only two of the sixty-
four groups active in 1980 could be classified as predominantly religious in
character and motivation: the Iranian-backed Shi'a organizations al-Dawa
and the Committee for Safeguarding the Islamic Revolution.

However, while the reemergence of modern religious terrorism was initially closely associated with the Islamic revolution in Iran, within a decade
of that event none of the world's major religions could claim to be immune
to the same volatile mixture of faith, fanaticism, and violence. Twelve
years later, in 1992, the number of religious terrorist groups had increased
exponentially (from two to eleven groups) and moreover had expanded to
embrace major world religions other than Islam, as well as various obscure
religious sects and cults.

Interestingly, as the number of religious terrorist groups was increasing,
the number of ethno-nationalist/separatist terrorist groups declined appreciably. One explanation for this trend may be that many ethno-national-
ist/separatist groups, suddenly finding themselves at the end of the cold
war enmeshed in bitter conflict and civil wars over their homelands (for
example, in Bosnia, Chechnya, Nagorno Karabakh, and other parts of Eastern Europe and the former Soviet Union), consequently had little time or
energy to engage in international terrorism. Another plausible explanation
is that at a time when the rigid bipolar structure of the cold war that had
throttled the United Nations for nearly half a century was breaking down
and new nations were obtaining sovereignty and rapidly gaining admission
to the international community, there was perhaps less reason to resort
to international terrorism in order to have one's own irredentist claims
recognized. Also, in circumstances where previous impediments to UN
membership no longer existed, many groups may have come to regard the
use of international terrorism not only as an embarrassment (that could
potentially vitiate their case for joining the community of nations) but as

counterproductive. Finally, it is also interesting to note that, notwithstanding the end of the cold war and the demise of the Soviet Union and the Warsaw Pact, the number of groups espousing Marxist-Leninist-Maoist dogma (or some idiosyncratic interpretation of those ideological elements) remained unchanged, thus further challenging the cold war myth of a global terrorist conspiracy directed by, and dependent upon, Moscow and its communist minions.

Significantly, during the 1990s the growth in the number of religious terrorist groups as a proportion of all active international terrorist organizations not only continued but increased appreciably. In 1994, for example, a third (sixteen) of the forty-nine identifiable international terrorist groups active that year could be classified as religious in character and/or motivation; and in 1995, their number grew yet again, to account for nearly half (twenty-six, or 46 percent) of the fifty-six known active international terrorist groups. A decade later, it is perhaps not surprising to find that this trend not only continued but solidified. In 2004, for instance, nearly half (fifty-two, or 46 percent) of the terrorist groups active that year were religious, while thirty-two (28 percent) were left-wing groups, and twenty-four (21 percent) were ethno-nationalist/separatist organizations.

It is perhaps not surprising also that religion should become a far more popular motivation for terrorism in the post–cold war era as old ideologies lie discredited by the collapse of the Soviet Union and communist ideology, while the promise of munificent benefits from the liberal-democratic, capitalist state, apparently triumphant at what Francis Fukuyama in his famous aphorism has termed the "end of history," fails to materialize in many countries throughout the world. The "public sense of insecurity" engendered by these changes[11]—which has affected in equal measure the most economically disadvantaged (e.g., the Gaza Strip and the former Soviet Union) and the most prosperous (e.g., Japan and the United States)—has been deepened by other societal factors, including accelerated population growth, rapid urbanization, and the breakdown of local services (e.g., medical care, housing, social welfare programs, and education), typically provided by the state.

The salience of religion as the major driving force behind international terrorism in the years preceding 9/11 is further evidenced by the fact that the most serious terrorist acts of the decade—whether reckoned in terms of political implications and consequences or numbers of fatalities caused—all had a significant religious dimension and/or motivation. They include:

- the March 1995 sarin nerve gas attack on the Tokyo subway system, perpetrated by an apocalyptic Japanese religious cult, which killed 12

people and wounded 3,796 others,[12] along with reports that the group
also planned to carry out identical attacks in the United States;[13]

- the August 1998 simultaneous suicide car and truck bombings of the U.S.
embassies in Nairobi, Kenya, and Dar es Salaam, Tanzania, by al Qaeda,
in which 301 people were killed and more than 5,000 wounded;
- the bombing of a shopping mall in Zamboanga, Philippines, that same
December by Muslim extremists belonging to the Abu Sayyaf Group,
wounding 60 Christians who were Christmas shopping;
- the bombing in April 1995 of an Oklahoma City federal office building, where 168 people perished;
- the 1993 bombing of New York City's World Trade Center by Islamic
radicals who deliberately attempted to topple one of the twin towers
onto the other;
- the assassination in November 1995, as previously mentioned, of
Israeli premier Yitzhak Rabin by a Jewish religious extremist, intended
as only the first step in a campaign of mass murder designed to disrupt the peace process;
- the June 1996 truck bombing of a U.S. Air Force barracks in Dhah-
ran, Saudi Arabia, where 19 people perished, by religious militants
opposed to the reigning al-Saud regime;
- the string of bloody attacks by Hamas suicide bombers that turned
the tide of Israel's national elections, killing 60 people, between February and March 1996;
- the brutal machine-gun and hand-grenade attack carried out by
Egyptian Islamic militants on a group of Western tourists, killing 18,
outside their Cairo hotel in April 1996;
- the massacre in November 1997 of 58 foreign tourists and 4 Egyptians
by terrorists belonging to the Gamat al-Islamiya (Islamic Group) at
the Temple of Queen Hatshepsut in Luxor, Egypt;
- the series of thirteen nearly simultaneous car and truck bombings
that shook Bombay, India, in February 1993, killing 400 people and
injuring more than 1,000 others, in reprisal for the destruction of an
Islamic shrine in that country;
- the December 1994 hijacking of an Air France passenger jet by Islamic
terrorists belonging to the Algerian Armed Islamic Group (GIA), who
plotted—as in the 9/11 attacks that would follow less than a decade
later—to crash the aircraft and the 283 passengers on board into
downtown Paris;[14]
- the wave of bombings unleashed by the GIA between the following
July and October, in metro trains, outdoor markets, cafes, schools,

and popular tourist spots, during which 8 people were killed and more than 180 others wounded;

• the unrelenting bloodletting by Islamic extremists in Algeria itself, which has claimed the lives of an estimated 100,000 people there since 1992.

As this list suggests, terrorism motivated in whole or in part by religious imperatives has often led to more intense acts of violence that have produced considerably higher levels of fatalities than the relatively more discriminating and less lethal incidents of violence perpetrated by secular terrorist organizations. Although religious terrorists committed only 6 percent of recorded terrorist incidents between 1998 and 2004, their acts were responsible for 30 percent of the total number of fatalities recorded during that time period.[15] The direct relationship between the religious motive for terrorism and higher numbers of deaths is even more dramatically depicted by the record of violence perpetrated by Shi'a Islamic terrorists during the 1980s and by al Qaeda specifically since 1998. Although Shi'a groups committed only 8 percent of all international terrorist incidents between 1982 and 1989, they nonetheless were responsible for 30 percent of the total number of fatalities arising from those incidents.[16] And while al Qaeda perpetrated only 0.1 percent of all terrorist attacks between 1998 and 2004, it was responsible for nearly 19 percent of total fatalities from terrorist attacks during that time period.[17]

Core Characteristics of Religious Terrorism

The reasons that terrorist incidents perpetrated for religious motives result in so many more deaths may be found in the radically different value systems, mechanisms of legitimation and justification, concepts of morality, and worldviews embraced by the religious terrorist and his secular counterpart.

For the religious terrorist, violence is first and foremost a sacramental act or divine duty executed in direct response to some theological demand or imperative. Terrorism thus assumes a transcendental dimension, and its perpetrators therefore often disregard the political, moral, or practical constraints that may affect other terrorists. Whereas secular terrorists, even if they have the capacity to do so, rarely attempt indiscriminate killing on a truly massive scale because such tactics are not consonant with their political aims and therefore are regarded as counterproductive, if not immoral, religious terrorists often seek the elimination of broadly defined categories of enemies and accordingly regard such large-scale violence not only as morally justified but as necessary expedients for the attainment of their goals. Religion—conveyed by sacred text and imparted via clerical authorities claiming to speak for the divine—therefore critically serves as a means to explain contemporary events and, in turn, as a legitimating force justifying violence. This explains why clerical sanction is so important to religious terrorists and why religious figures are often required to "bless" (i.e., approve or sanction) terrorist operations before they are executed.

Finally, religious and secular terrorists also have starkly different perceptions of themselves and their violent acts. Whereas secular terrorists regard violence either as a way of instigating the correction of a flaw in a system that is basically good or as a means to foment the creation of a new system, religious terrorists see themselves not as components of a system worth preserving but as "outsiders" seeking fundamental changes in the existing order. This sense of alienation also enables the religious terrorist to contemplate far more destructive and deadly types of terrorist operations than secular terrorists, indeed to embrace a far more open-ended category of "enemies" for attack—that is, anyone who is not a member of the terrorists' religion or religious sect. This explains the rhetoric common to "holy terror" manifestos describing those outside of the terrorists' religious community in denigrating and dehumanizing terms as, for example, "infidels," "dogs," "children of Satan," and "mud people." The deliberate use of such terminology to condone and justify terrorism is significant, for it further erodes constraints on violence and bloodshed by portraying the terrorists' victims as either subhuman or unworthy of living.

Islamic Groups

These core characteristics, while common to religious terrorists of all faiths, have nonetheless often been most closely associated with Islamic terrorist groups in general and Iranian-inspired ones and al Qaeda and its associates in particular.

The revolution that transformed Iran into an Islamic republic in 1979 played a crucial role in the modern advent of religious terrorism. At the root of the Iranian-backed Islamic terrorist campaign was the aim of extending the fundamentalist interpretation of Islamic law espoused in Iran to other Muslim countries. "We must strive to export our Revolution throughout the world," the Ayatollah Khomeini declared on the occasion of the Iranian new year in March 1980, just over a year after the establishment of the Islamic Republic in Iran, and must abandon all idea of not doing so, for not only does Islam refuse to recognize any difference between Muslim countries, it is the champion of all oppressed people. . . . We must make plain our stance toward the powers and superpowers and demonstrate to them despite the arduous problems that burden us. Our attitude to the world is dictated by our beliefs.[18]

The Iranian revolution in Iran has been held up as an example to Muslims throughout the world, exhorting them to reassert the fundamental teachings of the Qur'an and to resist the intrusion of Western—particularly United States—influence into the Middle East. This stance reflects the beliefs and history of Shi'a Islam as interpreted by Khomeini and subscribed to by his followers in Iran and other Middle Eastern countries. It begins with the notion of the Shi'a as a centuries-old minority within Islam, persecuted because of its special, revealed knowledge, but it further entails an unswerving conviction of the inherent illegitimacy of all secular government. Under this rationale, legitimacy can be conferred only through the adoption of Islamic law in order to facilitate the return of the Prophet Mohammed to earth as the Messiah. Accordingly, since Iran is the only state to have begun the process of redemption by creating a "true" Islamic state, it must be the advocate for the oppressed and aggrieved everywhere. Not only are violence and coercion permissible in order to achieve the worldwide spread of Islamic law, but they are also a necessary means to this divinely sanctioned end.

The sense of alienation and of the necessity for far-reaching changes in the world order is apparent in the works of a number of Shi'a theologians. "The world as it is today is how others shaped it," wrote Ayatollah Baqer al-Sadr. "We have two choices: either to accept it with submission, which means letting Islam die, or to destroy it, so that we can construct the world as Islam requires." Mustafa Chamran has stated: "We are not fighting within the rules of the world as it exists today. We reject all those rules." Hussein Mussawi, the former leader of Lebanon's Hezbollah who was the victim of an Israeli helicopter-borne assassination in 1992, once remarked, "We are not fighting so that the enemy recognizes us and offers us something. We are fighting to wipe out the enemy."[19]

These statements also reflect the Shi'a perception of encirclement and concomitant predatory defensiveness. "We, the sons of the community of Hezbollah [the Party of God],"[20] a 1985 communiqué from the Lebanese Shi'a terrorist group of the same name declared, "consider ourselves a part of the world Islamic community, attacked at once by the tyrants and the arrogant of the East and the West. . . . Our way is one of radical combat against depravity, and America is the original root of depravity."[21] That Hezbollah perceives itself as fighting an entirely self-defensive struggle, sanctioned if not commanded by God, is also evident in the pronouncements of the group's spiritual leader, Sheikh Muhammad Hussein Fadlallah. "We do not hold in our Islamic belief that violence is the solution to all types of problems," he once told an interviewer. "Rather, we always see violence as a kind of surgical operation that a person should use only after trying all other means, and only when he finds his life imperiled. . . . The violence began as the people, feeling themselves bound by impotence, stirred to shatter some of that enveloping powerlessness for the sake of liberty." In this context, Fadlallah pointed out, Israel's invasion of Lebanon in 1982 was the embodiment of the West's hostility to revolutionary Islam:

> This invasion was confronted by the Islamic factor, which had its roots in the Islamic Revolution in Iran. And throughout these affairs, America was the common denominator. America was generally perceived as the great nemesis behind the problems of the region, due to its support for Israel and many local reactionary regimes, and because it distanced itself from all causes of liberty and freedom in the area.[22]

Fadlallah unhesitatingly justifies Islamic terrorism on the grounds of self-defense. "We are not preachers of violence," he declared in a 1996 interview. "Jihad [literally "striving," but in this context "holy war"] in Islam is a defensive movement against those who impose violence."[23] For Hezbollah, then, the struggle against Israel's occupation of southern Lebanon was nothing less than divinely ordained. "The Resistance is not led by commanders," one local cleric proclaimed. "It is directed by the tenets of Islam."[24]

The role of clerical authority in sanctioning terrorist operations has always been critical to both Shi'a and Sunni organizations. The fatwa (a legal ruling or statement of legal issues, given by a mufti—a qualified jurist—at the request of a religious court)[25] issued in 1989 by the Ayatollah Khomeini imposing the death sentence on the author Salman Rushdie is precisely a case in point. Similarly, the Sunni extremists who bombed New York City's World Trade Center in 1993 specifically obtained a fatwa from Sheikh Omar Abdel-Rahman (the blind Egyptian cleric who is now imprisoned in the United States) before planning their attack. Muslim clerics have also lent their support and encouraged as well as given their blessing even to self-martyrdom—though suicide is forbidden by Islamic law. For example, immediately after the 1983 suicide attacks on the U.S. Marines and French paratroop headquarters, Hussein Mussawi said: "I proclaim loud and clear that the double attack of Sunday is a valid act. And I salute, at Death's door, the heroism of the kamikazes, which they are; they are now under the protection of the All Powerful one and of the angels."[26]

Nor are such sentiments restricted to radical Shi'a only. Militant Sunni fundamentalist organizations portray their struggle in similarly uncompromising terms. According to Antar Zouabri, a leader of the GIA's struggle in the 1990s to establish an Islamic republic in Algeria, there can never be either dialogue or truce in his organization's struggle against the illegitimate, secular Algerian government. The word of God, he argued, is immutable on this point: God, Zouabri explained to an interviewer in 1996, does not negotiate or engage in discussion. Zouabri further couched the GIA's campaign in terms of an "all-out war." Its ineluctable mission, he said, is to "found a true Islamic state": should innocents perish in the course of achieving this divinely commanded aim, then so be it. In the first instance, Zouabri explained, the killing of "apostates," or those not a part of the Islamic movement, is a duty for him and his followers. In any event, the Prophet excuses the murder of innocents, as revealed in a verse from the Qur'an that Zouabri quoted: "I am innocent of those killed because they were associated with those who had to be fought."[27]

The struggle being waged against Israel by the Islamic Resistance Movement (Harakat al-Muqawama al-Islamiya), better known by its Arabic acronym, Hamas (which also means "zeal"),[28] is similarly cast in terms of an all-out war from which there can be no respite until the enemy is vanquished. The Hamas Covenant, for example, bluntly states: "Israel will exist and will continue to exist until Islam will obliterate it, just as it obliterated others before it,"[29] a view reflected in the words of a leader of the group's political wing, who told American scholar Mark Juergensmeyer that "Palestine is not completely free"—not in reference to the truncated sovereignty exercised over seven Palestinian urban centers by Mahmoud Abbas's (Abu Mazen) Palestine Authority (PA),[30] but "until it is an Islamic state."[31] Moreover, the Hamas Covenant's article 7 displays clear millenarian overtones, declaring: "The time [of Redemption] will not come until the Muslims fight the Jews and kill them, and until the Jews hide behind rocks and trees when the call is raised: 'Oh Muslim, here is a Jew hiding! Come and kill him.'"[32] The religious terrorist's preoccupation with the elimination of an almost open-ended category of enemies is further illustrated in the sermon preached at a Gaza City mosque in 1987 by Hamas's founder and spiritual leader, Imam Sheikh Ahmad Ibrahim Yassin (who was killed in 2004 by an Israeli air strike). Driving home the point that Hamas's war is not only against Israel, but against all Jews, Yassin reportedly declared, "Six million descendants of monkeys [i.e., Jews] now rule in all the nations of the world, but their day, too, will come. Allah! Kill them all, do not leave even one."[33]

Bin Laden has deliberately framed al Qaeda's struggle in similarly stark, uncompromisingly theological terms. At a time when the impersonal forces of economic determinism and globalization were thought to have submerged the ability of a single man to affect the course of history, bin Laden has effectively melded the strands of religious fervor, Muslim piety, and a profound sense of grievance into a powerful ideological force. "All men dream: but not equally," T. E. Lawrence, the legendary Lawrence of Arabia, once wrote. "Those who dream by night in the dusty recesses of their minds wake in the day to find that it was vanity: but the dreamers of the day are dangerous men, for they may act their dream with open eyes, to make it possible."[34] Bin Laden is indeed one of the dangerous men that Lawrence described. He has repeatedly defined al Qaeda's fundamental raison d'être in terms of the "clash of civilizations" religious typology that America and its allies in the war on terrorism have labored so hard to avoid. "These events," bin Laden declared in his October 7, 2001, statement, quoted at the beginning of this chapter, "have divided the world into two sides—the side of believers and the side of infidels. . . . Every Muslim has to rush to make his religion victorious. The winds of faith have come."[35] In a videotaped speech broadcast over al-Jazeera television on November 3, 2001, he reiterated this message, stating: "This is a matter of religion and creed, it is not what Bush and Blair maintain, that it is a war against terrorism. There is no way to forget the hostility between us and the infidels. It is ideological, so Muslims have to ally themselves with Muslims."[36]

During the late 1990s bin Laden set the stage for this clash as the author/architect of two major fatwas.[37] The first, issued on August 23, 1996, was a lengthy and turgid diatribe. Titled "Declaration of War Against the Americans Occupying the Land of the Two Holy Places: A Message from Usama bin Muhammad bin Laden Unto his Muslim Brethren All Over the World Generally, and in the Arab Peninsula Specifically," it presented bin Laden's seminal analysis of Islam under siege. In this respect, it also evidenced the perennial terrorist characteristic, described in chapter 1, of the reluctant warrior, thrown perpetually on the defensive with no option but to embrace violence in response to the transgressions of some aggressive, predatory enemy. "Praise be to Allah," bin Laden began.

We seek His help and ask for his pardon. We take refuge in Allah from our wrongs and bad deeds. . . . I bear witness that there is no God except

Allah, no associates with Him and I bear witness that Muhammad is His slave and messenger. . . .

It should not be hidden from you that the people of Islam had suffered from aggression, inequity and injustice imposed on them by the Zionist-Crusaders alliance and their collaborators; to the extent that the Muslims blood became the cheapest and their wealth as loot in the hands of the enemies. Their blood was spilled in Palestine and Iraq. The horrifying pictures of the massacre of Qana, in Lebanon are still fresh in our memory. Massacres in Tajikistan, Burma, Cashmere [Kashmir], Assam, Philippine, Fatani, Ogadin [sic], Somalia, Eritrea, Chechnya and in Bosnia and Herzegovina took place, massacres that send shivers in the body and shake the conscience. All of this and the world watch and hear, and not only didn't respond to these atrocities, but also with a clear conspiracy between the USA and its allies and under the cover of the iniquitous United Nations the dispossessed people were even prevented from obtaining arms to defend themselves. . . .

The walls of oppression and humiliation cannot be demolished except in a rain of bullets. . . .

Without shedding blood no degradation and branding can be removed from the forehead I remind the youths of the Islamic world, who fought in Afghanistan and Bosnia Herzegovina with their wealth, pens, tongues and themselves that the battle had not finished yet [sic].[38]

Although widely dismissed and ignored at the time as inflated rhetoric or posturing braggadocio, the 1996 fatwa was an unambiguous clarion call to battle for Muslims everywhere. "My Muslim Brothers of The World," bin Laden concluded,

Your brothers in Palestine and in the land of the two Holy Places are calling upon your help and asking you to take part in fighting against the enemy your enemy and their enemy the Americans and the Israelis. [T]hey are asking you to do whatever you can, with one['s] own means and ability, to expel the enemy, humiliated and defeated, out of the sanctities of Islam. Exalted be to Allah [sic].[39]

The second fatwa, styled as a "Statement of the World Islamic Front: Jihad Against Jews and Crusaders," was issued on February 23, 1998. Although the basic message was the same, it differed from the 1996 iteration in that bin Laden was now only one of five signatories. The others were Ayman al-Zawahiri, emir of the Jihad Group in Egypt; Abu Yasir Rifa'I Ahmad Taha, head of the Egyptian Islamic Group; Sheikh Mir Hamza, secretary of the Jamiat-ul-Ulema-e-Pakistan; and Fazlur Rahman, emir of the Jihad Movement in Bangladesh. After obeisantly paying homage to "God, who revealed the Book, controls the clouds, defeats factionalism . . . and peace be upon our Prophet, Muhammad Bin-'Abdallah, who said: I have been sent with the sword between my hands to ensure that no one but God is worshipped, God who put my livelihood under the shadow of my spear and who inflicts humiliation and scorn on those who disobey my orders ,"[40] the fatwa explained how the

crimes and sins committed by the Americans are a clear declaration of war on God, his messenger, and Muslims. And ulema ["the legal scholars of Islam, 'guardians of the faith' "[41]] have throughout Islamic history agreed that the jihad is an individual duty if the enemy destroys the Muslim countries. . . .

On that basis, and in compliance with God's order, we issue the following fatwa to all Muslims:

The ruling to kill the Americans and their allies—civilians and military—is an individual duty for every Muslim who can do it in any country in which it is possible to do it, in order to liberate the al-Aqsa Mosque and the holy mosque [Mecca] from their grip, and in order for their armies to move out of all the lands of Islam, defeated and unable to threaten any Muslim. This is in accordance with the words of Almighty God, "and fight the pagans all together as they fight you all together," and "fight them until there is no more tumult or oppression, and there prevail justice and faith in God."[42]

It was duly executed six months later with the simultaneous suicide attacks on the U.S. embassies in Kenya and Tanzania. A statement released that same day by the "International Islamic Front," reiterated and justified the previous calls for jihad.

Oh Muslims, the Israeli cancer in Palestine and the American cancer in the land Hijaz (i.e., Saudi Arabia) must be uprooted. Islam obliges us to liberate all Muslim land from occupiers whoever they may be whether American, Israeli or other forces. . . .

Oh Muslims, yours is an Ummah [worldwide community of Muslims] for whom jihad is the spearhead of its ideology whose creed is built upon a firm foundation with unshakeable belief that victory is from Allah and that Allah has promised authority, victory and domination which will undoubtedly be fulfilled God willing.[43]

The February 1998 fatwa also exemplified one of bin Laden's major theological accomplishments: interpreting the imperative of jihad as an individual responsibility incumbent upon Muslims everywhere.[44] This henceforth became a familiar theme of bin Laden's declarations, articulated with increasing fervor in a succession of uncompromising exhortations. In his "Message to the Youth of the Muslim Ummah" of December 9, 2001, for instance, bin Laden detailed how jihad

> has become fard-ain [obligatory] upon each and every Muslim. . . . The time has come when all the Muslims of the world, especially the youth, should unite and soar against the kufr [nonbeliever] and continue jihad till these forces are crushed to naught, all the anti-Islamic forces are wiped off the face of this earth and Islam takes over the whole world and all other false religions.[45]

The above statement, in fact, encapsulates precisely bin Laden's preeminent objective: the restoration of a pan-Islamic caliphate that is at once as idealized as it is venerated.[46] The caliphate, which disappeared with the demise of the Turkish Ottoman Empire in 1924, is recalled by Muslims as a "golden age of Islam,"[47] when the theocratic "structure of law and governance bequeathed by the Mohammed to his successors" reigned and divinely revealed Sacred Law took precedence over secular "arbitrary or natural law."[48] Ayman al-Zawahiri, cosigner of the February 1998 fatwa and a physician by training who was the founder and leader of Egyptian Islamic Jihad[49] and is seen as both al Qaeda's chief strategist and bin Laden's deputy,[50] also invoked this long-lamented desideratum in a fatwa he personally issued that same year. Al Qaeda's goal, al-Zawahiri wrote, was as immutable as it was straightforward: to "unite all Muslims and establish a government that follows the rule of the Caliphs."[51] Three years later, as he fled with bin Laden from Afghanistan, pursued by the Afghani Northern Alliance and the combined might of the American and coalition militaries, al-Zawahiri stubbornly clung to his belief that that day would still come. While the "establishment of a Muslim state in the heart of the Islamic world," he conceded, "is not an easy goal or an objective that is close at hand . . . it constitutes the hope of the Muslim nation to reinstate its fallen caliphate and regain its lost glory."[52]

The United States is seen by both bin Laden and al-Zawahiri as willfully impeding this goal. They describe the United States as the "far enemy" that must be defeated both because of America's alleged opposition to Islam and the active support that its gives to the so-called near enemy—the corrupt, reprobate, and authoritarian anti-Islamic regimes in the Middle East, Central Asia, South Asia, and South-East Asia that could not otherwise remain in power.[53] In a May 1998 interview with ABC News, bin Laden explained his profound enmity toward the United States: "We believe that the worst thieves in the world today and the worst terrorists are the Americans. . . . We do not differentiate between those dressed in military uniforms and civilians: they are all targets."[54] On al-Jazeera television the following year, bin Laden used similar words to make the same point: "Our enemy . . . is every American male, whether he is directly fighting us or paying taxes."[55] Indeed, during the years immediately preceding the 9/11 attacks, bin Laden often lauded the men who bombed the New York City World Trade Center in 1993 as "role models" and repeatedly beseeched Muslims to "take the fighting to America."[56]

Jewish Terrorism

Significantly, the same characteristics attributed to Islamic terrorist groups—the legitimation of violence by reference to religious precepts, the sense of alienation, the existence of a terrorist movement in which the activists are the constituents, and a preoccupation with the elimination of a broadly defined category of "enemies"—are equally apparent among the Jewish terrorist movements that have surfaced in Israel since the early 1980s. To a great extent, many of the members of these groups draw their inspiration from the late Rabbi Meir Kahane.[57] A native of New York, Kahane preached a liturgy of virulent hatred of Arabs that simultaneously extolled the virtues of Jewish aggressiveness and combativeness. He was a prolific author,[58] sermonizer, public speaker, and newspaper columnist[59] who founded his own (now outlawed) Israeli political party/vigilante organization, Kach (Thus), to disseminate his extreme, uncompromising views.[60] Kahane's overriding obsession was to reverse the mythical image of the Jews as victim. From this flowed his conviction that the Jews were enmeshed in a continual struggle against an inherently anti-Semitic world, surrounded by hatemongers and closet anti-Semites in the United States and predatory, bloodthirsty Arabs both inside and encircling Israel. "And, above all," he wrote in 1971 and reiterated throughout his life, "let us understand that people, in the very best of times, do not like Jews."[61] Kahane's prescription in the face of this eternally bleak Jewish condition was simple: a militant aggressiveness, portrayed as nothing more than the inalienable right of self-defense, that evoked images of Frantz Fanon's philosophy of the catharsis of violence.[62] "Never again," Kahane declared, "means that we have had it in the concept of being beaten and not hitting back. No one will respect us, and no one in the end will love us, if we don't respect ourselves."[63]

When Kahane and his family emigrated to Israel in 1971, he began to apply his program of strident self-assertion to the "Palestinian problem." This entailed repeated and vitriolic denunciations of governmental policies with respect both to the peace and to its alleged "soft" approach to countering Palestinian terrorism. In 1980, for example, Kahane openly called upon the Israeli government to establish an official "Jewish terrorist group" whose sole purpose would be to "kill Arabs and drive them out of Israel and the Occupied Territories."[64] For more than a decade afterward, he unceasingly called for the forced expulsion of all Arabs from Eretz Israel (the Land of Israel—that is, the biblical lands of Greater Israel, embracing both the current state's territory and the occupied West Bank) or for their physical annihilation if they refused to leave. In a speech before university students in a Los Angeles suburb in 1988, Kahane described the Arabs as "dogs," as people who "multiply like fleas" who must be expelled from Israel or eliminated.[65] In this manner Kahane sought to dehumanize Arabs completely and thus make his odious policy prescriptions more tolerable and acceptable to Jews. "I don't intend to sit quietly by while Arabs intend to liquidate my state—either by bullets or by having babies," he declared. "It's important that you know what the name 'Kahane' means to the Arabs. It means terror."[66]

Kahane's concerns, however, went far beyond practical matters of security to embrace mystical Judaic notions that condoned and justified ill treatment of—even violence against—the Arabs. In this respect, the responsibility of all Jews to work actively to hasten redemption became immutably aligned with the "sin" of returning to the Arabs the biblical lands (the West Bank) that God gave to Israel. "Is there no longer a G-d in Israel?" Kahane asked in 1981

> Have we so lost our bearings that we do not understand the ordained historical role of the State of Israel, a role that ensures that it can never be destroyed and that no further exile from it is possible? Why is it that we do not comprehend that *it is precisely our refusal to deal with the Arabs according to halakhic* [Jewish religious law] *obligation that will bring down on our heads terrible sufferings, whereas our courage in removing them will be one of the major factors in the hurrying of the final redemption?*[67]

When a Jewish yeshiva (Jewish religious school) student was murdered by Arabs two years later, a group of Kahane's followers in the ultranationalist West Bank settler movement Gush Emunim (Bloc of the Faithful) decided to take action. Their plan was to attack an Islamic college in Hebron in the Israeli-occupied West Bank at a time of day calculated to inflict the maximum casualties. Significantly, like their Islamic counterparts, the Jewish settlers sought the specific approval and sanction of their own clerical authorities for the operation. Indeed, among the group it was axiomatic that they would not—indeed, that they could not—act without rabbinical blessing. Having secured this dispensation, the terrorists struck: opening fire with machine guns on the Islamic students as they emerged from their classrooms for the noontime recess, they killed three and wounded another thirty-three.

Emboldened by the success of this operation—and armed once again with rabbinical sanction—the terrorists set in motion plans for an even more ambitious attack. They now plotted the simultaneous bombings of five Arab buses at a day and time when they were guaranteed to be packed with passengers but the roads were likely to be empty of Jews. The plan was to attach explosive devices to the gas tanks of the buses, setting them to detonate on a Friday evening, after the Jewish Sabbath had begun. However, just as the group was about to act, they were all arrested. Only then did information come to light that for the preceding four years the group had also been plotting to blow up Jerusalem's Dome of the Rock—the third holiest shrine of Islam—which occupies the same grounds as the most sacred site in the Jewish religion, the Second Temple, which was destroyed in A.D. 70.[68]

The so-called Temple Mount operation represented a dramatic escalation in the terrorists' campaign, propelling it on a violent trajectory from simple vengeance wrought against mere mortals to genuine millenarian dimensions. The twenty-eight precision bombs that the terrorist cell had constructed were to them not mere instruments of death and destruction but the means by which miracles were to be attained.[69] Their goal was not just to destroy a Muslim holy place for reasons of blind hatred or petulant revenge but to facilitate the resurrection of a Jewish Third Temple and thereby enable the Messiah's return. They were convinced that through their actions they could themselves hasten redemption. Even more alarming, though, was the terrorists' ancillary motive. By obliterating so venerated an Islamic shrine, they also sought to spark a cataclysmic war between Israel and the Muslim world. The terrorists' vision was that a beleaguered Jewish state, attacked on all sides by enraged, unrelenting, savage forces, would have no option but to unleash its nuclear arsenal. The result would be the complete annihilation of Israel's Arab enemies,[70] and the establishment on earth of a new "Kingdom of Israel"—a theocracy governed by a divinely anointed Jewish king and held in judgment by a true "Supreme Court."[71] As with the terrorists' previous operations, this grand scheme was again entirely dependent on obtaining clerical approval.

The same volatile combination—messianic visions of redemption, legitimated by clerical dispensation and achieved through direct action entailing indiscriminate mass murder—was also evident a decade later in the 1994 Cave of the Patriarchs massacre and the assassination of Rabin the following year.[72] The first incident occurred on February 25, 1994, at a holy site revered (and shared) by both Judaism and Islam. Dr. Baruch Goldstein, an American-born, ultranationalist, orthodox Jew and ardent disciple of Kahane, entered the Ibrahim (Abraham) Mosque, located at the Cave, and opened fire on Muslim worshipers who had gathered there for Friday (Sabbath) services. His attack was timed to coincide not only with the middle of Islam's holy month of Ramadan (when the mosque was certain to be filled to capacity) but also with the Jewish festival of Purim. Purim celebrates how a Jew named Mordecai, living in fifth-century B.C. Persia, single-handedly saved his people from their archenemy, Haman. Seeking to play the role of a modern-day savior, Goldstein fired 119 bullets from his American-manufactured M-16 assault rifle into the crowd, killing 29 and wounding 150 before he was set upon by the stunned congregants, who beat him to death. Goldstein's grave is now a shrine, guarded and revered by the ultrareligious nationalists who share his intense animus toward secular Israeli government and regard the peace accords as a blasphemous plan to hand over to the Palestinians the biblical lands that God gave to the Jewish people. Like the Temple Mount plotters, Goldstein had sought to place himself in the vanguard of the actualization of the Jews' destiny. His mission, like theirs, was no less than to hasten redemption through the cataclysmic forces that his violent act was meant to unleash. This, Goldstein was certain, would ensure not only Israel's perennial possession of its biblical birthright but the coming of the Messiah as foretold by Kahane.

The assassination in 1995 of Prime Minister Rabin exuded the same uncompromising blend of religious fervor coupled with intense enmity toward Israel's secular government, its elected leaders, and the peace process that would return God-given lands to the Jews' most implacable opponents. Like Goldstein, Amir believed that he was fulfilling God's will. Invoking the *halakhic* decree of the "law of the pursuer" (*Din Rodef*), he explained to his police interrogators that he was completely justified in murdering the person he considered the architect of the Jewish people's doom. "The minute a Jew betrays his people and country to the enemy," Amir maintained, "he must be killed."[73] Amir appears to have been greatly influenced by extremist rabbis who had repeatedly condemned Rabin to death as a mortal enemy of the Jewish people.[74] Amir, accordingly, felt a moral obligation—what he himself described as a "mystical" urge—to kill a person declared by his religious authorities to pose so grave a danger to the Jewish people. "Perhaps physically I acted alone," Amir proclaimed during his trial, "but it was not only my finger on the trigger but the entire nation which for two thousand years dreamed about this country and spilled its blood for it."[75] Indeed, information that came to light after the assassination revealed that Amir had tried to murder Rabin on at least two previous occasions. The assassination, moreover, was intended by Amir and his alleged confederates to be only the first step in a campaign of mass murder, including car bombings to avenge Palestinian suicide attacks as well as the murder of Palestinian terrorists released from Israeli jails as part of the peace process.

Any hope that these uncompromisingly violent sentiments—backed and indeed encouraged by clerical decree—might have dissipated in the furor and national soul-searching that followed Rabin's assassination was dispelled by the call from an extremist rabbi in April 1997 for Jews to emulate Hamas and launch suicide attacks of their own against Arabs. "Suicide during wartime is permissible for the sake of the victory of Israel," wrote the rabbi from the West Bank settlement of Tapuah, advocating Jewish self-martyrdom in an article titled "Sacrificing Oneself for God." "A man who volunteers for such operations," he proclaimed, "will be called a hero and a martyr."[76]

American Christian White Supremacists

Half a world away from the Middle East in the heartland of America, the use of violence is similarly justified by theological imperative as a means to overthrow a reviled secular government and attain both racial purification and religious redemption. The bombing of the Alfred P. Murrah Federal Office Building in Oklahoma City in April 1995 suddenly shed unaccustomed light on an indigenous, violent, Christian white supremacist movement that had been active long before this tragedy.

In June 1997 Timothy McVeigh, a twenty-eight-year-old U.S. Army veteran, was convicted in a Denver federal court of perpetrating the attack. Sentenced to death by lethal injection, McVeigh was executed four years later. An antigovernment, right-wing extremist, McVeigh engineered the attack with the help of a friend, Terry L. Nichols, to commemorate the second anniversary of the FBI's bloody assault on the Branch Davidians' compound in

Waco, Texas, in the course of which seventy-four people, including twenty-one children, were killed.[77] He and his alleged accomplice(s) were apparently obsessed by the idea that the Waco assault—and a similar FBI siege of an alleged white supremacists' rural cabin at Ruby Ridge, Idaho, the previous year[78]—represented the opening salvo in U.S. government plans to outlaw and seize all privately held firearms. There were other motivations as well—including vengeance, protest, and armed resistance[79]—which, it transpired, are shared by the members of the well-armed, militantly antigovernment "citizens' militias" with whom McVeigh mixed. Zealous exponents, like those linked to the Oklahoma City bombing, of the American Constitution's Second Amendment, which provides for a well-regulated civilian militia and upholds the right to bear arms, many of these groups also evince the same combination of seditious, anti-Semitic, and racist views that is common to the broader American Christian Patriot (white supremacist) movement. In this respect, the militias have been described as part of a longer "conveyor belt," in a phrase coined by Leonard Zeskind (the director of the Atlanta-based Center for Democratic Renewal, an organization that monitors militia activity). The metaphor is intended to depict a process whereby individuals are initially recruited into groups like the militias on the basis of their opposition to legislation outlawing firearms but gradually come to embrace increasingly extreme and violent positions that, in turn, are legitimated by appeals to scripture and theological imperatives.

Although organized hate groups and other bodies similarly preoccupied with far-fetched conspiracy theories have existed in the United States for decades, the advent of extremist white supremacist "citizens' militias" and related Christian Patriot paramilitary groups oriented toward "survivalism," outdoor skills, guerrilla training, and outright sedition is a more recent development. Thus, while the various militia movements have surfaced only within the past fifteen years or so, they are in fact but the latest manifestations of a radical right-wing and white supremacist movement that has repeatedly "repackaged" itself in a bid to attract new recruits and a larger number of adherents and supporters. With the militias, the wider antigovernment movement discovered a powerful way of attracting people—like McVeigh—who were not only vehemently opposed to gun control but also subscribed to a variety of fantastic conspiracy theories that invariably involved the Clinton administration in some master plan to seize all firearms held by American citizens and thereby proscribe fundamental individual liberties. According to Michael Fortier, a close friend of McVeigh's, who testified for the prosecution at McVeigh's trial, "We both believed that the United Nations was actively trying to form a one-world government, disarm the American public, take away our weapons."[80] The Michigan Militia, an allegedly twelve-thousand-strong paramilitary survivalist organization to which McVeigh and Nichols are believed to have been linked,[81] believes that the U.S. government has already initiated a program to control completely the life of every American. "The Government is [already] in control," explains Ray Southwell, the group's cofounder and information officer. "And if you push back, if you cross the Government, they will come down on you hard. We are preparing to defend our freedom. The way things are going, I think bullets might be as valuable as gold and silver one day soon."[82] Accordingly, through training in guerrilla warfare and survivalist techniques, the militia prepares to resist what it maintains were plans by the Clinton administration to deploy UN forces armed with cast-off Soviet military equipment or hordes of communist Chinese troops, backed by Latino and black inner-city American street gangs, to crush any opposition. Stripped bare of its conspiratorial explanations, the Michigan Militia's purpose is sedition, plain and simple: its other cofounder and commander, Norman E. Olson, made no bones about that. "My goal is not to plan a revolution," he boasted in a 1994 message posted over the Internet (the favored means of communication of militia members and other white supremacists), "for revolution will come. . . . My goal is to establish the Republican Provisional Government."[83]

At one time, an estimated eight hundred other similarly oriented militias—with a total membership claimed to be more than five million, though more realistically put at no more than one hundred thousand—had reportedly organized in almost every state of the Union.[84] The difficulty in gauging even the rough dimensions of the American militia movement at what would have been its height in the mid-1990s is a product not only of its geographical pervasiveness and its then-unimpeded growth but also of critical differences between the two different types of militias that had emerged. On the one hand, there are the so-called talking militias (also known as "out-front" militias), to which the vast majority of the movement's adherents belong. The members of these groups are primarily concerned with opposing antigun legislation rather than with fomenting revolution, and consequently they are neither especially nor explicitly violent. Their politics therefore tend to reflect the entirely secular conspiracy theories that have long been associated with various far-right American groups parodied in films such as Stanley Kubrick's *Dr. Strangelove*. The "marching" militias (also referred to as "up-front" militias), on the other hand, were actively involved in violent, seditious activities, embracing the combination of revolutionary, racist, and anti-Semitic doctrines inherent in the wider American Christian Patriot movement today. It is this more radical element of the militia phenomenon—whose members perhaps number no more than a dedicated hard core of ten thousand people—who fervently believe in the impending UN invasion and takeover of America and therefore resolved to take violent action to prevent it from occurring.[85]

Among the more prominent of the "marching" militia groups that have come to light since the Oklahoma bombing is the Militia of Montana, or MOM. This organization embraces the same ineluctable revolutionary principles and harbors the same profound fears as its counterparts in Michigan and elsewhere. "Gun control is people control,"[86] its founders, brothers John and David Trochmann, declared in a 1995 interview. MOM's more than twelve thousand claimed members accordingly train in guerrilla warfare, survivalist techniques, and other unconventional tactics in preparation for withstanding the inevitable federal government onslaught to seize their weapons and deprive them of their inalienable right to bear arms, presaged by the Branch Davidian raid. The group also markets its own range of do-it-yourself manuals and tapes that not only explain how to manufacture bombs but exhort listeners to prepare for the coming apocalypse that is sure to engulf the United States in retribution for its "sins against God."[87] A more recent posting on its Web site explains in ambiguous language that

> We, at the Militia of Montana, are dedicated to ensuring that all Americans are educated to make an informed decision as to which direction America should go. Along with being physically prepared to withstand the onslaught which will erupt no matter where we end up, we must at all costs, keep reaching those who have not had the opportunity to decide for themselves. The Militia of Montana has been, and continues to be, a national focal point for assisting [sic] Americans in forming their own grass roots organization dedicated to American's [sic] sovereignty and status as an independent nation among the nations of the world.[88]

Montana is also home to other far-right groups, including the North American Volunteer Militia and the Almost Heaven "survivalist" compound. While the North American Volunteer Militia railed against the "mess" created by the U.S. government and warns, "We need cleansing ... we need blood to cleanse us,"[89] the millenarian Almost Heaven residents await the inevitable Armageddon. Founded and led by James "Bo" Gritz, formerly a presidential candidate for an extreme right-wing party and a U.S. Special Forces Vietnam veteran (supposedly the model for Sylvester Stallone's

"Rambo" character), this group embraces the same zealous advocacy of fire-arms possession and antigovernment sentiments as the militias, but also believes in a coming apocalypse, for which it prepares by stockpiling weapons, food, and valuables and training in survivalist techniques and guerrilla warfare.[90] Security is provided by Gritz's specially created elite SPIKE (Specially Prepared Individuals for Key Events) teams, which according to one knowledgeable observer bear as much resemblance to the mainstream militia organizations as the U.S. Army's Special Forces (Green Berets) do to the "weekend warriors" of the local National Guards (the American equivalent of Britain's Territorial Army).[91] In April 1996 a tense standoff between the FBI and yet another Montana militia, known as the Freemen, was defused and a repetition of the Branch Davidian debacle avoided when eighty-one days of negotiations led to the voluntary surrender of two of the group's members for whom federal arrest warrants had been issued.

To the south, the Texas-based Big Star One claimed a decade ago to have a military "division-sized" following, with separate "units" deployed across the northern part of the state and into Oklahoma and New Mexico; the Texas Constitutional Militia boasted a membership in the thousands and chapters in some forty counties; and a third militia, known as the Republic of Texas, prosecuted what it described as a "campaign of paper terrorism"—attempting to throttle state courts with bogus land claims and bad checks—claiming that the United States illegally annexed Texas in 1845 and therefore has no jurisdiction over the state.[92] The Indiana Militia is described by observers as a particularly militant anti-gun-control organization; its members proudly once proclaimed that they were "sick and tired of being raped and pillaged by the bunch of thieves that run the federal government"[93] and clamor to take matters into their own hands.

The militia movement's violent ambitions have been clearly illuminated by at least thirteen separate known conspiracies uncovered by federal authorities in the decade since the Oklahoma City bombing, among them the following:

- In 1995, seven members of the West Virginia Mountaineer Militia were arrested and charged with plotting to blow up the FBI's computer center in that state.
- Twelve members of an Arizona group known as the Viper Militia were arrested in 1996,[94] of whom six were later charged with illegal possession of explosives and machine guns along with conspiracy to promote civil disorder. The group is alleged to have plotted for more than two years to blow up seven federal office buildings in Phoenix

and to this end had carried out detailed reconnaissance, including videotaping of potential target sites. It was in the process of building up a stock of ammonium nitrate fertilizer—such as that used to construct the bomb that destroyed the Murrah Building—for this purpose. At the time of the arrest, the Vipers had amassed 1,900 pounds of the fertilizer;[95] the Oklahoma City bomb contained an estimated 4,800 pounds mixed with high-powered racing fuel.[96]

- Agents of the Bureau of Alcohol, Tobacco, and Firearms (BATF) arrested three members of the so-called Militia-at-Large for the Republic of Georgia in 1996. The three were subsequently convicted of conspiring to "wage war with the government," with plans including the assassination of senior elected officials and possibly even attacks at the then forthcoming Olympic Games in Atlanta.
- A group of white supremacists, describing themselves as members of the "Phineas Priesthood," were also arrested in 1996 in connection with a string of bombings and bank robberies in Spokane, Washington. Four either pled guilty or were convicted.
- Four Ku Klux Klansmen were arrested in 1997 and subsequently convicted of plotting to blow up a natural-gas processing plant to divert attention from a robbery that they were planning to finance seditious activities.
- Members of a militia group based in both Kansas and Texas were also arrested in 1997 and convicted on weapons charges pertaining to a series of planned attacks on U.S. military bases.
- A plot by members of the Michigan-based North American Militia to kill federal agents and unleash a bombing campaign was uncovered during 1997–98 and the conspirators arrested and convicted on explosives, weapons, and conspiracy charges.
- In 1998, members of a white supremacist group, the New Order, were convicted of plotting to "bomb public buildings around the country, rob banks, poison water supplies, and assassinate federal judges and others."
- Two white supremacists were convicted of planning to instigate a "race war" in 2001 by destroying Jewish and African American landmarks.
- In 2003, two antigovernment extremists were convicted of amassing a "huge arsenal of illegal weapons and explosives in Tyler, Texas, including suitcase bombs and a working chemical weapon."[97] They apparently possessed sufficient quantities of sodium cyanide to kill some six thousand people and had stockpiled half a million rounds of ammunition and sixty pipe bombs.[98]

Finally, American law enforcement agencies uncovered three separate plots in 1995 that involved people who had connections to various American Christian white supremacist organizations that sought to obtain deadly toxins and contaminants, presumably to use in terrorist attacks. In March, two members of the Minnesota Patriots Council, a militia group, were convicted of stockpiling enough ricin to kill at least 129 people,[99] allegedly as part of a plan to murder IRS agents, U.S. marshals, and local deputy sheriffs. According to the FBI, ricin is ranked as the third most toxic known substance, behind only plutonium and botulism: a minute amount can kill in minutes if inhaled, ingested, or absorbed through the skin. Two months later, a man described as a certified microbiologist—who also had links to the Aryan Nations—was able to order a quantity of bubonic plague agent through the mail from a Maryland chemical supply firm. He had obtained three vials of *Yersinia pestis*—a bacterium credited with having wiped out one-third of the population of fourteenth-century Europe. In addition to the bacterium, police found in his home a dozen M-1 carbines, smoke grenades, blasting caps—and white supremacist literature.[100] And in December, an Arkansas resident with reputed ties to white supremacist survivalist groups in that state was arrested at his farm on charges of having attempted to smuggle 130 grams of ricin into the United States from Canada. Canadian customs officials also discovered in the man's car four guns and more than twenty thousand rounds of ammunition. When U.S. authorities searched the man's Arkansas farm, they found copies of the (commercially available) *Poisoner's Handbook*, which explains how to extract ricin from castor beans, and *Silent Death*, which describes how to use toxic compounds to poison people.[101]

The members of all these groups, it should be noted, are not full-time, "professional" terrorists—like the more familiar Irish, Basque, Middle Eastern, and left-wing extremists active in Europe throughout the past few decades—but consider themselves "minutemen": ordinary citizens and patriots ready to take up arms at a moment's notice to defend their inalienable rights, self-styled heirs of the tradition of the American Revolution. It is therefore significant that the Oklahoma City bombing took place on the date that the American Revolution commenced in Boston 220 years earlier. Indeed, McVeigh actually used this analogy to describe himself and the reasons behind his actions. "Any able-bodied adult male, any patriot," he told a British journalist, "is responsible for defending his liberty. Just like the Minutemen of the revolution."[102]

Although the militias are a relatively recent phenomenon, their pedigree can be traced back to the Posse Comitatus (Latin for "power of the county") movement founded during the 1970s and its 1980s offshoot—with which

McVeigh is also believed to have had ties—the Arizona Patriots. These groups strenuously reject any form of government above the county level and specifically oppose federal and state income taxes, the existence of the Federal Reserve system, and the supremacy of the federal judiciary over local courts. Over the past two decades, local chapters of the Posse Comitatus have been founded in almost every state in this country. The group became increasingly violent, particularly in the American Midwest and the far Northwest, with members attacking local, state, and federal law enforcement officers who were attempting to serve subpoenas or otherwise enforce the law. An attempt to serve a subpoena on North Dakota Posse Comitatus member Gordon Kahl in 1983 resulted in the first of many armed confrontations between the radical right and the authorities. In the ensuing shoot-out, Kahl killed two federal marshals before he himself was shot to death.[103] Undeterred by Kahl's death, in December 1986 six members of the Arizona Patriots were arrested and subsequently convicted on charges of plotting to bomb an Internal Revenue Service (IRS) office in Ogden, Utah, the Los Angeles Federal Building (specifically, the FBI offices located there), and a synagogue in Phoenix, Arizona. Now a new generation of Arizona Patriots is carrying on their predecessors' campaign. Nightly shortwave radio broadcasts by Patriot leader William Cooper exhort members to resist forcibly the imposition of the "new world order" epitomized by institutions like the United Nations and treaties such as the General Agreement on Tariffs and Trade.

It would be a mistake, however, to view either the militias or the older Posse Comitatus and Arizona Patriots organizations as simply militant antifederalist or extremist tax-resistance movements. The aims and motivations of many of these extremist groups in fact span a broad spectrum of antifederalist and seditious beliefs coupled with religious hatred and racial intolerance, masked by a transparent veneer of religious precepts. Those that also embrace religious and racial intolerance are bound together by the ethos of the broader Christian Patriot movement, which includes:

- hostility to any form of government above the county level;
- the vilification of Jews and nonwhites as children of Satan;
- an obsession with achieving the religious and racial purification of the United States;
- belief in a conspiracy theory of powerful Jewish interests controlling the government, banks, and the media;
- advocacy of the overthrow of the U.S. government, or the ZOG (Zionist Occupation Government), as the Patriot/militia groups disparagingly refer to it.

Many militia groups' "field manuals" (literally recycled and repackaged versions of U.S. military training handbooks and genuine field manuals) and other literature quote liberally from Christian scripture in support of their violent activities and use biblical liturgy to justify their paranoid call to arms. A militia recruit recalled in an interview his initiation into the movement in a rural Missouri church: "It was odd. It was extremely religious. There were people standing along the aisles carrying weapons, rifles, a few with pistols. We all stood up and walked to the front of the church in this strange procession. We were told that it was part of the ritual of becoming 'God's soldiers' in this 'holy war.' One of the organizers of the event then mounted the pulpit declaring, 'Soon we will be asked to kill, but we will kill with love in our hearts because God is with us.'"[104]

The connecting thread in this seemingly diverse and disparate collection of citizens' militias, tax resisters, antifederalists, bigots, and racists is the white supremacist religious dogma espoused by the Christian Identity movement, itself based on the "Anglo-Israelism" movement that emerged in Britain during the mid-nineteenth century. The core belief of Anglo-Israelism was that the ten lost tribes of ancient Israel were composed of Anglo-Saxons, not Jews. However, in marked contrast to the present-day Christian Identity movement in the United States, nineteenth-century Anglo-Israelism embraced an entirely pacifist doctrine. The basic tenets of the contemporary American version of the Identity movement include the beliefs that:

- Jesus Christ was not a Semite but an Aryan;
- the lost tribes of Israel are composed not of Jews but of "blue-eyed Aryans";
- white Anglo-Saxons and not Jews are the true "Chosen People"; and
- the United States is the "Promised Land."

In this context, Jews are viewed as impostors and children of Satan who must be exterminated.

Identity theology, combined with militant tax resistance and a form of regressive populism, figures prominently in the Christian Patriotism doctrine subscribed to by the "marching" militia groups today. The ideological heir to the Posse Comitatus with its hard-line antifederalist principles, Christian Patriotism goes one step further by embracing a salient theological component that combines Identity interpretation of scripture with the myth of the Illuminati—the global conspiracy theory first promulgated in the late eighteenth century with respect to Freemasons and later adapted to include the Jews, worldwide banking interests, and other dark, mystical forces. According to its modern-day American interpretation, the "two seed" theory embraced by Christian Patriotism, there are two races on earth: one godly and one satanic—the former comprising white Anglo-Saxon Christians and the latter Jews and all nonwhites. The movement further believes in the moral and legal force of a form of "common law" derived from a synthesis of the Magna Carta, the original articles of the U.S. Constitution, and the American Bill of Rights, and it also regards all paper money as "fraudulent" and holds that gold and silver are the only legitimate means of trade. McVeigh, it should be noted, openly admitted to interviewers his belief in Christian Patriotism and involvement in Patriot activities.[105]

At the nexus of Identity, Christian Patriotism, and the militia movements for the past three decades has been the organization called the Aryan Nations. An extremist, anti-Semitic, neo-Nazi group of white supremacists, survivalists, and militant tax resisters, the Aryan Nations has its headquarters on a secluded, fenced-in forty-acre site at the edge of the Coeur d'Alene National Forest in Hayden Lake, Idaho. It was founded in 1974 by the Reverend Richard Girnt Butler, a former aeronautical engineer from California who had moved to Idaho the previous year. Under his direction, the Aryan Nations performs a function similar to that of the PLO, acting as an umbrella group for like-minded organizations, among which it provides a coordinating and liaison function. To this end, Aryan Nations congresses were held almost every year between 1973 and the 1990s—except for 1985, when widespread arrests of members of a radical splinter group, calling itself the Order, dealt a stunning, albeit temporary blow to the white supremacist movement. MOM's leader, John Trochmann, for example, was a featured speaker at the 1990 event.

Today, the Aryan Nations is a shadow of its former self. It is still reeling from the dual blows of Butler's death in 2004 and a lawsuit four years earlier that forced the movement to pay $6.3 million in damages to Victoria and Jason Keenan. The Keenans, who had been assaulted by Aryan Nations security guards, also took possession of the organization's Hayden Lake compound. They subsequently sold the property to a philanthropist, who then donated it to a local community college.[106] Nonetheless, the Aryan Nations still continues to oversee at least seventeen local chapters across the United States.[107] Its hate-filled Web site remains up and running as well. One recent statement, for instance, declares that "all means are justified to restore Aryan honor," calling for a racial "holy war" that "can only end in total victory or total defeat,"[108] while another statement elucidates how

Christian theology justifies its own variant of "jihad," citing biblical text in support of its theological arguments for a religious war.[109]

The Aryan Nations ideology evidences the same mixture of racist and seditious dicta as is common throughout the American Christian Patriot movement. "WE BELIEVE," a 1980s-era brochure titled *This Is Aryan Nations* explained,

> there is a battle being fought this day between the children of darkness (today known as Jews) and the children of light (God), the Aryan race, the true Israel of the Bible. . . .
>
> WE BELIEVE in the preservation of our race individually and collectively as a people as demanded and directed by God. We believe a racial nation has a right and is under obligation to preserve itself and its members. . . . As His divine race, we have been commissioned to fulfill His divine purpose and plans. . . .
>
> WE BELIEVE that there is a day of reckoning. The usurper will be thrown out by the terrible might of Yahweh's people as they return to their roots and their special destiny.[110]

Indeed, the "Aryan National State Platform" cites as article 8: "A ruthless war must be waged against any whose activities are injurious to the common interest."[111]

This "cleansing" of the United States forms an immutable point of reference for the Christian Patriots' ideology. "Aliens are pouring over as a flood into *each* of our ancestral lands," Butler warned, "threatening dispossession of the heritage, culture, and very life blood of our posterity. . . . We know that as we return to our Father's natural Life Order, all power, prosperity, and liberty again comes to us as our possession, to establish justice forever on earth."[112] In promotional literature from its heyday in the 1980s, the group proclaims its desire to "make clear to ourselves and our enemies what we intend to do: We will have a national racial state at whatever price in blood is necessary. Just as our forefathers purchased their freedom in blood, so must we." The leaflet went on to decry "the leadership of malicious, bastardizing politicians . . . [in] modern, decadent America [where] millions of whites watch in abject dismay and hopelessness as their great culture, heritage and civilization evaporates in the steaming stinking, seething milieu of so many alien races, cultures and gods."[113] Robert Matthews, the deceased leader of the Order, once declared that in order to stem this tide, all Jews, blacks, Hispanics, and other "mud people," along with white "race traitors," must be exterminated in what he described as "a racial and religious Armageddon."[114]

It is particularly alarming that the Christian Patriots' expressed raison d'être—the cocktail of racism, anti-Semitism, and sedition—is justified and legitimated on theological grounds. It is at once a political and a grassroots religious movement. The leaders of individual groups within it are indeed often themselves clergymen—like the Michigan Militia's founder and "general," *Pastor* Norman Olson; the Idaho-based Aryan Nations' leader, *Reverend* Richard Girnt Butler; and the Ku Klux Klan's *Pastor* Thorn Robb—who deliberately flaunt their clerical titles in order to endow their organizations with a theological veneer that condones and justifies violence. In an article from the 1980s titled "An All White Nation?—Why Not?" *Reverend* Roy B. Masker, for example, explains how Aryan Nations members "are in disobedience to our Father and God, Yahwey, for allowing the Nation He gave us to become the mongrelized cesspool in which we now find ourselves. . . . Indeed, it is incumbent upon us to BUILD A NEW, ALL-WHITE NATION! We are under command to do so! All scripture demands it!" Masker concludes with the admonition "Woe to those who stand in the way of the Aryan juggernaut!"[115]

The Christian Patriots do not appear to recognize any of the political, moral, or practical considerations that constrain most other terrorist groups from causing mass death and destruction. There are, in fact, striking parallels between these groups and religiously motivated Islamic Shi'a and messianic Jewish fanatics in the Middle East. All of these groups transform abstract political ideologies and objectives into a religious imperative. Violence is not merely sanctioned; it is divinely decreed. The killing of those described as "infidels" by the Shi'a, "dogs" by the Jews, or "children of Satan" by the Christian Patriots becomes a sacramental act.

Although the Christian Patriots have so far caused far less death, destruction, and bloodshed than their Islamic terrorist counterparts, evidence has come to light that at least some of the movement's key figures had laid plans to engage in indiscriminate mass killing. For example, an indictment handed down by a U.S. federal grand jury in 1987 alleged that fifteen representatives of groups from throughout the United States and Canada met at the Aryan Nations headquarters in Idaho in 1983 to plot the forcible overthrow of the federal government and the creation of a separate Aryan nation within the United States. The indictment stated that they planned to "carry out assassinations of federal officials, politicians and Jews, *as well as bombings and polluting of municipal water supplies* [emphasis added]."[116] Any doubts of their seriousness of purpose were dispelled when police and federal agents raided a white supremacist compound in rural Arkansas in April 1984 and discovered a stockpile of some thirty gallons of cyanide to be used to poison reservoirs in Chicago, Illinois, and Washington, D.C.[117]

An identical scenario, in fact, is detailed in the novel *The Turner Diaries*,[118] written by William Pierce under the pseudonym Andrew MacDonald, which has been cited both as "the Bible" of the Christian Patriots[119] and as a major influence on McVeigh in his planning of the Murrah Building bombing.[120] The book describes a chain of events that begins with a white supremacist revolution in 1991 and culminates two years later in "an all-out race war" and worldwide nuclear conflagration. A terrorist group called the Order embarks on a ruthless campaign of violence involving the assassination of public officials and prominent Jews, the shooting down of commercial airliners, the poisoning of water supplies, and bombings of public utilities. The book reaches its climax when the terrorists seize the U.S. nuclear arsenal and obliterate several American cities before turning the weapons on targets in Israel and the Soviet Union.

Turner's tale, although fictional, is in many ways of a kind with Adolf Hitler's *Mein Kampf*, which was not taken seriously at the time, only to be turned into terrible reality a mere ten years after its publication. In fact, as incredible and lunatic as the events described in *The Turner Diaries* may seem, the strategy of the inchoate terrorist campaign waged in the United States between 1983 and 1984 by Robert Matthews and the real-life Order was based entirely on the battle plan detailed in the book. In another example of life imitating art, MOM's two-hundred-page manual reportedly reads exactly like a blueprint for battle copied out of *The Turner Diaries*, detailing plans for how to:

- paralyze America's entire economy, including its agricultural and industrial sectors and transport and communications systems;
- assassinate prominent "artists and sports figures" and other leading personalities as a "useful form of propaganda for the revolutionary and patriot principles";
- eliminate spies and traitorous government officials; and
- generally foment "an air of nervousness, discredit, insecurity, uncertainty, and concern on the part of government."[121]

The bizarre apocalyptic vision of *The Turner Diaries* has long formed an integral part of the beliefs of white supremacists, Christian Patriots, and militia adherents. Whereas most people, for example, harbor deep fears of a nuclear war, many white supremacists appear to welcome the prospect as an opportunity to eliminate their avowed "enemies" and permit the fulfillment of their objectives to create a new world order peopled exclusively by the white race. The self-described purpose of the Covenant, the Sword, and the Arm of the Lord's former compound at Mountain Home, Arkansas (where the cyanide was discovered), was "to build an Ark for God's people during the coming tribulations on the earth."[122] Accordingly, the hundred or so men, women, and children who lived in the compound prepared themselves for the coming Armageddon by stockpiling weapons, food, and valuables and undergoing training in survivalist techniques and guerrilla warfare. As *Pastor* Terry Noble, a spokesman for the group, once explained, "We are Christian survivalists who believe in preparing for the ultimate holocaust. . . . The coming war is a step toward God's government."[123]

The influence that apocalyptic revelations and millenarian imperatives exerted over many of these groups may be seen in the "DIY [do-it-yourself] apocalypse kit" marketed by MOM. The kit reportedly contained such detailed instructions as the need to build at least two concealed and well-protected "fall-out" shelters, stockpile enough food to last for at least a year, and arm oneself with, at the very minimum, a Colt AR-15 assault rifle and six hundred rounds of .223 ammunition as well as at least one 9 mm–type Beretta automatic pistol with no fewer than two hundred bullets. A can opener, a toothbrush, and thermal underwear are the other recommended essentials—with MOM offering for sale such additional optional gear as a military surplus NBC (nuclear, biological, and chemical) protective suit (available in green only) for fifty dollars.[124]

These beliefs involving the inevitability of Armageddon are actively encouraged by proselytizers of Dominion theology, the most recent reinterpretation of Christian Identity doctrine circulating among the Christian Patriots. Dominion theology has been described by one knowledgeable observer as a "post-millennial Bible-based doctrine" incorporating the main tenets of Identity dogma. Thus, in addition to anti-Semitism and racism, Dominionists believe that it is incumbent upon each individual to hasten redemption by working actively to ensure the return of the Messiah (in the Dominionists' vision, Christ). Only by accelerating the inevitable apocalypse, Dominionists contend, will the tribulations that currently afflict the American Christian white man end. The apocalypse will be followed by a thousand-year period of rule by Christians, at the end of which Christ will return to earth.[125]

The abiding link between religion and violence was most clearly demonstrated at the conference sponsored by a leading Identity and Dominionist figure, *Reverend* Pete Peters,[126] in Estes Park, Colorado, in October 1992.[127] At that meeting, Louis Beam—one of the preeminent figures in American white supremacism—defined the violent strategy of "leaderless resistance" for the militia movement. Beam, a Vietnam veteran and former Grand Dragon of the Texas Ku Klux Klan, whose close ties with Butler led to his appointment as the Aryan Nations' ambassador-at-large, has long been at the cutting edge of white supremacist violent activism. It was he who, in the early 1980s, pioneered the use of computer bulletin boards as a means for like-minded hatemongers both to communicate with one another and to circulate literature and information otherwise outlawed by the U.S. and Canadian postal services. Beam was thus well positioned to take the American white supremacist movement into the twenty-first century, making full use of the advanced capabilities of the Internet and the World Wide Web. Information and literature from obscure organizations that was once difficult to obtain therefore has been made readily available over the Internet to millions; for example, the Aryan Nations can offer its materials to a huge audience via its Web site. Beam's concept of "leaderless resistance" was designed to avoid the mistakes of the past, when traditional-type terrorist groups like the Order were created to prosecute the white-race revolution, only to be undermined and ultimately neutralized by arrests and informants. Accordingly, Beam proposed that "phantom cell networks" or "autonomous leadership units" (ALUs) be established that would operate completely independently of one another but, through their individual terrorist acts, would eventually join together to create a chain reaction leading to a nationwide white supremacist revolution.

The object of "leaderless resistance," Beam has explained, is to "defeat state tyranny."[128] The concept is taken from the white supremacist adventure novel *Hunter*, William Pierce's sequel to *The Turner Diaries* (again written under the pseudonym Andrew MacDonald). The impact of the strategy on the militia movement has been profound. For example, the "field manual" produced by "the Free Militia" in Wisconsin—typical of the genre—states the following:

THE FUNDAMENTAL RULE GUIDING THE ORGANIZATION OF THE FREE MILITIA IS [NOT] GENERALIZED PRINCIPLES AND PLANNING BUT DECENTRALIZED TACTICS AND ACTION.

What is meant by this key statement is that the whole Militia must be committed to the same cause and coordinated in their joint defense of a community. . . . The way a balance between these competing concerns is achieved in the Free Militia is to organize all elements into "cells."[129]

Similarly, in an address to a meeting of the Washington State Militia in January 1996, MOM's John Trochmann was quoted as saying: "If the enemy forces have no idea what's . . . in store for them if they come to our back-yard . . . leave the element of surprise on your side. Not everyone has to stand up publicly. Go with the cell structure in some of your areas—have a ball. Let them guess what's going on for a change, instead of us."[130]

The latest incarnation of the fusion of religion and hate is believed to be the previously mentioned shadowy militant Christian Patriot activist-warriors known as the Phineas Priesthood. The name is taken from the Old Testament (Numbers 25), which recounts how a man named Phineas became an avenger priest by murdering a Midianite woman (named Zimri) whom he discovered having sex with her Israelite (Jewish) lover. The biblical tale is taken by some modern-day Christian anti-abortion extremists cum Identity adherents as a decree against "race-mixing" and a summons to "strike down those who are viewed as enemies of the pure white race."[131] The Phineas Priests' self-appointed mission is allegedly to impose what they believe is "God's law" on earth: that is, the enforcement of prohibitions against interracial marriage, homosexual-ity, and abortion and an end to the federal banking system. They are reported to be highly secretive: so little is known about the Priests that it is not even certain whether they are an actual group or organization or a loose association of like-minded individuals adhering to the wider movement's "leaderless resis-tance" or "phantom cells" strategy, or whether the name is simply a mysterious title adopted by individual Christian Patriot groups to confuse and mislead the authorities.[132] Joe Roy, the director of Klanwatch (a group that monitors hate crimes in America), believes that the Priests do genuinely exist, describing them as "zealots who truly believe they are commanded by God to carry out a revolution in the United States to restore 'God's law.'"[133]

Whatever the actual status of the Priesthood, a clear convergence of reli-gious terrorism and violence against homosexuals and abortion clinics and their staffs has been evident on several occasions in recent years.[134] In 1994, for example, a Christian fundamentalist minister named Paul Hill shot to death a clinic doctor and his escort in Pensacola, Florida. In his book *Should We Defend Born and Unborn Children with Force?* Hill cites Phineas's bibli-cal mission and writes of the need for a vigilante underground to punish all who "disobey God's law" on abortion or homosexuality and engage in other forms of blasphemous behavior.[135] The Priesthood was also invoked by Christian Patriots in defense of the slaying of three customers at a gay book-store in Shelby, North Carolina, in 1991, and it surfaced again in connection with a series of bank robberies and bombings that took place between April and July 1996 in Spokane, Washington. Three men were subsequently convicted for bombing a Planned Parenthood clinic (where abortions are performed), a local newspaper's offices, and a bank, as well as twice robbing the same bank to the tune of $108,000 (a sum that was never recovered). At the scene of some of their attacks the gang left a two-page printed document, signed with the mark of the "Phineas Priests." The document espouses both Dominionist and Identity liturgy, before concluding with the warning:

> Let the high praises of Yahweh [God] be in their mouth, and a two-edged sword in their hand; to execute vengeance upon the heathen, and punishments upon the people: To bind their kings with chains, and their nobles with fetters of iron: To execute upon them the judgement written . . .
> Flee you usurer from the face of our land, and all that would not that the Master should reign over them, for the end of Babylon is come. Praise Yahweh![136]

It should be noted that the uncompromising antigovernment fervor, aggressive racism, and strident anti-Semitism espoused by the American Christian Patriot movement has not been restricted to the United States. The racist British group Combat 18 (which takes its name from the first and eighth letters of the alphabet—Adolf Hitler's initials), for example, apparently openly emulates the American militias and Christian Patriot movements, advocating attacks on the police and other symbols of governmental authority. Its founder, Harold Covington, is, however, an American, and the group's mailing address is a post office box number in Raleigh, North Carolina.[137] And in Australia, militia groups patterned on the American model have reportedly been established using an organizational blueprint provided by MOM.[138]

Today, the American white supremacist movement seems a spent force. The National Alliance, which is reputed to be the largest remaining organization, currently has only about 1,500 members,[139] and the number of militia groups has declined appreciably, from the 900 or so thought to have existed around the time of the Oklahoma City bombing in 1995 to just 150 today. Moreover, the deaths of both Butler and William Pierce in 2002 denuded the movement of perhaps its two best-known leaders. In addition, Robert Millar, another prominent figure in the American white supremacist universe, who headed a white supremacist/survivalist compound in northeastern Oklahoma called Elohim City, passed away in 2001. And the subsequent conviction and imprisonment of Matthew Hale, whose World Church of the Creator was founded on the premise that only "white people are the creators of all worthwhile culture and civilization," removed from contention at least one would-be successor to Butler et al.[140]

At the same time, however, the movement has long demonstrated a remarkable resiliency and durability—combined with a proclivity for sharp, sudden spasms of violence—that cannot easily be discounted. Indeed, the deaths and imprisonment of these leaders and the declines in the number of nationwide chapters and overall membership do not appear to have been accompanied by a diminution in fervor or commitment among hardcore followers. According to MOM's David Trochmann, the remaining organizations are no less resolute and are still just as determined: they are just "much more private" and careful in expressing their views and organizational affiliations.[141] The National Alliance, for example, may have fewer members than before, but it still maintains chapters in some thirty states across the country.[142] Further, as noted in chapter 1, the FBI today is especially concerned about the threat from "lone wolves" like Timothy McVeigh and Eric Rudolph, neither of whom actually belonged to a white supremacist group, much less any existing terrorist group, but who were nevertheless clearly motivated and inspired by these organizations and their leaders to engage in violence.[143] Rudolph pled guilty in April 2005 to killing 2 people and injuring 150 others in a series of bombings that included the 1996 Olympics and a gay club in Atlanta, Georgia, as well as an abortion clinic in Birmingham, Alabama.[144] Like McVeigh, Rudolph was not himself a white supremacist, but he shared the beliefs and positions of that movement in this instance on issues such as legalized abortion and hatred of global institutions like the Olympic Games that, to Rudolph's mind, promoted the "despicable ideals [of] global socialism."[145]

Cults

The special potential of terrorism motivated by a religious imperative to cause mass indiscriminate killing has been perhaps most clearly demonstrated by the ominous activities of various religious cults and sects in the United States, Japan, and elsewhere since the 1980s. While the attention of law enforcement officials, government intelligence agencies, and security services was focused firmly on the more visible threat presented by familiar terrorist adversaries in the traditional ideological and ethno-nationalist/separatist groups, members of these organizations were already poised to cross the threshold of terrorist use of either weapons of mass destruction (WMD) or mass annihilation.

In 1984, for example, a nonlethal but disturbingly portentous incident occurred in the small Oregon town of Dalles. Followers of the Bhagwan Shree Rajneesh (an ascetic Indian mystic who, in addition to amassing a collection of ninety-three Rolls-Royce automobiles, had established a large religious commune nearby) contaminated the salad bars of ten restaurants with salmonella bacteria in hopes of debilitating the local populace and thereby rigging a key municipal election in the cult's favor. Although the plot to "take over the county" failed,[146] 751 people became ill, and 45 of them required hospitalization. Moreover, evidence subsequently came to light that the restaurant contaminations were in fact a test run for a more ambitious plot to poison the town's water supply.[147] The Rajneeshis'[148] successful cultivation and effective dispersal of the bacteria clearly suggested the ease with which lethal agents could potentially be produced and disseminated in even larger population centers.[149]

The release of deadly nerve gas on the Tokyo underground in March 1995 not only confirmed those fears but also marked a significant historical watershed in terrorist tactics and weaponry. Previously, most terrorists had shown an aversion to the esoteric and exotic weapons of mass destruction popularized in fictional thrillers or depicted in action-hero films and television shows. Radical in their politics, the majority of terrorists were equally conservative in their methods of operation. Indeed, from the time of the late-nineteenth-century Russian revolutionaries and the Fenian dynamiters who terrorized Victorian-era London, terrorists have continued to rely almost exclusively on the same two weapons: the gun and the bomb. The sarin-induced deaths of a dozen Tokyo commuters and the injuries inflicted on nearly four thousand others may have changed that forever.

The Aum Shinrikyo (Aum "Supreme Truth" sect)[150] arguably represents a new kind of terrorist threat, posed not by traditional secular adversaries but by a mass religious movement motivated by a mystical, almost transcendental, divinely inspired imperative. The group was founded in 1987 by Shoko Asahara. A partially blind, hitherto unexceptional purveyor of supposedly medicinal herbs (who in 1982 was fined eight hundred dollars and sentenced to twenty days' incarceration after conviction for selling fake cures) and owner of a chain of yoga schools in Japan, Asahara had emerged as a self-anointed prophet after a trip to the Himalayas the previous year. His messianic inclinations were subsequently encouraged by a vision he had while meditating on a beach after returning to Japan. According to Asahara, the Shiva God sent a "message" to him that he had been chosen to "lead God's army." Ashara believed that he had been ordained an *Abiraketsu no mikoto*, an ancient "light god," and given the divine task of establishing the "Kingdom of

Shambhala"—a utopian community populated only by those who had achieved psychic powers.[151] Not long after this experience, Asahara fortuitously fell into conversation with an eccentric historian he met at a mountainside spiritual retreat. The historian told him that Armageddon would come at the end of the century, that "only a merciful, godly race will survive," and that "the leader of this race will emerge in Japan." Asahara immediately knew that he was the person destined to be that leader. Transformed by this revelation, he changed his name from the plain-sounding Chizuo Matsumoto to the apparently more suitably spiritual Shoko Asahara.[152]

Shortly afterward, with just ten followers, Asahara opened the first Aum office. The new sect grew rapidly, tapping into the peculiarly Japanese fascination with mystical, obscure religious sects that combine the spiritual with the supernatural. Indeed, according to one account, at that time approximately 183,000 different religious cults already existed in Japan.[153] Aum's highly idiosyncratic mixture of Buddhism and Hinduism fused with notions of apocalyptic redemption exerted a powerful attraction for young, intelligent Japanese alienated by society's preoccupation with work, success, technology, and making money. Hence, by the end of 1987 Aum had fifteen hundred members with branches in several Japanese cities,[154] and by 1989 double that number.[155] In less than a decade, it would have some ten thousand members, organized within twenty-four branches scattered throughout Japan, alongside an estimated twenty to thirty thousand followers in Russia alone,[156] with an additional ten to twenty thousand converts in at least six other countries[157] and offices in New York, Germany, Australia, and Sri Lanka.

From the start, Asahara preached about the inevitability of an impending apocalypse, stressing his unique messianic mission and variously describing himself as "Today's Christ," "the saviour of This Century,"[158] and "the one and only person who had acquired supreme truth."[159] By 1994 these delusions of power and authority had led Asahara to believe that he should be king of Japan, claiming the mantle of Zhu Yuanzhang, a fourteenth-century Chinese religious leader who created the Ming dynasty.[160] Particular emphasis was given to the Hindu god of destruction and subsequent regeneration, Shiva, whose fifteen-foot visage dominated the entrance to the Satian-7 laboratory where the group manufactured the sarin nerve gas used in the subway attack. To round out his preoccupation with prophesied cataclysmic events, Asahara also borrowed Judeo-Christian notions of Armageddon and frequently cited the apocalyptic predictions of the sixteenth-century French astrologer Nostradamus, whose recently translated works had become best sellers in Japan. According to Asahara, the world would end—but he was never sure exactly when, variously fixing 1993, 1997, 1999, 2000, and 2003 as likely times. Whatever the date, Asahara was certain that Armageddon would be caused by a Third World War. Citing his otherworldly abilities of both "astral vision and intuitive wisdom," he proclaimed before an Aum conference in 1987 that nuclear war was "sure to break out" between 1999 and 2003. This catastrophe could be averted, Asahara assured his followers, provided that they worked actively to establish an Aum branch in every country in the world. "Spread the training system of Aum on a global scale and scatter Buddhas over the world," he advised. "Then we can avoid World War III for sure. I guarantee it."[161] From these apocalyptic predictions sprang Asahara's obsession with American enmity toward the Japanese in general and himself in particular. "As we move toward the year 2000," an Aum pamphlet warned, "there will be a series of events of inexpressible ferocity and terror. The lands of Japan will be transformed into a nuclear wasteland. Between 1996 and January 1998, America and its allies will attack Japan, and only 10 percent of the population of the major cities will survive."[162] Indeed, Asahara regularly blamed the United States for all of Japan's economic and social problems, as well as for attempting to destroy his own health. According to the testimony of Aum's former "Director of Intelligence," Yoshihiro Inoue, Ashara had stated that after overthrowing the Japanese government and seizing power, the movement's real challenge would be to deal with the U.S. military forces stationed in the country.[163] An intrinsic element of all these claimed plots was Asahara's fascination with nerve gas. "I come under a gas attack wherever I travel," he reportedly once declared, drawing a connection between the "jet fighters from the US forces [that] fly for exercises around Mt Fuji" and his alleged medical problems.[164]

Asahara thus deliberately fostered a climate of paranoiac expectation within the cult, driven by the same Manichean worldview embraced by other religious terrorist movements, with its conviction of the world as a battleground between good and evil. The sect's avowed enemies gradually expanded to include not only the predatory U.S. government and its minions in the Japanese government (who, Asahara alleged, were responsible for causing the January 1995 Kobe earthquake), but also a mysterious international cabal of Freemasons, Jews, and financiers. Asahara's adherence to the same far-fetched conspiracy theories promulgated by the American Christian Patriot movement is perhaps not entirely surprising given that he was also an unabashed admirer of Hitler and a fervent believer in the conspiratorial fantasies spun by such well-known anti-Semitic works as the turn-of-the-century forgery *Protocols of the Elders of Zion*.

In books such as *Disaster Approaches the Land of the Rising Sun: Shoko Asahara's Apocalyptic Predictions*, Asahara warned that Armageddon would be precipitated by a poisonous gas cloud dispatched from the United States that would engulf Japan.[165] Thereafter, a cataclysmic global conflict would erupt—involving both nerve gas and nuclear weapons—that, in words reminiscent of Hitler's proclaimed "thousand-year Reich," would lead to a thousand years of peace, after which the appearance of a new messiah would create a "paradise on earth."[166] In 1993, however, Asahara suddenly began to proclaim that the forthcoming apocalypse could be averted if Aum took proper action. "We need a lot of weapons to prevent Armageddon," he reportedly told his closest aides. "And we must prepare them quickly."[167]

Thus Aum embarked on its program to acquire an array of conventional and nonconventional weaponry that would effectively dwarf the arsenals of most established nation-states' standing forces. To achieve this goal, the group recruited scientists and technical experts from Japan, Russia (including two nuclear scientists), and other countries. In contrast to Asahara's lack of higher education—in 1977 he failed to win a place at Japan's best university, the University of Tokyo, and therefore immersed himself more fervently in yoga and his Oriental medical practice[168]—these individuals brought to Aum's projects superb credentials, including advanced degrees from their respective countries' most prestigious universities and research institutions. Among the Japanese recruited to Aum, for instance, was Seiichi Endo, Aum's "Minister of Public Health." Endo was a veterinarian and then a Ph.D. student at Kyoto University, considered the country's best university in the natural sciences, where he studied virology and genetic engineering. At Aum, he led the team of scientists tasked with developing biological weapons, including botulinum and anthrax.[169] Ikuo Hayashi, the "Minister of Medicine" and one of the five perpetrators of the subway nerve gas attack, had studied medicine at Keio University, one of Japan's best private universities. He subsequently held appointments as a heart specialist at the Keio University hospital and at the Henry Ford Heart and Vascular Institute in Detroit, Michigan. Hayashi was director of the Department of Circulatory Organs at the Japanese National Sanatorium when he joined the cult and was made director of Aum's own hospital. His responsibilities included administering drugs—including powerful hallucinogens and electroshock therapy—to "brainwash" recalcitrant group members and make them more compliant.[170] Another prominent Aum physician, Tomomasa Nakagawa, according to Robert J. Lifton, "became a visionary planner of large-scale killing" for Asahara. And Fumihiro Joyu, a telecommunications specialist who had been employed by Japan's space agency, became the cult's spokesman.[171] What all the Japanese recruits had in common, according to Mayuka Yamazaki, was that

> before joining Aum, they had questions about their lives. Some of them knew they were not outstanding enough to reach the pinnacle of Japanese society, some realized the limitations of their occupation and some were frustrated with their surroundings which [were] either boring or unfair. Aum effectively approached these young, intelligent but depressed elites, proposing to provide status, money, facilities and the tremendous opportunities to allow them to explore their potential capability to the maximum, and made them believe they could find themselves in Aum.[172]

Moreover, with its vast financial reserves (Aum's assets exceeded an estimated $1 billion,[173] and when the police searched Asahara's office, they reportedly discovered 22 pounds of gold and about £5 million in cash),[174] the sect was able to purchase whatever additional knowledge and resources its members lacked. Prime contractors in this respect were the Russian KGB's elite Alpha Group, the equivalent of the British SAS or American Delta Force, whose expertise in counterterrorist tactics (the group was established as a direct result of the Munich Olympics incident) and clandestine warfare (including sabotage, assassination, kidnapping, and intelligence and counterintelligence techniques) was imparted to Aum activists. Additional personnel from Russia's other military special operations force, known as Spetsnaz, reportedly provided further training in martial arts, escape and evasion techniques, and the use of various small arms, including rocket launchers and assault rifles. Aum is also thought to have purchased large quantities of small arms from KGB stocks and to have been in the market for such advanced weaponry as T-72 tanks, MiG-29 jet fighters, an SL-13 Proton rocket launcher and even a nuclear bomb. What is known is that Aum succeeded in obtaining a surplus twin-turbine Mi-17 helicopter, complete with chemical spray dispersal devices. The group had ambitious plans—and had already acquired sophisticated robotic manufacturing devices—to produce at least one thousand "knock-off versions" of Russia's world-famous AK-47 assault rifle, along with one million bullets. It had also perfected the manufacture of TNT and the central component of plastic explosives, RDX.[175] The group spent 90 million yen (about $9 million) on its manufacturing facilities for automatic weapons and another 34 million yen (about $3.4 million) to construct the Satian-7 facility.[176]

Aum's intentions, however, went far beyond a revolution facilitated by conventional armaments alone: it also armed itself with a panoply of chemical and biological warfare agents and had (unrequited) nuclear aspirations. When the police raided the sect's laboratories after the nerve gas attack on the Tokyo underground, they found enough sarin to kill an estimated 4.2 million people. In addition, Aum either had already produced or had plans to develop other nerve gases such as VX, tabun, and soman; chemical warfare agents such as mustard gas and sodium cyanide; and biological warfare agents that included anthrax, the highly contagious disease known as Q-fever, and possibly the deadly Ebola virus as well.[177] Authorities also found 100 grams of the psychedelic drug LSD—the equivalent of one million doses—and 3 kilograms of mescaline, among other hallucinatory and stimulant drugs.[178] As previously noted, these drugs, as well as electroshock therapy, were administered to punish cult members either for attempting to leave the cult or for even making contact with outsiders. These "brainwashing" treatments involved massive doses of LSD, which in some instances resulted in severe memory loss and other psychological dysfunction.[179] Aum's most ambitious project was without doubt its attempt to develop a nuclear capability. To this end, the group had purchased a 500,000-acre sheep station (known as Banjawarn Station) in a remote part of Western Australia. There, they hoped to mine uranium, which was to be shipped back to Aum's laboratories in Japan, where scientists using laser enrichment technology would convert it into weapons-grade nuclear material. The reason for a massive explosion that occurred near Aum's Australian holdings on May 28, 1993, which lit up the sky for miles and caused shock waves felt hundreds of miles away, is still unexplained but may have been related to Aum's nuclear research and development activities.

"With the use of sarin we shall eradicate major cities," Asahara had declared, and on the morning of March 20, 1995, his disciples put his deadly plan into action. The date was much sooner than had been expected, but Aum informants inside the National Police Agency had warned that the police were about to search the cult's compounds, and so Asahara suddenly ordered the planned attack to be brought forward in hopes of thwarting the impending raids and completely derailing the intensifying police investigation into Aum's activities.[180] At approximately eight o'clock on Monday morning, in the midst of rush hour, selected Aum cadres placed eleven packages containing sarin nerve gas on five subway trains on the Eidan Chiyoda, Hibiya, and Marunouchi lines. The trains were scheduled to converge within four minutes of one another at Kasumigaseki central station: the terminus at the heart of the Japanese government, used daily by the thousands of office workers employed in the country's most important ministries—including the National Police Agency. Eyewitnesses reported that some of the containers appeared to be ordinary lunch boxes or soft-drink flasks, while others were nylon trash bags wrapped in newspaper. In at least one instance, a man was observed stabbing his package with the sharpened tip of an umbrella, thus releasing the nerve gas. Almost immediately, passengers were affected by the noxious fumes: some were quickly overcome, others were afflicted with nosebleeds, oral hemorrhaging, uncontrollable coughing fits, or convulsions. In all, fifteen stations and three separate subway lines were affected. The casualties might even have been far greater had not favorable weather conditions fortuitously combined with hastened—and therefore perhaps botched—preparations that likely reduced the sarin's potency.

Amazingly, this was neither the first nor the last Aum attack to employ chemical or biological warfare agents. In April 1990 the group had attempted to realize one of Asahara's dire prophecies of an impending catastrophe by staging an attack with botulinum toxin. Using an aerosol device developed by Aum's scientists to disperse the poison over a wide area, the sect targeted downtown Tokyo and specifically the Diet (parliament) building. The toxin, however, proved ineffective. Another attempt to disperse botulinum in downtown Tokyo failed in June, as did a suspected Aum plot to spread anthrax the following month. Then, in June 1994, the group had tried to kill three judges presiding over a civil suit brought against Aum in the rural resort town of Matsumoto. The plan was to spray sarin into a block of flats where the judges were sleeping. Seven people were killed, and more than 250 others were admitted to the hospital with nerve-gas-induced symptoms. Though taken seriously ill, the judges survived. Incredible as it seems, a report previously issued by a special unit of the Tokyo metropolitan police department's criminal investigation laboratory pointing to the presence of the nerve gas apparently went ignored—despite repeated local complaints of strange odors emanating from the sect's nearby compound, alongside various unexplained disappearances of former Aum members and individuals who had attempted to investigate the sect's activities. Instead, the man who first reported the incident was branded as the culprit and accused of accidentally mixing some noxiously fatal concoction of weed killer.[181] Finally, in a last spasm of activity designed to avert the governmental onslaught directed at Aum in the wake of the underground attacks, members of the sect attempted to stage a chemical attack using hydrogen cyanide—more infamously known as Zyklon B, the same type of gas used by the Nazis at Auschwitz during the Second World War to murder tens of thousands of people—on May 5, the national "Children's Day" holiday.

Aum's objective, however, was not, as many have described it, wanton, mass indiscriminate murder as an end in itself, but the acquisition and unimpeded exercise of political power. Theological treatise and religious imperatives clearly played a preeminent role in the justification behind and motivation for Aum's campaign of violence and subversion. But killing for the sake of killing was not the engine driving Asahara's and the movement's grandiose ambitions. Indeed, it was Asahara's frustrations in pursuing legal, democratic means of change and influence that arguably drove him to embrace terrorism. As an adolescent, he had boasted of his desire one day to become the prime minister of Japan.[182] And in 1989 he presaged his entry into politics, explaining in *Mahayana*, Aum's magazine, "We have to complement what we cannot achieve religiously by [a] political approach."[183] In 1990, accordingly, together with twenty-five other Aum members, Asahara stood for election to Japan's House of Representatives as members of the Shinri Tou (Supreme Truth) Party.[184] Asahara was certain that he would win,[185] and he became deeply embittered by his defeat, claiming that the Japanese government had interfered to deprive him of the victory he had rightly won. Thereafter he became obsessed with exacting revenge by seizing power.[186]

On December 15, 1995, the Japanese prime minister, invoking a 1952 anti-subversion law, ordered Aum disbanded and seized all its assets. Although a court later ruled that the Anti-Subversive Activities Act did not apply to religious movements like Aum, new legislation—the "Regulation Against the Group Which Conducted Indiscriminate Massive Murder Attack" (*Dantai Kisei Ho*)—was enacted in 1999 that provided the authorities with new, strengthened powers to monitor and curtail the activities of groups like Aum.[187] Asahara and his lieutenants were charged with a variety of crimes, and in February 2004 a Tokyo district court sentenced Asahara to death. The Aum movement, however, astonishingly not only still exists but is reportedly thriving. In 2000 Aum renamed itself Aleph, and under a new leader, Fumhiro Joyu, its former spokesman, the group has attracted some fifteen hundred members.[188] Aleph has sought to distance itself from Aum's infamous past, portraying Asahara as its spiritual founder only, eschewing any theology that could be interpreted as justifying violence and murder, and making reparations payments to victims of the sarin attack.[189] A letter from the Aleph executive posted on the group's Web site in March 2005 evidenced this remorse:

> It is 10 years since that tragic day. The world has gone through great changes which people could not have imagined and so has our group. However, whenever we think of the people who have lived with sorrow, our mind always go back to the day. Here, again, we express our deepest

condolence on the people who died of the incident and give our greatest apology to what we did. As the best we can do, we will continue paying reparation from now. We will never repeat such a mistake.[190]

Conclusion

The emergence of obscure, idiosyncratic millenarian movements, zealously nationalist religious groups, militantly antigovernment, far-right paramilitary organizations, and a transnational network of religious extremists that seeks the restoration of theocratic rule over what was once a vast pan-Islamic empire arguably represents a different and potentially far more lethal threat than traditional terrorist adversaries—certainly a far more amorphous and diffuse one. The members of the Aum sect in Japan, the fanatical Jewish groups in Israel, the Christian Patriots in America, some of the radical Islamic organizations active in Algeria, Lebanon, and Palestine, and what is often described as the al Qaeda "nebula" do not conform to our traditional stereotypes of the secular terrorist organization. These groups had a defined set of conventional—and thereby potentially attainable—political, social, or economic objectives, and however disagreeable or distasteful their aims and motivations may have been, their ideology and intentions were at least comprehensible—albeit politically radical and personally fanatical.

In terms of the countermeasures that the government, military, police, and intelligence and security services can employ against these new types of adversaries, the first and most immediate challenge is simply identifying them. These ethereal, amorphous entities will often lack the "footprint" or modus operandi of an actual, existing terrorist organization, making it more difficult for intelligence, law enforcement, and other security specialists to get a firm idea or build a complete picture of their intentions and capabilities, much less their capacity for violence, before they strike. A second challenge is unraveling why mainstream religious traditions become radicalized and co-opted by violent extremists and why "fringe" movements or hitherto peaceful religious cults suddenly embark on lethal campaigns of indiscriminate terrorism. These primarily investigative, intelligence, and academic research issues need to be addressed before countervailing and deterrent measures can be considered. Traditional counterterrorism approaches and policies may not be relevant, much less effective, in the face of religious terrorism. Strategies that have been used successfully in the past—such as political concessions, financial rewards, amnesties, and other personal inducements—would be not only irrelevant but impractical, given both the religious terrorists' fundamentally alienated worldviews and their often extreme, resolutely uncompromising demands. Above all, the profound sense of alienation and isolation of these cults and religious movements needs to be vigorously counteracted. A bridge needs to be found between mainstream society and these militants so that they do not feel threatened and forced to withdraw psychologically into aggressive defensive stances used to justify violence or physically into heavily armed, seething compounds or into preemptive acts of violence directed against what they regard as a menacing, predatory society.

Demonstrable progress arguably has been made along these lines within the United States. The nonviolent resolution of the eighty-one-day standoff between the Freemen, a Montana militia organization, and the FBI in April 1996 provides a marked contrast to the debacle three years before involving the assault on the Branch Davidians' compound in Waco, Texas. By skillfully employing the tactics of negotiation and the nonconfrontational approaches developed during previous encounters with antigovernment and white supremacist groups, the authorities defused a potentially explosive situation, obtained the surrender of sixteen heavily armed Freemen who had barricaded themselves in the isolated ranch they had dubbed "Justus Township," and avoided the bloodshed that had accompanied previous incidents.[191]

But while patient negotiation and minimum force have an important role to play in specific instances, particularly sieges, there is a more widespread problem of intense, often paranoiac, antigovernment sentiments in many pockets of the American hinterland. Here, the challenge is surely one of developing preemptive educational programs to mitigate grassroots alienation and polarization and to stop the spread of seditious and intolerant beliefs before they take hold and become exploited by demagogues and hatemongers. Across the United States, progress can also be seen in this respect. A number of community groups and political action committees are attempting to counter the spread of ignorance, hate, and simplistic conspiracy theories that are used to explain complex economic phenomena and thus acquire new recruits to the antifederalist movement. Through a series of "town hall" meetings featuring plainspoken commonsense presentations that communicate important lessons in a vernacular as accessible and relevant to the local populace as that peddled by the conspiracy theorists, people gain a more critical perspective from which they can challenge the assertions of the sophists and refute the homespun ideologies that lie at the core of their odious belief systems.

The immense challenge of countering religious and religion-inspired terrorism among homegrown groups in the United States is eclipsed, of course, by that of ameliorating anti-American sentiment abroad. The tremendous international outpouring of sympathy and support that followed the 9/11 attacks has been vitiated to a great extent since by opposition to the United States–led invasion of Iraq and more general complaints over the Bush administration's prosecution of the war on terrorism.[192] The revelations about prisoner abuse at Abu Ghraib and the indefinite detention of "enemy combatants" at the Guantánamo Bay U.S. military base[193] have further sharpened friction between the United States and the Muslim world. Bin Laden's astonishing popularity among the populations of such key American allies in the war on terrorism as Pakistan (where in 2004 he was viewed favorably by 65 percent of those polled), in Jordan (55 percent), and in Morocco (45 percent) attests to the intense antipathy felt toward the United States in North Africa, the Middle East, and South and South-East Asia, as well as in other regions with large Muslim populations. This perception of Islam under attack by an incontestably predatory, aggressive U.S.-dominated West is of course eagerly exploited and expertly manipulated by bin Laden and his minions. "This is the most dangerous, fiercest, and most savage crusade war launched against Islam," bin Laden said in a statement broadcast by al-Jazeera on December 27, 2001. "God willing the end of America is imminent."[194]

The rise of bin Laden and his worldwide Islamic revolutionary movement, al Qaeda, is of course just such a case in point. The movement flows from a widespread perception of Islam under seige: threatened by an ineluctably bellicose Western-dominated world order and therefore portrays al Qaeda as the true defender of Islam and protector of Muslims everywhere. In this respect, the use of U.S. military force—even in self-defense or to prevent terrorist attacks—is seen not only by Muslims but by many others too as symptomatic of a heavy-handed foreign policy. This realization may account for the shift in U.S. foreign policy proposed in Washington, D.C., during the spring of 2005. The change would move away from the global war on terrorism declared by President Bush after 9/11 to a more subtle approach and mix of policy options now dubbed a "strategy against violent extremism." Although details remain sketchy, this reconfigured effort would specifically seek to ameliorate Muslim antipathy toward the United States by undercutting support for radical Islam.[195]

The above proposed policy adjustment notwithstanding, the resurgence of this ancient breed of adversary, the religious terrorist, actually means that nothing less than a sea change is required in our thinking about terrorism and the policies needed to counter it. Perhaps the most sobering realization in confronting religious terrorism is that the threat—and the problems that fuel it—can never be eradicated completely. The complexity, diversity, and often idiosyncratic characteristics of religious terrorism imply that there is no "magic bullet"—no single superior solution—that can be applied to all cases. Yet this fact only reinforces the need for multiple creative solutions, if not to resolve, then at least to ameliorate both the underlying causes of religious terrorism and its violent manifestations. Only by expanding our range of possible responses will we be able to target our resources prudently and productively in ways that will have the greatest positive effect.[196]

Chapter 5

Suicide Terrorism

In no area of contemporary terrorism has religion had a greater impact than in propelling the vast increase of suicide attacks that have occurred since 9/11. The years from 2001 to 2005 alone account for 78 percent of all the suicide terrorist incidents perpetrated between 1968 and 2005. And the dominant force behind this trend is religion.[1] Indeed, of the thirty-five terrorist organizations employing suicide tactics in 2005, 86 percent (thirty-one of thirty-five) were Islamic. These movements, moreover, have been responsible for 81 percent of all suicide attacks since 9/11.[2]

As of 2005, more than 350 suicide attacks had taken place in at least twenty-four countries—including the United Kingdom, Israel, Sri Lanka, Russia, Lebanon, Turkey, Italy, Indonesia, Pakistan, Colombia, Argentina, Kenya, Tanzania, Croatia, Morocco, Singapore, the Philippines, Saudi Arabia, Kuwait, and Iraq.[3] By comparison, at the dawn of the modern era of religious terrorism some twenty years ago, this was a phenomenon confined exclusively to two countries: Lebanon and Kuwait. Toward the end of the 1980s, however, suicide terrorism began to spread beyond the Middle East: first to Sri Lanka but then, as the 1990s unfolded, to India, Argentina, Israel, Saudi Arabia, Kenya, and Tanzania. It was also initially embraced by only a couple of terrorist groups: al Dawa, an Iraqi Shi'a group, and the Lebanese

Shi'a organization Hezbollah (mostly using its cover name, Islamic Jihad). Hezbollah's example of successfully driving the United States out of Lebanon with suicide attacks (which will be discussed) subsequently inspired other groups to adopt this tactic, specifically: the Liberation Tigers of Tamil Eelam (LTTE or the Tamil Tigers), Hamas, the Palestine Islamic Jihad, and al Qaeda. Even secular, ethno-nationalist movements that later resorted to suicide attacks have either deliberately cultivated religious imagery—such as al-Fatah in calling its special suicide unit the al-Aqsa Martyrs Brigade (combining "al-Aqsa," referring to the mosque in Jerusalem that, together with the adjacent Dome of the Rock, is Islam's third holiest shrine, and the word "martyr," among the most potent religious images)—or, like the Tamil Tigers, evidenced characteristics like the single-minded devotion to, and veneration of, a leader (in this case its founder and supreme commander for some three decades, Velupillai Prabhakaran) that arguably have more in common with a religious cult like Aum than with stereotypical nationalist-separatist groups such as the IRA or the Basque ETA.

Core Characteristics of Suicide Terrorism

Terrorists have become increasingly attracted to suicide attacks because of their unique tactical advantages compared to those of more conventional terrorist operations. Suicide tactics are devastatingly effective, lethally efficient, have a greater likelihood of success, and are relatively inexpensive and generally easier to execute than other attack modes. The terrorist decision to employ this tactic therefore is neither irrational nor desperate, as is sometimes portrayed; rather it is an entirely rational and calculated choice, consciously embraced as a deliberate instrument of warfare—the "strategic logic" to which Robert Pape refers.[4] For radical Islamic terrorist groups in particular, religious and theological justification plays an additionally critical role: it ensures a flow of recruits to these organizations that is needed to sustain suicide operations.

Suicide terrorism differs from all other terrorist operations because the perpetrator's own death is an essential requirement for the attack's success.[5] The suicide terrorist is the "ultimate smart bomb," a human missile relentlessly homing in on its target but with flexibility in timing and access. The suicide terrorist thus has the ability to effect last-minute changes in his or her attack plan, on the basis of ease or difficulty of approach, the paucity or density of people in or around the target, and whether or not security personnel are present or other countermeasures are visible. Suicide terrorist operations are also inexpensive to mount. According to one estimate, the total cost of a typical Palestinian suicide operation, for example, is about one hundred fifty dollars.[6] Yet this modest sum yields a very attractive return: on average, suicide operations worldwide kill about four times as many people as other kinds of terrorist attacks. In Israel the average is even higher, inflicting six times the number of deaths and roughly twenty-six times more casualties than other acts of terrorism.[7] These attacks are also less complicated and compromising than other terrorist operations, since no escape plan is needed: if the attack is successful, there is no assailant to capture and interrogate. The very fact that it is a suicide attack obviates the need to formulate a plan for the perpetrator(s) to get away—often the most complicated and complex aspect of a terrorist operation—and therefore greatly enhances its simplicity.

Suicide terrorism, moreover, is guaranteed to provide media coverage, given its irresistible combination of savagery and bloodshed. Suicide terrorist attacks are also an especially powerful psychological weapon. With the exception perhaps of only weapons of mass destruction (WMD) terrorism, no other terrorist tactic arguably induces the same fear and paralysis in the terrorists' target audience. This is of course precisely the terrorists' purpose: to intimidate government and citizens alike and create a climate of profound fear and insecurity that the terrorists seek to manipulate and exploit to their advantage. The suicide terrorist attack is thus deliberately conceived by its practitioners to have far-reaching and profound psychological effects and repercussions well beyond the immediate victims or object of the attack.

These core characteristics of suicide terrorism were all clearly evident on 9/11. First, the operation's success, of course, was completely dependent on the nineteen hijackers' willingness to martyr themselves.[8] Each, accordingly, not only was handpicked by bin Laden himself but also was then asked to swear an oath of loyalty, pledging to carry out a suicide operation. Then, in addition to the training that the hijackers underwent in preparation for the attack, each was filmed for a martyrdom video to be released after his death.[9] According to Khalid Sheikh Mohammed (KSM), all but one of the nineteen hijackers made such a tape. The lone exception (whom KSM did not name) was excused after he explained his fear that "it might be hypocritical and Allah, then, might not accept his sacrifice."[10]

Second, the plan itself was a masterful act of deception that sought to turn ordinary passenger aircraft into "human cruise missiles" and hence the ultimate smart bomb.[11] The 9/11 Commission Report specifically noted this aspect of the operation, describing its chief architect, KSM, as having used "his imagination, technical aptitude, and managerial skills to hatching and planning an extraordinary array of terrorist schemes," including the "use of aircraft as missiles guided by suicide operatives."[12]

Third, the 9/11 attacks were relatively inexpensive to mount. According to the 9/11 Commission, al Qaeda spent between $400,000 and $500,000 to finance the operation.[13] Its effects on both the U.S. and the global economy and the vast expenditures on security measures worldwide that have followed have of course been disproportionately immense. Bin Laden himself specifically lauded the cost-effectiveness of the 9/11 attacks in the video-taped message released just before the U.S. national elections on October 29, 2004. After citing a statement made at a conference held by the venerable London-based Royal Institute of International Affairs that al Qaeda "spent $500,000 on the event while America, in the incident and its aftermath lost—according to the lowest estimate—more than $500 billion," bin Laden crowed that this meant "every dollar of al-Qaida defeated a million dollars by the permission of Allah, besides the loss of a huge number of jobs." He then credited the attacks with setting in motion America's current budget-deficit problems, stating that this sum "has reached record astronomical numbers estimated to total more than a trillion dollars."[14] Previous major al Qaeda attacks reflected an equally handsome return on investment. According to the CIA, for example, the 1998 East Africa embassy bombings required no more than $10,000—and succeeded in killing 301 people and injuring 5,000 others.[15] And the leader of a radical Egyptian jihadist terrorist group was quoted a month after the October 2000 maritime suicide attack on the USS *Cole*, a U.S. Navy destroyer anchored in Aden, Yemen, as stating that that operation similarly cost al Qaeda no more than $10,000.[16] In addition to claiming the lives of 17 American sailors and wounding 39 others, it resulted in $250 million in damage to the vessel.[17]

Fourth, the 9/11 operation exceeded in terms of lethality and destruction even al-Qaeda's grandest expectations. "I was the most optimistic of them all," bin Laden boasted in a videotape discovered by American troops in Kandahar, Afghanistan. "I was thinking that the fire from the gas in the plane would melt the iron structure of the building and collapse the area where the plane hit and all the floors above it only. This is all that we had hoped for."[18] Al-Zawahiri also credited the attack's suicide dimension with its astonishing infliction of death and destruction. "It was the mujahideen's desire for martyrdom that was the unique advantage," he explained in an audiotape released on the first anniversary of the attack, "which resulted in the stealthy raids on New York and Washington—by the grace of Allah. Nineteen mujahideen who desired death were able to inflict damage upon America, such as it had never before witnessed in its history."[19]

Fifth, the 9/11 attacks had an indisputably powerful psychological impact on the American psyche. They shattered the country's sense of well-being and invulnerability that had been founded on both America's unrivaled superpower status and its relative geographical isolation, separated from the rest of the world by two vast oceans.[20] With the attacks, al Qaeda sought to depict the United States not only as the "paper tiger" that bin Laden called it[21] but also as dangerously exposed and therefore vulnerable in the face of continued suicide onslaught.[22] "We love this kind of death for Allah's cause as much as you like to live," bin Laden warned CNN's Peter Arnett in a 1997 interview. "We have nothing to fear. [Death] is something we wish for."[23] Less than a month after the 9/11 attacks, al Qaeda's chief spokesman, Suleimain Abu Ghaith, invoked exactly the same image of unrelenting, future attacks to torment the United States. "The Americans must know that the storm of airplanes will not stop, God willing," he said. "And there are thousands of young people who are as keen about death as Americans are about life."[24] Al-Zawahiri similarly raised the specter of endless waves of suicide attackers a year later. "It is the love of death in the path of Allah," he declared, "that is the weapon that will annihilate this evil empire of America by the permission of Allah. The mujahid youth will compete with each other to die in the path of Allah, to destroy the myth of 'great' America, by the permission of Allah."[25] The fact that these threatened follow-on attacks have yet to materialize has done little to mitigate the fears of many Americans about likely future attack.

Finally, that no escape plan was required and that the 9/11 attacks were doubtless the most media-covered news story of our time are both self-evident. It remains only to consider briefly the role that religion played in inspiring and motivating the hijackers. This is most clearly evidenced by the suicide note that Mohammad Atta, the operation's ringleader and one of the four pilots, wrote to his confederates. It was found at Boston's Logan Airport seven days after the attack, in a flight bag belonging to Atta that had missed its connecting flight from Portland, Maine, onto the ill-fated Los Angeles–bound American Airlines Flight 11.[26] "Be happy, optimistic, calm," Atta advised his fellow hijackers,

because you are heading for a deed that God loves and will accept [as a good deed]. It will be the day, God willing, you spend with the women in paradise.

Smile in the face of hardship young man / For you are heading toward eternal paradise. . . .

Pray for yourself and all of your brothers that they may be victorious and hit their targets and . . . ask God to grant you martyrdom facing the enemy, not running away from it, and for him to grant you patience and the feeling that anything that happens to you is for him.[27]

This same unflinching dedication and determination to martyring oneself can be seen in the pre-attack videotape made by Ibrahim Ahmed al-Haznawi, one of the terrorists who provided the "muscle" aboard American Airlines Flight 77, which crashed into the Pentagon shortly after departing from Washington, D.C.'s Dulles Airport. "O Allah, I sacrifice myself for your sake, accept me as a martyr," al-Haznawi pleads. "We shall meet in the eternal Paradise with the prophets, honest people, martyrs, and righteous people."[28]

Although al Qaeda is the first terrorist group to have successfully conducted suicide attacks on land, at sea, and in the air, the LTTE and Palestinian terrorist movements—such as Hamas,[29] the Palestine Islamic Jihad (PIJ),[30] the al-Aqsa Martyrs Brigade,[31] and some of the Palestinian Popular Front organizations[32]—have in fact emerged as this tactic's foremost exponents. They have not only eclipsed the earlier record established by Hezbollah but each has perpetrated more suicide attacks than all other terrorist groups combined—including al Qaeda. Indeed, since the LTTE adopted this tactic in 1987, its suicide cadres are reported to have been responsible for as many as two hundred attacks.[33] The LTTE's elite suicide units comprise men, women[34] and children,[35] operate on both land and sea,[36] and, according to some reports, have also aspired to develop an airborne suicide attack capability.[37] Although this record of suicide attacks by a single terrorist organization has yet to be surpassed,[38] the various Palestinian terrorists organizations employing this tactic have together been credited with carrying out more than two hundred suicide attacks since 1993.[39] More than 70 percent of these attacks have occurred since the start in September 2000 of what has been called both the al-Aqsa Intifada (Arabic for "uprising" or more literally, "shaking off") and the Second Intifada.[40]

The resort to suicide terrorism by the Tamils and the Palestinians has often been portrayed in terrorist propaganda and world press accounts alike as two sides of the same coin: intense outbursts of violence born of frustration, desperation, and humiliation, caused by the intransigence and brutality of the Sri Lankan and Israeli governments. Such explanations, however, give a distorted view of the rationale that underlies suicide terrorism. While such grievances are real and help ensure a steady stream of recruits, the organizational employment of suicide operations, as previously described, is an instrumental decision. Suicide terrorism in this respect is seen by its adherents as a particularly effective way to communicate a violent message. High-profile attacks are thus conducted for the purpose of demonstrating the terrorist organization's ability and determination to use violence to achieve its political objectives.[41] This motivation was particularly strong in the case of the LTTE and Hamas, which, as upstart organizations challenged by older, well-entrenched political rivals, were forced to distinguish themselves—in the eyes of both their state opponents and their would-be supporters—in an already crowded political field. Suicide terrorism thus became the chosen instrument for achieving this objective, designed to impress their friends, strike fear into the hearts of their enemies, and catapult them to the forefront of their respective national struggles.

Given that the LTTE and these Palestinian movements account for the vast majority of suicide terrorist incidents committed respectively before and since 9/11, both case studies are well suited to closer examination in order to better comprehend the dynamics of and motivations behind suicide terrorism.

The "Tamil Tigers" and Suicide Terrorism

From its founding, the LTTE has sought to develop the image of an elite, professional, and ruthlessly dedicated fighting force. This image was designed initially as much to distinguish the LTTE from other, better-established Tamil separatist groups as to intimidate its principal set of opponents: the government of Sri Lanka and the country's predominantly Buddhist ethnic Sinhalese majority. During its opening period of operations, the organization's tactic of choice was assassination. The LTTE's targeting efforts were directed principally against rival Tamils and Tamil and Sinhala government officials and security forces. Later, as an almost logical extension of these calculated political killings, suicide bombing became the LTTE's signature mode of attack, further reinforcing its image as a distinctive and elite strike force. In this, as in every other aspect of the group's existence, the overriding influence and vision of its founder and leader, Velupillai Prabhakaran, reigns supreme. The histories of Prabhakaran and the LTTE are inextricably linked. It is therefore necessary to know the one to understand the other.

The LTTE emerged in the mid-1970s in the midst of a period of renewed intercommunal tensions that was rapidly descending into violence. Twenty years earlier, the recently formed Ceylonese government had enacted highly discriminatory legislation that gave preference to Sinhalese over Tamils in government hiring, university admissions, and the attainment of key professional qualifications.[42] Although these laws were deeply resented, Tamil opposition was largely kept in check until 1972, when the legislation was reinforced and further institutionalized in the Republican Constitution of the newly renamed state of Sri Lanka.[43] The Sinhala ascendancy over the Tamils was now complete. Long-standing sectarian tensions resurfaced as Tamil anger mounted over this latest act of discrimination and disenfranchisement. Among the comparatively well-educated Tamil youth living in and around Jaffna, the historical center of the community's cultural heritage, the passage of the Standardization of Education Act two years before had already triggered intense resentment and acts of civil disobedience. In the face of growing discrimination in university admissions quotas, a group of activists formed the Tamil Students Front in 1970, one of the first groups to specifically advocate violence in order to regain Tamil civil rights. In a relatively short span of time, this single movement initiated a militant ethnonationalist awakening that eventually resulted in the creation of thirty-six different extremist Tamil separatist groups.[44]

One of these groups was a new Tamil political party called the Tamil United Liberation Front (TULF). The TULF quickly emerged as the leading political force within the Tamil community. Its hard-line nationalist platform, which called for the establishment of an independent, ethnically separate Tamil state in the northern and adjacent northeastern and eastern regions of Sri Lanka, helped distinguish it from its more conciliatory parent organization, the Tamil United Front (TUF). A more important distinction, however, was the fact that in addition to engaging in legal, overt political activities, as the TUF did, the TULF was also preparing for war. Unwilling to put its trust in a political system that had long demonstrated its bias against basic Tamil civil rights, the TULF sought to hedge its bets by establishing a parallel, clandestine organization to recruit radical young Tamils who believed that the only solution to their political problems would be found at the point of a gun. Prabhakaran, who joined the TULF in 1972, was among these recruits.[45]

Little is known conclusively about Prabhakaran's background. Most commentators agree, however, that he was born in 1954 and was the son of a tax commissioner—not the progeny of a smuggler, as is sometimes reported.[46] His grandfather is believed to have been a postman. Unlike many rural Tamils at the time, his family would thus have had both an interest in learning and the means to acquire at least some formal, if rudimentary, education. Prabhakaran has claimed that his own political and ethnic consciousness was awakened when he was nine or ten years old, after hearing stories told to him by his relatives about the bloody history of Tamil-Sinhalese relations over the course of the previous decade.[47] The increasing militancy of Tamil nationalism unfolding during the mid-1970s closely mirrored the development of Prabhakaran's own strident views. Given his developing radicalism, it might have been expected that he would be gradually drawn toward one of the more extreme offshoots of the TULF, the Tamil New Tigers (TNT).[48] The TNT at that time was led by its founder, Chetti Thanabalsingham, who had established the organization in 1974 for the purpose of silencing pro-government Tamils,[49] eliminating Tamil police informants and their Sinhalese police handlers, and staging armed demonstrations against the Sinhalese government. Prabhakaran was quickly promoted to serve as Thanabalsingham's deputy.[50]

The TNT gained particular notoriety in 1975, when its gunmen murdered the Tamil mayor of Jaffna, Alfred Duraiyappah.[51] The group suffered a mortal blow the following year, however, when Thanabalsingham was arrested. Never one to repine, Prabhakaran immediately stepped in and assumed command on May 5, 1976. He renamed the group the Liberation Tigers of Tamil Eelam and set about reshaping it in his own image. Prabhakaran's immediate challenge was to distinguish the LTTE from its thirty-plus rivals.[52] His solution was to refashion the old TNT/new LTTE into an elite, ruthlessly efficient, and highly professional fighting force. According to Rohan Gunaratna, an expert on the LTTE, "Prabhakaran insisted on keeping [his] numbers small, maintaining a high standard of training, [and] enforcing discipline at all levels."[53] The end result was a cadre that was unswervingly dedicated to winning a Tamil homeland, Tamil Eelam. The groundwork was thus laid early in LTTE's history for the culture of individual self-sacrifice that eventually manifested itself in the employment of suicide tactics. At the time, this culture proved especially successful not only as a means of attracting popular support but also as a means of intimidating the group's Tamil and Sinhalese opponents. As the LTTE's reputation—and its leader's appetite for power—grew, so did its strength. Actual and potential rivals were now systematically eliminated both within and outside the Tiger organization. Power was ruthlessly and relentlessly consolidated to ensure the movement's preeminence.[54] By the end of the decade Prabhakaran had completed his ascent to power, and the LTTE had become the preeminent political and military force within the Tamil community.[55]

The next watershed in the development of the LTTE was the widespread ethnic riots that convulsed Sri Lanka in July 1983.[56] The riots were sparked by an LTTE land mine ambush that killed thirteen SLAF (Sri Lanka Armed Forces) soldiers in Jaffna. The disorders escalated rapidly throughout the country into the bloodiest attacks perpetrated by Sinhalese mobs against Tamils since Sri Lanka (then Ceylon) had achieved its independence from

Britain in 1948. Hundreds of Tamils were killed and thousands injured. Destruction of homes, businesses, and other property was especially wide-spread. The riots proved to be a boon to the LTTE and other militant groups, for thousands of young Tamils who previously had shunned violence now flocked to the various guerrilla movements. LTTE propaganda hammered home the point that the Tamil community could feel truly secure only if they had a land of their own. In the wake of the devastation, many who had previously resisted the group's entreaties now found themselves drawn to Prabhakaran's uncompromising message. Attempts by moderates from both communities to restore ethnic amity were rebuffed. This was reinforced by unthinking government policies that in the riots' aftermath were viewed as unresponsive, nonconciliatory, and even hostile.[57]

The LTTE meanwhile worked actively to continue to sow discord in an effort to complete the isolation of the Tamil population from the central government. These acts included allegedly provoking the government into carrying out misdirected retaliatory attacks against Tamil targets in order to reinforce the growing ethnic divide. One way in which the LTTE sought to capitalize on these developments was to draw recruits from the families of those who had suffered at the hands of the security forces or the Sinhalese mobs, offering them a venue through which to strike back. Later on, the LTTE's efforts to recruit individuals into its suicide units would also focus specifically on the families of those who had been victimized by the authorities.[58] According to Father Harry Miller, a Jesuit priest who directs a private NGO (nongovernment organization) that is engaged in peace and reconciliation work in Sri Lanka, "The abuse that ordinary people suffer at the hands of the army [is] the primary motivating factor to join the Tigers." One such candidate, quoted in the same article, was a twenty-two-year-old man named Mahendran. "I am thinking of joining [the LTTE]," he explained. "The harassment that I and my parents have suffered at the hands of the army makes me want to take revenge."[59] The Tamil Tigers were only too happy to oblige.

In 1983, in an effort to capitalize on the momentum generated by these events, as well as to further distinguish the group from its nationalist rivals, Prabhakaran decreed that henceforth every LTTE fighter—male and female alike—would be required to wear a glass capsule containing potassium cyanide around his or her neck. Prabhakaran's order was unambiguous: any LTTE cadre who was in danger of being arrested was obligated to bite down on the glass vial, which would lacerate the gums and send the deadly poison into the system, for a quick death. Prabakaharan thus commanded his fighters to kill themselves rather than risk capture and subsequent interrogation by the authorities.[60] The LTTE's rank and file responded with alacrity. The cyanide capsule, which is suspended on a leather thong around each fighter's neck, has become a badge of honor[61] and a source of pride among LTTE cadres, each of whom receives the capsule amid great ceremony at passing out exercises. Prabhakaran and other senior LTTE commanders also adopted the practice. Photographs of the Tigers' supreme leader have often revealed the capsule worn prominently around his own neck.

The most significant turning point in the LTTE's history, however, was still to come. Sometime around the mid-1980s, Prabhakaran decided to steer the group down an even more violent path that would greatly increase its international notoriety. Hezbollah's 1983 suicide attack on the U.S. Marine compound in Lebanon reportedly made a deep impression on Prabhakaran and the Tigers' senior leadership.[62] A small and little-known terrorist group was able to offset its relative weakness and in a single devastating attack strike decisively at the world's leading superpower. The same tactic, Prabhakaran is believed to have concluded, could be employed by the LTTE to offset its own numerical and material disadvantages against the Sri Lankan state. Indeed, it has been suggested that Prabhakaran became convinced that if the LTTE did not significantly step up its campaign by resorting to suicide attacks it would never achieve its goal of winning a Tamil homeland in his lifetime. "With perseverance and sacrifice," Prabhakaran is said to have argued, "Tamil Eelam can be achieved in 100 years. But if we conduct Black Tiger [suicide] operations, we can shorten the suffering of the people and achieve Tamil Eelam in a shorter period of time."[63]

Prabhakaran's real genius, however, was in creating a historical narrative for the LTTE and the Tamil people that was tailored to support suicide terrorism. Two themes, in particular, were actively incorporated into Tiger lore. The first, as illustrated by Prabhakaran's own words just quoted, was the belief that extreme sacrifices would have to be made to secure an independent future for the Tamil nation. The cornerstone of the LTTE's self-identity became the principle of self-sacrifice and, ultimately, martyrdom, for the greater good of the Tamil race. This principle is today reflected in the Tamil word *thatkodai* (to give yourself), which is used in lieu of the word *thatkolai* (suicide) to describe the group's suicide operations. In the words of S. Thamilchelvam, the political head of the LTTE, these operations are regarded by the movement's suicide cadres as a "gift of the self," a "self-gift," an "oath to the nation," that is offered in the name of Tamil Eelam.[64]

The second theme that Prabhakaran incorporated into the movement's constructed mythology was that of "determination and invincibility."[65] This theme both supported and was, in turn, supported by his decision to turn to suicide operations in 1987. The first of the attacks was carried out on May 5 by "Captain Millar," who subsequently became one of the movement's most important martyrs. The target, in this case, was a former Tamil high school that had been taken over by elements of the Sri Lankan army.[66] It was a textbook vehicular assault, closely resembling Hezbollah's attack on the Marine barracks four years earlier. Seventy-five people were killed in the attack, the news of which radiated throughout Sri Lanka, generating widespread shock and horror. The incident not only represented a significant military and political setback for the Sri Lankan government, it also proved to be a significant psychological blow to the Sinhalese population, endowing the LTTE with an aura of unstoppable fanaticism. The group has worked to reinforce and capitalize on that fanatical image ever since.

Since the organization was intent on cultivating an image of invincibility, it was natural that the LTTE confer a special status on its "Black Tiger" suicide units. Those who volunteer to join the Black Tigers are required to demonstrate an even higher level of skill, dedication, and motivation than traditional LTTE cadres. While everyone must be willing to fight, in Prabhakaran's view only a very few have what it takes to intentionally sacrifice themselves to destroy the enemy.[67] "Our strength is our willingness to make the supreme sacrifice," declared Gena, the thirty-year-old leader of the female "Black Tigresses" (also known as the Birds of Freedom) in a 1998 interview.[68] "This is the most supreme sacrifice I can make," said a seventeen-year-old Tamil recruit named Vasantha. "The only way we can achieve our eelam [homeland] is through arms. That is the only way anybody will listen to us. Even if we die."[69] Proof of this commitment may be found in the laminated identification cards carried by suicide cadres on missions in Colombo. The cards show a photograph of the suicide bomber and his or her name. Written in both English and Sinhala and emblazoned with the symbolic warning of a skull and crossbones, the card states: "I am filled with a huge explosive. If my journey is blocked I will explode it. Let me go."[70] Although decades of fighting and combat losses have forced the group to adopt a much more liberal—even coercive—recruitment policy, the elite units within the LTTE (e.g., reconnaissance and intelligence cadres as well as the group's various suicide squads) continue to be carefully selected and trained to a high mental and physical standard.[71]

From its inception, the development and strategic evolution of the LTTE has been inexorably guided by Prabhakaran's domineering leadership and omnipresent influence. Prabhakaran exercises direct control over virtually every aspect of organizational life, imposing a strict, ascetic regimen on LTTE cadres that is based on unquestioned loyalty to their leader and the goal of Tamil Eelam.[72] This subjugation of individual will is evidenced by the degree of control that the LTTE exerts over the personal affairs of its rank and file. Sexual contact or relationships among unmarried cadres, for example, are strictly forbidden and harshly punished. LTTE cadres may marry only after they have reached a specific age determined by Prabhakaran and then only with their commanders' approval.[73] Prabhakaran's pivotal role and unchallenged influence over the organization are reinforced in a daily ceremony in which cadres pledge allegiance to Prabhakaran the man, rather than to the organization or to the Tamil people or their homeland.[74] These and similar internal policies have further contributed to the group's carefully cultivated "brand" as an elite fighting force.

Although Prabhakaran is not believed to have ever received any formal military training, he is thought by many of his followers to be a military genius. His knowledge of strategy, tactics, weapons, logistics, and military administration is reportedly derived from his voracious reading in history and military affairs. Prabhakaran's idea to create a maritime guerrilla commando unit, for example, is reported to have come from reading a history of the famed Special Boat Squadron (SBS), an elite unit of the Royal Marines that is Britain's counterpart to the U.S. Navy SEALs.[75] It was his own idea to turn the unit into a suicide force, which he named the Sea Tigers.[76] Prabhakaran is also described as a film buff, with a strong preference for war movies and other action thrillers. Once again, he is prepared to borrow a good idea when he sees one. Prabhakaran's idea to design a suicide vest that would allow an attacker to approach his or her target without being detected is said to have come from viewing a *Death Wish*–like movie, released for the South Asian film market. In the movie, a beautiful girl apparently presents a bouquet of flowers to the president of the United States. As she offers the bouquet, she kills herself and the president with a bomb concealed beneath her clothing.[77] The 1991 assassination of former Indian prime minister Rajiv Gandhi by a female LTTE suicide terrorist was carried out in a similar manner.

Whatever the source of Prabhakaran's strategic insights, it is clear that the LTTE has waged a determined and, at times, quite successful military campaign. The group's estimated eight to ten thousand fighters (based on an "active duty" cadre of three to six thousand[78] men and women) constitute one of the best trained and equipped nonstate military forces in the world today—complete with armored and artillery units, its own blue- and brown-water navies, a reportedly embryonic air capability, comprising micro-light aircraft, a commando and special reconnaissance force, many portable surface-to-air missiles, and last but not least, the aforementioned suicide attack units. As of 2005, the LTTE had fought the Sri Lankan government to a standstill in a conflict that has cost more than sixty thousand lives since its inception in 1983. In the face of this battlefield deadlock, Colombo decided to enter negotiations with the LTTE in 2001. In the view of many knowledgeable observers, however, it was the threat posed by LTTE's suicide campaign that finally drove the regime to the bargaining table. Such attacks, one former Sri Lankan official has argued, have had their intended effect. "We have been cowed. We have been intimidated by suicide terrorism. It is that simple. The fear caused by this tactic has made us cave in to them."[79]

Over the years, LTTE suicide attacks have been carried out to support two distinctly different campaigns: a rural campaign and an urban campaign. In the case of the group's rural operations, suicide tactics have been employed primarily against the Sri Lanka Armed Forces, often as part of a larger operational plan involving guerrilla and semi-conventional forces. In the case of the group's urban campaign, numerous and often highly dramatic suicide attacks have been carried out against critical national infrastructure and what the Tigers refer to expansively as VIPs, such as senior elected government leaders, prominent political figures, other high-level government officials, senior military and police commanders, and even lower-ranking military and police intelligence officers whose competence attracts the attention of the Tigers.[80] Since many of these latter actions take place in and around Colombo and at times have caused significant numbers of collateral casualties, LTTE attacks against nonmilitary targets are never claimed.

The Tigers continue to insist that "it is not the policy of the LTTE to attack civilian targets."[81] "By adopting such a position," Gunaratna explains, the group "seeks to project to the international community that it is a liberation movement that targets only military personnel, and not a terrorist group."[82] The LTTE, for example, has never taken credit for the suicide truck bombing of the Central Bank of Sri Lanka in January 1996, that killed ninety people and wounded fourteen hundred others or for the November 1994 assassination of presidential candidate Gamini Dissanayake, which claimed the lives of fifty-four people and injured seventy-two. In 1991, as previously noted, the group also used a suicide bomber to assassinate former Indian prime minister Rajiv Gandhi. Two years later, a deep penetration mole wearing a suicide bodysuit similar to that worn by the female cadre who killed Gandhi, succeeded in killing Sri Lankan president Ranasinghe Premadasa. Neither assassination was ever claimed. Government efforts to ascribe such attacks to the LTTE result in denials and the counterclaim that the regime is trying to whip up anti-Tamil sentiment.

In summary, suicide terrorism has become a central tactic in LTTE planning. The purpose of adopting this tactic was twofold: first, to distinguish the group from its many better-established political challengers within the Tamil resistance and attract a solid base of popular support, and second, to achieve a perceptual force multiplier that would allow the LTTE to level the playing field with the Sri Lankan government. To achieve these objectives, the LTTE has worked very deliberately to cultivate an image of elitism, professionalism, invincibility, and fanatical single-mindedness. The use of suicide tactics to demonstrate these qualities has been an important part of this policy. Prabhakaran and his senior commanders, as we have seen, were inspired to experiment with this tactic in the wake of Hezbollah's stunning attack against the U.S. Marine barracks in Lebanon in 1983. Since then, the use of suicide operations has been institutionalized to the point that they have become a signature tactic of the Tamil Tigers, symbolizing the determination of the organization, its membership, and its supreme leader. An uneasy truce reigns today in Sri Lanka. Whether the latest round of negotiations will lead to a lasting peace is unclear. Should these efforts fail, as is widely predicted, we can expect the LTTE to once again resume the use of suicide operations as a means of impressing its friends and intimidating its enemies.

The Palestinian Use of Suicide Terrorism

From its inception in 1987, Hamas faced the same problem that had confronted the LTTE: devising a means of carving out a distinctive niche in an already crowded field of competing militant groups. Hamas's challenge, however, was considerably more formidable. As a latecomer to an already well-established Palestinian liberation movement with deep popular roots, Hamas not only had to distinguish itself from competing terrorist organizations, some of which had been fighting for decades,[83] but it also had to differentiate itself from a long-standing and powerful representative body— the Palestine Liberation Organization (PLO)—which had become the preeminent force in Palestinian politics. That in 2005 Hamas reportedly could claim the support of upwards of 70 percent of the Palestinians on the West Bank and Gaza[84] is a testament to the group's success in overcoming its initial disadvantages. As in the case of the LTTE, Hamas's eventual adoption of suicide terrorism as a signature mode of attack was pivotal to this process.

Although Hamas can trace its ideological lineage to the Muslim Brotherhood,[85] the group itself arguably owes its existence to a fatal traffic accident that took place in the Gaza Strip on December 8, 1987. That day, an otherwise unremarkable collision involving an Israeli truck and some other vehicles resulted in the deaths of several Palestinian workers. Without warning, the mishap triggered an explosion of Palestinian rioting. The disorders were initially dismissed by Palestinians and Israelis alike as an ephemeral outburst of frustration. Within days, however, it was clear that events had taken on a dynamic of their own and that the riots were spreading throughout the occupied areas. Palestinians began to describe this outpouring of popular anger as an intifada. The uprising was not even a week old when, on December 14, the Muslim Brotherhood distributed a leaflet calling for sustained resistance.[86] This leaflet is credited as marking the birth of Hamas.

From the beginning, Hamas's young, predominantly university-educated leadership[87] consciously sought to distance themselves and their new organization from the mainstream, secular PLO and its affiliated terrorist and nationalist groups. Most had attended Palestinian universities where the Muslim Brotherhood had been particularly active and were greatly influenced by the movement's doctrine combining religion with politics.[88] Accordingly, Hamas's fundamental raison d'être became the liberation of Palestine and the establishment of an Islamic state in all Palestine (that is, Israel as well as the West Bank and Gaza Strip). Such a liberation could be achieved, they argued, only by means of a popular jihad. "Jihad," in this context, referred not only to a collective struggle, as it is commonly understood, but also to the belief that the use of organized violence was the "sole legitimate way to retrieve Palestine in its entirety." Once this territorial imperative was achieved, Islamic social and moral norms would then be rigorously enforced in the new state.[89] Hamas's religious ideology and "maximalist" political aims were thus resolutely opposed to the "minimalist" aims pursued by the PLO.

To more clearly define its agenda and delineate itself from its mainstream Palestinian competitors, Hamas also adopted the motto of "not [ceding] one inch" of land, thus further emphasizing its uncompromising opposition to dialogue, much less a negotiated settlement, with Israel.[90] One leaflet, distributed during the intifada's first year, neatly encapsulated the group's doctrinal platform. Titled "Islamic Palestine from the [Mediterranean] Sea to the [Jordan] River," it declared: "Muslims have had a full—not a partial—right to Palestine for generations, in the past, present and future. . . . No Palestinian generation has the right to concede the land, steeped in martyr's blood. . . . You must continue the uprising and stand up against the usurpers wherever they may be, until the complete liberation of every grain of the soil of . . . Palestine, all Palestine, with God's help."[91] In both word and deed, from its inception, Hamas disdained in equal measure the PLO and the traditional, local Palestinian ruling elite in Gaza and the West Bank along with its declared enemy, Israel. The group, moreover, was neither impressed nor intimidated by the strength of the much-vaunted IDF (Israel Defense Forces).[92]

Nonetheless, the intifada's early years were characterized more by Palestinian youths' throwing stones and general rioting and popular unrest than by any sustained campaign of outright terrorism.[93] The use of *bayanat*, the Arabic word for leaflets, was one of the principal ways in which Hamas publicized itself and sought to differentiate itself and its fundamentalist religious orientation from the secular groups involved in the intifada.[94] In addition to declaring its own strike days—apart from those proclaimed by the United National Command of the Intifada-UNC (the umbrella organization directing the uprising)—Hamas also endeavored to set itself up as a social welfare organization. Accordingly, Hamas leaflets during this period dealt as much with the range of issues affecting Palestinian daily life—such as work, health, transport, education, and religious instruction—as they did with the need for resistance and rebellion.[95]

By 1989, however, the intifada was losing momentum.[96] Hamas, moreover, was losing ground to its rivals, which now included not only the secular nationalist Palestinian groups but a religious group—the Palestine Islamic Jihad (PIJ). In the face of this situation, as Shaul Mishal and Avraham Sela have noted, "Hamas's turn to violence was a matter of necessity." Its opening actions, however, were unimpressive. Lacking a bona fide military wing with the attendant organizational ability to recruit and train fighters, obtain arms, and plan and control serious operations, Hamas activists were able to carry out just ten attacks during its first year of dedicated operations. While the movement managed to increase this number to thirty-two attacks in its second year, it still had little effect on its targeted constituents, who continued to favor the group's better-established, secular rivals.[97] The only significant attention Hamas seems to have attracted during this opening period was from Israeli security forces, which came down hard on the organization in a series of operations between late 1990 and early 1991, effectively stripping it of its emerging military potential.[98]

This all changed, however, with the establishment of a proper military wing in 1991, the Battalions of Izz al-Din al-Qassam.[99] The new unit began modestly enough, with the systematic execution of Palestinian collaborators in the Gaza Strip. By the following year it had graduated to the assassination of Israeli settlers and the use of car bombs and was well on its way to becoming a force in Palestinian politics. Hamas's increasingly violent successes spawned both imitation and competition from other Palestinian militants, especially those who shared the group's religious orientation. The PIJ in particular was driven to strike out in new directions, forging ties with Hezbollah and participating in attacks on IDF forces in south Lebanon.[100] The climax to this phase of the intifada came between October and December 1992, when a series of terrorist attacks claimed the lives of five Israeli soldiers and a member of the Border Police. The incident proved to be the last straw for Israeli prime minister Itzhak Rabin, who ordered the deportation to Lebanon of 415 Islamic Palestinian activists (the vast majority of whom belonged to Hamas).[101] The deportation proved to be a serious miscalculation. Deposited in the middle of rough country in south Lebanon, in the middle of winter, the deportees quickly became a cause célèbre, attracting international media attention and sympathy.[102] Hamas bore the fruits of its leaders' suffering, attaining a level of support among both Palestinians and foreigners that it might not otherwise have achieved. Included among the exiles were doctors, clerics, teachers, engineers, judges, and professors, thus supporting Hamas's claims that it was a true community and social welfare organization and not a terrorist group.[103]

More significantly, during the nearly ten months they were in Lebanon, the Hamas exiles were able to establish the organization's first ties to Hezbollah. The PIJ, for its part, benefited doubly, forging tighter relations with Iran while significantly enhancing its military capabilities under Hezbollah's tutelage.[104] The impact of this exile on Hamas, however, was ultimately more profound. Mishal and Sela are unequivocal in stating that the "deportation of 415 Islamic activists by Israel to Lebanon in December 1992 was a milestone in Hamas's decision to use car bombs and suicide attacks as a major modus operandi against Israel." A direct cause and effect, they argue, is clearly evident in the exiles' return to Gaza and the West Bank the following year and Hamas's decision to adopt suicide tactics. "Thus it was no coincidence," they write, "that Hamas's first suicide operation was carried out shortly after the deportees had returned to the occupied territories."[105]

The deportations also had a third major unintended consequence: with almost the entire established Hamas political leadership in exile the movement did not collapse, as Israel hoped it would. Instead, the leadership vacuum was filled by the exiles' more violent-minded, younger followers. This new generation was concerned less with the Islamization of Palestinian society, which had been the focus of much of the organization's initial efforts, than with the active promotion of the military dimension of Hamas's struggle. Emulating the militarism of historical Palestinian guerrilla groups like al-Fatah, they pushed an even harder line of no compromise/no surrender with Israel and focused their efforts on increased attacks in the hope of pressuring Israel to withdraw from the Occupied Territories.[106] The net result was that the influence of the al-Qassam wing grew within Hamas while the group's overall prestige among Palestinians similarly increased.[107]

Hamas was now well positioned to escalate its military campaign against Israel and consolidate the political gains it was beginning to achieve over the PLO and other rivals. These imperatives acquired new urgency in the fall of 1993 with the conclusion of the Oslo Accords and the commencement of formal negotiations between the PLO and Israel. The entire process was anathema to Hamas. Not only did negotiations entail de facto recognition of Israel and the cessation of the Palestinian military struggle, but also the parameters of the Israeli-Palestinian Declaration of Principles (DOP) guiding the discussions called for the eventual implementation of UN Security Council Resolutions 242 and 338, leading to formal Palestinian recognition of Israel's right to exist.[108] According to Mishal and Sela, the implications of this unprecedented breakthrough in Palestinian-Israeli relations

> dramatically changed Hamas's strategic situation. Indeed, as a movement whose military activity against Israel now outweighed that of Fatah and the other Palestinian national organizations, the PLO-Israel agreement confronted Hamas with nothing less than an existential problem. To begin with, the agreement put an end to the Intifada, which had provided Hamas with ideal conditions to become a genuine political alternative to the PLO. In addition, the PLO's agreement to desist from hostile actions against Israel, a commitment to be imposed by the future self-governing Palestinian Authority (PA) in the occupied territories, clearly threatened to curtail Hamas's freedom of military action.[109]

In response, Hamas decided to challenge simultaneously the entire DOP framework, Arafat's leadership, and the PLO's authority within the Occupied Territories.[110] As Hamas's greatest concern was the deleterious effect that any peace process would have on the continuation of a popular jihad against Israel,[111] the movement arguably had no option but to further step up its armed operations. The Israeli decision to allow the Hamas and PIJ deportees to return to the West Bank and the Gaza Strip in late 1993 greatly strengthened Hamas just as it was poised to strike.[112]

Hamas initiated a new round of bombings within a month of the signing of the Oslo Accords. Three major attacks killed twenty-six Israelis and wounded scores of others. The message Hamas was communicating to Israel and the PLO alike was clear: there would be no peace and security[113] "unless and until Hamas [was] recognized and its demands [were] met."[114] While these incidents were impressive in their own right, they did little to change the basic correlation of forces between either Hamas and the PLO or between Hamas and Israel. Indeed, in the context of this decades-old conflict, the newest round of attacks was neither particularly significant nor extraordinary. Both sides in the struggle had become conditioned to worse. Hamas was still nothing more than a nuisance—an increasingly violent nuisance, to be sure, but a nuisance nevertheless. At this critical juncture, Hamas's challenge—much as it had been only a few years earlier for Prabhakaran and the LTTE—was to find an operational profile that was sufficiently dramatic and extraordinary to alter the strategic balance in Palestine and Israel once and for all. The solution that Hamas, like the LTTE, embraced was the use of suicide tactics.[115]

Hamas carried out its first suicide attack on April 6, 1994. The incident, which killed eight people and wounded thirty-four others, occurred in the northern Israeli city of Afula. It was timed to coincide with the end of the Islamic period of mourning that had begun on February 25 when, as previously mentioned, Dr. Baruch Goldstein, an ultranationalist orthodox Jew, had killed twenty-nine Palestinian worshipers at the Ibrahim Mosque in Hebron. The attack was also meant to derail the talks then in progress between Israel and the PLO on implementing the Oslo Accords.[116] Thereafter a series of suicide bombings followed, including attacks in Hadera on April 13 (which killed five people), at the Dizengoff Shopping Center in Tel Aviv in October (in which twenty-two people died), and at Nezarim Junction less than a month later (where three people were killed).[117] According to the late professor Ehud Sprinzak, an Israeli scholar and one of the world's foremost authorities on terrorism, these incidents were decisive in "erod[ing] Israel's collective confidence in the peace process," which, in turn, "played right into the hands of extremist Hamas clerics who opposed negotiations with Israel."[118]

Hamas's inauguration of suicide tactics sharpened its rivalry with the numerically inferior and less consequential PIJ. Fearing its own complete eclipse, the PIJ got into the act, killing twenty Israeli soldiers in a suicide attack near Netanya on January 22, 1995. In all these incidents—for Hamas and the PIJ alike—Hezbollah's influence, example, and training are evident.[119] Khaled Meshal, Hamas's political leader, was quite candid about this during an interview he gave in July 2000. "We always have the Lebanese experiment before our eyes," he explained. "It was a great model of which we are proud."[120] Indeed, according to Mishal and Sela, these early suicide operations were textbook Hezbollah attacks—both groups, they point out, adopted the "same procedure [for] finding a candidate for a suicide operation, training and preparing him psychologically, writing a farewell letter, and making a videotape before his mission."[121] At least seven years before, Dr. Fathi Shiqaqi, the PIJ's founder and leader, had developed a plan for what he termed, "exceptional" martyrdom operations involving human bombs that was based on Hezbollah's theological justification.[122] Within the context of suicide terrorism as deception, Hamas also appears to have borrowed a leaf from LTTE's book on the subject, similarly insisting publicly that, despite its attacks on shopping malls and buses, the group "opposed any action that hurt civilians."

The suicide attacks and the carnage that they wrought elicited an aggressive response from Israel, one element of which was the Israeli decision to target Palestinian leaders who were believed to be directly engaged in planning suicide operations. In October of that year Israeli agents are thought to have assassinated Fathi Shiqaqi in Malta. Three months later they achieved an even more important success when they managed to kill Hamas's master bomb maker, Yahya Ayyash. Ayyash, whose expertise had earned him the sobriquet "the Engineer" (bestowed by no less a personage than Israeli prime minister Rabin), is credited with having first proposed that Hamas engage in suicide bombing.[123] He also reputedly built the bombs that were used in the 1994 Afula and Hadera attacks. Altogether, he was believed to have been responsible for the deaths of 130 Israelis and injuries to nearly 500 others.[124] Rather than ending the suicide attacks, however, Ayyash's assassination triggered the most dramatic escalation in this campaign to date. After six months of relative quiet, Hamas bombers struck five times in two weeks, killing a total of 59 Israelis. Their targets included public buses, populated bus stops, and Tel Aviv's Dizengoff Shopping Center—for the second time in seventeen months.

The death toll from these attacks alone was nearly half the total amassed by suicide bombers over the preceding two years.[125] The bombings are also widely credited with affecting the outcome of Israel's national elections in May 1996. The right-wing Likud coalition's Benjamin Netanyahu was elected prime minister over the Labor Party candidate and sitting premier, Shimon Peres. In the wake of this new wave of attacks, Netanyahu's hard-line stance on negotiations and promise of security proved to be more attractive to Israeli voters than Peres's pledge to continue the peace process begun by his assassinated predecessor, Itzhak Rabin. Even at the time it was clear that this was precisely what Hamas intended: to use suicide attacks to polarize the Israeli polity and scuttle the peace process. The election of Netanyahu, it was calculated, not only would serve to undermine the Oslo Accords but would have the secondary advantage of undermining the political ascendancy of the PLO.[126] For the IDF, Hamas's violent retribution, despite the loss of one of its key operatives, provided unwelcome and disquieting evidence of the group's newfound strategic depth and organizational resiliency. The IDF now judged Hamas to be "militarily the strongest Palestinian organization."[127] The head of military intelligence, Brigadier General Ya'acov Amidor, was forced to concede at this time that Hamas had become a serious challenge to Israeli security. "You can trim its branches," he suggested, but it was going to be difficult to "pull out its roots."[128]

Thereafter, however, the pace of Palestinian terrorist attacks began to wane. Two suicide attacks were conducted in August and September 1996, and three attacks were carried out between March and September 1997. Hamas's relative quiescence during this period, until the collapse of the Oslo Accords that followed the abortive Camp David meetings in the summer of 2000, was a reflection of several factors. The first appears to have been the establishment of a tenuous modus vivendi with the governing Palestinian Authority (PA). Hamas attacks on Israeli targets were deliberately restricted in return for the Palestinian Authority's refusal to cave in to Israeli pressure to proscribe Hamas's political activities. The second reason was a function of the times. This was a period of unbridled optimism in Israel and Palestine about the possibilities for a stable peace. The newly elected Labor government's energetic efforts to reach a comprehensive settlement contrasted sharply with the hard-line stance of its predecessors in the Likud Party and had an overwhelming calming effect on the conflict. It was also a time of close cooperation between PA security forces and their Israeli counterparts.[129] Not only were Hamas and PIJ terrorists apprehended and imprisoned by the PA, but even leading Hamas commanders such as Muhammad Daif were swept up in the dragnet (brokered and overseen by U.S. government representatives) and jailed.

Finally, and most relevant for our purposes, was Hamas's own policy of "controlled violence."[130] The rational basis of this policy was clearly articulated in late 1995 by one of the group's senior leaders based in Gaza, Mahmud al-Zahar. In an interview given to the East Jerusalem daily al-Quds, al-Zahar made a point of explaining how Hamas's use of violence was a carefully calculated means to an end. It was not, as its critics suggested, an end in itself. In every case, he argued, the group's decision to use force was subordinated to its larger political objectives. If the prevailing political climate made it necessary for Hamas to put its military option on the shelf, it was prepared to do so, at least for a period of time. "We must calculate the benefit and cost of continued armed operations," al-Zahar said. "If we can fulfill our goals without violence, we will do so. Violence is a means, not a goal. Hamas's decision to adopt self-restraint does not contradict our aims, including the establishment of an Islamic state instead of Israel. . . . We will never recognize Israel, but it is possible that a truce could prevail between us for days, months, or years."[131]

That self-restraint ended on October 30, 2000, when a Hamas suicide bomber killed fifteen people in Jerusalem. Less than a month before, as previously discussed, the visit of prime ministerial candidate Ariel Sharon to Jerusalem's al-Haram al-Sharif triggered what has come to be known as the al-Aqsa Intifada and the escalation of violence that has followed since. The appreciably greater number of suicide attacks during the most recent phase of this long-standing conflict attests to the growing importance of this tactic. According to the database maintained by Haifa University's National Security Studies Center, there were a total of twenty-three suicide attacks between December 31, 1993, and September 30, 2000 (e.g., the start of the al-Aqsa Intifada)—an average of 0.24 per month. During the first fifteen months of the al-Aqsa Intifada, that is, from October 1, 2000, to December 31, 2001, there were thirty-nine attacks—an average of 2.6 per month. And during the entirety of 2002, when, as of January, the Second Intifada entered a far more violent and dangerous phase as the al-Aqsa Martyrs Brigade began its own campaign of suicide bombings, a total of fifty-nine incidents were recorded—an average of 4.9 per month. Viewed from another perspective, there were nearly as many suicide attacks carried out against Israeli targets during 2002 as during the previous eight years combined (sixty-two).[132]

Four explanations account for this dramatic upsurge of suicide attacks:

- first, the terrorist belief that the sustained and unrelenting use of suicide attacks will achieve results that cannot be matched by using other tactics;
- second, the inverted sense of normality that the Palestinian terrorist organizations have created within the Palestinian community and the resulting approval that has been bestowed on suicide operations;
- third, the use of religion and theological justification—communicated and encouraged by Muslim clerical authorities—both to sustain support of these tactics among Palestinians and other Muslims and to ensure a continued flow of new recruits for suicide operations into the ranks of the terrorist organizations; and
- fourth, entrenched rivalries between the Palestinian terrorist organizations that have resulted in a deadly competition to determine which group is able to mobilize and deploy the largest number of suicide

terrorists in an effort to win the support of the Palestinian population and undermine its rivals.

Suicide Terrorism as an Instrument of War

It is clear that the leadership of Hamas and the PIJ entered the al-Aqsa Intifada with the belief that a sustained suicide bombing campaign would have the desired political effect on both the Israeli government and their own political base that would be significantly greater than what they could expect to achieve through "conventional" terrorist attacks. The Hezbollah model again loomed large. Only four months earlier, the IDF had completed its withdrawal from south Lebanon. The primary reason for this policy reversal, in the opinion of both Hezbollah[133] and Palestinian[134] observers, was Israel's inability to deal effectively with the new threat posed by suicide tactics. As the leader of the PIJ, Ramadan Shalah, explained in late 2001,

> The shameful defeat that Israel suffered in southern Lebanon and which caused its army to flee in terror was not made on the negotiations table but on the battlefield and through jihad and martyrdom, which achieved a great victory for the Islamic resistance and Lebanese People. . . . We would not exaggerate if we said that the chances of achieving victory in Palestine are greater than in Lebanon. . . . If the enemy could not bear the losses of the war on the border strip with Lebanon, will it be able to withstand a long war of attrition in the heart of its security dimension and major cities?[135]

Moreover, to Hamas at least, suicide attacks were seen as the next step in a logical progression. "Like the intifada in 1987," Hamas's Khaled Meshal told the BBC, "the current intifada has taught us that we should move forward normally from popular confrontation to the rifle to suicide operations. This is the normal development."[136]

The decision to rely on suicide bombings during the new intifada, in this regard, was neither irrational nor desperate,[137] but rational and calculated. As the terrorists themselves have pointed out, suicide bombings are both inexpensive and effective. "It is easy and costs us only our lives," Shallah told one interviewer. "Human bombs," he further averred, "cannot be defeated, not even by nuclear bombs."[138] The logic behind the operations was explained by a leading Gaza Muslim activist interviewed on Israeli television in 1994. His exposition of this phenomenon accurately captured the logic or strategy of suicide terrorism as an especially effective weapon of the weak, of the powerless, in confronting a stronger and exponentially more powerful opponent. "We lack the arms possessed by the enemy," he said.

> We have no planes or missiles, not even artillery with which to fight evil. The most effective instrument for inflicting harm with a minimum of losses is this type of operation. This is a legitimate technique based on martyrdom. Through such action, the "martyr" acquires the right to enter heaven and liberate himself from all the pain and suffering of this world.[139]

Using almost identical terminology, a member of Hamas's al-Qassam brigades explained to Nasra Hassan, an international relief worker posted to Gaza who has been studying the phenomenon of suicide terrorism since 1996: "We do not have tanks or rockets, but we have something superior— our exploding Islamic human bombs. In place of a nuclear arsenal, we are proud of our arsenal of believers."[140]

As these quotes also attest, suicide attacks are considered to be a means of offsetting a numerically superior, better-armed, and better-equipped opponent. Indeed, the material and technological inferiority of the Palestinian resistance is often used as a justification for employing suicide tactics. The Palestinians, as Meshal has claimed, "are fighting with the only tools they possess."[141] Shalah offered an identical justification for PIJ suicide operations: "Our enemy possesses the most sophisticated weapons in the world and its army is trained to a very high standard. We have nothing with which to repel killing and thuggery against us except the weapon of martyrdom."[142] Another PIJ official has argued that suicide terrorism is necessary to achieve a "balance of terror"[143]—a logic expressed by a fellow militant who declared, "If our wives and children are not safe from Israeli tanks and rockets, theirs will not be safe from our human bombs."[144]

Part and parcel of these justifications are two ancillary, but critical, beliefs. The first is related to the "effectiveness" argument cited. According to this line of reasoning, suicide terrorism is the only way to convince Israeli decision makers that the Palestinian people will never yield to coercion. The second, derivative belief is that in adopting suicide tactics, the Palestinian resistance has finally discovered Israel's Achilles' heel. Drawing again on the Hezbollah model, Meshal, for instance, claims, "The Zionist enemy . . . only understands the language of Jihad, resistance and martyrdom; that was the language that led to its blatant defeat in South Lebanon and it will be the language that will defeat it on the land of Palestine."[145] Similarly, more than a decade earlier, Shiqaqi had argued that suicide tactics would prove to be the most efficacious means of wearing down Israel's will. This would be achieved, he explained, "through the explosion, which forces the mujahid not to waver, not to escape; to execute a successful operation for religion and jihad; and to destroy the morale of the enemy and plant terror in the people."[146]

Suicide terrorism is thus embraced by the Palestinians as a psychological weapon that is capable of paralyzing their hated opponent. "The Israelis . . . will fall to their knees," said Sheikh Ahmad Yassin, the spiritual leader of Hamas[147] until his death in an Israeli air strike in 2004. "You can sense the fear in Israel already; they are worried about where and when the next attacks will come. Ultimately, Hamas will win."[148] The reason, according to another Hamas leader, Ismail Haniya, who was famously quoted in both a *Washington Post* article and a Thomas Friedman *New York Times* column in March 2002, is that in suicide attacks the Palestinian people—after years of struggle—have finally discovered Israel's point of greatest vulnerability. In words reminiscent of bin Laden, Haniya said that Jews "love life more than any other people, and they prefer not to die."[149] Lest such claims be dismissed as terrorist hyperbole or braggadocio, no higher authority than the preeminent Muslim religious figure in Palestine, the Mufti of Jerusalem, Ikrama Sabri, has explicitly endorsed this view. "Look at the society of the Israelis," he told Jeffrey Goldberg, a *New Yorker* magazine correspondent. "It is a selfish society that loves life. These are not people who are eager to die for their country and their God. The Jews will leave this land rather than die, but the Muslim is happy to die."[150]

This is what is known in the Middle East as the "spiderweb" theory. It is the conclusion drawn by Hezbollah about Israel's withdrawal from south Lebanon and is today embraced by the Palestinians as well. The phrase itself is derived from a verse of the Qur'an about the inherent weakness of non-believers. "The parable of those who take guardians besides Allah," verse 29.41 states, "is as the parable of the spider that makes for itself a house; and surely the frailest of the houses is the spider's house did they but know." It was applied in the context of Israel's frailty by Hezbollah's spiritual leader, Sheikh Hassan Nasrallah, who described the Jewish state as a formidable military power, but one that is rooted in a civil society that has become materialistic and lazy, its citizens self-satisfied, comfortable, and pampered to the point that they have gone soft. This view was echoed by the IDF chief of staff, Lieutenant General Moshe "Boogie" Ya'alon, who explained in an interview published in *Ha'Aretz* in August 2002 the perception on the part of the country's enemies that the Israeli army is strong, Israel has technological superiority and is said to have strategic capabilities, but its citizens are unwilling any longer to sacrifice lives in order to defend their national interests and national goals. Therefore, Israel is a spider-web society: it looks strong from the outside, but touch it and it will fall apart.[151]

The IDF high command, for its part, does not dispute Hezbollah's explanation for why the IDF withdrew from Lebanon or the influence of the "spider-web" theory on Palestinian thinking. "If you ask why this crisis [the al-Aqsa Intifada] erupted four months after IDF withdrew from Lebanon," one senior IDF strategist explains, "the answer is yes. There was clear encouragement. . . . Lebanon is not the West Bank, but the Palestinians were influenced."[152]

Inverted Sense of Normality and Societal Imprimatur

The Palestinian terrorists have also worked hard to endow suicide operations with a positive social imprimatur and to build support for this tactic among their political constituents. In the process, they have fostered an inverted sense of normality throughout much of Palestinian society whereby suicide—the senseless taking of one's life, an act that is usually negatively regarded as aberrant, if not abnormal—becomes accepted and commonplace, with demonstrably positive connotations. This view is facilitated through the terrorist organizations' attendant efforts to attach a positive societal imprimatur to the suicide terrorist act. The veneration routinely accorded martyrs reinforces this view. The images of suicide terrorists emblazoned on murals and wall posters, calendars and key chains, postcards and pennants throughout Palestine are but one manifestation of this deliberate process.[153] Similarly, the suddenly elevated and now highly respected status accorded their families—is another.[154] The proud parents of Palestinian martyrs, for instance, publish announcements of their progeny's accomplishments in local newspapers not on the obituaries page but in the section announcing weddings.[155] Finally, the terrorist organizations (and their supporters through financial contributions) provide material (as well as spiritual) encouragement to both the suicide terrorists and their families. According to one authoritative account, until at least 2001 Hamas paid the families of suicide terrorists a death benefit of $3,000 to $5,000[156]—more than double the financial compensation paid to families of terrorists killed in other, nonsuicidal attacks.[157] Later, during the al-Aqsa

Intifada, this amount increased to $10,000 and then, courtesy of Saddam Hussein's largesse, to $25,000.[158] There are reportedly additional, significant material benefits as well, including far nicer living accommodation and a wealth of consumer goods—"appliances, rugs and stuffed furniture . . . gaudy wall clocks, even . . . [a] bracelet and rings"[159]—that are bestowed on the martyr's family.

Videos of martyrs before their operations are of course routinely made by Hamas and the PIJ and circulated as a means to call attention to the organization and its determined fighters, to cultivate an image of invincibility and the inevitability of victory, and, not least, to attract further recruits.[160] The wedding announcements cited earlier are further evidence of the pervasiveness of the recalibration of Palestinian societal values engineered by the terrorist organizations. Far from regarding the suicide bombers as people with psychological problems, as other societies would, Palestinian society lauds martyrs for their bravery and selflessness.[161] The reaction in Palestinian neighborhoods in Gaza when news of a successful suicide strike is broadcast illustrates this. According to one report, typically candy is distributed in the streets and women respond with traditional shrieks of joy. "Martyrdom has become an ambition for our children," Sadl Abu Hein, a psychology lecturer from Gaza, has sadly observed.[162] It is not surprising, therefore, to find that opinion polls taken in 2002 reported that more than 70 percent of Palestinians support suicide attacks against Israel.[163]

Use of Religion and Theological Justification

Religion and theological justification, in particular, that is communicated and encouraged by Muslim clerical authorities has played an important role in framing popular attitudes toward suicide operations and encouraging their followers to carry out acts of self-sacrifice on behalf of their community. Characteristic of this role was a sermon given by Sheikh Ibrahim Madhi on April 12, 2001, at the Gaza City mosque, which was broadcast live on Palestinian television. "Anyone who does not attain martyrdom in these days," the sheikh declared, "should wake in the middle of the night and say: 'My God, why have you deprived me of martyrdom for your sake? For the martyr lives next to Allah.'" He then called on Allah to "accept our martyrs in the highest heavens . . . show the Jews a black day . . . annihilate the Jews and their supporters . . . [and] raise the flag of Jihad across the land."[164]

Such messages are reinforced by Palestinian television channels, which regularly air promotional spots extolling the virtues of martyrdom operations and actively encouraging Palestinian youth to volunteer. One such segment broadcast in 2003 depicts the image of a young Palestinian couple out for a walk when suddenly IDF troops open fire, shooting the woman in the back and killing her. While visiting her grave, her boyfriend is also shot dead by the IDF. He then is shown ascending to heaven, where he is welcomed by his girlfriend, who is seen dancing with dozens of other female martyrs, portraying the seventy-two virgins—the promised "Maidens of Paradise"—who reputedly await the male martyr in heaven.[165] The clip is thus cleverly designed to appeal to would-be male and female martyrs alike.[166] In fact, just two days before the August 18, 2003, suicide bombing of a bus in Jerusalem by a Hamas terrorist that killed eighteen people, a music video version of this same spot aired on the Palestinian Authority's television station. In commentary provided on the same station the day before the blast, an Islamic scholar explained:

When the Shahid [martyr] meets his Maker, all his sins are forgiven from the first gush of blood. He is exempted from the "torments of the grave" (Judgment); he sees his place in paradise, he is shielded from the great shock, and marries Dark Eyed Virgins. He is an heavenly advocate for 70 members of his family, on his head is placed a crown of honor, one stone of which, is worth more than all there is in this world.[167]

Theological arguments are regularly invoked both by the organizations responsible for the attacks and by the community that approvingly supports them. The Qur'an, however, expressly forbids suicide. It is considered as one of the "greatest wrong-doings" a Muslim can commit, according to Brother Abu Ruqaiyah, an Islamic philosopher and author of a detailed treatise addressing the religious legitimacy of suicide terrorism.[168] Accordingly, a semantical distinction has been devised, similar to that used by the Tamil Tigers, that differentiates suicide—the taking of one's own life—from martyrdom, in which the perpetrator's death is a requirement for the attack's success and is thus justified and accepted. Suicide terrorism therefore becomes the ultimate expression of selflessness and altruism. "The ideal of sacrificing one's life for the sake of the community or God," Dr. Eyad Sarraj, a Gaza-based Palestinian psychiatrist, writes,

is deeply rooted and glorified in this part of the World. . . . A person who would die for his country or tribe is glorified, even sanctified and blessed.
    Islam is a powerful message and the Quran is the most beautifully Arab written script with overwhelming appeal. In the Quran God says:

"and don't think that those who are killed in the battle for God, are dead. Sure they are alive and looked after by God." Our life on earth life [*sic*] is the lower one, but the life after is the higher and the true. . . .

In the next life you will be rewarded for your goodness or will be punished for your badness. You will either go to heaven or you to hell [*sic*]. Heaven is profusely described through Quran as the place of eternal joy, beauty and happiness. The quest of Muslims in this earthly life is to secure a place in heaven through total surrender to God.[169]

The perpetrators of this violence are thus accorded a special status and are revered as *shaheed batal*—"martyr heroes"[170] or *istishahadi*—"he who martyrs himself."[171] As Ruqaiyah notes, "It is important to know that suicide is forbidden [in Islam] because of its evil objectives; such as impatience, desperation or any other bad and evil objects." In the context of the *istishahadi*, however, he explains, "The Qur'an evidences that such assaults are Islamically legitimate." Ruqaiyah goes on to cite ten Islamic theologians/ philosophers who similarly support this argument and the four essential motivations that justify such attacks:

1. Seeking for Martyrdom
2. Hurting the enemy
3. Encouraging Muslims
4. Weakening the spirit of the enemy

In conclusion, Ruqaiyah states that "evidences from the Qur'an and the Sunnah . . . [have] clearly demonstrated that the 'Islamic-bombing assault' or the 'martyrdom attack' is Islamically legitimate as far as it is within the framework of Islam."[172] Similar pronouncements have been made by prominent Muslim clerics and in some instances have been promulgated as fatwas.[173] Among the most prominent was the declaration by the Ayatollah Khomeini, who once declared that he knew of no command "more binding to the Muslim than the command to sacrifice life and property to defend and bolster Islam."[174]

In the specific context of Palestine, Sheikh Yusuf al Qardawi, a well-known theologian, published an article in 1996 that began: "Suicide bombings in occupied Palestine represent one of the highest forms of jihad in the name of Allah." He argued further that

to call these operations suicide attacks would be a mistake and misleading. These are examples of heroic sacrifice, as utterly outside the bounds of suicide as the acts of martyrs. A suicide takes his life. . . . But what we are talking about is killing yourself for your religion and your people. A suicide is someone tired of himself and Allah, but a mujahadin [holy warrior] is imbued with faith in Allah's grace and generosity.[175]

Indeed, Sheikh Yassin had reportedly justified suicide terrorism by citing Sura 2, verses 190–91 of the Qur'an, which state: "Fight in the way of Allah against those who fight against you. . . . And slay them wherever ye find them and drive them out of the place when they drove you out, for persecution is worse than slaughter."[176] The U.S.-based Anti-Defamation League of B'nai B'rith has compiled a list of "Arab Leaders [Who] Glorify Suicide Terrorism," along with these leaders' similarly effusive panegyrics to the exalted *istishahadi*.[177]

The language and terminology are, of course, reminiscent of the medieval Assassins' doctrine, invoking the paradise that awaits the holy terrorists. This heaven is described today just as it was more than seven hundred years ago, as a place replete with "rivers of milk and wine . . . lakes of honey, and the services of seventy-two virgins," where the martyr will see the face of Allah and later be joined by seventy chosen relatives.[178] Indeed, the pleasures of alcohol—which all Muslims are forbidden in their lives on earth— and sex, according to some accounts of interpretations, are permitted in this glorious afterlife, in which the commandments of the Shari'a (Islamic law) supposedly do not apply.[179] Not surprisingly, perhaps, from the time of the first Islamic suicide bomb attacks in the early 1980s, witnesses and survivors have often recounted how the bombers were seen smiling just before blowing themselves and their victims up. The U.S. Marine corporal standing guard outside the barracks at Beirut International Airport on the morning of October 23, 1983, for example, recalled how the truck-bomb's driver, a young man with bushy black hair and a moustache, "looked right at me . . . and smiled."[180] This is known as the *bassamat al-Farah*, the "smile of joy"—a tradition of the Shi'a denoting the joy of martyrdom. It is just as prevalent among Sunni terrorists. The statement issued by Hamas following the Israeli assassination of the group's master bomber, Yahya Ayyash, "the Engineer," attests to the virtues of self-sacrifice.[181] "Our valiant Palestinian people," it declared,

> Your militant movement, Hamas, while bringing you glad tidings that its leader hero Yahya Ayyash has ascended to heaven, congratulates its hero leader on winning the honor of martyrdom for the sake of God, and recalls the long series of sacrifices which were given as cheap offerings for the sake of God and the freedom of the homeland and the people. . . .

Martyrdom has been Yahya's long-pursued wish. It is the hope pursued by Hamas's heroes every hour.[182]

These sentiments were confirmed by Ayyash's own father, who observed, "If he is dead, then God bless his soul. If he has acquired martyrdom, then congratulations."[183] The Pulitzer Prize winner and *New York Times* reporter and editor Joseph Lelyveld recounts a conversation he had with the mother of a twenty-three-year-old Palestinian suicide bomber who, only days before his university graduation, had killed himself and two IDF soldiers. Asked how she reacted to news of her son's death, the mother similarly replied, "I was very happy when I heard. To be a martyr, that's something. Very few people can do it. I prayed to thank God. In the Koran it's said that a martyr does not die. I know my son is close to me. It is our belief."[184]

One reason perhaps that the parents (and other relatives) of suicide bombers applaud and praise the violent deaths of their progeny (relations) may be because of their own impending salvation. For instance, it is widely believed that by becoming a martyr the suicide terrorist is able to intercede with God and ensure that seventy members of his family enter heaven.[185] Barbara Victor, an American journalist, recounts in her book on female Palestinian suicide bombers a conversation she had in January 2003 with Sheikh 'Abd-Salan Abu Shukheudem, the chief mufti of the Palestine Authority Police Force—a position akin to the official chaplain of a British or American police force. Sheikh Abu Shukheudem detailed for Victor the seven rewards that, according to Islamic tradition, are bestowed on the martyr for his or her act of self-sacrifice. "From the moment the first drop of blood is spilled," he explained,

> the martyr does not feel the pains of his injury, and is absolved of all his bad deeds; he sees his seat in Paradise; he is saved from the torture of the grave; he is saved from the fear of the Day of Judgment; he marries seventy-two beautiful black-eyed women; he is an advocate for seventy of his relatives to reach Paradise; he earns the Crown of Glory, whose precious stone is better than all this world and everything in it.[186]

In an interview four years earlier in the Palestinian Authority's newspaper, *al Hayat al Jadida,* Sheikh Abu Shukheudem had made the exact same point.[187]

Nasra Hassan recalled a meeting she had in 1999 with a young Hamas-affiliated imam, a graduate of Cairo's prestigious al Azhar University, who was similarly eloquent in his depiction of the afterlife that awaits the martyr.

"He explained," Hassan wrote, "that the first drop of blood shed by a martyr during jihad washes away his sins instantaneously. On the Day of Judgment, he will face no reckoning. On the Day of Resurrection, he can intercede for seventy of his nearest and dearest to enter Heaven; and he will have at his disposal seventy-two houris, the beautiful virgins of Paradise."[188] Indeed, an almost identical formulation was used by Sheikh Isma'il al-Radhwan, who was quoted in a sermon he delivered in 2001 promising:

> The martyr, if he meets Allah, is forgiven with the first drop of blood; he is saved from the torments of the grave; he sees his place in Paradise; he is saved from the Great Horror (of the day of judgment); he is given 72 black-eyed women; he vouches for 70 of his family to be accepted to Paradise; he is crowned with the Crown of glory, whose precious stone is better than all of this world and what is in it.[189]

As these various quotes and statements illustrate, such ethereal promises, repeated by Muslim clerics, are readily accepted by the martyrs and would-be martyrs and doubtless believed by parents and other family members who, though saddened by the death of their relatives, arguably are nonetheless comforted by their own likely ascension to heaven.[190] Thus the Palestinian terrorist organizations have created a recruitment and support mechanism of compelling and attractive incentives, based on theological justification and interpretation of sacred text, that sustains their suicide bombing campaign by appealing both to the would-be bomber and to his or her family. While male recruits, for instance, are promised the proverbial seventy-two virgins in paradise, the families of both male and female bombers are co-opted into supporting—if not encouraging—their relations' homicidal self-destruction by the promise of an assured place in heaven as well.[191]

Rivalry and Competition Between Terrorist Groups

Finally, the rivalries between the various Palestinian terrorist organization groups has often spawned intense competition. The struggle for both political preeminence and popular support that has long characterized Hamas-PLO/PA relations[192] has already been discussed. A new element was introduced into this equation in November 2001 with the formation within Fatah and the irregular militias under its aegis, known as the Tanzim, of the al-Aqsa Martyrs Brigade—a specially dedicated suicide terrorist unit. Fears of Hamas's growing popularity and prestige among Palestinians had persuaded the PLO/PA that it could not afford not to have its own suicide cadre.[193] External as well as internal considerations likely dictated this decision. First was the erosion of morale among the PLO/PA's fighters, who were witnessing the eclipse of the power and influence of the organization they belonged to because of the actions of their rivals. Second was the hope that suicide attacks would not only reinvigorate the PLO/PA but also advance its aims and strengthen its stature vis-à-vis Hamas and the PIJ. Third was the hope that by resorting to suicide tactics, it too would experience the surge in recruits that Hamas especially and the PIJ to a lesser extent had experienced.[194] And finally, there was the belief that through sustained suicide attacks the PLO/PA could accrue the power and prestige that had attended Hamas's and the PIJ's use of this tactic. Indeed, Fatah's creation of the al-Aqsa Martyrs harked back thirty years, to the similar decision to establish the previously discussed Black September Organization as a means to counteract the success and publicity generated by the PFLP's brazen airline hijackings and that upstart movement's newfound power and popularity.

In November 2001 Fatah signaled its entry into the realm of suicide terrorism by launching a joint operation with the PIJ. Two terrorists from each group—one of whom was a member of the Palestinian Authority's police force, based in Jericho—blew themselves up on a bus near Hadera.[195] Israel's seizure two months later of the *Karine-A*, a cargo ship transporting some fifty tons of arms and explosives to the PLO,[196] doubtless accelerated the frequency of al-Aqsa Martyrs Brigades attacks. Now deprived of the means to wage a more conventional terrorist campaign perhaps of its choosing and even more fearful of being eclipsed by Hamas with the loss of this weaponry, al-Fatah was driven to escalate al-Aqsa Martyrs operations. Indeed, it is probably not entirely coincidental that within weeks of the loss of the *Karine-A* shipment, the first female suicide bomber appeared. Her name was Wafa Idris, a twenty-eight-year-old divorcée who worked as a medical secretary for the Palestinian Red Crescent. She was recruited and deployed on a suicide bombing mission to Jerusalem in the name of the al-Aqsa Martyrs Brigade. One person, an eighty-one-year-old man, was killed, and 114 others were wounded.[197] Since then, according to retired IDF colonel Gal Luft, "Al-Aqsa has capitalized on the Islamists' opposition to the participation of women and established squads of willing female suicide bombers named after Wafa Idris, the Palestinian woman who blew up herself."[198]

The al-Aqsa Martyrs operations challenged Hamas and the PIJ and set in motion an almost macabre competition among them of who could mobilize and deploy the largest number of and the most effective "martyrs." The succession of terrorist incidents that convulsed Israel during the first part of

2002 was likely fueled by this competition. Indeed, by any measure, 2002 was an astonishing year for Israel in terms of suicide bombings. There were on average five successful suicide attacks per month in 2002, nearly double the number of successful attacks during the first fifteen months of the al-Aqsa Intifada—which itself is a figure more than ten times the monthly average since 1993. The distribution of groups claiming credit for suicide attacks during 2002 is revealing. Of the fifty-nine incidents recorded that year, the al-Aqsa Martyrs Brigade lead with twenty-five (42 percent), followed by Hamas with sixteen (27 percent), and the PIJ with twelve (2 percent). Significantly, this intergroup competition was so febrile that in just one year the al-Aqsa Martyrs Brigades staged nearly two-thirds the number of suicide attacks that Hamas had perpetrated during the previous three years combined.[199]

Conclusion

As this discussion of Tamil and Palestinian "martyrdom" operations demonstrates, suicide terrorism is an instrumental strategy. The resort to suicide operations has significantly less to do with the presumed anger, desperation, or frustration of those who actually carry out these attacks than with the strategic requirements of the organizations that send the bombers on their way.[200] In a widely read account of Palestinian martyrs, for example, published shortly after 9/11 in the *New Yorker*, Nasra Hassan observed that none of the 250 or so suicide bombers and their handlers that she interviewed conformed to the typical suicidal personality. "None of them were uneducated, desperately poor, simple-minded, or depressed. Many were middle class and, unless they were fugitives, held paying jobs." They included, in fact, the sons of two millionaires.[201] Suicide tactics have been adopted by a growing number of terrorist organizations around the world because they are shocking, deadly, cost-effective, secure, and very difficult to stop. There are only two basic operational requirements that an organization must be able to satisfy to get into the game: a willingness to kill and a willingness to die.

Suicide terrorism, it bears repeating, is not simply a product of intense personal frustration or desperation but an organizational imperative that on the one hand increases the likelihood of a successful terrorist attack and on the other is intrinsically appealing to terrorists because of its profoundly unsettling psychological effects on the societies against which it is directed. The suicide aspect of the 9/11 attacks on the World Trade Center and the Pentagon, as previously noted, was essential to the success of those operations and, indeed, to their undeniably stunning impact. Moreover, the increased likelihood of success that attracts terrorists to suicide attacks is precisely what prompted Timothy McVeigh to consider turning his 1995 bombing of the Alfred P. Murrah Federal Office Building in Oklahoma City into a suicide operation. Not once, but four times in his quasi-autobiography, *American Terrorist*, McVeigh discusses how he contemplated employing this tactic for this very reason until he identified a plan that satisfied his intentions but did not require him to surrender his life in the process.[202]

Accordingly, the suicide attackers who struck the World Trade Center and the Pentagon on 9/11 will likely be followed by other suicide attacks on targets in the United States. The debate over whether suicide attacks in the United States are an "if" or a "when" proposition has in fact already been answered. Four years before 9/11, two Palestinians had plotted a suicide bombing attack on the New York City subway. Their plans to bomb the B subway line, running from the northern tip of Manhattan to Coney Island on the south shore of Brooklyn, were foiled only because an informant told the police. When they were arrested, the terrorists were probably less than a day away from attacking; according to law-enforcement authorities, five bombs had been primed. Although the pair were never formally linked to any identifiable terrorist organization, and appeared to have concocted the plot on their own, there was no doubting their determination. "I always dreamed to be a martyr," one of the would-be bombers declared.[203] Both men resisted arrest when police officers and FBI agents raided their apartment, and both were shot and wounded in the struggles that ensued, one while attempting to detonate the explosives. "I wouldn't call them sophisticated," Howard Safir, the commissioner of the New York City police at the time, observed, "but they certainly were very dangerous."[204] That suicide bombers don't need to be sophisticated is precisely what makes them so dangerous. Indeed, it is the ease and simplicity of suicide bombings that makes it so appealing to terrorists. The means of attack, moreover, can vary widely:

- using aircraft as human cruise missiles (as in the 9/11 attacks) or boats as human torpedoes (as in the 2000 attack on the USS *Cole*);
- involving vehicular bombs with a driver and explosive-laden cars or trucks (as in the 1998 simultaneous attacks on the U.S. embassies in Kenya and Tanzania); or
- using pedestrians—individual attackers wearing a specially designed vest or belt or carrying a backpack or small handheld bag containing explosives and connected to a manual or remote-control detonator.

Similarly, the potential targets of these attacks can be equally diverse, embracing

- high-value symbolic targets such as buildings or installations (e.g., the World Trade Center and the Pentagon on 9/11) that necessarily involve the infliction of mass casualties;
- high-value human targets with the goal of assassination (e.g., of the president and/or vice president of the United States, Cabinet officers, Supreme Court justices, senators, congressmen, mayors, and other prominent individuals, whether in government office or not); and
- deliberately lethal attacks specifically targeting the public (e.g., on buses, trains, and subways, shopping malls, cinema, sports stadiums, pedestrian malls, or any public venue where people gather).

The potential perpetrators of such attacks in the United States could range from domestic right-wing extremists (such as McVeigh) to militant nationalists (such as the two Palestinians involved in the 1997 New York City subway attack plot) to radical Islamic jihadists (such as the nineteen al Qaeda operatives who hijacked the four commercial airline flights on 9/11) and even to lone individuals without any organizational affiliation (such as the gunman who staged a suspected suicide attack at Los Angeles International Airport on July 4, 2002). As the last incident suggests, bombs and explosives are not the only weapons in an act of suicide terrorism; firearms, knives, and other weapons can be involved. The most consequential suicide attacks, however, in terms of casualties and effect, would doubtless be those involving a weapon capable of causing mass casualties, most likely a bomb or explosive device or a means of attack designed to generate some wider conflagration (e.g., crashing an aircraft laden with combustible jet fuel into a building, such as on 9/11).

The challenge in responding to suicide terrorism is not to fall victim to the psychological paralysis and sense of defenselessness or powerlessness that the terrorists hope to achieve. A myth is only as strong as you believe it is. As Ehud Sprinzak had long argued, "Contrary to popular belief, suicide bombers can be stopped—but only if security authorities pay more attention to their methods and motivations." The experience of a country like Israel, for example, shows that despite the significant death toll inflicted by suicide attacks initially, with the proper attention, focus, preparations, and training, this threat can be effectively countered. Israel in fact has achieved remarkable success in dramatically reducing the number of successful suicide attacks. Various authoritative Israeli government sources maintain that the countermeasures adopted since 2002 have prevented at least 80 to 85 percent of all attempts.[205] A special report produced by the Israeli security establishment summarizing that country's war on terrorism, for example, cites a 30 percent decrease in the number of Palestinian terrorist attacks—including suicide attacks—against Israeli targets in 2003, compared with 2002, as well as a 50 percent decrease in the number of casualties.[206] Israeli authorities specify three reasons behind the decline:

> First, quite good intelligence and understanding of the situation as well as analysis of information in a fast and effective way.
>
> Second, . . . when we have intelligence we can send units and engage quickly.
>
> And, third, we have been able to close up the "operational circle"—that is, when we have information, we are able to deploy the right unit and weapons quickly.[207]

Although the challenges of defending against and effectively countering this threat are vastly more complex for countries that, unlike Israel, are not enmeshed in what is considered a perpetual state of war, with potential enemies, poised immediately across national borders, and that have exponentially larger territory and populations, precautions based on Israel's experience can be taken with the confidence that the threat of suicide terrorism is reduced. Perhaps most important is the realization that suicide terrorism is an instrument of war that is not going to suddenly end, so we need to accept that a long struggle faces us. Suicide terror attacks are rational acts undertaken as part of a deliberately calculated and orchestrated campaign to undermine confidence in government and leadership, crush popular morale, and spread fear and intimidation. Responding to suicide terrorism must therefore be equally calculated and planned and instrumental in its reactions. Only by preparing to respond to this threat before terrorists prepare to launch it can we effectively defend ourselves against both the psychological and the physical damage that such acts are designed to unleash. The police, the military, and intelligence agencies can take steps that work from the outside in, beginning far ahead in time and distance from a potential attack and ending at the moment and the site of an actual attack. Although the importance of these steps is widely recognized, they have been implemented unevenly by many countries, including the United States. Among the key lessons are:

- *Understand the terrorists' mind-set and their operational environment.* Know their modus operandi and targeting patterns. Suicide bombers are rarely lone outlaws; they are preceded by long logistical trails. Focus not just on suspected bombers but on the infrastructure required to launch and sustain suicide bombing campaigns. This is the essential spadework. It will be for nothing, however, if concerted efforts are not made to circulate this information quickly and systematically within police forces, across regional jurisdictions (especially the adjacent and surrounding suburbs of a metropolitan area), and among other government authorities charged with protection and defense against terrorist attack.

- *Develop strong confidence-building ties with the communities from which terrorists are most likely to come or hide in, and mount communications campaigns to eradicate support from these communities.* The most effective and useful intelligence comes from places where terrorists conceal themselves and seek to establish and hide their infrastructure. Law enforcement officers should actively encourage and cultivate cooperation by building strong ties with community leaders, including elected officials, civil servants, clerics, businessmen, and teachers, among others, and thereby enlist their assistance and support.

- *Encourage businesses from which terrorists can obtain bomb-making components to alert authorities if they notice large or unusual purchases—the acquisition, for example, of ammonium nitrate fertilizer or of pipes, batteries, and wires or chemicals commonly used to fabricate explosives.* Information about customers who simply inquire about any of these materials can also be extremely useful to police officers. Companies that either sell or distribute materials that can be used in the construction of a terrorist device must be made aware and instructed on identifying and reporting suspicious activity to the authorities.[208]

- *Force terrorists to pay more attention to their organizational and personal security than to planning and carrying out attacks.* Terrorist groups do not attack people or places without planning and reconnaissance. The greatest benefit is in disrupting pre-attack operations. Given the highly fluid international threat that the United States faces alongside the potential for entirely homegrown adversaries (like Timothy McVeigh) to launch such attacks, specialized counterterrorism units, dedicated specifically to identifying and targeting the intelligence-gathering and reconnaissance activities of terrorist organizations, should be established within existing law enforcement agencies. These units should be especially aware of places at which organizations frequently recruit new members and bombers themselves, such as community centers, social clubs, schools, and religious institutions.

- *Make sure that ordinary materials don't become shrapnel. Some steps to build up physical defenses were taken after 9/11—reinforcing park benches, erecting Jersey barriers around vulnerable buildings, and the like.* More precautions are needed, such as ensuring that windows on buses and subway cars are shatterproof and that seats and other accoutrements are not easily dislodged or splintered. Buses can be outfitted, as in Israel, with barriers to make entry through rear exit doors impossible and to enable the driver to stop a suspicious person from entering the bus from the front door. Explosives sensors can also be installed at the point where passengers step up into the bus from the street.

- *Civil defense and public efforts that enlist the help and support of citizens in remaining alert for strange or suspicious behavior of people in areas in and around likely attack sites (i.e., on buses and subways, at historical landmarks, near embassies or consulates, or particularly well-known buildings) and being aware of packages or bags left unattended at public venues.* During the IRA's bombing campaign in London from the 1970s to the 1990s, residents and visitors to that city were reminded of the need for vigilance through posters and other advertisements containing basic instructions on both what to look for and whom to contact. Israel's populace is similarly indoctrinated on the need for eternal vigilance and the appropriate action to take when suspicion is aroused or a terrorist attack occurs. Although public awareness campaigns of this type have been instituted in some cities in the United States, in many cases they are either insufficiently advertised or simply warn citizens to be aware and provide a toll-free telephone number but do not advise specifically what citizens should be aware of or sufficiently educate them to the extent that is done in Israel today and that was done in London in the past.[209]

- *Teach law enforcement awareness—what to do at the moment of an attack or an attempt.* Prevention comes first from the cop on the beat, who will be forced to make instant life-and-death decisions affecting those nearby. Rigorous training is needed for identifying a potential suicide bomber, confronting a suspect, and responding and securing the area around the attack site in the event of an explosion. Is the officer authorized to take action upon sighting a suspected bomber, or must he or she call a supervisor or special unit first? Policies and procedures must be established. In the aftermath of a blast the police must determine whether emergency medical crews and firefighters may enter the site; concerns about a follow-up attack can dictate that first responders be held back until the area is secured. The ability to make such lightning-quick determinations requires training—and, tragically, experience.[210]

An effective defense against suicide terrorism must be nimble, flexible, and adaptive. It must be as dynamic and fluid as terrorist operational planning, reconnaissance, and attack execution are. Accordingly, law enforcement plans, procedures, and policies cannot rest on past laurels or previous successes achieved in deterring, preventing, or responding to terrorist threats and/or attacks but must be familiar with existing, historical, emergent, and probable future terrorist targeting patterns and modi operandi.

In this respect, that our enemies are marshaling their own resources to continue the struggle that crystallized on 9/11 is beyond doubt. Whether it will materialize in the same shape or form as the suicide bombing campaigns directed against Sri Lanka and Israel—or as occurred in July 2005 in London—remains to be seen. But in his 2001 book, *Knights Under the Prophet's Banner*, al-Zawahiri laid down a blueprint for how al Qaeda envisions this struggle will unfold: "We must move the battle to the enemy's ground to burn the hands of those who ignite fire in our countries," he wrote. This entails, al-Zawahiri continued:

1. The need to inflict the maximum casualties against the opponent, for this is the language understood by the west, no matter how much time and effort such operations take.

2. The need to concentrate on the method of martyrdom operations as the most successful way of inflicting damage against the opponent and the least costly to the mujahidin in terms of casualties.

3. The targets as well as the type and method of weapons used must be chosen to have an impact on the structure of the enemy and deter it enough to stop its brutality, arrogance, and disregard for all taboos and customs. It must restore the struggle to its real size.[211]

At a time when the greatest military onslaught in history against a terrorist movement is still being prosecuted, in February 2004 al-Zawahiri defiantly proclaimed: "Bush, reinforce your security measures. . . . The Islamic nation which sent you the New York and Washington brigades has taken the firm decision to send you successive brigades to sow death and aspire to paradise."[212]

Chapter 6

The Old Media, Terrorism, and Public Opinion

The goals and motivations of terrorists, as we have seen in previous chapters, vary widely, from such grand schemes as the total remaking of society along fundamentalist religious or doctrinaire ideological lines, and even the fulfillment of some divinely inspired millenarian imperative, to comparatively more distinct aims such as the reestablishment of a national homeland or the unification of a divided nation. Still other terrorists are motivated by very issue-specific causes, such as the banning of abortion, animal rights, or environmental concerns, and seek to apply direct pressure on both the public and its representatives in government to either enact or repeal legislation directly affecting their particular interest. Despite these many differences, however, all terrorist groups have one trait in common: they do not commit actions randomly or senselessly. Each wants maximum publicity to be generated by its actions and, moreover, aims at intimidation and subjection to attain its objectives. In the words of the late Dr. Frederick Hacker, a psychiatrist and noted authority on terrorism, terrorists seek to "frighten and, by frightening, to dominate and control. They want to impress. They play to and for an audience, and solicit audience participation."[1]

Terrorism, therefore, may be seen as a violent act that is conceived specifically to attract attention and then, through the publicity it generates, to communicate a message. "There is no other way for us," a leader of the United Red Army (the "parent group" of the Japanese Red Army) terrorist group once explained. "Violent actions . . . are shocking. We *want* to shock people, everywhere. . . . It is our way of communicating with the people."[2] The modern news media, as the principal conduit of information about such acts, thus play a vital part in the terrorists' calculus. Indeed, without the media's coverage the act's impact is arguably wasted, remaining narrowly confined to the immediate victim(s) of the attack rather than reaching the wider "target audience" at whom the terrorists' violence is actually aimed. Only by spreading the terror and outrage to a much larger audience can the terrorists gain the maximum potential leverage that they need to effect fundamental political change. "Terrorism is theatre," Brian Jenkins famously declared in his seminal 1974 paper, explaining how "terrorist attacks are often carefully choreographed to attract the attention of the electronic media and the international press."[3]

Just as often, the media respond to these overtures with almost unbridled alacrity, proving unable to ignore what has been accurately described as "an event . . . fashioned specifically for their needs."[4] The American media coverage of the hijacking of TWA Flight 847 by Lebanese Shi'a terrorists in 1985 amply confirms that observation. Three terrorists belonging to Hezbollah had hijacked the aircraft en route from Rome to Cairo on June 14. The hijackers originally demanded the release of 776 Shi'a held in Israeli jails, although they later reduced that number. The commandeered aircraft was flown first to Beirut, then to Algiers, then back to Beirut. At each stop passengers who were not U.S. citizens, along with the women and children on board, were released, until only thirty-nine American men remained. After the aircraft landed in Beirut for the second time, the hostages were spirited into hiding and scattered throughout the city to thwart any attempted rescue operation by U.S. military forces. During the seventeen-day crisis, while the Americans were held hostage in Beirut, nearly 500 news segments—an average of 28.8 per day[5]—were broadcast by the three major U.S. television networks (ABC, the American Broadcasting Corporation; NBC, the National Broadcasting Corporation; and CBS, the Columbia Broadcasting System). Indeed, on average, two-thirds of their daily early-evening "flagship" news shows (fourteen out of twenty-one minutes) focused on the hostage story,[6] and their regularly scheduled programs were interrupted at least eighty times over those seventeen days with special reports or news bulletins.[7] This intense coverage was made possible by the small army of reporters, field producers, editors, camera crews, and sound technicians that the three networks rushed to the scene of the breaking story: within days, a total of eighty-five people representing the three networks were in Beirut.[8] The message that they imparted to their viewers was clear: no news of any significance was occurring anywhere except that which concerned the hostages and their anxious families back home.

More disconcerting, perhaps, was the tenor of the coverage. As the hostage crisis dragged on day after day, at times with seemingly little or no progress toward a resolution, the vast media resources deployed for just this one story had to find or create "news" to justify the expense and continued presence of the media personnel, even if no "real news" was occurring. A gross imbalance therefore emerged: "soft," human-interest feature stories predominated (mostly interviews with the hostages and their families), accounting for slightly more than a third of all reports, with fewer than half as many stories addressing "real" issues, such as the U.S. government's reactions to various developments in the crisis or the Reagan administration's persistent efforts to reach a resolution.[9] The cloying and meretricious content of the reporting was clearly revealed in a contemporary *Washington Post* article. "In the race for on-the-air scoops, which ABC-TV News seems to have won to date," it began, "the interview Friday morning between anchorman [news presenter] Dan Rather of 'CBS Evening News' and TWA flight 847's hostage media star, Allyn Conwell, was distinctive."[10] In possibly the most egregious perversion of news reporting during this episode, the "news presenters" rather than the "news makers" had become the story!

However, the most pernicious effect of the crisis was its validation of terrorism as a tactic. The Reagan administration, driven by intense domestic pressure generated by the hostages' plight, in turn compelled Israel to accede to the hijackers' demands and release 756 imprisoned Shi'a. The terrorists, in return, duly freed their thirty-nine American captives. The line of distraught hostage family members that paraded before the three networks' cameras ensured that there was no letup of pressure. "Should the Reagan administration press Israel to release its Shi'a prisoners?" the son of one hostage was asked on a morning news show. "That's what I'd like to see," came the reply.[11] The networks professed little or no concern that they had moved beyond reporting the news to actively helping to determine policy. At times, presenters assumed for themselves the responsibility of negotiating with the terrorists. "Any final words to President Reagan this morning?" the congenial host of ABC's *Good Morning America* asked the leader of one Lebanese group.[12] Justifying this type of active intervention in a story, CBS White House correspondent Lesley Stahl explained, "We are an instrument for the hostages. . . . We force the Administration to put their lives above policy."[13]

Those responsible for determining and implementing that policy under-standably took a very different view. Reflecting on a state of affairs where public emotions were seen to determine government policy, Congressman Tom Lantos lamented that "focusing on individual tragedies, interview-ing the families of people in anguish, in horror, in nightmare, completely debilitates national policymakers from making rational decisions in the national interest."[14] His complaint was echoed by former U.S. secretary of state Henry Kissinger and Zbigniew Brzezinski, President Carter's national security adviser during the Tehran hostage crisis. Both agreed that there was little doubt that the febrile television coverage afforded to hijackings and hostage situations involving American citizens complicates and under-mines governmental efforts to obtain their release.[15]

That terrorism had indeed become a perverted form of show business is borne out by the experiences of other journalists who dealt with the hos-tage-takers' "spin doctors" and therefore witnessed at first hand the terror-ists' polished PR campaign. "These guys are so sophisticated about the way they are getting through to the American viewer," a senior Associated Press editor marveled. "These guys are street fighters [yet] they're making ground rules for the media."[16] According to John Bullock, a British journalist who covered the story, throughout the crisis the terrorists knew exactly what they were doing. Their deft manipulation of the U.S. networks, he recalls, "was done quite consciously. There were graduates of media studies from American colleges at meetings at Nabih Berri's house in West Beirut while ['spin doctoring'] tactics were being worked out."[17]

The fruit of the hijackers' labors may be seen in the abject capitulation of the American TV networks to the terrorists' point of view. On-air commentary repeatedly and unthinkingly equated the wanton kidnapping of entirely inno-cent airline passengers (who were singled out only because of the nationality of the passport they carried) with Shi'a militiamen and suspected terrorists detained by Israeli troops during fighting in southern Lebanon. These invidi-ous and inaccurate comparisons were all the more odious considering that one of the hostages, a U.S. Navy diver named Robert Dean Stethem, had been mercilessly beaten to death on board the aircraft shortly after the hijacking began. As one critic noted, "It's a cliché now that the Shi'ites got the networks to carry their political message back to America. When the TV coverage is replayed, it's clear just how well the Shi'ite line was delivered." Indeed, so obvi-ous was this perceived bias on the part of some reporters that it was said to be a standing joke among journalists in Beirut that the initials "ABC" stood for the "Amal Broadcasting Company" (in recognition of the attention it show-ered on one of the Lebanese militias purportedly helping to effect the hostages' release), while "NBC" denoted the "Nabih Berri Company" (the name of that militia's leader).[18] While the American networks' response to the TWA Flight 847 crisis is doubtless the most glaring example of terrorism's ability to capture media attention and manipulate and exploit it in ways amenable to the terrorists' cause, the problem is endemic to all democratic countries with open and unrestricted press reporting. So pervasive was the influence exerted by West German terrorists over coverage of the 1972 deal that freed a kidnapped West Berlin politician, Peter Lorenz, in exchange for five imprisoned terrorists, that one executive was driven to admit that "for seventy-two hours we lost control of our medium."[19] In 1978 the same blanket coverage, to the exclusion of almost all other news, that would later be afforded the TWA hijacking was evident in Italy throughout the fifty-five-day state crisis engendered by the Red Brigades' kidnapping of former prime minister Aldo Moro. According to one analysis, during that time only two articles appeared on the front pages of that country's newspapers that did not have to do with the Moro case.[20] During the 1990s, complaints were voiced in Britain over the stranglehold exercised by Sinn Fein spin doctors on behalf of their IRA masters over reporting in Northern Ireland. Henry McDonald, BBC Northern Ireland security correspondent between 1994 and 1996, contends that the terrorists and their apologists orchestrated a public relations campaign that imposed a "politically correct culture" on the reporting of both British and Irish print and electronic media. "It is a culture," McDonald claims, "where the commentators and opinion-formers blame [then British prime minister] John Major for resumed IRA violence, rather than the IRA itself."[21]

Given that terrorism is inherently about attracting attention and publicity, and that in even its earliest manifestations centuries ago the Zealots and the Assassins deliberately played to an audience far beyond the immediate victims of their attacks, why is it only comparatively recently that the media have been blamed for serving as the terrorists' willing apologists? The answer may be found in two technological advances in mass communication that occurred nearly one hundred years apart, respectively altering the way that news is transmitted and making it accessible to exponentially larger audiences. These developments, in turn, have been ruthlessly and successfully exploited by terrorists.

Terrorism and the Transformation of Reporting

The invention of the steam-powered printing press in 1830 began the modern era of mass media and communication: within three years the first mass-circulation newspaper was being produced in the United States. Subsequent technological refinements led to the introduction of the even more efficient rotary press the following decade. News became more timely (because of the speed with which newspapers could now be printed) and more accessible (as the economics of technological innovation created a more widely affordable product). By the 1870s the newspaper business had been completely transformed by the advent of electric power coupled with the development of curved stereotype printing plates, together resulting in the automatic rotary cylinder press—and the capability to print on both sides of a continuous roll of paper. The revolution in mass communication, begun less than fifty years earlier, was now complete, offering abundant new opportunities to communicate on a vaster scale than ever before. I have already noted that terrorists were quick to recognize the potential of this new mass communications technology. It suffices simply to add here that the symbiotic relationship between terrorism and the media was forged during this era by both the Russian constitutionalists in the Narodnaya Volya and their anarchist contemporaries who, through "propaganda by deed," deliberately sought to communicate their revolutionary message to a wide audience.

The second great revolution in mass communication that directly affected terrorism occurred in 1968. That year marked not only, as previously noted, the birth of international terrorism—when Palestinian terrorists began to hijack airliners in Europe—but also the launching by the United States of the first television satellite. Now stories could be transmitted from local studios back to network news headquarters for editing and broadcast far more rapidly than was previously possible. It is perhaps not entirely coincidental that from this time forward, the United States became the number one target of terrorists throughout the world. Throughout the following thirty years, terrorists attacked American citizens and interests more than those of any other country.[22] While there are various reasons why terrorists find American targets so attractive,[23] a salient consideration has always been the unparalleled opportunities for publicity and exposure that terrorists the world over know they will get from the extensive U.S. news media. This was made especially clear during the TWA Flight 847 crisis when a British correspondent assigned to the story discovered that the hostage-takers paid no attention to "non-American and non-television journalists."[24] In retrospect, therefore, the U.S. satellite launch was the first, critical step in facilitating the American news media's worldwide predominance through its ability to reach a numerically vast audience. Ironically, it was also this development that made the same audience exponentially more attractive to terrorists than that of any other nation.

By the early 1970s the effect of this technological leap was further enhanced by the availability of three critical pieces of television equipment that made possible the reporting of events in "real time." These were the Minicam (the portable, lightweight video camera), the equally portable battery-powered video recorder, and the time-base corrector (which converts video footage into transmittable output that in turn can be broadcast over the airwaves). With this combination of technologies, live television transmissions could now be made directly from remote locations throughout the world and beamed instantaneously into the homes of viewers everywhere.[25] The dramatic potential of this breakthrough was, as previously described, spectacularly demonstrated at the 1972 Munich Olympics when Palestinian terrorists were able to monopolize the attention of a global television audience who had tuned in expecting to watch the Games.

The emergence of these broadcast technologies has had equally profound consequences for the content of the news and its impact on government. The ability to transmit a breaking story live spawned intense competition among rival networks to "scoop" one another (as was illustrated by the *Washington Post* article that commented on the network news organizations during the TWA Flight 847 hostage situation). This could be accomplished basically in one of two ways: by being the first on the scene or by being the first to report some hitherto undisclosed information. The main problem with the former is that even though it is the most sought-after prize of TV journalism, it is also an inherently evanescent advantage. Hence, having broken the story and captured viewers' attention, the priority becomes to hold that attention with equally gripping follow-on reports. Accordingly, for the duration of an important story's life, the media's focus invariably shifts from the reporting of the limited and often dwindling quantity of "hard" news to more human-interest-type "feature" stories, mostly involving exclusive interviews (e.g., the aforementioned Rather-Conwell exchange) or the breathless revelation of some previously unknown or undocumented item of related news—no matter how trivial or irrelevant.

For the media-savvy terrorist, these conditions are ripe for exploitation. The networks' capability to broadcast instantaneously, coupled with the intense pressure to scoop competitors, has meant that the responsibilities once exercised by a studio editor—with the attendant opportunities for sober reflection or considered judgment—have long since passed in the rush to "go live on air."[26] The television medium thus presents itself as a vacuum waiting to be filled; a void of rolling cameras and open mikes susceptible to terrorist exploitation and manipulation. Indeed, in this key respect, the terrorists' and the networks' interests are identical: having created the story, both are resolved to ensure its longevity. The overriding objective for the terrorists is to wring every last drop of exposure, publicity, and coercive power from the incident, while the networks' goal is to squeeze from the story every additional ratings point that their coverage can provide. "Capturing the audience's attention may be easy," political psychologists Jeffrey Z. Rubin and Nehemia Friedland note, "but terrorist organizations need a flair for the dramatic to sustain that interest."[27] Precisely the same can be said of television correspondents and field producers.

The quest to keep a story alive leads inevitably to a disproportionate fixation on the "human-interest angle": most often, the grief and anguish of family and friends of terrorist victims and/or hostages. In this manner, the vicarious dimension of a terrorist incident—the stimulation of thoughts in the minds of millions of television viewers and newspaper readers everywhere that "there but for the grace of God go I"—is effectively and efficiently mined by terrorist and journalist alike. Beyond any doubt, the American networks during the TWA crisis served this diet on a platter to a waiting and watching public at home, made hungry both for every scrap of information on the hostages themselves and for each morsel doled out on the plight of their worried loved ones back home. This sort of coverage dovetailed perfectly with the terrorists' wish to apply the maximum pressure possible on the Reagan administration to force Israel to accede to the hijackers' demands. Day in and day out, as the hostages' uncertain fate was played out in the glare of the camera's lens, the administration was progressively compelled to abandon its publicly stated policy of refusing to negotiate with terrorists, undermine its relations with a close regional ally, embrace the recovery of the hostages as its only goal, and believe that its sole option was the safe return of the thirty-nine American hostages in exchange for the release of the more than seven hundred Shi'a imprisoned in Israel. "What the Shi'ite terrorists in Beirut achieved is spin control beyond the wildest dreams of any politician," the American columnist Fred Barnes wrote in the wake of the crisis. "How did this happen?" he asked rhetorically. "Easy," came the reply:

> The terrorists exploited the normal lust of the media—particularly TV—for breaking events of international impact, and for high drama and a human dimension to the news. . . . Media competition, always brutal, is especially fierce in this atmosphere, partly because the public is more attentive, partly because media stardom may be at stake for some.[28]

It will be recalled that the leading late-night American television news show *Nightline* grew out of the need to report at the end of each day, as viewers prepared for sleep, some new tidbit of information from Tehran during the previous 444-day hostage crisis of 1979–80. This approach not only made the show's presenter, Ted Koppel, a media star[29] but also spawned dozens of imitators in other countries.

One additional, even paramount, consideration influencing television news coverage that has emerged in recent years is its cost. A once finite number of privately owned or state-run broadcasting corporations now must contend with heightened competition not only from their traditional network rivals but also from a virtually unlimited array of upstart cable and satellite channels. Moreover, news is now broadcast over such diverse media as the Internet, e-mail, and faxes, and via local telephone servers. Therefore today, on top of increasingly constrained news budgets (an issue that was emerging more than a decade ago), foreign network news coverage, especially, must increasingly justify itself and its vast expense by winning larger audience shares. According to one veteran network foreign correspondent writing in the late 1990s, the daily cost of the typical international television news team "begins at around $3,000 a day. Air fare and excess baggage charges can easily reach $12,000"—in addition to the costs of satellite uplinks and transmittal time.[30] Accordingly, network executives exhibit a discernible proclivity to look more to the "bottom line" than to journalistic priorities for guidance and hence to emphasize entertainment value over good reporting. "They've got us putting more fuzz and wuzz on the air," Dan Rather lamented in a 1993 speech, "cop show stuff, so as to compete not with other news programs but with entertainment programs—including those posing as news programs—for dead bodies, mayhem and lurid tales."[31] This view was reiterated by one of Rather's colleagues, Garrick Utley, the chief foreign correspondent for NBC and ABC TV news and a contributor to CNN, in a lead article in the prestigious American journal *Foreign Affairs*.[32] Immediacy, exclusivity, and drama (the more violent or life-threatening, the better) thus become the essential "hooks" with which to reel in viewers and ensure a flow of advertising revenue. Terrorist incidents, inherently dramatic, replete with human interest, and often of prolonged duration (whether the wrenching daily ordeal of hostages or reports on post-attack cleanup and repercussions in the aftermath of bombings), thus occupy center stage in network television's entertainment/news calculations. The result is a trivialization of television news that inevitably emphasizes aspects of the story that the wider viewing audience can "relate to,"[33] rather than genuine analysis or probing to gain an understanding of the background to a particular issue. The camera becomes tightly focused on the human drama at the expense of the "bigger picture" that is what the story is really about. In essence, what is broadcast is the "big picture" writ so small that the average television viewer can understand it, the story deliberately "packaged" to suit the typical audience's short attention span.[34] "Mindless gaga and emotional gush seem the mainstays of the moment," the *Washington Post's* television critic, Tom Shales, opined in the midst of the TWA crisis, bemoaning the debasement of broadcast news.[35]

This trend in American television news is by no means an inconsequential development, given that by 1978 television had become the primary source of news information for a majority (67 percent) of Americans and the *only* source of news for 34 percent.[36] The emphasis on entertainment and, in turn, the violence and "blood and guts" aspects of news stories were demonstrated in a study of the three major American networks' reporting on Armenian terrorism between 1975 and 1983. It concluded that while the coverage had indeed (as noted in chapter 3) provided unparalleled exposure to the terrorists and their cause, the "networks tended to reduce Armenians to terrorists (not freedom fighters) shooting an American woman in the back as she tried to flee, taunting the police by holding a small child at gun point, and killing a young French boy with a gasoline bomb." In this respect, virtually no attention was paid to the historical background, political context, or attendant wider issues that would have shed light on the terrorists' reasoning and motivations.[37]

Unfortunately, the approach to terrorism coverage embraced by broadcast journalists is often emulated by their print counterparts. "As the television media trivialise the news," James Adams, former CEO of United Press International and past *Sunday Times* Washington Bureau chief, foreign editor, and defense editor, argues, "so newspapers have to seek ways of presenting their information in a lively and exciting way to their audience. That has meant not just a narrowing of the focus but a concentration on the trivial, the marginal and the irrelevant in the search for excitement."[38] Color photos, lurid images, and sensational headlines splashed across the front pages of tabloids and their more serious counterparts are what now sells newspapers (and advertising copy) as much as commercial airtime. Accordingly, there is often the same abandonment in print as over the airwaves of any effort to understand the "bigger picture." Instead, an obsession with voyeuristic detail now predominates in many newspapers. It is an outcome dictated by the same financial pressures and declining revenues that have ravaged network television news, even while the broadcast media continue to erode the news-reading public. Adams, for example, draws a comparison between his stint at the *Sunday Times* as foreign manager during the 1980s and that of one his predecessors, Ian Fleming (the creator of the fictional spy James Bond), in the 1950s. While Fleming could call on the services of 150 correspondents throughout the world, thirty years later Adams had only 8 at his disposal. "What that means today," he writes, "is that media coverage is highly selective and driven not necessarily by the importance of a story, but by the cost of covering it, or even by something as simple as who happens to be in the area at the time."[39]

Under these circumstances, news reporting is driven primarily by the imperative of speed in getting on air or into print and subsequently by the search for additional material to justify the initial expense and attention and thereby to continue to fill a broadcast slot or a printed page. This situation is, however unwittingly, tailor-made for terrorist manipulation and contrivance. "'Don't shoot, Abdul! We're not on prime time!'" is how terrorism expert J. Bowyer Bell described the conscious efforts of terrorists to play to the modern media and the media's eagerness to respond. Sadly, this jocular observation is closer to reality than exaggeration. During the 1975 seizure of OPEC headquarters in Vienna and kidnapping of the oil ministers, for example, Carlos "the Jackal" obligingly waited for the arrival of the television camera crews before dramatically fleeing the building with his hostages.[40] Four years later, a sullen mob outside the American embassy in Tehran, where the fifty-two hostages were being held, suddenly came to life when a Canadian Broadcasting Company camera team showed up, turned on its klieg lights, and began filming. As A. P. Schmid recounts, "As soon as the cameras were on, the demonstrators began shouting 'Death to Carter,' raised their fists, looked angry and burned American flags. After two minutes, the cameraman signalled the end of the 'take.' Then the same scene was done once more for the French-speaking Canadians, with the crowd shouting 'Mort a Carter.'"[41]

Cause and Effect? Terrorism, the Media, and Public Opinion

Clearly, terrorism and the media are bound together in an inherently symbiotic relationship, each feeding off and exploiting the other for its own purposes. The real issue, however, is not so much the relationship itself, which is widely acknowledged to exist, but whether it actually affects public opinion and government decision making, as the media's critics claim, in a manner that favors or assists terrorists. The answer is far more complex and ambiguous than the conventional wisdom on this subject suggests.

In the view most commonly, if somewhat reflexively, advanced by statesmen,[42] scholars,[43] and other critics the media are either "the terrorists' best friends"[44] or, in former British prime minister Margaret Thatcher's well-worn metaphor, supplying "the oxygen of publicity on which [terrorists] depend."[45] The media are condemned for having "made the terrorists' task all too easy"[46] or accused of having "become the unwilling—and in some cases, willing— amplifier of the terrorists' publicity campaign."[47] Indeed, Benjamin Netanyahu, a former Israeli prime minister who subsequently became that country's finance minister, maintains that "unreported, terrorist acts would be like the proverbial tree falling in the silent forest."[48] The obvious implication being made in all these assertions is that if the terrorists could somehow be "starved" of the publicity on which they "thrive,"[49] both their malignant influence and the frequency with which they act would be greatly reduced.[50]

This argument, while seductive in its simplicity, nonetheless ignores the fact that, for all the attention and sensationalist coverage that the media lavish on terrorism, rarely is it positive. "I have seen no evidence," Lawrence K. Grossman, the president of NBC News, wrote in an article defending the media's coverage of the TWA hostage crisis, "that audiences are ever taken in by the propaganda of terrorists who have blackmailed their way on to the television screen."[51] However self-serving or self-exculpatory Grossman's argument may be, it is not without foundation. Even scholars like Walter Laqueur, who in one breath criticize the media for its unstinting coverage of terrorism, concede in the next that this has not led to more favorable public attitudes toward either terrorists or their causes.[52]

A study conducted during 1988 and 1989 by the renowned American think tank, the RAND Corporation, reached precisely the same conclusion. By surveying a nationally representative sample, it sought to identify empirically public perceptions of both terrorism and terrorists and analyze how public opinion is affected by terrorist acts. The timing of the survey was particularly significant: it immediately followed a prolonged period of heightened international terrorist activity, characterized by repeated attacks on American targets abroad. These incidents (including the 1985 TWA hijacking) had also been heavily reported by the American press and broadcast media. Public awareness of the issue was therefore high. Indeed, terrorism had been a major news item throughout the five years preceding the study, and it had already been cited in a 1986 CBS News/*New York Times* opinion poll as the most important problem facing the United States by a margin of 15 percentage points above any other problem, domestic or international. Despite the media's continual and often intense attention to terrorist activities over a period of years, however, the RAND study found that public approval for terrorists "*was effectively zero* [emphasis added]."[53]

At the same time, the study also revealed that even though the vast majority of Americans have little sympathy toward groups that sponsor or commit terrorist acts,[54] they nonetheless evince a profound and abiding fascination with both terrorists and terrorism. As Konrad Kellen explained, "People [may not] approve of terrorists any more than they approve of murderers. . . . But people are clearly intrigued by them."[55] This was made abundantly clear on May 5, 1986, when NBC's *Nightly News* broadcast an in-depth interview with Abul Abbas, the leader of the Palestine Liberation Front (PLF). Just seven months earlier, the PLF had shocked the world when it had seized an Italian cruise ship, the *Achille Lauro*, and then attempted to trade the vacationing passengers on board for fifty Palestinian terrorists imprisoned in Israel. In the course of the hijacking, the terrorists brutally murdered an American tourist confined to a wheelchair, Leon Klinghoffer, and cast his body into the Mediterranean. Eventually, the head of the PLO, Yasir Arafat, intervened and brokered a deal whereby the terrorists would allow the ship to dock at Alexandria and would release their hostages in return for receiving safe passage back to the PLF's base in Tunisia. U.S. Navy fighters, however, intercepted the EgyptAir plane carrying the four hijackers and forced it to land at a NATO air base in Sicily, where the terrorists were arrested by Italian police officers. The U.S. State Department subsequently announced a $250,000 reward for Abbas's capture and launched an international manhunt. In tracking down the fugitive terrorist leader and obtaining an "exclusive interview" with him, NBC had therefore succeeded where the U.S. government hitherto had failed. More to the point, the network disingenuously implied that its news staff had accomplished this feat entirely on their own and without Abbas's encouragement or assistance.[56] The extent of the media's symbiotic relationship with terrorism, no less than the public fascination to which both media and terrorists actively cater, could hardly have been more blatant. What was particularly striking about the NBC interview, however, was not simply the "statesmanlike" status that the network promiscuously accorded to a man whose hands, as the hijacking's mastermind, were arguably drenched in Klinghoffer's blood, but the preening self-importance that attended NBC's broadcast of this spectacle. "We like to interview all leaders," Grossman boasted. "I think it is important for the American people to understand, be informed and make their own judgements."[57] Yet by no stretch of the imagination could (or should) Abbas be ranked with those world "leaders" whose views merit the most coveted prize on American television—a dedicated slot on a major prime-time news show. Abbas, in fact, was one of the least successful PLO commanders; his group's previous operations had featured episodes reminiscent of the Keystone Kops, with terrorists flying hot-air balloons and hang gliders, all of which had failed as miserably as the attempt to free the fifty prisoners through hijacking a luxury liner. Nevertheless, while Abbas may have been a failure as a terrorist, he certainly had a flair for a form of macabre showmanship that suited NBC and its audience's interests perfectly. In the incandescent glare of the camera's lights, the public and media fascination with terrorism transformed Abbas into the "media star of the moment" rather than the kidnapper and murderer that he really was.[58] Indeed, so far as many—perhaps most—viewers were concerned, the interview was doubtless more "entertainment" than news. Tasteless or inappropriate as the NBC broadcast may have been, then, it probably had little or no impact on most viewers' attitudes toward terrorists or terrorism, except perhaps to reaffirm their overwhelming negative impressions.

The phenomenon of public fascination with terrorism is by no means confined to American news audiences only. A Royal Ulster Constabulary (RUC) divisional commander quoted at a conference on terrorism and the media by his boss at the time, Chief Constable Sir John Hermon, rhetorically asked whether "a rapist in Hampshire or a burglar in Berkshire [would] be accorded the freedom through the [British] media to justify rape and burglary and be allowed to threaten more of the same."[59] The answer, as we all know, is obviously that he would not. However, the point is less the publicity "showered" on terrorism by the media than that terrorism patently *is* "news"—often in an international as well as a national context—in a way that these other crimes, mostly, are not. Perhaps we should feel grateful that even after nearly forty years of violence and strife in Northern Ireland, terrorism remains so—relatively—infrequent an occurrence that it is indeed still "news." But there is also an undeniably inherent element of drama in terrorism that seems to enable it genuinely to transcend the mundane and stimulate among audiences an almost insatiable interest, which the media of course actively encourage and feed. Thus, while the media may be guilty of constantly—perhaps at times even shamelessly—scrambling to fill a vacuum created by twenty-four-hour news channels, rolling news shows, and intense competition, the media neither exist nor function in a vacuum, and, like any business, they respond naturally to "consumer demand." Whether this makes for good reporting or sound professional behavior on the part of print and broadcast journalists is another question. On this issue, too, the opinions of critics and audiences differ considerably.

As the lightning rod for much of the criticism directed at the media over its coverage of terrorism, the TWA crisis epitomizes for many the corrosive effect of terrorism on journalistic standards.[60] Reagan administration officials railed against the "media extravaganza" in Beirut that one senior political appointee claimed "gave irresponsibility and tastelessness a new meaning."[61] Even veteran newsmen, like NBC's Roger Mudd, cringed at what they too regarded as something of a "media circus."[62] Yet the American public disagreed completely. An ABC News/*Washington Post* poll conducted shortly after the TWA hostage crisis ended, for instance, found that more than two-thirds of Americans approved of the way television had reported the story,[63] while a Gallup poll from the same period revealed an even higher proportion in favor: 89 percent.[64] Nor were these strongly positive ratings ephemeral aberrations of opinion. Three-quarters of Americans surveyed a year later in a poll conducted by Gallup and the Times Mirror Corporation (which publishes the *Los Angeles Times*, among other newspapers) similarly expressed satisfaction with both television and the print media's reporting of terrorist incidents. Moreover, 71 percent of respondents regarded their country's news organizations as "highly professional."[65] These unequivocal responses, flying in the face of mostly genuinely deserved, if sometimes overheated, criticism, seem to confirm viewers' interest in terrorism stories primarily for their entertainment value—and their lack of interest in the terrorists or their broader "message."

The media were further excoriated by both senior government officials and distinguished elder statesmen for the excessive attention focused on individual hostages and their families. "TV is probably going to cost the lives of a number of people in a dangerous situation like this sometime in the future,"[66] one unidentified presidential aide declared, echoing the frequently heard criticism that the intense coverage compromised administration efforts to free the hostages. However, nearly half of those surveyed in the Gallup/Times Mirror poll regarded the unrelenting attention devoted to the hostages as a positive development that ensured the hostages' safety and eventual release. As the wife of one hostage explained on a morning news show, "If we like it or not, television is a way . . . to put pressure where pressure needs to be put."[67] More than a few hostages wholeheartedly agreed. "Thank the Lord we're on our way," one declared as he boarded the flight that was to take him back to the United States, flashing the thumbs-up sign to a CNN camera crew filming his departure, and "thanks for all the coverage."[68] The American CNN reporter Jeremy Levin, who himself was kidnapped in Beirut by Hezbollah terrorists in March 1984, has made the exact same point. Levin maintains that the extensive media attention focused on his plight during the eleven months he was held captive actually deterred his captors from killing him.[69] He also makes the discomforting argument that the longest hostage crisis— that of the Americans and other Western nationals (including Terry Waite, the Archbishop of Canterbury's special envoy) kidnapped by terrorists in

Lebanon between 1984 and 1992—was also the one that had the least sustained media coverage.[70]

Seen in the light of the above discussion, the accepted wisdom about the symbiotic relationship between terrorism and the media appears far less self-evident than is commonly assumed. While most terrorists certainly crave the attention that the media eagerly provide, the publicity that they receive cuts both ways. On the one hand, terrorists are indeed assured of the notoriety that their actions are designed to achieve, but, on the other, the public attitudes and reactions that they hope to shape by their violent actions are both less predictable and less malleable than either the terrorists or the pundits believe. For example, one of the IRA's main aims in abandoning its cease-fire in February 1996 was to convince the British public that the government was to blame for the breakdown of negotiations and thereby to put pressure on the prime minister to grant concessions to the nationalist position that the government was hitherto unwilling or unable to make. The result was equivocal—in large measure, perhaps, because of the unanimous condemnation heaped on the IRA and Sinn Fein by the British (and, arguably, the world) press for the Friday evening blast at London's Canary Wharf, which killed two people and injured hundreds of others. While 63 percent of people polled a week later thought that the government should still be willing to talk with Sinn Fein in order to find a way to restore the cease-fire, 89 percent nonetheless "overwhelmingly blamed" the IRA for wrecking the peace process. Sinn Fein and the IRA's well-oiled public relations machine in Northern Ireland were eventually able to put their spin (as noted above) on the reporting of this issue in the province. Their failure to achieve the same result on the mainland, however, was notable. As one analysis noted, "In isolation, those figures suggest television appearances since last weekend of [Gerry] Adams and other prominent Sinn Fein leaders have had little success in deflecting criticism."[71] This may also explain why the IRA was driven to escalate its bombing campaign throughout England during the weeks and months following the cease-fire's collapse. Indeed, until the change of government in May 1997, the IRA was resorting to the naked use of terrorism as a means to coerce the government back to the negotiating table, rather than to manipulate public attitudes in a manner usefully sympathetic to the nationalists' frustrations.

There are two areas in particular, however, where a clear causal relationship between terrorism and the attention it receives from the media has a negative effect on public and governmental behavior. The first is the public's perception of personal risk from terrorism, and the consequent effect on willingness to travel; the second is the time pressure imposed by the media, under which governments confronted with terrorist-created crises labor.

Action and Reaction: The Impact on Travel and Government Decision Making

When the RAND survey asked members of the public how likely they thought it that they might be involved in several low-probability events, the results on terrorism were revealing. Although the majority of respondents were able accurately to gauge the relative risk involved—realizing that they were more likely to be involved in an automobile accident than a terrorist incident—the perceived difference in the likelihood of the two eventualities was far smaller than the actual difference in probabilities. For example, 71 percent thought it likely that they would be involved in a car crash—although the estimated actual probability is just 19.2 per 100,000 people. By comparison, while only 14 percent thought that they were likely to be flying on a plane that is hijacked or the victim of a terrorist bombing, the actual chances of being hijacked are fewer than one in 100,000 (no similar statistics for bombings were available). Viewed from another perspective, 47,087 persons were killed in automobile accidents in the United States during 1988 and 45,582 during 1989 (the two years during which the RAND study was conducted), while 203 Americans were killed in terrorist incidents throughout the world in 1988 (93 percent of them perishing in a single incident, the December in-flight bombing of Pan Am Flight 103 over Lockerbie), and 23 in 1989. Indeed, an American was just as likely to be killed by a dog as by a terrorist in 1989; yet nearly a third of those surveyed that year stated that they would refuse the opportunity to travel abroad because of the threat of terrorism. There is no statistical evidence whether an identical percentage had similarly concluded that it was now equally dangerous to keep dogs as pets.[72]

The distortion in perception that results in higher probabilities' being accorded to terrorism than to other life-threatening acts is in large measure doubtless a direct reflection of the disproportionate coverage accorded terrorism by the American media. Indeed, at one time during the 1980s the American television networks were devoting more attention to terrorism than to poverty, unemployment, and crime combined—despite the fact that these were arguably more important political issues since they had a far greater and more immediate impact on the daily lives of most Americans.[73] The role of media coverage in fueling viewing and reading audiences' irrational fears of terrorism was dramatically demonstrated by the wave of cancellations of travel plans by Americans immediately following the TWA hijacking. Some 850,000 people canceled their travel and holiday reservations—both foreign and domestic—because of fears of becoming enmeshed in some terrorist incident (much as, in the wake of the November 1997 terrorist attack on foreign tourists at Luxor, many travelers were reported to be canceling planned trips to Egypt). An additional 200,000 Americans rebooked their foreign holidays to U.S. destinations, on the assumption that their own country, at least, was still safe from terrorism.[74] The attack also had severe secondary consequences for local economies in foreign countries that were dependent on the tourist trade; for example, 50 percent of American bookings to Italy and 30 percent to Greece were lost. While the reluctance of Americans to visit the country from which the ill-fated TWA flight had departed (Italy) is understandable, as, perhaps, are their reservations about traveling to and from a nearby country whose airports at the time were widely criticized for their poor security (Greece), it is more difficult to explain why the peaceful Netherlands experienced an only slightly less startling drop in the number of American visitors (20 percent).[75]

To put the actual terrorist threat to Americans during 1985 into perspective: 6.5 million U.S. citizens traveled abroad that year, of whom 6,000 died from a variety of natural causes, accidents, and violence. Only 17 of these 6,000 people perished as a result of terrorist-related acts.[76] The chances of dying abroad were thus only one in 150,000 to begin with, and an almost infinitesimally small number so far as the risk from terrorism was concerned. Yet despite these overwhelmingly low probabilities, by February 1986 a total of 1.8 million Americans had changed their plans to go on vacation outside the United States.[77] Cancellations of Greek holidays booked by Americans more than doubled from the previous year[78]—even while British and Scandinavian tourism to Greece increased by 22 percent and 25 percent, respectively.[79] The number of American visitors to Britain itself fell by an astonishing 40 percent compared to the previous year's figure.[80] Indeed, 76 percent of Americans surveyed in April 1986 (following the in-flight bombing of a TWA passenger aircraft en route from Rome to Athens and the bombing of a West Berlin discotheque by Libyan agents) stated that the threat of terrorism had made it too dangerous to travel overseas that year—compared with 67 percent who had felt that way the previous July.[81] By the end of 1986, some 80 percent of Americans who had planned to travel abroad that year had canceled[82]—despite the fact that the fears generated by the threat of terrorism were grossly divergent from the real risk.

The effects of the nexus between the news media and terrorism on decision making go far beyond the question of U.S. citizens' overseas travel plans. A third revolution in the communication of news unfolded throughout the closing decades of the twentieth century to transform not only the way the world now gets its news but also the manner in which political leaders make decisions. This revolution has been less dependent than its two predecessors upon some new major technological breakthrough, deriving more from a concatenation of technological advances that have cumulatively changed the style rather than the mechanics of news presentation. The "CNN Syndrome"—a catchphrase coined in recognition of the Atlanta-based Cable News Network—has revolutionized news broadcasting through the emergence of dedicated round-the-clock "all the news all the time" television stations on both satellite and cable. More recently, these have spawned a myriad of attendant, often connected, communications outlets—Internet news providers (e.g., CNN interactive), automated e-mail and fax news services, and so on—that feed a worldwide audience with an insatiable appetite for information transmitted in real time and furnish immediate access to the actual locations and the people on the spot making the news.

The power of this latest expansion of the communications mass media is attested to by the multitude of television sets that can now be found in the office of virtually every functionary and politician in official Washington, D.C.—from mid-ranking civil servants to Pentagon flag officers, CIA spymasters to Commerce Department officials, congressmen to the president—their screens glowing silently throughout the day until some event of sufficient magnitude occurs to warrant both the attention of their owners and the adjustment of the volume knob upward. "Our best intelligence is invariably the media," confessed Noel Koch, the deputy assistant secretary of defense responsible for counterterrorism during the Reagan administration, even as long ago as the mid-1980s. The ultimate accolade, however, was offered by Lieutenant Colonel Oliver North, the former National Security Council aide made famous for his pivotal role in the 1986 arms-for-hostages deal, who said that "CNN runs ten minutes ahead of NSA"—comparing the privately owned cable company to the National Security Agency, America's super-secret electronic- and signals-gathering intelligence agency.[83]

The effects of this immediacy, however, are such that television becomes not just an opinion shaper but a policy driver, its presenters and on-air analysts racing to define the range of options at a government's disposal or to interpret likely public reaction—and its repercussions. As the late Lloyd Cutler, adviser to President Carter during the 1979–80 Iran hostage crisis, once explained, "If an ominous foreign event is featured on TV news, the

President and his advisers feel bound to make a response in time for the next evening news program."[84] Debate is not just precipitously joined, but abruptly rushed and then quickly truncated, depriving policymakers, government officials, and military commanders of the time needed to analyze critical issues thoroughly, reach well-thought-out decisions, craft coherent responses, and act with confidence based on exhaustive deliberation.[85] Governments are consequently increasingly pressured to respond to events before they can be evaluated fully, taking their cue from the "spin" that the media give them rather than working toward decisions made on the basis of all the available information. When asked in a 1993 interview specifically about the impact of the "CNN Syndrome" on government decision making, Prime Minister John Major replied: "I think it is bad for government. I think the idea that you automatically have to have a policy for everything before it happens and respond to things before you have had a chance to evaluate them isn't sensible."[86]

The Clinton administration's experience during the last months of America's involvement in Somalia is a salutary reminder of both the overpowering influence of images flashed across the television screen and the hazards of decisions made on the basis of initial impressions and incomplete information. On October 3, 1993, a U.S. military operation to arrest Somali warlord General Mohammed Farah Aideed's paymaster and chief lieutenants went disastrously awry. Fifteen U.S. Rangers were killed and seventy-seven others wounded. In some of the most gripping footage broadcast on American television, an injured U.S. army helicopter pilot was seen being paraded through the streets of Mogadishu by a chanting, gun-wielding Somali mob. Reacting quickly to the incident—while scrambling to preempt criticism by Congress, the media, and the American public—President Clinton announced within days the immediate dispatch of military reinforcements to Somalia, but set March 31, 1994, as the firm date for the withdrawal of all American forces there—regardless of whether the multinational UN-led humanitarian aid mission to that country had in fact been successfully completed by that date. A *USA Today*/CNN/Gallup poll taken shortly after the incident validated the president's fears that a majority of Americans would hold him and his administration responsible for pursuing an ill-conceived humanitarian aid mission that had now cost the lives of more than a dozen troops. Fifty-two percent of those polled thought it was a mistake to have become involved in Somalia in the first place (a decision, in fact, made by the outgoing Bush administration), with 57 percent opposing Clinton's decision to send reinforcements.[87] An ABC News poll revealed similar results.[88]

However, upon closer—and more sober—inspection, many of these "results" appear less conclusive. For example, according to the *USA Today/CNN/Gallup* poll, 50 percent of those questioned in their survey who stated that they wanted U.S. troops immediately withdrawn had watched the television coverage of the injured helicopter pilot being led by Somali militiamen past jeering crowds and had been particularly incensed by the spectacle. But among those polled who hadn't seen the broadcasts, only 33 percent favored withdrawal.[89] In addition, 49 percent of Americans surveyed in a subsequent ABC-TV poll actually disapproved of the president's decision to set a withdrawal date, compared with 45 percent who approved it,[90] while a poll conducted later that same week by the University of Maryland's Program on International Policy Attitudes found that only 28 percent of its nationwide sample favored immediate withdrawal, with 43 percent stating that they thought U.S. forces should remain in Somalia "until we have stabilized the country"—even, if necessary, beyond the stated withdrawal deadline.[91] Accordingly, in retrospect it appears that because of the raw emotions generated by the widely televised scenes depicting the brutal treatment of the captive helicopter pilot, the president may well have been stampeded into a decision that did not necessarily reflect public opinion. John Chancellor, senior commentator on NBC News and doyen of American network news, tried to distinguish between television's perennial search for dramatic footage and the responsibilities incumbent upon reporters. "You have journalism, which is thoughtful and considered," Chancellor observed, "and you have what I call 'electronics,' which is the use of our facilities to transmit pictures and words, but does not have a lot to do with journalism."[92] It is the convergence of the two that has fundamentally altered the context and content of the news today and has also at times exercised a distorted influence over both public opinion and official decision making. In this new era of mass media, where the "information revolution" has transformed communication worldwide as a result of breakthroughs in real-time, rapid communication, the rush to meet airtime and print deadlines, and the attendant inevitably hurried judgments and immediate decisions, may present still further opportunities for manipulation and influence by terrorists than have hitherto existed.

Conclusion

We live today in an age of sound bites and "spin," in which arresting footage or pithy phrases are valued above considered analysis and detailed exegesis—and are frequently mistaken for good journalism. One of the enduring axioms of terrorism is that it is designed to generate publicity and attract attention to the terrorists and their cause. It is, accordingly, an activity custom-tailored to mass media communication in the twenty-first century. Terrorist acts are only too easily transformed into major international media events—precisely because they are often staged specifically with this goal in mind. Their dramatic characteristics of sudden acts of violence exploding across the screen or the printed page, rapidly unfolding into crises and pitting enigmatic adversaries against the forces of law and order make these episodes as ideal for television as they are irresistible for broadsheet and tabloid journalist alike.

In Britain, the media (and public) fascination with terrorists is second perhaps only to that with the country's royal family. How else can one explain the small article that was featured on page 4 of the London *Times* on September 3, 1997, as part of its coverage of the Princess of Wales's tragic death, and the repetition of its content the following day as part of a larger article on page 6? Both described how Leila Khaled—the Palestinian terrorist who gained international notoriety as a result of her involvement in the in-flight hijacking of a TWA flight in 1969 and of an El Al passenger jet the following year—had been touched by the princess, to whom she dedicated a poem that she sent to the princess's two sons.[93] Apart from the fact that there could be no two people more different than a former terrorist, whose actions on those two occasions deliberately endangered the lives of hundreds of innocent airline passengers, and a woman who is remembered in part for ameliorating the suffering of the innocent and infirm, that Khaled and her thoughts should be considered newsworthy is testimony to the powerful magnetic attraction exercised by terrorists and terrorism for the media in even the most unlikely (and absurd) circumstances.

For terrorists, media coverage of their activities is, as we have seen, something of a double-edged sword, providing them with the attention and publicity that they invariably seek, but not always in a particularly useful or even helpful manner. In this respect, while the 1985 TWA hostage crisis provides a clear lesson of how terrorists exploit and prompt the media for their own advantage, the denouement of the so-called Unabomber's seventeen-year terrorist campaign arguably demonstrates the opposite. The anonymous Unabomber—the name coined by the FBI in reference to his targeting of people associated with either universities or the airline industry—who killed three people and wounded twenty-three others using simple yet ingeniously constructed homemade bombs sent through the post, had promised in June 1995 to restrict his lethal terrorist campaign provided that either the *New York Times* or the *Washington Post* printed his entire manuscript and three annual follow-up messages. As a result of the publication in September of his 35,000-word diatribe against technology, modernity, and the destruction of the environment in the *Washington Post*,[94] information subsequently came to light that led directly to the arrest of Theodore Kaczynski, a former University of California at Berkeley mathematician, who was charged with the bombings. Had the alleged "Unabomber" not been as obsessed with publicity as he was, he might never have been unmasked and arrested. As David Rapoport has observed,

> The relationship between publicity and terror is indeed paradoxical and complicated. Publicity focuses attention on a group, strengthening its morale and helping to attract recruits and sympathizers. But publicity is pernicious to the terrorist groups too. It helps an outraged public to mobilize its vast resources and produces information that the public needs to pierce the veil of secrecy all terrorist groups require.[95]

While that bizarre case was not terrorism as most commonly understood, in that the Unabomber was a lone individual acting from a frustration and animus so profound that no other person could share them, it nonetheless demonstrates the complexity of terrorism's symbiotic relationship with the media. Moreover, it poses yet another formidable challenge to the almost unthinkingly accepted conventional wisdom about this relationship and underscores the need for critical, but subtle, distinctions to be made in this area.

Chapter 7

The New Media, Terrorism, and the Shaping of Global Opinion

B in Laden's dramatic television appearance on October 7, 2001, as recounted in chapter 4, provided stunning confirmation of just how sophisticated terrorist communications in the twenty-first century have become. In contrast to the jerky, often amateurish videos or the older Super 8 film recordings typical of even the more communications-savvy terrorists of the past, bin Laden's pre-recorded statement was remarkable for both its excellent quality and its masterful timing. Professionally produced, shot, and edited, the clip was masterfully packaged and queued to go on air as soon as the anticipated U.S. air strikes commenced that fateful Sunday.[1]

For bin Laden and his followers—and no less for other terrorists around the globe—the weapons of terrorism are no longer simply the guns and bombs that they always have used. Now those weapons include the Minicam and videotape; editing suite and attendant production facilities; professionally produced and mass-marketed CD-ROMs and DVDs; and, most critically, the laptop and desktop computers, CD burners and e-mail accounts, and Internet and World Wide Web access that have defined the information revolution today. Indeed, in recent years, the art of terrorist communication has evolved to a point at which the terrorists themselves can now control the entire production process: determining the content, context, and medium over which their message is projected and targeting precisely the audience (or multiple audiences) they seek to reach. The implications of this development are enormous, challenging the monopoly on mass communication of the terrorist message that has long been exercised by commercial and state-owned broadcasting outlets. Hence, much like previous information revolutions—such as the invention of the rotary press in the mid-nineteenth century and the advances in television equipment that made possible the reporting of events in "real time" in the 1960s—that also profoundly affected terrorist and insurgent external communications, a new information revolution has occurred to empower these movements with the ability to shape and disseminate their own message in their own way, enabling them to completely bypass traditional, established media outlets. As Tina Brown, the doyenne of postmodern media, has pointed out, the "conjunction of 21st-century Internet speed and 12th-century fanaticism has turned our world into a tinderbox."[2]

Violence as Communication

One of the enduring axioms of terrorism is that it is designed to generate publicity and attract attention to the terrorists and their cause. Terrorism, as was discussed in chapter 6, is widely seen as a violent act that is conceived specifically to attract attention and then, through the publicity it generates, to communicate a message.[3] The terrorist must parlay this illumination (e.g., publicity) into a more effective vehicle of elucidation (propaganda). The centrality of propaganda[4] to this communications process and its importance to the terrorist are self-evident.[5] As a 1991 RAND study on this subject observed,

> Propaganda grants authority to its makers. In the first place, simply by demonstrating its ability to disseminate information that the government has banned, a guerrilla group proves that it is a viable force. Second, once a group has the people's ears and eyes it can manipulate their minds, causing them to act as they might not otherwise; or if it does not work as effectively as this, its messages at least command the attention of those who read, hear or see them. In words and pictures, those whose plans are hidden from public view can portray themselves any way they please. Furthermore, if appearing to play a particular role can win support, propaganda will help these guerrillas to become in fact the powerful forces that they claim to be.[6]

Through propaganda, terrorists seek to communicate a particular message to a particular target audience. The exact purpose of these communications can vary, depending upon the message and the target audience(s) to whom it is directed. It can be didactic—designed to inform, educate, solicit support (whether material, financial, or spiritual), and ultimately rally the masses behind the insurgents or terrorists. It can be a vehicle for recruitment—meant to win new converts to the cause or replenish the ranks of depleted fighters. But it can also be deliberately coercive—conceived to promote or ensure compliance through threat or blandishment. Further, its intents can transcend mere tactical coercion and seek to intimidate strategically—that is, to undermine popular confidence in government and leadership and thereby attempt to paralyze opponents with fear by trumpeting the terrorists' ability to strike at will and the inability of the government and security forces to provide effective defense or protection. Finally, it can serve an entirely internal function—what has been termed "auto propaganda"—when it is directed toward members of the terrorist group in order to strengthen morale, dampen dissent, or justify and legitimate or explain particularly controversial decisions or operations.[7]

In sum, propaganda is directed toward a committed audience to strengthen resolve or toward an uncommitted audience to win sympathy and support. It can be variously focused on the terrorists' or insurgents' actual or would-be constituents, the public at large, the enemy government and its bureaucratic minions and security forces, or even inwardly on the underground fighters themselves as a means to promote and enhance internal cohesion and morale.

The terrorist of the past used three principal means of facilitating this communications process:

- clandestine, rebel radio stations
- underground newspapers, posters, flyers, and other publications
- conventional, commercial, or state-owned mass media (e.g., television, radio, and the press)

Each of the above had its own attractions and limitations, dependent primarily on the degree of direct control and influence it provided the terrorist or insurgent group over a particular audience. For instance, the two means over which terrorists had the most control—their own clandestine radio stations and newspapers and other periodicals and publications—also generally had the most limited impact. They had either inherent technical and geographical constraints that inhibited reception and restricted the listening audience or publication problems that made mass production and wide distribution difficult, if not impossible.

The now totally anachronistic multimedia efforts of one of the cold war era's more sophisticated Marxist-Leninist insurgent-cum-terrorist movements of the time, El Salvador's FMLN (Farabundo Marti Liberation Front) is a case in point. Its flagship newspaper, *Venceremos* (We will win) had a limited press run and thus a fairly narrow readership. Its usefulness, accordingly, was confined to reinforcing or guiding the political activities of already committed FMLN activists and supporters.[8] Its clandestine radio station of the same name was hardly more technically sophisticated or expansive in audience reach. Broadcasting over standard shortwave band radio transmission, with varying audio quality and mostly only to a loyal, nearby listening audience, ensured that the impact of Radio Venceremos was perennially both localized and limited.[9] Even less impressive were the external communications capabilities of the FMLN's U.S.-backed, anti-communist counterparts in neighboring Nicaragua. Radio Quince de Septiembre (Radio Fifteenth of September), the putative "voice" of the United States–backed Nicaraguan Contras (Nicaraguan Democratic Front), for example, was then bluntly described by one contemporary U.S. government observer as a "joke because of its basic broadcasting technology, amateurish copy, and numerically inconsequential listening audience."[10]

Given the constrained communications resources available to terrorists only a generation ago, it is not surprising that emphasis was often given to exploiting traditional mass media. But because of the limitations over control discussed in chapter 6, this was always at best a Hobson's choice: gaining exposure but only partially serving the terrorists' wider communication needs. By the mid-1980s, moreover, the latent romanticism of the underground fighter that at times had surfaced in some reporting was rapidly ebbing. In addition, the opportunities for terrorist exploitation were diminishing as new guidelines were imposed and more-stringent self-policing was practiced in response to the wave of criticism leveled at the media.[11] Finally, for many terrorist and insurgent groups there was no escaping the fundamental bias toward the status quo evidenced by most commercial and especially Western and state-owned media. So long as editorial power was vested ultimately in the pro-establishment, capitalist elite, many revolutionaries concluded, their message would always be diluted, misconstrued, or seized upon for its "entertainment" value rather than its didactic purposes.[12]

Then, in the 1990s, the advent of three new technological developments afforded terrorists the opportunity to break the stranglehold over mass communications hitherto enjoyed by commercial and state-owned media. These were

- the Internet,
- affordable, if not extraordinarily cheap, video production and duplication processes, and
- private, terrorist-owned television stations.

Terrorist and Insurgent Use of the Internet

Few technological innovations have had the impact of the Internet and the World Wide Web. Beyond any doubt, in a comparatively short span of time, they have revolutionized communications, enabling the rapid (often in real time), pervasive, and—most important—inexpensive exchange of information worldwide. In terms of political activism, they have been something of a godsend, providing an effective way for groups to promote what some observers call a "global dialectic," a situation in which awakening, awareness, activism, and radicalism can be stimulated at a local level and then mobilized into a wider process of dissent and protest.[13] "Groups of any size, from two to millions," Dorothy E. Denning, of the Naval Postgraduate School, points out, "can reach each other and use the Net to promote an agenda. Their members and followers can come from any geographical region on the Net, and they can attempt to influence foreign policy anywhere in the world."[14] That sort of reach is one dramatic advantage that the Internet provides; speed is another. As a human rights activist working for an East Timor refugee NGO explained in a 1996 interview:

Using "old" communications, vital information could take weeks before it reached us. Often we had to wait for the first refugees to arrive. Then their accounts were written down and sent by mail. It could take days and weeks before they reached Australia or the USA. So, when the "news" of a massacre finally arrived at the newsdesk, the so called news was already old. With the arrival of new media and in particular, the Internet, this whole process might take just a few hours.[15]

Indeed, as is described below, a variety of terrorist and insurgent groups were quick to exploit this feature as a means of mobilizing international support and pressure and actively enlisting international humanitarian relief organizations and other NGOs on their behalf.

In addition to ubiquity and timeliness, the Internet has other advantages. It can circumvent government censorship, messages can be sent anonymously and also quickly and almost effortlessly, and it is an especially cost-effective means of mass communication.[16] It also enables terrorists to undertake what Denning has termed "perception management"[17]: in other words, they can use it to portray themselves and their actions in precisely the light and context they wish—unencumbered by the filter, screening, and spin of established media.[18] The Internet also facilitates their engagement in what has been referred to as "information laundering," taking an interesting or provocative video clip and/or sound bite, and featuring it and focusing on it and creating an "Internet buzz" about it in the hope that it will move into the mainstream press.[19] Finally, the Internet carries with it new and significantly enhanced fund-raising capabilities for otherwise illegal or underground entities. Financial contributions, in essence, are now "just a click away," with many sites providing banking details for cash transfers.[20] In this respect, the Internet has proved to be an especially beneficial communications medium for terrorists—a key means for both external (propaganda) and internal (command and control and information) purposes.

The first group to successfully harness the power of the Internet was arguably the Zapatista National Liberation Army (EZLN), known more familiarly simply as the Zapatistas.[21] The group, it should be emphasized, is *not* a terrorist organization but an insurgent movement. Nonetheless, its effective exploitation of the Internet at the beginning of the 1990s was subsequently emulated by other insurgent movements and terrorist groups alike. As the Zapatistas themselves boast in a Web posting accessed in June 2005:

> The international circulation through the Net of the struggles of the Zapatistas in Chiapas, Mexico has become one of the most successful examples of the use of computer communications by grassroots social movements. That circulation has not only brought support to the Zapatistas from throughout Mexico and the rest of the World, but it has sparked a world wide discussion of the meaning and implications of the Zapatista rebellion for many other confrontations with contemporary capitalist economic and political policies.[22]

The EZLN's insurrection commenced on New Year's Day 1994 in Mexico's rural and southernmost state, Chiapas. The government responded as it had countless times in the past: deploying military and police force to suppress the rebellion and hunt down the EZLN guerrillas. And, like countless peasant uprisings before it, the Zapatistas' revolt was likely to go mostly unnoticed by a world preoccupied with more pressing matters than the grievances of a couple of hundred landless indigenous Indians and mestizos in a long-impoverished and largely inconsequential corner of the country. As it turned out, the Zapatistas were not to be so easily brushed aside.[23] In addition to repulsing initial government efforts to dislodge them from the five towns and one city they occupied, the Zapatistas quickly demonstrated an unusual flair for external communications.[24] In Subcomandante Marcos, the articulate and charismatic, ski-mask-clad, pipe-smoking spokesman for the group, the EZLN pursued a novel tactic. Rather than calling only on the support, solidarity, and armed assistance of revolutionaries and guerrillas elsewhere, they appealed directly to Mexican civil society and specifically to peace activists, human rights groups, international humanitarian relief organizations, and other nongovernment organizations to join the Zapatistas' struggle by lobbying the Mexican government to implement the socioeconomic and political changes that the group demanded and to travel to Chiapas to observe and monitor the conflict. As David E. Ronfeldt and colleagues note, "This was not at all a conventional way to mount an insurrection."[25]

Over the next fifteen months or so, the Zapatistas' mobilization strategy proved pivotal in halting government efforts to defeat the rebellion. Legend has it that, using a laptop computer that he carried in a backpack, Subcomandante Marcos plugged into the cigarette lighter socket of a Jeep or a truck and simply dialed up to log on to the Internet, enabling him to dispatch messages in real time to activists and supporters in Mexico City, the United States, Canada, and Europe. Although, as Thomas Olesen notes in his authoritative work on the Zapatistas, "there is no evidence as such that either the EZLN or Subcomandante Marcos [had] direct access to the Internet through modem or cellular phones,"[26] Marcos, however *indirectly*, was nonetheless able to communicate quickly and effectively to reach a larger national and international audience than pre–Internet era insurgents could ever have hoped.[27] Indeed the group's communication strategy was critical in blunting a major 1995 government offensive. "Information flooded out of the conflict zone," one account of the information counteroffensive reported. "The smallest of details, the slightest harassment of the civilian population, was spread to thousands of sympathisers and journalists all over the world. The result saw demonstrations and protests against the army offensive and concerned reports from human rights groups."[28]

Through both their pioneering use of the "floodgate" tool and other denial-of-service measures[29] and the forging of effective connections with their peaceful activist supporters and sympathizers around the world, the Zapatistas were able to orchestrate a campaign of e-mail and fax bombardment directly to Mexican president Ernesto Zedillo and the minister of the interior, Esteban Moctezuma, that resulted in the suspension of the offensive. "Before, we used faxes and telephones," one peace activist rallied by the group gushed, "and it took forever. Now the information arrives [with the snap of a finger]. The feedback is instantaneous."[30] So successful were the Zapatistas' mobilization efforts that in January 1995, President Zedillo proclaimed a truce and agreed to enter negotiations with the EZLN. As Mexico's foreign minister, Jose Angel Gurría, later reflected: "Chiapas . . . is a place where there has not been a shot fired in the last fifteen months. . . . The shots lasted ten days and ever since the war has been a war of ink, of written word, a war on the Internet."[31] Indeed, when Mexican security forces raided a series of EZLN safe houses in Mexico City and Veracruz they reportedly discovered "as many computer diskettes as bullets."[32] For Marcos the message and significance of the Zapatistas' Internet strategy was clear. "This is a new type of warfare," he declared in an interview published in a British Internet magazine in 1996.[33] Since that time, the Zapatistas have regularly used Internet-based "collective manifestations" that they themselves variously call or describe as "electronic civil disobedience," "net strikes," and "mail bombs." As one observer of the EZLN's networking phenomenon explains, "The idea of these computer-mediated actions is to go beyond the sending of emails to figures such as politicians. The purpose, instead, is disruptive: for example, to flood mailboxes and overwork websites to the extent that they break down or become defunct for periods of time."[34] A 1998 Internet posting by the "New York Zapatistas" advocated "electronic civil disobedience," describing it as

applying the principles and tactics of traditional civil disobedience—like trespass and blockade—to the electronic systems of communication upon which Mexican government officials and their supporters depend. . . . We therefore urge that the following tactics be used against governmental, financial, and corporate sites responsible for the ongoing genocide in Chiapas. 1) Phone Zaps: Repeated calling to disrupt normal operations. 2) Fax Jams: Repeated faxing to overload fax machines. 3) Email Jams: Massive emailing to overload email inboxes and servers. 4) Virtual Sit-Ins: trespassing and blockading of web sites.[35]

Although it is impossible to detect a direct causal connection between the Zapatistas' success and the spread of Internet usage to other insurgent and terrorist groups throughout the world, it is clear that around this time other groups began rapidly to awake to the power of electronic external communications and the distinct advantages that they offered over other, older propaganda vehicles. Among the first were the LTTE (Tamil Tigers). The group established TamilNet.com in 1995,[36] and its success has since spawned

several additional sites, including www.eelam.com,[37] www.eelam.net, www.
eelamweb.com, www.tamiltigers.net, www.cantam.com, and www.canadat-
amils.net.[38] These servers are based in India, the United Kingdom, Norway,
Canada, and Australia, among other places—that is, often in countries with
sizable existing Tamil émigré communities. Like the Zapatistas, the Tigers'
initial presence on the Internet was motivated by a desire to present an
alternative news and information source to the Sri Lankan state-controlled
media.[39] The Sri Lankan government's imposition of press censorship coupled with the announcement of a major new military offensive was what
had specifically prompted the creation of TamilNet. As a Tiger spokesperson explained: "We all knew what would happen if the government started
a large scale offensive in the heavily populated Jaffna region. At the same
time, the Sri Lankan government and its media were engaged in a massive
stream of propaganda trying to justify the war against the People of Tamil
Eelam."[40]

The site's purpose was conceived (and remains) to mobilize the support
of the 450,000-member Tamil diaspora by providing them with breaking
news from Eelam, the historical Tamil homeland in the north and north-
east of Sri Lanka, where the fighting between the rebels and Sri Lanka
Armed Forces has mostly been confined.[41] Like the Zapatistas, the Tiger
site also sought to link up with international humanitarian relief organizations and various Tamil and non-Tamil NGOs. A recent look at www.eelam.
com's home page, for example, shows links to topics such as the tsunami
that devastated parts of Sri Lanka's coast in December 2004 and attendant
LTTE-sponsored relief efforts ("Tsunami Disaster Relief: please contact
your nearest Tamils Rehabilitation Organisations office").[42] Home pages for
other Tiger sites encourage readers to "link to us" and provide instructions
on how to do so. Like that of most other terrorist and insurgent organization's sites, the Tiger's Web presence is primarily information-oriented,[43]
with navigational bars that provide background and history about the Tamil
people and the LTTE's struggle. These sites often also contain a map of the
historical Tamil homeland in Sri Lanka; a history tab with further information on the Tamil people's long struggle for self-determination; a biography of the Tiger's founder and leader, Velupillai Prabhakaran; audio buttons
through which recordings of "VOT: Voice of the Tigers" can be downloaded
and listened to; LTTE press releases; daily news clips and links to other
news sources; and a gallery of photographs of alleged atrocities inflicted by
the Sri Lankan military on Tamil civilians. Features include profiles of the
LTTE's feared women fighters, "freedom poems," and even an "online quiz."
Finally, as on many other sites, merchandising—serving the dual purposes

of fund-raising and morale boosting cum solidarity building—occupies a prominent place on the site. A variety of terrorist kitsch, including flags, calendars, videos, books, pamphlets, is available for sale.[44]

TamilNet scored a huge public relations coup in the summer of 1996 when it convincingly refuted Sri Lankan army claims of having repulsed a Tiger attack on an important base at Mullaitivu at the cost of only about seventy government casualties. With credible reports from LTTE cadres coming directly from the scene via satellite telephones, TamilNet posted dispatches and stories that painted a totally different picture. Not only had the camp *not* been captured, but more than a thousand Sri Lankan soldiers had been killed in the failed assault. As one observer noted,

> It's not unusual that two parties in a war have vastly differing stories. As it turned out, the Tamil Tigers were more accurate. A week later, the Sri Lankan Army admitted to losing the camp. Twelve hundred soldiers were also lost. This was a major breakthrough for TamilNet and the alternative news channels. Newspapers such as the *Washington Post* and the *International Herald Tribune* began quoting bulletins from the LTTE statements and were extremely suspicious of the official Sri Lankan Army news dispatches.[45]

Not surprisingly, the success of the Tiger Web sites prompted determined government attempts to shut them down.[46] One such effort in November 1997, however, backfired completely and resulted instead in denial-of-service attacks launched against Sri Lankan diplomatic facilities worldwide.[47] The embassies in Seoul, Ottawa, and Washington, D.C., were reportedly the worst affected, with e-mail unavailable in each for at least a week.[48]

Today, almost without exception, all major (and many minor) terrorist and insurgent groups have Web sites.[49] As a researcher at the U.S. government's Foreign Broadcast and Information Service (FBIS) who focuses on the Internet has observed, "These days, if you're not on the web, you don't exist."[50] Indeed, according to perhaps the preeminent expert in the field of terrorist communication and the Internet, Gabriel Weimann, "the story of the presence of terrorist groups in cyberspace has barely begun to be told." He notes that in 1998 fewer than half of the thirty groups that the U.S. State Department designates as Foreign Terrorist Organizations (FTOs) had Web sites, but by the end of 1999 nearly all of them did.[51]

Despite the multiplicity and diversity of terrorist Web sites, they share a number of key characteristics. These sites are often notable for their colorful, well-designed, and visually arresting graphic content. In this respect, they seem intended particularly to appeal to a computer-savvy, media-saturated, video-game-addicted generation. Most of the sites chart the terrorist group's history, its aims and objectives, and the depredations inflicted by an enemy state(s) or people(s) upon the constituency it purports to represent. The sites also often contain biographies of the group's leadership, its founders, and key personalities; up-to-date news and accompanying feature stories; speeches, ideological treatises, and especially the organization's communiqués and other important statements. Ethno-nationalist/separatist movements will also generally have maps of the contested territory they claim to represent or be fighting for. Virtually without exception, all sites studiously avoid focusing on or drawing any attention to either violence or death and destruction that they are responsible for. Instead, issues such as freedom of expression and the plight of imprisoned comrades are highlighted.[52] In the case of the more sophisticated organizations, such as the LTTE and Hezbollah, multiple sites are maintained in different languages. Arab and Islamic groups, Basque and Irish national-separatist movements, religious cults, Marxist-Leninist and Maoist movements, European neo-Nazi groups, and even al Qaeda can all be found on the Web.[53] Nonetheless, Arab and Islamic groups are regarded by knowledgeable observers to have the largest presence there.[54] According to one,

That Internet usage by Islamists is growing is obvious. What is also obvious is that they will use it to promote their views, advance the strategies of the "global Islamic movement" and organize their activities, which experience has shown are sometimes inimical to western security, and in a wider sense might also seek to subvert the security of the state.[55]

Middle East Arab terrorist organizations in particular are seen as being on the "cutting edge of organizational networking," having demonstrated an ability to harness information technology for offensive operations, as well as using the more typical propaganda, fund-raising, and recruiting purposes of other groups.[56]

Perhaps the preeminent group in this respect, and one of the first to harness fully the communications power of the Web, is Hezbollah. The group has often maintained as many as twenty different sites,[57] in three different languages: English, French, and Arabic.[58] Each site has a different purpose, orientation, and intended audience. The movement's Central Press Office and main Web page site, for instance, in the past could be accessed directly at www.hizbollah.org.[59] It had the requisite background account of the struggle and history of the organization that is found on other terrorist

and insurgent sites, as well as tabs presenting "statements on the resistance," "political declarations," press clips and releases, special focuses on
the "occupied zone" (e.g., Israel) and on "hostages and wounded," as well
as "speeches of the S.G."—that is, the movement's secretary general and
spiritual leader, Sheikh Hassan Nasrallah.[60] Nasrallah, in fact, also maintains his own dedicated site containing postings in French,[61] English, and
Arabic.[62] Readers were encouraged to contact the Web site and post their
own views and opinions on the anti-Zionist struggle and alleged crimes
committed by Israel and its armed forces.[63] This feature is apparently especially valued by Hezbollah. According to a group spokesman, "The service
is very important for the morale of the resistance fighters. They are always
very happy to know that people around the world are backing them."[64]
Hezbollah in 2001 claimed that it was receiving forty thousand visitors to
its sites per month.[65]

A more circuitous route is required to find the current Hezbollah Central
Press Office site, at http://almashriq.hiof.no/lebanon/300/320/324/324.2/
hizballah.[66] While it is not dissimilar to the previous iteration, it does
more obviously reflect the movement's redoubled bid for political legitimacy outside Lebanon.[67] For instance, the home page features a long statement titled "Hizballah—*social radicals* [my emphasis]," which describes the
group's background and history with an emphasis on its social-welfare and
political activities. Resistance, much less the movement's terrorist legacy
and continuing armed operations, is prominently absent. The series of links
to other Hezbollah documents, institutions, and sites that it offers includes
such ostensibly benign topics as

- the movement's 1996 electoral platform,
- a 1997 message Hezbollah received from Pope John Paul II,
- the Emdad Committee for Islamic Charity,
- Al Manar TV, and
- the Al Jarha Association ("Getting by with a little help from a friend:
  Beirut's al-Jarha Association helps wounded resistance fighters build
  themselves").

The "Hizbullah: Views and Concepts" section is similarly anodyne, addressing issues like "Hizbullah and Dialogue," "Hizbullah and the Political System in Lebanon," and, of course, "Hizbullah and Human Rights," among
other subjects.

Other prominent Hezbollah Web sites include www. moqawama.org,
which specifically focuses on attacks against Israeli targets, and www.

almanar.com.lb (*manar* is Arabic for "the Beacon"), the movement's television and radio station, which contains news reports, access to video clips, and other information.[68] Hezbollah also uses the Internet and its television station, as well as other media outlets to promote and sell a video game called *Special Force* that its Central Internet Bureau labored for "two long years" to create.[69] "Pursue your enemy from position to position," one spot on al-Manar beckoned prospective purchasers. "Take part in making victory."[70] That Hezbollah intuitively understood the market for such a game is evidenced by the claim that some ten thousand copies were reportedly sold in Lebanon, Syria, Bahrain, the United Arab Emirates, Canada, Germany, and Australia during the eight weeks following its release in March 2003.[71] An advertisement for the game, easily located on the Internet in June 2005, explains:

"SPECIAL FORCE" IS BASED ON REALITY, MEANING THAT THE GAME IS BASED ON EVENTS THAT TOOK PLACE IN A LAND CALLED LEBANON. LEBANON WAS INVADED BY "ISRAEL" IN 1978 & 1982, AND WAS FORCED TO WITHDRAW AND DID WITHDRAW IN THE YEAR 2000. AFTER THAT WE DECIDED TO PRODUCE A GAME THAT WILL BE EDUCATIONAL FOR OUR FUTURE GENERATIONS AND FOR ALL FREEDOM LOVERS OF THIS WORLD OF OURS.

"Special Force game," it concludes, "will render you a partner of the resistance."[72] Features include a training simulation, where players can hone their shooting skills by firing at targets of Israeli prime minister Sharon and minister of defense and former IDF chief of staff Shaul Mofaz. The qualification medal for excellent marksmanship that follows is then awarded by a simulated Sheikh Nasrallah. The game's main attraction, however, is doubtless the assaults on IDF positions and tanks that test a player's skill at avoiding land mines and snipers and shooting down attack helicopters to accomplish the mission. "Thank you," states the registration card that comes with *Special Force*. "The Designers of 'Special Force' are very Proud to provide you with this special product which embodies objectively the defeat of the Israeli enemy and the heroic actions taken by the heroes of the Islamic Resistance in Lebanon."[73] As Bilal Zain, a member of the game's design team, explained, through the medium of entertainment *Special Force* seeks to convey Hezbollah's "values, concepts and ideas."[74] Accordingly, instructions for play are available in Arabic, English, French, and Farsi. "Be A Partner In The Victory . . . ," the liner notes on the video case state. "Fight, Resist, Destroy Your Enemy In The Game Of Force And Victory."[75]

The Palestinian group Hamas has had a similarly strong presence on the Internet. Although its original Web site did refer to the group by name (www.hamas.org), like Hezbollah, in recent years Hamas has also relied on another, more generic, moniker—in this case, "Palestinian Information Center."[76] Additional links have in the past been provided through such general Muslim information sites as the Ohio-based MSANews (originating at Ohio State University) and from groups such as the Islamic Association for Palestine.[77] Observers often cite the professionalism, excellent content, and clean and fluid English and Arabic prose found on the site. Indeed, for these reasons, Israeli authorities reportedly consider the Web site to be a very effective communications vehicle for the group.[78] In the past, the site has very adroitly featured interviews with the father of Muhammad al-Dura, the twelve-year-old Palestinian boy who was allegedly shot to death shortly after the al-Aqsa Intifada began in October 2000 at an Israeli-Palestinian border crossing as the father vainly attempted to shelter him from the bullets flying around them,[79] along with photographs of wounded Palestinian babies in hospital and other depictions of IDF mistreatment of Palestinian youths.[80] The site also posted copies of the Hamas Covenant in what was reported to be an excellent, verbatim English translation, various communiqués of attacks and messages from Hamas's military wing, the Iss al-Din al-Kassam brigades, and a daily account or running diary of the wing's operations.[81] A more nefarious purpose has also been reported by observers of terrorist Internet usage: the reported communication of operational instructions through steganography (the clandestine concealment of messages and other information embedded in images and other visual displays)[82] and other activities meant to facilitate terrorist endeavors, fund-raising, and further logistical and support endeavors.[83]

Today, Hamas's presence on the Web is maintained through sites such as IntifadaOnline.com,[84] which has been active since 1988[85] and "brings you the Palestinian side of the story. We also advise you on how to help." Its home page formerly contained the familiar image of Muhammad al-Dura, wounded Palestinian babies in the hospital, Palestinian children being beaten and dragged through the street by IDF soldiers, IDF troops restraining a Palestinian teenager in a choke hold, and the ubiquitous image of a youthful Palestinian demonstrator facing an Israeli tank. Scrolling farther down the page revealed photographs of Palestinian martyrs (including suicide bombers) and additional images of Palestinian babies injured in Israeli violence.[86] The site now features the no less familiar but still compelling image of a Palestinian youth hurling a stone at an IDF tank, thus deliberately evoking the enduring memory of the lone Chinese pro-democracy demonstrator who faced down a Chinese tank at Tiananmen Square in 1989. Under the headline "Justice, Freedom, and Peace," alongside banners the color of the Palestinian national flag, additional links are provided to translations in twenty-two languages—including Arabic, Danish, Dutch, English, Farsi French, German, Greek, Japanese, Korean, Malay, Norwegian, Russian, Spanish, Turkish, and Urdu.[87] Links are provided to Web sites providing additional news and information on the Palestinian struggle, poetry, and the Web sites of mainstream established news media, such as the BBC (British Broadcasting Corporation) and CNN. Navigational bars also direct viewers to

- stories and pictures,
- explanations such as "Why Intifada?"
- other news items about the Intifada,
- a discussion of the nefarious "silencing of the Intifada," and
- information on how to "be part of Intifada."

The last link encouraged visitors to participate in demonstrations, write letters to their elected officials and newspapers, and boycott Israeli goods. Instructions were also given on how to add Hamas links and banners to one's own site.[88]

Until the summer of 2002, an affiliated Hamas site, www.qassam.net, actively solicited donations for the explicit purpose of purchasing AK-47 assault rifles, dynamite, and bullets with which "to assist the cause of jihad and resistance until the [Israeli] occupation is eliminated and Muslim Palestine is liberated." Donations in the amount of US$3 for bullets, US$100 per kilogram of dynamite, US$2,000 for an AK-47, and US$12,000 for a rocket-propelled grenade launcher were reportedly suggested. Prospective donors were invited to contact an address on a Web site that provided instructions for transferring money to a Gaza-based bank account. The name on the account and the account number were said to change every forty-eight to seventy-two hours. A message addressed to the would-be donor stated: "Dear Donor: Please tell us the field in which you prefer your money to be spent on such as: martyrdom attacks; buying weapons for the mujahadeen; training the youth; or inventing and developing missiles, mortars [and] explosives."[89]

Hamas reportedly maintained some twenty active sites at the end of 2004.[90] Among them was a site in Arabic, www.sabiroon.net, extolling terrorist operations, including suicide bombings; another for a radio station associated with Hamas (al-Aqsa Voice), at www.aqsavoice.com; and one featuring the movement's children's magazine, *al-Fateh*, at www.al-fateh-net.[91] Like Hezbollah, for a time Hamas also maintained a dedicated site for its leader, Abd al Aziz al Rantisi (www.rantisi.net), who succeeded Sheikh Yasin following his assassination in March 2004. The site for Rantisi, who was killed shortly after Yasin, was hosted by an American server.[92] It could not be accessed as of June 2005. The PIJ, Hamas's counterpart, has a considerably less extensive presence on the Internet—but nonetheless still maintains six sites.[93]

In addition, Muslim—but non-Arabic and non–Middle Eastern—sites have also had an active presence on the Internet. The most sophisticated have been Web sites of various radical Pakistani organizations such as Lashkar-e-Taiba (Army of the Pure), Harakat ul Mujahideen (Movement of Warriors), Harakat al-Ansar (Movement of the Partisans), and the London-based Hizb ut Tahrir (Party of Liberation),[94] which itself has maintained upwards of twenty different sites. According to the aforementioned FBIS analysts, Hizb ut Tahrir has a "bigger presence on the Web than in life." Nonetheless, the multiplicity of its sites and the sophistication of its Web design and content have made it an important resource on radical Islamic ideology. Although the majority of the Pakistani-based groups have had relatively anemic and poorly designed sites (e.g., Hizb ul Mujahideen, Harakat al-Ansar), Lashkar-e-Taiba was an exception. Its Web designers were not only proficient but also capable of posting content in multiple languages—English, Arabic, and Urdu.[95] Audio links on the site provided connections to Radio al-Jihad and Mercaz al-Dawa.[96] Fund-raising was a prominent feature on the Web for Lashkar and other groups, with banking details and instructions provided for direct deposits into the group's account.[97] An entreaty on the site described how the group's holy warriors were engaged in fighting the "oppressive Hindu Army in the snow covered valleys, mountains and jungles of Kashmir. These Mujadhideen best deserve your charity."[98] The site was visceral in its enmity toward what its authors defined as Islam's triumvirate of most-hated opponents: India, the United States, and Israel.[99] According to Jessica Stern, in the past one of Lashkar's sites included a "list of purported Jews working for the Clinton administration," listing staff such as Robert Nash, who was then director of presidential personnel (a non-Jewish African American), and George Tenet, the former director of the Central Intelligence Agency (a Greek American).[100]

Finally, the generic Web sites for radical Islamic ideology maintained in past years out of London and other places in the United Kingdom provided an additional vehicle for the dissemination of propaganda and solicitation of philanthropic contributions. Principal among these were the now difficult to find www.azzam.com and www. kawkaz.com (now www.kavkaz.com or www.kavkazcenter.com). Azzam.com's real sponsor is unknown. It was posted in the name of Azzam Publications, a reference to Abdullah Azzam, a Palestinian who was among the first Arabs to go fight in Afghanistan against the Soviet occupation in the early 1980s and who later achieved fame as a colleague and patron of Osama bin Laden and with bin Laden, as the cofounder of the entity that eventually became known as al Qaeda. Azzam was assassinated in Peshawar in 1989.[101] The azzam.com site was essentially dedicated to global jihad and actively solicited contributions for the Taliban and Chechen guerrillas fighting against Russian forces. A message in early 2001 stated how an "Appeal for cash donations" to the Taliban "is especially urgent." It suggested a minimum US$20,000 contribution and provided advice on how to deliver it personally to the Taliban consul general in Karachi, Pakistan.[102] This site also had long served as a mouthpiece for bin Laden and al Qaeda.[103] Indeed, azzam.com postings in 2002 urged Muslims to come to Pakistan and Afghanistan to fight against the "Jewish-backed American Crusaders" (e.g., U.S. soldiers). It also provided these would-be recruits with useful practical travel information on how to unobtrusively leave one's job and how to avoid arousing suspicion from employers, diplomats issuing visas, and inquisitive border and immigration officials.[104]

The kawkaz web site was similarly devoted to fund-raising for both the Taliban and the Chechens—as well as encouraging volunteers to travel to Afghanistan and Chechnya to fight for Islam. The goal of raising US$10 million per month for the Taliban was once trumpeted. As large sums had already been successfully raised for the Chechens, the aforementioned FBIS analysts did not regard this pretension as entirely "unrealistic." The site contained translations in some sixteen different languages and was sophisticated in design and message. According to the FBIS analysts, the Chechen site provided an "example par excellence of where we are in a new era of propaganda."[105] Today, it operates as www.kavkaz.org.uk, under the banner "News—Facts—Analysis," with postings in three languages (Russian, English, and Turkish). In addition to its focus on Chechnya and Chechen mujahideen issues, the new site also presents information and news about the insurgency in Iraq. Other tabs link to a photo gallery, videos, sections titled "Analysis," "Talking Points," "Chat," and opportunities for cooperation. Among the recent postings on its home page were articles such as "Russians turn Chechen orphans into zombies" and "21 invaders, collaborators eliminated in Chechnya." Online polls also ask readers whether the alleged energy crisis in Moscow is the result of: (a) an "Act of sabotage," (b) "Technical problems," or (c) "Human error." In addition, there are links to six other sites, including www.kavkaz.tv, www.kavkazcenter.com, www.kavkazcenter.net, and www.kavkazcenter.info.[106] As one U.S. government observer of the terrorism Internet phenomenon has noted in the context of the kavkaz sites, "Never in history has there been an opportunity where propaganda is so effective."[107]

Al Qaeda, in fact, is unique among all terrorist groups in this respect: from the start its leadership seems to have intuitively grasped the enormous communicative potential of the Internet and sought to harness this power both to further the movement's strategic aims and to facilitate its tactical operations. The priority that al Qaeda accorded to external communications is evidenced by its pre-9/11 organizational structure. One of the original four al Qaeda operational committees was specifically charged with media and publicity (the others were responsible for military operations, finance and business, and fatwa and Islamic study).[108] Egyptian computer experts who had fought alongside bin Laden in Afghanistan against the Red Army during the 1980s were reportedly specifically recruited to create the extensive network of Web sites, e-mail capabilities, and electronic bulletin boards[109] that continues to function today despite al Qaeda's expulsion from Afghanistan, the destruction of its operational base in that country, and the ongoing prosecution of the United States–led global war on terrorism.

The Internet has long facilitated three critical functions for al Qaeda:

1. propaganda for recruitment and fund-raising and to shape public opinion in the Muslim world,
2. terrorist training and instruction,
3. operational planning for attacks through both e-mail communication and the access it provides to an array of useful open source information.

Each has assumed even great importance in the post-9/11 era and since the loss of Afghanistan as a physical sanctuary. For al Qaeda, the Internet therefore has become something of a virtual sanctuary, providing an effective, expeditious, and anonymous means through which the movement can continue to communicate with its fighters, followers, sympathizers, and supporters worldwide. For example, before 9/11, al Qaeda had only one Web site: www.alneda.com. Today, the movement is present on more than fifty different sites.[110] "The more Web sites, the better it is for us," a jihadist statement posted on azzam.com in 2002 proclaimed. "We must make the Internet our tool."[111]

Initially, as already stated, www.alneda.com fulfilled this requirement.[112] The site, which was published in the Arabic language only (as indeed are all the hardcore jihadist sites), emphasized three core messages that remain the basic staple of al Qaeda and other jihadist Web sites today:

- first, that the West is implacably hostile to Islam;
- second, that the only way to address this threat and the only language that the West understands is violence;
- third, that jihad, therefore, is the only option.[113]

In support of these arguments, the theory of jihad was elaborated upon in great theological and legalistic detail. The obligation of all Muslims both to protect and to spread Islam by the sword was a particular focus of online treatises. In addition, summaries of news affecting the Islamic struggle against the West, al Qaeda's own accounts of ongoing fighting and skirmishing with American and allied forces both in Afghanistan and in Pakistan, and suggested readings—including books by authors approved by al Qaeda theoreticians—could be found on the site.[114] Lengthy justifications for the 9/11 attacks were also posted. Video clips and other messages extolling the operation were featured, accompanied by Islamic juridical arguments sanctioning the killing of innocents. Like other terrorist sites, poems glorified the sacrifices of al Qaeda martyrs and waxed eloquent on the unrelenting defensive struggle being fought against Islam's enemies. During the period immediately following the 9/11 attacks, when al Qaeda suffered a series of stunning reverses, culminating in the loss of Afghanistan as a base, alneda.com also performed an invaluable morale-boosting purpose by trying to lift the spirits of al Qaeda fighters and shore up support among its sympathizers. According to British journalist Paul Eedle, a February 2002 Internet posting contained the names and home phone numbers of eighty-four al Qaeda fighters being held by Pakistani authorities "presumably with the aim that sympathizers would contact their families and let them know that they were alive."[115]

The alneda.com site was also used to call Muslims' attention to the alleged control, suppression, and censorship of information about the jihadist struggle by the West and established media outlets. "The U.S. enemy, unable to gain the upper hand over the mujahadeen on the battlefield," one June 2002 statement explained, "has since Sept. 11 been trying to gag the world media. The more the United States tries to stifle freedom of expression, the more determined we will become to break the silence. America will lose the media war, too."[116] Another, titled "America Nears the Abyss," compared the damage wrought to the U.S. economy by the 9/11 attacks to the struggle prosecuted by the mujahideen in Afghanistan during the 1980s that, it maintained, had set in motion the chain of events that led to the collapse of the Soviet Union and the demise of communism. The same fate, it predicted, would befall the United States, and it cited the weakening American dollar, the parlous state of the U.S. stock market, and the erosion of confidence both at home and abroad in the American economy.[117] Indeed, as previously noted, bin Laden has long argued that the United States is poised on the verge of financial ruin and total collapse much as the USSR once was—with the force of Islam ensuring America's demise much as it achieved that of the Soviet Union more than a decade ago. Indeed, when bin Laden addressed his fighters as they fled Afghanistan in December 2001, he struck the same defiant note. "America is in retreat by the grace of God Almighty and economic attrition is continuing up to today," he declared. "But it needs further blows. The young men need to seek out the nodes of the American economy and strike the enemy's nodes."[118]

The alneda.com site continued to function sporadically throughout 2002, repeatedly moving from one Internet service provider to another to circumvent the efforts of the United States and other governments to shut it down completely. In its death throes that summer, it shifted during one eight-week period from a provider in Malaysia to one in Texas and then to one in Michigan before disappearing completely.[119] Since then, a variety of online magazines have maintained al Qaeda's presence on the Net. The first appeared shortly after 9/11 and featured a series of articles titled "In the Shadow of the Lances." Initially written by the movement's putative spokesman, Suleimain Abu Ghaith, the first five issues were mostly theological or ideological treatises. Typical were discussions reiterating how "America does not understand dialogue. Nor peaceful coexistence. Nor appeals, nor condemnation, nor criticism. America," Abu Ghaith argued, "will only be stopped by blood."[120] In February 2003, however, as the U.S.-led invasion of Iraq loomed imminent, authorship of the series abruptly changed from Abu Ghaith, the theoretician and philosopher, to Saif al-Adel, the warrior. Al-Adl, one of the movement's most senior operational commanders and a former Egyptian Army Special Forces officer who joined al Qaeda as a result of the 1998 merger with Ayman Zawahiri's Egyptian Islamic Jihad, implored jihadists to descend upon Iraq—not to support Saddam Hussein but to defend Muslims against this latest instance of U.S. and Western aggression. He also dispensed detailed, practical advice on guerrilla operations and urban warfare tactics with which to engage—and ultimately defeat—the invading American and British forces in Iraq.[121] The virtues of guerrilla warfare were again lavishly extolled in a posting that appeared on alneda.com on April 9, 2003. Clearly written sometime after American forces had entered Baghdad, it cited prominent historical cases where numerically smaller and less powerful forces using guerrilla tactics had successfully challenged larger, better-equipped adversaries. Under the caption "Guerrilla Warfare Is the most Powerful Weapon Muslims have, and It is The Best Method to Continue the Conflict with the Crusader Enemy," the statement foreshadowed the current insurgency in Iraq, presciently explaining how

with guerilla warfare, the Americans were defeated in Vietnam and the Soviets were defeated in Afghanistan. This is the method that expelled the direct Crusader colonialism from most of the Muslim lands, with Algeria the most well known. We still see how this method stopped Jewish immigration to Palestine, and caused reverse immigration of Jews from Palestine. The successful attempts of dealing defeat to invaders using guerilla warfare were many, and we will not expound on them. However, these attempts have proven that the most effective method for the materially weak against the strong is guerrilla warfare.[122]

This mixture of ideology and propaganda alongside practical guidance on guerrilla warfare and related terrorist operations has come to typify al Qaeda's current Internet profile.[123] With respect to the former, a new Internet magazine named *Sawt al-Jihad* (Voice of Jihad) appeared in February 2004, published by al Qaeda's Saudi organization. Its message was less one of attacking U.S. and other Western targets than the importance of mobilizing Muslim public opinion and support of jihad.[124] Nonetheless, according to Reuven Paz, an editorial titled "Belief First: They Are the Heretics, the Blood of Each of Them Is the Blood of a Dog" implicitly justified the slaughter of Americans. "My fighting brother," its author, Sheikh Naser al-Najdi, wrote,

kill the heretic; kill whoever his blood is the blood of a dog; kill those that Almighty Allah has ordered you to kill. . . .
Bush son of Bush. . . . a dog son of a dog . . . his blood is that of a dog. . . .
Shut your mouth and speak with your other mouth—the mouth of the defender against his attacker.[125]

In Islam, dogs are considered to be among the most impure creatures, and true believers are forbidden to even touch one. Thus, the equating of President Bush with a dog is meant to be especially damning.

With respect to practical guidance, another new online publication, also published by the al Qaeda organization in Saudi Arabia, *Mu'askar al-Battar* (Camp of the Sword) seeks to provide operational information. Its first issue, published in January 2004, explained how "in order to join the great training camps you don't have to travel to other lands. Alone, in your home or with a group of your brothers, you too can begin to execute the training program. You can all join the Al-Battar Training Camp."[126] The power of this particular communications vehicle appears to have been demonstrated by the influence that the March 2004 edition had on subsequent patterns of terrorist activities in Saudi Arabia and Iraq. Reportedly written by Abdul Azziz al-Moqrin,[127] the reputed commander of al Qaeda's operations on the Arabian Peninsula until he was killed by Saudi security forces in May 2005, it singled out economic targets, especially those connected with the region's oil industry, as priorities for attack. "The purpose of these targets," Moqrin wrote,

is to destabilize the situation and not allow the economic recovery such as hitting oil wells and pipelines that will scare foreign companies from working there and stealing Muslim treasures. Another purpose is to have foreign investment withdrawn from local markets. Some of the benefits of those operations are the effect it has on the economic powers like the one that had happened recently in Madrid where the whole European economy was affected.[128]

In the weeks that followed, al-Moqrin's strategy seemed to bear fruit. The U.S. State Department, for instance, advised American citizens to leave Saudi Arabia. After the murder in April 2004 of five expatriate workers at a petrochemical complex in the Saudi industrial city of Yanbu, foreign companies there were reported to have evacuated employees from the country.[129] These fears acquired new urgency with the attack in May on a housing complex in Khobar, where twenty-two foreigners were killed, and the execution by beheading in June of an American defense contractor, Paul M. Johnson Jr.[130]

This same targeting guidance also explains the spate of kidnappings and tragically similar executions of foreign contractors, diplomats, and aid workers in Iraq that commenced within a week of its release. The first victim was Mohammed Rifat, a Canadian, who was seized on April 8. During the following three months, more than sixty others were kidnapped. Although the majority were eventually released, five hostages were brutally murdered—most often by beheading, with the act itself filmed and posted on jihadist Web sites.[131] Among the dead was a young Jewish American businessman, Nicholas Berg. Al-Moqrin had deemed as a special priority "assassinating Jewish businessmen and teach lessons to those who cooperate with them [*sic*]." Indeed, al-Moqrin provided additional "practical examples" of how his targeting guidance should be implemented. The preferred hierarchy of targets were:

- "American and Israeli Jews first, the British Jews and then French Jews and so on."
- "Christians: Their importance is as follows: Americans, British, Spanish, Australians, Canadians, Italians."

Within these categories there were further distinctions:

- "Businessmen, bankers, and economists, because money is very important in this age"
- "Diplomats, politicians, scholars, analysts, and diplomatic missions"
- "Scientists, associates and experts"; "Military commander and soldiers"; and
- "Tourists and entertainment missions and anybody that was warned by mujahideen not to go to step in the lands of Moslems."[132]

Finally, along with propaganda and training, al Qaeda has also made extensive use of the Internet for intelligence-gathering purposes and targeting. The so-called Manchester Manual, the compendium of terrorist tradecraft assembled by al Qaeda sometime during the 1990s, advises explicitly that "openly and without resorting to illegal means, it is possible to gather at least 80% of information about the enemy."[133] Indeed, *The 9/11 Commission Report* cites four specific instances in which KSM and the nineteen hijackers accessed information from the Internet to plan or facilitate the 9/11 attacks.[134] An al Qaeda computer found by American military forces in Afghanistan contained architectural models of a dam in the United States and software with which to simulate various catastrophic failures, as well as programming instructions for the digital switches that operate American power, water, transport, and communications grids.[135] And more recently, in March 2005, three British al Qaeda operatives were indicted by a U.S. federal court on charges of having carried out detailed reconnaissance of financial targets in lower Manhattan, Newark, New Jersey, and Washington, D.C. In addition to videotaping the Citigroup Center and the New York Stock Exchange in New York City, the Prudential Financial building in

Newark, and the headquarters of the International Monetary Fund and the World Bank in Washington, D.C., the men were alleged to have amassed more than five hundred photographs of the sites—many of which had simply been downloaded from the Internet.[136]

Video Production and Duplication Processes

Al Qaeda and other terrorist groups have also made use of a variety of contemporary technologies to project their message—including computer CD-ROMs, DVDs, and the professionally produced video clips cited at the beginning of this chapter. Indeed, a two-hour al Qaeda recruitment video that bin Laden had circulated throughout the Middle East during the summer of 2001—and that Peter Bergen argues subtly presaged the September 11 attacks—is just such an example.[137] The video, with its graphic footage of infidels attacking Muslims in Chechnya, Kashmir, Iraq, Israel, Lebanon, Indonesia, and Egypt; children starving under the yoke of United Nations economic sanctions in Iraq; and, most vexatiously, the accursed presence of "Crusader" military forces in the holy land of Arabia was subsequently converted to CD-ROM and DVD formats for ease in copying onto computers and loading onto the World Wide Web for still wider, global dissemination. Titled *The Destruction of the American Destroyer USS Cole*, the DVD version, except for the misspellings, choppy English translation, and tendentious message, has a color jacket sleeve and liner notes that appear little different from the commercial videos one rents or purchases at the local video store.[138] "This tape are real life scenes that potray [sic]," the liner notes state, "with blood and tears, the sorry state of the Muslim Nation. after [sic] revealing the illness, it goes on to discribe [sic] the cure, whils [sic] giving the glad tiding and hopes for the future as a means of encouragement to remain firm and be steadfast for the sake of the future generation."[139]

Other video productions that either al Qaeda or its affiliated groups have distributed evidence the same sophisticated production capabilities and accomplished editing. A particularly revealing sign of their professionalism is the way that videos depicting scenes such as the repugnant execution of the journalist Daniel Pearl[140] or the last will and testament of Ahmed Ibrahim A. al-Haznawi, one of the September 11 hijackers, are all shot with a blue background. This technique enables an editor to insert contemporary news footage or evocative images at a later time and thereby enhance or put in a particularly powerful context the video's message.[141] The video clip of Daniel Pearl's brutal execution, for example, is intercut simultaneously with footage in the left and right corners of the screen depicting the widely televised alleged shooting death in October 2000 of the Palestinian child Muhammad al-Dura, as well as similar scenes of Israeli Defense Force operations involving Palestinian civilians. The tape of al-Haznawi, one of the hijackers aboard the American Airlines flight that crashed into the Pentagon on September 11, contained a date and place name beside his reproduced signature indicating that it was recorded in Khandahar, Afghanistan, around March 2001. Broadcast first by the Qatar-based Arab language news network al-Jazeera in mid-April, the clip was similarly interspersed with contemporary footage showing Ayman Zawahiri, bin Laden's chief lieutenant, lauding the 9/11 attacks as a "gift from God" with additional voice-over referring to the Arab League summit in Beirut that had been held two weeks earlier.[142] Both videos—like much al Qaeda propaganda—are noteworthy for the repeated references to, and depictions of, the suffering of Muslim children, whether in Palestine, Iraq, or elsewhere. It is hard to imagine a more potent propaganda tool, recruiting vehicle, or means to justify and legitimate violence than to focus on the maltreatment and abject condition of children.

It was not surprising, therefore, to find another professionally produced al Qaeda recruitment video circulating around the Middle East in the spring of 2002 in an effort to attract new martyrs to bin Laden's cause. The seven-minute tape, seized from an al Qaeda member by American authorities, reportedly opens with the image of a spinning globe with still pictures of dead men floating by and the words in Arabic:

> They are the ones that say, (of their brethren slain), while they themselves sit (at ease:) "If only they had listened to us, they would not have been slain." Say: "Avert death from your own selves if you speak the truth." Think not of those who are slain in Allah's way as dead. Nay, they live, finding their sustenance in the presence of their Lord.

This is then followed by footage of mujahideen in battle, with depictions of the fighters' death and beneath it text reading: "Say not the martyr had died, for he is alive and happy lodged in eternal paradise." The video goes on to show more combat scenes, followed by the images of twenty-seven martyrs shown in rapid succession with the name of each listed, where he or she is from, and where he or she died. The narrator explains that they hailed from Algeria, Chechnya, Egypt, Jordan, Kuwait, Libya, Mecca (Saudi), Medina (Saudi), Morocco, Najd (presumably Saudi), Pakistan, Palestine, United Arab Emirates, and Yemen and that they perished while fighting in Afghanistan,

Bosnia, Chechnya, Dagestan, Pakistan, and Tajikistan, circa the early and mid-1990s. Twelve of the martyrs are then featured in a special segment accompanied by a voice-over saying, "They rejoice in the bounty provided by Allah: And with regard to those left behind who have not yet joined them (in their bliss), the martyrs glory in the fact that on them is no fear, nor have they (cause to) grieve." The video concludes with a message of greeting from the "Black Banner Center for Islamic Information" along with accompanying contact details and the Qur'anic invocation "There is no god but Allah, and Muhammad is Allah's messenger."[143]

Al Qaeda, however, cannot claim credit for having pioneered the filming of jihadist attacks for propaganda, recruitment, and marketing purposes. That distinction is credited by one source to the infamous Jordanian-born commander of Chechen fighters known by the nom de guerre Khattab. Khattab reportedly began to film his group's attack on Russian military forces under the assumption that "if they killed a few Russian soldiers in an ambush along a road the impact of the strike was limited, however if the operation was filmed and then shown to the Russian people that impact was multiplied manifold." Khattab and his men thus videotaped any assault—whether involving ambushes, roadside bombings, kidnappings, or rocket attacks—and soon had enough footage to produce a forty-minute video titled *Russian Hell 1*.[144] Khattab's successors have continued this policy. During the August 2005 siege of a school in Beslan, Ossetia, by Chechen terrorists, one of the attackers was reported by a hostage to have "constantly filmed us."[145]

Insurgent Television

Perhaps the most startling advance in terrorist communications over the past decade, however, has been the emergence of the terrorists' own television stations. In this respect, the video production and duplication capabilities already cited that have facilitated the customization of sophisticated messages on the Internet are a product of a growing sophistication among terrorists in the television studio and the editing booth as well. Among the pioneers in this process has been Hezbollah, whose al-Manar television station along with its news Web site on the Internet, have afforded this movement an unprecedented ability to shape and tailor its external communications. In this way terrorist groups have been able to assume complete control over the content, context, footage, and voice-overs depicting their organization and its activities.

Al-Manar began broadcasting as a small terrestrial station in 1991 with limited on-air time and programming content.[146] Within a decade, however, it was transmitting via satellite on a 24/7 basis.[147] Today, al-Manar provides eight news bulletins daily in Arabic and one each in English and French. In addition to its headquarters operations in Beirut, the station has bureaus in Egypt, Iran, Jordan, and the United Arab Emirates (UAE) and correspondents stationed in Belgium, France, Iraq, Kosovo, Kuwait, Morocco, the Occupied Territories (Palestine), Russia, Sweden, Syria, Turkey, and, until recently, even the United States.[148] Al-Manar's Web site describes the station's mission as

> motivated by the ambitions of participation in building a better future for the Arab and Muslim generations by focusing on the tolerant values of Islam and promoting the culture of dialogue and cooperation among the followers of the Heavenly religions and human civilizations. It focuses on highlighting the value of the human being as the center of the Godly messages which endeavor to save his dignity and freedom and develop the spiritual and moral dimensions of his personality [sic].
>
> Al-Manar avoids cheap incitement in dealing with developments and activities, and it stresses objectively on the adoption of the fair and just causes of the whole nation [sic].[149]

However, according to Avi Jorisch, the author of a detailed study of the station and its programming content,

> Today, Hizballah [sic] continues to use al-Manar as a means of publicly offering its services to Palestinians fighting for the destruction of Israel and the total liberation of historic Palestine (e.g., all territory west of the Jordan River). . . . Accordingly, one of al-Manar's major objectives is to inspire resistance. . . .
>
> With regard to the United States, al-Manar has broadcast anti-American propaganda since its inception, often using the same propaganda methods it employs against Israel. Various programs have focused on distorting U.S. history, lambasting U.S. Middle East policy, propagating conspiracy theories about the September 11 attacks, and demonizing the relationship between Washington and the "Zionist entity," Israel. With the start of Operation Iraqi Freedom in 2003, both Hizballah and al-Manar renewed their vitriol toward their old, reliable foe, the "Great Satan."[150]

The station's primetime programming clearly reflects its biases. Shows such as *The Spider's House* (see the previous allusion to the significance of this Qur'anic verse with respect to Israel, in chapter 5) detail Israel's inherent weaknesses and its inevitable defeat through the use of suicide attacks and other terrorist tactics. More recently, the same attributes and eventuality have been ascribed to the United States as a result of its occupation of Iraq. *What's Next* is a talk show that hosts guests with particularly "vitriolic anti-American views." Another show, called *Terrorists*, details the alleged depredations inflicted throughout history by Israel on the Arab world, while *My Blood and the Rifle* is a panegyric to Hezbollah's fighters, extolling their victory over Israel in south Lebanon and their heroic sacrifices.[151] That this format is tremendously appealing is indisputable. A Gallup poll of Middle Eastern audience viewing preferences for news taken in March 2002 revealed that al-Manar was the fifth most popular station watched in the past week and was ranked as the third most popular station to which viewers turn to first to catch up on current world affairs.[152] It is reportedly one of the most watched stations in the Palestine territories.[153] Lebanese television officials boast that al-Manar is the third most popular station in that country, and at times of crisis with Israel it is often the first.[154]

During the 1990s Hezbollah created field units of combat camera crews that accompanied the organization's operational units into battle in order to provide al-Manar with the compelling footage it required.[155] Footage of Hezbollah fighters, attired in fatigues, with body armor and helmets, carrying out textbook military assaults on Israeli positions in South Lebanon and those of their South Lebanon Army (SLA) allies were a regular feature of al-Manar's television broadcasts and Internet Web site from the mid-1990s until the Israeli withdrawal in May 2000.[156] As one United Nations official explained, "For Hezbollah, 60 per cent of the success of an operation depends on getting some good footage."[157] Indeed, Hezbollah propaganda efforts, directed at Israeli audiences back home—and specifically at the mothers of IDF troops serving in southern Lebanon—are widely regarded as having been influential in generating public pressure on the Israeli government to withdraw from Lebanon.[158] "By means of the Internet," Ibrahim Nasser al-Din, a Hezbollah military leader, claimed, "Hezbollah has succeeded in entering the homes of Israelis, creating an important psychological breakthrough."[159] This quote appeared in an article published in a leading Israeli newspaper, which further reported how parents of IDF soldiers serving in Lebanon regularly visited the Hezbollah site to get a version of the news unvarnished by Israeli military censors. "I regard these sites as a legitimate source of information," one father was quoted as saying.[160] Much as the efforts of Sri Lankan authorities to suppress news of military defeats backfired disastrously in public relations terms, the same occurred with

Israel in 1999. Contradicting IDF reports that Hezbollah had returned the body of only one member of a team of Israeli marine commandos killed in a Hezbollah ambush, the group publicized on its Web site that the coffin contained the body parts of other soldiers as well. The statement generated a nasty confrontation between the commando's families and the IDF, with accusations of cover-up and duplicity undermining trust and confidence among the Israelis in its armed forces.[161]

Hezbollah, however, is not the only terrorist group to use its own television for propaganda and mobilization purposes. The widespread protests unleashed throughout Europe immediately following the arrest by Turkish authorities of the Kurdish terrorist leader Abdullah Ocalan, in February 1999, provides further proof of the reach and rapidity with which modern communications technology can rally the masses. Within hours of the announcement of his arrest, demonstrators swarmed onto the streets of Paris, Moscow, London, Frankfurt, Milan, Bern, Sydney, and more than a dozen other cities in response to pleas issued by the PKK (Kurdish Workers Party) over both its Internet site and its London-based television station, Med-TV.[162] The television station, founded in 1995, mirrors the ambitions of terrorists and insurgents throughout the globe today. "Our aim," in the words of the station manager, Sami Abdurahman, "is to present our Kurdish brothers across the world with the objective facts."[163] Or, as the American statesman Hiram W. Johnson, would have said: "The first casualty when war comes is truth."

Conclusion

In the final analysis, a terrorist movement's longevity ultimately depends upon its ability to recruit new members as well as appeal to an expanding pool of both active supporters and passive sympathizers. The role of effective communication in this process is pivotal: ensuring the continued flow of fighters into the movement, binding supporters more tightly to it, and drawing sympathizers more deeply into its orbit. "Without communication," Schmid and de Graaf presciently argued more than twenty years ago, "there can be no terrorism."[164] The revolution in terrorist communications described in this chapter has facilitated this process in hitherto unimaginable ways. Virtually every terrorist group in the world today, as previously noted, now has its own Internet Web site and, in many instances, maintains multiple sites in different languages with different messages tailored to specific audiences. The ability to communicate in real time via the Internet, using a variety of compelling electronic media—including dramatic video footage, digital photographs, and audio clips accompanied by visually arresting along with savvy and visually appealing Web design—has enabled terrorists to reach a potentially vast audience faster, more pervasively, and more effectively than ever before. Indeed, the changing face of terrorism in the twenty-first century is perhaps best exemplified by the items recovered by Saudi security forces during a raid on an al Qaeda safe house in Riyadh in late spring 2004. In addition to the traditional terrorist arsenal of AK-47 assault rifles, explosives, rocket-propelled grenades, hand grenades, and thousands of rounds of ammunition that the authorities expected to find, they also discovered an array of electronic consumer goods, including video cameras, laptop computers, CD burners, and the requisite high-speed Internet connection. According to CNN investigative journalist Henry Schuster, the videos

> had been part of an al Qaeda media blitz on the Web that also included two online magazines full of editorials and news digests, along with advice on how to handle a kidnapping or field-strip an AK-47 assault rifle. The videos mixed old appearances by bin Laden with slick graphics and suicide bombers' on-camera last wills and testaments. They premiered on the Internet, one after the other, and were aimed at recruiting Saudi youth.[165]

The widespread availability of these sophisticated but inexpensive communications technologies, as this chapter also argued, has effectively shattered the monopoly on readily accessible information formerly wielded by conventional commercial and state-owned television and radio broadcasting outlets and the print media. The extent of the transformation is evidenced by the fact that today terrorist Web sites are as regularly consulted as they are cited (and publicized) by the mainstream press.[166] For some audiences, moreover, the sites maintained by terrorist movements and their sympathizers alarmingly present an increasingly compelling and indeed accepted alternative point of view. This was of course al Qaeda's purpose in creating its first Web site, www.alneda.com, and in maintaining a variety of successor sites since: to provide an alternative source for news and information over which the movement itself could exert total control. Identical arguments—claiming distortion and censorship by Western and other mainstream media—have also been voiced by sites either created by the Iraqi insurgent groups themselves or entities sympathetic to them.[167] "Western Propaganda Media Try to Shut Down albasrah.net! [sic]," the banner on one such site, www.albasrah.net, asserts. "Once again," it argued, "the propaganda media have begun to spew stupid accusations against al-Basrah, the true aim of which is to smother the voice of Iraqi people and smother one of the few sources of information on the unprecedented massacres that are taking place inside occupied Iraq in the name of 'international law'."[168]

Indeed, the insurgency in Iraq has arguably emerged as the cynosure of contemporary, cutting-edge terrorist communications. For instance, according to analysts at the Alexandria, Virginia–based IntelCenter, to date, more than a dozen terrorist groups have produced their own videos.[169] At least half, however, are either indigenous Iraqi insurgent organizations or foreign jihadists fighting there. Since late 2003, a growing number of "mujahideen films" have been marketed for sale (mostly in DVD format) at souks and bazaars in Iraq and posted either in part or in whole on the Internet. The films variously

- depict scenes of insurgents using roadside bombs to ambush U.S. military forces on patrol in Humvees or firing handheld surface-to-air missiles (SAMs) at U.S. military aircraft flying overhead;
- impart practical, tactical advice to insurgents (for example: advising insurgents "to vacate the area no later than 10 minutes after launching an attack, before US forces zero in on their position") and instruction in the use of weaponry and the planning and execution of attacks;
- transmit the last words of kidnapped Iraqis and foreigners about to be executed[170] and, in many instances, display gory footage of the executions themselves;[171]
- appeal for financial contributions;[172] and
- perhaps most important, solicit recruits from the Middle East, South and Central Asia, North Africa, Europe, and even North America to come to Iraq to become "lions from the martyr's brigade."[173]

These mujahideen films are but one manifestation of a much broader and highly sophisticated communications strategy. The more prominent insurgent organizations fighting in Iraq, for instance, have themselves established dedicated information offices that in essence function as "online press agencies," issuing communiqués, developing and posting new content for their Web sites (often several times a day), and generally updating and regularly replenishing news and other features. "The Iraqi armed opposition appear to make a priority of communication," two particularly knowledgeable observers of the insurgency in that country have written,

in ways that go far beyond the unique intention of terrorising the adversary. Combatant groups produce an astonishingly large and varied range of texts and images, which it would be wrong to reduce to their most brutal types. Besides the threatening tracts there is an impressive body of strategic analysis, cold-blooded, lucid and detailed. Similarly, the most monstrous video sequences eclipse a wealth of films, sometimes of professional quality, extending from "lectures" in classical Arabic on the manufacture of explosives to "advertising" material put out by new groups making their first public appearance.

The insurgents' intent is to explain and legitimate their use of violence (employing theological arguments and treatises, for example, to differentiate between "illicit terrorism" and "licit terrorism" and thereby justify their attacks); drive a wedge between the Iraqi people and the so-called collaboration authorities (e.g., the Iraqi interim government); undermine popular confidence in the ability of the Iraqi government and Iraqi security forces and the U.S. and coalition militaries to maintain order throughout the country; and, last, to facilitate communications between and among various groups in order to forge new alliances and cooperative arrangements, however tactical or short-lived.[174]

Indeed, the IntelCenter analysts who both collect and study the aforementioned mujahideen films and also monitor the Internet for Iraqi insurgent communications believe that we are on the cusp of an emergent and potentially even more extensive phenomenon. "As video editing software, video compression, computer power, camera technology and Internet bandwidth continue to improve," they argue,

the speed, sophistication and quantity of jihadi videos will continue to increase. This is also currently being driven by the sheer volume of jihadi operations in Iraq, which are providing an ample supply of material for new releases.[175]

Thus the revolution in terrorist communications that has rapidly unfolded within the past few years is certain to continue. Its capabilities and products will likely also become increasingly more sophisticated in quality, content, and transmission capacity—and more numerous and pervasive than ever. The implications of this phenomenon are perhaps only now beginning to be understood. What is clear, though, is that as terrorist communications continue to change and evolve, so will the nature of terrorism itself. While one cannot predict what new forms and dimensions terrorism will assume during the rest of the twenty-first century, this evolutionary process will continue and will doubtless be abetted—and accelerated—by new communications technologies—as has been the case over the past decade.

Chapter 8

The Modern Terrorist Mind-set:
Tactics, Targets, Tradecraft,
and Technologies

The wrath of the terrorist is rarely uncontrolled. Contrary to both popular belief and media depiction, most terrorism is neither crazed nor capricious. Rather, terrorist attacks are generally both premeditated and carefully planned. As shown in chapter 6, the terrorist act is specifically designed to communicate a message. But, equally important, it is also conceived and executed in a manner that simultaneously reflects the terrorist group's particular aims and motivations, fits its resources and capabilities, and takes into account the "target audience" at which the act is directed. The tactics and targets of various terrorist movements, as well as the weapons they favor, are therefore ineluctably shaped by a group's ideology, its internal organizational dynamics, and the personalities of its key members, as well as a variety of internal and external stimuli.

The Nexus of Ideological and Operational Imperatives

All terrorist groups seek targets that are rewarding from their point of view and employ tactics that are consonant with their overriding political aims. Whereas left-wing terrorists like the German Red Army Faction

(RAF) and the Italian Red Brigades (RB) have selectively kidnapped and assassinated people whom they blamed for economic exploitation or political repression in order to attract publicity and promote a Marxist-Leninist revolution, terrorists motivated by a religious imperative have engaged in more indiscriminate acts of violence, directed against a far wider category of targets encompassing not merely their declared enemies but anyone who does not share their religious faith. The actions of ethno-nationalist/separatist groups arguably fall somewhere in between these two models. On the one hand, the violent campaigns waged by groups like the PLO, the IRA, and the Basque separatist organization ETA have frequently been more destructive and have caused far greater casualties than those of their left-wing counterparts. But, on the other hand, their violence has largely been restricted to a specifically defined "target set"—namely, the members of a specific rival or dominant ethno-nationalist group.[1] Perhaps the least consequential of all these terrorist group categories (in terms both of frequency of incidents and of impact on public and governmental attitudes) has been the disparate collection of recycled Nazis, racist "political punk rockers," and other extreme right-wing elements that has emerged over the years in various European countries. But even their sporadic and uncoordinated, seemingly mindless violence—fueled as much by beer and bravado as by a discernible political agenda—is neither completely random nor unthinkingly indiscriminate. Indeed, for all these categories, the point is less their inherent differences than the fact that their tactical and targeting choices correspond to, and are determined by, their respective ideologies and attendant mechanisms of legitimation and justification, and, perhaps most critically, by their relationship with the intended audience of their violent acts.

The overriding tactical—and, indeed, ethical—imperative for left-wing terrorists, for example, has been the deliberate tailoring of their violent acts to appeal to their perceived "constituencies." In a 1978 interview, the German left-wing terrorist Michael "Bommi" Baumann denounced the hijacking of a Lufthansa passenger plane the previous year by terrorists seeking the release of imprisoned RAF members as "madness . . . you can't take your life and place it above that of children and Majorca holiday-makers and say: *My* life is valuable! That is elitarian madness, bordering on Fascism."[2] For Baumann, the deliberate involvement of innocent civilians in that terrorist operation was not only counterproductive but wrong. It was counterproductive in that it tarnished the left-wing terrorists' image as a true "revolutionary vanguard"—using violence to draw attention to themselves and their cause and "educate" the public about what the terrorists perceived as the inequities of the democratic-capitalist state. It was also wrong in itself because innocent people—no matter what the political justification—should not be the victims of terrorist acts directed against the state.

For this reason, left-wing terrorists' use of violence historically has been heavily constrained. Their self-styled crusade for social justice is typically directed against governmental or commercial institutions, or specific individuals who they believe represent capitalist exploitation and repression. They are therefore careful not to undertake actions that might alienate potential supporters or their perceived constituency. Accordingly, left-wing violence tends to be highly discriminate, selective, and limited. Individuals epitomizing the focus of the terrorists' ideological hostility—wealthy industrialists like Hans Martin Schleyer (who was kidnapped and later murdered by the RAF in 1977) or leading parliamentarians like Aldo Moro (who similarly was kidnapped and subsequently murdered by the RB)—are deliberately selected and meticulously targeted for their intrinsic "symbolic" value. "You know that we did not kidnap Moro the man, but [rather] his function," explained Mario Moretti, the leader of the RB Rome column who masterminded the operation, during his trial in November 1984. For Moretti, Moro was first and foremost a powerful symbol: a former prime minister and reigning Christian Democratic Party chief; a political wheeler-dealer par excellence; and architect of the impending historic compromise with the Italian Communist Party that would fundamentally alter the country's political landscape and further marginalize the RB. He was, in the terrorists' eyes, the "supreme manager of power in Italy" and had been for the previous twenty years, a man whom Moretti described as the "demiurge of bourgeois power." By abducting so important a leader and so profound a symbol, the RB sought to galvanize the Italian left and thereby decisively transform the political situation in its favor.[3]

Even when less discriminate tactics such as bombing are employed, the violence is meant to be equally "symbolic." That is, while the damage inflicted is real, the terrorists' main purpose is not to destroy property or obliterate tangible assets but to dramatize or call attention to a political cause. The decision-making process of the left-wing terrorist group is perhaps depicted most clearly in Baumann's description of the planning of a 1969 terrorist attack by the group known as the Tupamaros West Berlin (a precursor of both the Second of June Movement and the original RAF). Baumann and his colleagues wanted to stage an operation that would simultaneously attract attention to themselves and their cause, publicize the plight of the Palestinian people, and demonstrate the West German left's solidarity and sympathy with the Palestinians' struggle. "We sat down and pondered what would be a story that nobody could miss, that everyone would have to talk about and everyone would have to report," Baumann recalled. "And we came up with the right answer—a bomb in the Jewish Community Centre—and on the anniversary of the 'Crystal Night'[4] during the Third Reich. . . . Though it didn't explode, the story [still] went round the world."[5] By striking on this particular date, against this specific target, with its deep—and unmistakable—symbolic significance, the group sought to draw a deliberate parallel between Israeli oppression of the Palestinians and Nazi persecution of the Jews.[6]

The use by left-wing terrorists of "armed propaganda" (i.e., violent acts with clear symbolic content) is thus a critical element in their operational calculus. It is also the principal means by which these organizations "educate" the masses through their self-anointed role as "revolutionary vanguard." The first official "strategic resolution" of the RB, for example, stressed exactly this theme. "It is not a question of organizing the class movement within the area of armed struggle," the 1975 document stated, "but of entrenching the organization of the armed struggle and the political realization of its historical necessity within the class movement."[7] A less turgid explanation of this strategy was later offered by Patrizio Peci, leader of the group's Turin column, when he reflected how, "as crazy as it might seem, the plan in a few words was this: First phase, armed propaganda. . . . Second phase, that of armed support. . . . Third phase, the civil war and victory. In essence, we were the embryo, the skeleton of the future . . . the ruling class of tomor-row in a communist society."[8] The RAF drew similar parallels in its exegesis of the relationship between the terrorist vanguard and "the people." "Our original conception of the organization implied a connection between the urban guerrilla and the work at the base," explained the document, titled "Sur la Concepcíon de la Guerilla Urbaine":

> We would like it if each and all of us could work at the neighborhoods and factories, in socialist groups that already exist, influence discussion, experience and learn. This has proved impossible. . . .
>
> Some say that the possibilities for agitation, propaganda and organi-zation are far from being eradicated and that only when they are, should we pose the question of arms. We say: it will not really be possible to profit from any political actions as long as armed struggle does not appear clearly as the goal of the politicization.[9]

This approach is not entirely dissimilar to that of many ethno-national-ist/separatist groups. These terrorist movements also see themselves as a revolutionary vanguard—if not in classic Marxist-Leninist terms, at least as a spearhead, similarly using violence to "educate" fellow members of their national or ethnic group about the inequities imposed upon them by the ruling government and the need for communal resistance and rebellion. As one Basque nationalist bluntly told an interviewer, "ETA is the vanguard of our revolution."[10] Accordingly, like all ethno-nationalist/separatist terrorists, ETA uses demonstratively symbolic acts of violence to generate publicity and rally support by underscoring the powerlessness of the government to withstand the nationalist expression that it (ETA) champions, and thereby to embarrass and coerce the government into acceding to the group's irredentist demands. ETA's "target audience," however, is not just the local, indigenous population but often the international community as well. These groups, accordingly, recognize the need to tightly control and focus their operations in such a manner as to ensure both the continued support of their local "constituencies" and the sympathy of the international community. What this essentially means is that their violence must always be perceived as both purposeful and deliberate, sustained and omnipresent. Gerry Adams, the president of Sinn Fein, the Irish nationalist political party linked to the IRA, himself expressed precisely this point in an article he wrote in 1976 to commemorate the sixtieth anniversary of the 1916 Easter Uprising. "Rightly or wrongly, I am an IRA Volunteer," Adams explained,

and, rightly or wrongly, I take a course of action as a means to bringing about a situation in which I believe the people of my country will prosper. . . . The course I take involves the use of physical force, but only if I achieve the situation where my people can genuinely prosper can my course of action be seen, by me, to have been justified.[11]

Indeed, as the veteran Northern Ireland correspondent David McKittrick points out, "Sinn Fein, in its efforts to build a political machine in both parts of Ireland, has [always] been concerned to project IRA violence as the clinical and carefully directed use of force."[12]

The more successful ethno-nationalist/separatist terrorist organization will be able to determine an effective level of violence that is at once "tolerable" for the local populace, tacitly acceptable to international opinion, and sufficiently modulated not to provoke massive governmental crackdown and reaction. The IRA has demonstrably mastered this synchronization of tactics to strategy. Since the mid-1980s, according to Patrick Bishop and Eamonn Mallie, the organization's military high command has clearly recognized that "Republican strategy required a certain level of violence—but only enough to distort the private and public life of the North, and to make sure that the military arm was properly exercised."[13] What this has often resulted in is the targeting of members of the security forces (ordinary policemen and soldiers) in preference to the terrorists' avowed enemies in some rival indigenous community. This is true in Northern Ireland, where fewer than 20 percent of the IRA's victims between 1969 and 1993 were Protestant civilians,[14] and in Spain, where more than 60 percent of fatalities inflicted by the Basque ETA have been members of the Spanish security forces.[15]

Certainly, "traitors," informants, and other collaborators among their own brethren are regularly targeted, but here the terrorist group must be careful to strike another balance between salutary, if sporadic, "lessons" that effectively intimidate and compel compliance from their own communities and more frequent and heavy-handed episodes that alienate popular support, encourage cooperation with the security forces, and therefore prove counterproductive. By the same token, highly placed government officials and security force commanders will, when the opportunity presents itself and the political conditions are propitious, be attacked. But given the combination of uncertain—and possibly undesirable—political and security repercussions, the difficulties involved in gaining access to these VIPs, and the considerable effort required of such operations, they are generally eschewed in favor of more productive, if less spectacular, operations that, moreover, conform to the terrorists' perceptions of what are regarded as "legitimate" or "acceptable" targets—however abhorrent the attacks may seem to the outside world.

The terrorist campaign is like a shark in the water: it must keep moving forward—no matter how slowly or incrementally—or die. Hence, when these more "typical" targets fail to sustain the momentum of a terrorist campaign, or when other, perhaps even totally unrelated, events overshadow the terrorists and shunt their cause out of the public eye, terrorists often have to resort to more violent and dramatic acts to refocus attention back upon themselves. But it would be a mistake to see these acts—which often involve the bombing of public gathering places or the hijacking of airliners—as random or senseless. For example, the discussion in chapter 3 showed how, following the Palestinian terrorists' failure to mount a concerted guerrilla campaign against Israel in the occupied West Bank and Gaza Strip after the 1967 Six Day War, the PFLP began hijacking international airliners. The purpose of these operations was not necessarily wantonly to kill or otherwise harm innocent persons (in contrast to many subsequent terrorists' targeting of civil aviation) but to use the passengers as pawns in pursuit of publicity and the extraction of concessions from unsympathetic governments. As one of the group's most famous hijackers, Leila Khaled, once explained, "Look, I had orders to seize the plane, not to blow it up. . . . I care about people. If I had wanted to blow up the plane no one could have prevented me."[16]

Even when terrorists' actions are not as deliberate or discriminating, and when their purpose is in fact to kill innocent civilians, the target is still regarded as "justified" because it represents the terrorists' defined "enemy." Although incidents may be quantitatively different in the volume of death or destruction caused, they are still qualitatively identical in that a widely known "enemy" is being specifically targeted. This distinction is often accepted by the terrorists' constituents and at times by the international community as well. The recognition that the Palestinians obtained in the wake of the 1972 Munich Olympics massacre is a particularly prominent case in point. The poignant message left behind by the terrorist team struck precisely the sympathetic chord they had intended. "We are neither killers nor bandits," their letter stated. "We are persecuted people who have no land and no homeland. . . . We are not against any people, but why should our place here be taken by the flag of the occupiers . . . why should the whole world be having fun and entertainment while we suffer with all ears deaf to us?"[17] As the PFLP's Bassam Abu Sharif explained, "For violence to become fruitful, for it to get us to our aims, it should not be undertaken without a proper political base and intention."[18] While the logic in such a case may well be contrived, there is nonetheless a clear appreciation both that violence has its limits and that, if used properly, it can pay vast dividends. In other words, the level of violence must be kept within the bounds of what the terrorists' "target audience" will accept.

But acts of terrorism, like battles in conventional wars, are difficult to limit and control once they are started, and often result in tragedy to civilians who are inadvertently caught up in the violence. One well-known example is the tragic bombing that occurred at Enniskillen, Northern Ireland, in November 1987, causing the deaths of eleven innocent bystanders attending a memorial ceremony and injuries to sixty-three others. The IRA was quick to describe the incident as an accident resulting from the "catastrophic consequences" of an operation against British troops gone awry.[19] In this instance, there was an acceptance that some grievous wrong had been done, albeit clothed in layers of self-serving justifications. Eamon Collins, a former IRA terrorist, describes the organization's reaction to another botched attack that also accidentally claimed the lives of innocent civilians some years later:

The IRA—regardless of their public utterances dismissing the condemnations of their behaviour from church and community leaders—tried to act in a way that would avoid severe censure from within the nationalist community; they knew they were operating within a sophisticated set of informal restrictions on their behaviour, no less powerful for being largely unspoken.[20]

The Basque ETA is no different—alternately threatening and remorseful in communiqués that seek simultaneously to absolve it of responsibility for its violent deeds and to reap the rewards of introspection and self-criticism. "We claim responsibility for the failed action against a member of the Spanish police," reads one, "following the placing of an explosive charge under his car. We very much deplore the accidental injuries involuntarily caused to his neighbor . . . and we wish his prompt and complete recovery."[21]

Right-wing terrorism has often been characterized as the least discriminating, most senseless type of contemporary political violence. It has earned this reputation mostly as a result of the seemingly mindless "street" violence and unsophisticated attacks that in recent years have increasingly targeted immigrants, refugees, guest workers, and other foreigners in many European countries, especially in eastern Germany and other former communist-bloc states,[22] but also from an inchoate bombing campaign that briefly convulsed Western Europe in the early 1980s. If the means of the right-wing terrorists sometimes appear haphazardly planned and often spontaneously generated, their ends are hardly less indistinct. Essentially, their ostensible goal is the destruction of the liberal-democratic state to clear the way for a renascent National Socialist ("Nazi") or fascist one. But the extent to which this is simply an excuse for the egocentric pleasure derived from brawling and bombing, preening or parading in 1940s-era Nazi regalia, is hard to judge, given that the majority of right-wing groups do not espouse any specific program of reform, preferring to hide behind vague slogans of strident nationalism, the need for racial purity, and the reassertion of governmental strength. In sum, the democratic state is somewhat reflexively assailed for its manifold weaknesses—notably its liberal social welfare policies and tolerance of diverse opinion—alongside its permitting of dark-skinned immigrants in the national labor force and of Jews and other minorities in positions of power or influence. The right-wing terrorists believe that their nation's survival is dependent upon the exorcism of these elements from its environs; only by becoming politically, racially, and culturally homogeneous can the state recover its strength and again work for its natural citizens rather than the variegated collection of interlopers and parasites who now sap the nation of its strength and greatness.

It should be noted that while the European groups share many similarities (racism, anti-Semitism, xenophobia, and a hatred of liberal government) with their American counterparts, they differ fundamentally in their mechanisms of legitimation and justification. Whereas the U.S. groups may be more accurately categorized as religious—rather than strictly as right-wing—terrorists because of the pivotal roles that liturgy, divine inferences, and clerical sanction play in underpinning and motivating their violence, the foundations of the European right are avowedly secular, with neither theological imperatives nor clerics exerting any significant influence. Indeed, the ill-defined, amorphous contours of the contemporary European extreme right's political philosophy can be summed up by the refrain from a popular song by the British white power band White Noise: "Two pints of lager and a packet of crisps. Wogs out! White Power!"[23] or the folk song composed by Gottfried Küssel, Führer of an Austrian neo-Nazi organization: "Do you see his nose, no? Do you know his nose? His nose you do not know? It is crooked and ugly? Then hit him in the face. He is a Jew, a damned Jew, bloodsucker of the European race."[24] By comparison, the lunatic and far-fetched millenarian views of American Christian white supremacists appear to be deeply profound theological treatises.

It is for this reason, perhaps, that European right-wing terrorism has rarely transcended the boundaries of street brawls or the Molotov cocktail hurriedly tossed into a refugee shelter or a guest workers' dormitory (even though, of course, such crude acts of violence possess just the same tragic potential to kill and maim as much more sophisticated terrorist operations). Nonetheless, it would be a mistake to see right-wing violence as completely indiscriminate or entirely irrational. Indeed, the few occasions on which the neo-Nazis have attempted more ambitious types of operations have sent shock waves throughout the Continent. In August 1980, for instance, a powerful explosion tore through the crowded rail station in Bologna, Italy, in the midst of the summer holiday crush. At the time, the total of 84 people killed (and 180 wounded) was second only to the record 91 who had perished in a single terrorist act in the Irgun's bombing of the King David Hotel thirty-four years before. When it was followed less than a month later by a bombing at the popular Munich Oktoberfest celebration, killing 14 and injuring another 215, fears were raised of a new terrorist onslaught more lethal and indiscriminate than that waged by either the European leftist terrorist organizations or the Continent's various ethno-nationalist/separatist groups. But it did not materialize. Instead, the pattern of right-wing terrorism in Europe has remained largely the same since the 1970s: one of sporadic attacks, albeit specifically directed against particular types of targets—primarily refugee shelters and immigrant workers' hostels, anarchist houses and political party offices, and Arab and African immigrants walking along the street, as well as Jewish-owned property or businesses.

As crude and relatively unsophisticated and, indeed, intellectually depraved as this terrorist category may appear, then, right-wing violence, like all forms of terrorism, is based not on some pathological obsession to kill or beat up as many people as possible but rather on a deliberate policy of intimidating the general public into acceding to specific demands or pressures. The right-wing terrorists see themselves, if not as a revolutionary vanguard, then as a catalyst of events that will lead to the imposition of an authoritarian form of government. Thus, like other terrorist movements, they too tailor their violence to appeal to their perceived constituency—be it fellow extreme nationalists, intransigent racists and xenophobes, reactionary conservatives, or militant anti-communists—and, with the exception of a handful of noteworthy, but isolated, indiscriminate bombings, they seek to keep the violence they commit within the bounds of what the ruling government will tolerate without undertaking massive repressive actions against the terrorists themselves.

Moreover, the phenomenon by which terrorists consciously learn from one another, discussed in chapter 2, is evident in the case of at least some German right-wing terrorist elements, suggesting aspirations toward a more planned and coherent campaign of violence than has hitherto existed and raising the possibility of a more serious future threat. As long ago as 1981, Manfred Roeder, for a time Germany's leading neo-Nazi, advocated the emulation of left-wing terrorist targeting and tactics in hopes of endowing the movement with a clearer purpose and attainable goal. For the rightists, however, there was another factor: envy of the attention, status, and occasional tactical victories won by left-wing terrorists in groups such as the RAF, alongside the realization that indiscriminate terrorist attacks would not result in the attainment of the neo-Nazis' goals. "The RAF had brought terrorism to modern Europe," Ingo Hasselbach, one of Roeder's successors, recalled, "and even though they could not have been more opposed to our ideology, we respected them for their fanaticism and skill." Hasselbach therefore advocated for his *Kameradschaft* (Nazi "brotherhood"), before his own disillusionment forced him to break completely with the movement he had once so enthusiastically championed, a lethally discriminate campaign of terrorism mirroring that pursued by the RAF. Like the original founders of the Baader-Meinhof Group twenty years before, Hasselbach believed that his National Alternative Berlin (NA) neo-Nazi organization could not achieve its political objectives by attempting to operate as a legal political party. Accordingly, he sought to mold the group into a terrorist organization modeled on the RAF and laid plans to assassinate prominent Jews and communists and leading politicians. "We wanted to bring neo-Nazi terrorism up to the level of that carried out by the radical Left," Hasselbach later explained,

> striking at targets that would be both better guarded and more significant—targets that would do serious damage to the democratic German state while driving home our racial message. There was, for instance, talk of assassinating Gregor Gusi, the head of the reformed Communist Party, the PDS; he was East Germany's most prominent Jew and leader of the Communists to boot. He was not only a major politician but the political representative of the former GDR system. We also considered hitting Ignatz Bubis, the new head of the Jewish community, as well as a number of politicians in Bonn—including the interior minister and Chancellor Kohl himself.[25]

Like other terrorist organizations, the more sophisticated right-wing groups also seek targets that are likely to advance their cause. In this respect, their terrorist acts are as calculated as those of the left-wing organizations they try to emulate. Publicity and attention are, of course, paramount aims, but at the same time there is a conscious recognition that only if their violence is properly calculated and at least in some (however idiosyncratic) way regulated will they be able to achieve the effects they desire and the political objectives they seek. As an IRA terrorist once said, "You don't bloody well kill people for the sake of killing them."[26] This is not, however, the case with many of the religious terrorist movements discussed in chapter 4. For them, though violence does still have an instrumental purpose, it is also often an end in itself—a sacred duty executed in direct response to some theological demand or imperative. A 1990 study of Lebanese Shi'a terrorists, for example, revealed that none of those in the sample were interested in influencing an actual or self-perceived constituency or in swaying popular opinion; their sole preoccupation was serving God through the fulfillment of their divinely ordained mission.[27] Hence, for religious terrorists there are demonstrably fewer constraints on the actual infliction of violence, and the category of targets/enemies is much more open-ended. The leader of an Egyptian terrorist cell, for instance, professed absolutely no remorse when he was told that an attack he had planned against visiting Israeli Jews had instead killed nine German tourists. His matter-of-fact response was that "infidels are all the same."[28] Indeed, how else can one explain the mad plots of the American Christian white supremacists? Or the Aum sect's wanton and repeated attempts to use chemical warfare nerve agents indiscriminately in populous urban centers? Or the cataclysmic aim of the Jewish Temple Mount bombers in Israel? The willingness of religious terrorists to contemplate such wholesale acts of violence is a direct reflection of the fact that they, unlike their secular counterparts, see in violence a demonstrably divine or transcendental purpose, committed in the service or upon the commandment of their own god or religious figures, and therefore they feel little need to regulate or calibrate that violence. Al Qaeda's repeated calls for unconstrained violence against Americans, Jews, and others clearly underscores the elasticity of the movement's defined "enemy." "All those who oppose U.S. policy," Suleimain Abu Ghaith suggestively warned in October 2001, should "not ride planes or live in high buildings."[29] With only slightly more specificity, Abu Musab al-Zarqawi, the Jordanian-born leader of the Tanzim Qa'idat al-Jihad fi Bilad al Rafidaya (Organization of Jihad's Base in the Country of the Two Rivers, or QJBR), al Qaeda's operations arm in Iraq, attempted in May 2005 to justify the suicide terrorist attacks in that country that have claimed the lives of Muslims and non-Muslims alike—including in some cases women and children. "There is no doubt," Zarqawi expostulated,

> that Allah commanded us to strike the Kuffar (unbelievers), kill them, and fight them by all means necessary to achieve the goal. The servants of Allah who perform Jihad to elevate the word (laws) of Allah, are permitted to use any and all means necessary to strike the active unbeliever combatants for the purpose of killing them, snatch their souls from their body, cleanse the earth from their abomination, and lift their trial and persecution of the servants of Allah. The goal must be pursued even if the means to accomplish it affect both the intended active fighters and unintended passive ones such as women, children and any other passive category specified by our jurisprudence. This permissibility extends to situations in which Muslims may get killed if they happen to be with or near the intended enemy, and if it is not possible to avoid hitting them or separate them from the intended Kafirs.
>
> Although spilling sacred Muslim blood is a grave offense, it is not only permissible but it is mandated in order to prevent more serious adversity from happening, stalling or abandoning Jihad that is [sic].[30]

The Organizational Dynamics of Terrorist Groups

All terrorists, however, have one trait in common: they live in the future, for that distant—yet imperceptibly close—point in time when they will assuredly triumph over their enemies and attain the ultimate realization of their political destiny. For the religious groups, this future is divinely decreed and the terrorists themselves are specifically anointed to achieve it. The inevitability of their victory is taken for granted, as a 1996 communiqué issued by the Egyptian Gamat al-Islamiya (Islamic Group) reveals. Citing the Qur'an, the document brusquely dismisses even the possibility that its secular opponents might succeed. "They plot and plan and God too plans," it declares, "but the best of planners is God." Therefore the group must faithfully and resolutely "pursue its battle . . . until such time as God would grant victory—just as the Prophet Mohammed did with the Quredish [his most implacable enemies] until God granted victory over Mecca."[31]

For the secular terrorists, too, eventual victory is as inevitable as it is predetermined. Indeed, the innate righteousness of their cause itself assures success. "Our struggle will be long and arduous because the enemy is powerful, well-organised, and well-sustained from abroad," Leila Khaled wrote in her autobiography, published in 1973. "We shall win because we represent the wave of the future . . . because mankind is on our side, and above all because we are determined to achieve victory."[32] Comparatively small in number, limited in capabilities, isolated from society, and dwarfed by both the vast resources of their enemy and the enormity of their task, secular terrorists necessarily function in an inverted reality where existence is defined by the sought-after, ardently pursued future rather than the oppressive, angst-driven, and incomplete present. "You convince yourself that to reach this Utopia," the Red Brigades' Adriana Faranda later recalled of the group's collective mind-set, "it is necessary to pass through the destruction of society which prevents your ideas from being realised."[33] By ignoring the present and literally "soldiering on" despite hardship and adversity, terrorists are able to compensate for their abject weakness and thereby overcome the temporal apathy or hostility of a constituency whom they claim to represent. "We made calculations," Faranda's comrade-in-arms Patrizio Peci explained in his memoirs. "The most pessimistic thought that within twenty years the war would be won, some said within five, ten. All, however, thought that we were living through the most difficult moment, that gradually things would become easier."[34] The left-wing terrorists thus console themselves that the travails and isolation of life underground are but a mere transitory stage on the path to final victory.

The longevity of most modern terrorist groups, however, would suggest otherwise. David Rapoport, for example, estimates that the life expectancy of at least 90 percent of terrorist organizations is less than a year and that nearly half of the ones that make it that far cease to exist within a decade.[35]

Thus the optimistic clarion calls to battle issued by terrorist groups the world over in communiqués, treatises, and other propaganda have a distinctly hollow ring given the grim reality of their organizational life cycles. "NEVER BE DETERRED BY THE ENORMOUS DIMENSIONS OF YOUR OWN GOALS," proclaimed a communiqué issued by the left-wing French terrorist group Direct Action in 1985,[36] yet less than two years later the group had effectively been decapitated by the capture of virtually its entire leadership, and shortly afterward it fell into complete lassitude. Similarly, in 1978 the RB leader, Renato Curio, bragged about a struggle that he envisioned would last forty years, but within a decade even this terrorist organization—for a time one of Europe's most formidable—had collapsed under the weight of arrests and defections.[37]

Some categories of terrorist groups admittedly have better chances of survival—and perhaps success—than others. Historically, although religious movements like the Assassins persisted for nearly two centuries and the Thugs remained active for more than six hundred years, in modern times ethno-nationalist/separatist terrorist groups have typically lasted the longest and been the most successful. Al-Fatah, the Palestinian terrorist organization led by the late Yasir Arafat, for example, was founded in 1957. The PLO itself is now more than forty years old. The Basque group ETA was established in 1959, while the current incarnation of the IRA, formally known as the Provisional Irish Republican Army, is nearly forty years old and is itself the successor of the older official IRA that was founded nearly a century ago and can in turn be traced back to the various Fenian revolutionary brotherhoods that had surfaced periodically since Wolfe Tone's rebellion in 1789. However, except in the immediate postwar era of massive decolonization, success for ethno-nationalist terrorist organizations has rarely involved the actual realization of their stated long-term goals of self-determination or nationhood. More often it has amounted to a string of key tactical victories that have sustained prolonged struggles and breathed new life into faltering—and in some instances, geriatric—terrorist movements.

The resilience of these groups is doubtless a product of the relative ease with which they are able to draw sustenance and support from an existing constituency—namely, the fellow members of their ethno-nationalist group. By contrast, both left- and right-wing terrorist organizations must actively proselytize among the politically aware and radical, though often uncommitted, for recruits and support, thus rendering themselves vulnerable to penetration and compromise. The ethno-nationalists derive a further advantage from their historical longevity by being able to appeal to a col-

lective revolutionary tradition and even at times a predisposition to rebellion. This assures successive terrorist generations both a steady stream of
recruits from their respective communities' youth and a ready pool of sympathizers and supporters among their more nostalgic elders. These groups'
unique ability to replenish their ranks from within already close, tight-knit
communities means that even when a continuing campaign shows signs
of flagging, the torch can be smoothly passed to a new generation. Abu
Iyad, Arafat's intelligence chief, can therefore dismiss as mere ephemeral
impediments the cul-de-sacs and roundabouts that have long hampered
the advance of the Palestinian liberation movement. "Our people will bring
forth a new revolution," he wrote in 1981. "They will engender a movement
much more powerful than ours, better armed and thus more dangerous to
the Zionists. . . . And one day, we will have a country."[38]

The ethno-nationalists' comparative success, however, may have as much
to do with the clarity and tangibility of their envisioned future—the establishment (or reestablishment) of a national homeland from within some
existing country—as with these other characteristics. The articulation of so
concrete and comprehensible a goal is by far the most potent and persuasive rallying cry. It also makes the inevitable victory appear both palpable
and readily attainable, even though the path to it be prolonged and protracted. Few would have doubted Martin McGuinness's 1977 pledge that
the IRA would keep "blattering on until Brits leave,"[39] or Danny Morrison's
declaration twelve years later that "when it is politically costly for the British
to remain in Ireland, they'll go. . . . It won't be triggered until a large number
of British soldiers are killed and that's what's going to happen."[40]

Left-wing terrorist movements, by comparison, appear doubly disadvantaged. Not only do they lack the sizable existing pool of potential recruits
available to most ethno-nationalist groups, but among all the categories of
terrorists they have formulated the least clear and most ill-defined vision
of the future. Prolific and prodigious though their myriad denunciations of
the evils of the militarist, capitalist state may be, precious little information
is forthcoming about its envisioned successor. "That is the most difficult
question for revolutionaries," replied Kozo Okamoto, the surviving member of the three-man Japanese Red Army (JRA) team that staged the 1972
Lod Airport massacre, when asked about the postrevolutionary society that
his group sought to create. "We really do not know what it will be like."[41]
The RAF's Gudrun Ensslin similarly brushed aside all questions about the
group's long-term aims. "As for the state of the future, the time after victory," she once said, "that is not our concern. . . . We build the revolution,
not the socialist model."[42] This inability to articulate coherently, much less

cogently, their future plans may explain why the left-wing terrorists' campaigns have historically been the least effectual.

Even when left-wing terrorists have attempted to conceptualize a concrete vision of the future, their efforts have rarely produced anything more lucid or edifying than verbose disquisitions espousing an idiosyncratic interpretation of Marxist doctrine. "We have applied the Marxist analysis and method to the contemporary scene—not transferred it, but actually applied it," Ensslin wrote in a collection of RAF statements published by the group in 1977 (and subsequently banned by the German government). Yet no further elucidation of the desired result is offered, except the belief that Marxism will be rendered obsolete when the revolution triumphs and the "capitalist system has been abolished."[43] Slightly more reflective is the exposition offered by the American radical Jane Alpert, who in her memoir explains how she and her comrades-in-arms

> believed that the world could be cleansed of all domination and submission, that perception itself could be purified of the division into subject and object, that power playing between nations, sexes, races, ages, between animals and humans, individuals and groups, could be brought to an end. Our revolution would create a universe in which all consciousness was cosmic, in which everyone would share the bliss we knew from acid [LSD], but untainted by fear, possessiveness, sickness, hunger, or the need for a drug to bring happiness.[44]

Nonetheless, this vision comes across as so vague and idyllic as to appear almost completely divorced from reality, an effect, perhaps, of its drug-induced influence. That drugs played a part in the formulation of other leftist terrorist strategies is an interesting, though perhaps exaggerated, sidelight. Baumann, for example, also recounts the centrality of drugs to the would-be revolution. "We said integrate dope into praxis too," he recalled. "No more separate shit, but a total unification around this thing, so that a new person is born out of the struggle."[45] It should be noted, though, that a study commissioned by the Italian secret services in the 1970s discovered (somewhat counterintuitively) that right-wing terrorists were in fact more likely to abuse[46] and, indeed, to use drugs than their left-wing counterparts. Two Italian psychiatrists conducting a related study attributed this tendency to the rightists' innate psychological instability, at least compared to Italian left-wing terrorists. "In the right-wing terrorism," wrote Drs. Franco Ferracuti and Francesco Bruno, "the individual terrorists are frequently psychopatho-logical and the ideology is empty; in left-wing terrorism, ideology is outside of reality and terrorists are more normal and fanatical."[47]

But it would be a grave error to dismiss the left-wing terrorists as either totally feckless and frivolous or completely devoid of introspection or seriousness of purpose. For them, the future was simply too large and abstract a concept to comprehend; instead, action—terrorist attacks specifically designed to effect the revolution—was embraced as a far more rewarding pursuit. Accordingly, it was Fanon, and not Marx, who arguably exerted the greater influence. For example, Susan Stern, a member of the 1970s-era American left-wing terrorist group the Weathermen, recalled the dynamic tension between thought and action that permeated the group and affected all internal debate. "Once we tore down capitalism, who would empty the garbage, and teach the children and who would decide that?" she and her comrades would often consider.

> Would the world be Communist? Would the Third World control it? Would all whites die? Would all sex perverts die? Who would run the prisons—would there be prisons? Endless questions like these were *raised* by the Weathermen, but we didn't have the answers. *And we were tired of trying to wait until we understood everything* [emphasis added].[48]

The RAF's seminal treatise, "Sur la Concepcíon de la Guerilla Urbaine," reflects the same frustration. Quoting fellow revolutionary Eldridge Cleaver, a leader of the Black Panther Party, an African American radical political organization active during the 1960s, it states: "For centuries and generations we have contemplated and examined the shit from all sides. 'Me, I'm convinced that most things which happen in this country don't need to be analysed much longer,' said Cleaver. The RAF put the words of Cleaver into practice."[49]

Indeed, all terrorists are driven by this burning impatience, coupled with an unswerving belief in the efficacy of violence. The future that they look forward to is neither temporal nor born of the natural progression of mankind; rather, it is contrived and shaped, forged and molded, and ultimately determined and achieved by violence. "What use was there in writing memoranda?" Begin rhetorically inquired to explain the Irgun's decision to resume its revolt in 1944.

> What value in speeches? . . . No, there was no other way. If we did not fight we should be destroyed. To fight was the only way to salvation.
>
> When Descartes said: "I think, therefore, I am," he uttered a very profound thought. But there are times in the history of peoples when

thought alone does not prove their existence. . . . There are times when everything in you cries out: your very self-respect as a human being lies in your resistance to evil.

We fight, therefore we are![50]

Thirty years later, Leila Khaled similarly invoked the primacy of action over talk and bullets over words: "We must act, not just talk and memorise the arguments against Zionism," she counseled.[51] This view was echoed by Yoyes, an ETA terrorist who lost faith in the endless promises that "independence can be won by peaceful means. It's all a lie. . . . The only possibility we have of gaining our liberty is through violence."[52] As the former neo-Nazi Ingo Hasselbach recalled of his own experience, "The time for legal work and patience was through. The only thing to do was to turn our *Kameradschaft* into a real terrorist organization."[53]

For some terrorists, however, the desire for action can lead to an obsession with violence itself. Abu Nidal, for example, was once known and admired for his "fiery and unbending nationalism," whereas today he is recalled and almost universally disdained as little more than an "outlaw and killer."[54] Eamon Collins described a similar transformation in his PIRA-gunman cousin Mickey, who, Collins realized, had gradually "lost any sense of the wider perspective, and was just obsessively absorbed by the details of the next killing."[55] Andreas Baader is perhaps a different type altogether. From the very start of the RAF's campaign, he never wavered from his conviction that the terrorist's only "language is action."[56] Baumann, who knew Baader well, remembers the RAF's founder as a "weapons maniac, [who] later developed an almost sexual relationship with pistols (the Heckler and Koch type in particular)."[57] Indeed, according to Baader himself, "Fucking and shooting [were] the same thing."[58] Unquestionably a man of action and not words, he preferred, in the terrorist vernacular, "direct actions"—bank robberies, vandalism and arson, bombings, and armed attacks—to debate and discourse. "Let's go, then!" was Baader's immediate response, for example, when his lover and co-leader Ensslin suggested that the group bomb an American military base in retaliation for the U.S. Air Force's mining of North Vietnam's Haiphong harbor in 1972. Despite being the leading figure of an organization dedicated to achieving profound political change, he had absolutely no time for politics, which he derisively dismissed as a load of "shit."[59] Baader's whole approach can be summed up in the advice he gave to a wavering RAF recruit. "Either you come along [and join the revolution and fight]," he said, "or you stay forever an empty chatterbox."[60]

Although Baader may perhaps be an extreme example of this phenom-enon, action is the undeniable cynosure for all terrorists—perhaps even more so, the thrill and heady excitement that accompany it. Far more of Peci's 222-page account of his life as a Red Brigadist, for instance, is devoted to recounting in obsessive detail the types of weapons (and their technical specifications) used on particular RB operations and which group members actually did the shooting than to elucidating the organization's ideological aims and political goals.[61] Baumann is particularly candid about the cathar-tic relief that an operation brought to a small group of individuals living underground, in close proximity to one another, constantly on the run and fearful of arrest and betrayal. The real stress, he said, came from life in the group—not from the planning and execution of attacks.[62] Others, like Stern, Collins, the RAF's Silke Maier-Witt and the RB's Susana Ronconi, are even more explicit about the "rush" and the sense of power and accomplishment they derived from the violence they inflicted. "Nothing in my life had ever been this exciting," Stern enthused as she drifted deeper into terrorism.[63] Collins similarly recalls how he led an "action-packed existence" during his six years in the IRA, "living each day with the excitement of feeling I was playing a part in taking on the Orange State."[64] For Maier-Witt, the intoxi-cating allure of action was sufficient to overcome the misgivings she had about the murder of Schleyer's four bodyguards in order to kidnap the man himself. "At the time I felt the brutality of that action. . . . [But it] was a kind of excitement too because something had happened. The real thing," she consoled herself, had "started now."[65] Ronconi is the most expansive and incisive in analyzing the terrorist's psychology. "The main thing was that you felt you were able to influence the world about you, instead of experi-encing it passively," thereby combining intrinsic excitement with profound satisfaction. "It was this ability to make an impact on the reality of everyday life that was important," she explained, "and obviously still is important."[66]

For the terrorist, success in having this impact is most often measured in terms of the amount of publicity and attention received. Newsprint and air-time are thus the coin of the realm in the terrorists' mind-set, the only tangi-ble or empirical means they have by which to gauge their success and assess their progress. In this respect, little distinction or discrimination is made between good and bad publicity. The satisfaction of simply being noticed is often regarded as sufficient reward. "The only way to achieve results," boasted the JRA in its communiqué claiming credit for the 1972 Lod Airport massacre, in which twenty-six people were slain (including sixteen Puerto Rican Christians on a pilgrimage to the Holy Land), "is to shock the world right down to its socks."[67] The archterrorist Carlos "the Jackal" reportedly meticulously clipped and had translated newspaper accounts about him and his deeds.[68] "The more I'm talked about," Carlos once explained to his terrorist colleague—later turned apostate—Hans Joachim Klein, "the more dangerous I appear. That's all the better for me."[69] Similarly, when Ramzi Ahmed Yousef, the alleged mastermind behind the 1993 bombing of New York's World Trade Center, was apprehended in Pakistan two years later, police found in his possession two remote-control explosive devices, along with a collection of newspaper articles detailing his exploits.[70]

For Carlos and Yousef as for many other terrorists, however, this equation of publicity and attention with success and self-gratification has the effect of locking them into an unrelenting upward spiral of violence in order to keep the eye of the media and the public on them.[71] Yousef, for example, planned to follow the World Trade Center bombing with the assassinations of Pope John Paul II and the prime minister of Pakistan, Benazir Bhutto, and the nearly simultaneous in-flight bombings of eleven U.S. passenger airliners. Klein in fact describes escalation as a "force of habit" among terrorists, an intrinsic product of their perennial need for validation, which in turn is routinely assessed and appraised on the basis of media coverage. The effect is that terrorists today often feel driven to undertake ever more dramatic and destructively lethal deeds in order to achieve the same effect that a less ambitious or bloody action may have had in the past. To their minds at least, the media and the public have become progressively inured or desensitized to the seemingly endless litany of successive terrorist incidents; thus a continuous upward ratcheting of the violence is required in order to retain media and public interest and attention. As Klein once observed, the "more violent things get, the more people will respect you. The greater the chance of achieving your demands."[72] Timothy McVeigh, the convicted Oklahoma City bomber, seemed to be offering the same explanation when responding to his attorney's question whether he could not have achieved the same effect of drawing attention to his grievances against the U.S. government without killing anyone. "That would not have gotten the point across," McVeigh reportedly replied. "We needed a body count to make our point."[73] In this respect, although the Murrah Building bombing was doubtless planned well in advance of the portentously symbolic date of April 19 deliberately chosen by McVeigh, he may nonetheless have felt driven to surpass in terms of death and destruction the previous month's dramatic and more exotic nerve gas attack on the Tokyo subway in order to guarantee that his attack too received the requisite media coverage and public attention.

The terrorists' ability to attract—and, moreover, to continue to attract—attention is most often predicated on the success of their attacks. The most feared terrorists are arguably those who are the most successful in translating thought into action: ruthless and efficient, demonstrating that they are able to make good on their threats and back up their demands with violence. This organizational imperative to succeed, however, in turn imposes on some terrorist groups an operational conservatism that makes an ironic contrast with their political radicalism, decreeing that they adhere to an established modus operandi that, to their minds at least, minimizes the chances of failure and maximizes the chances of success. "The main point is to select targets where success is 100% assured," the doyen of modern international terrorism, George Habash, once explained.[74] For the terrorist, therefore, solid training, sound planning, good intelligence, and technological competence are the essential prerequisites for a successful operation. "I learned how to be an effective IRA member," Collins reminisced about his two-year training and induction period: "how to gather intelligence, how to set up operations, how to avoid mistakes."[75] Similarly, an unidentified American left-wing radical who specialized in bombings described in a 1970 interview the procedures and extreme care that governed all his group's operations. The "first decision," he said, is

> political—determining appropriate and possible targets. Once a set of targets is decided on, they must be reconnoitered and information gathered on how to approach the targets, how to place the bomb, how the security of the individuals and the explosives is to be protected. Then the time is chosen and a specific target. Next there was a preliminary run-through—in our case a number of practice sessions. . . . The discipline during the actual operation is not to alter any of the agreed-upon plans or to discuss the action until everyone's safe within the group again. Our desire is not just for one success but to continue as long as possible.[76]

Good intelligence, therefore, is as critical for the success of an operation as it is for the terrorists' own survival. Perhaps for this reason, bin Laden and his minions spent five long years planning and plotting the 1998 suicide bombings of the U.S. embassies in Nairobi, Kenya, and Dar es Salaam, Tanzania.[77] The seaborne attack on the USS *Cole* took them two years to plan, while the monumental operations that would become 9/11 began to take shape as early as 1995, when KSM first began to speculate about crashing aircraft into the World Trade Center's twin towers and the Central Intelligence Agency headquarters in Langley, Virginia.[78] Indeed, *Mu'askar al-Battar* (*Camp al-Battar*) magazine, for instance, published multiple special issues such as "Covert Work Groups," "Intelligence: How to Set-up an Intelligence

Network," "Outlines for Planning a Surveillance Operation," and "Military Sciences: The Planning of Operations." Typical of detailed instruction provided is guidance on how the

> mujahideen need a strong Islamic Intelligence apparatus in order to counter the dangers that surround their secret operations in towns. . . . The members of this group must be chosen with extreme care . . . [and] all members [must] be trained in the gathering of field intelligence by all methods, in the writing of intelligence reports, in photography (still and video) and in the correct evaluation of information found in the filed (the surveillance site) . . . [so] that if security is compromised, perhaps by the arrest of a cell member, that the remaining cell member are not endangered [sic].[79]

An almost Darwinian principle of natural selection also seems to affect terrorist organizations, whereby (as noted above) every new terrorist generation learns from its predecessors, becoming smarter, tougher, and more difficult to capture or eliminate. In this respect, terrorists also analyze the "lessons" to be drawn from mistakes made by former comrades who have been either killed or apprehended. Press accounts, judicial indictments, courtroom testimony, and trial transcripts are meticulously culled for information on security force tactics and methods, which is then absorbed by surviving group members. The third generation of the RAF that emerged in the late 1980s is a classic example of this phenomenon. According to a senior German official, group members routinely studied "every court case against them to discover their weak spots." Having learned about the techniques used against them by the authorities from testimony presented by law enforcement personnel in open court (in some instances having been deliberately questioned on these matters by sympathetic attorneys), the terrorists are consequently able to undertake the requisite countermeasures to avoid detection. For example, learning that the German police could usually obtain fingerprints from the bottom of toilet seats or the inside of refrigerators, surviving RAF members began to apply a special ointment to their fingers that, after drying, prevented fingerprints and thus thwarted their identification and incrimination.[80] As a spokesperson for the Bundeskriminalamt (BKA or Federal Investigation Department) lamented in the months immediately preceding the RAF's unilateral declaration of a cease-fire in April 1992, the "'Third Generation' learnt a lot from the mistakes of its predecessors—and about how the police works. . . . They now know how to operate very carefully."[81] Indeed, according to a former member of the group, Peter-Jürgen Brock, now serving a life sentence for murder, the RAF before the cease-fire had "reached maximum efficiency."[82]

Similar accolades have also been bestowed on the IRA. At the end of his tour of duty in 1992 as general officer commanding British forces in Northern Ireland, General Sir John Wilsey described the IRA as "an absolutely formidable enemy. The essential attributes of their leaders are better than ever before. Some of their operations are brilliant in terrorist terms."[83] By this time, too, even the IRA's once comparatively unsophisticated loyalist terrorist counterparts had absorbed the lessons of their own past mistakes and had consciously emulated the IRA to become disquietingly more "professional" as well. One senior Royal Ulster Constabulary (RUC) officer noted this change in the loyalist terrorists' capabilities, observing in 1991 that they too were increasingly "running their operations from small cells, on a need to know basis. They have cracked down on loose talk. They have learned how to destroy forensic evidence. And if you bring them in for questioning, they say nothing."[84]

Finally, the pre-9/11 al Qaeda also evidenced the absorption of "lessons" from previous experience in order to help its operatives blend in in Western environments and avoid attracting attention. Manuals found in the movement's training camps in Afghanistan purported to provide a list of "dos and don'ts" that amounted to a "Tips for the Traveling Terrorist" list. Included among the proffered advice were such pointers as:

- Don't wear short pants that show socks when you're standing up. The pants should cover the socks, because intelligence authorities know that fundamentalists don't wear long pants. . . .
- Underwear should be the normal type that people wear, not anything that shows you're a fundamentalist.
- Not long before traveling—especially from Khartoum—the person should always wear socks and shoes to [get] rid of cracks [in the feet that come from extended barefoot walking], which take about a week to cure. . . .
- You should differentiate between men and women's perfume. If you use women's perfume, you are in trouble.[85]

More recently, this learning process is evident in the operational tradecraft of the bombers responsible for the simultaneous explosions that tore through three London subway trains and a bus on July 7, 2005. The attacks on mass transit during the morning rush hour in London have inevitably been compared with the similar incident involving the bombing of four commuter trains in Madrid, Spain, on March 11, 2004, that killed 191 people. According to counterterrorism experts, a pattern has emerged whereby "radical cells learn from each attack and refine their operations, making preventive measures and police investigations more difficult." As one German police officer lamented, "Terrorists discover our tactics and respond. The competition is continuous."[86]

The Technological Treadmill

Finally, success for the terrorists is dependent on their ability to keep one step ahead of not only the authorities but also counterterrorist technology. The terrorist group's fundamental organizational imperative to act also drives this persistent search for new ways to overcome or circumvent or defeat governmental security and countermeasures. The IRA's own relentless quest to pierce the armor protecting both the security forces in Northern Ireland and the most senior government officials in England illustrates the professional evolution and increasing operational sophistication of a terrorist group. The first generation of early-1970s IRA devices were often little more than crude anti-personnel bombs, consisting of a handful of roofing nails wrapped around a lump of plastic explosive and detonated simply by lighting a fuse. Time bombs from the same era were hardly more sophisticated. Typically, they were constructed from a few sticks of dynamite and commercial detonators stolen from construction sites or rock quarries attached to ordinary battery-powered alarm clocks. Neither device was terribly reliable and often put the bomber at considerable risk. The process of placing and actually lighting the first type of device carried with it the potential to attract undesired attention while affording the bomber little time to effect the attack and make good his or her escape. Although the second type of device was designed to mitigate precisely this danger, its timing and detonation mechanism was often so crude that accidental or premature explosions were not infrequent, thus causing some terrorists inadvertently to kill themselves—what was known in Belfast as "own goals." About 120 IRA members were killed in this way between 1969 and 1996.[87]

In hopes of obviating, or at least reducing, these risks, the IRA's bomb makers invented a means of detonating bombs from a safe distance using radio controls for model aircraft, which could be purchased at hobby shops. Scientists and engineers working in the scientific research and development division of the British Ministry of Defence (MoD) in turn developed a system of electronic countermeasures and jamming techniques for the army that effectively thwarted this means of attack. However, rather than abandon the tactic completely, the IRA began to search for a solution to the problem. In contrast to the state-of-the art laboratories, huge budgets, and academic credentials of their government counterparts, the IRA's own "R&D" department toiled in cellars beneath cross-border safe houses and the back rooms of urban tenements for five years before devising a network of sophisticated electronic switches for their bombs that would ignore or bypass the army's electronic countermeasures. Once again, the MoD scientists returned to their laboratories, emerging with a new system of electronic scanners able to detect radio emissions the moment the radio is switched on—and, critically, just tens of seconds before the bomber can actually transmit the detonation signal. The almost infinitesimal window of time provided by this "early warning" of impending attack was just sufficient to allow army technicians to activate a series of additional electronic measures to neutralize the transmission signal and render detonation impossible.

For a time, this mechanism proved effective. But then the IRA discovered a means to outwit even this countermeasure. Using radar detectors like those used by motorists in the United States to evade speed traps, in 1991 the group's bomb makers fabricated a detonating system that can be triggered by the same type of handheld radar gun used by police throughout the world to catch speeding drivers. Since the radar gun can be aimed at its target before being switched on, and the signal that it transmits is nearly instantaneous, no practical means currently exists either to detect or to intercept the transmission signal. Moreover, shortly after making this breakthrough the IRA's "R&D" units developed yet another means to detonate bombs, using a photo-flash "slave" unit that can be triggered from a distance of up to eight hundred meters by a flash of light. This device, which sells for between sixty and seventy pounds, is used by commercial photographers to produce simultaneous flashes during photo shoots. The IRA bombers attach the unit to the detonating system on a bomb and then simply activate it with an ordinary commercially available flashgun.

Not surprisingly, therefore, the IRA bombers earned a reputation for their innovative expertise, adaptability, and cunning. "There are some very bright people around," the British Army's chief ammunitions technical officer (CATO) in Northern Ireland commented in 1992. "I would rate them very highly for improvisation. IRA bombs are very well made."[88] A similar accolade was offered that same year by the staff officer of the British Army's 321 Explosives and Ordnance Disposal Company: "We are dealing with the first division," he said. "I don't think there is any organization in the world as cunning as the IRA. They have had twenty years at it and they have learned from their experience. We have a great deal of respect for their skills . . . not as individuals, but their skills."[89] While not yet nearly as good as the IRA, the province's loyalist terrorist groups have themselves been on a "learning curve" with regard to bomb-making and are said to have become increasingly adept in the construction, concealment, and surreptitious placement of bombs.

In certain circumstances, even attacks that are not successful in conventionally understood military terms of casualties inflicted or assets destroyed can still be counted a success for the terrorists provided that they are technologically daring enough to garner media and public attention.[90] Although the IRA failed to kill the prime minister, Margaret Thatcher, at the Conservative Party's 1984 conference in Brighton, the technological ingenuity of the attempt, involving the bomb's placement at the conference site weeks before the event and its detonation timing device powered by a computer microchip, nonetheless succeeded in capturing the world's headlines and providing the IRA with a platform from which to warn Mrs. Thatcher and all other British leaders: "Today we were unlucky, but remember we only have to be lucky once—you will have to be lucky always."[91] Similarly, although the remote-control mortar attack staged by the IRA on No. 10 Downing Street as Mrs. Thatcher's successor, John Major, and his cabinet met at the height of the 1991 Gulf War failed to hit its intended target, it nonetheless successfully elbowed the war out of the limelight and shone renewed media attention on the terrorists, their cause, and their impressive ability to strike at the nerve center of the British government even at a time of heightened security. "The Provies are always that step ahead of you," a senior RUC officer has commented. "They are very innovative."[92] Although the technological mastery employed by the IRA is arguably unique among terrorist organizations, experience has nonetheless demonstrated repeatedly that when confronted by new security measures, terrorists will seek to identify and exploit new vulnerabilities, adjusting their means of attack accordingly and often carrying on despite the obstacles placed in their path.

Conclusion

"All politics is a struggle for power," wrote C. Wright Mills, and "the ultimate kind of power is violence."[93] Terrorism is where politics and violence intersect in the hope of delivering power. All terrorism involves the quest for power: power to dominate and coerce, to intimidate and control, and ultimately to effect fundamental political change. Violence (or the threat of violence) is thus the sine qua non of terrorists, who are unswervingly convinced that only through violence can their cause triumph and their long-term political aims be attained. Terrorists therefore plan their operations in a manner that will shock, impress, and intimidate, ensuring that their acts are sufficiently daring and violent to capture the attention of the media and, in turn, of the public and government as well. Often erroneously seen as indiscriminate or senseless, terrorism is actually a very deliberate and planned application of violence. It may be represented as a concatenation of five individual processes, designed to achieve, sequentially, the following key objectives:

1. *Attention.* Through dramatic, attention-riveting acts of violence, terrorists seek to focus attention on themselves and their causes through the publicity they receive, most often from news media coverage.
2. *Acknowledgment.* Having attracted this attention, and thrust some otherwise previously ignored or hitherto forgotten cause onto the state's—or, often more desirably, the international community's—agenda, terrorists seek to translate their newfound notoriety into acknowledgment of (and perhaps even sympathy and support for) their cause.
3. *Recognition.* Terrorists attempt to capitalize on the interest and acknowledgment that their violent acts have generated by obtaining recognition of their rights (i.e., acceptance of the justification of their cause) and of their particular organization as *the* spokesperson of the constituency whom the terrorists purport to, or in some cases actually do, represent.
4. *Authority.* Armed with this recognition, terrorists seek the authority to effect the changes in government and/or society that lie at the heart of their movement's struggle. This may involve a change in government or in the entire state structure, or redistribution of wealth, readjustment of geographical boundaries, assertion of minority rights, imposition of theocratic rule, etc.
5. *Governance.* Having acquired authority, terrorists seek to consolidate their direct and complete control over the state, their homeland and/or their people.

While some terrorist movements have been successful in achieving the first three objectives, rarely in modern times has any group attained the last two. Nonetheless, all terrorists exist and function in hopes of reaching this ultimate end. For them, the future rather than the present defines their reality. Indeed, they can console themselves that in 1987 the British prime minister, Margaret Thatcher, said of the African National Congress, "Anyone who thinks it is going to run the government in South Africa is living in cloud-cuckoo land."[94] Exactly ten years after that remark was uttered, Queen Elizabeth II greeted President Nelson Mandela on his first official state visit to London.

Chapter 9

Terrorism Today and Tomorrow

Terrorism today is dominated by several different trends that in recent years have become increasingly intertwined—with often unsettling consequences. The reemergence in the early 1980s of terrorism motivated by a religious imperative set in motion profound changes in the nature, motivations, and capabilities of terrorists that are still unfolding. The proliferation during the 1990s of so-called amateur terrorists (with little or no formal connection to an existing terrorist group) continued this process, transforming terrorism into the arguably more diffuse and amorphous phenomenon that it indisputably has now become. Meanwhile, the end of the cold war and the demise of the Soviet bloc did not end state sponsorship of terrorism, and the emergence of a professional subculture of terrorist "guns for hire" added yet another destabilizing dimension to a phenomenon that arguably was becoming increasingly more difficult to neatly categorize. This concluding chapter discusses some of the implications of these trends within the context of the rise and persistence of both religious and state-sponsored terrorism, in an effort to shed some light on likely future developments, including potential terrorist use of weapons of mass destruction. It also considers the current and future trajectory of the threat posed by al Qaeda, affiliated and associated

movements, and the independent network of sympathizers and supporters it has spawned and inspired.

The Emergence of Modern State-Sponsored Terrorism

Certainly, governments have long engaged in various types of illicit,
clandestine activities—including the systematic use of terror—against their
enemies, both domestic and foreign. The Nazis' victimization of Jews, gyp-
sies, communists and homosexuals, political rivals, and other "enemies of
the state" in Germany and the Serbian military's intimate involvement in
fomenting anti-Hapsburg unrest in Bosnia on the eve of the First World
War are two clear examples of past state sponsorship of or, indeed, outright use of terrorism. But what sets these (and many other historical) cases
apart from the type of state-sponsored terrorism that has emerged since
the early 1980s is the way in which some governments have now come to
embrace terrorism as a deliberate instrument of foreign policy: a cost-effective means of waging war covertly, through the use of surrogate warriors or
"guns for hire"—terrorists.

The pivotal event in the emergence of state-sponsored terrorism as a
weapon of the state and an instrument of foreign policy was doubtless
the seizure in November 1979 of fifty-two American hostages at the U.S.
embassy in Tehran by a group of militant Iranian "students." For 444 days
these so-called students—who claimed to have acted independently, without government support or encouragement—held the world's most powerful country at bay. Throughout that protracted episode they focused
unparalleled worldwide media attention on both themselves and their anti-
American cause, ultimately costing an American president his reelection
to office. As events would later show, this incident was only the beginning
of an increasingly serious and extensive state-sponsored terrorist campaign directed by the Khomeini regime in Iran against the United States
as well as other Western countries. Its lessons, moreover, were absorbed
not only by Iran's clerical rulers, who sought to expunge Western (and
especially American) influence from the Middle East, but by the leaders of
the region's other "pariah states"—Libya, Syria, and Iraq—and by foreign
governments elsewhere. Acts of violence, perpetrated by terrorists secretly
working for governments, were shown to be a relatively inexpensive and,
if executed properly, potentially risk-free means of anonymously attacking
stronger enemies and thereby avoiding the threat of international punishment or reprisal.

For the terrorist, the benefits of state sponsorship were even greater. Such a relationship appreciably enhanced the capabilities and operational capacity of otherwise limited terrorist groups, placing at their disposal the resources of an established nation-state's entire diplomatic, military, and intelligence apparatus and thus greatly facilitating planning and intelligence. The logistical support provided by states assured the terrorists of otherwise unobtainable luxuries, such as the use of diplomatic pouches for the transport of weapons and explosives, false identification in the form of genuine passports, and the use of embassies and other diplomatic facilities as safe houses or staging bases. State sponsorship also afforded terrorists greater training opportunities; thus some groups were transformed into entities more akin to elite commando units than to the stereotypical conspiratorial cell of anarchists wielding Molotov cocktails or radicals manufacturing crude pipe bombs. Finally, terrorists were often paid handsomely for their services, turning hitherto financially destitute entities into well-endowed organizations with investment profiles and healthy balance sheets.

For all these reasons, it was not necessary for the state-sponsored terrorist to identify with his patron's cause. Nor did he necessarily have to be the rabid ideologue, religious zealot, or extreme nationalist common to ideologically and religiously motivated groups or ethno-nationalist/separatist organizations. All the state-sponsored terrorist needed to do was to be willing to perform a service for a price, as an independent mercenary—a mere "hired gun." The Abu Nidal Organization (ANO) is a prominent case in point. This group, founded and led by the Palestinian terrorist Sabri al-Banna, had been variously employed by Syria, Iraq, and Libya (three countries that have been on the U.S. State Department's list of state sponsors of terrorism since the list was established in 1979).[1] As the group has profited from its mercenary role, so it has progressively relinquished its original revolutionary/political motivations in favor of activities devoted almost entirely to making money. The ANO, accordingly, reputedly amassed a considerable fortune: initially through its "for hire" terrorist activities, but then through exploiting its gains from these deals in shrewd commercial and real estate investments, including the profitable operation of a multinational arms trading company that had been based in Poland. In 1988 the ANO's assets were said to be worth an estimated $400 million. Given the vast profits involved, it is not surprising that the group's financial portfolio is administered by a separate "finance directorate" within the organization—with Abu Nidal himself at its head.[2]

Even supposedly ideologically "pure" Marxist-Leninist organizations, like the Japanese Red Army (JRA), built up a fortune during the 1980s through commissioned terrorism. The JRA, which has been based in Lebanon's Bekaa valley since its founding in 1971 by a former Meiji University student named Fusako Shigenobu, has in fact always sought outside patrons. Initially, the PFLP filled this role, with the JRA performing operations—such as the 1972 suicide machine-gun and hand-grenade attack on Israel's Lod Airport, in which twenty-six people were killed and eighty others wounded—on the PFLP's behalf. Later, the group was taken under the wing of the world's legendary master terrorist, Carlos "the Jackal," for whom it carried out operations including the takeover of the French embassy in The Hague in 1974 and the bombing that same year of a popular discotheque on rue St. Germain in Paris, where two people were killed and thirty-five injured. In 1986 Shigenobu decided to diversify the JRA's income stream still further by cutting a lucrative deal with Libyan leader Muammar Qaddafi. Only a few months earlier, U.S. Air Force jets had bombed Tripoli and Benghazi in retaliation for Libya's alleged involvement in a terrorist attack on a West Berlin nightclub popular with American GIs that had killed two people and wounded some two hundred others. Qaddafi was desperate for revenge; fearing further American retaliatory air strikes were he to take direct action, he turned to the JRA for help. The group was only too happy to oblige, adopting the alias Anti-Imperialist International Brigades (AIIB) as a cover for those operations executed specifically on Libya's behalf.

The JRA mounted the first AIIB attack in June 1986, targeting the American and Japanese embassies in Jakarta, Indonesia, with remote-controlled mortars positioned in a nearby hotel room. The following year the group "commemorated" the first anniversary of the U.S. air strike with an identical attack on three U.S. diplomatic facilities in Madrid. They struck again in June, detonating a car bomb outside the U.S. embassy in Rome, and shortly afterward launched rocket attacks against both the same target and the British embassy nearby. To mark the second anniversary of the 1986 U.S. air strike, the JRA/AIIB initiated its most ambitious plan: simultaneous attacks against American military targets in the United States and Europe. The American arm of the plan, however, went seriously awry a month before the attacks were to commence when a veteran JRA terrorist, Yu Kikumura, was arrested by a New Jersey state police officer in March while en route to New York. In the backseat of Kikumura's car the police officer found several hollowed-out fire extinguishers, packed with explosive material and roofing nails. Kikumura had planned to place these crude but effective anti-personnel bombs outside a U.S. Navy recruiting station on Thirty-fourth Street in Manhattan.[3] Kikumura was subsequently convicted and sentenced to thirty years in prison.

The other JRA/AIIB attacks scheduled for that day in Europe, however, went off almost as planned. In Naples a car bomb exploded outside a U.S. military club, killing five people and wounding seventeen others, while in Spain the group bombed a U.S. air base. Then, in July, the AIIB attacks suddenly ended, with a failed remote-controlled rocket attack on the U.S. embassy in Madrid. Thereafter, the JRA itself mysteriously ceased active terrorist operations, its twenty or so members presumably having "retired" to the group's base in the Bekaa valley or to its sanctuary in North Korea to live off the sizable nest egg that Shigenobu had accumulated for herself and her followers.

State-sponsored terrorism has had a profound and more broad impact on patterns of terrorism. Since state-sponsored terrorism is geared less to obtaining publicity than to pursuing specific foreign policy objectives by covertly bringing pressure to bear on the sponsor's opponents through acts of violence, it operates under fewer constraints than does ordinary terrorism. In addition, because state-sponsored terrorists do not depend on the local population for support, they need not concern themselves with the risk of alienating popular support or provoking a public backlash. Thus the state-sponsored terrorist and his patron can engage in acts of violence that are typically more destructive and bloodier than those carried out by groups acting on their own behalf. Indeed, given the enhanced resources that state-supported groups can command, it is not surprising to find that identifiable state-sponsored terrorist attacks during the 1980s were overall eight times more lethal than those carried out by groups without state support or assistance. Among them were:

- the April 1983 suicide car bomb explosion outside the U.S. embassy in Beirut that killed 69 people and was claimed by Islamic Jihad (Islamic Holy War), a cover name used by Iranian-backed Lebanese Shi'a terrorists;
- the simultaneous suicide truck bombings of the U.S. Marine headquarters at Beirut International Airport and the French paratroop headquarters in that city, which killed 241 Marines and 58 paratroopers, respectively, in October 1983, and for which Islamic Jihad also took credit, boasting in a communiqué how "two martyr *mujahidin* [holy warriors] set out to inflict upon the U.S. Administration an utter defeat not experienced since Vietnam, and a similar one upon the French Administration";[4]
- the identical attack carried out by Islamic Jihad on the Israeli military government building in Sidon the following month that resulted in the deaths of 67 people;

• the coordinated car bomb attacks in Karachi, Pakistan, carried out by agents of Afghanistan's secret intelligence service, WAD, in July 1987, killing 72 people and wounding more than 250 others;
• the bomb placed by two North Korean agents on a Korean Air Lines plane en route from Baghdad to Seoul that killed all 115 people on board in November 1987;
• the sabotage of a munitions dump in Islamabad, Pakistan, in April 1988 by Afghani WAD operatives that killed more than 100 people and wounded 1,100;
• the midair explosion aboard Pan Am Flight 103 in December 1988 over Lockerbie, Scotland, that claimed the lives of all 259 passengers as well as of 11 people on the ground and has been linked to two Libyan intelligence agents, acting not only with official Libyan state sanction but possibly at the behest of Iran as well;
• the in-flight bombing of a French UTA passenger jet over Chad in August 1989 that killed 171 people and was claimed by Islamic Jihad.

State-sponsored terrorism has also been employed on a far more discriminating scale to stifle external dissent. Exiled opposition figures, political dissidents, human rights activists, journalists, political cartoonists, and others have been intimidated and, in some instances, murdered at the behest of various foreign governments. In one especially notorious case, Bulgarian agents used a poison-tipped umbrella to murder dissident exile Georgi Markov on a London bridge in 1978.[5] Libyan, Iranian, and Iraqi agents have also allegedly carried out operations against opponents of their respective regimes residing in the United States, France, Germany, Italy, Switzerland, Austria, South Africa, and the United Kingdom. In 1991, for example, an Iranian "hit team," using diplomatic cover, assassinated former prime minister and outspoken critic of the Khomeini regime Shahpur Baktiar in Paris; and since 1989 Salman Rushdie, the Pakistani-born British author of *The Satanic Verses*, has lived under the fatwa (religious edict) death sentence imposed on him and his publishers for blasphemy by the Ayatollah Khomeini, in pursuit of which a group of Iranian clerics have offered a $2.5 million bounty to whoever fulfills the ayatollah's decree. Thus far, the book's Japanese translator has been stabbed to death, its Norwegian publisher shot, and its Italian translator knifed, while Rushdie himself continues to lead a life on the run, protected around the clock by Scotland Yard's Special Branch at a cost to the British taxpayer of more than one million pounds, as of 1997.[6] The most serious—and daring—state-sponsored terrorist incident of the 1980s was the attempt on the life of Pope John Paul II as he greeted the crowd gathered in St. Peter's Square on May 13, 1981. Although a young Turkish terrorist, Mehmet Ali Agca, was apprehended on the spot and subsequently convicted of the attack, it is widely believed that the Bulgarian secret service was behind the assassination plot—allegedly acting on instructions from KGB head and later premier of the Soviet Union Yuri Andropov.[7]

A Persistent Phenomenon

Today, state sponsorship of terrorism continues unabated. In 2004, for example, the U.S. State Department designated six countries as terrorism sponsors: Cuba, Iran, Libya, North Korea, Sudan, and Syria. With the exception of Sudan, which was added in 1993, and Iraq, which was removed in 2004,[8] each of these countries has remained on the list of terrorism's patron states for more than a decade. The reason, as noted above, is that neither economic sanctions nor military reprisals have proved completely successful in effecting positive changes to these countries' policies on terrorism. Even seasoned U.S. government counterterrorist analysts are somewhat dismissive of their effects. A high-level discussion paper circulated within the American intelligence community in 1996, for instance, noted:

In theory, the threat or imposition of embargoes and sanctions would appear to be a powerful leveraging tool in the conduct of foreign relations between countries. In practice, no state sponsor of international terrorism against which the U.S. has enacted an embargo or sanctions has renounced it[s] role of sponsorship or denounced terrorism as a tool of its foreign policy. Nor has any state once placed on the state sponsors list ever been removed.[9]

Since that time, of course, Iraq has been dropped from the list—but as the result of invasion and regime change. More-limited military reprisals against state sponsors of terrorism have arguably not proved effective; worse still, in some respects they have been counterproductive. For example, the aforementioned 1986 U.S. air strike against Libya is frequently cited as proof of the effectiveness of military retaliation; yet, rather than deterring the Qaddafi regime from engaging in state-sponsored terrorism, it appears that it may have had precisely the opposite effect. In the first place, far from stopping Libyan-backed terrorism, the U.S. air strike goaded the Libyan dictator to undertake even more serious and heinous acts of terrorism against the United States and its citizens. Indeed, after a brief lull, Libya not only resumed but actually increased its international terrorist activities. According to the RAND Terrorism Incident Database, at least fifteen identifiable state-sponsored terrorist incidents in 1987 and eight in 1988—including the previously cited "for hire" incidents perpetrated by the JRA/AIIB—have been conclusively linked to Libya.[10] The incident involving Kikumura is especially noteworthy as evidence that Qaddafi was not only continuing his terrorist campaign against the United States but significantly escalating it in dispatching the veteran JRA terrorist to New York on the (failed) bombing mission. The United States was not the only country to suffer continued acts of Libyan-sponsored international terrorism. In retaliation for Britain's role in allowing the U.S. warplanes that bombed Tripoli and Benghazi to take off from bases in that country, Qaddafi deliberately increased his supply of weapons to the IRA. During the months following the air strike, the Irish terrorist group reportedly took delivery of some five to ten tons of Semtex-H plastic explosive (investigators believe that about eight ounces of Semtex-H was used in the bomb that exploded aboard Pan Am Flight 103), in addition to one hundred twenty tons of other arms and explosives, including twelve SAM-7 ground-to-air missiles, stocks of RPG-7 rocket-propelled grenades, and anti-aircraft and anti-tank guns.[11] British authorities largely credit the Libyan weapons shipments with having appreciably facilitated the IRA's terror campaign over the following months and years.

As for the air strikes' sending a powerful deterrent message to other terrorists elsewhere, as the Reagan administration claimed at the time, the evidence is similarly wanting. Indeed, more terrorist attacks against American targets occurred during the three-month period following the U.S. action (fifty-three) than during the three months preceding it (forty-one).[12] In fact, the U.S. State Department admitted in the 1996 edition of its *Patterns of Global Terrorism* that Libya had continued throughout the period to provide support for the most "rejectionist" (that is, the most vehemently opposed to the Israeli-Palestinian peace process and dialogue) and extreme of the Palestinian terrorist groups, including the ANO, the Palestine Islamic Jihad (PIJ), and Ahmed Jibril's PFLP-GC (General Command). And Abu Nidal reportedly made his home—and had his organization's headquarters—in Libya.[13]

Finally, even the oft-repeated claims of the attack's surgical precision and the immense technological sophistication of American precision-guided air-delivered ordnance fail to hold up under examination. Despite the particularly careful selection of military targets for the U.S. fighter-bombers, thirty-six civilians were killed in the air strike and ninety-three others wounded. These civilian deaths and injuries not only were tragic in themselves but they deprived the United States of the moral high ground it often claims to occupy with respect to terrorists and terrorism and thereby engendered further domestic and international criticism. Perhaps the most incontrovertible—and obvious, if ignored—refutation of "the myth of military retaliation," however, is the 1988 in-flight bombing of Pan Am Flight 103. After what has been described as "the most extensive criminal investigation in history,," the joint FBI and Scottish police investigation resulted in the indictment of two Libyan employees of that country's national airline, Abdel Basset Ali al-Megrahi and Lamen Khalifa Fhimah, who were alleged to have been agents of Qaddafi's intelligence service.[14] In January 2001, a special Scottish court sitting in the Netherlands convicted al-Megrahi, and he was sentenced to life imprisonment. Fhimah was acquitted of the charges against him and released.[15]

In 2005, though, it is not Libya but Iran that is deemed by the U.S. State Department to be the "most active state sponsor of terrorism." Iran is specifically faulted for failing "to bring to justice" or to extradite for trial elsewhere senior al Qaeda members—including, reportedly, Sa'ad bin Laden (Osama bin Laden's eldest son), Saif al-Adl, and Suleimain Abu Ghaith—all of whom Iran detained in 2003; for "encouraging anti-Israeli activity, both rhetorically and operationally"; for continuing to provide sanctuary, material support, and assistance to Hezbollah and Palestinian terrorist organizations such as Hamas, the Palestinian Islamic Jihad, the al-Aqsa Martyrs Brigade, and the PFLP-GC; and for having "pursued a variety of policies in Iraq during 2004, some of which appeared to be inconsistent with Iran's stated objectives regarding stability in Iraq as well as those of the Iraqi Interim Government (IIG) and the Coalition."[16]

In previous years, Iran was accused of actively planning and facilitating the execution of attacks by both its agents and surrogates in groups such as the Lebanese Hezbollah.[17] According to Israeli and American intelligence sources, for example, during 1996 at least three 747 jumbo cargo jets were landing in Damascus every month ferrying weapons sent by Tehran to its minions in Hezbollah. Among the armaments were long-range Katyusha rockets, Russian-made Sagger anti-tank weapons, and other sophisticated ordnance. Mixed in with the weapons were humanitarian supplies for the nascent political party to dispense to its Lebanese Shi'a constituents, thereby strengthening its political position.[18] At the time, Iran was alleged to have provided a total of about $100 million a year to various Islamic terrorist organizations across the world, with the lion's share going to Hezbollah.[19] Tehran was also believed to have been behind subversive activities in several Gulf states, including a planned coup in Bahrain that was foiled in

June 1996. The authorities arrested nearly thirty members of the Bahraini branch of Hezbollah, who confessed to plotting since 1993 to overthrow the emirate's al-Khalifa ruling family, which belongs to the minority Sunni branch of Islam.

Conclusive proof of Iran's continued sponsorship of international terrorism was revealed in a Berlin court in April 1997, when convictions were obtained for an Iranian and four Lebanese accused of the killing in 1992 of three Iranian Kurdish dissidents and their translator, murders carried out on instructions from Tehran. As a result of evidence presented during the trial, which lasted nearly four years, the German authorities issued an arrest warrant for Ali Fallahian, the Iranian minister of intelligence, for his role in the murders and accused the Iranian government's Committee for Special Operations—which reportedly comprised the highest echelon of Iran's ruling elite, including President Hashemi Rafsanjani and the country's supreme religious leader, the Ayatollah Ali Khamenei—of actually having issued orders for the dissidents' murder. Exile sources maintained that Tehran is directly responsible for the murder of at least twenty Iranian opposition figures in Europe between 1979 and 1997.[20] And yet American efforts over the years to dissuade Iran from sponsoring terrorism have proved largely ineffective. In 1995, for example, the CIA's deputy director for intelligence testified before Congress that the U.S. economic embargo imposed the previous April had been "a failure" and would be unlikely ever to have any impact without more widespread international support. At the time, only Israel, El Salvador, and the Ivory Coast had answered President Clinton's call for sanctions.[21]

Even those countries on the State Department's list that may not be current active sponsors of international terrorism—Syria, Cuba, and North Korea—nevertheless play a critical role in abetting terrorist operations. Without their provision of training facilities, sanctuary, safe havens, and other "passive" forms of support, many groups would find it far more difficult to continue to operate. For example, although there is no evidence that either Syria or Syrian government officials have been directly involved in the planning or execution of international terrorist attacks since 1986, that country continues to provide sanctuary and assistance to terrorists. The PFLP-GC, a Palestinian faction firmly opposed to the Arab-Israeli peace process, which was implicated just before the 1988 bombing of Pan Am Flight 103 in a plot to bomb American and Israeli commercial aircraft flying from Europe,[22] has had its headquarters in Damascus for nearly forty years. Other groups, such as Hamas, the PIJ, and the PFLP, also maintain bases in Syria. In addition, the Bashar Assad regime is accused of continuing to allow Iran to use Damascus as a transit point for supplies destined for Hezbollah in neighboring Lebanon.[23] The United States in June 2005 also criticized Syria for allowing Iraqi insurgents—former Ba'athist Party members and regime loyalists as well as foreign fighters affiliated with Abu Musab Zarqawi's organization—to use that country as a base from which to mount attacks in Iraq.[24] Finally, Syria has been blamed for the car bomb assassination of former Lebanese prime minister Rafik Hariri in February 2005 (twenty others were also killed), as well as for the subsequent murder of other outspoken Lebanese politicians and journalists opposed to Syrian domination of Lebanon.[25]

For countries like Syria, then, terrorism remains a useful and integral tool of foreign policy: a clandestine weapon to be wielded whenever the situation is appropriate and the benefits tangible, but one to be kept sheathed when the risks of using it appear to outweigh the potential gains and the possible repercussions are likely to prove counterproductive. For the state sponsor, much as for the terrorist group itself, terrorism—contrary to popular perception—is not a mindless act of fanatical or indiscriminate violence; rather it is a purposefully targeted, deliberately calibrated method of pursuing specific objectives at acceptable cost. In this respect, the attractions of terrorists as "surrogate warriors" or mercenaries for various renegade regimes may in fact have increased. Future aggressors may prefer to accomplish clandestinely with a handful of armed men and a limited amount of weaponry what traditionally whole armies, navies, and air forces have been deployed to achieve. Not only could such small bands facilitate the conquest of neighboring or rival states, but if such action is carried out covertly—and successfully—the state sponsor might escape identification, and hence international military response and economic sanction. Accordingly, terrorists may in the future come to be regarded by the globe's rogue states as the "ultimate fifth column"—a clandestine, cost-effective force used to wage war covertly against more powerful rivals or to subvert neighboring countries or hostile regimes.

Terrorist Use of Nonconventional Weapons

Meanwhile, the face of terrorism is changing in other ways. New adversaries, new motivations, and new rationales have emerged over the past decade to challenge at least some of the conventional wisdom on both terrorists and terrorism. In the past, terrorist groups were recognizable mostly as collections of individuals belonging to an organization with a well-defined command and control apparatus, who had been previously trained (in however rudimentary a fashion) in the techniques and tactics of terrorism, were engaged in conspiracy as a full-time avocation, lived underground while constantly planning and plotting terrorist attacks, and at times were under the direct control, or operated at the express behest, of a foreign government (as, for example, in the case of Libya's sponsorship of JRA operations claimed in the name of the Anti-Imperialist International Brigades). Radical leftist organizations such as the JRA, the Red Army Faction, the Red Brigades, and so on, as well as ethno-nationalist/separatist terrorist movements like the PLO, the IRA, and ETA, conformed to this stereotype of the "traditional" terrorist group. These organizations engaged in highly selective and mostly discriminate acts of violence. They targeted for bombing various "symbolic" targets representing the source of their hostility (e.g., embassies, banks, national airline carriers) or kidnapped and assassinated specific people whom they considered guilty of economic exploitation or political repression in order to attract attention to themselves and their causes.

However, as radical or revolutionary as these groups were politically, the vast majority were equally conservative in their operations. These types of terrorists were said to be demonstrably more "imitative than innovative," having a very limited tactical repertoire directed against a similarly narrow target set.[26] They were judged as hesitant to take advantage of new situations, let alone to create new opportunities. What little innovation was observed lay more in the terrorists' choice of targets (e.g., the 1985 hijacking of the Italian cruise ship *Achille Lauro* by Palestinian terrorists as opposed to the more typical terrorist hijacking of passenger aircraft) or in the methods used to conceal and detonate explosive devices than in their tactics or their interest in using nonconventional weapons—specifically CBRN[27]— chemical, biological, radiological,[28] or nuclear weapons.

Although some terrorist groups had occasionally toyed with the idea of using such indiscriminately lethal weapons, few had ever crossed the critical psychological threshold of actually implementing their heinous daydreams or executing their half-baked plots. Admittedly, in 1979 Palestinian terrorists poisoned some Jaffa oranges exported to Europe in hopes of sabotaging Israel's economy; in 1984 followers of the Bhagwan Shree Rajneesh contaminated the salad bars of ten restaurants with salmonella bacteria; and six years later the LTTE used chlorine gas in an attack on a Sri Lankan military camp at East Kiran.[29] But these three isolated incidents represented virtually the total extent of either *actual* use or serious *attempts* at the use by terrorists of such nonconventional weapons and tactics. Instead, most terrorists seemed relatively content with the limited killing potential of their handguns and machine guns and the slightly higher casualty rates that their bombs achieved. Like most people, terrorists themselves appeared to fear powerful contaminants and toxins about which they knew little and which they were uncertain how to fabricate and safely handle, much less effectively deploy and disperse. Indeed, of more than eight thousand international terrorism incidents recorded in the RAND Terrorism Incident Database between 1968 and 1998, fewer than sixty offer any indication of terrorists plotting such attacks, attempting to use chemical or biological agents, or intending to steal or fabricate their own nuclear devices.[30]

Accordingly, until 9/11, the conventional wisdom held that terrorists were interested not in killing but in publicity. Violence was employed less as a means of wreaking death and destruction than as a way to appeal to and attract supporters, focus attention on the terrorists and their causes, or attain tangible political aims or concessions—for example, the release of imprisoned brethren, some measure of political autonomy or independence for a historical homeland, or a change of government. Terrorists, it was thus argued, themselves believed that only if their violence was calculated or regulated would they be able to obtain the popular support or international recognition they craved or achieve the political ends that they desired. They therefore would neither carry out mass casualty attacks using conventional weapons nor use CBRN weapons simply because there was little reason for them to kill en masse when the death of a handful of people often sufficed.[31] In the case of CBRN weapons, this logic was taken further with the argument that there were few realistic demands that terrorists could make by threatening the use of such indiscriminate weapons and little that they could accomplish by using them that they could not achieve otherwise. In other words, the terrorists' aims and objectives could just as easily be realized through less extreme measures than the detonation of a nuclear device, the dispersal of radioactive materials, or attacks employing either biological or chemical warfare agents. In perhaps the most important book written on terrorism in the 1970s, Walter Laqueur articulated this school of thought, concluding unambiguously: "It can be taken for granted that most of the terrorist groups existing at present will not use this option, either as a matter of political principle or because it would defeat their purpose."[32]

There was also general acceptance of Brian Jenkins's well-known formulation from 1975 that "terrorists want a lot of people watching and a lot of people listening and not a lot of people dead."[33] Even after the events of the mid-1980s, when a series of high-profile and particularly lethal suicide car and truck bombings were directed against American diplomatic and military targets in the Middle East (in one instance resulting in the deaths of 241 U.S. Marines), there appeared to many to be no reason to revise this assumption. Indeed, reflecting the prevailing view, Jenkins continued to argue that "simply killing a lot of people has seldom been one terrorist objective. . . . Terrorists operate on the principle of the minimum force necessary. They find it unnecessary to kill many, as long as killing a few suffices for their purposes."[34] This maxim was further applied to the question of potential terrorist use of CBRN and cited to explain the paucity of actual known plots, much less verifiable incidents. As Jenkins explained in another influential 1975 paper on potential terrorist use of radiological or nuclear weapons,

> Scenarios involving the deliberate dispersal of toxic radioactive material . . . do not appear to fit the pattern of any terrorist actions carried out thus far. . . . Terrorist actions have tended to be aimed at producing immediate dramatic effects, a handful of violent deaths—not lingering illness, and certainly not a population of ill, vengeance-seeking victims. . . . If terrorists were to employ radioactive contaminants, they could not halt the continuing effects of their act, not even long after they may have achieved their ultimate political objectives. It has not been the style of terrorists to kill hundreds or thousands. To make hundreds or thousands of persons terminally ill would be even more out of character.[35]

During the past decade, however, these long-standing assumptions increasingly have been called into question either by terrorist attacks that did employ an unconventional weapon, such the 1995 sarin nerve gas attack on the Tokyo subway, or that resulted in large numbers of casualties, such as the 1993 bombing of New York City's World Trade Center, where the terrorists sought to topple one of the 107-story twin towers onto the other in hopes of killing 250,000 people;[36] the massive explosion at a U.S. government office building in Oklahoma City two years later; the bombings in 1998 of the American embassies in Kenya and Tanzania; the 9/11 attacks, of course; and the litany of aborted or averted attacks both before and since that might possibly have produced mass carnage had they been executed (e.g., the 1994 plot to crash a hijacked Air France passenger aircraft into the heart of Paris and the al Qaeda plan revealed in 2004 to attack simultaneously New York City's financial district in lower Manhattan, a business center in nearby Newark, New Jersey, and the offices of the World Bank and International Monetary Fund in Washington, D.C., as well as a variety of mass transit and infrastructure targets in London). This array of actual, thwarted, and aborted incidents has challenged the conventional wisdom that the self-imposed constraints that hitherto had prevented terrorists either from employing CBRN weapons or undertaking mass casualty attacks with less exotic weaponry are still relevant. And, most of all, these incidents have shown that the more "traditional" and familiar types of ideological and ethno-nationalist and separatist organizations who dominated terrorism for the past thirty years—and upon which in the 1970s analysts like Laqueur, Jenkins, and others based many of our most fundamental assumptions about terrorists and their behavior—have been joined by a variety of rather different terrorist entities with arguably less comprehensible nationalist or ideological motivations.

This new generation of terrorists, as was discussed in chapter 4, is not only characterized by more salient theological influences, but in some cases has embraced millenarian, if not apocalyptic aims. They are themselves also less cohesive organizational entities, with a deliberately more diffuse structure and membership with distinctly more opaque command and control relationships.[37] Accordingly, they represent a different and potentially more lethal threat than the above-mentioned more familiar, "traditional" terrorist adversaries. In contrast to the stereotypical terrorist group of the past, this new generation of terrorists evidences a number of characteristics that affect their operations, decision making, and targeting in profoundly different ways. Rather than the pyramidal, hierarchical organizational structures that were dominant among terrorist organizations during the 1970s and 1980s, these terrorists are part of far more amorphous, indistinct, and broad movements. Moreover, as illustrated in chapter 1, they tend to operate on a linear rather than hierarchical basis. Hence, instead of the classic cellular structure that was common to previous generations of terrorist organizations, many of these newer movements are more loosely connected or indirectly linked through networks comprising both professionals (e.g., trained, full-time terrorists) and "amateurs" (hangers-on, supporters, sympathizers, and would-be terrorists who may lack the expertise or experience of their better-established counterparts). This phenomenon, variously termed "leaderless resistance," "phantom cell networks," "autonomous leadership units," "autonomous cells," "networks of networks," or "lone wolves," as was also discussed in chapter 1, has become one of the most important trends in terrorism today.

The absence of any existing, publicly identified central command authority is especially significant in that it may remove any inhibitions on the terrorists' desire to inflict widespread, indiscriminate casualties. These individual networks may be less sophisticated or less technically competent, but they could have greater freedom and independence in tactical decisions than traditional terrorist cells, given the absence of a central command structure or physical headquarters otherwise available to victim states to target in retaliation. Accordingly, this particular trend in terrorism potentially represents a very different and possibly far more lethal threat than that posed by more familiar, traditional terrorist adversaries. Further, the anonymity intrinsic to this type of operation coupled with the lack of a discernible organizational structure with a distinguishable command chain behind the attackers is deliberately designed to prevent easy identification and to facilitate the perpetrators' escape and evasion.

Finally, many terrorist movements today are also seen to have less easily defined aims or identified objectives. Some are motivated by unswerving hostility toward the West in general and the United States in particular or a desire for revenge and retaliation that is frequently fueled by powerful religious imperatives and justifications rather than abstract political ideologies. Thus, in contrast to the intelligible demands of the more familiar, predominantly secular terrorist groups of the past who mostly claimed credit for and explained their violent acts, some of the most heinous and lethal attacks perpetrated by terrorists over the previous two decades—primarily those directed against innocent civilians specifically and therefore designed to inflict the maximum casualties possible—have gone unclaimed.[38] By maintaining their anonymity, terrorists may believe that they are able to capitalize further on the fear and alarm intrinsically generated by their violence. Indeed, according to Raphael F. Perl, a well-respected terrorism analyst with the U.S. Congressional Research Service, only about 30 percent of all terrorist attacks in 2004 were claimed.[39]

The appearance of these new types of adversaries—with very different motivations and accordingly often a greater interest in acquiring an array of lethally more ambitious capabilities—at least compared to their secular counterparts—understandably has generated new concerns of potential CBRN terrorism. As Laqueur warned in a seminal reassessment of terrorism trends and thinking published in 1996, "Proliferation of weapons of mass destruction does not mean that most terrorists are likely to use them in the foreseeable future, but some almost certainly will, in spite of all the reasons militating against it."[40] In this respect, it was bin Laden's alleged development of chemical warfare agents for use against U.S. forces in Saudi Arabia that was cited just two years later to justify the controversial American cruise missile attack on the al-Shifa pharmaceutical plant in Khartoum, Sudan.[41] Moreover, since that time incontrovertible information has repeatedly come to light that clearly illuminates al Qaeda's long-standing and concerted efforts to develop a diverse array of chemical, biological, and even nuclear weapons capabilities.[42]

Bin Laden's interest in acquiring a nuclear weapon reportedly began as long ago as 1992. An al Qaeda agent subsequently attempted to purchase uranium from South Africa, either late the following year or early in 1994, without success.[43] Four years later, al Qaeda operatives were still engaged in this quest when Mamdouh Mahmud Salim, a senior official in the organization, was arrested in Germany while attempting to buy enriched uranium. Bin Laden, however, appears to have been undeterred by these initial failures. Indeed, in May 1998 he issued a proclamation in the name of the International Islamic Front for Fighting the Jews and Crusaders, titled "The Nuclear Bomb of Islam." In it, the al Qaeda leader unambiguously declared that "it is the duty of Muslims to prepare as much force as possible to terrorize the enemies of God."[44] When asked several months later by a Pakistani journalist whether al Qaeda was "in a position to develop chemical weapons and try to purchase nuclear material for weapons," bin Laden replied: "In answer, I would say that acquiring weapons for the defense of Muslims is a religious duty."[45]

Evidence of bin Laden's continued interest in nuclear weaponry again surfaced just six weeks after the 9/11 attacks with the arrests of two Pakistani nuclear scientists—Sultan Bashiruddin Mahmood and Abdul Majeed. In August 2001 the scientists had held three days of meetings with bin Laden, Zawahiri, and other top al Qaeda officials at its secret headquarters near Kabul, Afghanistan. Although their discussions ranged widely to include chemical and biological weapons, Mahmood told his interrogators that bin Laden was specifically interested in nuclear weapons. Al Qaeda supposedly had acquired some nuclear material from an affiliated jihadist movement in Central Asia, the Islamic Movement of Uzbekistan (IMU), and Mahmood's opinion was solicited on its suitability for use in an explosive device. According to Graham Allison,

Mahmood explained to his hosts that the material in question could be used in a dirty bomb but could not produce a nuclear explosion. Al-Zawahiri and the others then sought Mahmood's help in recruiting other Pakistani nuclear experts who could provide uranium of the required purity, as well as assistance in constructing a nuclear weapon. Though Mahmood characterized the discussions as "academic," Pakistani officials indicated that Mahmood and Majeed "spoke extensively about weapons of mass destruction" and provided detailed responses to bin Laden's questions about the manufacture of nuclear, biological, and chemical weapons.[46]

Al Qaeda's desire to develop at least some kind of nuclear weapons capability was again revealed in January 2002 when CNN reporters discovered in a Kabul office that al Qaeda had been using a twenty-five-page document containing designs for such a device.[47] Further, more recent evidence suggests that bin Laden has not completely abandoned his quest to acquire a nuclear weapon. In a 2004 interview broadcast on the CBS investigative news show *60 Minutes*, Michael Scheuer, the former head of the CIA's bin Laden unit and author of the seminal work on bin Laden, *Through Our Enemies' Eyes*, disclosed that the al Qaeda leader had received permission in May 2003 from an influential Saudi cleric, Sheikh Nasir bin Mahid al-Fahd, to use precisely such a weapon against the United States.[48]

In addition to its nuclear ambitions, al Qaeda has also actively sought to develop a variety of chemical and biological weaponry. These efforts appear to have begun in earnest with a memo written by al-Zawahiri on April 15, 1999, to Muhammad Atef, who was then deputy commander of al Qaeda's military committee. Citing articles published in *Science*, the *Journal of Immunology*, and the *New England Journal of Medicine*, as well as information gleaned from books such as *Tomorrow's Weapons* (1964), *Peace or Pestilence* (1949), and *Chemical Warfare* (1924), Zawahiri outlined his thoughts on the particular attraction of biological weapons ad seriatim:

a) The enemy started thinking about these weapons before WWI. Despite their extreme danger, we only became aware of them when the enemy drew our attention to them by repeatedly expressing concerns that they can be produced simply with easily available materials. . . .

b) The destructive power of these weapons is no less than that of nuclear weapons.

c) A germ attack is often detected days after it occurs, which raises the number of victims.

d) Defense against such weapons is very difficult, particularly if large quantities are used. . . .

I would like to emphasize what we previously discussed—that looking for a specialist is the fastest, safest, and cheapest way [to embark on a biological- and chemical-weapons program].[49]

One of the specialists thus recruited was a U.S.-trained Malaysian microbiologist named Yazid Sufaat. A former captain in the Malaysian army, Sufaat graduated from California State University in 1987 with a degree in biological sciences. He later joined al-Jemaah al-Islamiya (the Islamic Group), an al Qaeda affiliate operating in South-East Asia, and worked closely with its military operations chief, Riduan Isamuddin, better known as Hambali—and with Hambali's al Qaeda handler, Khalid Sheikh Mohammed (KSM).

In January 2000, Sufaat had also played host to two of the 9/11 hijackers, Khalid Almihdar and Nawaf Alhazmi, who stayed in his Kuala Lumpur condominium. Later that year, Zacarias Moussaoui, the alleged "twentieth hijacker," who is currently on trial in a federal district court in Alexandria, Virginia, stayed with Sufaat, too. Under KSM's direction, Hambali and Sufaat set up shop at an al Qaeda camp in Kandahar, Afghanistan, where their efforts focused on the weaponization of anthrax.[50] Although the two made some progress, biowarfare experts believe that on the eve of 9/11 al Qaeda was still at least two to three years away from producing a sufficient quantity of anthrax to use as a weapon.[51] Sufaat's arrest in late 2001, however, may not have entirely derailed al Qaeda's bioterror efforts. When KSM himself was apprehended two years later, he was found hiding in the Rawalpindi home of a Pakistani bacteriologist—who has since disappeared.[52]

Before 9/11, a separate team of al Qaeda operatives had been engaged in a parallel R&D effort to produce ricin and chemical warfare agents at the movement's Derunta camp, near the eastern Afghan city of Jalalabad. The Derunta facility reportedly included laboratories and a school that trained a handpicked group of terrorists in the use of chemical and biological weapons. Its director was an Egyptian, Midhat Mursi, known as Abu Kebab, and the school's teachers included Sufaat and a Pakistani microbiologist. When U.S. military forces overran the camp, they found castor oil (ricin is derived from castor beans) and the equipment required to produce the toxin. Both Mursi and a colleague named Menad Benchellali managed to avoid capture. Although Mursi remains at large, Benchellali, a French national of Algerian heritage, was arrested in 2002. After fleeing Afghanistan, he had initially settled in the Pankisi Gorge, an area in Georgia that borders Chechnya, but he became homesick. Once back in France, Benchellali became involved in a terrorist cell that had planned to bomb the Russian embassy in Paris. Acting on information provided by French authorities following Benchellali's arrest, police in Britain and Spain detained twenty-nine suspects from North African countries suspected of ties to al Qaeda and an affiliated Kurdish-Iraqi terrorist group, Ansar al-Islam.[53] Evidence seized by British police in the search of one suspect's apartment in North London included both recipes and ingredients for several toxins—including ricin, cyanide, and botulinum.[54] British authorities believe that the ricin production instructions had been downloaded from an American white supremacist Web site and then photocopied on a machine at a well-known radical London mosque.[55] A police raid the previous year on a house in Norfolk used by another cell of Northern Africans also found recipes for ricin and other poisons, along with information about explosives and instructions for making bombs.[56]

A common thread in all these cases—whether involving actual al Qaeda operatives or others with potential links to the movement—is a strong interest in, and clear willingness to use, these nonconventional weapons; that interest, however, was not always matched by the capabilities required either to fabricate or to effectively disseminate them. As John Parachini, a CBRN terrorism expert, had argued,

> Demonstrating interest in something is far different both from, first, experimenting with it and, second, mastering the procedures to execute an attack. Gaining access to materials is certainly a major barrier, but it is not the only one. Delivering toxic materials to targets in sufficient quantities to kill in the same fashion as explosives is not easy.[57]

Indeed, as mesmerizingly attractive as these nonconventional weapons are to some terrorists, they have historically proved frustratingly disappointing to whoever has tried to use them. Despite the extensive use of poison gas during World War I, for instance, that weapon accounted for only 5 percent of all casualties in that epic conflict. Even in more recent times, such as during the 1980s when Iraq used chemical weapons in its war against Iran, less than one percent (5,000) of the 600,000 Iranians who perished were killed by gas. The wartime use of biological weapons has a similarly checkered record. On at least eleven occasions before and during World War II, the Imperial Japanese Army employed germ agents as diverse as cholera, dysentery, bubonic plague, anthrax, and paratyphoid, disseminated in both water and air. Not only did these fail to kill as many Chinese soldiers as the Japanese had hoped, but on at least one occasion—the 1942 assault on Chekiang—10,000 Japanese soldiers themselves were affected, of whom some 1,700 died. "The Japanese program's principal defect, a problem to all efforts so far," David Rapoport concluded, was "an ineffective delivery system."[58] The difficulties of using germs as weapons is further substantiated by the work of Seth Carus, a researcher at the National Defense University in Washington, D.C. Carus has compiled perhaps the most authoritative accounting of the use of biological agents by a wide range of adversaries, including terrorists, government operatives, ordinary criminals, and the mentally unstable. His exhaustive database, which begins in 1900, reveals that during the twentieth century a grand total of 10 people were killed and fewer than 900 made ill as a result of some 180 acts of either bioterrorism or bio-crime. The majority of these incidents, moreover, involved the selective poisoning of specific people rather than the wholesale, indiscriminate attacks most often imagined.[59]

As the previously recounted experience of Aum also demonstrated, delivery remains a significant technological hurdle for terrorists, whether they are using chemical or biological weapons. On at least nine occasions Aum attempted to disseminate botulinum toxin (*Clostridium botulinum*) or anthrax (*Bacillus anthracis*) using aerosol means; each time the terrorists failed, either because the botulinum agents they grew and enriched were not sufficiently toxic or because the mechanical sprayers used to dissemi-nate the anthrax spores became clogged and hence inoperative.[60] These multiple failures with biological weapons prompted the cult's scientists to concentrate on developing chemical ones instead.[61] But even the use of chemical agents in an enclosed environment like a subway car in an under-ground tunnel proved problematic. Far more people would likely have died in the London subway attack from the explosive force and smoke inhalation caused by conventional bombs—as occurred in the July 11, 2005, attacks on the London Underground that killed more than fifty people—than the sarin nerve gas that killed twelve (including, inadvertently, one of the per-petrators). In addition, nearly three-quarters (73.9 percent) of the nearly five thousand reported casualties were in fact treated for shock, emotional upset, or some psychosomatic symptom.[62] In other words, the actual num-ber of people physically injured or harmed in the sarin attack was far lower than is widely believed.

In sum, these continuing technical constraints notwithstanding, com-pelling motives, such as those raised by religious terrorism, coupled with potential opportunity, e.g., ease of access to both the information and mate-rial required to fabricate and employ CBRN weapons—could portend for a bloodier and more destructive era of terrorism in the future. Certainly the combination of motive and opportunity has already fueled al Qaeda's quest to develop a range of CBRN weapons capabilities. Indeed, a combination of unforeseen developments and unexpected technological breakthroughs could launch terrorism on a higher trajectory toward greater levels of lethal-ity and destruction, perhaps involving even CBRN weapons.

The most salient motive—as the al Qaeda and Aum cases demonstrate—remains one involving some religious or theological imperative, whereby a group animated by a desire to decisively attack an enemy state and its popu-lation (perhaps in order to deliver a stunning knockout blow) or, in the case of a millenarian movement, to hasten redemption through acts of violence or to attempt or implement Armageddon by the apocalyptic use of a nuclear weapon, deliberately embarks on such a course of action. But it would be a mistake to see such motivations involving CBRN terrorism as exclusively within the purview of religious terrorists. One can readily envision similar scenarios involving secular terrorist groups. For example, the LTTE (as previously noted) is the first nonstate entity known to have carried out a chemical weapons attack. In the case of already extremely violent, seemingly intractable, and increasingly stalemated ethno-nationalist conflicts, for example, one has to consider whether eventually one side might finally seek to inflict a crushing defeat—whether in actual physical terms or in psychological terms—on an opponent using some form of CBRN against its civilian population. One possible scenario would thus involve an ethno-nationalist minority on the verge of either experiencing a military defeat or having some political settlement imposed on them employ such a weapon in a final act of desperation. Given the typical "winner-takes-all" stakes of these conflicts,[63] terrorism might also logically be employed against countries contributing military contingents to international peacekeeping forces charged with enforcing contested political agreements or even separating belligerents just as one side is on the verge of vanquishing its opponent. Further, the prospect that these conflicts might be continued or carried on by other means—for reasons exclusively of vengeance or retaliation—beyond their ostensible political and/or military endgames cannot be dismissed. Indeed, revenge and retaliation as age-old motivations of intense bloodletting and carnage therefore could also be considered as possibly leading to terrorist use of some CBRN weapon. Hence, one can imagine some group turning to such weapons in a desperate gamble to stave off final military defeat, derail the imposition of a political settlement inimical to its parochial interests, or simply strike out against an opponent in either simple petulance or base vengeance.

In terms of opportunities, the obsolescence of the control that regimes erected during the cold war to prevent states from acquiring strategic nuclear materials and developing even very basic chemical and biological warfare capabilities has been illustrated by how al Qaeda as well as Aum—both nonstate actors—set out to acquire or produce chemical, biological, and even nuclear weapons. Future efforts by other nonstate actors in this realm may well be abetted by the proliferation of fissile materials from the former Soviet Union states or rogue states like Iran and North Korea or by the emergence of an illicit market hawking bona fide nuclear materials.[64] Admittedly, while much of the material that has been offered during the past decade as part of this "black market" cannot be classified as SNM (strategic nuclear material, that is, suitable for the construction of a fissionable explosive device), highly toxic radioactive agents can potentially be paired with conventional explosives and turned into a crude "dirty" bomb. Hence, in terms of capabilities, a combination of a large fertilizer truck bomb with even a smaller amount of radioactive material, for example, could not only destroy an iconic landmark commercial or government building but also render a considerable chunk of prime real estate surrounding it indefinitely unusable because of radioactive contamination. The disruption to commerce and the shattering of the public's sense of security and well-being that likely would result is fundamentally disquieting. Even a small "dirty" bomb, detonated within an enclosed space such as an office building or a subway car and resulting in commensurately smaller loss of life and actual physical destruction, could have devastating psychological consequences, given the attendant publicity and the enhanced coercive power accorded to the terrorists. In either instance, the indefinite prolongation of the terrorist incident because of the radioactive contamination caused could last for years. Not only would the primary target of the attack have been destroyed or seriously damaged, but a much larger secondary target area surrounding it would also be contaminated and therefore need to be isolated and cordoned off from further access or use. Such an attack, though using chemical weapon, rather than a radioactive one, paired with conventional explosives, in fact has already been attempted. In April 2004 authorities in Jordan disrupted a plot orchestrated by Abu Musab Zarqawi to use twenty tons of chemicals and explosives to attack the prime minister's office, the General Intelligence Department's headquarters, and the U.S. embassy in Amman. An estimated eighty thousand people reportedly could have been killed or seriously injured both from the initial explosions and from the chemical toxins that would have been released into the air.[65]

Even a limited terrorist attack involving not a WMD per se but an unconventional radiological weapon—or a chemical or biological weapon—could have disproportionately enormous psychological consequences, generating unprecedented fear and alarm and thus serving the terrorists' purpose(s) just as well as a larger weapon or a more ambitious attack with massive casualties could. Accordingly, the issue here may not be ruthless terrorist use of some WMD as much as it is calculated terrorist use of some unconventional weapon to achieve far-reaching psychological effects in a particular target audience. A key lesson in this respect from the October 2001 anthrax letters was that terrorists don't have to kill three thousand people to create panic and foment fear and insecurity: five people dying under mysterious circumstances is quite effective at unnerving an entire nation. Moreover, the extended closures of three sites of the attacks—the Hart Senate Office Building and the Brentwood postal station, both in Washington, D.C., and another mail facility in Hamilton Township, New Jersey—as well as the indefinite closure of a fourth site in Florida, underscore the same challenges of decontamination with respect to biological weapons as were cited in the context of a "dirty bomb." Although the Hart Building finally reopened in January 2002, the Brentwood and Hamilton Township stations were not declared fit for human occupancy until 2003 and 2004, respectively. The American Media building in Boca Raton remains sealed to this day. Moreover, it cost $41.7 million to decontaminate the Hart Building, where the anthrax contagion was smallest and the most contained; the actual figure was nearly double the initial projection of $23 million. Estimates as high as $100 million have been posited to clean up the American Media structure.[66] Accordingly, the future nonconventional weapons threat may not be as much the ruthless terrorist use of some weapon of mass destruction in an attempt to destroy an entire city and affect its entire population as the discrete, calculated terrorist use of some chemical, biological, or radiological device to achieve far-reaching psychological effects or provoke a specific reaction from the targeted country.

In this critical respect, American counterterrorism efforts before 9/11 may have been focused too exclusively on extremes that, paradoxically, may have indirectly contributed to the success of the 9/11 attacks. Attention was also arguably focused too exclusively on either the low-end threat posed by car and truck bombs against buildings or the more exotic high-end threats, against entire societies, involving chemical, biological, and nuclear weapons, and cyber-attacks.[67] The implicit assumptions of many American planning scenarios on mass casualty attacks were that they would involve germ or chemical agents or result from widespread electronic attacks on critical infrastructure. It was therefore assumed that any conventional or less extensive incident could be addressed simply by planning for the most catastrophic threat. This approach left a painfully vulnerable gap in our antiterrorism defenses, in which a traditional and long-proved tactic—like airline hijacking—was neglected in favor of other, less conventional threats and in which the consequences of using an aircraft as a suicide weapon seemed to have been ignored. Indeed, according to one estimate, of more than 201 federal planning exercises conducted in the United States up until 9/11, at least two-thirds were concerned only with defending against biological or chemical attacks and thus ignored the possibility that other kinds of attacks—such as those at the World Trade Center and the Pentagon—might result in large numbers of casualties and might present unique challenges of their own in terms of emergency response and rescue.[68]

In retrospect, it was not the 1995 sarin nerve gas attack on the Tokyo subway and the nine attempts to use bio-weapons by Aum that should have been the dominant influence on our counterterrorist thinking, but a 1986 hijacking of a Pan Am flight in Karachi, where the terrorists' intention was reported to have been to crash it into the center of Tel Aviv, and the 1994 hijacking in Algiers of an Air France passenger plane by Armed Islamic Group (GIA) terrorists, who similarly planned to crash the fuel-laden aircraft with its passengers into downtown Paris. The lesson, accordingly, is not that we need to be unrealistically omniscient but rather that we need to be able to respond across a broad technological spectrum of potential adversarial attacks. CBRN terrorism is, of course, a salient threat. But it is only one of many threats we face, and not necessarily the most likely or—the widespread perception notwithstanding—even the most effective. As undeniably potent a psychological weapon as chemical, biological, and radiological weapons certainly are, terrorists arguably can kill more effectively—and sufficiently plentifully—by relying on more-conventional weapons. Indeed, as the 9/11 attacks clearly demonstrated, terrorists can readily achieve their dual aims of fear and intimidation simply by blowing things up.

In sum, new combinations could produce new and deadlier adversaries. Terrorism today already reflects such a potentially lethal mixture: it is frequently perpetrated by "amateurs," motivated by religious enmity, blind hatred, or a mix of individually idiosyncratic motivations, and in some instances it is deliberately exploited or manipulated by "professional" terrorists and at times by state sponsors as well. Hence, the increasing availability of fissile materials coupled with the relative ease with which chemical or biological warfare agents can be manufactured (however more problematically their effective dissemination could be achieved) suggests that terrorists possessing this constellation of characteristics would be the most likely and would have the least trouble—at least with respect to their motivation and mind-set—crossing into the domain of employing such a weapon.

There is sometimes a thin line between prudence and panic. The challenge, therefore, in responding to the potential threat of terrorist use of chemical, biological, radiological, and nuclear weapons is to craft a comprehensive defense that is not only cost-effective and appropriate to the threat but also sufficiently dynamic that it can respond as effectively as possible under the most difficult circumstances. Because of the extreme consequences that potentially could result from an attack involving nuclear material or a chemical or biological agent, even the remotest likelihood of one cannot be completely dismissed as insignificant. The challenge, therefore, is to avoid overreaction while still preparing adequately for a threat that remains highly uncertain but would nonetheless clearly have profound consequences.

The al Qaeda Movement Today: An Enduring Threat

The al Qaeda movement today is best described as a networked transnational constituency rather than the monolithic, international terrorist organization with an identifiable command and control apparatus that it once was. This development is a product of the transformation that al Qaeda has undergone since 9/11 from an essentially unitary entity to a less tangible transnational movement true to its name—as previously discussed—the "base of operation" or "foundation," or, as other translations more appropriately describe it, the "precept" or "method." The result is that today there are many al Qaedas rather than the single al Qaeda of the past. The current al Qaeda therefore exists more as an ideology that has become a vast enterprise—an international franchise with like-minded local representatives, loosely connected to a central ideological or motivational base but advancing the remaining center's goals at once simultaneously and independently of each other.

Since 9/11 al Qaeda has clearly shown itself to be a nimble, flexible, and adaptive entity. Because of its remarkable durability, the progress that the United States and its allies achieved during the first phase of the global war on terrorism (GWOT)—when al Qaeda's training camps and operational bases, infrastructure, and command-and-control nucleus in Afghanistan were destroyed and uprooted—has thus far proved elusive during subsequent phases. In retrospect, too, the loss of Afghanistan does not appear to have affected al Qaeda's ability to mount terrorist attacks to the extent we had perhaps hoped to achieve when "Operation Enduring Freedom" began.[69] In fact, al Qaeda rebounded from its Afghanistan setbacks within weeks of the last set-piece battles that were fought in the White Mountains along the Pakistani border at Shoh-e-Kot, Tora Bora, and elsewhere between December 2001 and March 2002. The attacks in Tunisia in April 2002 and in Pakistan the next month provided the first signs of the movement's resiliency. Those were followed in turn by the attacks in Bali, Yemen, and Kuwait the following October, and then by the coordinated, nearly simultaneous incidents against an Israeli hotel and a charter passenger jet in Kenya that November.[70]

Al Qaeda's capacity to continue to plan and execute new terrorist strikes despite the loss of Afghanistan as a base shouldn't come as a surprise. Previous "high-end" attacks, for example, predated its comfortable relationship with the Taliban in Afghanistan and had already demonstrated that the movement's strength is not in geographical possession or occupation of a defined geographical territory but in its fluidity and impermanence.

The activities of the peripatetic Ramzi Ahmed Yousef, reputed mastermind of the 1993 World Trade Center bombing, during his sojourn in the Philippines in 1994 and 1995 is a case in point. Yousef's grand scheme to bomb simultaneously eleven American commercial aircraft in midflight over the Pacific Ocean (the infamous "Bojinka" plot),[71] for example, did not require extensive operational bases and command and control headquarters in an existing country to facilitate its planning and execution.

Perhaps al Qaeda's greatest achievement, though, has been the make-over it has given itself since 2001.[72] On the eve of 9/11, al Qaeda was a unitary organization, assuming the dimensions of a lumbering bureaucracy. The troves of documents and voluminous data from computer hard disks captured in Afghanistan, for example, revealed as much mundane paperwork as grandiose plots: complaints about expensive cell phone bills and expenditures for superfluous office equipment,[73] as well as crude designs for dreamt-about nuclear weapons.[74] Because of its logistical bases and infrastructure in Afghanistan, that now-anachronistic version of al Qaeda had a clear, distinct center of gravity. As we saw in the systematic and rapid destruction inflicted during the military operations as part of Operation Enduring Freedom during the global war on terrorism's first phase, that structure was not only extremely vulnerable to the application of conventional military power but played precisely to the American military's vast technological strengths. In the time since 9/11, however, al Qaeda in essence has transformed itself from a bureaucratic entity that could be destroyed and an irregular army that could be defeated on the battlefield to the clearly less powerful, but nonetheless arguably more resilient, amorphous entity it is today.

Amazingly, al Qaeda also claims that it is stronger and more capable now than it was on 9/11.[75] Al Qaeda propagandists on Web sites and in other forums, for instance, repeatedly point to a newfound vitality that has facilitated an operational capacity able to carry out at least two major attacks per year since 9/11, compared to the one attack every two years that it could implement before then. "We are still chasing the Americans and their allies everywhere," al-Zawahiri crowed in December 2003, "even in their homeland."[76] Irrespective of whether our definition of a major attack and al Qaeda's are the same, propaganda doesn't have to be true to be believed: all that matters is that it is communicated effectively and persuasively—precisely the two essential components of information operations that al Qaeda has mastered.

That al Qaeda can continue to prosecute this struggle is a reflection not only of its transformative qualities and communications skills but also of the deep well of trained jihadists from which it can still draw. According to the 2004 edition of the authoritative annual *Strategic Survey*, published by the London-based International Institute for Strategic Studies (IISS), a cadre of at least eighteen thousand individuals who trained in al Qaeda's Afghanistan camps between 1996 and 2001 are today theoretically positioned in some sixty countries throughout the world.[77] Moreover, al Qaeda's management reserves seem to be similarly robust—at least to an extent perhaps not previously appreciated. A "corporate succession" plan of sorts has seemed to function even during a time when al Qaeda has been relentlessly tracked, harassed, and weakened. Al Qaeda thus appears to retain at least some depth in managerial personnel, as evidenced by its abilities to produce successor echelons for the mid- and senior-level operational commanders who have been killed or captured. It also still retains some form of a centralized command and control structure responsible for gathering intelligence, planning, and perhaps even overseeing spectacular attacks against what are deemed the movement's most important, high-value targets in the United States, the United Kingdom, Pakistan, and doubtless elsewhere. The computer records, e-mail traffic, and other documents seized by Pakistani authorities when a computer savvy al Qaeda operative named Mohammed Naeem Noor Khan was apprehended in July 2004 point to the continued existence of a more robust, centralized entity than had previously been assumed.[78] The investigations of the July 2005 London attacks may yet reveal a similar chain of command extending from London and the British Midlands to a surviving, rump al Qaeda leadership still situated in Pakistan or some other country.[79]

Moreover, despite the vast inroads made in reducing terrorist finances, especially monetary contributions, al Qaeda doubtless also has sufficient funds with which to continue to prosecute its struggle. According to one open source estimate, as of 2003 some $120 million of *identifiable* al Qaeda assets had been seized or frozen.[80] Given that bin Laden reputedly amassed a war chest in the billions of dollars, ample funds may still be at the disposal of his minions. At one point, for example, bin Laden was reputed to own or control some eighty companies around the world. In the Sudan alone, he owned all of that country's most profitable businesses, including construction, manufacturing, currency trading, import-export, and agricultural enterprises. Not only were many of these well managed to the extent that they regularly turned a profit, but this largesse in turn was funneled to local al Qaeda cells that in essence became entirely self-sufficient, self-reliant terrorist entities in the countries within which they operated.[81] The previously cited IISS report focused on this issue as well. "While the organization and its affiliates and friends do not enjoy the financial fluidity that they did before the post–11 September counterterrorism mobilization," the report noted, "neither do they appear shorn of resources." The analysis disquietingly also explained how "since the Afghanistan intervention forced al-Qaeda to decentralize and eliminated the financial burden of maintaining a large physical base, al-Qaeda has needed less money to operate."[82]

Finally, and above all, despite the damage and destruction and key leadership losses that it has sustained over the past three years, al Qaeda stubbornly adheres to its fundamental strategy and objectives: continuing to inspire the broader radical jihadist movement. As discussed in chapter 4, bin Laden and al-Zawahiri years ago defined this strategy as a two-pronged assault on both the "far enemy" (the United States and the West) and the "near enemy" (those reprobate, authoritarian, anti-Islamic regimes in the Middle East, Central Asia, South Asia, and South-East Asia against whom the global jihadist movement is implacably opposed).[83] In recent years, for example, terrorist strikes have rocked London, Madrid, and Istanbul—representing the "far enemy" (although Turkey is a Muslim country, its long-standing membership in NATO makes it part of the Western power structure in the jihadists' eyes), as well as Riyadh, Casablanca, and Baghdad and Islamabad and Jakarta—the "near enemies." The periodic release of fresh targeting guidance and operational instructions through the aforementioned *Mu'askar al-Battar* (Camp of the Sword) and *Sawt al-Jihad* (Voice of Jihad) online magazines has helped to give renewed focus and sustain this strategy.

The al Qaeda Movement's Organizational and Operational Resiliency

Unlike the hierarchical, pyramidal structure that typified terrorist groups of the past, the al Qaeda movement is in the main flatter, more linear, and more organizationally networked. Nonetheless, it still retains some important characteristics and aspects of a more organized entity, mixing and matching organizational and operational styles as dictated by particular missions or imposed by circumstances. The al Qaeda movement, accordingly, can perhaps be usefully conceptualized as comprising four distinct, but not mutually exclusive, dimensions. In descending order of sophistication, they are:

1. Al Qaeda Central encompasses the remnants of the pre-9/11 al Qaeda organization. Although its core leadership includes some of the familiar,

established commanders of the past, there are a number of new players who have advanced through the ranks as a result of the death or capture of key al Qaeda senior-level managers such as KSM, Abu Atef, Abu Zubayda, and Hambali, and most recently, Abu Faraj al-Libi. It is believed that this hard core remains centered in or around Pakistan and continues to exert some coordination, if not actual command capability, in terms of commissioning attacks, directing surveillance and collating reconnaissance, planning operations, and approving their execution. This category comes closest to the al Qaeda operational template or model evident in the 1998 East Africa embassy bombings and the 9/11 attacks. Such high-value, "spectacular" attacks are entrusted only to al Qaeda's professional cadre: the most dedicated, committed, and absolutely reliable element of the movement. Previous patterns suggest that these "professional" terrorists are deployed in predetermined and carefully selected teams. They are also provided with very specific targeting instructions. In some cases, such as the East Africa bombings, they may establish contact with, and enlist the assistance of, local sympathizers and supporters, but solely for logistical and other attack-support purposes or to enlist these locals in the actual execution of the attack(s). The operation, however, will be planned and directed by the "professional" element, with the locals clearly subordinate and playing strictly a supporting role (albeit a critical one).

2. Al Qaeda Affiliates and Associates embraces formally established insurgent or terrorist groups who over the years have benefited from bin Laden's largesse and/or spiritual guidance and/or have received training, arms, money, and other assistance from al Qaeda. Among the recipients of this assistance have been terrorist groups and insurgent forces in Uzbekistan and Indonesia, Chechnya and the Philippines, Bosnia and Kashmir, as well as other places. By supporting these groups, bin Laden had a threefold intention. First, he sought to co-opt these movements' mostly local agendas and channel their efforts toward the cause of global jihad. Second, he hoped to create a jihadist "critical mass" from these geographically scattered, disparate movements that would one day coalesce into a single, unstoppable force. And third, he wanted to foster a dependency relationship whereby as a quid pro quo for previous al Qaeda support, these movements would either undertake attacks at al Qaeda's behest or provide essential local, logistical, and other support to facilitate strikes by the al Qaeda "professional" cadre noted above.

This category includes such groups as: al-Ittihad al-Islami (AIAI), Abu Musab Zarqawi's al Qaeda in Mesopotamia (formerly Jamaat al Tawhid wa'l Jihad), Asbat al-Ansar, Ansar al Islam, Islamic Army of Aden, Islamic Movement of Uzbekistan (IMU), Jemaah Islamiya (JI), Libyan Islamic Fighting Group (LIFG), Moro Islamic Liberation Front (MILF), Salafist Group for Call and Combat (GSPC), and the various Kashmiri Islamic groups based in Pakistan—e.g., Harakat ul Mujahidin (HuM), Jaish-e-Mohammed (JeM), Laskar-e-Tayyiba (LeT), and Laskar I Jhangvi (LiJ).

3. Al Qaeda Locals are amorphous groups of al Qaeda adherents who are likely to have had some previous terrorism experience, will have been blooded in battle as part of some previous jihadist campaign in Algeria, the Balkans, Chechnya, and perhaps more recently in Iraq, and may have trained in some al Qaeda facility before 9/11. They will therefore have had some direct connection with al Qaeda—however tenuous or evanescent. Their current relationship, and even communication, with a central al Qaeda command and control apparatus may be equally tenuous, if not actually dormant. The distinguishing characteristic of this category, however, is that there is a previous connection of some kind with al Qaeda. Specific examples of this adversary include Ahmed Ressam, who was arrested in December 1999 at Port Angeles, Washington State, shortly after he had entered the United States from Canada. Ressam had a background in terrorism, having belonged to Algeria's Armed Islamic Group (GIA). After being recruited to al Qaeda, he was provided with a modicum of basic terrorist training in Afghanistan. In contrast to the professional cadre detailed above, however, Ressam was given very nonspecific, virtually open-ended targeting instructions before being dispatched to North America. Also unlike the well-funded professional cadre, Ressam was given only $12,000 in "seed money" and instructed to raise the rest of his operational funds from petty thievery. He was also told to recruit members for his terrorist cell from among the expatriate Muslim communities in Canada and the United States.[84]

4. Al Qaeda Network consists of homegrown Islamic radicals—from North Africa, the Middle East, and South and South-East Asia—as well as local converts to Islam mostly living in Europe, Africa, and perhaps Latin America and North America as well, who have no direct connection with al Qaeda (or any other identifiable terrorist group) but who nonetheless are prepared to carry out attacks in solidarity with or support of al Qaeda's radical jihadist agenda. They are motivated by a

shared sense of enmity and grievance toward the United States and the West in general and their host nations in particular. In this case, the relationship with al Qaeda is more inspirational than actual, abetted by profound rage over the U.S. invasion and occupation of Iraq and the oppression of Muslims in Palestine, Kashmir, Chechnya, and elsewhere. Critically, these people are neither part of a known, organized group nor even a very cohesive entity unto themselves. Examples of this category, which comprises small cells of like-minded locals who gravitate toward the cell to plan and mount terrorist attacks completely independently of any direction provided by al Qaeda, include the group of mostly Moroccan Islamic radicals based in Spain who carried out the March 2004 Madrid bombings and their counterparts in the Netherlands who were responsible for the November 2004 murder of Theo Van Gogh, among others.

The most salient threat posed by these four categories continues to come from al Qaeda Central and then from its affiliates and associates. However, an additional and equally challenging threat is now posed by less discernible and more unpredictable entities drawn from the vast Muslim diaspora in Europe. As far back as 2001, the Netherlands' intelligence and security service detected increased terrorist recruitment efforts among Muslim youth living in the Netherlands who it was previously assumed had been completely assimilated into Dutch society and culture.[85] Representatives of Muslim extremist organizations had already succeeded in embedding themselves in, and drawing new sources of support from, receptive elements within established diaspora communities. In this way, new recruits who likely had not previously come under the scrutiny of local or national law enforcement agencies could be brought into the movement.

This new category of terrorist adversary, moreover, has also proved more difficult for the authorities in these countries to track and anticipate. They constitute often previously unknown cells, which it is difficult, if not impossible, to effectively profile. Although the members may be marginalized individuals who work in menial jobs, are from the lower socioeconomic strata of society, and possibly have long criminal records or histories of juvenile delinquency, others may well come from solidly middle- and upper-middle-class backgrounds with university and perhaps even graduate degrees and previous passions for cars, sports, rock music, and other completely secular, more ethereal interests. What they will have in common is a combination of a deep commitment to their faith—perhaps recently rediscovered; admiration of bin Laden for the cathartic blow struck against America on 9/11;

hatred of the United States and the West; and a profoundly shared sense of alienation from their host countries. These new recruits are the anonymous cogs in the worldwide al Qaeda enterprise and include both long-standing residents and new immigrants found across in Europe, but specifically in countries with large expatriate Muslim populations such as Britain, Spain, France, Germany, Italy, the Netherlands, and Belgium.

The al Qaeda Movement's Ideological Resiliency and Continued Resonance

Despite the damage and destruction and losses of key leaders and personnel that al Qaeda has suffered since 2001, it stubbornly adheres to its fundamental raison d'être: continuing to inspire and motivate the broader radical jihadist community. The principle of jihad is the ideological bond that unites this amorphous movement, transcending its loose structure, diverse membership, and geographical separation. The requirement to engage in jihad is relentlessly expounded in both video- and audiotapes of bin Laden, al-Zawahiri, and other senior al Qaeda personalities, on myriad jihadist Web sites, and by radical clerics and lay preachers speaking in mosques or addressing informal circles of adherents in more private settings. The struggle is cast in narrow, defensive terms: extolling the duty of the faithful to defend Islam by the sword. Imitation by example is encouraged through the depiction of the sacrifices of past martyrs (suicide terrorists and others who perished in battle against the infidel) coupled with messages about the importance of continuous battle against Islam's enemies. "It is no secret that warding off the American enemy is the top duty after faith and that nothing should take priority over it," bin Laden wrote in his seminal 1996 declaration of war.[86] Such exhortations continue to resonate today, when many Muslims harbor a deep sense of humiliation and resentment over the invasions of Afghanistan and Iraq, the continued bloodletting of their coreligionists in Palestine, Chechnya, and Kashmir, among other places,[87] the ill treatment of detainees at Abu Ghraib and Guantánamo alongside the myriad other reasons jihadists have for hating the United States. Indeed, the expostulated theological requirement to avenge the shedding of innocent Muslim blood—and particularly that of Muslim children who have been killed in Iraq and Palestine—has repeatedly been invoked by bin Laden.[88] These calls for revenge, coupled with the terrorists' own abiding faith in the potential regenerative power of even a single, dramatic terrorist attack to breathe new life into the jihadist movement, ensure that the war on terrorism will be won neither easily nor soon.

Terrorist morale is also sustained by propaganda portraying the 9/11 attacks as a great victory and America's involvement in Iraq as a quagmire that will ultimately bring about the downfall of the United States. The connection between the destruction of the World Trade Center and the blow struck against the U.S. economy by the 9/11 attacks has been a persistent jihadist theme.[89] It was repeated by bin Laden himself in the videotape broadcast on October 29, 2004, when he explained, "So we are continuing this policy in bleeding America to the point of bankruptcy. Allah willing, and nothing is too great for Allah."[90] Parallels are also drawn with the mujahideen's defeat of the Red Army in Afghanistan, the alleged chain reaction it set in motion that led to the demise of the Soviet Union and the collapse of communism with the current travails the United States faces in Iraq, and the inevitability of our defeat there at the hands of contemporary jihadists. Indeed, al Qaeda propaganda has long described the United States as a "paper tiger,"[91] on the verge of financial ruin and total collapse much as the USSR once was, with the power of Islam poised similarly to push America over the precipice.[92] Bin Laden emphasized this very point in his last publicly known address to his fighters in December 2001, when he declared, "America is in retreat by the grace of God Almighty and economic attrition is continuing up to today. But it needs further blows. The young men need to seek out the nodes of the American economy and strike the enemy's nodes."[93] And he repeated it again in the aforementioned videotape, released just days before the 2004 American presidential elections. "This is in addition to our having experience in using guerrilla warfare and the war of attrition to fight tyrannical superpowers, as we, alongside the Mujahideen, bled Russia for ten years, until it went bankrupt and was forced to withdraw in defeat. All Praise is due to Allah."[94] This strategy thus continues to guide jihadist target selection and tactics today.

The ability of the al Qaeda movement to continue to prosecute this struggle is also a direct reflection of its capacity to attract new recruits and replenish expended resources. Hence, the main challenge for al Qaeda and the wider jihadist movement is to promote and ensure its durability as an ideology and concept. It can achieve this only by staying in the news, elbowing itself into the limelight through dramatic and bloody attack and thereby promoting its continued relevance as the defender and avenger of Muslims everywhere.[95] Violence will thus continue to be key to ensuring its continued presence as an international political force. Hence, al Qaeda and the wider movement's resiliency, if not longevity, will be predicated on its continued ability to recruit new cadre, mobilize the Muslim masses, and marshal support—both spiritual and practical—for jihad.

Repercussions of Iraq on the Broader Terrorist Threat

Iraq had already emerged as an important rallying cry for al Qaeda and the radical jihadist movement even before the actual invasion began. The call to arms that al Qaeda issued, however, was not in support of Saddam Hussein or his regime but in resistance to what was—and is still—perceived as continued U.S. and Western aggression against Muslims and neo-colonialist encroachment on Muslim lands. In fact, the idea that al Qaeda wanted to make Iraq the central battlefield of jihad was first suggested by al Qaeda itself. In February 2003, a month before the U.S.-led coalition even invaded Iraq, the movement's information department released the fifth and sixth installments of a series of online articles titled *In the Shadow of the Lances* that had begun to appear shortly after the 9/11 attacks. Although the previous installments had been written by al Qaeda's chief spokesman, Suleimain Abu Ghaith, who had been trained as a theologian and a Muslim cleric, these two new issues were authored by Saif al-Adl,[96] the movement's chief of military operations, one of its most senior commanders and a warrior by training who had been an officer in the Egyptian Army's Special Forces and a military trainer at al Qaeda's al-Farook camp in Afghanistan.[97] In these two issues, al-Adl imparted practical advice to Iraqis and foreign jihadists on how guerrilla warfare tactics could be used against the American and British troops. "Turn the mujahedin military force into small units with good administrative capabilities," he suggested, since this "will spare us big losses. Large military units pose management problems. They occupy large areas which are difficult to conceal from air reconnaissance and air attack."[98] His exhortations echoed previous statements made by bin Laden since at least 1996 about the asymmetric virtues of guerrilla warfare. Indeed, the al Qaeda leader has often cited the victory he claims was achieved with this tactic against American forces in Mogadishu, Somalia, during October 1993—when eighteen U.S. Army Rangers and Delta Force commandos were killed in fighting with Somali militiamen and, according to bin Laden, al Qaeda fighters too.[99] "It must be obvious to you," bin Laden had stated in his 1996 declaration of war, that, "due to the imbalance of power between our armed forces and the enemy forces, a suitable means of fighting must be adopted i.e. using fast moving light forces that work under complete secrecy. In other words to initiate a guerrilla warfare, were [*sic*] the sons of the nation, and not the military forces, take part in it."[100] For bin Laden, the withdrawal of American military forces that followed is proof that terrorism and guerrilla warfare can defeat more powerful opponents.

Al Qaeda's entreaties to jihadists to descend on Iraq and confront the United States and coalition military forces only intensified after the fall of Baghdad. For example, a statement posted on the movement's alneda.com Web site on April 9, 2003, which was clearly written after American forces had entered the Iraqi capital, lauded the virtues of guerrilla warfare against conventional military opponents. Under the heading "Guerrilla Warfare Is the most Powerful Weapon Muslims have, and It is The Best Method to Continue the Conflict with the Crusader Enemy," these lessons of history were cited to rally jihadists for renewed battle. "With guerilla warfare," it explained,

> the Americans were defeated in Vietnam and the Soviets were defeated in Afghanistan. This is the method that expelled the direct Crusader colonialism from most of the Muslim lands, with Algeria the most well known. We still see how this method stopped Jewish immigration to Palestine, and caused reverse immigration of Jews from Palestine. The successful attempts of dealing defeat to invaders using guerilla warfare were many, and we will not expound on them. However, these attempts have proven that the most effective method for the materially weak against the strong is guerrilla warfare.[101]

The clearest explication of al Qaeda's strategy in Iraq was provided by Zawahiri himself on the occasion of the second anniversary of the 9/11 attacks. "We thank God," he declared, "for appeasing us with the dilemmas in Iraq and Afghanistan. The Americans are facing a delicate situation in both countries. If they withdraw they will lose everything and if they stay, they will continue to bleed to death."[102] On the attacks' third anniversary, he issued a slightly different version of the same statement, now proclaiming that U.S. defeat in Iraq and Afghanistan "has become just a question of time" and explaining, "The Americans in both countries are between two fires. If they continue, they will bleed until death, and if they withdraw, they will lose everything."[103] Indeed, what U.S. military commanders optimistically described in late 2003 as the jihadist "magnet" or terrorist "flytrap" orchestrated by the U.S. invasion of Iraq is thus viewed very differently by al Qaeda. "Two years after Tora Bora," Zawahiri observed in December 2003, "the American bloodshed [has] started to increase in Iraq and the Americans are unable to defend themselves."[104] For al Qaeda, accordingly, Iraq has proved to be both an important battleground and an effective means of preoccupying American military forces and distracting U.S. attention while al Qaeda and its confederates make new inroads and strike elsewhere. On a personal level, it may have also provided bin Laden and al-Zawahiri with the breathing space that they desperately needed to further obfuscate their trail. But most important, Iraq has figured prominently in al Qaeda and jihadist plans and propaganda as a way to reinvigorate the jihadist cause and sustain its momentum as well as engage U.S. forces in battle and thus perpetuate the image of Islam cast perpetually on the defensive with no alternative but to take up arms against American and Western aggressors. In addition, the ongoing violence in Iraq, coupled with the inability of U.S. and coalition and Iraqi security forces to maintain order and the Abu Ghraib revelations along with other disadvantageous developments, have all doubtless contributed to America's poor standing in the Muslim world.

Finally, whatever the outcome of the current conflict in Iraq, its consequences will likely be felt for years to come. Much like Afghanistan after the struggle against the Soviet occupation ended in that country, the surviving foreign jihadists who fought in Iraq will eventually return to their home countries or the émigré communities that they came from. Having been blooded in battle in Iraq, they will possess experience, cachet, and credibility that will be useful for both jihadist recruitment and operational purposes elsewhere. Moreover, in contrast to the mujahideen who returned home from Afghanistan a decade and a half ago, trained mostly in rural guerrilla warfare, this new generation of jihadists will have acquired in Iraq invaluable firsthand experience in urban warfare—including the construction of vehicular and roadside IEDs, the use of standoff weaponry like mortars and similar remote-control-fired devices, assassination and kidnapping techniques, and sniper and ambush tactics.[105] The application of these newly learned capabilities to urban centers in Europe, North Africa, the Middle East, South Asia, and elsewhere could result in a precipitous escalation of bloodshed and destruction, reaching into countries and regions that hitherto have experienced little, if any, organized jihadist violence. While the threat to Europe is perhaps the most serious, the danger may be greatest in Saudi Arabia—the country from which the overwhelming majority of jihadists (61 percent) fighting in Iraq hail.[106]

The al Qaeda Movement Today and Tomorrow

Al Qaeda's obituary has been written too often since 9/11. "Al-Qa'ida's Top Primed to Collapse, U.S. Says," trumpeted a *Washington Post* headline two weeks after KSM's arrest in March 2003. "I believe the tide has turned in terms of al-Qa'ida," Congressman Porter J. Goss, then-chairman of the U.S. House of Representatives Intelligence Committee and himself a former

CIA case officer who became its director a year later, was quoted as saying. "We've got them nailed," an unidentified intelligence expert was quoted as saying, and still more expansively declared, "We're close to dismantling them."[107] These upbeat assessments continued the following month with the nearly bloodless capture of Baghdad and the failure of al Qaeda to make good on threats of renewed attack in retaliation for invasion.[108] Citing administration sources, an article in the *Washington Times* on April 24, 2003, reported the prevailing view in official Washington that al Qaeda's "failure to carry out a successful strike during the U.S.-led military campaign to topple Saddam Hussein has raised questions about their ability to carry out major new attacks."[109] Despite major terrorist attacks in Jakarta and Istanbul during the latter half of the year and the escalating insurgency in Iraq, this optimism carried into 2004. "The Al Qaida of the 9/11 period is under catastrophic stress," Ambassador Cofer Black, at the time the U.S. State Department's counterterrorism coordinator, declared. "They are being hunted down, their days are numbered."[110] Then came the Madrid bombings six weeks later and the deaths of 191 people. The most accurate assessment, perhaps, was therefore the one offered by al Qaeda itself. "The Americans," Thabet bin Qais, a spokesperson for the movement, said in May 2003, "only have predications and old intelligence left. It will take them a long time to understand the new form of al-Qaida."[111] Admittedly, while the first part of bin Qais's assertion is not correct, there is more than a grain of truth to the second part: we are indeed still struggling to understand the changing character and nature of al Qaeda and the shifting dimensions of the terrorist threat as it has evolved since 9/11.

Whatever the future holds for bin Laden and al Qaeda, it is indisputable that the war on terrorism will likely be longer than many believed when it began more than four years ago. It has already surpassed the amount of time that the United States fought World War II. And, by any measure, it has already had a seismic effect on the United States and the entire world. Bin Laden is in fact one of the few people alive who can claim to have fundamentally changed the course of history. And, in this respect, the epic battle that he launched is not over yet. Even bin Laden's death is unlikely to collapse the movement he created. The al Qaeda cofounder and leader has in fact long prepared for his death and has likely formulated a succession plan of his own, not necessarily with regard to who specifically will replace him as leader, but in order to ensure the continuation of the movement and revolution that he set in motion. On several occasions, bin Laden has spoken of his own martyrdom and warmly welcomed it. In August 1998, for instance, he declared, "I am fighting so I can die a martyr and go to heaven to meet

God. Our fight is now against America. I regret having lived this long. I have nothing to lose." And again, four months later, he proclaimed, "I am not afraid of death. Rather, martyrdom is my passion because martyrdom would lead to the birth of 1,000s of Osamas."[112] Although much of what bin Laden says is a mixture of bravado and braggadocio, in the past when we have failed to take him at his word, it has often been to our detriment. Given the immense patience, elongated time frames, and meticulous planning that have long characterized bin Laden's oversight of al Qaeda's major tactical operations, we can be sure he has devoted the requisite thought and effort to safeguarding his legacy and his movement's longevity.

What bin Laden also doubtless understands is that in the post-9/11 world, terrorism's power to coerce and intimidate, to force changes in our daily lives, and to influence our policies and affect how and on what we spend money has increased enormously. In this respect, not only the stakes have grown, but so have public fears and expectations. More and more, the measure of success in the war on terrorism is defined as the ability of intelligence agencies and law enforcement organizations to prevent, preempt, and deter attacks. Conversely, the measure of success for the terrorists has become simply the ability to act. Although there is a world of difference between bombing a bar on a Saturday night in Bali and laying waste to the World Trade Towers and severely damaging the Pentagon, the impacts are no longer completely dissimilar. The tragic loss of innocent life in any attack linked to al Qaeda is calculated by its masterminds to rekindle worldwide the same profound fears and anxieties that the attacks on 9/11 ignited. Al Qaeda's stature and reception in parts of the world today is a product of the extraordinary success achieved and attention generated by the attacks that day. Under these circumstances, we must be careful to avoid impatience and the temptation to declare victory in the war on terrorism—and not least, we must guard against precipitous optimism.

Countering terrorism is akin to taking a series of time-lapse photographs. The image captured on film today is not the same as the image yesterday, nor will it be the same tomorrow.[113] Terrorism, similarly, is constantly changing, evolving—indeed, far more rapidly and consequentially during the period of time since 9/11. In February 2006, we face a different enemy than we confronted on 9/11. Winning the war on terrorism will take decades, not years, to accomplish. If we are to succeed, our efforts must be as tireless, innovative, and dynamic as those of our opponents.

Notes

1. Defining Terrorism

1. *The Oxford English Dictionary, Compact Edition* (Oxford: Oxford University Press, 1971), p. 3268, col. 216.

2. Ibid.

3. David Rapoport, "Terrorism," in Mary Hawkesworth and Maurice Kogan, eds., *Routledge Encyclopedia of Government and Politics* (London: Routledge, 1992), 2:1061.

4. Quoted in R. R. Palmer, *The Age of the Democratic Revolution*, vol. 2, *The Struggle* (Princeton, N.J.: Princeton University Press, 1970), p. 126.

5. Quoted in ibid., p. 124.

6. Walter Laqueur, *The Age of Terrorism* (Boston: Little, Brown, 1987), p. 11.

7. Quoted in *Oxford English Dictionary*, p. 3268, col. 216.

8. It should be noted that the phrase itself was popularized by Paul Brousse, the French physician turned anarchist, in the newspaper he founded and edited, *L'Avant-Garde*. See David Stafford, *From Anarchism to Reformism: A Study of the Political Activities of Paul Brousse Within the First International and the French Socialist Movement, 1870–90* (Toronto: University of Toronto Press, 1971), pp. 76–88, 123–24. The text of the article may be found on pp. 256–59.

9. Quoted in George Woodcock, ed., *The Anarchist Reader* (Glasgow: Fontana, 1977), pp. 43–44.

10. Interestingly, the group was staunchly opposed to terrorism in democratic, open societies such as the United States. In 1881, for example, the executive committee of Narodnaya Volya publicly denounced for this reason the alleged anarchist political motive behind the assassination that year of U.S. president James Garfield. As Grant Wardlaw explains, Narodnaya Volya believed that terrorism could be justified only in extreme circumstances, and it denounced all such actions in countries that permitted "normal political activity." See *Political Terrorism: Theory, Tactics, and Counter-measures* (Cambridge: Cambridge University Press, 1990), p. 23.

11. Lavrov, quoted in Zeev Ivianksi, "Fathers and Sons: A Study of Jewish Involve-ment in the Revolutionary Movement and Terrorism in Tsarist Russia," *Terrorism and Political Violence* 1, no. 2 (April 1989): 146.

12. An interesting account of the assassination and the context that gave rise to Narodnaya Volya can be found in Franklin L. Ford, *Political Murder: From Tyran-nicde to Terrorism* (Cambridge, Mass.: Harvard University Press, 1985), pp. 224–30.

13. The successor group active in 1905 has already been described. In 1887 another group—which included Vladimir Lenin's older brother—attempted to assassinate Alexander III. They too were arrested and hanged. See Vera Broido, *Apostles Into Terrorists: Women and the Revolutionary Movement in the Russia of Alexander II* (London: Maurice Temple Smith, 1977), pp. 198–203.

14. The anarchist, it should be noted, was neither necessarily nor exclusively vio-lent. Indeed, many remained simply intellectuals, advocating freedom of all types, while abjuring and condemning the use of violence.

15. For example, in addition to McKinley, anarchists attempted to assassinate the German Kaiser in 1878, murdered the president of Italy in 1894, King Umberto I of Italy in 1900, Empress Elizabeth of Austria-Hungary in 1898, and the prime ministers of Spain in 1897 and 1912, and were implicated in the 1886 Haymarket Square bombing in Chicago and in other incidents such as François-Claudius Ravachol's bombings of Paris's rue St. Germain in 1892, and Emile Henry's bombing of the Café Terminus in 1894.

16. As James Joll recounts: "The violence of this propaganda and the explicit incitement contained in pamphlets like [Johann] Most's . . . *Science of Revolution-ary Warfare* ('a manual of instruction in the use and preparation of Nitro-glycerine, Dynamite, Gun-cotton, Fulminating Mercury, Bombs, Fuses, Poisons, etc.') all con-tributed to the anarchists' being held responsible for any violent disturbances." *The Anarchists* (Boston: Little, Brown, 1964), p. 141.

17. Quoted in Patrick Bishop and Eamonn Mallie, *The Provisional IRA* (London: Corgi, 1989), p. 21.

18. Walter Laqueur, *Terrorism* (London: Weidenfeld and Nicolson, 1977), p. 106.

19. Tim Pat Coogan; *The IRA: A History* (Niwot, Colo.: Roberts Rinehart, 1993), p. 11.

20. Bishop and Mallie, *The Provisional IRA*, p. 21.

21. See, for example, Ingrid Bazinet, "British Ex-Detainees See Link Between Guantanamo, Iraq Torture," *Agence France Presse*, May 14, 2004; Kate Zernike and David Rhode, "Forced Nudity of Iraqi Prisoners Is Seen as a Pervasive Pattern, Not Isolated Incidents," *New York Times*, June 8, 2004; David Rose, *Guantanamo: Amer-ica's War on Human Rights* (London: Faber and Faber, 2004), pp. 97–99; and R. Jef-frey Smith, "Justice Redacted Memo on Detainees: FBI Criticism of Interrogations Was Deleted," *Washington Post*, March 22, 2005.

22. Coogan, *The IRA*, p. 12.

23. Quoted in Lindsay Clutterbuck, "The Progenitors of Terrorism: Russian Rev-olutionaries or Extreme Irish Republicans?" *Terrorism and Political Violence* 16, no. 1 (Spring 2004): 163.

24. See "O'Donovan Rossa's Dynamiters," from *Irish World*, August 28, 1880, in Walter Laqueur, ed., *Voices of Terror: Manifestos, Writings, and Manuals of Al Qaeda, Hamas, and Other Terrorists from Around the World and Throughout the Ages* (New York: Reed Press, 2004), pp. 117–18.

25. See the calculator at http://minneapolisfed.org/Research/data/us/calc/histor1800.cfm.

26. Quoted in Clutterbuck, "The Progenitors of Terrorism," p. 163.

27. Laqueur, *Terrorism*, p. 113.

28. Clutterbuck, "The Progenitors of Terrorism," p. 165.

29. Lindsay Clutterbuck, "Countering Irish Republican Terrorism in Britain: Its Origin as a Police Function" (unpublished manuscript, 2005; made available courtesy of Dr. Clutterbuck).

30. Laqueur, *Terrorism*, p. 69.

31. Clutterbuck, "The Progenitors of Terrorism," p. 169.

32. Coogan, *The IRA*, p. 12.

33. Clutterbuck, "Countering Irish Republican Terrorism in Britain," p. 10.

34. Clutterbuck, "The Progenitors of Terrorism," p. 176.

35. Kachig Toloyan, "Martyrdom as Legitimacy: Terrorism, Religion, and Symbolic Appropriation in the Armenian Diaspora," in Paul Wilkinson and A. M. Stewart, eds., *Contemporary Research on Terrorism* (Aberdeen: Aberdeen University Press, 1987), pp. 90–91.

36. See Roland Gaucher, *Les Terroristes* (Paris: Editions Albin Michel, 1965), pp. 181–89.

37. The second is Hitler's "Final Solution" involving the Jews, and the third, Pol Pot's reign of terror in Cambodia after 1975.

38. Laurence Lafore, *The Long Fuse: An Interpretation of the Origins of World War I* (London: Weidenfeld and Nicolson, 1966), p. 180.

39. Ibid.

40. The names of both the Black Hand and Dmitrievich were again invoked in July 1997 in threats issued against British peacekeeping forces stationed in Bosnia as part of the NATO-led Stabilization Force, SFOR.

41. Imanuel Geiss, ed., *July 1914: The Outbreak of the First World War* (New York: Norton, 1967), p. 52.

42. Ibid., pp. 52–53. See also Vladimir Dedijer, *The Road to Sarajevo* (London: MacGibbon and Kee, 1967), pp. 393–95.

43. Quoted in Laqueur, *The Age of Terrorism*, p. 66.

44. Quoted in Alan Bullock, *Hitler: A Study in Tyranny* (New York: Harper, 1958), pp. 239–40.

45. Robert Conquest, *The Great Terror* (Harmondsworth: Penguin, 1971), p. 14.

46. Robert C. Tucker, *Stalin in Power: The Revolution from Above, 1928–1941* (New York: Norton, 1990), p. 271.

47. See the brilliant exegesis of terrorism's history of imprecise definition in Conor Gearty, *The Future of Terrorism* (London: Phoenix, 1997), pp. 11–13.

48. Yasir Arafat, "Address to the UN General Assembly (November 13, 1974)," in Walter Laqueur, ed., *The Israel-Arab Reader: A Documentary History of the Middle East Conflict* (New York: Bantam, 1976), p. 510.

49. Claire Sterling, *The Terror Network: The Secret War of International Terrorism* (New York: Holt, Rinehart, and Winston, 1981). See also Ray S. Cline and Yonah Alexander, *Terrorism: The Soviet Connection* (New York: Crane Russak, 1984), and, by far the least polemical of this genre, Roberta Goren, *The Soviet Union and Terrorism*, ed. Jillian Becker (London: Allen and Unwin, 1984).

50. See, e.g., Brian Michael Jenkins, *New Modes of Conflict* (Santa Monica, Calif.: RAND Corporation, R-3009-DNA, June 1983), pp. 13–14; Brian Michael Jenkins, *International Terrorism: The Other World War* (Santa Monica, Calif.: RAND Corporation, R-3302-AF, November 1985), pp. 19–20; and David C. Martin and John Walcott, *Best Laid Plans: The Inside Story of America's War Against Terrorism* (New York: Harper and Row, 1988), p. 46.

51. The term was first coined by the French criminologist and terrorism expert Xavier Raufer, in 1991.

52. Rachel Ehrenfeld, *Narco-Terrorism* (New York: Basic Books, 1990), pp. ix, xiii.

53. Two particularly informative discussions about the myth of "narco-terrorism" and the political baggage the term carried with it can be found in Grant Wardlaw, "Linkages Between the Illegal Drugs Traffic and Terrorism," *Conflict Quarterly* 8, no. 3 (Summer 1988): 5–26, and Abraham H. Miller and Nicholas A. Damask, "The Dual Myths of 'Narco-Terrorism': How Myths Drive Policy," *Terrorism and Political Violence* 8, no. 1 (Spring 1996): 114–31. See also Mark Bowden, *Killing Pablo: The Hunt for the World's Greatest Outlaw* (New York: Atlantic Monthly Press, 2001).

54. See, for example, Bowden, *Killing Pablo*.

55. Peter Lupsha, "Gray Area Phenomenon: New Threats and Policy; Dilemmas," unpublished paper quoted by Ambassador Edwin G. Corr in introduction to Max G. Manwaring. ed., *Gray Area Phenomena: Confronting the New World Disorder* (Boulder, Colo.: Westview, 1993), p. xiii.

56. Xavier Raufer, "Gray Areas: A New Security Threat," *Political Warfare*, no. 19 (Spring 1992): 1.

57. Bruce Hoffman, "Low-Intensity Conflict: Terrorism and Guerrilla Warfare in the Coming Decades," in Lawrence Howard, ed., *Terrorism: Roots, Impact, Responses* (New York: Praeger, 1992), p. 140.

58. The exact number of deaths caused by the 9/11 attacks is believed to be 2,976. Of these, the New York City Medical Examiner's Office concluded that 2,752 were killed by American Airlines Flight 11 and United Airlines Flight 75, which struck the World Trade Center towers. Forty people were killed when United Airlines Flight 93 crashed into a rural field in Somerset County, Pennsylvania, and 184 people were killed when American Airlines Flight 77 struck the Pentagon. The numbers of people seriously injured were surprisingly low and defied initially dire expectations. According to a RAND Corporation estimate, no more than about 250 people

required hospitalization for one day or more as a result of the attacks. See Lloyd Dixon and Rachel Kaganoff Stern, *Compensation Losses from the 9/11 Attacks* (Santa Monica, Calif.: RAND Corporation, MG-264-ICJ, 2004), pp. 15–16. The RAND report cites New York City Medical Examiner's Office, Office of Chief Medical Examiner, "World Trade Center Operational Statistics," April 2004, as the source from which these data were obtained. See also National Commission on Terrorist Attacks Upon the United States, *The 9/11 Commission Report: Authorized Edition* (New York: Norton, 2004), p. 552, n. 188.

59. Brian Michael Jenkins, "The Organization Men: Anatomy of a Terrorist Attack," in James F. Hoge Jr. and Gideon Rose, eds., *How Did This Happen? Terrorism and the New War* (New York: Public Affairs, 2001), p. 5.

60. Some 440 people perished in a 1978 fire deliberately set by terrorists at a movie theater in Abadan, Iran.

61. See the White House, President George W. Bush, Office of the Press Secretary, "President Declares 'Freedom at War with Fear': Address to a Joint Session of Congress and the American People," September 20, 2001, http://www.whitehouse. gov/news/releases/2001/09/print/20010920–8.html. Interestingly, neither conclusive data nor complete agreement exists on this figure. A U.S. State Department publication produced shortly after the attacks, for instance, cites 78 countries. See U.S. Department of State, *The Network of Terrorism* (Washington, D.C.: U.S. State Department, 2001), p. 6; while the New York Times, *A Nation Challenged: A Visual History of 9/11 and Its Aftermath* (New York: Callaway, 2002), p. 234, states that among the victims were the citizens of 115 countries. And a Web site dedicated to the victims of the 9/11 attacks, http://www.september11victims.com/ september11victims/COUNTRY_CITIZENSHIP.htm, cites a much lower figure of citizens of only 36 countries.

62. Bruce Hoffman, *Lessons of 9/11: Statement Submitted for the Committee Record to the United States Joint September 11, 2001 Inquiry Staff of the House and Senate Select Committees on Intelligence, 8 October 2002* (Santa Monica, Calif.: RAND Corporation, 2002), p. 2.

63. Quoted in Ken Herman, "After the Assault: U.S. Braces for Crusade Against 'Evil,'" *Atlanta Journal-Constitution*, September 17, 2001.

64. *Oxford English Dictionary*, p. 3268, col. 216.

65. Quoted in U.S. Department of State, *Patterns of Global Terrorism 2001* (Washington, D.C.: U.S. Department of State, Publication 10940, May 2002), p. i.

66. White House, "President Declares 'Freedom at War with Fear,'" September 20, 2001. See also the 2002 State of the Union Address, in which President Bush stated, "Iraq continues to flaunt its hostility toward America and to support terror." White House, "The President Delivers State of the Union Address," January 29, 2002, http://www.whitehouse.gov/news/releases/2002/01/20020129–11.html.

67. See White House, "The President Delivers State of the Union Address," in which President Bush declared: "States like these, and their terrorist allies, constitute an axis of evil, arming to threaten the peace of the world. By seeking weapons

of mass destruction, these regimes pose a grave and growing danger. They could provide these arms to terrorists, giving them the means to match their hatred. They could attack our allies or attempt to blackmail the United States. In any of these cases, the price of indifference would be catastrophic."

68. Michael Howard, "What Friends Are For," *National Interest*, no. 69 (Fall 2002): 8.

69. See Richard A. Clarke, *Against All Enemies: Inside America's War on Terrorism* (New York: Free Press, 2004), pp. 30–33, 241–42, 264–65, 268–69.

70. See the White House, "President Bush Discusses Iraq: Remarks by the President to the Pool Before and After Golf—Crawford, Texas," August 10, 2002, http://www.whitehouse.gov/news/releases/2002/08/20020810–3.html, in which the president explains: "I described them [Iraq] as the axis of evil once. I described them as an enemy until proven otherwise. They obviously, you know, desire weapons of mass destruction. I presume that he [Saddam Hussein] still views us as an enemy. I have constantly said that we owe it to our children and our children's children to free the world from weapons of mass destruction in the hands of those who hate freedom. . . . What I do believe the American people understand is that weapons of mass destruction in the hands of leaders such as Saddam Hussein are very dangerous for ourselves, our allies. They understand the concept of blackmail. They know that when we speak of making the world more safe, we do so not only in the context of al Qaeda and other terrorist groups, but nations that have proven themselves to be bad neighbors and bad actors."

71. Quoted in Walter Pincus, "British Intelligence Warned Blair of War," *Washington Post*, May 13, 2005.

72. Michael Howard, "Smoke on the Horizon," *Financial Times* (London), September 7, 2002.

73. Quoted in Bob Woodward, *Bush at War* (New York: Simon and Schuster, 2003), p. 94. The acute sensitivity that this particular word arouses among Muslims is explained by medieval historian Hugh Kennedy as follows: "The word 'crusade' is used by Western politicians almost without thought to describe a war fought for idealistic and ideological motives, rather than for naked gain. For many Muslims, brought up to see themselves as innocent victims and the idea of the crusade as essentially anti-Islamic, the apparent survival of the crusading ideal is threatening and sinister." See Hugh Kennedy, "Holy Warriors: Telling the Story of the Crusades as History, Not Metaphor," *New York Times Book Review*, April 3, 2005, p. 24.

74. Geoffrey Nunberg, "The War of Words: 'Terror' and 'Terrorism,'" *International Herald Tribune* (Paris), July 22, 2004.

75. See, e.g., John [Johann] Most, "Advice for Terrorists," in Walter Laqueur and Yonah Alexander, eds., *The Terrorism Reader* (New York: Meridian, 1987), pp. 100–109, and David Rapoport, "The Politics of Atrocity," in Yonah Alexander and Seymour Maxwell Finger, eds., *Terrorism: Interdisciplinary Perspectives* (New York: John Jay Press, 1977), p. 46.

76. See, e.g., the treatises written by two group members, Nikolai Morozov's

"The Terrorist Struggle" and G. Tarnovski's "Terrorism and Routine," in Laqueur and Alexander, *The Terrorism Reader*, pp. 72–79; also see Broido, *Apostles Into Terrorists*, p. 180.

77. See, for example, Committee for the Publication of Lehi Writings, *B'Ha'Machterot* [In the Underground] (Tel Aviv: Yair Press, 1959), vol. D, pp. 45–46; ibid., vol. A, p. 357; ibid., vol. B, pp. 141–44; Gerold Frank, *The Deed* (New York: Simon and Schuster, 1963), pp. 131, 133–34; Joseph Heller, *The Stern Gang: Ideology, Politics, and Terror, 1940–1949* (London: Frank Cass, 1995), pp. 104, 115, and 125; and Yitzhak Shamir, *Summing Up: An Autobiography* (London: Weidenfeld and Nicolson, 1994), pp. 151–52.

78. Martha Crenshaw, *Terrorism and International Cooperation*, Occasional Paper Series 11 (New York: Institute for East-West Security Studies, 1989), p. 5.

79. Carlos Marighela, *For the Liberation of Brazil*, trans. John Butt and Rosemary Sheed (Harmondsworth: Penguin, 1971), pp. 62, 89.

80. Peter Bergen, *Holy War, Inc.: Inside the Secret World of Osama bin Laden* (New York: Free Press, 2001), p. 29.

81. As Jason Burke notes, "'Al-Qaeda' is a messy and rough designation. . . . The word itself is critical. 'al-Qaeda' comes from the Arabic root *qaf-ayn-dal*. It can mean a base, as in a camp or a home, or a foundation, such as what is under a house. It can mean a pedestal that supports a column. It can also mean a precept, rule, principle, maxim, formula, method, model or pattern." Jason Burke, *Al-Qaeda: Casting a Shadow of Terror* (London: I. B. Tauris, 2003), p. 7. See also Jason Burke, "Think Again: Al Qaeda," *Foreign Policy* (May/June 2004), http://www.foreign policy.com.

82. Quoted in Julian Nundy, "Wounded Jackal Defends Record of Family Values," *Independent* (London), August 31, 1994.

83. Rohan Gunaratna, "Khalid Sheikh Mohammed: The Brain," *Playboy* 52, no. 6 (June 2005): 80, 170.

84. Quoted in Hala Jaber, *Hezbollah: Born with a Vengeance* (New York: Columbia University Press, 1997), p. 130.

85. Konrad Kellen, *On Terrorists and Terrorism* (Santa Monica, Calif.: RAND Corporation, N-1942-RC, December 1982), p. 10.

86. Quoted in Alison Jamieson, *Terrorism* (Hove, East Sussex: Wayland, 1991), p. 33.

87. See Judith Palmer Harik, *Hezbollah: The Changing Face of Terrorism* (London: I.B. Tauris, 2004), pp. 2–5, and Amal Saad-Horayeb, *Hizbu'llah: Politics and Religion* (London: Pluto, 2002), pp. 95–97, 145–47.

88. See Hassan M. Fattah, "Hezbollah Declares Full Support for Syria," *New York Times*, March 6, 2005, and Neal MacFarquhar, "Leader of Hezbollah Discovers a New Fray: Lebanese Politics," *New York Times*, March 13, 2005.

89. See, e.g., Crenshaw, *Terrorism and International Cooperation*, p. 5; Brian Michael Jenkins, *The Study of Terrorism: Definitional Problems* (Santa Monica, Calif.: RAND Corporation, P-6563, December 1980), p. 10; Gary Sick, "The Political Underpinnings of Terrorism," in Charles W. Kegley Jr., ed., *International Terrorism:*

Characteristics, Causes, Controls (New York: St. Martin's, 1990), p. 52; and Paul Wilkinson, "Terrorism," in Michael Foley, ed., *Ideas That Shape Politics* (Manchester: Manchester University Press, 1994), p. 189.

90. Jenkins, *The Study of Terrorism*, p. 10.

91. Quoted in Harris O. Schoenberg, *A Mandate for Terror: The United Nations and the PLO* (New York: Shapolsky Books, 1989), p. 71.

92. Quoted in Frederick J. Hacker, *Crusaders, Criminals, Crazies: Terror and Terrorism in Our Time* (New York: Norton, 1976), p. 174.

93. Quoted in Schoenberg, *A Mandate for Terror*, pp. 75–76.

94. Quoted in Hacker, *Crusaders, Criminals, Crazies*, p. 274.

95. Quoted in Abraham D. Sofaer, "Terrorism and the Law," *Foreign Affairs* 64, no. 5 (Summer 1986): 904.

96. Quoted in Albert Parry, *Terrorism: From Robespierre to Arafat* (New York: Vanguard, 1976), p. 552.

97. North Atlantic Assembly Papers, Sub-committee on Terrorism, *Terrorism* (Brussels: International Secretariat, January 1989), p. 34.

98. See UNGA Resolution 52/164, http://www.unodoc.org/unodoc/terroris_convention_terrorist_bombing.html.

99. See http://www.cns.miis.edu/pubs/inven/pdfs/bomb.pdf.

100. Jenkins, *The Study of Terrorism*, p. 2.

101. For a particularly insightful discussion of this dichotomy, see Gearty, *The Future of Terrorism*, pp. 10–11. See also "What Is Terrorism?" *Economist* (London), March 2, 1996, pp. 23–25.

102. Quoted in Sofaer, "Terrorism and the Law," p. 904.

103. Alex P. Schmid, Albert J. Jongman, et al., *Political Terrorism: A New Guide to Actors, Authors, Concepts, Data Bases, Theories, and Literature* (New Brunswick, N.J.: Transaction Books, 1988), p. 12.

104. Quoted in Christopher Dobson, *Black September: Its Short, Violent History* (London: Robert Hale, 1974, 1975), pp. 62–63.

105. The RAND Terrorism Incident Database.

106. "Arab Leaders Join World in Assailing Terrorists' Attack," *Los Angeles Times*, December 19, 1973.

107. "The Arab Terrorists," *New York Times*, December 18, 1973.

108. Juan de Onis, "Guerrilla Unit Attacks Cairo Proposal," *New York Times*, June 21, 1973.

109. John K. Cooley, "New Arab Unity Hits Palestinian Guerrillas," *Christian Science Monitor* (Boston), September 19, 1973; Joseph Fitchett, "Guerrillas Seeking Leverage," *Christian Science Monitor* (Boston), November 27, 1973.

110. "Syrian Clampdown on Fatah Guerrillas Told," *Los Angeles Times*, September 20, 1973.

111. Jonathan C. Randal, "Guerrillas Fear Trade-off of Interests," *Washington Post*, October 12, 1973; Jim Hoagland, "Palestinian Guerrillas Say They Reject Cease-fire," *Washington Post*, October 23, 1973.

112. Rapoport, "The Politics of Atrocity," p. 46.

113. "30 More Slain by 'Terrorists' near Algiers," *International Herald Tribune* (Paris), April 15, 1997.

114. James F. Clarity, "Obscure Doctor Again Faces Sinn Fein Chief," *International Herald Tribune* (Paris), April 15, 1997.

115. "In Our Pages: 100, 75, and 50 Years Ago—1947: Zionists' Suicide," *International Herald Tribune* (Paris), April 22, 1997.

116. "39 Killed in Jerusalem Headquarters," *The Times* (London), July 23, 1946; "41 Dead, 53 Injured, 52 Missing in Terrorist Attack on Secretariat," *Palestine Post* (Jerusalem), July 23, 1946.

117. Rapoport, "The Politics of Atrocity," p. 46.

118. Peter Baker and Susan B. Glasser, "Hundreds Held Hostage at School in Russia," *Washington Post*, September 2, 2004; and Peter Baker and Susan B. Glasser, "Russia School Siege Ends in Carnage," *Washington Post*, September 4, 2004.

119. C. J. Chivers and Stephen Lee Meyers, "Insurgents Seize School in Russia and Hold Scores," *New York Times*, September 2, 2004.

120. C. J. Chivers and Stephen Lee Meyers, "Terror in Russia; Battle in Beslan," *New York Times*, September 4, 2004.

121. Edward Cline, "Terrorists, Period," *Washington Post*, September 11, 2004.

122. Daniel Okrent, "The War of the Words: A Dispatch from the Front Lines," *New York Times*, March 6, 2005.

123. Quoted in U.S. Department of State, Office of the Coordinator for Counterterrorism, *Patterns of Global Terrorism 2003* (Washington, D.C.: U.S. Department of State, Publication 11124, April 2004), p. xii.

124. Quoted in Counterterrorism Threat Assessment and Warning Unit, *Terrorism in the United States 2000/2001* (Washington, D.C.: U.S. Department of Justice, FBI Publication #0308, 2002), p. 3.

125. One Hundred Seventh Congress of the United States of America, *Homeland Security Act of 2002*, January 23, 2002, o. HR 5005–7, http://www.dhs.gov/dhspublic/public/display?theme = 46&content = 410.

126. See Department of Defense Dictionary of Military and Associated Terms, http://www.dtic.mil/doctrine/jel/dodict/data/t/05373.html.

127. Department of State, Office of the Coordinator for Counterterrorism, *Patterns of Global Terrorism 2003*, p. xii.

128. Brian M. Jenkins, "International Terrorism: A New Mode of Conflict," in David Carlton and Carlo Schaerf, eds., *International Terrorism and World Security* (London: Croom Helm, 1975), p. 16.

129. See, for example, the explanation in Counterterrorism Threat Assessment and Warning Unit, *Terrorism in the United States 1999* (Washington, D.C.: U.S. Department of Justice, FBI Publication #0308, 2000), pp. 1, 5–7.

130. Alex P. Schmid, *Political Terrorism: A Research Guide* (New Brunswick, N.J.: Transaction Books, 1984), p. x.

131. Schmid, Jongman, et al., *Political Terrorism*, p. 1.

132. Walter Laqueur, *Terrorism* (London: Weidenfeld and Nicolson, 1977), p. 7; Laqueur, *The Age of Terrorism*, pp. 11, 142–56.

133. The "study of terrorism," Laqueur further argued, "can manage with a minimum of theory." Quoted in Schmid, Jongman, et al., *Political Terrorism*, p. 3.

134. Ibid., p. 6.

135. As Laqueur notes, "The distinction is of more than academic importance; there have been guerrilla units of ten thousand men and women but an urban terrorist unit seldom, if ever, comprises more than a few people and urban terrorist 'movements' rarely consist of more than a few hundred members." See Walter Laqueur, *Guerrilla: A Historical and Critical Study* (Boston: Little, Brown, 1976), p. xi.

136. Ian F. W. Beckett, *Encyclopedia of Guerrilla Warfare* (New York: Checkmark Books, 2001), p. xiii.

137. Laqueur, *Guerrilla*, p. x. Laqueur goes on to note: "What is now commonly called 'urban guerrilla' warfare is, of course, terrorism in a new dress" (p. xi).

138. Beckett, *Encyclopedia of Guerrilla Warfare*, p. ix.

139. Central Intelligence Agency, *Guide to the Analysis of Insurgency* (Washington, D.C.: U.S. Government Printing Office, no date), p. 2.

140. U.S. Department of State, Office of the Coordinator for Counterterrorism, *Patterns of Global Terrorism 2003*, p. 113.

141. Ibid., p. 89.

142. Ibid. At the same time, it should be emphasized that the situation in Iraq is often so fluid and opaque, with secular Ba'athists and other former regime elements, for instance, who have been conducting insurgent attacks against U.S. and coalition forces, at times allying themselves tactically and operationally with foreign terrorists and Islamic extremists. See Bruce Hoffman, *Insurgency and Counterinsurgency in Iraq* (Santa Monica, Calif.: RAND Corporation, OP-127, 2004), p. 17.

143. Also known by its acronym, QJBR, literally Tanzim Qa'idat al-Jihad fi Bilad al Rafidaya (Organization of Jihad's Base in the Country of the Two Rivers).

144. Kellen, *On Terrorists and Terrorism*, p. 9.

145. See Ford, *Political Murder*, p. 362.

146. Kellen, *On Terrorists and Terrorism*, p. 10.

147. John Arquilla and David Ronfeldt. "A New Epoch—and Spectrum—of Conflict," in John Arquilla and David Ronfeldt, eds., *In Athena's Camp: Preparing for Conflict in the Information Age* (Santa Monica, Calif.: RAND Corporation, MR-880-OSD/RC, 1997), p. 3.

148. Quoted in Dan Barry and Al Baker, "Getting the Message from 'Eco-Terrorists': Mystery Group Takes Its Campaign East," *New York Times*, January 8, 2001.

149. *Igniting the Revolution: An Introduction to the Earth Liberation Front*, distributed by the North American Earth Liberation Front Press Office, Portland, Oregon (no date).

150. Quoted in Barry and Baker, "Getting the Message from 'Eco-Terrorists.'"

151. Ayman al-Zawahiri, *Knights Under the Prophet's Banner*, translated and published in FBIS, "Al-Sharq Al-Awsat Publishes Extracts from Al-Jihad Leader al-Zawahiri's New Book," Document ID: GMP20020108000197, January 8, 2002, p. 86. See also the excerpt reprinted in Laqueur, *Voices of Terror*, pp. 431–32.

152. These three concepts, most commonly used by or associated with the American white supremacist/far-right militia movements, are discussed in chapter 4.

153. The phrase now often used to describe al Qaeda's vast international network appears to have been coined first by John Arquilla and David Ronfeldt. See Francis Pisani, "How to Fight the Terror Network," *Le Monde Diplomatique*, February 6, 2002, http://mondeodiplo.com/2002/06/02network.

154. John Arquilla and David Ronfeldt, "The Advent of Netwar (Revisited)," in John Arquilla and David Ronfeldt, eds., *Networks and Netwars: The Future of Terror, Crime, and Militancy* (Santa Monica, Calif.: RAND Corporation, MR-1382-OSD, 2001), p. 6.

155. John Arquilla and David Ronfeldt, "The Advent of Netwar," in Arquilla and Ronfeldt, *In Athena's Camp*, p. 280.

156. See *FBI Strategic Plan, 2004–2009*, http://www.fbi.gov/publications/strategicplan/strategicplantext.htm.

2. The End of Empire and the Origins of Contemporary Terrorism

1. B. H. Liddell Hart, *History of the Second World War* (New York: Paragon, 1979), p. 233.

2. See, e.g., General George Grivas's observations concerning the impact of these promises on postwar Greek-Cypriot nationalist aspirations, in Charles Foley, ed., *The Memoirs of General Grivas* (London: Longmans, 1964), p. 12.

3. David Thomson, *Europe Since Napoleon* (Harmondsworth: Penguin, 1978), p. 778.

4. Text of the "Joint Declaration by the President and the Prime Minister, August 12, 1941," in Winston S. Churchill, *The Second World War*, vol. 3, *The Grand Alliance* (London: Reprint Society, 1956), p. 352.

5. Winston S. Churchill, *The Second World War*, vol. 4, *The Hinge of Fate* (London: Reprint Society, 1956), p. 705.

6. Quoted in Alistair Horne, *A Savage War of Peace: Algeria 1954–1962* (Harmondsworth: Penguin, 1977), p. 42.

7. Quoted in Foley, *The Memoirs of General Grivas*, p. 13.

8. Menachem Begin, *The Revolt: Story of the Irgun* (Jerusalem: Steimatzky, 1977), p. 52.

9. Quoted in Bruce Hoffman, "Jewish Terrorist Activities and the British Government in Palestine 1939 to 1947" (D.Phil. thesis, Oxford University, 1986), pp. 327–28.

10. Begin, *The Revolt*, pp. 52–54.

11. Ibid., p. 56.

12. Carlos Marighela, *For the Liberation of Brazil*, trans. John Butt and Rosemary Sheed (Harmondsworth: Penguin, 1971), pp. 61–97.

13. Begin, *The Revolt*, p. 52.

14. Hansard, *House of Commons*, vol. 441, col. 2342 (Oliver Stanley), August 12, 1947.

15. Begin, *The Revolt*, pp. 54–45.

16. See texts of 80th Congress, House Joint Resolution 196, introduced by Andrew Somers on May 15, 1947, and Senate Resolution 149, introduced by Warren Magnusson et al. on July 17, 1947, in Isaac Zaar, *Rescue and Liberation: America's Part in the Birth of Israel* (New York: Bloch, 1954), pp. 230, 243, and House Joint Resolution 237, introduced by Somers on 11 July 1947, quoted in Hoffman, "Jewish Terrorist Activities," p. 370.

17. Quoted in Michael J. Cohen, *Palestine and the Great Powers, 1945–1948* (Princeton, N.J.: Princeton University Press, 1982), p. 250.

18. Elizabeth Monroe, "Mr Bevin's 'Arab Policy,'" in Albert Hourani, ed., *St. Antony's Papers no. 11: Middle Eastern Affairs No. 2* (London: Chatto and Windus, 1961), p. 34.

19. For details of UNSCOP's visit and deliberations, see Jorge García-Granados, *The Birth of Israel: The Drama as I Saw It* (New York: Knopf, 1948). García-Granados was the Guatemalan representative on the committee.

20. The special committee issued its report on August 31, 1947, and unanimously recommended that Palestine should be granted its independence. See "Summary of the Report of UNSCOP," in Walter Laqueur, ed., *The Israel-Arab Reader: A Documentary History of the Middle East Conflict* (New York: Bantam, 1976), pp. 108–12.

21. Creech-Jones to Munro [*sic*], October 23 and November 30, 1961, boxes 32/3 and 32/6, Letters, Creech-Jones Papers, Rhodes House, Oxford.

22. "Only Thus" was the Irgun's motto. See "Speech of the Commander-in-Chief of the Irgun Zvai Le'umi, 15 May 1948," in Eli Tavin and Yonah Alexander, eds., *Psychological Warfare and Propaganda: Irgun Documentation* (Wilmington, Del.: Scholarly Resources, 1982), pp. 240–41.

23. Foley, *The Memoirs of General Grivas*, p. 47.

24. Quoted in Horne, *A Savage War of Peace*, p. 95.

25. Foley, *The Memoirs of General Grivas*, p. 208.

26. Quoted in Horne, *A Savage War of Peace*, p. 95.

27. General Grivas, *Guerrilla Warfare and Eoka's Struggle*, trans. A.A. Pallis (London: Longmans, 1964), p. 19.

28. Foley, *The Memoirs of General Grivas*, appendix 1, p. 204.

29. Ibid., p. 31.

30. Grivas, *Guerrilla Warfare and Eoka's Struggle*, p. 19.

31. Ibid., p. 38.

32. Foley, *The Memoirs of General Grivas*, p. 53.

33. Ibid., pp. 56–57; Michael Dewar, *Brush Fire Wars: Minor Campaigns of the British Army Since 1945* (New York: St. Martin's, 1984), p. 80.

34. Foley, *The Memoirs of General Grivas*, p. 71.

35. Charles Foley and W.I. Scobie, *The Struggle for Cyprus* (Stanford, Calif.: Hoover Institution Press, 1975), p. 160.

36. Quoted in Alan Hart, *Arafat: A Political Biography. The Definitive Biography Written in Co-operation with Yasser Arafat* (London: Sidgwick and Jackson, 1994), pp. 112–13. See also John K. Cooley, *Green March, Black September: The Story of the*

Palestinian Arabs (London: Frank Cass, 1973), p. 91; David Hirst, *The Gun and the Olive Branch* (London: Futura, 1977), pp. 273, 276, 306–7; Edgar O'Ballance, *Arab Guerilla Power* (London: Faber, 1974), pp. 23, 26; and Zeev Schiff and Raphael Rothstein, *Fedayeen: The Story of the Palestinian Guerrillas* (London: Valentine, Mitchell, 1972), pp. 8 and 60.

37. Nelson Mandela, *Long Walk to Freedom* (London: Abacus, 1994), pp. 326, 355.

38. Quoted in Roland Gaucher, *Les Terroristes* (Paris: Editions Albin Michel, 1965), p. 262.

39. Quoted in Horne, *A Savage War of Peace*, p. 186.

40. Quoted in ibid., p. 194.

41. Quoted in George Armstrong Kelly, *Lost Soldiers: The French Army and Empire in Crisis, 1947–1962* (Cambridge, Mass.: MIT Press, 1965), p. 201.

42. Florence Beauge, "'If France Recognized and Condemned These Practices, I Would Take That as a Step Forward,'" *Le Monde* (Paris), November 23, 2000.

43. Florence Beauge, "'I Am Resolute on Torture . . . I Myself Have Proceeded with Summary Executions . . . '" *Le Monde* (Paris), November 23, 2000.

44. Paul Aussaresses, *The Battle of the Casbah: Terrorism and Counter-Terrorism in Algeria, 1955–1957* (New York: Enigma Books, 2002), p. 126.

45. Ibid., p. 129.

3. The Internationalization of Terrorism

1. Quoted in Alex P. Schmid and Janny de Graaf, *Violence as Communication: Insurgent Terrorism and the Western News Media* (Beverly Hills, Calif.: Sage, 1982), p. 32.

2. Between 1968 and 1980, Palestinian groups were responsible for 331 incidents, compared with the 170 incidents attributed to the next most active group, the anti-Castro Cuban terrorist movements, and Irish and Turkish groups were in third position with 115 incidents each (RAND Chronology of Terrorism Incidents: see note 14).

3. Michael B. Oren, *Six Days of War: June 1967 and the Making of the Modern Middle East* (Oxford: Oxford University Press, 2002), p. 2.

4. Quoted in David Hirst, *The Gun and the Olive Branch* (London: Futura, 1977), p. 304.

5. Quoted in Schmid and de Graaf, *Violence as Communication*, p. 30.

6. Simon Reeve, *One Day In September: The Story of the 1972 Munich Olympics Massacre* (London: Faber and Faber, 2000), pp. 95–103.

7. Abu Iyad with Eric Rouleau, *My Home, My Land: A Narrative of the Palestinian Struggle*, trans. Linda Butler Koseoglu (New York: Times Books, 1981), pp. 111–12.

8. John K. Cooley, *Green March, Black September: The Story of the Palestinian Arabs* (London: Frank Cass, 1973), p. 126; Hirst, *The Gun and the Olive Branch*,

p. 311. The American ABC network alone had four hundred broadcast staff present. See James W. Hoge, "The Media and Terrorism," in Abraham Miller, ed., *Terrorism: The Media and the Law* (New York: Transnational, 1982), p. 96.

9. Peter Taylor, *States of Terror: Democracy and Political Violence* (London: Penguin, 1993), p. 8.

10. Guy R. Sanan, "Olympic Security, 1972–1996: Threat, Response, and International Cooperation" (Ph.D. diss., St. Andrews University, 1997), p. 77.

11. Quoted in Christopher Dobson and Ronald Payne, *The Carlos Complex: A Study in Terror* (London: Coronet/Hodder and Stoughton, 1978), pp. 17–18.

12. *Al-Sayad* (Beirut), September 13, 1972, quoted in Sanan, "Olympic Security 1972–1996," p. 77. The same communiqué, attributed to George Habash, is quoted in part in Taylor, *States of Terror*, p. 8.

13. Schmid and de Graaf, *Violence as Communication*, p. 31.

14. The RAND Terrorism Incident Database defines and categorizes terrorist incidents in order to help analysts, policymakers, and practitioners understand general trends in the threat. It is based on more than thirty years of research by analysts at the RAND Corporation who have both regional expertise and relevant language skills. The database is divided into two different data sets. The incidents collected between 1968 and 1998 account only for international terrorism. International terrorism includes incidents in which the perpetrators go abroad to strike their targets, select domestic targets associated with a foreign state, or create an international incident by attacking airline passengers or equipment. This data set has been continuously maintained since 1972 by the RAND Corporation, in Santa Monica, California, between 1994 and 1998 by the Centre for the Study of Terrorism and Political Violence at St. Andrews University, Scotland, in association with RAND, and since 1998 by RAND alone. The more recent database (2001 to the present) includes both international and domestic terrorist incidents. Domestic terrorism is defined as incidents perpetrated by local nationals against a purely domestic target. See "Terrorism Update: Understanding the Terrorism Database," in Oklahoma City National Memorial Institute for the Prevention of Terrorism, *MIPT Quarterly Bulletin* (First Quarter 2002): 4n.

15. "Interview with ASALA," *Panorama Magazine* (Milan), September 1, 1980, pp. 62–65.

16. Armenian Secret Army for the Liberation of Armenia, *The Reality* (Armenian Secret Army for the Liberation of Armenia, no date), p. 4; reprinted as "Booklet Giving History of ASALA's Existence Gives New Insight Into the Revolutionary Movement," *Armenian Reporter* (New York), January 10, 1985.

17. Moorad Mooradian, "Terrorists Speak: Interviews with ASALA Members" (unpublished manuscript, no date), pp. 15–16.

18. "Armenians Turning to Terrorism," *Los Angeles Times*, January 25, 1981.

19. "The Portrait of an Armenian Terrorist Leader," *Le Matin* (Paris), quoted in "French Paper Provides Information on ASALA Leader Hagopian," *Mamara* (Istanbul), January 16, 1985.

20. Gerard Chaliand and Yves Ternon, *The Armenians: From Genocide to Resistance*, trans. Tony Berrett (London: Zed, 1983), p. 6.

21. Andrew Corsun, *Research Papers on Terrorism: Armenian Terrorism, 1975–1980* (Washington, D.C.: Office of Security Threat Analysis Group, U.S. Department of State, 1982), p. 1.

22. Mark Armen Ayanian and John Z. Ayanian, "Armenian Political Violence on American Network News: An Analysis of Content," *Armenian Review* 40, no. 1–157 (Spring 1987): 28.

23. Alex P. Schmid and Janny de Graaf, *Insurgent Terrorism and the Western News Media: An Exploratory Analysis with a Dutch Case Study* (Leiden: Center for the Study of Social Conflicts [COMT], Dutch State University, The Netherlands, November 1980), quoted in Brian Michael Jenkins, *The Psychological Implications of Media-Covered Terrorism* (Santa Monica, Calif.: RAND Corporation, P-6627, June 1981), p. 7.

24. "The Palestinians of the 1990s," *Foreign Report* (London), no. 2202 (April 2, 1992).

25. Quoted in I. Fetscher and G. Rohrmoser, *Analysen zum Terrorismus* [Analyses on the subject of terrorism], vol. 1, *Ideologien und Strategien* [Ideologies and strategies] (Bonn: Westdeutscher Verlag, 1981), p. 301.

26. Christoph Wackerngel, "Transcript of a Talk by Christoph Wackerngel," September 14, 1995 (unpublished manuscript), p. 1.

27. Eileen MacDonald, *Shoot the Women First* (New York: Random House, 1991), p. 210.

28. Michael "Bommi" Baumann, *Terror or Love? Bommi Baumann's Own Story of His Life as a West German Urban Guerrilla*, trans. Helene Ellenbogen and Wayne Parker (New York: Grove Press, 1979), pp. 19–20. The book was originally published in Germany in 1971 under the title *Wie alles anfing* [How it all began].

29. Klein had first gained notoriety for his role in the 1975 seizure of the OPEC ministers' meeting in Vienna masterminded by the infamous Carlos "the Jackal," the Venezuelan terrorist Ilich Ramirez Sanchez. Seriously wounded during the attack, in 1978 Klein broke with his former comrades and completely disavowed armed struggle as a means to achieve political change.

30. Quoted in Jean Marcel Bougereau, "Memoirs of an International Terrorist: Conversations with Hans Joachim Klein," in *The German Guerrilla: Terror, Reaction, and Resistance* (Sanday, Orkney: Cienfuegos Press, no date), p. 12. See also the similar statements on pp. 9, 14, and 15.

31. See especially "CHANGE YOUR HATRED INTO ENERGY" (issued by the BLACK FRONT); "SHALOM & NAPALM" (issued by the BLACK RATS, T.W.); and "STATION TW," quoted in Baumann, *Terror or Love?* pp. 56–57, 67–69. For the wider influence of the Vietnam War on German terrorism, see especially the communiqués claiming credit for the attempted assassination of the American commander in chief of NATO (and future secretary of state) General Alexander Haig in Obourg, Belgium, on June 25, 1979, and the "Hunger Strike Declaration of 4 December

1984 by Imprisoned Members of the Red Army Faction," both quoted in Dennis Pluchinsky, "Western Europe's Red Terrorists: The Fighting Communist Organizations," in Yonah Alexander and Dennis Pluchinsky, eds., *Europe's Red Terrorists: The Fighting Communist Organizations* (London: Frank Cass, 1992), pp. 24, 62.

32. Quoted in Stefan Aust, *The Baader-Meinhof Group: The Inside Story of a Phenomenon* (London: Bodley Head, 1987), p. 366.

33. Baumann, *Terror or Love?*, p. 60. See also p. 59 and the "SHALOM & NAPALM" communiqué on pp. 67–68.

34. Baumann, *Terror or Love?* p. 5.

35. David C. Rapoport, "The International World as Some Terrorists Have Seen It: A Look at a Century of Memoirs," *Journal of Strategic Studies* 10, no. 4 (December 1987): 45.

36. David Th. Schiller, "From a National to an International Response," in H. H. Tucker, ed., *Combating the Terrorists: Democratic Responses to Political Violence* (New York: Facts on File, 1988), p. 188.

37. James Adams, *The Financing of Terror* (New York: Simon and Schuster, 1986), p. 49.

38. Ibid., p. 243.

39. Ibid., p. 104.

40. Iyad, *My Home, My Land*, p. 221.

41. Christopher Walker, "£194m 'Missing' as Arafat Seeks Aid from Britain," *The Times* (London), July 14, 1997.

4. Religion and Terrorism

1. "Broadcast by Usama bin Ladin (October 7, 2001), Al-Jazira television. Translation by BBC News," in Barry Rubin and Judith Colp Rubin, eds., *Anti-American Terrorism and the Middle East: A Documentary Reader* (Oxford: Oxford University Press, 2002), pp. 249–51.

2. Quoted in John Kifner, "Israelis Investigate Far Right: May Crack Down on Speech," *New York Times*, November 8, 1995.

3. See Gregory Crouch, "Suspect in Killing of Dutch Filmmaker Maintains His Silence," *New York Times*, July 12, 2005; Gregory Crouch, "Man on Trial in Dutch Killing Says He'd Do 'Same Again,'" *New York Times*, July 13, 2005; and Associated Press, "Extremist Admits to the Slaying of Dutch Filmmaker," *Washington Post*, July 13, 2005.

4. *Oxford English Dictionary, Compact Edition* (Oxford: Oxford University Press, 1971), p. 3868, col. 87.

5. See David C. Rapoport, "Fear and Trembling: Terrorism in Three Religious Traditions," *American Political Science Review* 78, no. 3 (September 1984): 668–72, and Walter Laqueur, *The Age of Terrorism* (Boston: Little, Brown, 1987), pp. 7–8.

6. *Oxford English Dictionary*, p. 3311, col. 388.

7. Rapoport, "Fear and Trembling," pp. 660–64. If one accepts that upwards of a million people may have been murdered by the Thugs, then on average they killed 833.333 people a year.

8. *Oxford English Dictionary*, p. 125, col. 499.

9. Rapoport, "Fear and Trembling," p. 659.

10. Numbers of active, identifiable terrorist groups from 1968 to the present are derived from the RAND Terrorism Incident Database.

11. Mark Juergensmeyer, "Terror Mandated by God," *Terrorism and Political Violence* 9, no. 2 (Summer 1997): 20.

12. Murray Sayle, "Martyrdom Complex," *New Yorker*, May 13, 1996.

13. Nicholas D. Kristof, "Japanese Cult Planned U.S. Attack," *International Herald Tribune* (Paris), March 24, 1997; Robert Whymant, "Cult Planned Gas Raids on America," *The Times* (London), March 29, 1997.

14. The hijackers' plans were foiled, however, after the French authorities learned of their intentions and ordered commandos to storm the aircraft after it had landed for refueling in Marseilles.

15. RAND Terrorism Incident Database.

16. According to the RAND Terrorism Incident Database, between 1982 and 1989 Shi'a terrorist groups committed 247 terrorist incidents and were responsible for 1,057 deaths.

17. According to the RAND Terrorism Incident Database, there were a total number of 11,769 terrorist attacks recorded between 1998 and 2004. Al Qaeda was responsible for 22 of those incidents but caused a total of 3,457 fatalities.

18. Imam Khomeini, *Islam and Revolution*, trans. Hamid Algar (London: KPI, 1981), pp. 286–87.

19. Quoted in Amir Taheri, *Holy Terror: The Inside Story of Islamic Terrorism* (London: Sphere, 1987), pp. 7–8.

20. Hezbollah was the product of several splits within the Lebanese Shi'a movement. Its origins can be traced back to 1974, when a Lebanese Shi'a cleric, Imam Musa al-Sadr, who had studied in the Iranian holy city of Qom, organized the "Movement of the Underprivileged" to advance Shi'a interests and improve the community's lowly socioeconomic conditions. This movement was subsequently reorganized as the principal Shi'a political party in Lebanon, Amal, which formed its own militia during the civil war that racked Lebanon a year later. In 1979, however, al-Sadr vanished during a visit to Libya. The disappearance of the imam created a vacuum within Amal that made the party fertile ground for Iranian influence and rendered the movement susceptible to the fundamentalist call of the revolution that had brought Khomeini to power earlier that year. Nabih Berri, a lawyer, was appointed head of Amal the following year. Hussein Mussawi, the person quoted above and the alleged mastermind behind the terrorist campaign against Libya to recover the imam, was named Berri's deputy and commander of the militia. A fanatical supporter of Khomeini, Mussawi sought to place Amal in the vanguard of a regional revolution based on the new Iranian Islamic Republic. Berri, on the other

hand, clung to a moderate line and advocated a new deal for the Shi'a community within the confines of the existing Lebanese state structure. By this time, however, the radicalization of the Shi'a in Lebanon had gone far beyond the narrow national-ist and social aims of Amal. In 1981, Mussawi broke with Berri and founded his own organization, Islamic Amal. Shortly after, another faction split from Amal and under the leadership of Abbas Mussawi (a nephew of Hussein) and the "spiritual guidance" of Sheikh Muhammed Hussein Fadlallah, it soon came to be known as Hezbollah. Like Islamic Amal, Hezbollah embraced Khomeini's summons for a pan-Islamic revolt designed to turn Lebanon into an Iranian-style Islamic republic.

21. "Open Letter from the Party of God to the Disinherited of Lebanon and the World Revealing the Way and the Intentions which are their Own on the Occa-sion of the First Anniversary of Ragheb Harb, Symbol of the Islamic Resistance and Exemplary Martyr," issued by Hezbollah, Beirut, Lebanon, February 16, 1985.

22. Ayatollah Muhammed Hussein Fadl Allah [sic], "Islam and Violence in Political Reality," *Middle East Insight* 4, nos. 4–5 (1986): 4–13. See also the quote from Fadlallah's book *Invisible Armies* in Alison Jamieson, *Terrorism* (Hove, East Sussex: Wayland, 1991), p. 33: "We don't see ourselves as terrorists, because we don't believe in terrorism. . . . We don't see resisting the occupier as a terrorist action. We see ourselves as mujihadeen who fight a Holy War for the people. Faith, whether religious or political, is all. To the individual terrorist, or supporter of terrorism, a murder can be an expression of the defence of freedom; a car-bomb which kills civilians can be a blow struck in a war of liberation; a kidnapping and murder can be a step towards justice. The intensity of conviction that justifies one man's justice at any price almost inevitably means that the freedom or justice of others will be ignored, or at worst trampled and destroyed."

23. Quoted in Laura Marlowe, "A Fiery Cleric's Defense of Jihad," *Time*, January 15, 1996.

24. Quoted in Hala Jaber, *Hezbollah: Born with a Vengeance* (New York: Colum-bia University Press, 1997), p. 23.

25. See H. A. R. Gibb, *Islam* (Oxford: Oxford University Press, 1978), p. 71, and Malise Ruthven, *A Fury for God: The Islamist Attack on America* (London: Granta, 2002), p. xvii.

26. Quoted in draft copy of the *United States Department of Defense Commission on the Beirut International Airport (BIA) Terrorist Act of October 23, 1983* (known as "The Long Commission" in reference to its chairman, retired Admiral Robert L. J. Long, U.S. Navy, no date), p. 38.

27. Armed Islamic Group communiqué, containing a twelve-page interview with Antar Zouabri, September 1996.

28. Hamas was founded in 1987 by Sheikh Amid Ibrahim Yassin. Its estimated $70 million annual budget is derived mostly from contributions by Iran and Saudi Arabia, although Palestinians and Arabs in countries throughout the world (includ-ing the United States and Britain) also donate funds to the movement. In addition to its violent activities, Hamas provides social services to Palestinian communities in the Gaza Strip and West Bank, including schools, medical assistance, and related

welfare activities. In this respect, Hamas is consciously emulating the success of both the PLO and Hezbollah in providing social services while simultaneously waging a violent terrorist campaign.

29. Quoted in Anti-Defamation League of B'nai B'rith, *ADL Special Background Report: Hamas, Islamic Jihad, and the Muslim Brotherhood: Islamic Extremists and the Terrorist Threat to America* (New York: Anti-Defamation League of B'nai B'rith, 1993), p. 4.

30. As Fathi Shiqaqi, the general secretary of Palestine Islamic Jihad, whom it is believed was assassinated by the Israeli secret services in Malta in 1995, once explained: "Our struggle with the enemy in Palestine is meant to open every possible form of jihad, including suicide attacks. The enemy thought he had closed the Palestine file when he signed the Oslo Agreements and thus could eliminate us. That requires us to make a special effort to foil his plot. That is why suicide bombers are important." Quoted in Rafi Yisra'eli, "Islamikaze: Suicide Terrorism Examined," *Nativ* (Tel Aviv), January–April 1997, p. 3.

31. Imad Saluji, quoted in Mark Juergensmeyer, "The Worldwide Rise of Religious Nationalism," *Journal of International Affairs* 50, no. 1 (Summer 1996): 1.

32. Quoted in Yisra'eli, "Islamikaze," p. 3.

33. Quoted in *ADL Special Background Report: Hamas, Islamic Jihad, and the Muslim Brotherhood*, p. 4.

34. T. E. Lawrence, *Seven Pillars of Wisdom* (Harmondsworth: Penguin Books, 1977), p. 23.

35. "Text of Bin Laden Remarks: 'Hypocrisy Rears Its Ugly Head,'" *Washington Post*, October 8, 2001.

36. Neal MacFarquhar with Jim Rutenberg, "Bin Laden, in a Taped Speech, Says Attacks in Afghanistan Are a War Against Islam," *New York Times*, November 4, 2001, p. B2.

37. See Anonymous, *Through Our Enemies' Eyes: Osama bin Laden, Radical Islam, and the Future of America* (Dulles, Va.: Brassey's, 2002), pp. 55–59. This book, written by Michael Scheuer, a veteran Central Intelligence Agency analyst who headed its bin Laden Unit in the late 1990s, is without doubt the preeminent work on bin Laden and al Qaeda.

38. Quoted in Yonah Alexander and Michael S. Swetnam, *Usama bin Laden's al-Qaida: Profile of a Terrorist Network* (Ardsley, N.Y.: Transnational, 2001), appendix 1A, pp. 1–2, 19.

39. Quoted in ibid., appendix 1A, p. 21.

40. Quoted in ibid., appendix 1B, p. 1.

41. Ruthven, *A Fury for God*, p. xxii.

42. Quoted in Alexander and Swetnam, *Usama bin Laden's al-Qaida*, appendix 1B, pp. 1–2.

43. Quoted in Ben Venzke and Aimee Ibrahim, *The al-Qaeda Threat: An Analytical Guide to al-Qaeda's Tactics and Targets* (Alexandria, Va.: Tempest Publishing, 2003), pp. 158–59.

44. Anonymous, *Through Our Enemies' Eyes*, pp. 53–54, 69–70, 72.

45. Quoted in Venzke and Ibrahim, *The al-Qaeda Threat*, p. 160.

46. U.S. Department of State, *Patterns of Global Terrorism 2001* (Washington, D.C.: U.S. Department of State, Publication 10940, May 2002), p. 105.

47. National Commission on Terrorist Attacks Upon the United States, *The 9/11 Commission Report: Authorized Edition* (New York: Norton, 2004), pp. 49–51.

48. Gibb, *Islam*, pp. 2–3, 10–11. See also Ruthven, *A Fury for God*, pp. xvi, xix.

49. Counter Terrorism Center, *Counter Terrorism 2005* (Washington, D.C.: Central Intelligence Agency, 2004), p. 214.

50. See Rohan Gunaratna, *Inside Al Qaeda: Global Network of Terrorism* (London: Hurst, 2002), p. 26.

51. Quoted in Alexander and Swetnam, *Usama bin Laden's al-Qaida*, p. 2.

52. Ayman al-Zawahiri, *Knights Under the Prophet's Banner: Meditations on the Jihadist Movement*, translated and published in FBIS, "Al-Sarq Al-Aswat Publishes Extracts from Al-Jihad Leader Al-Zawahiri's New Book," Document ID GMP20020108000197, December 2, 2001, p. 87.

53. Jason Burke, "Think Again: Al Qaeda," *Foreign Policy* (May/June 2004), http://www.foreign policy.com. This concept of the "far and near" enemies was first articulated by al-Zawahiri in an article titled "The Way to Jerusalem Passes Through Cairo," published in *Al-Mujahideen*, April 1995. See Montasser Al-Zayyat, *The Road to Al-Qaeda: The Story of Bin Laden's Right-Hand Man* (London: Pluto, 2004), p. 62.

54. Quoted in National Commission on Terrorist Attacks Upon the United States, *The 9/11 Commission Report*, p. 47.

55. Quoted in U.S. Department of State, *The Network of Terrorism* (Washington, D.C.: U.S. Department of State, 2001), p. 8.

56. Quoted in ibid.

57. Kahane was assassinated in New York City in November 1990 by El Sayyid A. Nosair, one of the men convicted of conspiring to bomb the World Trade Center (while he was serving a prison term in connection with Kahane's assassination) as well as the follow-on plot to blow up bridges and tunnels linking New York with New Jersey in hopes of obtaining the release of the Trade Center bombers.

58. See, e.g., books such as *Never Again! A Program for Survival* (Los Angeles: Nash Publishing, 1971) and *They Must Go* (New York: Grosset and Dunlap, 1981), and pamphlets such as *Viewpoint Kahane: There Is No More Tal* (no date) and *Uncomfortable Questions for Comfortable Jews* (no date).

59. His "Rabbi Kahane Speaks" column was regularly featured in the American-Jewish newspaper the *Jewish Press*.

60. See Ami Pedahzur, *The Israeli Response to Jewish Extremism and Violence: Defending Democracy* (Manchester: Manchester University Press, 2002), pp. 34–37, and Ehud Sprinzak, *Brother Against Brother: Violence and Extremism in Israeli Politics from Altalena to the Rabin Assassination* (New York: Free Press, 1999), pp. 2–3.

61. Kahane, *Never Again!*, p. 110.

62. Ehud Sprinzak, "Violence and Catastrophe in the Theology of Rabbi Meir Kahane: The Ideologization of Mimetic Desire," in Mark Juergensmeyer, ed., *Violence and the Sacred in the Modern World* (London: Frank Cass, 1992), pp. 51, 64–66. In his book, written at the height of the Algerian war, Fanon, a psychiatrist, wrote of the "liberating" effects of violence on the oppressed. See Frantz Fanon, *The Wretched of the Earth* (London: Penguin, 1990).

63. Quoted in Janet L. Dolgin, *Jewish Identity and the JDL* (Princeton, N.J.: Princeton University Press, 1977), p. 69.

64. *New York Times*, 15 May 1980, quoted in Bruce Hoffman, "The Jewish Defense League," *Terrorism, Violence, and Insurgency Journal* 5, no. 1 (Summer 1984): 13.

65. Kahane speaking at California State University at Northridge, California, March 1988 (attended by author).

66. Ibid.

67. Kahane, *They Must Go*, p. 272 (emphasis in original).

68. Ehud Sprinzak, *The Ascendance of Israel's Radical Right* (Oxford: Oxford University Press, 1991), pp. 98–99.

69. Ehud Sprinzak, "Fundamentalism, Terrorism, and Democracy: The Case of the Gush Emunim Underground," Wilson Center Occasional Paper no. 4 (Washington, D.C.: Smithsonian Institution, 1986), p. 11.

70. See Thomas L. Friedman, "Jewish Terrorists Freed by Israel," *New York Times*, December 9, 1984; Grace Halsell, "Why Bobby Brown of Brooklyn Wants to Blow Up Al Aqsa," *Arabia*, August 1984; Martin Merzer, "Justice for All in Israel?" *Miami Herald*, May 17, 1985; and "Jail Term of Jewish Terrorist Reduced," *Jerusalem Post* (international edition), October 12, 1985. The information pertaining to the terrorists' desire to provoke a cataclysmic holy war between Muslims and Jews was verified by an American law enforcement officer, involved with the investigation of Jewish terrorist incidents in the United States and knowledgeable about the Jerusalem incident, in conversation with the author.

71. Sprinzak, "Fundamentalism, Terrorism, and Democracy," pp. 11–13.

72. Pedahzur, *The Israeli Response to Jewish Extremism and Violence*, p. 84.

73. Quoted in Joel Greenberg, "Israeli Police Question Two Rabbis in Rabin Assassination," *New York Times*, November 22, 1995.

74. Michael Karpin and Ina Friedman, *Murder in the Name of God: The Plot to Kill Yitzhak Rabin* (New York: Metropolitan, 1998), p. 4. See also Pedahzur, *The Israeli Response to Jewish Extremism and Violence*, pp. 5–6, 94–95, 253–58, 281.

75. Quoted in Greenberg, "Israeli Police Question Two Rabbis in Rabin Assassination."

76. Quoted in Marie Colvin, "Rabbi Calls for Suicide Bombings," *Sunday Times* (London), April 13, 1997.

77. The assault came at the end of a fifty-one-day standoff between the Branch Davidian cult, led by Reverend David Koresh, and agents of both the Bureau of Alcohol, Tobacco, and Firearms (BATF) and the FBI. The crisis began when BATF agents attempted to arrest Koresh and some of his followers on charges of illegal possession

of firearms (specifically of converting single-shot AR-15 assault rifles into full automatic machine guns). There had also been reports of the cult's bizarre sexual practices and abuse of its members' children that had prompted increased law enforcement interest in the Davidians' Mount Carmel compound. Koresh believed that he
was God's special messianic messenger, sent to earth, he claimed, to "reveal the
hidden meaning of the entire biblical prophetic corpus." Through his charismatic
and persuasive personality, Koresh inculcated in his followers a sense of imminent
redemption and apocalyptic visions that culminated in the deaths of Koresh and
his followers on April 19, 1993. See James D. Tabor and Eugene V. Gallagher, *Why
Waco? Cults and the Battle for Religious Freedom in America* (Berkeley: University
of California Press, 1995).

78. In 1992, one U.S. marshal was killed attempting to arrest Randy Weaver for
the sale of illegal sawed-off shotguns. Weaver's son was shot to death in the initial
confrontation, and his wife was subsequently killed by an FBI sniper before the tense
standoff was defused six days later. The incident became a cause célèbre for the
militias and other extremist groups and is widely believed to have "lit the fuse" for
the 1995 Oklahoma City bombing.

79. See Lou Michel and Dan Herbeck, *American Terrorist: Timothy McVeigh and
the Oklahoma City Bombing* (New York: Regan, 2001), pp. 166–69.

80. Quoted in Associated Press, "McVeigh Aimed to Spark Revolt, Ex-Buddy
Says," *International Herald Tribune* (Paris), May 13, 1997.

81. Mike German, "Behind the Lone Terrorists, a Pack Mentality," *Washington
Post*, June 5, 2005.

82. Quoted in Keith Schneider, "Fearing a Conspiracy, Some Heed a Call to
Arms," *New York Times*, November 14, 1994.

83. Quoted in Jo Thomas, "Militias Hold a Congress, and Not a Gun Is Seen," *New
York Times*, November 1, 1994.

84. The U.S. Anti-Defamation League of B'nai B'rith, one of the most authoritative of the groups monitoring the militia phenomenon, puts the number of active
members at a considerably lower figure of fifteen thousand people in forty states
(see Anti-Defamation League of B'nai B'rith, *ADL Special Report: The Militia Movement in America* [New York: Anti-Defamation League of B'nai B'rith, 1995], p. 1),
while the Southern Poverty Law Center reports some 809 militia organizations that
have been active in all fifty states plus the District of Columbia (see *False Patriots:
The Threat of Antigovernment Extremists* [Montgomery, Ala.: Southern Poverty Law
Center, 1996], pp. 58–68). Meanwhile, another authority, Paul de Armond, the director of the Public Good, a Washington State grassroots community organization,
claims that the total number of militia members plus other Americans involved
in the wider Christian white supremacist movement exceeds five million (Paul de
Armond, "The Anti-Democratic Movement—More Than Militias," August 1995,
http://www.nwcitizen.com/publicgood.

85. There is reportedly also a "bridge" faction, believed to consist of extreme
right-wing Mormons associated with the racist (but not anti-Semitic) splinter of the

far right Libertarian Party, known as the Constitution Party, attempting to reconcile these two factions. I am indebted to Paul de Armond, of the Public Good in Bellingham, Washington State, for drawing my attention to these critical distinctions and providing me with information on these groups.

86. Quoted in David Harrison, "Jackboot Stamp of the New Right," *Observer* (London), April 23, 1995.

87. See John Carlin, "DIY Apocalypse," *Independent* (London), April 30, 1995, and Timothy Egan, "Trying to Explain Contacts with Paramilitary Groups," *New York Times*, May 2, 1995.

88. "Militia of Montana: Statement of Purpose," http://www.militiaofmontana. com.

89. Quoted in John Carlin, "'We Need Blood to Cleanse Us,'" *Independent* (London), May 2, 1995.

90. Gritz's millenarian preparatory plans suffered a grievous setback when he was arrested on kidnapping charges in Connecticut involving his part in an ugly child-custody battle.

91. Personal communication between the author and Paul de Armond, director of the Public Good, Bellingham, Washington State, July 25, 1995.

92. The group was itself also involved in a weeklong siege with law enforcement authorities that was resolved peacefully despite threats by the militia to "wage an Alamo-style fight to the death." Sam Howe Verhovek, "Showdown at the 'Republic of Texas' Ends in Surrender," *International Herald Tribune* (Paris), May 5, 1997.

93. Quoted in Harrison, "Jackboot Stamp of the New Right."

94. The group's name is believed to be derived from the "Operation American Viper"—a 68-page "war plan" cum strategy document that is circulated among U.S. militias inciting them to revolution and guerrilla war against the "global conspiracy" orchestrated by the U.S. federal government and the United Nations in league with international bankers, Jews, and others. See Steven A. Holmes, "U.S. Charges 12 in Arizona Plot to Blow Up Government Office," *New York Times*, July 2, 1996.

95. James Brooke in the *New York Times*: "Agents Seize Arsenal of Rifles and Bomb-Making Material in Arizona Militia Inquiry," July 3, 1996; "Volatile Mix in Viper Militia: Hatred Plus a Love for Guns," July 4, 1996; and "As Trial Nears for Militia, Some Charges Are Dropped," October 9, 1996.

96. McVeigh, however, claims that he used 5,400 pounds (108 fifty-pound bags) of ammonium nitrate that he bought for $540. He paid about $3,000 for the racing fuel. See James Brooke, "Newspaper Says McVeigh Described Role in Bombing," *New York Times*, March 1, 1997.

97. "Threats from Within," *Washington Post*, April 19, 2005.

98. Lois Romano, "Domestic Extremist Groups Weaker but Still Worrisome," *Washington Post*, April 19, 2005.

99. Associated Press, "Man Accused of Possessing Lethal Toxin Hangs Himself," *Los Angeles Times*, December 24, 1995.

100. Karl Vick, "Man Gets Hands on Bubonic Plague Germs, but That's No Crime," *Washington Post*, December 30, 1995.

101. Associated Press, "Man Accused of Possessing Lethal Toxin Hangs Himself"; John Kifner, "Antiterrorism Law Used in Poison Smuggling Case," *New York Times*, December 23, 1995, and John Kifner, "Man Arrested in Poison Case Kills Himself in Jail Cell," *New York Times*, December 24, 1995.

102. Quoted in Tim Kelsey, "The Oklahoma Suspect Awaits Day of Reckoning," *Sunday Times* (London), April 21, 1996.

103. See James Corcoran, *Bitter Harvest: The Birth of Paramilitary Terrorism in the Heartland* (New York: Penguin, 1995), passim.

104. Quoted in Flo Conway and Jim Siegelman, "Identity and the Militia," *Arkansas Democrat-Gazette* (Little Rock), December 3, 1995.

105. Quoted in Kelsey, "The Oklahoma Suspect Awaits Day of Reckoning." See also German, "Behind the Lone Terrorists, a Pack Mentality."

106. "Legal Action: Keenan v. Aryan Nations," Southern Poverty Law Center Web site, http://www.splcenter.org/legal/docket/files.jsp?cdrID = 30&sortID = 3.

107. Bob Moser, "Alabama Getaway," Southern Poverty Law Center Web site, http://www.splcenter.org/legal/intel/intelreport/article.jsp?aid = 506.

108. Aryan Nations Web site, http://www.aryan-nation.org.

109. Ibid., http://www.aryan-nation.org/holyorder.Jihad.htm.

110. *This is Aryan Nations* brochure distributed by the Aryan Nations [no date]. This document can also be accessed from the World Wide Web at http://www.stormfront.org/aryan_nations/platform.html.

111. Aryan Nations, *Calling Our Nation*, no. 53 (no date), p. 2. This document can also be accessed from the World Wide Web at http://www.stormfront.org/aryan_nations/platform.html.

112. "To Our New People," open letter from Reverend Richard G. Butler, *Aryan Nations* (no date).

113. *This Is Aryan Nations.*

114. *Washington Post*, December 26, 1984, quoted in Bruce Hoffman, *Terrorism in the United States and the Potential Threat to Nuclear Facilities* (Santa Monica, Calif.: RAND Corporation, R-3351-DOE, January 1986), p. 42.

115. Roy B. Masker, "An All White Nation? Why Not?" *Calling Our Nation*, no. 53, p. 23.

116. See Rodney Bowers, "White Radicals Charged with Sedition," *Arkansas Gazette* (Little Rock), April 25, 1987.

117. Joseph M. Melnachak, "A Chronicle of Hate: A Brief History of the Radical Right in America," *Terrorism, Violence, and Insurgency Report* 6, no. 4 (no date): 41–42. This was also confirmed to the author by an FBI agent present at the raid.

118. Andrew MacDonald, *The Turner Diaries* (Arlington, Va.: National Alliance/National Vanguard Books, 1985). For a biography of MacDonald/Pierce see Michael Janofsky, "One Man's Journey from Academia to Extremism," *New York Times*, July 5, 1995.

119. *New York Times*, December 27, 1984, quoted in Hoffman, *Terrorism in the United States*, p. 42.

120. McVeigh, quoted in interviews with Patrick E. Cole, "'I'm Just Like Anyone Else,'" *Time*, April 15, 1996, and Kelsey, "The Oklahoma Suspect Awaits Day of Reckoning."

121. Quoted in Conway and Siegelman, "Identity and the Militia."

122. Quoted in Anti-Defamation League of B'nai B'rith, *Hate Groups in America: A Record of Bigotry and Violence* (New York: Anti-Defamation League of B'nai B'rith, 1982), p. 52.

123. Quoted in ibid., pp. 51, 53.

124. Carlin, "DIY Apocalypse."

125. Paul de Armond, "Christian Patriots at War with the State," Public Good home page, http://www.nwcitizen.com/publicgood.

126. Among the congregants of Peters's church in Laporte, Colorado, were members of the 1980s terrorist group "the Order"; Jeffrey Kaplan, "Right-Wing Violence in North America," *Terrorism and Political Violence* 7, no. 1 (Spring 1995): 54; Conway and Siegelman, "Identity and the Militia."

127. See Morris Dees with James Corcoran, *Gathering Storm: America's Militia Threat* (New York: HarperCollins, 1996), pp. 1–2 and passim, and Paul de Armond, "Leaderless Resistance: The Two-Pronged Movement Consolidates Under Identity," Public Good home page, http://www.nwcitizen.com/publicgood.

128. Louis Beam, Leaderless Resistance (text from Cyberspace Minuteman BBS 312-275–6326), quoted in Tom Burghardt, "Leaderless Resistance and the Oklahoma City Bombing," Public Good home page, http://www.nwcitizen.com/publicgood.

129. *Field Manual Section 1: Principles Justifying the Arming and Organizing of a Militia* (Wisconsin: Free Militia, 1994), p. 78, quoted in ibid.

130. Quoted in de Armond, "Leaderless Resistance."

131. Quoted in James Ridgeway, "Arms and the Men: Are Far Right Militia Cells Using Robbery to Fund Their Cause?" *Village Voice* (New York), May 9, 1995.

132. Ibid.; James Brooke, "Arrests Add to Idaho's Reputation as a Magnet for Supremacists," *New York Times*, October 27, 1996; Loretta J. Ross, "Using the Bible to Justify Killing," *Baltimore Sun*, August 8, 1994; personal communication between Paul de Armond and the author, August 1997.

133. Quoted in "Klanwatch, a Project of the Southern Poverty Law Center," *Intelligence Report* (Montgomery, Alabama), no. 84 (November 1996): 1, 4.

134. Similarly, although not invoking the Phineas Priesthood name, a group calling itself the Army of God claimed credit in April 1997 for two unsolved bombings in Atlanta that wounded a total of twelve people. The first explosion occurred outside an abortion clinic in January, the second outside a gay nightclub.

135. Quoted in Ross, "Using the Bible to Justify Killing."

136. "Spokane Robbery Document" on Public Good home page, http://www.nwcitizen.com/publicgood.

137. Leonard Doyle, "US Militias Show Way for British Fascists," *Independent* (London), April 27, 1995.

138. Personal communication with Paul de Armond, April 1996.

139. Anti-Defamation League of B'nai B'rith, "Extremism in America: National Alliance," http://www.adl.org/learn/ext_us?N_Alliance.asp?LEARN_Cat = Extremism& Lean_SubCat = Extremism_in_America&picked = 3&item = na.

140. Quoted in Romano, "Domestic Extremist Groups Weaker but Still Worrisome."

141. Ibid.

142. Anti-Defamation League, "Extremism in America: National Alliance."

143. German, "Behind the Lone Terrorists, a Pack Mentality."

144. Henry Schuster, "Lone Wolves: Solitary Threats Harder to Hunt," http://www.cnn.com/2005/US/02/01/schuster.column/index.html.

145. See Henry Schuster, "Why Did Rudolph Do It? Question Lingers After Plea Deal Reached," http://www.cnn.com/2005/US/04/11/schuster.column/index.html, and Shalila Dewan, "Bomber Offers Guilty Pleas, and Defiance," *New York Times*, April 14, 2005.

146. Quoted in Mary Thornton, "Oregon Guru Disavows Rajneeshism, Vows to Survive Investigations," *Washington Post*, October 20, 1985; Peter H. King, "Guru Revels in Revelation of a 'Paradise' Defiled," *Los Angeles Times*, September 22, 1985.

147. W. Seth Carus, "The Rajneeshees" (1984), in Jonathan B. Tucker, ed., *Toxic Terror: Assessing Terrorist Use of Chemical and Biological Weapons* (Cambridge, Mass.: MIT Press, 2000), p. 131.

148. For the most complete and authoritative accounts of this incident, see ibid., pp. 115–37. and Judith Miller, Stephen Engelberg, and William Broad, *Germs: Biological Weapons and America's Secret War* (New York: Simon and Schuster, 2001), pp. 15–33.

149. Miller, Engelberg, and Broad, *Germs*, pp. 32–33.

150. In revising this discussion of Aum Shinrikyo, I benefited from the research and translations from original Japanese sources done by Ms. Mayuka Yamazaki, a graduate student in the Security Studies Program at Georgetown University, Washington, D.C.

151. Manabu Watanabe, "Religion and Violence in Japan Today: A Chronological and Doctrinal Analysis of Aum Shinrikyo," *Terrorism and Political Violence* 10, no. 4 (Winter 1998): 83.

152. Quoted in David E. Kaplan and Andrew Marshall, *The Cult at the End of the World: The Incredible Story of Aum* (London: Hutchinson, 1996), pp. 7–12.

153. Shoichi Okawa, "Aum Shinrikyo," http://www.guardian.co.uk/cults/a-z-cults. html.

154. Kaplan and Marshall, *The Cult at the End of the World*, p. 18.

155. "Aum Shinrikyo Special Edition: Expanded Leveraging 'Supernatural Power,'" *Asahi Shimbun* (Tokyo), May 21, 1998.

156. See National Police Agency, "Aum Shinrikyo," *Shoten* (Tokyo), no. 269,

chapter 2, http://www.npa.go.jp/kousi/biki2/seco2/seco2_09.htm; Andrew Pollack, "Japanese Sect May Struggle to Get By Without Its Leader," *New York Times*, May 17, 1995; and Alessandra Stanley, "Russians Shut Down Branch of Japanese Sect," *New York Times*, March 30, 1995.

157. William J. Broad, "Seismic Blast: Bomb or Quake?" *New York Times*, January 23, 1997.

158. Quoted in James Walsh, "Shoko Asahara: The Making of a Messiah." *Time*, April 3, 1995.

159. Quoted in National Police Agency, "Aum Shinrikyo: An Alarming Report on the Terrorist Group's Organization and Activities," *Shoten* (Tokyo), no. 252 (1995): 6.

160. "Special Edition: The First Aum Case Will Start on April 24th," *Yomiuri Shimbun* (Tokyo), April 20, 1996.

161. Quoted in Kaplan and Marshall, *The Cult at the End of the World*, pp. 16–17.

162. Quoted in Nicholas D. Kristof with Sheryl WuDunn, "The Seer Among the Blind: Japanese Sect Leader's Rise," *New York Times*, March 26, 1995.

163. "Special Edition: 1998 Aum Case—Matsumoto [Asahara] Was a Ringleader," *Yomiuri Shimbun* (Tokyo), December 31, 1998.

164. Quoted in James K. Campbell, "Excerpts from Research Study 'Weapons of Mass Destruction and Terrorism: Proliferation by Non-State Actors'" (paper presented at International Conference on Aviation Safety and Security in the 21st Century, White House Commission on Aviation Safety and Security and George Washington University, Washington, D.C., January 13–15, 1997), p. 14.

165. See David Van Biema, "Prophet of Poison," *Time*, April 3, 1995.

166. Quoted in Juergensmeyer, "The Worldwide Rise of Religious Nationalism," p. 17.

167. Quoted in Kaplan and Marshall, *The Cult at the End of the World*, p. 85. See also "Special Edition: Summary of Aum Case," *Yomiuri Shimbun* (Tokyo), June 14, 1996.

168. Watanabe, "Religion and Violence in Japan Today," p. 82.

169. "Aum Shinrikyo Special Edition: Targeted Elites—They Were Brainwashed and Became Aum's Robot," *Asahi Shimbun* (Tokyo), May 28, 1995. See also Robert Jay Lifton, *Destroying the World to Save It: Aum Shinrikyo, Apocalyptic Violence, and the New Global Terrorism* (New York: Metropolitan Books, 1999), p. 30.

170. Haruki Murakami, *Underground* (Tokyo: Kodansha bunko, 1999), p. 35.

171. Lifton, *Destroying the World to Save It*, pp. 28–31.

172. Mayuka Yamazaki, "Aum Shinrikyo" (unpublished manuscript, April 2005), p. 4.

173. Broad, "Seismic Blast: Bomb or Quake?"

174. Okawa, "Aum Shinrikyo."

175. As a result of the raids on Aum facilities in March 1995, Japanese police found a notebook belonging to a senior Aum executive listing this weaponry and associated purchase and production costs. See "Aum Shinrikyo Special Edition: Transforming Into a 'Terrorist' Cult," *Asahi Shimbun* (Tokyo), June 16, 1996.

176. "Aum Shinrikyo Special Edition: Targeted Elites."

177. Richard Lloyd Parry, "Sect's Poisons 'Could Kill 4.2m,'" *Independent on Sunday* (London), March 26, 1995; Andrew Pollack, "Japanese Police Say They Found Germ-War Material at Cult Site," *New York Times*, March 29, 1995.

178. National Police Agency, "Aum Shinrikyo," p. 11.

179. "Special Edition: Examination of Aum's Other Crime—Illegal Drug Production," *Yomiuri Shimbun* (Tokyo), February 28, 1996.

180. Reuters, "Tokyo Cult Leader Said to Have Made Gas Confession," *The Times* (London), October 5, 1995.

181. Jonathan Annells and James Adams, "Did Terrorists Kill with Deadly Nerve Gas Test?" *Sunday Times* (London), March 19, 1995. Interestingly, this news account was published only a day before the nerve gas attack on the Tokyo underground took place.

182. Watanabe, "Religion and Violence in Japan Today," p. 82.

183. "Special Edition: The Arrest of Guru Shoko Asahara, and the History of Asahara's Analects," *Yomiuri Shimbun* (Tokyo), May 16, 1995.

184. National Police Agency, *Keisatsu Hakusyo 1996* (Police White Paper 1996), http://www.pdc.npa.go.jp/halusyo/h08/h080101.html.

185. Testimony by a former member of Aum in "Special Edition: 1998 Aum Case—Matsumoto [Asahara] Was a Ringleader," *Yomiuri Shimbun* (Tokyo), December 31, 1998.

186. "Special Edition: The First Aum Case Will Start on April 24th."

187. Ibid.; National Police Agency, *Keisatsu Hakusyo* (Police White Paper 2000), chapter 5, http://www.pdc.npa.go.jp/hakusyo/h12h120500.html.

188. Joyu was not implicated in the cult's violence and was convicted only of charges involving fraudulent real estate transactions. Accordingly, he served only a brief prison term. Lifton, *Destroying the World to Save It*, p. 31.

189. See Aleph's Web site, http://www.aleph.to/info/2000c.html#991201.

190. See Aleph's Web site, http://www.aleph.to/news/200503.html#01.

191. See, for example, "No Flames, No Guns in Montana," *New York Times*, June 15, 1996; David Johnston, "Surrender Is a Victory for a Strategy of Patience," *New York Times*, June 13, 1996; Brad Knickerbocker, "Patience Is a Virtue in Freeman Standoff," *Christian Science Monitor* (Boston), June 14, 1996; and Lucinda Franks, "Annual of Law Enforcement: Don't Shoot—In the New FBI, Patience Comes First," *New Yorker*, July 22, 1996, http://www.threatlink.com/pr/articles/Don't%20Shoot.pdf.

192. See Pew Research Center for People and the Press, "Summary of Findings: A Year After the Iraq War—Mistrust of America in Europe Even Higher, Muslim Anger Persists," March 16, 2004, http://people-press.org/reports/display.php3?ReportID = 206.

193. See "Biden Says Prison at Guantanamo Bay Should Be Closed," *Washington Post*, June 6, 2005; Seymour M. Hersh, *Chain of Command: The Road from 9/11 to Abu Ghraib* (New York: HarperCollins, 2004), pp. 1–72; and David Rose, *Guantanamo: America's War on Human Rights* (London: Faber and Faber, 2004), passim.

194. "Interview with Usama bin Ladin (December 27, 2001), in Rubin and Colp Rubin, *Anti-American Terrorism and the Middle East*, p. 266.

195. See Susan B. Glasser, "Review May Shift Terror Policies," *Washington Post*, May 29, 2005, and Jim Hoagland, "A Shifting Focus on Terrorism," *Washington Post*, April 24, 2005.

196. Bruce Hoffman, "Old Madness, New Methods: Revival of Religious Terrorism Begs for Broader U.S. Policy," *RAND Review* 22, no. 2 (Winter 1998): 12–17.

5. Suicide Terrorism

1. That there has been a significant rise in the incidence of suicide terrorism since 9/11 is not disputed by scholars. See, for instance, Robert A. Pape, "The Strategic Logic of Suicide Terrorism," *American Political Science Review* 97, no. 3 (August 2003): 343–61, and Robert A. Pape, *Dying to Win: The Strategic Logic of Suicide Terrorism* (New York: Random House, 2005), p. 1, as well as Mia A. Bloom, *Dying to Kill: The Allure of Suicide Terror* (New York: Columbia University Press, 2005). The role of religion behind this increase, however, is debated. Pape argues in his seminal article that "religious fanaticism does not explain why the world leader in suicide terrorism is the Tamil Tigers in Sri Lanka," while conceding that "although religious motives may matter, modern suicide terrorism is not limited to Islamic Fundamentalism" ("The Strategic Logic of Suicide Terrorism," p. 343). In his book, however, Pape is more explicit, writing that the "presumed connection between suicide terrorism and Islamic fundamentalism is misleading. . . . There is little connection between suicidal terrorism and Islamic fundamentalism, or any of the world's religions. In fact, the leading instigators of suicide attacks are the Tamil Tigers" (*Dying to Win*, pp. 1–2). While I fully agree with Pape on this point that the Tigers are responsible for the largest number of suicide terrorist attacks between 1968 and 2001, they are *not*, however, the driving force behind the increasing use of this tactic *since* 9/11. In fact, since 2002 an uneasy truce between the Tigers and the Sri Lankan government has meant that the Tigers have largely abjured from engaging in any terrorist operations, much less suicide attacks. Moreover, Pape is not accurate in categorizing the Tamil Tigers as a "Marxist Leninist" group. They are more appropriately described as an ethno-nationalist/separatist movement. Further, as is discussed below, while the Tigers are not a religious terrorist organization, they nonetheless share some characteristics more commonly seen in religious cults than in their secular ethno-nationalist/separatist counterparts. For a particularly incisive critique of Pape's fundamental arguments about suicide terrorism, see Bloom, *Dying to Kill*, pp. 83–84.

2. The RAND Terrorism Incident Database. As Mia Bloom also concludes in her exhaustive study of suicide terrorism, "There is an increasing and disturbing trend towards Islamic suicide terrorism." Bloom, *Dying to Kill*, p. 2.

3. RAND Terrorism Incident Database. See also Israeli Security Agency, "Security

Seminar on Combating the Threat of Suicide Bombers," Israeli Embassy, Washington, D.C., September 16, 2003.

4. Pape, "The Strategic Logic of Suicide Terrorism," pp. 345–47. See also Bruce Hoffman, "The Logic of Suicide Terrorism: Lessons from Israel that America Must Learn," *Atlantic Monthly* 291, no. 5 (June 2003): 40–47.

5. See Yoram Schweitzer, "Suicide Terrorism: Development and Main Characteristics," in International Policy Institute for Counter-Terrorism at the Interdisciplinary Center, Herzilya, *Countering Suicide Terrorism: An International Conference* (Jerusalem: Gefen, 2001), p. 76.

6. Nasra Hassan, "Letter from Gaza: An Arsenal of Believers," *New Yorker*, November 19, 2001, p. 39.

7. The RAND Terrorism Incident Database.

8. See Yosri Fouda and Nick Fielding, *Masterminds of Terror: The Truth Behind the Most Devastating Terrorist Attack the World Has Ever Seen* (New York: Arcade, 2003), p. 136; Rohan Gunaratna, "Khalid Sheikh Mohammed: The Brain," *Playboy* 52, no. 6 (June 2005): 168; and National Commission on Terrorist Attacks Upon the United States, *The 9/11 Commission Report: Authorized Edition* (New York: Norton, 2004), p. 156.

9. *The 9/11 Commission Report*, p. 235.

10. Quoted in Fouda and Fielding, *Masterminds of Terror*, p. 141.

11. Ibid., p. 99.

12. *The 9/11 Commission Report*, p. 154.

13. Ibid., p. 172.

14. Al Jazeera.Net, "NEWS: Arab World—Full Transcript of bin Laden's Speech," November 1, 2004, http://Englishaljazeera.net/NR/exeres/79C6AF22–98FB-4A1C-B21F-2BC36E87F61F.htm.

15. *The 9/11 Commission Report*, p. 498, n. 127.

16. "Militant Islamist: Attack on Cole Cost 10,000 Dollars," *Deutsche Presse-Agentur* (Nicosia), November 12, 2000.

17. *The 9/11 Commission Report*, pp. 212–13.

18. "Videotape of a Private Meeting (December 13, 2001: Usama Bin Ladin)," in Barry Rubin and Judith Colp Rubin, eds., *Anti-American Terrorism and the Middle East: A Documentary Reader* (Oxford: Oxford University Press, 2002), p. 245.

19. "Ayman al-Zawahiri Interview September 2002 Audio Interview by Unknown Interviewer," quoted in Ben Venzke and Aimee Ibrahim, *The al-Qaeda Threat: An Analytical Guide to al-Qaeda's Tactics and Targets* (Alexandria, Va.: Tempest Publishing, 2003), p. 173.

20. See "Americans and 9/11: The Personal Toll," Pew Research Center for the People and the Press Survey Reports, September 5, 2002, http://people-press.org/reports/dislay.php3?PageID = 633, and "Introduction. One Year Later: New Yorkers More Troubled, Washingtonians More on Edge," September 5, 2002, http://people-press.org/reports/display.php3?PageID = 160.

21. Quoted in John Miller, "Interview: Osama Bin Laden (May 1998)," http://www.pbs.org/wgbh/pages/frontline/shows/binladen/who/interview.html.

22. See, for example, the excerpts from bin Laden statements collected in the chapter titled "Martyrdom" in Venzke and Ibrahim, *The al-Qaeda Threat*, pp. 169–72.

23. "Osama bin Laden Interview March 1997 Peter Arnett Interview for CNN," quoted in Venzke and Ibrahim, *The al-Qaeda Threat*, p. 170.

24. "Sulaiman Abu Ghaith Video 9 October 2001 Video Aired on al-Jazeera," quoted in Venzke and Ibrahim, *The al-Qaeda Threat*, p. 171.

25. "Ayman al-Zawahiri Interview September 2002 Audio Interview by Unknown Interviewer," quoted in Venzke and Ibrahim, *The al-Qaeda Threat*, p. 173.

26. The Reporters, Writers, and Editors of *Der Spiegel* Magazine, *Inside 9–11: What Really Happened* (New York: St. Martin's, 2001), p. 304.

27. "Suicide Note (September 18, 2001): Muhammad Atta," in Rubin and Colp Rubin, *Anti-American Terrorism and the Middle East*, p. 236.

28. "Pre-Attack Videotape (Summer 2001): Ahmad Al-Haznawi Al-Ghamidi," in Rubin and Colp Rubin, *Anti-American Terrorism and the Middle East*, p. 276.

29. See Shaul Mishal and Avraham Sela, *The Palestinian Hamas: Vision, Violence, and Coexistence* (New York: Columbia University Press, 2000), p. 66.

30. Although the idea to use suicide terrorist tactics originated with the PIJ in 1988, Hamas was the first Palestinian to actually carry out such an attack.

31. The suicide attack unit controlled by both al-Fatah, the Palestinian terrorist group founded by PLO leader and Palestine Authority (PA) head Yasir Arafat in 1957 and still closely linked to him and its popular militia, the Tanzim. See Dani Naveh et al., Minister of Parliamentary Affairs, *The Involvement of Arafat, PA Senior Officials, and Apparatuses in Terrorism Against Israel, Corruption, and Crime* (Jerusalem: Ministry of Foreign Affairs, 2002), passim.

32. Principally, the Popular Front for the Liberation of Palestine (PFLP) and the Popular Front for the Liberation of Palestine-General Command (PFLP-GC), both of whose headquarters are located in Damascus.

33. No precise, widely accepted total is easily accessible. Dr. Rohan Gunaratna claims that the total was 168 as of the year 2000 (see Rohan Gunaratna, "Suicide Terrorism: A Global Threat," *Jane's Intelligence Review*, October 20, 2000, http://www.janes.com/security/international_security/news/usscole/ jir001020_1_ n.shtml). A *New York Times* article, however, puts the total at 220 attacks (see Amy Waldman, "Suicide Bombing Masters: Sri Lankan Rebels," *New York Times*, January 14, 2003). The Tigers themselves claim that as of 1999 the LTTE had conducted 147 suicide attacks. However, this figure does not include operations involving nonmilitary targets—including politicians and other prominent people, ordinary civilians, and infrastructure and economic targets (see Rohan Gunaratna, "The LTTE and Suicide Terrorism," *Frontline*, February 2000, pp. 5–8). Interestingly, while a private study undertaken by a serving Sri Lankan Armed Forces officer does not cite total incident numbers, this officer has tallied the number of Tamil suicide cadre killed. As LTTE suicide attacks are mainly (but not exclusively) executed by one perpetrator only, the total of 239 LTTE Black Tigers (special suicide cadre) killed in action that this officer claims (including 60 male Black Tigers and 18 female Tigers who died in land attacks and 115 and 46, respectively, in maritime operations) dovetails with

the Gunaratna and Waldman figures. See "LTTE Declared Total Numbers of Killed During the Last 20 Years" (unpublished manuscript, no date).

34. See, for example, Radika Coomaraswamy, "Women of the LTTE: The Tiger's and Women's Emancipation," *Frontline* (Chennai, India), January 10, 1997, pp. 61–64; Dexter Filkins, "Sri Lanka Women at War: Tamil Rebel Group Is Now One-Third Female," *International Herald Tribune* (Paris), March 13, 2000; Rohan Gunaratna, "Suicide Terrorism," p. 53; and Jenny Kay, "Dying for Their Cause," *Eva* (London), June 1998, pp. 18–19.

35. The LTTE maintains so-called Baby Brigade and Tiger Cub units composed of children reputedly as young as 13–15 who are groomed for later service in the movement's elite military units. See Barbara Crossette, "Sri Lanka's Army Is Hitting Last Guerrilla Group," *New York Times*, May 2, 1991; Barbara Crossette, "Tamil Rebels Said to Recruit Child Soldiers," *New York Times*, July 17, 2000; Celia W. Dugger, "Rebels Without a Childhood in Sri Lanka War," *New York Times*, September 10, 2000; Guy Goodwin-Gill and Ilene Cohn, *Child Soldiers: The Role of Children in Armed Conflict* (Oxford: Clarendon, 1994), pp. 29, 31, 40; Rohan Gunaratna, "Tiger Cubs and Childhood Fall as Casualties in Sri Lanka," *Jane's Intelligence Review* (July 1998), pp. 32–37; and Lindsay Murdoch, "Reign of Terror by Sir Lanka's Pol Pot," *Sydney Morning Herald* (Australia), June 15, 1995.

36. See, for example, Anthony Foster, "An Emerging Threat Shapes Up as Terrorists Take to the High Seas," *Jane's Intelligence Review* (July 1998), p. 44, and Rohan Gunaratna, "Sea Tiger Success Threatens the Spread of Copycat Tactics," *Jane's Intelligence Review* (March 2001), pp. 12–16.

37. Using so-called ultralights (small, single-pilot aircraft also known as microlights) a special LTTE unit reportedly planned to attack the Sri Lankan prime minister's official residence at Temple Trees on the Galle Road in Colombo. This airborne option was pursued after attempts to target the residence by ground attack were deterred by heavy security surrounding the compound. Interview with retired Sri Lankan Air Force officer, subsequently confirmed by Sri Lankan authorities, December 1997. See also Chris Kamalendran, "LTTE's Aircraft: Yes, No," *Sunday Times* (Colombo), December 6, 1998, and Rohan Gunaratna, "Case Study: The Liberation Tigers of Tamil Eelam," *Jane's Intelligence Review* (October 2001), p. 8.

38. Pape, *Dying to Win*, p. 4.

39. The Sherut Ha-Bitachon Ha-Klali, also known as the Shabak or Shin Bet. According to their figures, 61 suicide bombings occurred between 1993 and September 2000 and 145 between October 2000 and September 2002. See Amos Harel, "Shin Bet: 145 Suicide Bombers Since the Start of the Intifada," *Ha'aretz* (Tel Aviv), September 29, 2002, www.haartezdaily.com.

40. Shaul Mishal and Reuben Aharoni, *Speaking Stones: Communiqués from the Intifada Underground* (Syracuse, N.Y.: Syracuse University Press, 1994), p. xiii. The First (and less violent) Palestinian Intifada is most commonly said to have erupted in 1987 and ended in 1993 with the signing of the Oslo Accords. The al-Aqsa Intifada takes its name from the mosque on the al-Haram al-Sharif (Holy

Precinct or Noble Sanctuary), the thirty-five-acre plaza built atop the site of the destroyed Jewish Second Temple where both the mosque and the Dome of the Rock are located. The name for the uprising is derived from the riots there that followed Ariel Sharon's well-publicized visit to the Temple Mount (the Jewish name for the Holy Precinct) in September 2000. See James Bennet, "Jerusalem Holy Site a Tense Crossroads Again," *New York Times,* August 29, 2003, and David Eshel, "The Al-Aqsa Intifada: Tactics and Strategies," *Jane's Intelligence Review* (May 2001), p. 36.

41. For a detailed discussion of suicide terrorism's instrumental purpose in this respect, see Bruce Hoffman and Gordon H. McCormick, "Terrorism, Signaling, and Suicide Attack," *Studies in Conflict and Terrorism* 27, no. 4 (July–August 2004): 243–81.

42. See Rohan Gunaratna, *War and Peace in Sri Lanka* (Sri Lanka: Institute of Fundamental Studies, 1987), pp. 16–18, and Rohan Gunaratna, "The Conflict in Sri Lanka, 1982–Present" (unpublished paper prepared as part of a project on how terrorism escalates conducted at the Centre for the Study of Terrorism and Political Violence, University of St. Andrews [Scotland]), March 1997, pp. 1–2. See also Patrick Brogan, *The Fighting Never Stopped* (New York: Vintage, 1990), pp. 228–29, and Mackenzie Briefing Notes, "Funding Terror: The Liberation Tigers of Tamil Eelam and Their Criminal Activities in Canada and the Western World" (Toronto: Mackenzie Centre, December 1995), p. 2.

43. The renaming added insult to injury of the country's Tamil population, as "Lanka" refers to the island's ancient *Sinhalese* name, ignoring the Tamil minority, and the word *sri* meaning "auspicious" or "resplendent" in the Sinhalese language. See Christine Niven et al., *Sri Lanka: A Lonely Planet Travel Survival Kit* (Victoria, Australia: Lonely Planet, 1996), pp. 9–10.

44. Gunaratna, *War and Peace in Sri Lanka,* p. 27.

45. Interviews with LTTE suicide cadre, Colombo, Sri Lanka, December 1997 and February 2003.

46. Brogan, *The Fighting Never Stopped,* p. 228.

47. Interview with LTTE suicide cadre, Colombo, Sri Lanka, December 1997.

48. The adoption of the tiger as the TNT's—and subsequently the LTTE's—identifying symbol was meant to evoke the powerful Cholas dynasty of ancient times, which had once conquered Sri Lanka and other parts of Asia and had used the tiger as its symbol as well. See Rohan Gunaratna, "The Rebellion in Sri Lanka: Sparrow Tactics to Guerrilla Warfare (1971–1996)" (unpublished manuscript, no date), p. 10.

49. Significantly, attention was drawn precisely to this LTTE policy in a 1988 analysis by the U.S. Department of Defense. Included in a synopsis of the LTTE's "political objectives" was "Eliminate moderate Tamils and other Tamil militant groups that compete with the LTTE for influence and power within the Sri Lankan Tamil community." See U.S. Department of Defense, *Terrorist Group Profiles* (Washington, D.C.: U.S. Government Printing Office, 1988), p. 120.

50. Gunaratna, "The Rebellion in Sri Lanka," p. 11, and Rohan Gunaratna, *Implications of the Sri Lankan Tamil Insurgency* (Colombo: Alumni Association of the Bandaranaike Centre for International Studies and London: International Foundation of Sri Lankans United Kingdom, 1997), pp. 8–9.

51. "Masked Gunmen Kill Jaffna Mayor," *Daily News* (Colombo), July 28, 1975.

52. For a list of these groups, see Gunaratna, *War and Peace in Sri Lanka*, p. 27.

53. Gunaratna, "The Rebellion in Sri Lanka," p. 13.

54. Interview with LTTE suicide cadre, Colombo, Sri Lanka, December 1997. See also, for example, "Three Former TULF MPs Shot Dead in Jaffna," *The Hindu* (Chennai), April 9, 1985; K. P. Sunil, "The Midnight Massacre," *Illustrated Weekly of India*, June 8, 1986; "Amir, Yoheswaran Shot Dead, Siva Serious," *Daily News* (Colombo), July 14, 1989; and "Yogasangari—MP Killed in Madras," *Daily News* (Colombo), June 21, 1990.

55. Interview with former senior LTTE cadre, Colombo, Sri Lanka, December 1997.

56. Manoj Joshi, "On the Razor's Edge: The Liberation Tigers of Tamil Eelam," *Studies in Conflict and Terrorism* 19, no. 1 (January–March 1996): 21.

57. See Gunaratna, *Implications of the Sri Lankan Tamil Insurgency*, pp. 10–12, and Gunaratna, *War and Peace in Sri Lanka*, pp. 32–33.

58. Interview with LTTE suicide cadre, Colombo and Batticaloa, Sri Lanka, December 1997. See also Sri Lankan Armed Forces briefing, "Suicide Terrorism in Sri Lanka," no date, slide 5.

59. Quoted in Charu Lata Joshi, "Ultimate Sacrifice—Sri Lanka: Suicide Bombers," *Far Eastern Economic Review*, June 1, 2000, accessed at www.feer.com/006 01/p64current.html.

60. Interviews conducted with former LTTE cadre in Colombo, Jaffna, and Batticoloa, Sri Lanka, December 1997. See also Rohan Gunaratna, "Suicide Terrorism in Sri Lanka and India: LTTE Suicide Capability, Likely Trends, and Response" (unpublished manuscript, expanded version of a paper presented at the First International Conference on Countering Suicide Terrorism, Herzilya, Israel, February 20–23, 2000), p. 1.

61. Gunaratna, *War and Peace in Sri Lanka*, p. 20.

62. In discussions with his followers, Prabhakaran has reportedly often cited Hezbollah's 1983 attack on the Marine barracks as the main inspiration for the group's use of suicide attack. Interview with former senior LTTE cadre, Colombo, Sri Lanka, December 1997 and February 2003.

63. Quoted in Gunaratna, "The LTTE and Suicide Terrorism."

64. Quoted in Waldman, "Suicide Bombing Masters."

65. The LTTE's reputation and prowess were greatly enhanced by its success in compelling the 1990 withdrawal of the Indian Peace Keeping Force (IPKF) sent to restore order in the predominantly Tamil northern and northeastern parts of the island. After three years of persistent LTTE attack and harassment, the Indians left Sri Lanka—a singularly dramatic achievement for any terrorist group or insurgent movement, given India's military power and prowess.

66. See "The Black Tiger Unit of the LTTE" (unpublished report written by a Sri Lankan Army intelligence officer known to one of the authors), p. 1, and Waldman, "Suicide Bombing Masters," January 14, 2003.

67. Gunaratna, "Suicide Terrorism in Sri Lanka and India," p. 9.

68. Quoted in Kay, "Dying for Their Cause," p. 19.

69. Quoted in Charu Lata Joshi, "Ultimate Sacrifice—Sri Lanka."

70. A photocopy of such a card is in the author's possession. It dates from the 1998–99 time period. See also interviews with senior Sri Lankan intelligence officials, Colombo, Sri Lanka, February 2003.

71. Interviews conducted with former LTTE cadre in Colombo, Jaffna, and Batticoloa, Sri Lanka, December 1997. See also Gunaratna, "Suicide Terrorism in Sri Lanka and India," p. 9.

72. Waldman, "Suicide Bombing Masters."

73. Interviews conducted with former LTTE cadre in Colombo, Jaffna, and Batticoloa, Sri Lanka, December 1997. See also Filkins, "Sri Lanka Women at War."

74. Interviews conducted with former LTTE cadre in Colombo, Jaffna, and Batticoloa, Sri Lanka, December 1997. See also Gunaratna, "Suicide Terrorism in Sri Lanka and India," p. 9.

75. Ibid.

76. Sea-borne operations have included surface attacks involving Jet Skis, high-speed rubber rafts, and specially designed radar-evading vessels constructed of fiberglass, as well as mini-submarines and other underwater-propulsion devices along with underwater demolition missions carried out by well-trained frogmen. See Rohan Gunaratna, "Maritime Terrorism: Future Threats and Responses" (briefing presented to the International Research Group on Political Violence and Terrorism, Washington, D.C., May 2001), and Gunaratna, "Suicide Terrorism in Sri Lanka and India," p. 1. According to one account, Sea Tiger attacks have destroyed a third of the Sri Lankan Navy. Al Qaeda's sea-borne attack on the USS *Cole* in Aden harbor in October 2000 is believed to have been copied from Sea Tiger assaults. See Waldman, "Suicide Bombing Masters."

77. Interview conducted with former LTTE cadre in Colombo, December 1997.

78. Office of the Coordinator for Counterterrorism, *Patterns of Global Terrorism 2001* (Washington, D.C.: U.S. Department of State, Publication 10940, May 2002), p. 100.

79. Interview, Colombo, Sri Lanka, February 2003.

80. The U.S. Department of State classifies the LTTE as a terrorist organization, explaining that the group "has an integrated battlefield insurgent strategy with a terrorist program that targets not only key personnel in the countryside but also senior Sri Lankan political and military leaders in Colombo." See Office of the Coordinator for Counterterrorism, *Patterns of Global Terrorism 1996* (Washington, D.C.: U.S. Department of State, Publication 10433, April 1997), p. 54. The LTTE was also classified as a terrorist group by the U.S. Department of Defense in its *Terrorist Group Profiles*, pp. 120–21.

81. Christopher Thomas, "Appeal for Calm as Tamils Deny Train Bombing," *The Times* (London), July 26, 1996.

82. Gunaratna, "The LTTE and Suicide Terrorism."

83. Among the best-known, if not most significant, of these groups are al-Fatah, the Palestinian guerrilla group founded by Yasir Arafat in 1957; the Popular Front for the Liberation of Palestine (PFLP), established in 1967; the Popular Front for the Liberation of Palestine–General Command (PFLP-GC), established in 1967; and at least ten other secular organizations. See Directorate of Intelligence, Central Intelligence Agency, *Palestinian Organizations: A Reference Aid* (Washington, D.C.: Central Intelligence Agency, LDA 90–11155, March 1990), passim.

84. The Gaza percentage is likely to be even higher given the militancy and more entrenched religious orientation of its Palestinian population.

85. The Muslim Brotherhood was founded in Egypt by Hassan al-Banna in 1929. Its goal is to "impose the laws of Islam upon the social, political and constitutional life of the Muslim nations." See Evyatar Levine and Yaacov Shimoni. eds., *Political Dictionary of the Middle East in the Twentieth Century* (London: Weidenfeld and Nicolson, 1972), pp. 262–63.

86. See Ziad Abu-Amr, "Hamas: A Historical and Political Background," *Journal of Palestinian Studies* 23, no. 4 (Summer 1993): 10; Phyllis Bennis, *From Stones to Statehood: The Palestinian Uprising* (New York: Olive Branch Press, 1990), p. 27; and Michael Theodoulu, "New Attacks Feared After Defiant Vow by Hamas," *The Times* (London), August 22, 1995.

87. Interview with Roni Shaked, *Yedioth Ahronoth* (Tel Aviv) reporter and an expert on Hamas. See also Joe Stork, *Erased in a Moment: Suicide Bombing Attacks Against Israeli Civilians* (New York: Human Rights Watch, October 2002), p. 64.

88. Rex Brynen and Neil Caplan, "Israel and Palestine: Implications of the Intifada," in Rex Brynen, ed., *Echoes of the Intifada: Regional Repercussions of the Palestinian-Israeli Conflict* (Boulder, Colo.: Westview, 1992), p. 7.

89. Mishal and Sela, *The Palestinian Hamas*, p. 50.

90. In recent years, however, Hamas has conceded that a *hudna*—a cease-fire or truce—with Israel is permissible.

91. Quoted in Mishal and Aharoni, *Speaking Stones*, p. 31.

92. Brynen and Caplan, "Israel and Palestine," p. 7.

93. Mishal and Sela, *The Palestinian Hamas*, pp. 56–57.

94. Mishal and Aharoni, *Speaking Stones*, p. 26.

95. Hisham H. Ahmad, *Hamas from Religious Salvation to Political Transformation: The Rise of Hamas in Palestinian Society* (Jerusalem: Passia, 1994), p. 51.

96. Ali Jarbawi and Roger Heacock, "The Deportations and the Palestinian-Israeli Negotiations," *Journal of Palestinian Studies* 22, no. 3 (Spring 1993): 32.

97. Mishal and Sela, *The Palestinian Hamas*, p. 57.

98. Ibid., p. 64.

99. The unit is named after a Syrian-born sheikh who became an iconic figure in the history of the Palestinian nationalist resistance movement. Sheikh al-Qassam

was the spiritual head of a collection of villages in the area around Haifa during the 1920s and 1930s, populated mostly by landless peasants who had been displaced by the Zionists. A militant nationalist and devout Muslim, al-Qassam organized a Palestinian guerrilla unit that in 1931 began to raid Jewish settlements in the Jezreel Valley. In a clash with British police in November 1935 al-Qassam was killed. The loss of their leader did not deter al-Qassam's followers, who continued fighting, setting the stage for the countrywide revolt against British rule, known as the Arab Rebellion, which erupted the following year and continued until 1939. See Y. Porath, *The Palestinian Arab National Movement, 1929–1939: From Riots to Rebellion* (London: Frank Cass, 1977), pp. 132–39. See also Abu-Amr, "Hamas," p. 6, and Stork, *Erased in a Moment*, p. 65, n. 158.

100. Mishal and Sela, *The Palestinian Hamas*, p. 65.

101. Stork, *Erased in a Moment*, p. 73.

102. Jarbawi and Heacock. "The Deportations and the Palestinian-Israeli Negotiations," p. 32. See also Mishal and Sela, *The Palestinian Hamas*, pp. 96–97.

103. The deportees included, for example, Dr. Ab al-Azziz al-Rantisi, Husayn Abu Kuwik (a West bank union official), Fadil Salih (an imam), and Hasan Yusuf (a schoolteacher). See Abu-Amr, "Hamas," p. 26, and Ahmad, *Hamas from Religious Salvation to Political Transformation*, p. 77.

104. Scott Atran, "Genesis of Suicide Terrorism," *Science* 299 (March 7, 2003): 1535. See also Stork, *Erased in a Moment*, p. 73.

105. Mishal and Sela, *The Palestinian Hamas*, pp. 65–66.

106. Jarbawi and Heacock, "The Deportations and the Palestinian-Israeli Negotiations," p. 40.

107. Ehud Ya'ari, "The Metamorphosis of Hamas," *Jerusalem Report*, January 14, 1993, p. 25.

108. The two Security Council resolutions in essence call for Israel to return to the boundaries that existed before the 1967 Six Days' War and therefore for Israeli withdrawal from the West Bank and the Gaza Strip in return for the unqualified recognition by both Israel and Palestinians of one another's legitimate right to statehood. Jeffrey Michels, "National Vision and the Negotiation of Narratives: The Oslo Agreement," *Journal of Palestinian Studies* 24 (Autumn 1994): 37.

109. Mishal and Sela, *The Palestinian Hamas*, pp. 66–67.

110. Abu-Amr, "Hamas," p. 13.

111. Mishal and Sela, *The Palestinian Hamas*, p. 67.

112. Boaz Ganor, "Suicide Attacks in Israel," in International Policy Institute for Counter-Terrorism, *Countering Suicide Terrorism*, p. 136.

113. Mark Juergensmeyer, "The Worldwide Rise of Religious Nationalism," *Journal of International Affairs* 50, no. 1 (Summer 1996): 7.

114. Abu-Amr, "Hamas," p. 13.

115. See Walter Laqueur, *The New Terrorism: Fanaticism and the Arms of Mass Destruction* (Oxford: Oxford University Press, 1999), p. 139, and Walter Laqueur, *No End to War: Terrorism in the Twenty-first Century* (New York: Continuum, 2003), p. 107.

334 5. Suicide Terrorism

116. Stork, *Erased in a Moment*, p. 66, n. 158.

117. "Record of Suicide Attacks," *The Times* (London), March 5, 1996.

118. Ehud Sprinzak, "Rational Fanatics," *Foreign Policy*, no. 120 (September/October 2000): 71.

119. Ganor, "Suicide Attacks in Israel," p. 136, and Theodoulu, "New Attacks Feared After Defiant Vow by Hamas."

120. BBC Summary of World Broadcasts, July 23, 2000, quoted in Pape, "The Strategic Logic of Suicide Terrorism," p. 355.

121. Mishal and Sela, *The Palestinian Hamas*, p. 66.

122. Shiqaqi reportedly borrowed the distinction used by Hezbollah between suicide and martyrdom. While Islam disdains suicide, it extols martyrdom: hence Shiqaqi's formulation that "Allah may cause to be known those who believe and may make some of you martyrs, and Allah may purify those who believe and may utterly destroy the disbelievers . . . [however] no one can die except by Allah's leave." Quoted in Atran, "Genesis of Suicide Terrorism," p. 1535.

123. According to a Hamas activist, in the early 1990s Ayyash sent a letter to the Hamas leadership that reportedly argued, "We paid a high price when we used only slingshots and stones. We need to exert more pressure, make the cost of the occupation that much more expensive in human lives, that much more unbearable." Quoted in Hassan, "Letter from Gaza," p. 38.

124. Ayyash was assassinated with a small bomb concealed in a mobile telephone. For the most complete account of Ayyash and Israel's hunt for him, see Samuel M. Katz, *The Hunt for the Engineer: How Israeli Agents Tracked the Hamas Master Bomber* (New York: Fromm, 1999), passim. See also Marie Colvin and Andy Goldberg, "Israel on Alert for Wave of 'Sleeper' Bombers," *Sunday Times* (London), March 10, 1996.

125. "Record of Suicide Attacks," *The Times* (London), March 5, 1996.

126. See Serge Schmemann, "Bus Bombing Kills Five in Jerusalem, 100 Are Wounded," *New York Times*, August 22, 1995.

127. Quoted in Israel Shahak, "Hamas and Arafat: The Balance of Power," *Middle East International*, no. 468 (February 4, 1996): 17.

128. Quoted in Serge Schmemann, "Terror Isn't Alone as a Threat to Middle East Peace," *Jerusalem Post*, March 4, 1996.

129. Sprinzak, "Rational Fanatics," p. 71.

130. Mishal and Sela, *The Palestinian Hamas*, p. 50.

131. From *al-Quds* (East Jerusalem), October 12, 1995, quoted in Mishal and Sela, *The Palestinian Hamas*, p. 71.

132. "Database of Terrorism Attacks Against Israel, 1948–Present," maintained by the National Security Studies Center (NSSC), Haifa University, Mt. Carmel, Haifa, Israel. Information courtesy of Dr. Ami Pedahzur and Mr. Arie Perliger of the NSSC staff.

133. See Yariv Tsfati and Gabriel Weimann, "www.terrorism.com: Terror on the Internet," *Studies in Conflict and Terrorism* 25, no. 5 (September–October 2001): 315–16. See also Edward Lucas, "Deadly Image Which Could Give Hezbollah the

Edge," *Scotsman* (Edinburgh), April 14, 2000; Bill Maxwell, "Good Women Help Bring War's End," *Albany Times Union*, June 5, 2000; and Tanya Willmer, "Soldiers' Mothers Pray Their Own Battle Over After Israel Ends Its Vietnam," *Agence France Presse*, May 24, 2000.

134. Pape, "The Strategic Logic of Suicide Terrorism," p. 355.

135. BBC Summary of World Broadcasts, November 3, 2001 quoted in ibid.

136. BBC Summary of World Broadcasts, July 23, 2000, quoted in Pape, "The Strategic Logic of Suicide Terrorism," p. 355.

137. See General (Ret.) Amnon Lipkin-Shahak, Introduction to International Policy Institute for Counter-Terrorism, *Countering Suicide Terrorism*, p. 5, where he writes: "I believe that these [suicide] attacks were motivated by desperation."

138. Quoted in Sprinzak, "Rational Fanatics," p. 68.

139. Abdallah Shami, interviewed on Israeli television Channel 1 on December 9, 1994, quoted in Rafi Yisra'eli, "Islamikaze: Suicide Terrorism Examined," *Nativ* (Tel Aviv), January–April 1997, p. 3.

140. Quoted in Hassan, "Letter from Gaza," p. 38.

141. "Hamas' Mishal: Jihad Palestinians' Sole Option," *al-Zaman*, November 23, 2000, FBIS-NES, Document ID: GMP 20001123000110, p. 4.

142. Quoted in Sprinzak, "Rational Fanatics," p. 68.

143. Quoted in Anders Strindberg, "'The Ultimate Sacrifice': The Social and Political Dynamics of Suicide Operations in Palestine," *MIPT Quarterly Bulletin* (Second Quarter, 2002): 4.

144. Quoted in Hassan, "Letter from Gaza," p. 39.

145. Quoted in ibid.

146. Quoted in ibid., p. 38.

147. Yassin was assassinated in 2004 by the Israeli Air Force in what the Israeli authorities described as a "targeted killing."

148. Quoted in Burhan Wazis, "Suicide Bombing Is Democratic Right, Says the 'Soul' of Hamas," *Observer* (London), August 19, 2001.

149. Quoted in Thomas L. Friedman, "Strategy of Suicide Bombings," *New York Times*, March 31, 2002.

150. Quoted in Jeffrey Goldberg, "The Martyr Strategy: What Does the New Phase of Terrorism Signify?" *New Yorker*, July 9, 2001.

151. Quoted in Ari Shavit, "The Enemy Within," *Ha'Aretz, Friday Magazine*, August 20, 2002, p. 3, http://www.freeman.org/m_online/sept02/shavit.htm.

152. Interview with senior IDF officers, the Kirya, Tel Aviv, Israel, December 2002.

153. See, for example, the poster jointly produced by Hamas and the al-Aqsa Martyrs Brigade (circa 2002–03) of three martyrs, two of whom are brothers (also in the author's collection).

154. See Mark Juergensmeyer, *Terror in the Mind of God* (Berkeley: University of California Press, 2000), p. 166, for another discussion of this phenomenon.

155. One such announcement, for a young Palestinian suicide terrorist, pro-

claimed, "The Wedding of the Martyr Ali Khadr Al-Yassini to the Black-Eyed in Eternal Paradise"—one of the reputed seventy-two virgins whom Muslim martyrs are promised in Heaven—in *Al-Hayat Al-Jadida*, which was described as an "Arafat-controlled paper." See Joseph Lelyveld, "All Suicide Bombers Are Not Alike: A Journey to Gaza, Cairo, and Hamburg in Search of What Really Made Sept. 11 Possible," *New York Times Magazine*, October 28, 2001, p. 51.

It should be noted that an important recruiting incentive is indeed the promise—allegedly according to Islamic mythology—that the would-be martyr would feel no pain in the commission of his sacred act and would then ascend immediately to a glorious heaven, described as a place replete with "rivers of milk and wine . . . lakes of honey, and the services of 72 virgins," where the martyr will see the face of Allah and later be joined by seventy chosen relatives. See "Wedded to Death in a Blaze of Glory—Profile: The Suicide Bomber," *Sunday Times* (London), March 10, 1996, and Christopher Walker, "Palestinian 'Was Duped Into Being Suicide Bomber,'" *The Times* (London), March 27, 1997.

156. Hassan, "Letter from Gaza," p. 39.

157. Gal Luft, "The Palestinian H-Bomb: Terror's Winning Strategy," *Foreign Affairs* 81, no. 4 (July/August 2002): 6.

158. Hamza Hendawi, "Cult Evolves Around Suicide Bombers," Associated Press, April 28, 2002, http://www.news.findlaw.com/ap_stories/i/1107/4–28–2002/20020 428102000255505.html.

159. Lelyveld, "All Suicide Bombers Are Not Alike," p. 50.

160. See the series of martyrdom videos collected and distributed by the IntelCenter, *Hamas Audio/Video Files*, vol. 1 (Alexandria, Va.: www.intelcenter.com), no date.

161. Lelyveld, "All Suicide Bombers Are Not Alike," p. 51.

162. Quoted in Hendawi, "Cult Evolves Around Suicide Bombers," April 28, 2002.

163. Ibid. Lelyveld cites a 78 percent approval. See Lelyveld, "All Suicide Bombers Are Not Alike," p. 50.

164. Anti-Defamation League of B'nai B'rith, "Arab Leaders Glorify Suicide Terrorism," April 17, 2002, http://www.adl.org/israel/Israel-suicide-terror.asp.

165. This clip was shown to participants at the International Policy Institute for Counter-Terrorism's (ICT) Third International Conference, Herzilya, Israel, September 7–10, 2003. Among them was one of the authors of this paper.

166. FBIS, Near East/South Asia, "Israel: Palestinian Television Broadcasts Clip Encouraging Martyrdom," *Ma'ariv* (Tel Aviv) (Hebrew), August 11, 2003, p. 8.

167. Itmar Marcus, "PA Music Video Promising 'Maidens of Paradise' to Shahids—2 Days Before Suicide Bombings," *Palestinian Media Watch Multi-media Bulletin*, August 12, 2003, http://www.pmw.org.il.

168. See the Qur'an, for example, Sura 4, verse 29: "And do not kill yourselves; verily God is compassionate unto you," http://lexicorient.com/eo/texts/Qur'an/ Qur'an004.htm, and especially the treatise by Brother Abu Ruqaiyah, "The Islamic

Legitimacy of the 'Martrydom Operations,'" originally published in the sixteenth issue of *Nida'ul Islam* (December–January 1996–97), http://www.islam.org.au/articles/16martyrdom.htm.

169. Eyad Sarraj, "The Making of a Suicide Bomber," March 10, 1996, e-mail dated March 23, 1997, sent by news@baraka.baraka.org. Dr. Reuven Paz, one of Israel's leading authorities on Islamic terrorism, has advanced the same argument. See Reuven Paz, "The Islamic Legitimacy of Suicide Terrorism," in International Policy Institute for Counter-Terrorism, *Countering Suicide Terrorism*, pp. 87–88.

170. Hassan, "Letter from Gaza," p. 38.

171. Mouin Rabbani, "Suicide Attacks Fueled by Alienation and Futility," *Philadelphia Inquirer Commentary*, April 3, 2001, http://inq.philly.com/content/inquirer/2001/04/03/opinion/RABBANI03.htm.

172. Ruqaiyah, "The Islamic Legitimacy of the 'Martrydom Operations.'"

173. According to journalist Joyce M. Davis, other leading Islamic authorities, such as Mohammed Sayed Tantawi of al Azhar University in Cairo and Sheikh Hamed al-Midawi, a cleric at Jerusalem's al-Aqsa mosque and the chairman of the (Muslim) Legal Appeals Court in that city, "believe Islamic teachings clearly support suicide bombings, but only against Israeli military targets. Suicide bombings are merely a form of jihad, one of the pillars of Islam, these jurists say. And they say Palestinian suicide bombers are helping to defend their land from Israeli aggression." See Joyce M. Davis, *Martyrs: Innocence, Vengeance, and Despair in the Middle East* (New York: Palgrave/Macmillan, 2003), p. 113.

174. Quoted in Mark Juergensmeyer, *The New Cold War? Religious Nationalism Confronts the Secular State* (Berkeley: University of California Press, 1993), p. 153.

175. Quoted in Rafi Yisra'eli, "Islamikaze: Suicide Terrorism Examined."

176. Quoted in Davis, *Martyrs*, p. 113.

177. Anti-Defamation League of B'nai B'rith, "Arab Leaders Glorify Suicide Terrorism."

178. "Wedded to Death in a Blaze of Glory," and Walker, "Palestinian 'Was Duped Into Being Suicide Bomber.'"

179. Yisra'eli, "Islamikaze," p. 3.

180. Lance Corporal Eddie DiFranco, quoted in David C. Martin and John Walcott, *Best Laid Plans: The Inside Story of America's War Against Terrorism* (New York: Harper and Row, 1988), p. 125.

181. The Israeli secret service reportedly planted a small bomb comprising an estimated two ounces of plastic explosive in a cellular phone used by Ayyash that was detonated by radio signal on January 5, 1996, when he answered a telephone call from his father. See Joel Greenberg, "Slaying Blended Technology and Guile," *New York Times*, January 10, 1996, and Serge Schmemann, "Palestinian Believed to Be Bombing Mastermind Is Killed," *New York Times*, January 6, 1997.

182. "Hamas Issues Statement on Ayyash Killing," al-Quds Palestinian Radio (in Arabic), 1755 GMT, January 5, 1996.

183. Quoted in Harvey W. Kushner, "Suicide Bombers: Business as Usual," *Studies in Conflict and Terrorism* 19, no. 4 (October–December 1996): 335.

184. Quoted in Lelyveld, "All Suicide Bombers Are Not Alike," p. 50.

185. Davis, *Martyrs*, p. 154.

186. Quoted in Barbara Victor, *Army of Roses: Inside the World of Palestinian Woman Suicide Bombers* (New York: Rodale, 2003), pp. 111–12.

187. *Al Hayat al Jadida*, September 17, 1999, quoted in Aluma Solnick, "The Joy of the Mothers of Palestinian 'Martyrs,'" *MEMRI: Inquiry and Analysis Series*, no. 61 (June 25, 2001): 1, www.memri.org.

188. Hassan, "Letter from Gaza," p. 39.

189. *Jerusalem Post Internet Editor*, September 6, 2001, quoted in Steven Stalinsky, "Palestinian Authority Sermons, 2000–2003," *MEMRI Special Report*, no. 24 (December 26, 2003), http://www.memri.org.

190. Davis, *Martyrs*, p. 154. See also Ibn Warraq, "Virgins? What Virgins?" *Guardian* (London), January 12, 2002, http://www.guardian.co.uk/saturday_review/story/0%2C3605%2C631332%2Coo.html.

191. Davis, *Martyrs*, p. 154. See also *Al Hayat Al Jadida* (Palestine Authority), September 17, 1999, quoted in Solnick, "The Joy of the Mothers of Palestinian 'Martyrs,'" p. 1, and *The Jerusalem Post Internet Edition*, September 6, 2001, quoted in Stalinsky, "Palestinian Authority Sermons, 2000–2003," p. 2.

192. As one analyst notes of the 1995–96 Hamas suicide bombing campaign: "The bombings were not directed to effect change in Israel; rather, they were intended to undermine the PA." See Ori Slonim, "The Hamas and Terror: An Alternative Explanation for the Use of Violence," *Strategic Assessment* 2, no. 3 (Ramat Aviv: Jaffee Center for Strategic Studies at Tel Aviv University, December 1999): 17.

193. See Naveh et al., *The Involvement of Arafat, PA Senior Officials, and Apparatuses in Terrorism Against Israel, Corruption, and Crime*, passim. See also Matthew Levitt, "Designating the Al-Aqsa Martyrs Brigades," *Peacewatch*, no. 371 (Washington, D.C.: Washington Institute for Near East Policy, March 25, 2002), pp. 1–2, and Stork, *Erased in a Moment*, pp. 77–79.

194. See Hassan, "Letter from Gaza," p. 39. See also William Drozdiak, "Extremes Squeeze Arafat as Hamas's Power Swells," *International Herald Tribune* (Paris), August 25, 1997, and Neal MacFarquhar, "Portrait of a Suicide Bomber: Devout, Apolitical, and Angry," *New York Times*, March 18, 1996.

195. Luft, "The Palestinian H-Bomb," pp. 4–5.

196. The *Karine-A* was intercepted in the Red Sea on January 3, 2002, by Israeli commandos and the Israeli Navy while en route from Iran to Gaza. See Gal Luft, "Special Policy Forum Report: The *Karine-A* Affair: A Strategic Watershed in the Middle East?" *Peacewatch*, no. 361 (Washington, D.C.: Washington Institute for Near East Policy, January 30, 2002), pp. 1–2; David Makovsky, "The Seizure of Gaza-Bound Arms: Political Implications," *Peacewatch*, no. 358 (Washington, D.C.: Washington Institute for Near East Policy, January 8, 2002), pp. 1–2; Robert Satloff, "*Karine-A*: Strategic Implications of Iranian-Palestinian Collusion," *Policywatch*, no.

539 (Washington, D.C.: Washington Institute for Near East Policy, January 15, 2002), pp. 1–2; and "Caught Red-Handed: The Inside Story of an Arms Shipment," *Jane's Foreign Report*, no. 2672, January 17, 2002, p. 1.

197. Among the injured was a Woodmere, Long Island, resident named Mark Sokolow, who on September 11 had escaped unharmed from the second tower of the World Trade Center, only to find himself enmeshed in another life-threatening terrorist incident, this time in Jerusalem.

198. Luft, "The Palestinian H-Bomb," p. 5.

199. Database of Terrorism Attacks Against Israel, 1948–Present, maintained by the National Security Studies Center, Haifa University, Mt. Carmel, Haifa, Israel.

200. See, for example, Sarraj, "The Making of a Suicide Bomber," and Rabbani, "Suicide Attacks Fueled by Alienation and Futility."

201. Hassan, "Letter from Gaza," p. 38.

202. Lou Michel and Dan Herbeck, *American Terrorist: Timothy McVeigh and the Oklahoma City Bombing* (New York: Regan, 2001), pp. 102, 144–45, 332, and 358.

203. Quoted in Daniel Pipes, *Militant Islam Reaches America* (New York: Norton, 2002), pp. 201–2.

204. Quoted in MacNeil/Lehrer Productions, *Transcript of "The News Hour with Jim Lehrer,"* August 1, 1997.

205. Interviews and discussions with senior Israeli military, intelligence, and law enforcement officers in Tel Aviv, Jerusalem, Haifa, and Herzilya during December 2002, July 2003, and September 2003.

206. Margot Dudevitch, "2003 Terror Report: 50% Decrease in Israeli Casualties," *Jerusalem Post*, January 9, 2004. See also Patrick Bishop, "Have the Suicide Bombers Been Defeated?" *Daily Telegraph* (London), May 26, 2004.

207. Interview with senior Israel Defense Officer responsible for counterterrorism planning and operations, Tel Aviv, December 2002. Moreover, both Israeli and Palestinians "agree that the main factor in the decline in activity is Israel's success in killing or capturing leaders of the most militant [Palestinian terrorist] groups." See Bishop, "Have the Suicide Bombers Been Defeated?"

208. The New York City Police Department (NYPD) has already developed and implemented in the New York metropolitan area an ambitious program precisely along these lines. Discussions with and presentations by NYPD Intelligence Division officers, November 2003 and February 2004.

209. Ehud Sprinzak, "Outsmarting Suicide Terrorists," *Christian Science Monitor* (Boston), October 24, 2000.

210. Interview with NYPD officer, February 2004.

211. Ayman al-Zawahiri, *Knights Under the Prophet's Banner: Meditations on the Jihadist Movement*, translated and published in FBIS, "Al-Sarq Al-Aswat Publishes Extracts from Al-Jihad Leader al-Zawahiri's New Book" (Document ID GMP20020108000197, December 2, 2001), pp. 90–91.

212. "Al-Qaeda Firebrand Threatens New Attacks on US, Taunts Bush: Television," *Agence France Presse*, February 24, 2004.

6. The Old Media

1. Frederick J. Hacker, *Crusaders, Criminals, Crazies: Terror and Terrorism in Our Time* (New York: Norton, 1976), p. xi.

2. Quoted in Gerald McKnight, *The Mind of the Terrorist* (London: Michael Joseph, 1974), p. 168.

3. Brian Michael Jenkins, "International Terrorism: A New Mode of Conflict," in David Carlton and Carlo Schaerf, eds., *International Terrorism and World Security* (London: Croom Helm, 1975), p. 16.

4. J. Bowyer Bell, "Terrorist Scripts and Live-Action Spectaculars," *Columbia Journalism Review* 17, no. 1 (1978): 50.

5. Tony Atwater, "Network Evening News Coverage of the TWA Hostage Crisis," *Terrorism and the News Media Research Project* (Boston: Emerson College, no date), p. 5.

6. Ibid., p. 7.

7. John Dillin, "NBC News President Defends, but Revises, Terrorism Coverage," *Christian Science Monitor* (Boston), August 5, 1985.

8. ABC dispatched forty people, NBC sent twenty-five, and CBS sent twenty. See Roderick Townley and John Weisman, "The Reporters' Rat Race: Danger, Chaos, and Rumors of Payoffs," *TV Guide*, September 21, 1985.

9. Atwater, "Network Evening News Coverage of the TWA Hostage Crisis," p. 6.

10. Eleanor Randolph, "Networks Turn Eye on Themselves," *Washington Post*, June 30, 1985.

11. Quoted in Fred Barnes, "Shiite Spin Control," *New Republic* (Washington, D.C.), July 15 and 22, 1985, p. 12.

12. Quoted in Edwin Diamond, "The Coverage Itself—Why It Turned Into 'Terrorvision,'" *TV Guide*, September 21, 1985, p. 13.

13. Quoted in ibid., p. 10.

14. Quoted in A. P. Schmid, "Terrorism and the Media: The Ethics of Publicity," *Terrorism and Political Violence* 1, no. 4 (October 1989): 564.

15. Joseph Fromm, "TV: Does It Box in [the] President in a Crisis? *U.S. News and World Report*, July 5, 1985.

16. Walter Mears, quoted in Randolph, "Networks Turn Eye on Themselves."

17. Quoted in Walter Laqueur, *The Age of Terrorism* (Boston: Little, Brown, 1987), p. 125.

18. Diamond, "The Coverage Itself," pp. 10, 12.

19. As part of the deal, West German television was forced to broadcast footage of each of the five freed terrorists being released and boarding the aircraft that would take them to freedom, as well as present communiqués prepared by the Second of June terrorist group. Daniel Schorr, "The Encouragement of Violence," in Benjamin Netanyahu, ed., *Terrorism: How the West Can Win* (New York: Avon, 1986), p. 114.

20. Notes from the International Seminar on Terrorism and the Mass Media

held in Sicily, April 3–5, 1981; archival material in the RAND Terrorism Incident Database.

21. Henry McDonald, "How the BBC Dances to an IRA Tune," *Sunday Times* (London), January 19, 1997.

22. Followed by Israel, France, Britain, Germany, the former Soviet Union/Russia, Turkey, Cuba, Spain, and Iran. RAND Terrorism Incident Database.

23. Including the geographical scope and diversity of America's overseas commercial interests, its numerous military bases on foreign soil, and the United States' stature as the leader of the free world during the Cold War and as the lone remaining superpower today.

24. Quoted in Laqueur, *The Age of Terrorism*, p. 125.

25. Grant Wardlaw, *Political Terrorism: Theory, Tactics, and Counter-measures* (Cambridge: Cambridge University Press, 1990), p. 80.

26. Ibid.

27. Jeffrey Z. Rubin and Nehemia Friedland, "Theater of Terror," *Psychology Today* 20, no. 3 (March 1986): 24.

28. Barnes, "Shiite Spin Control," p. 10.

29. David C. Martin and John Walcott, *Best Laid Plans: The Inside Story of America's War Against Terrorism* (New York: Harper and Row, 1988), p. 189.

30. Garrick Utley, "The Shrinking of Foreign News," *Foreign Affairs* 76, no. 2 (March–April 1997): 6.

31. Quoted in James Adams, "The Role of the Media," in Robert L. Pfaltzgraff Jr. and Richard H. Schultz Jr., eds., *Ethnic Conflict and Regional Instability: Implications for U.S. Policy and Army Roles and Missions* (Carlisle, Pa.: U.S. Army Strategic Studies Institute, 1994), p. 163.

32. Utley, "The Shrinking of Foreign News," p. 2.

33. Ibid., p. 6.

34. T. E. Pattern and R. D. McClure, *The Unseeing Eye: The Myth of Television Power in National Elections* (New York: G. P. Putnam's Sons, 1976), quoted in Sandra Wurth-Hough, "Network News Coverage of Terrorism: The Early Years," *Terrorism* 6, no. 3 (Summer 1983): 410.

35. Tom Shales, "America's Ordeal by Television," *Washington Post*, July 2, 1985.

36. Burns W. Roper, *Public Perceptions of Television and Other Mass Media: A Twenty Year Review, 1959–1978* (New York: Roper Organization, Inc., 1979), pp. 1–5, quoted in Mark Armen Ayanian and John Z. Ayanian, "Armenian Political Violence on American Network News: An Analysis of Content," *Armenian Review* 40, no. 1–157 (Spring 1987): 16.

37. See Aryanian and Ayanian, "Armenian Political Violence on American Network News," pp. 28–29.

38. Adams, "The Role of the Media," p. 162.

39. Ibid., p. 166.

40. Neil Hickey, "Terrorism and Television," *TV Guide*, July 31, 1976, p. 6.

41. Schmid, "Terrorism and the Media," p. 559.

42. In addition to Kissinger and Brzezinksi, mentioned above, the U.S. attorney general at the time, Edwin Meese, Secretary of Defense Caspar Weinberger, and the U.S. State Department legal adviser Abraham D. Sofaer also called for greater press restraint in the aftermath of the TWA hostage crisis.

43. See, e.g., the discussions in Yonah Alexander and Richard Latter, eds., *Terrorism and the Media* (McLean, Va.: Brassey's, 1990), passim, and Netanyahu, *Terrorism*, pp. 109–29, 229–39.

44. Laqueur, *The Age of Terrorism*, p. 121.

45. Quoted in R.W. Apple Jr., "Meese Suggests Press Code on Terrorism," *New York Times*, July 18, 1985.

46. Paul Wilkinson, "Terrorism and Propaganda," in Alexander and Latter, *Terrorism and the Media*, p. 30.

47. Margaret Thatcher, quoted in Karen DeYoung, "U.S. Considering Talks on Hijacking Coverage," *Washington Post*, July 18, 1985.

48. Netanyahu, *Terrorism*, p. 109.

49. Ibid.

50. Perhaps the most far-reaching legislation enacted in this regard was the ban imposed by Britain between 1988 and 1994 on the broadcast of all interviews with terrorists or their supporters. According to the home secretary at the time the ban was introduced, Douglas Hurd, this extreme measure was not an attempt to impose censorship of the media but simply to deny members of the IRA, Sinn Fein, and other paramilitary groups "this easy platform for those who use it to propagate terrorism" (*Guardian* [London], October 20, 1988). Its effects, however, were perhaps more farcical than efficacious. Although the terrorists or spokespeople themselves were prevented from appearing on air, their statements were nonetheless still broadcast: by actors "standing in" for the proscribed individuals, in essence, reading scripts prepared by the terrorists. The result went beyond even the obvious circumvention and dilution of the legislation's intent, but mocked the government—completely destroying its efforts to control the dissemination of terrorist views. For a contrasting view, see the analysis in Shane Kingston, "Terrorism, the Media, and the Northern Ireland Conflict," *Studies in Conflict and Terrorism* 18, no. 3 (July–September 1995): 203–32.

51. Lawrence K. Grossman, "Television and Terrorism: A Common Sense Approach," *TVI Report* 6, no. 4 (1986): 3.

52. Laqueur, *The Age of Terrorism*, p. 127.

53. Theo Downes-LeGuin and Bruce Hoffman, *The Impact of Terrorism on Public Opinion, 1988 to 1989* (Santa Monica, Calif.: RAND Corporation, MR-225-F.F/RC, 1993), p. 16.

54. It should be noted, however, that a small percentage of the respondents who expressed relevant ethnic identification with a specific group were found to have slightly more ambivalent attitudes (mainly Jewish Americans and Irish Americans, respectively, with regard to the Jewish Defense League and the IRA). Ibid.

55. Konrad Kellen, quoted in ibid.

56. Philip Geyelin, "NBC: How to Protect a Terrorist," *Washington Post*, May 19, 1986.

57. Quoted in ibid. See also the editorial by Mortimer B. Zuckerman, the chairman and editor in chief of *U.S. News and World Report*, "Playing the Terrorists' Game," *U.S. News and World Report*, June 9, 1986.

58. As John O'Sullivan of the *London Daily Telegraph* remarked in a 1985 interview, "We mishandle [terrorists] because . . . we treat them in effect as politicians rather than . . . criminals." "Do Terrorists Need Television, TV Guide Asks," *United Press International*, February 18, 1985.

59. Quoted in Sir John Hermon, "The Police, the Media, and the Reporting of Terrorism," in Alexander and Latter, *Terrorism and the Media*, p. 39.

60. See Martin and Walcott, *Best Laid Plans*, pp. 188–92.

61. Abraham D. Sofaer, quoted in DeYoung, "U.S. Considering Talks on Hijacking Coverage."

62. Quoted in Diamond, "The Coverage Itself."

63. Margaret Genovese, "Terrorism: Newspapers Grapple with the Extraordinary Challenges of Covering Worldwide Terrorist Incidents," *Presstime*, (New York) August 1986.

64. Grossman, "Television and Terrorism," p. 1.

65. Donald Bremner, "Media Given Mixed Reviews on Terrorism," *Los Angeles Times*, September 26, 1986.

66. Quoted in Fromm, "TV: Does It Box in [the] President in a Crisis?"

67. Quoted in Barnes, "Shiite Spin Control," p. 12.

68. Quoted in Fromm, "TV: Does It Box in [the] President in a Crisis?"

69. Patrick Clawson, "Why We Need More but Better Coverage of Terrorism," *Orbis* 80, no. 4 (Winter 1987): 702. It should be noted, however, that Sir Geoffrey Jackson, the British ambassador to Uruguay who was kidnapped by the Tupamaros in 1971 and held for eight months, maintains that the absence of media publicity was critical in the terrorists' decision to release him.

70. Martin and Walcott, *Best Laid Plans*, p. 191.

71. "Public Support Adams Talks," *Sunday Times* (London), February 18, 1996.

72. Downes-LeGuin and Hoffman, *The Impact of Terrorism on Public Opinion*, pp. 14–15. Information on dog bites provided courtesy of Dr. Andrew Rowan, researcher at Tufts University, Medford, Massachusetts.

73. See David Rapoport, "Terrorism," in Mary Hawkesworth and Maurice Kogan, eds., *Routledge Encyclopedia of Government and Politics* (London: Routledge, 1992), 2:1073.

74. Graham Norton, "The Terrorist and the Traveller: A Gulf Aftermath Assessment," *World Today* (London), May 1991, p. 81.

75. Desmond Balmer, "U.S. Tourists React to Terrorism Fear," *New York Daily News*, March 2, 1986.

76. Stuart I. Feiler, "Terrorism: Is Tourism Really the Target? *Hotel and Restaurants International*, October 1986.

77. Survey conducted by the U.S. Travel Data Center (a national nonprofit travel and tourism trade organization), cited in Harvey J. Iglarsh, "Fear of Flying: Its Economic Costs," *Terrorism* 10, no. 1 (Winter 1987): 46.

78. Feiler, "Terrorism: Is Tourism Really the Target?."

79. Ralph Blumenthal, "Peak Season of American Travel to Europe Ends Showing Little Recovery," *New York Times*, September 14, 1986.

80. Norton, "The Terrorist and the Traveller," p. 81.

81. ABC News/Washington Post poll, cited in "Views on National Security," *National Journal* (Washington, D.C.), October 25, 1986.

82. Norton, "The Terrorist and the Traveller," p. 81.

83. Quoted in Martin and Walcott, *Best Laid Plans*, p. 191.

84. Quoted in Fromm, "TV: Does It Box in [the] President in a Crisis?"

85. Adams, "The Role of the Media," pp. 164–65.

86. Thomas Plate and William Tuohy, "Los Angeles Times Interview: John Major—Even Under Fire, Britain's Prime Minister Holds His Own," *Los Angeles Times*, June 20, 1993.

87. Tom Squiteri, "U.S.: Return Our Men," *USA Today* (Washington, D.C.), October 6, 1993.

88. B. Drummond Ayres Jr., "The Somalia Mission: Voices," *New York Times*, October 9, 1993.

89. Everett Carl Ladd, "U.S. Public and Somalia," *Christian Science Monitor* (Boston), October 15, 1993.

90. American Broadcasting Companies, Inc., *Nightline* (ABC, 11.30 p.m. ET), October 7, 1993.

91. Cited in Benjamin C. Schwarz, *Casualties, Public Opinion, and U.S. Military Intervention: Implications for U.S. Regional Deterrence Strategies* (Santa Monica, Calif.: RAND Corporation, MR-431-A/AF, 1994), p. 24.

92. Quoted in Fromm, "TV: Does It Box in [the] President in a Crisis?"

93. See "Khaled Tribute," *The Times* (London), September 3, 1997, and Christopher Walker, "Arabs Are Convinced Car Crash Was a Murder Plot," *The Times* (London), September 4, 1997.

94. See "Unabomber Manifesto," *Washington Post*, September 19, 1995.

95. David Rapoport, "The Media and Terrorism: Implications of the Unabomber Case," editorial in *Terrorism and Political Violence* 8, no. 1 (Spring 1996): viii.

7. The New Media

1. Mohammed El-Nawawy and Adel Iskandar, *Al-Jazeera: The Story of the Network That Is Rattling Governments and Redefining Modern Journalism* (Cambridge, Mass.: Westview, 2003), pp. 143, 146–47.

2. Tina Brown, "Death by Error," *Washington Post*, May 19, 2005.

3. Alex P. Schmid and Janny de Graaf, *Violence as Communication: Insurgent Terrorism and the Western News Media* (Beverly Hills, Calif.: Sage, 1982), p. 9.

4. For the purposes of this study, the definition of propaganda used is that of the Institute for Propaganda Analysis, cited in Jacques Ellul, *Propaganda: The Formation of Men's Attitudes*, trans. Konrad Kellen and Jean Lerner (New York: Knopf, 1965), pp. xi–xii: "Propaganda is the expression of opinion or actions carried out deliberately by individuals or groups with a view to influencing the opinions or actions of other individuals or groups for predetermined ends and through psychological manipulations."

5. As Ellul notes, "Propaganda is made, first of all, because of a will to action, for the purpose of effectively arming policy and giving irresistible power to its decisions." Ibid., p. x.

6. Christina Meyer, *Underground Voices: Insurgent Propaganda in El Salvador, Nicaragua, and Peru* (Santa Monica, Calif.: RAND Corporation, N-3299-USDP, 1991), p. 2.

7. See Bonnie Cordes, "When Terrorists Do the Talking: Reflections on Terrorist Literature," in David C. Rapoport, ed., "Special Issue: Inside Terrorist Organizations," *Journal of Strategic Studies* 10, no. 4 (December 1987): 164.

8. Meyer, *Underground Voices*, pp. 9–10.

9. Ibid., pp. 11–12.

10. Quoted in Stephen Engelberg, "Contras to Start New Radio Station, *New York Times*, November 5, 1986.

11. Yariv Tsfati and Gabriel Weimann, "www.terrorism.com: Terror on the Internet," *Studies in Conflict and Terrorism* 25, no. 5 (September–October 2001): 316.

12. See Schmid and de Graaf, *Violence as Communication*, pp. 223–24; Edward Herman and Gerry O'Sullivan, *The "Terrorism" Industry* (New York: Pantheon, 1989), pp. 191–93, 218; and Dorothy E. Denning, "Activism, Hacktivism, and Cyberterrorism: The Internet as a Tool for Influencing Foreign Policy," http://www.nautilus.org/info-policy/workshop/papers/denning.html (accessed April 16, 2002), p. 4.

13. "Militant Islamic Political Activism on the Worldwide Web" (seminar by two analysts with the Foreign Broadcast Information Service, presented at the RAND Corporation Washington, D.C., Office, December 19, 2000).

14. Denning, "Activism, Hacktivism, and Cyberterrorism," p. 3.

15. Charles Schreiner, coordinator of East Timor Action Network, quoted in Roy Krovel, "www.guerrilla.net," *Internet Today* (London), issue 25 (November 1996): 23.

16. Denning, "Activism, Hacktivism, and Cyberterrorism," p. 4.

17. Dorothy Denning, "Information Warfare and Cyber-Terrorism" (Women in International Security [WIIS] seminar, Washington, D.C., December 15, 1999).

18. As two observers have noted with respect to the perception management conducted by terrorists on the Web: "It is not surprising that networked terrorists have already begun to leverage IT for perception management and propaganda to

influence public opinion, recruit new members, and generate funding. Getting a message out and receiving extensive news media exposure are important components of terrorist strategy, which ultimately seeks to undermine the will of an opponent. In addition to such traditional media as television or print, the Internet now offers terrorist groups an alternative way to reach out to the public, often with much more direct control over the message." Michele Zanini and Sean J. A. Edwards, "The Networking of Terror in the Information Age," in John Arquilla and David Ronfeldt, eds., *Networks and Netwars: The Future of Terror, Crime, and Militancy* (Santa Monica, Calif.: RAND Corporation, MR-1382-OSD, 2001), p. 43.

19. "Militant Islamic Political Activism on the Worldwide Web."

20. Ibid.

21. For a detailed examination and analysis of the EZLN, see Thomas Olesen, *International Zapatismo: The Construction of Solidarity in the Age of Globalization* (London: Zed, 2005), and David F. Ronfeldt et al., *The Zapatista Social Netwar in Mexico* (Santa Monica, Calif.: RAND Corporation, MR-994-A, 1998).

22. "An Accion Zapatista Report—Zapatistas in Cyberspace: A Guide to Analysis and Resources," http://www.eco.utexas.edu/faculty/Cleaver/zapsincyber.html (accessed June 14, 2005). The EZLN's seven-year-old Web site could still be accessed as of 2002 at http://www.utexas.edu/students/nave (note the server's U.S.-based location at a Texas university site). Today, its official site can be accessed (as of June 14, 2005) at "Zapatista Network: A Clearinghouse of Zapatista Information and Support Worldwide." Another site, "EZLN—¡Ya Basta! [Enough already]," at http://www.ezln.org (accessed June 15, 2005), is not an official EZLN site, but, according to Olesen, it "was the first website devoted entirely to the issues of the EZLN and Chiapas." See Olesen, *International Zapatismo*, p. 190.

23. Note that in the global crackdown on terrorist fund-raising and related support activities that followed the September 11, 2001, attacks, the sites of many of the better-known terrorist and insurgent groups prominently featured on the Web either closed down completely or became accessible only on a sporadic basis. These include al Qaeda's www.alneda.com, Hezbollah's www.hizbollah.org, and Hamas's www.hamas.org, among others.

24. Tim Golden, "Mexico's New Offensive: Erasing Rebel's Mystique," *New York Times*, February 11, 1995.

25. Ronfeldt et al., *The Zapatista Social Netwar in Mexico*, p. 2.

26. Olesen, *International Zapatismo*, p. 190.

27. Ibid., p. 3; Tod Robberson, "Loaded Guns and Diskettes: Rebels Win Hearts and Minds on Internet," *International Herald Tribune* (Paris), February 21, 1995, and Krovel, "www.guerrilla.net," p. 23.

28. Krovel, "www.guerrilla.net," p. 23.

29. "Militant Islamic Political Activism on the Worldwide Web."

30. Quoted in Robberson, "Loaded Guns and Diskettes."

31. Quoted in Ronfeldt et al., *The Zapatista Social Netwar in Mexico*, p. 4.

32. Robberson, "Loaded Guns and Diskettes."

33. Quoted in Krovel, "www.guerrilla.net," p. 23.

34. Olesen, *International Zapatismo*, pp. 84–85.

35. Quoted in ibid., p. 85.

36. Krovel, "www.guerrilla.net," p. 23.

37. Accessed on June 14, 2005.

38. Rohan Gunaratna, *International and Regional Security Implications of the Sri Lankan Tamil Insurgency* (St. Albans, Herts: International Foundation of Sri Lankans, 1997), pp. 53–58. See also Denning, "Activism, Hacktivism, and Cyberterrorism," p. 8, and Tsfati and Weimann, "www.terrorism.com: Terror on the Internet," passim.

39. Reuters, "Propaganda to the People," Wired News.com, http://www.wired.com/news/print/0,1294,11363,00.html (accessed April 11, 2002).

40. Quoted in Krovel, "www.guerrilla.net," p. 24.

41. Gunaratna, *International and Regional Security Implications of the Sri Lankan Tamil Insurgency*, p. 58.

42. Accessed on June 14, 2005.

43. See the excellent content analysis of terrorist Web sites in Tsfati and Weimann, "www.terrorism.com: Terror on the Internet," pp. 319–21.

44. See http://www.eelam.web.com/ (accessed regularly between July and August 2002).

45. Krovel, "www.guerrilla.net," p. 25.

46. Ibid., p. 24.

47. Thailif Deen, "Tigers Try Electronic Terrorism," *Daily News* (Colombo), November 22, 1997.

48. Interview with foreign ministry and intelligence officials in Colombo, Sri Lanka, December 1997.

49. Zanini and Edwards, "The Networking of Terror in the Information Age," p. 43.

50. "Militant Islamic Political Activism on the Worldwide Web."

51. Gabriel Weimann, *Terror on the Internet: The New Arena, the New Challenges* (Washington, D.C.: U.S. Institute of Peace, forthcoming), p. 16 of the manuscript.

52. Ibid., pp. 49–51.

53. A survey conducted by two Israeli academicians, which examined sites in 1998 and again in 2002, showed that Hamas, Hizbollah, the Shining Path, Kahane Lives, the Basque separatist group ETA, the IRA, Aum Shinrikyo, the FARC, the ELN, Peru's MRTA (Tupac Amaru), the Turkish Marxist group DHKP/C, the PKK, the IMU, Egypt's Islamic Group, the Popular Front for the Liberation of Palestine, Palestine Islamic Jihad, and the cold war dinosaur Japanese Red Army, in addition to the EZLN and the LTTE, had a presence on the Internet. See Tsfati and Weimann, "www.terrorism.com: Terror on the Internet," pp. 328–30. See also Peter Victor, "Fascists Take to the Keyboards," *The Independent on Sunday* (London), April 7, 1995; Agence France Presse, "Eta Driven from Internet," *The Times* (London), February 20, 1996; "Intelligence Battle in Cyberspace," *Intelligence Newsletter*, no. 263 (April 27, 1995): 3; and www.alneda.com (al Qaeda's Web site, accessed on August 12, 2002).

54. "Militant Islamic Political Activism on the Worldwide Web"; Michael Whine, "Islamist Organizations on the Internet," *Terrorism and Political Violence* 11, no. 1 (Spring 1999): 125–26; Zanini and Edwards, "The Networking of Terror in the Information Age," p. 29.

55. Whine, "Islamist Organizations on the Internet," p. 131.

56. Zanini and Edwards, "The Networking of Terror in the Information Age," p. 29.

57. Whine, "Islamist Organizations on the Internet," pp. 125–26.

58. "Militant Islamic Political Activism on the Worldwide Web."

59. Efforts to access these and all other Hezbollah sites, except for the al-Manar television site (www.manartv.com.lb/news/aspx and www.manar.com), in June 2005 proved unsuccessful.

60. See www.hizbollah.org/english, accessed during July and August 2002.

61. Reportedly only one other terrorist or insurgent group, Algeria's Islamic Salvation Party (FIS), regularly posts content in the French language. See "Militant Islamic Political Activism on the Worldwide Web."

62. Ibid.

63. Zanini and Edwards, "The Networking of Terror in the Information Age," p. 26.

64. Quoted in Whine, "Islamist Organizations on the Internet," p. 126.

65. Charles Pillar, "Terrorists Taking Up Cyberspace: Web Sites Have Become Inexpensive, Easily Accessible Tools for Giving Instructions to Operatives and Raising Funds," *Los Angeles Times*, February 9, 2001.

66. http://almashriq.hiof.no/lebanon/300/320/324/324.2/hizballah/ (accessed June 15, 2005).

67. Ibid.

68. Accessed June 15, 2005. See also Zanini and Edwards, "The Networking of Terror in the Information Age," p. 43; Denning, "Activism, Hacktivism, and Cyberterrorism," pp. 7–8; Julia Scheeres, "Blacklisted Groups Visible on Web," Wired News. com, http://www.wired.com/news/print/0,1283,47616,00.html (accessed April 19, 2002); and James Kitfield, "The Hezbollah Model," *National Journal* 34, no. 20 (May 18, 2002).

69. Badih Chayban, "Hizbullah Rolls Out New Computer Game: Special Force Lets Players Use Sharon for Target Practice," *Daily Star* (Beirut), March 3, 2003, http://www.specialforce.net/english/news/dailystart.htm.

70. Quoted in Mariam Karouny, "Hizbollah Computer Game Recalls Israeli Battles," *Reuters Technology*, March 18, 2003, http://www.specialforce.net/english/news/reuters.htm.

71. Daniel J. Wakin, "Video Game Mounts Simulated Attacks Against Israeli Targets," *New York Times*, May 18, 2003.

72. See http://www.specialforce.net/english/indexeng.htm (accessed June 15, 2005).

73. Registration Card No. 336070, *Special Force Version 1* (no date).

74. Quoted in Wakin, "Video Game Mounts Simulated Attacks Against Israeli Targets."

75. Back cover, *Special Force Version 1* (no date).

76. See, for example, http://www.palestine-info.com (accessed in January 2002 and again on June 15, 2005). See also Scheeres, "Blacklisted Groups Visible on Web." The affiliated www.qassam.net was closed down in 2002.

77. See, for example, http://www.msanews-list (accessed August 2002). MSANews has also included links to, and communiqués from, other radical Islamic groups such as the FIS, GIA, etc. See also Whine, "Islamist Organizations on the Internet," p. 127.

78. "Militant Islamic Political Activism on the Worldwide Web."

79. Doubts about the authenticity of this entire episode have been raised. See especially James Fallows, "Who Shot Mohammed Al-Dura?" *Atlantic Monthly* 291, no. 5 (June 2003): 49–56.

80. See, for example, http://www.palestine-info.com (accessed in January 2002).

81. Whine, "Islamist Organizations on the Internet," p. 128. See also the discussion in Tsfati and Weimann, "www.terrorism.com: Terror on the Internet," pp. 319–20.

82. Bin Laden and al Qaeda have also been alleged to employ this means to communicate secretly over the Internet. See Reuters, "Extremists Post Hidden Messages," Wired News.com, February 6, 2001, http://www.wired.com/news/print/0,1294,41650,00.html (accessed April 19, 2002); Declan McCullagh, "Bin Laden: Steganography Master?" Wired News.com, February 7, 2001, http://www.wired.com/news/print/0,1283,41658,00.html (accessed April 19, 2002); Jack Kelley, "Terror Groups Hide Behind Web Encryption: Officials Say Sites Disguise Activities," *USA Today*, February 6, 2001; and Jack Kelley, "Militants Wire Web with Links to Jihad," *USA Today*, July 10, 2002.

83. See Whine, "Islamist Organizations on the Internet," p. 128, and Zanini and Edwards, "The Networking of Terror in the Information Age," p. 37.

84. http://www.IntifadaOnline.com (accessed in August 2002 and on June 15, 2005).

85. "Special Information Bulletin: Marketing of Terrorism Through the Internet," Intelligence and Terrorism Information Center at the Center for Special Studies (C.S.S.), November 2004, http://www.intelligence.org.il/eng/sib/1_05/n_t.htm (accessed June 16, 2005).

86. This image has regularly been featured on these sites since 2000.

87. http://www.IntifadaOnline.com (accessed June 15, 2005). See also, for example, http://www.palestine-info.com (accessed in January 2002).

88. http://www.IntifadaOnline.com (accessed in October 2000, January 2001, August 2002, and June 15, 2005).

89. Quoted in Kelley, "Militants Wire Web with Links to Jihad."

90. "Special Information Bulletin: Marketing of Terrorism Through the Internet," November 2004, and Part 2, December 2004, http://www.intelligence.org.il/eng/sib/1_05/n_t.htm (accessed June 16, 2005).

91. Only www.sabiroon.net could be accessed on June 16, 2005.

92. Weimann, *Terror on the Internet*, p. 80.

93. Only two—http://www.qudsway.com and http://www.palestineway.com— could be accessed on June 16, 2005.

94. Accessed at http://www.hizb-ut-tahrir.info/english/index.html on June 15, 2005.

95. www.lashkar-e-taiba.net (accessed in February 2001).

96. "Militant Islamic Political Activism on the Worldwide Web."

97. Jessica Eve Stern, "Pakistan's Jihad Culture," *Foreign Affairs* 79, no. 6 (November/December 2000): 120. See also Naill McKay, "Do Terrorists Troll the Net?" Wired News.com, http://www.wired.com/news/print/0,1294,15812,00.html (accessed April 16, 2002); Pillar, "Terrorists Taking Up Cyberspace"; Scheeres, "Blacklisted Groups Visible on Web"; and Zanini and Edwards, "The Networking of Terror in the Information Age," p. 38.

98. Quoted in Pillar, "Terrorists Taking Up Cyberspace."

99. www.lashkar-e-taiba.net (accessed February 2001).

100. Stern, "Pakistan's Jihad Culture," p. 124.

101. "Militant Islamic Political Activism on the Worldwide Web."

102. Quoted in Pillar, "Terrorists Taking Up Cyberspace."

103. Peter Bergen, *Holy War, Inc.: Inside the Secret World of Osama bin Laden* (New York: Free Press, 2001), p. 38.

104. Quoted in Kelley, "Militants Wire Web with Links to Jihad."

105. "Militant Islamic Political Activism on the Worldwide Web."

106. Accessed on June 15, 2005.

107. "Militant Islamic Political Activism on the Worldwide Web."

108. Rohan Gunaratna, *Inside Al-Qa'ida: Global Network of Terrorism* (London: Hurst), p. 57. Its director was known by the nom de guerre Abu Reuter—an obvious reference to the famous global news wire service.

109. Zanini and Edwards, "The Networking of Terror in the Information Age," p. 37.

110. Weimann, *Terror on the Internet*, p. 64.

111. "Information Security News: Militants Wire Web with Links to Jihad," *InfoSec News*, July 11, 2002, quoted in ibid., p. 27.

112. See www.alneda.com, accessed at http:www.swithun.demon.co.uk/markaz/homepage02jul22.htm, on August 12, 2002.

113. Paul Eedle, "Terrorism.com," *The Guardian* (London), July 17, 2002.

114. Presentation made by British journalist Paul Eedle, "The Language of Jihad" at the third annual conference of the Centre for the Study of Terrorism and Political Violence, Symposium on Islamic Extremism and Terrorism in the Greater Middle East, St. Andrews University, St. Andrews, Scotland, June 8, 2002.

115. Eedle, "Terrorism.com."

116. Quoted in Kelley, "Militants Wire Web with Links to Jihad."

117. Eedle, "Terrorism.com."

118. Translation by, and personal communication with, Eedle, July 31, 2002.

119. Kelley, "Militants Wire Web with Links to Jihad." Discussion and communications between the author and British journalist Paul Eedle, July and August 2002.

120. Quoted in Eedle, "Terrorism.com."

121. See "Al-Qa'ida Organization Addresses a Message to Iraqi, Islamic Peoples (Internet) www.alfjr.com in Arabic," March 5, 2003 (posting by "Ayn al-Haqiqah," titled "The al-Qa'ida Organization Writes a Letter to the Iraqi People" in the Issues of the Islamic Nation section of the chat room of http://www.alfjr.com, March 5, 2003). See also Ben Venzke and Aimee Ibrahim, *Al-Qaeda's Advice for Mujahideen in Iraq: Lessons Learned in Afghanistan*, vol. 1.0 (Alexandria, Va.: IntelCenter, April 14, 2003), passim.

122. *MEMRI Special Dispatch—Jihad and Terrorism Studies*, no. 493 (April 11, 2003), quoting http://www.cubezero.nt/vhsvideo/imagis/?subject = 2&rec = 1043.

123. Reuven Paz, "Who Wants to Email Al-Qaeda?" *Occasional Paper, PRISM (Project for the Study of Islamist Movements)* 1, no. 8 (October 2003); *Occasional Paper, PRISM (Project for the Study of Islamist Movements)* 2, no. 2 (July 2004), http:www.e-prism.org/images/PRISM_vol_2_no_2.doc.

124. Weimann, *Terror on the Internet*, p. 41.

125. Quoted in Reuven Paz, "Sawt al-Jihad: New Indoctrination of Qa'idat al-Jihad," *Occasional Paper, PRISM (Project for the Study of Islamist Movements)* 1, no. 8 (October 2003), http:www.e-prism.org/images/PRISM_no_9.doc.

126. Quoted in Weimann, *Terror on the Internet*, p. 105.

127. Moqrin was reportedly killed by Saudi security forces in Riyadh on June 18, 2004.

128. IntelCenter, *Al-Qaeda Targeting Guidance*, vol. 1.0, Thursday, April 1, 2004 (Alexandria, Va.: IntelCenter/Tempest Publishing, 2004), pp. 6–9.

129. See the following articles by Neal MacFarquhar in the *New York Times*: "As Terrorists Strike Arab Targets, Escalation Fears Arise," April 30, 2004; "Firm Pulls 100 from Saudi Arabia After 5 Deaths," May 2, 2004; "After Attack, Company's Staff Plans to Leave Saudi Arabia, May 3, 2004. See also Kim Ghattas and Roula Khalaf, "Shooting Spree in Saudi City Spreads Jitters Among Western Companies," *Financial Times* (London), May 3, 2004.

130. Craig Whitlock, "Islamic Radicals Behead American in Saudi Arabia," *Washington Post*, June 19, 2004.

131. See Sean Young, "Online Co. Shuts Down Site with Beheading," *Yahoo! News*, May 14, 2004, http://www.crime-research.org/news/14.05.2004/270; John F. Burns, "Video Appears to Show Insurgents Kill a Downed Pilot," *New York Times*, April 23, 2005; and Jonathan Finer and Anthony Faiola, "Insurgents Say They Have Killed Japanese: Video May Show Body of Hostage," *Washington Post*, May 29, 2005.

132. IntelCenter, *Al-Qaeda Targeting Guidance*, vol. 1.0, pp. 6–9.

133. *Declaration of Jihad Against the Country's Tyrants—Military Series* (no date). Also known as the Manchester Manual, this document was obtained by

British police during a raid in March 2000 of an al Qaeda safe house in Manchester. It was found on a computer left behind by Abu Anas al-Libi, a key al Qaeda operative wanted in connection with the 1998 East Africa embassy bombings, who fled Britain and is believed to be at large still. A version of the manual can be accessed at http://www.usdoj.gov/ag/manualpart1_3pdf.

134. *The 9/11 Commission Report*, pp. 157, 164, 495.

135. Barton Gellman, "Cyber-Attacks by Al-Qaeda Feared: Terrorists at Threshold of Using Internet as Tool of Bloodshed, Experts Say," *Washington Post*, June 27, 2002.

136. Dan Eggen, "Indictment Cites Plans to Target Financial Hubs: 3 Britons' Extradition to Be Sought," *Washington Post*, April 13, 2005.

137. Bergen, *Italy War*, Inc., p. 27.

138. Intended, in the version the author acquired, most likely for British Muslims in the United Kingdom.

139. *The Destruction of the American Destroyer USS Cole*, DVD version, produced by the Assahab (the Cloud) Foundation (no date).

140. See http://prohosters.com/pearl/#ogr or the link to the execution clip found on the site www.ogrish.com.

141. Eedle, "The Language of Jihad." Also, further discussion and communication between the author and Eedle in July and August 2002.

142. Howard Schneider and Walter Pincus, "Bin Laden Video Includes Sept. 11 Praise," *Washington Post*, April 16, 2002.

143. Transcript of video, April 3, 2002, p. 9.

144. IntelCenter, *Evolution of Jihadi Video* (EJV), vol. 1.0, May 11, 2005 (Alexandria, Va.: IntelCenter/Tempest Publishing, 2005), p. 4.

145. Quoted in Peter Finn and Peter Baker, "Hostages Were Helpless in the Face of Chaos," *Washington Post*, September 5, 2005.

146. It was initially on air only six hours a day. See Kitfield, "The Hezbollah Model."

147. See the "About Us" description at http://www.manartv.com.lb/aboutUS. aspx?Language = en (accessed on June 20, 2005).

148. Avi Jorisch, *Beacon of Hatred: Inside Hizballah's Al-Manar Television* (Washington, D.C.: Washington Institute for Near East Policy, 2004), p. xiv.

149. "About Us" description at http://www.manartv.com.lb/aboutUS.aspx? Language = en.

150. Jorisch, *Beacon of Hatred*, p. xiv. This report is noteworthy for an accompanying CD-ROM with video clips of fifty-seven actual al-Manar broadcasts to illustrate its central arguments. See especially pp. 52–61 for discussions of al-Manar's anti-American and Iraq coverage.

151. Ibid., p. xv.

152. According to the Gallup poll, in response to the question of television stations watched in the last seven days, the rankings were: MBC, 37.1 percent of total audience; LBC, 26.6 percent; Abu Dhabi, 25.8 percent; Future TV, 21.1 percent; and

al-Manar, 16.0 percent. In response to the question of which television channel is turned to first to catch up on current world affairs, the rankings were: al-Jazeera, 43.2 percent; MBC, 7.7 percent; and al-Manar, 5.4 percent. Communication between the author and an analyst in the U.S. State Department's Policy Planning Staff responsible for monitoring Middle Eastern media, August 12, 2002.

153. Kitfield, "The Hezbollah Model."

154. Jorisch, *Beacon of Hatred*, p. xiii.

155. Zanini and Edwards, "The Networking of Terror in the Information Age," p. 42.

156. Hizbollah video clips obtained by the author in 1999 that were packaged on the al-Manar Web site and related Hizbollah sites, for fund-raising purposes. See also Kitfield, "The Hezbollah Model."

157. Quoted in Edward Lucas, "Deadly Image Which Could Give Hezbollah the Edge," *Scotsman* (Edinburgh), April 14, 2000.

158. See ibid.; Tanya Willmer, "Soldiers' Mothers Pray Their Own Battle Over After Israel Ends Its Vietnam," *Agence France Presse*, May 24, 2000; and Bill Maxwell, "Good Women Help Bring War's End," *Albany Times Union*, June 5, 2000.

159. Quoted from the Hezbollah Web site, which appeared in the Israeli daily newspaper *Yediot Aharonot* on December 16, 1998, and is cited by Tsfati and Weimann, "www.terrorism.com: Terror on the Internet," p. 315.

160. Quoted in ibid., p. 325.

161. Ibid., pp. 325–26; "Hizbullah's Cyber-Success," *Foreign Report* (London), no. 2527 (January 14, 1999): 4–5.

162. Alessandra Stanley, "Top Kurd's Arrest Unleashes Rioting All Across Europe," *New York Times*, February 17, 1999; Thomas W. Lippman, "Capture of Kurd Spurs Rage in Europe," *Washington Post*, February 17, 1999.

163. Amberin Zaman, "Swords Into Rabbit Ears," *Washington Post*, February 4, 1999.

164. Schmid and de Graaf, *Violence as Communication*, p. 9.

165. Henry Schuster, "Studios of Terror: Al Qaeda's Media Strategy," http://www. cnn.com/2005/WORLD/MCAST/02/15/schuster.column/index.html (accessed February 15, 2005).

166. See, for instance, "Islamic Group Says It Set Off Dagestan Blast," *New York Times*, July 3, 2005; Andy Mosher, "Abducted Egyptian Envoy Killed in Iraq," *Washington Post*, July 8, 2005; and John F. Burns, "Rebels Kill Egyptian Diplomat, Adding Pressure on Others in Iraq," *New York Times*, July 8, 2005.

167. See, for instance, the "Iraq" tab at www.kavkazcenter.com and the "Iraqi Resistance Report" tab at www.jihadunspun.com, as well as such sites as www.islammemo.cc/taqrer/one_news.asp?Idnew = 292; www.la7odood.com; www.balagh.com/thaqafa/0604ggpz.htm; and www.albasrah.net, all accessed on July 6, 2005.

168. www.albasrah.net, accessed on July 6, 2005.

169. They include: al Qaeda, Ansar al-Islam, Ansar al-Sunnah, Islamic Army in

Iraq, Salafist Group for Call and Combat (GSPC), Sout al-Jihad in Iraq, Organization of Jihad's Base in the Country of the Two Rivers (QJBR), the al-Haramain Brigades, the Taliban, and groups in Chechnya, Bosnia, Kashmir, and Indonesia. See IntelCenter, *Evolution of Jihadi Video*, p. 5.

170. Awadh al-Taee and Steve Negus, "Now Showing (Despite Official Warnings): 'Mujahideen Movie,'" *Financial Times* (London), February 16, 2005.

171. See, for example, Finer and Faiola, "Insurgents Say They Have Killed Japanese," and Burns, "Rebels Kill Egyptian Diplomat, Adding Pressure on Others in Iraq."

172. David E. Kaplan, "National Security Watch: Eurolefties Fund Iraq Insurgency," *U.S. News and World Report*, June 23, 2005, http://www.usnews.com/usnews/news/articles/050623/23euroleft.htm.

173. Quoted in Susan B. Glasser, "'Martyrs' in Iraq Mostly Saudis: Web Sites Track Suicide Bombings,'" *Washington Post*, May 15, 2005.

174. David Baran and Mathieu Guidère, "Sons et images de l'opposition irakienne," [Sound and pictures of the Iraqi opposition], *Le Monde Diplomatique* (Paris), May 2005. An infelicitous translation, titled "Iraq: A Message from the Insurgents," was also published by *Le Monde Diplomatique*'s English edition. See also Robert F. Worth, "Jihadists Take Stand on Web, and Some Say It's Defensive," *New York Times*, March 13, 2005.

175. IntelCenter, *Evolution of Jihadi Video*, p. 5.

8. The Modern Terrorist Mind-set

1. Peter H. Merkl, Prologue to Peter H. Merkl, ed., *Political Violence and Terror* (Berkeley: University of California Press, 1986), p. 8.

2. Quoted in Peter Neuhauser, "The Mind of a German Terrorist," *Encounter* 51, no. 3 (September 1978): 81.

3. Quoted in Richard Drake, *The Aldo Moro Murder Case* (Cambridge, Mass.: Harvard University Press, 1995), pp. 118–19.

4. On the night of November 10, 1938, German storm troopers destroyed virtually every synagogue in Germany and set fire to some seven thousand Jewish businesses. About thirty thousand Jews were arrested and thrown into concentration camps. The event takes its name—Kristallnacht—from the broken plate-glass windows of the Jewish-owned stores.

5. Neuhauser, "The Mind of a German Terrorist," pp. 83–84.

6. Baumann's vignette, like the previously discussed 1972 Munich Olympics operation, again underscores how even attacks that fail to achieve their ostensible objective (the successful detonation of a bomb and attendant damage and destruction caused) can nonetheless still accomplish a terrorist group's immediate objectives and therefore just as effectively serve its wider intentions.

7. Quoted in Alison Jamieson, *The Heart Attacked: Terrorism and Conflict in the Italian State* (London: Marion Boyars, 1989), p. 89.

8. Patrizio Peci, *Io, l'infame* [I, the scoundrel] (Milan: Arnoldo Mondadori, 1983), p. 46.

9. "RAF Philosophy," in *The German Guerrilla: Terror, Reaction, and Resistance* (Sanday, Orkney: Cienfuegos Press, no date), pp. 98–99.

10. Quoted in Eileen MacDonald, *Shoot the Women First* (New York: Random House, 1991), p. 11.

11. Quoted in Peter Taylor, *Provos: The IRA and Sinn Fein* (London: Bloomsbury, 1997), p. 201.

12. David McKittrick, *Despatches from Belfast* (Belfast: Blackstaff Press, 1989), p. 77.

13. Patrick Bishop and Eamonn Mallie, *The Provisional IRA* (London: Corgi, 1989), p. 387.

14. Robert W. White, "The Irish Republican Army: An Assessment of Sectarianism," *Terrorism and Political Violence* 9, no. 1 (Spring 1997): 44.

15. "But Basques Aren't Irish," *Economist* (London), July 20, 1996.

16. Quoted in Gerald McKnight, *The Mind of the Terrorist* (London: Michael Joseph, 1974), p. 26.

17. Quoted in Christopher Dobson, *Black September: Its Short, Violent History* (London: Robert Hale, 1974, 1975), p. 95.

18. Quoted in McKnight, *The Mind of the Terrorist*, p. 26.

19. Quoted in Howell Raines, "With Latest Bomb, IRA Injures Its Own Cause," *New York Times*, November 15, 1987.

20. Eamon Collins, with Mick McGovern, *Killing Rage* (London: Granta, 1997), p. 296.

21. Quoted in MacDonald, *Shoot the Women First*, p. 5.

22. See, for example, the compelling autobiographical account of the German neo-Nazi Ingo Hasselbach (with Tom Reiss), *Führer-Ex: Memoirs of a Former Neo-Nazi* (London: Chatto and Windus, 1996).

23. Quoted in Bill Buford, *Among the Thugs* (London: Mandarin, 1992), p. 154.

24. Hasselbach, *Führer-Ex*, p. 119.

25. Ibid., pp. 274–75.

26. Quoted in McKnight, *The Mind of the Terrorist*, p. 179.

27. Ayla H. Schbley, "Religious Terrorists: What They Aren't Going to Tell Us," *Terrorism* 13, no. 3 (Summer 1990): 240.

28. Quoted in Agence France Presse, "Bomber 'Wanted to Kill Jews,'" *The Times* (London), October 15, 1997.

29. "Sulaimain Abu Ghaith—Statement—13 October 2001," quoted in Ben Venzke and Aimee Ibrahim, *The al-Qaeda Threat: An Analytical Guide to al-Qaeda's Tactics and Targets* (Alexandria, Va.: Tempest Publishing, 2003), p. 109.

30. "Zarqawi Statement May 20, 2005, Part 1," English Translation © *Jihad Unspun 2005*, May 26, 2005, http://www.jihadunspun.com/newsarchive/article_internal.php?article = 102833&list = /newsarchive/index.php&.

31. Islamic Group in Egypt, "Statement on U.S. Sentencing of Sheikh Rahman," January 19, 1996.

32. Leila Khaled, *My People Shall Live: The Autobiography of a Revolutionary* (London: Hodder and Stoughton, 1973), p. 209.

33. Quoted in Jamieson, *The Heart Attacked*, p. 271.

34. Peci, *Io, l'infame*, p. 46.

35. David Rapoport, "Terrorism," in Mary Hawkesworth and Maurice Kogan, eds., *Routledge Encyclopedia of Government and Politics* (London: Routledge, 1992), 2:1067.

36. Quoted in Bonnie Cordes, "When Terrorists Do the Talking: Reflections on Terrorist Literature," in David C. Rapoport, ed., "Special Issue: Inside Terrorist Organizations" *Journal of Strategic Studies* 10, no. 4 (December 1987): 155.

37. Quoted in "Inside the Red Brigades," *Newsweek*, May 15, 1978.

38. Abu Iyad with Eric Rouleau, *My Home, My Land: A Narrative of the Palestinian Struggle*, trans. Linda Butler Koseoglu (New York: Times Books, 1981), p. 226.

39. Quoted in David Blundy, "Inside the IRA," *Sunday Times* (London), July 3, 1977.

40. Quoted in M. L. R. Smith, *Fighting for Ireland? The Military Strategy of the Irish Republican Movement* (London: Routledge, 1995), p. 224.

41. Quoted in Patricia G. Steinhoff, "Portrait of a Terrorist: An Interview with Kozo Okamoto," *Asian Survey* 16, no. 9 (September 1976): 844–45.

42. Quoted in I. Fetscher and G. Rohrmoser, *Analysen zum Terrorismus* [Analyses on the subject of terrorism], vol. 1, *Ideologien und Strategien* [Ideologies and strategies] (Bonn: Westdeutscher Verlag, 1981), p. 327.

43. Gudrun Ensslin, "Statement of 19 January 1976," in *Red Army Faction, Texte der RAF* [RAF texts] (Malmo, Sweden: Verlag Bo Cavefors, 1977), p. 345.

44. Jane Alpert, *Growing Up Underground* (New York: William Morrow, 1981), pp. 141, 175.

45. Michael "Bommi" Baumann, *Terror or Love? Bommi Baumann's Own Story of His Life as a West German Urban Guerrilla*, trans. Helene Ellenbogen and Wayne Parker (New York: Grove Press, 1979), p. 49.

46. Anonymous, "Notes for the First Analysis of the Phenomenon of Terrorism of the Right" (unpublished study commissioned by the Italian secret services, no date), p. 2.

47. Franco Ferracuti and Francesco Bruno, "Psychiatric Aspects of Terrorism in Italy" (unpublished study commissioned by the Italian secret services, no date), pp. 18, 20.

48. Susan Stern, *With the Weathermen: The Personal Journey of a Revolutionary Woman* (Garden City, N.Y.: Doubleday, 1975), p. 90. Alpert, in her memoir, describes similar discussions and frustrations giving way to action. See *Growing Up Underground*, pp. 140–41, 155.

49. "RAF Philosophy," pp. 99–100. Alpert similarly recalls how her lover and fellow terrorist, Sam Melville, quickly reached the point at which he was fed up with talk and ready for action: "Sam, after a few days, dispensed with theorizing and got

down to what interested him: hideouts, disguises, dynamite, plastique, secret communiques." See Alpert, *Growing Up Underground*, p. 155.

50. Menachem Begin, *The Revolt: Story of the Irgun* (Jerusalem: Steimatzky, 1977), p. 46.

51. Khaled, *My People Shall Live*, p. 110.

52. Quoted in Peter Taylor, *States of Terror: Democracy and Political Violence* (London: Penguin, 1993), p. 159.

53. Hasselbach, *Führer-Ex*, p. 272.

54. Patrick Seale, *Abu Nidal: A Gun for Hire* (New York: Random House, 1992), p. 57.

55. Collins, *Killing Rage*, p. 177.

56. Quoted in Michael Seufert, "Dissension Among the Terrorists: Killing People Is Wrong," *Encounter* 51, no. 3 (September 1978): 84.

57. Neuhauser, "The Mind of a German Terrorist," pp. 82–83. Heckler and Koch is a leading German weapons manufacturer, producing "top of the line" handguns, submachine guns, and other small arms.

58. Quoted in Stefan Aust, *The Baader-Meinhof Group: The Inside Story of a Phenomenon* (London: Bodley Head, 1987), p. 97.

59. Quoted in Jillian Becker, *Hitler's Children: The Story of the Baader-Meinhof Gang* (London: Panther Books, 1978), p. 90.

60. Quoted in ibid., p. 244.

61. Observation of Dr. Sue Ellen Moran, a RAND consultant, in April 1985.

62. Neuhauser, "The Mind of a German Terrorist," p. 85.

63. Stern, *With the Weathermen*, p. 41.

64. Collins, *Killing Rage*, p. 363.

65. Quoted in Taylor, *States of Terror*, p. 125.

66. Quoted in MacDonald, *Shoot the Women First*, p. 198.

67. Quoted in McKnight, *The Mind of the Terrorist*, p. 180.

68. Klein specifically recalls that when the German newsmagazine *Der Spiegel* serialized a book about Carlos written by an English journalist—presumably Colin Smith's *Carlos: Portrait of a Terrorist* (London: Andre Deutsch, 1976)—he "kept all the articles and had them translated." Jean Marcel Bougereau, "Memoirs of an International Terrorist: Conversations with Hans Joachim Klein," in *The German Guerrilla: Terror, Reaction, and Resistance* (Sanday, Orkney: Cienfuegos Press, no date), p. 38.

69. Quoted in ibid., p. 36.

70. James Bone and Alan Road, "Terror by Degree," *The Times Magazine* (London), October 18, 1997.

71. See, e.g., David Hearst, "Publicity Key Element of Strategy," *Guardian* (London), July 31, 1990, and David Pallister, "Provos Seek to 'Play Havoc with British Nerves and Lifestyle,'" *Guardian* (London), July 31, 1990.

72. Quoted in Bougereau, "Memoirs of an International Terrorist," pp. 12, 39.

73. Quoted in James Brooke, "Newspaper Says McVeigh Described Role in Bombing," *New York Times*, March 1, 1997. See also the extended discussion of McVeigh's motivation in this respect in Lou Michel and Dan Herbeck, *American Terrorist: Timothy McVeigh and the Oklahoma City Bombing* (New York: Regan, 2001), p. 169.

74. Quoted in Oriana Fallaci, "Interview with George Habash," *Life Magazine*, June 12, 1970.

75. Collins, *Killing Rage*, pp. 65–66.

76. Quoted in "Bombs Blast a Message of Hate," *Life Magazine*, March 27, 1970.

77. Peter Bergen, *Holy War, Inc.: Inside the Secret World of Osama bin Laden* (New York: Free Press, 2001), pp. 86, 132; National Commission on Terrorist Attacks Upon the United States, *The 9/11 Commission Report: Authorized Edition* (New York: Norton, 2004), p. 261.

78. *The 9/11 Commission Report*, pp. 152–53.

79. Abdul Azziz al-Moqrin, "Covert Work Groups," *Mu'askar al-Battar*, issue 6; Saif al-Adl, "Outlines for Planning a Surveillance Operation," *Camp al-Battar Magazine*, issue 9; "Military Sciences: The Planning of Operations," issue 11; and "Intelligence: How to Set-up an Intelligence Network," issue 20 (accessed at www.mawsuat.com/index.html on June 14, 2005).

80. See Frederick Kempe, "Deadly Survivors: The Cold War Is Over but Leftist Terrorists in Germany Fight On," *Wall Street Journal*, December 27, 1991.

81. Quoted in Adrian Bridge, "German Police Search for Red Army Faction Killers," *Independent* (London), April 6, 1991.

82. Quoted in Kempe, "Deadly Survivors."

83. Quoted in Edward Gorman, "How to Stop the IRA," *The Times* (London), January 11, 1992.

84. Quoted in William E. Schmidt, "Protestant Gunmen Are Stepping Up the Violence in Northern Ireland," *New York Times*, October 29, 1991.

85. Alan Cullison, "Inside Al-Qaeda's Hard Drive," *Atlantic Monthly* 294, no. 2 (September 2004): 61.

86. Keith Johnson et al., "British Police Fear More Attacks by Terrorists: Lack of Clues, Hard Leads Suggests Bombers Learned from Madrid-Blast Arrests," *Wall Street Journal*, July 8, 2005.

87. "Terrorists Killed by Their Own Devices," *Independent* (London), February 20, 1996.

88. Quoted in Ian Graham, "Official: IRA Using 'Bigger, Better' Bombs," *London Press Association*, January 23, 1992.

89. Quoted in Edward Gorman, "Bomb Disposers Mark 21 Years in Ulster," *The Times* (London), November 7, 1992.

90. See, e.g., Maria McGuire, *To Take Arms: A Year in the Provisional IRA* (London: Macmillan, 1973), p. 62.

91. Quoted in "Outrage Not a Reason for Inaction," *Manchester Guardian* (international edition), October 21, 1984.

92. Interview, North Armagh, Northern Ireland, August 1992.

93. C. Wright Mills, *The Power Elite* (London: Oxford University Press, 1956), p. 171.

94. Quoted in "Don't Spoil the Party," *Economist* (London), July 13, 1996.

9. Terrorism Today and Tomorrow

1. This list of state sponsors of terrorism was mandated by the Export Administration Act of 1979 to identify and report to Congress "countries that have repeatedly provided state support for international terrorism." See U.S. Department of State, Office of the Coordinator for Counterterrorism, *Patterns of Global Terrorism 1996* (Washington, D.C.: U.S. Department of State, Publication 10433, April 1997), p. v.

2. Patrick Seale, *Abu Nidal: A Gun for Hire* (New York: Random House, 1992), pp. 202–5.

3. Counter Terrorist Unit, *New Jersey State Police: Kikumura Investigation—A Case Study* (no date).

4. Quoted in Magnus Ranstorp, *Hizb'allah in Lebanon: The Politics of the Western Hostage Crisis* (Basingstoke: Macmillan, 1997), p. 38.

5. The sharpened tip of the umbrella contained ricin, a poison derived from castor beans that is ranked third in toxicity, behind only plutonium (which is used in thermonuclear weapons) and botulism. Before he died, Markov told doctors that a man had bumped into him on Westminster Bridge and had casually apologized for poking Markov with his umbrella. Traces of the poison pellet concealed in the umbrella were discovered in Markov's thigh. See Christopher Andrew and Oleg Gordievsky, *KGB: The Inside Story* (New York: HarperCollins, 1990), pp. 64–65.

6. Michael Binyon and Michael Theodoulou, "Bounty on Rushdie Raised to $2.5M," *The Times* (London), February 13, 1997. In 1992 the bounty had been raised to $2 million. See Reuters, "$2 Million Reward for Death of Rushdie Repeated by Iran," *New York Times*, June 18, 1992.

7. For the most detailed accounts of the plot to kill the pope, who as a staunch Polish nationalist, head of the Roman Catholic Church, and ardent proponent of civil liberties and religious freedoms had supposedly incurred the unswerving enmity of the Kremlin, see Paul B. Henze, *The Plot to Kill the Pope* (New York: Scribner's, 1983), passim; Claire Sterling, *The Time of the Assassins* (New York: Holt, Rinehart, and Winston, 1983), passim. For a different interpretation, see Ugur Mumcu, *Papa-Mafya-Agca* [Pope, Mafia, Agca] (Ankara: Tekin Yayinevi, 1984), passim.

8. U.S. Department of State, Office of the Coordinator for Counterterrorism, *Country Reports on Terrorism 2004*, April 2005, p. 88, http://www.state.gov/s/ct/rls/c14813.htm.

9. "Discussion Paper on Preventing Terrorism: U.S. Government Prevention Capabilities" (unpublished paper), July 23, 1996, p. 6.

10. See Karen Gardela and Bruce Hoffman, *The RAND Chronology of International Terrorism for 1987* (Santa Monica, Calif.: RAND Corporation, R-4006-RC, 1991), p. 7.

11. See "IRA: The Libyan Connection," *Economist* (London), March 31, 1990. See also James Adams and Liam Clarke, "War Without End," *Sunday Times* (London), June 17, 1990; Edward Gorman, "Libyan Arms Shipments Allow IRA to Maintain Campaign of Violence," *The Times* (London), March 7, 1991; Robert Cottrell, "French Court Told of Huge Libyan Arms Run by IRA," *Independent* (London), January 8, 1991; and David McKittrick, "Voyage Into Business of Terror," *Independent* (London), January 12, 1991.

12. Gardela and Hoffman, *The RAND Chronology of International Terrorism for 1987*, p. 6.

13. Office of the Coordinator for Counterterrorism, *Patterns of Global Terrorism 1996*, p. 25.

14. A 193-count federal grand jury indictment presented in Washington, D.C., charged the two Libyans with specifically executing the bombing of Pan Am Flight 103 by placing a suitcase containing the bomb on board a flight originating in Malta that would be subsequently transferred to the ill-fated Pan Am aircraft. See U.S. District Court for the District of Columbia, *United States of America v. Abdel Basset Ali al-Megrahi and Lamen Khalifa Fhimah*, November 14, 1991.

15. Marlise Simons, "Lockerbie Bomber Loses Appeal and Begins Sentence," *New York Times*, March 15, 2002.

16. Office of the Coordinator for Counterterrorism, *Country Reports on Terrorism 2004*, pp. 95–96.

17. Office of the Coordinator for Counterterrorism, *Patterns of Global Terrorism 1996*, pp. 23–24.

18. Robin Wright, "Iran Supplies Lebanese Radicals Through Syria, U.S. Aides Say," *International Herald Tribune* (Paris), December 14–15, 1996.

19. Douglas Jehl, "Iran Tells the Europeans That It Doesn't Back Terrorism," *New York Times*, March 8, 1996.

20. William Drozdiak, "EU Recalls Envoys as Iran is Found Guilty of Terror," *International Herald Tribune* (Paris), April 11, 1997.

21. Quoted in Tom Rhodes, "Sanctions on Iran 'a Failure,'" *The Times* (London), October 13, 1995.

22. The remaining questions regarding the PFLP-GC and Syria's involvement in the Pan Am Flight 103 bombing are documented in Roy Rowan, "Pan Am 103: Why Did They Die?" *Time*, April 27, 1992. See also David Hoffman, "Reports Renew Suspicions of Iran, Syria Bomb Link," *Washington Post*, April 26, 1992; Kathy Evans and Richard Norton-Taylor, "Spain Checks Syrian Link to Lockerbie," *The Times* (London), June 6, 1992; and David Twersky, "The Risks of Cozying Up to Syria," *New York Times*, July 28, 1992.

23. Office of the Coordinator of Counterterrorism, *Country Reports on Terrorism 2004*, p. 90. See also John Ward Anderson, "7 Arrested in Tel Aviv Bombing: Syrian-

Based Leaders of Islamic Jihad Assert Responsibility," *Washington Post*, February 27, 2005.

24. See, for example, Eric Schmitt, "Don't Aid Zarqawi, U.S. Warns Iraqi Neighbors," *New York Times*, June 2, 2005; John Hendren, "Rumsfeld Tells Nations Not to Help Zarqawi," *Los Angeles Times*, June 2, 2005; John F. Burns, "Iraq's Ho Chi Minh Trail," *New York Times*, June 5, 2005; Ghaith Abdul-Ahad, "Outside Iraq but Deep in the Fight: A Smuggler of Insurgents Reveals Syria's Influential, Changing Role," *Washington Post*, June 8, 2005; and Steven R. Weisman, "White House Escalates Its Campaign to Isolate Syria," *New York Times*, June 23, 2005.

25. See, for example, Steven R. Weisman, "U.S. Has 'Credible' Word of Syrian Plot to Kill Lebanese," *New York Times*, June 10, 2005; Sam F. Ghattas, "Syria Foes to Control Lebanon's Parliament," *Washington Post*, June 21, 2005; and John Kifner, "Anti-Syria Alliance Claims Victory in Lebanese Voting," *New York Times*, June 20, 2005.

26. Brian Michael Jenkins, *International Terrorism: The Other World War* (Santa Monica, Calif.: RAND Corporation, R-3302-AF, November 1985), p. 12.

27. For reasons of clarity and precision, the term "CBRN" is preferred to the more commonly used yet potentially misleading term "weapons of mass destruction," or "WMD." With the exception of nuclear weapons, none of these unconventional weapons by itself is, in fact, capable of wreaking mass destruction, at least not in structural terms. Indeed, the terminology "weapons of mass casualties" may be a more accurate depiction of the potentially lethal power that could be unleashed by chemical, biological, or non-explosive radiological weapons. The distinction is more than rhetorical and is critical to understanding the vastly different levels of technological skills and capabilities, weapons expertise, production requirements, and dissemination or delivery methods needed to undertake an effective attack using either chemical or biological weapons in particular. See Advisory Panel to Assess Domestic Response Capabilities for Terrorism Involving Weapons of Mass Destruction, *First Annual Report to the President and the Congress* (Washington, D.C.: RAND Corporation, December 15, 1999), pp. ii–iii.

28. Radiological terrorism involves *contamination* with readily available radioactive materials, for instance those used in medicine and commerce, as compared with nuclear terrorism, which implies an explosion caused by the chain reaction created by fissionable materials.

29. The attack—like Aum's five years later—was relatively crude, again suggesting the impediments to mounting more-sophisticated operations employing CBRN weapons. In this instance, several large drums of the chemical were transported from a nearby paper mill and positioned around the camp's perimeter. When the wind currents were judged right, the attackers released the gas, which wafted into the camp. The use of this weapon was verified personally by the author, who visited the destroyed encampment in December 1997 and saw the drums of chlorine gas used in the attack, which had been left on the outskirts of the camp. It was further confirmed in the course of in-depth interviews with more than a dozen serving or retired senior Sri Lankan military commanders (including an officer who was pres-

ent at the East Kiran camp when the attack occurred), intelligence officials, police officers, and captured LTTE cadre conducted in Colombo, Jaffna, and Batticoloa, Sri Lanka, by the author in December 1997 and January 2000.

30. Admittedly, these are only those incidents or plots that we *definitely* know about and that have also been reported in open, published sources.

31. See, for example, the discussion in Peter deLeon, Bruce Hoffman, and Konrad Kellen, *The Threat of Nuclear Terrorism: A Reexamination* (Santa Monica, Calif.: RAND Corporation, N-2706, January 1988), pp. 4–6.

32. Walter Laqueur, *Terrorism* (London: Weidenfeld and Nicolson, 1977), p. 231.

33. Brian Michael Jenkins, "International Terrorism: A New Mode of Conflict," in David Carlton and Carlo Schaerf, eds., *International Terrorism and World Security* (London: Croom Helm, 1975), p. 15.

34. Brian Michael Jenkins, *The Likelihood of Nuclear Terrorism* (Santa Monica, Calif.: RAND Corporation, P-7119, July 1985), p. 6.

35. Brian Michael Jenkins, *Will Terrorists Go Nuclear?* (Santa Monica, Calif.: RAND Corporation, P-5541, November 1975), pp. 6–7.

36. Direct examination of Brian Parr, *United States of America v. Ramzi Ahmed Yousef and Eyad Ismoil*, S1293CR.180 (KTD), October 22, 1997, p. 4721, cited in John V. Parachini, "The World Trade Center Bombers (1993)," in Jonathan B. Tucker, ed., *Toxic Terror: Assessing Terrorist Use of Chemical and Biological Weapons* (Cambridge, Mass.: MIT Press, 2000), p. 202, n. 78.

37. See, for example, the analysis of the international terrorist campaign allegedly orchestrated by Osama bin Laden in Neil King Jr., "Moving Target: Fighting Terrorism Is Far More Perilous Than It Used to Be," *Wall Street Journal Europe*, August 25, 1998.

38. These include, among other incidents, the series of car bombings that convulsed Bombay in 1993, killing 317 people; the huge truck bomb that destroyed a Jewish community center in Buenos Aires in 1994, killing 96; the 1995 bomb that demolished the Alfred P. Murrah Building in Oklahoma City, leaving 168 dead; the 1996 bombing of a U.S. Air Force barracks at Khobar, Saudi Arabia; and the series of bombings of apartment buildings in Dagestan and Moscow in August and September 2004. Indeed, the 1988 in-flight bombing of Pan Am Flight 103 is an especially notorious example. Although we know—as a result of what has been described as the "most extensive criminal investigation in history"—that the two Libyan government airline employees were identified, and one of them was convicted of placing the suitcase containing the bomb that eventually found its way onto the flight, no believable claim of responsibility has ever been issued. Hence, we still don't know why the aircraft was targeted or who ordered or commissioned the attack. For a more detailed study of this issue, see Bruce Hoffman, "Why Terrorists Don't Claim Credit," *Terrorism and Political Violence* 9, no. 1 (Spring 1997): 1–6.

39. Craig Whitlock, "Terror Probes Find 'the Hands, but Not the Brains,'" *Washington Post*, July 12, 2005.

40. Walter Laqueur, "Postmodern Terrorism," *Foreign Affairs* 75, no. 5 (September–October 1996), p. 34.

41. See both the contemporary accounts of the explanation for the strike by Barbara Crossette et al., "U.S. Says Iraq Aided Production of Chemical Weapons in Sudan," *New York Times*, August 25, 1998; Michael Evans, "Iraqis Linked to Sudan Plant," *The Times* (London), August 25, 1998; James Risen, "New Evidence Ties Sudanese to Bin Laden, U.S. Asserts," *New York Times*, October 4, 1998; and Gregory L. Vistica and Daniel Klaidman, "Tracking Terror," *Newsweek*, October 19, 1998; and the "insider" account published by two members of President Clinton's National Security Council staff, Daniel Benjamin and Steven Simon, *The Age of Sacred Terror* (New York: Random House, 2002), pp. 259–62, 353–65.

42. John Parachini, "Putting WMD Terrorism Into Perspective," *Washington Quarterly* 26, no. 4 (Autumn 2003): 44.

43. See Graham Allison, *Nuclear Terrorism: The Ultimate Preventable Catastrophe* (New York: Times Books, 2004), p. 3; Peter Bergen, "The Bin Laden Trial: What Did We Learn?" *Studies in Conflict and Terrorism* 24, no. 6 (November–December 2001): 431; Benjamin Weiser, "U.S. Says Bin Laden Aide Tried to Get Nuclear Material," *New York Times*, September 26, 1998; and Michael Grunwald, "U.S. Says Bin Laden Sought Nuclear Arms," *Washington Post*, September 26, 1998.

44. Quoted in Ben Venzke and Aimee Ibrahim, *The al-Qaeda Threat: An Analytical Guide to al-Qaeda's Tactics and Targets* (Alexandria, Va.: Tempest Publishing, 2003), p. 52.

45. "Osama bin Laden—Interview—23 December 1998, Rahimullah Yusufzai Interview," in ibid., p. 53.

46. Allison, *Nuclear Terrorism*, pp. 20–23.

47. CNN.Com, "Live from Afghanistan—Was Al Qaeda Working on a Super Bomb?" January 24, 2004, http://www.isis-online.org/publications/terrorism/transcript.html.

48. See Dafna Linzer, "Nuclear Capabilities May Elude Terrorists, Experts Say," *Washington Post*, December 29, 2004, and "Bin Laden Seeking Nukes," *Toronto Star*, November 24, 2004.

49. Quoted in Alan Cullison, "Inside Al-Qaeda's Hard Drive," *Atlantic Monthly* 294, no. 2 (September 2004): 62.

50. Alan Sipress, "Key Player in Nuclear Trade Ring Found Hospitable Base in Malaysia," *Washington Post*, February 24, 2004; Judith Miller, "U.S. Has New Concerns About Anthrax Readiness," *New York Times*, December 28, 2003.

51. Eric Lipton, "Qaeda Letters Are Said to Show Pre-9/11 Anthrax Plans," *New York Times*, May 21, 2005.

52. Barton Gellman, "Al Qaeda Near Biological, Chemical Arms Production," *Washington Post*, March 23, 2003.

53. Ibid.; Joby Warrick, "An Al Qaeda 'Chemist' and the Quest for Ricin," *Washington Post*, May 5, 2004.

54. Alan Cowell, "One Conviction in Plot to Spread Deadly Toxins, but 8 Go Free," *New York Times*, April 13, 2005.

55. Information provided by British authorities.

56. Duncan Campbell and Rosie Cowan, "Ricin Plot: Terror Trail That Led from Algeria to London," *Guardian* (London), April 14, 2005.

57. Parachini, "Putting WMD Terrorism Into Perspective," p. 39.

58. David Rapoport, "Terrorism and Weapons of the Apocalypse," *National Security Studies Quarterly* 5, no. 3 (Summer 1999): 52–54.

59. W. Seth Carus, *Bioterrorism and Biocrimes: The Illicit Use of Biological Agents Since 1900* (Working paper) (Washington, D.C.: Center for Counterproliferation Research, National Defense University, February 2001 Revision), pp. v, 10, 11, 21.

60. Two attempts were made with anthrax and seven with botulinum toxin. W. Seth Carus, *Bioterrorism and Biocrimes: The Illicit Use of Biological Agents in the Twentieth Century* (Washington, D.C.: Center for Counterproliferation Research, National Defense University, March 1999), p. 62.

61. Chemical attacks are, however, arguably easier to detect and to contain (e.g., localize), because biological infection occurs without notice and is usually followed by an incubation period during which victims unknowingly spread the contagion.

62. Anthony G. Macintyre, MD, et al., "Weapons of Mass Destruction: Events with Contaminated Casualties—Effective Planning for Health Care Facilities, *JAMA* (Journal of the American Medical Association)*, no. 263 (January 2000): 242–49.

63. That is, conflicts that have been intrinsically oriented toward the elimination or subjugation of entire rival ethnic, nationalist, or religious groups (e.g., "ethnic cleansing") rather than the attainment of some negotiated power-sharing settlement between rival peoples who decide to "live happily ever after" in reconstituted multinational/multiethnic/religion-tolerant states.

64. See Graham T. Allison et al., *Avoiding Nuclear Anarchy: Containing the Threat of Loose Russian Nuclear Weapons and Fissile Material* (Cambridge, Mass.: MIT Press, 1996), pp. 57–61; Bruce Hoffman with David Claridge, "Illicit Trafficking in Nuclear Materials," *Conflict Studies*, nos. 314/315 (London: Research Institute for the Study of Conflict and Terrorism, January/February 1999): passim; and Robert S. Litwak, *Rogue States and U.S. Foreign Policy: Containment After the Cold War* (Washington, D.C.: Woodrow Wilson Center Press, 2000), pp. 158–238.

65. Video prepared by the Jordanian authorities, no date. See also Jamal Halaby, "Zarqawi Among 13 Indicted by Jordan in Plot: Officials Say Militants Planned to Attack Premier's Office, U.S. Embassy in Amman," *Washington Post*, October 18, 2004.

66. Leonard A. Cole, *The Anthrax Letters: A Medical Detective Story* (Washington, D.C.: Joseph Henry Press, 2003), pp. 215–17.

67. See, for example, White House, "Fact Sheet on Combating Terrorism: Presidential Decision Directive 62," May 22, 1998, http://cns.miis.edu/research/cbw/pdd-62.htm, which states that "easier access to sophisticated technology means that the destructive power available to terrorists is greater than ever. Adversaries may thus be tempted to use unconventional tools, such as weapons of mass destruction, to

target our cities and disrupt the operations of our government"; Statement for the record before the Senate Select Committee on Intelligence, January 28, 1998, http://www.fbi.gov/congress/98archives/threats.htm; "Remarks by the President [William Jefferson Clinton] to 17th Annual Legislative Conference of the International Association of Fire Fighters," Hyatt Regency Hotel, Washington, D.C., March 15, 1999, p. 3, http://www.usia.gov/topical/ pol/terror/99031502.html.

68. Joby Warrick and Joe Stephens, "Before Attack, U.S. Expected Different Hit: Chemical, Germ Agents Focus of Preparations," *Washington Post*, October 2, 2001.

69. See, for example, Associated Press, "Expert Warns of al-Qaida-Linked Groups," January 7, 2004; Ellen Nakashima, "Thai Officials Probe Tie to Al-Qa'ida in Attacks," *Washington Post*, January 9, 2004; and Associated Press, "Saudis Discover al-Qaida Training Camps," January 15, 2004, http://www.ap.org.

70. See William Wallis, "Kenya Terror Attacks 'Planned from Somalia,'" *Financial Times*, November 5, 2003.

71. See the particularly knowledgeable account of this plot in Maria A. Ressa, *Seeds of Terror: An Eyewitness Account of Al-Qaeda's Newest Center of Operations in Southeast Asia* (New York: Free Press, 2003), pp. 1–5, 21–44.

72. This point is also made in International Institute for Strategic Studies, *Strategic Survey 2003/4* (Oxford; Oxford University Press, 2004), p. 6, where the authors note: "The Afghanistan intervention offensively hobbled, but defensively benefited, al-Qaeda. While al-Qaeda lost a recruiting magnet and a training, command and operations base, it was compelled to disperse and become even more decentralized, 'virtual' and invisible."

73. See Cullison, "Inside Al-Qaeda's Hard Drive," pp. 63–64.

74. Mike Boetcher (CNN correspondent), "Al-Qa'ida's Nuclear Weapons Program," presentation at the Centre for the Study of Terrorism and Political Violence Symposium on Islamic Extremism and Terrorism in the Greater Middle East, University of St. Andrews, St. Andrews, Scotland, June 7–8, 2002.

75. See Dana Priest and Walter Pincus, "New Target and Tone: Message Shows Al-Qa'ida's Adaptability," *Washington Post*, April 16, 2004, and Geoffrey Nunberg, "Bin Laden's Low-Tech Weapon," *New York Times*, April 18, 2004.

76. Associated Press, "Purported al-Qaida Tape Warns of Attacks," December 19, 2003, http://www.ap.org.>

77. International Institute for Strategic Studies, *Strategic Survey 2003/4*, p. 6. As one commentary explained, "IISS's figure of 18,000 potential operatives is calculated by deducting the 2,000 suspects killed or captured since the September 11 2001 attacks from the estimated 20,000 recruits thought to have passed through al-Qaeda training camps in Afghanistan between 1996 and 2001." Mark Huband and David Buchan, "Al-Qaeda May Have Access to 18,000 'Potential Operatives,' Says Think-Tank," *Financial Times* (London), May 26, 2004. A figure of 20,000 is similarly cited in *Staff Report No. 15*, the National Commission on Terrorist Attacks Upon the United States ("9/11 Commission"), on p. 10.

Note that according to the report issued by the Joint Inquiry of the Senate and

House Intelligence Committees, an estimated 70,000–120,000 people trained in Afghanistan between 1979 and 2001, thus suggesting that the IISS estimate could be a conservative one. Joint Inquiry Into Intelligence Community Activities Before and After the Terrorist Attacks of September 11, 2001, *Report of the U.S. Senate Select Committee on Intelligence and U.S. House Permanent Select Committee on Intelligence Together with Additional Views* (December 2002), p. 38, and "Al-Qa'ida Trained at Least 70,000 in Terrorist Camps, Senator Says," *Los Angeles Times*, July 14, 2003.

78. See, for example, David Johnston and David E. Sanger, "New Generation of Leaders Is Emerging for Al-Qa'ida," *New York Times*, August 10, 2004; Josh Meyer and Greg Miller, "Fresh Details Back Threats," *Los Angeles Times*, August 3, 2004; Walter Pincus and John Mintz, "Pakistani-U.S. Raid Uncovered Terrorist Cell's Surveillance Data," *Washington Post*, August 2, 2004; and Glen Kessler, "Old Data, New Credibility Issues," *Washington Post*, August 4, 2004.

79. See, for example, Frederick Studemann et al., "Five Arrested as London Bomb Attack Probe Widens to Egypt and Pakistan," *Financial Times* (London), July 16–17, 2005, and Glenn Frankel and Craig Whitlock, "London Probe Extends Abroad: Egyptian Arrested; Pakistani Sought," *Washington Post*, July 16, 2005.

80. Electronic newsletter of the Orion Group, April 24, 2003.

81. Anonymous, *Through Our Enemies' Eyes: Osama bin Laden, Radical Islam, and the Future of America* (Dulles, Va.: Brassey's, 2002), p. 34.

82. International Institute for Strategic Studies, *Strategic Survey 2003/4*, p. 8. In its *Staff Report No. 16*, the National Commission on Terrorist Attacks Upon the United States ("9/11 Commission") notes on p. 16 that the 9/11 operation cost between $400,000 and $500,000 to mount.

83. Anonymous, *Imperial Hubris: Why the West Is Losing the War on Terror* (Washington, D.C.: Brassey's, 2004), pp. 138–39.

84. See U.S. District Court, Southern District of New York, 1734HA01, *United States of America v. Mokhtar Haouri*, S4 00 Cr. 15 (JFK), June 3, 2001, pp. 538, 548, 589, 622, 658, 697.

85. See General Intelligence and Security Service, *Recruitment for the Jihad in the Netherlands: From Incident to Trend* (The Hague: Ministry of the Interior and Kingdom Relations, December 2002).

86. "Declaration of War Against the Americans Occupying the Land of the Two Holy Places," in Yonah Alexander and Michael S. Swetnam, *Usama bin Laden's al-Qaida: Profile of a Terrorist Network* (Ardsley, N.Y.: Transnational, 2001), appendix 1A, p. 19.

87. See, for example, "Text of Bin Laden Remarks: 'Hypocrisy Rears Its Ugly Head,'" *Washington Post*, October 8, 2001.

88. Ibid. See also Anonymous, *Through Our Enemies' Eyes*, pp. 47, 197.

89. Paul Eedle, "Terrorism.com," *Guardian* (London), July 17, 2002.

90. Al Jazeera.Net, "NEWS: Arab World—Full Transcript of bin Laden's Speech," November 1, 2004, http://Englishaljazeera.net/NR/exeres/79C6AF22–98FB-4A1C-B21F-2BC36E87F61F.htm.

91. Quoted in John Miller, "Interview: Osama Bin Laden (May 1998)," http://www.pbs.org/wgbh/pages/frontline/shows/binladen/who/interview.html.

92. Anonymous, *Through Our Enemies' Eyes*, p. xix.

93. Translation by, and personal communication with, Eedle, July 31, 2002.

94. "Transcript: Full Text from the 18 Minute Tape Released by Al-Jazeera from Osama Bin Laden."

95. Bin Laden's October 29, 2004, statement also evidenced this understanding. See ibid.

96. Ben Venzke and Aimee Ibrahim, *Al-Qaeda's Advice for Mujahideen in Iraq: Lessons Learned in Afghanistan*, vol. 1.0 (Alexandria, Va.: IntelCenter, April 14, 2003), passim.

97. Jason Burke, *Al-Qaeda: Casting a Shadow of Terror* (London: I. B. Tauris, 2003), p. 105.

98. "Al-Qa'ida Organization Addresses a Message to Iraqi, Islamic Peoples (Internet) www.alfjr.com in Arabic," March 5, 2003 (posting by "Ayn al-Haqiqah," titled "The al-Qa'ida Organization Writes a Letter to the Iraqi People" in the Issues of the Islamic Nation section of the chat room of www.alfjr.com, March 5, 2003). See also Anonymous, *Imperial Hubris*, pp. 60–61, and Venzke and Ibrahim, *Al-Qaeda's Advice for Mujahideen in Iraq*.

99. These events are described in Mark Bowden, *Black Hawk Down: A Story of Modern War* (Boston: Atlantic Monthly Press, 1999), and in the Hollywood commercial film of the same name.

100. "Declaration of War Against the Americans Occupying the Land of the Two Holy Places," in Alexander and Swetnam, *Usama bin Laden's al-Qaida*, appendix 1A, p. 11.

101. *MEMRI Special Dispatch—Jihad and Terrorism Studies*, no. 493 (April 11, 2003), quoting http://www.cubezero.nt/vhsvideo/imagis/?subject = 2&rec = 1043.

102. Quoted in Anonymous, *Imperial Hubris*, p. xxi.

103. Quoted in Walter Pincus, "Al-Qa'ida Releases Tape Predicting U.S. Defeat," *Washington Post*, September 10, 2004.

104. Quoted in Associated Press, "Purported al-Qaida Tape Warns of Attacks."

105. See Douglas Jehl, "Iraq May Be Prime Place for Training of Militants, C.I.A. Report Concludes," *New York Times*, June 22, 2005.

106. Followed by Syria (10 percent) and Kuwait (7 percent). See Reuven Paz, "Arab Volunteers Killed in Iraq: An Analysis," *PRISM Series of Global Jihad* 3, no. 1 (March 2005): 2, www.e-prism.org/pages/4/index.htm.

107. Dana Priest and Susan Schmidt, "Al-Qa'ida's Top Primed to Collapse, U.S. Says," *Washington Post*, March 16, 2003.

108. See, for example, CNN, "Alleged bin Laden Tape a Call to Arms," http://cnn.com/2003/WORLD/meast/02/11/sprj.irq.wrap, and bin Laden's statement, "We want to let you know and confirm to you that this war of the infidels that the U.S. is leading with its allies . . . we are with you and we will fight in the name of God."

109. David R. Sands, "Al-Qa'ida's Credibility 'on the Line' as War in Iraq Winds

Down," *Washington Times*, April 24, 2003. See also Dennis Pluchinsky, "Al-Qa'ida Identity Crisis," *Washington Times*, April 28, 2003.

110. "U.S.: Al Qaida Is 70 Percent Gone, Their 'Days Are Numbered,'" *World Tribune.com*, January 23, 2004.

111. Sarah el Deeb, "Al-Qaida Reportedly Plans Big New Attack," Associated Press, May 8, 2003.

112. Quoted in Anonymous, *Through Our Enemies' Eyes*, pp. 6 and 31.

113. Analogy made by the renowned French terrorism expert and criminologist Xavier Raufer, April 2003.

Bibliography

Books, Articles, Reports, Statements, and Other Documents

Abdul-Ahad, Ghaith. "Outside Iraq but Deep in the Fight: A Smuggler of Insurgents Reveals Syria's Influential, Changing Role." *Washington Post*, June 8, 2005.

Abu-Amr, Ziad. "Hamas: A Historical and Political Background." *Journal of Palestinian Studies* 23, no. 4 (Summer 1993).

"An Accion Zapatista Report—Zapatistas in Cyberspace: A Guide to Analysis and Resources." http://www.eco.utexas.edu/faculty/Cleaver/zapsincyber.html (accessed June 14, 2005).

Adams, James. *The Financing of Terror*. New York: Simon and Schuster, 1986.

——. "The Role of the Media." In Robert L. Pfaltzgraff Jr. and Richard H. Schultz Jr., eds., *Ethnic Conflict and Regional Instability: Implications for U.S. Policy and Army Roles and Missions*. Carlisle, Pa.: U.S. Army Strategic Studies Institute, 1994.

——. *Secret Armies: Inside the American, Soviet, and European Special Forces*. New York: Atlantic Monthly Press, 1987.

Adams, James and Liam Clarke. "War Without End." *Sunday Times* (London), June 17, 1990.

Advisory Panel to Assess Domestic Response Capabilities for Terrorism Involving Weapons of Mass Destruction. *First Annual Report to the President and the Congress*. Washington, D.C.: RAND Corporation, December 15, 1999.

Agence France Presse. "Bomber 'Wanted to Kill Jews.'" *The Times* (London), October 15, 1997.

——. "Eta Driven from Internet." *The Times* (London), February 20, 1996.

Ahmad, Hisham H. *Hamas from Religious Salvation to Political Transformation: The Rise of Hamas in Palestinian Society*. Jerusalem: Passia, 1994.

al-Adl, Saif. "Intelligence: How to Set-up an Intelligence Network." *Camp al-Battar Magazine*, issue 20. www.mawsuat.com/index.html (accessed June 14, 2005).

———. "Military Sciences: The Planning of Operations." *Camp al-Battar Magazine*, issue 11. www.mawsuat.com/index.html (accessed June 14, 2005).

———. "Outlines for Planning a Surveillance Operation." *Camp al-Battar Magazine*, issue 9. www.mawsuat.com/index.html (accessed June 14, 2005).

Alden, Robert. "Terrorism Issue Taken Up at UN." *New York Times*, November 10, 1972.

Alexander, Yonah and Richard Latter, eds. *Terrorism and the Media*. McLean, Va.: Brassey's, 1990.

Alexander, Yonah and Michael S. Swetnam. *Usama bin Laden's al-Qaida: Profile of a Terrorist Network*. Ardsley, N.Y.: Transnational, 2001.

Al Jazeera.Net. "NEWS: Arab World—Full Transcript of bin Laden's Speech." November 1, 2004. http://Englishaljazeera.net/NR/exeres/79C6AF22–98FB-4A1C-B21F-2BC36E87F61F.htm.

Allen-Mills, Tony. "McVeigh Trial Leaves Militia Riddle Unsolved." *Sunday Times* (London), June 15, 1997.

———. "Real-Life Rambo Meets His Match in Schoolyard." *Sunday Times* (London), October 6, 1996.

Allison, Graham. *Nuclear Terrorism: The Ultimate Preventable Catastrophe*. New York: Times Books, 2004.

Allison, Graham T., Owen R. Cote Jr., Richard A. Falkenrath, and Steven E. Miller. *Avoiding Nuclear Anarchy: Containing the Threat of Loose Russian Nuclear Weapons and Fissile Material*. Cambridge, Mass.: MIT Press, 1996.

al-Moqrin, Abdul Azziz. "Covert Work Groups." *Mu'askar al-Battar*, issue 6. www.mawsuat.com/index.html (accessed June 14, 2005).

Alpert, Jane. *Growing Up Underground*. New York: William Morrow, 1981.

"Al-Qaeda Firebrand Threatens New Attacks on US, Taunts Bush: Television." *Agence France Presse*, February 24, 2004.

"Al-Qa'ida Organization Addresses a Message to Iraqi, Islamic Peoples (Internet) www.alfjr.com in Arabic." March 5, 2003. Posting by "Ayn al-Haqiqah," titled "The al-Qa'ida Organization Writes a Letter to the Iraqi People" in the Issues of the Islamic Nation section of the chat room of http://www.alfjr.com, March 5, 2003.

"Al-Qa'ida Trained at Least 70,000 in Terrorist Camps, Senator Says." *Los Angeles Times*, July 14, 2003.

Al-Taee, Awadh and Steve Negus. "Now Showing (Despite Official Warnings): 'Mujahideen Movie.'" *Financial Times* (London), February 16, 2005.

al-Zawahiri, Ayman. *Knights Under the Prophet's Banner: Meditations on the Jihadist Movement*. Translated and published in FBIS, "Al-Sarq Al-Aswat Publishes Extracts from Al-Jihad Leader al-Zawahiri's New Book." Document ID GMP20020108000197, December 2, 2001.

Al-Zayyat, Montasser. *The Road to Al-Qaeda: The Story of Bin Laden's Right-Hand Man*. London: Pluto, 2004.

Ambler, John Steward. *The French Army in Politics, 1945–1962*. Columbus: Ohio State University Press, 1966.

American Broadcasting Companies, Inc. *Nightline* (ABC, 11:30 p.m. ET), October 7, 1993.

"Americans and 9/11: The Personal Toll." Pew Research Center for the People and the Press Survey Reports, September 5, 2002. http://people-press.org/reports/display.php3?PageID = 633.

"Amir, Yoheswaran Shot Dead, Siva Serious." *Daily News* (Colombo), July 14, 1989.

Anderson, John Ward. "7 Arrested in Tel Aviv Bombing: Syrian-Based Leaders of Islamic Jihad Assert Responsibility." *Washington Post*, February 27, 2005.

Andrew, Christopher and Oleg Gordievsky. *KGB: The Inside Story.* New York: HarperCollins, 1990.

Annells, Jonathan and James Adams. "Did Terrorists Kill with Deadly Nerve Gas Test?" *Sunday Times* (London), March 19, 1995.

Anonymous. *Imperial Hubris: Why the West Is Losing the War on Terror.* Washington, D.C.: Brassey's, 2004.

——. "Notes for the First Analysis of the Phenomenon of Terrorism of the Right." Unpublished study commissioned by the Italian secret services. No date.

——. *Through Our Enemies' Eyes: Osama bin Laden, Radical Islam, and the Future of America.* Dulles, Va.: Brassey's, 2002.

Anti-Defamation League of B'nai B'rith. *ADL Special Background Report: Hamas, Islamic Jihad, and the Muslim Brotherhood: Islamic Extremists and the Terrorist Threat to America.* New York: Anti-Defamation League of B'nai B'rith, 1993.

——. *ADL Special Report: The Militia Movement in America.* New York: Anti-Defamation League of B'nai B'rith, 1995.

——. "Arab Leaders Glorify Suicide Terrorism." April 17, 2002. http://www.adl.org/israel/Israel-suicide-terror.asp.

——. "Extremism in America: National Alliance." http://www.adl.org/learn/ext_us?N_Alliance.asp?LEARN_Cat = Extremism& Lean_SubCat = Extremism_in_America&picked = 3&item = na.

——. *Hate Groups in America: A Record of Bigotry and Violence.* New York: Anti-Defamation League of B'nai B'rith, 1982.

Apple Jr., R. W. "Meese Suggests Press Code on Terrorism." *New York Times*, July 18, 1985.

"Arab Leaders Join World in Assailing Terrorists' Attack." *Los Angeles Times*, December 19, 1973.

"The Arab Terrorists." *New York Times*, December 18, 1973.

Armed Islamic Group communiqué, containing a twelve-page interview with Antar Zouabri. September 1996.

Armenian Secret Army for the Liberation of Armenia. *The Reality.* Armenian Secret Army for the Liberation of Armenia, no date.

"Armenians Turning to Terrorism." *Los Angeles Times*, January 25, 1981.

Armond, Paul de. "The Anti-Democratic Movement—More Than Militias." August 1995. The Public Good home page. http://www.nwcitizen.com/publicgood.

——. "Christian Patriots at War with the State." June 1997. The Public Good home page. http://www.nwcitizen.com/publicgood.

——. "Leaderless Resistance: The Two-Pronged Movement Consolidates Under Identity." June 1997. Public Good home page. http://www.nwcitizen.com/publicgood.

Arnold, Guy et al. *Revolutionary and Dissident Movements.* Harlow: Longman, 1991.

Arquilla, John and David Ronfeldt. "The Advent of Netwar." In John Arquilla and David Ronfeldt, eds., *In Athena's Camp: Preparing for Conflict in the Information Age.* Santa Monica, Calif.: RAND Corporation, MR-880-OSD/RC, 1997.

——. "The Advent of Netwar (Revisited)." In John Arquilla and David Ronfeldt, eds., *Networks and Netwars: The Future of Terror, Crime, and Militancy.* Santa Monica, Calif.: RAND Corporation, MR-1382-OSD, 2001.

——. "A New Epoch—and Spectrum—of Conflict." In John Arquilla and David Ronfeldt, eds., *In Athena's Camp: Preparing for Conflict in the Information Age.* Santa Monica, Calif.: RAND Corporation, MR-880-OSD/RC, 1997.

Aryan Nations. *Calling Our Nation,* no. 53 (no date). http://www.stormfront.org/aryan_nations/platform.html.

Aryan Nations Web site. http://www.aryan-nation.org.

Asprey, Robert B. *War in the Shadows: The Guerrilla in History.* Vol. 2. New York: Doubleday, 1975.

Associated Press. "Expert Warns of al-Qaida-Linked Groups." January 7, 2004. http://www.ap.org.

——. "Extremist Admits to the Slaying of Dutch Filmmaker." *Washington Post,* July 13, 2005.

——. "Man Accused of Possessing Lethal Toxin Hangs Himself." *Los Angeles Times,* December 24, 1995.

——. "McVeigh Aimed to Spark Revolt, Ex-Buddy Says." *International Herald Tribune* (Paris), May 13, 1997.

——. "Purported al-Qaida Tape Warns of Attacks." December 19, 2003. http://www.ap.org.

——. "Saudis Discover al-Qaida Training Camps." January 15, 2004. http://www.ap.org.

Associated Press and Agence France Presse. "Cult 'Studied Deadly Ebola Virus.'" *New York Times,* April 25, 1995.

Aston, Clive C. *A Contemporary Crisis: Political Hostage-Taking and the Experience of Western Europe.* Westport, Conn.: Greenwood, 1982.

Atran, Scott. "Genesis of Suicide Terrorism." *Science* 299 (March 7, 2003).

Atwater, Tony. "Network Evening News Coverage of the TWA Hostage Crisis." *Terrorism and the News Media Research Project.* Boston: Emerson College, no date.

"Aum Shinrikyo Special Edition: Expanded Leveraging 'Supernatural Power.'" *Asahi Shimbun* (Tokyo), May 21, 1998.

"Aum Shinrikyo Special Edition: Targeted Elites—They Were Brainwashed and Became Aum's Robot." *Asahi Shimbun* (Tokyo), May 28, 1995.

"Aum Shinrikyo Special Edition: Transforming Into a 'Terrorist' Cult." *Asahi Shimbun* (Tokyo), June 16, 1996.

Aussaresses, Paul. *The Battle of the Casbah: Terrorism and Counter-Terrorism in Algeria, 1955–1957*. New York: Enigma Books, 2002.

Aust, Stefan. *The Baader-Meinhof Group: The Inside Story of a Phenomenon*. London: Bodley Head, 1987.

Ayanian, Mark Armen and John Z. Ayanian. "Armenian Political Violence on American Network News: An Analysis of Content." *Armenian Review* 40, no. 1–157 (Spring 1987).

Ayres Jr., B. Drummond. "The Somalia Mission: Voices." *New York Times*, October 9, 1993.

Baker, Peter and Susan B. Glasser. "Hundreds Held Hostage at School in Russia." *Washington Post*, September 2, 2004.

——. "Russia School Siege Ends in Carnage." *Washington Post*, September 4, 2004.

Balmer, Desmond. "U.S. Tourists React to Terrorism Fear." *New York Daily News*, March 2, 1986.

Baran, David and Mathieu Guidère. "Sons et images de l'opposition irakienne" [Sound and pictures of the Iraqi opposition]. *Le Monde Diplomatique* (Paris), May 2005.

Barber, Noel. *The War of the Running Dogs: How Malaya Defeated the Communist Guerrillas 1948–60*. London: Fontana, 1972.

Barkun, Michael. "Millenarian Aspects of 'White Supremacist' Movements." *Terrorism and Political Violence* 1, no. 4 (October 1989).

——. "Millenarian Groups and Law Enforcement Agencies: The Lessons of Waco." *Terrorism and Political Violence* 6, no. 1 (Spring 1994).

——. "Racist Apocalypse: Millennialism on the Far Right." *American Studies* 31 (1990).

Barnaby, Frank. "Nuclear Accidents Waiting to Happen." *World Today* (London) 52, no. 4 (April 1996).

Barnes, Fred. "Shiite Spin Control." *New Republic* (Washington, D.C.), July 15 and 22, 1985.

Barry, Dan and Al Baker. "Getting the Message from 'Eco-Terrorists': Mystery Group Takes Its Campaign East." *New York Times*, January 8, 2001.

Bauer, Yehuda. *From Diplomacy to Resistance: A History of Jewish Palestine, 1939–1945*. New York: Atheneum, 1973.

Baumann, Michael "Bommi." *Terror or Love? Bommi Baumann's Own Story of His Life as a West German Urban Guerrilla*. Translated by Helene Ellenbogen and Wayne Parker. New York: Grove Press, 1979.

Bazinet, Ingrid. "British Ex-Detainees See Link Between Guantanamo, Iraq Torture." *Agence France Press*, May 14, 2004.

Beauge, Florence. "'I Am Resolute on Torture . . . I Myself Have Proceeded with Summary Executions . . . '" *Le Monde* (Paris), November 23, 2000.

——. "'If France Recognized and Condemned These Practices, I Would Take that as a Step Forward.'" *Le Monde* (Paris), November 23, 2000.

Becker, Jillian. *Hitler's Children: The Story of the Baader-Meinhof Gang.* London: Panther Books, 1978.

Beckett, Ian F. W. *Encyclopedia of Guerrilla Warfare.* New York: Checkmark Books, 2001.

Begin, Menachem. *The Revolt: Story of the Irgun.* Jerusalem: Steimatzky, 1977.

——. *White Nights: The Story of a Prisoner in Russia.* Jerusalem: Steimatzky, 1977.

Bell, J. Bowyer. *The Secret Army: The IRA, 1916–1979.* Dublin: Poolbeg, 1989.

——. "Terrorist Scripts and Live-Action Spectaculars." *Columbia Journalism Review* 17, no. 1 (1978).

——. *Terror Out of Zion: The Violent and Deadly Shock Troops of Israeli Independence, 1929–1949.* New York: St. Martin's, 1977.

——. *A Time of Terror: How Democratic Societies Respond to Revolutionary Violence.* New York: Basic Books, 1978.

Benjamin, Daniel and Steven Simon. *The Age of Sacred Terror.* New York: Random House, 2002.

Bennet, James. "Jerusalem Holy Site a Tense Crossroads Again." *New York Times,* August 29, 2003.

Bennett, Will. "Simple Bombs Improved but Lack Accuracy." *Independent* (London), February 8, 1991.

——. "Terrorists Keep Changing Tactics to Elude Security Forces." *Independent* (London), December 17, 1991.

Bennis, Phyllis. *From Stones to Statehood: The Palestinian Uprising.* New York: Olive Branch Press, 1990.

Bergen, Peter. "The Bin Laden Trial: What Did We Learn?" *Studies in Conflict and Terrorism* 24, no. 6 (November–December 2001).

——. *Holy War, Inc.: Inside the Secret World of Osama bin Laden.* New York: Free Press, 2001.

Bernstein, Richard. "Chemist Can't Pinpoint Bomb Contents at Trial." *New York Times,* January 12, 1994.

"Biden Says Prison at Guantanamo Bay Should Be Closed." *Washington Post,* June 6, 2005.

"Bin Laden Seeking Nukes." *Toronto Star,* November 24, 2004.

Binyon, Michael and Michael Theodoulou. "Bounty on Rushdie Raised to $2.5M." *The Times* (London), February 13, 1997.

Bishop, Patrick. "Have the Suicide Bombers Been Defeated?" *Daily Telegraph* (London), May 26, 2004.

Bishop, Patrick and Eamonn Mallie. *The Provisional IRA.* London: Heinemann, 1987; paperback ed., London: Corgi, 1989.

"The Black Tiger Unit of the LTTE." Unpublished report. No date.

Bloom, Mia A. *Dying to Kill: The Allure of Suicide Terror.* New York: Columbia University Press, 2005.

Blumenthal, Ralph. "Peak Season of American Travel to Europe Ends Showing Little Recovery." *New York Times*, September 14, 1986.

Blundy, David. "Inside the IRA." *Sunday Times* (London), July 3, 1977.

"Bombs Blast a Message of Hate." *Life Magazine*, March 27, 1970.

Bone, James and Alan Road. "Terror by Degree." *The Times Magazine* (London), October 18, 1997.

"Booklet Giving History of ASALA's Existence Gives New Insight Into the Revolutionary Movement." *Armenian Reporter* (New York), January 10, 1985.

"Bosnia Serb 'Black Hand' Group Threatens to Kill Peace Force." *BBC Summary of World Broadcasts*, July 17, 1997.

Bougereau, Jean Marcel. "Memoirs of an International Terrorist: Conversations with Hans Joachim Klein." In *The German Guerrilla: Terror, Reaction, and Resistance*. Sanday, Orkney: Cienfuegos Press, no date.

Bowden, Mark. *Black Hawk Down: A Story of Modern War*. Boston: Atlantic Monthly Press, 1999.

———. *Killing Pablo: The Hunt for the World's Greatest Outlaw*. New York: Atlantic Monthly Press, 2001.

Bowers, Rodney. "White Radicals Charged with Sedition." *Arkansas Gazette* (Little Rock), April 25, 1987.

Bremner, Donald. "Media Given Mixed Reviews on Terrorism." *Los Angeles Times*, September 26, 1986.

Bridge, Adrian. "German Police Search for Red Army Faction Killers." *Independent* (London), April 6, 1991.

Brinton, Crane. *The Anatomy of Revolution*. New York: Vintage, 1965.

British Broadcasting Corporation. "Leaflet in Banja Luka Vows Revenge on British Forces 'Soon.'" *BBC Summary of World Broadcasts*, July 19, 1997.

Broad, William J. "Seismic Blast: Bomb or Quake?" *New York Times*, January 23, 1997.

Brogan, Patrick. *The Fighting Never Stopped*. New York: Vintage, 1990.

Broido, Vera. *Apostles Into Terrorists: Women and the Revolutionary Movement in the Russia of Alexander II*. London: Maurice Temple Smith, 1977.

Brooke, James. "Agents Seize Arsenal of Rifles and Bomb-Making Material in Arizona Militia Inquiry." *New York Times*, July 3, 1996.

———. "Armed Group Under Siege Has Sown Anger and Hate." *New York Times*, March 31, 1996.

———. "Arrests Add to Idaho's Reputation as a Magnet for Supremacists." *New York Times*, October 27, 1996.

———. "As Trial Nears for Militia, Some Charges Are Dropped." *New York Times*, October 9, 1996.

———. "Newspaper Says McVeigh Described Role in Bombing." *New York Times*, March 1, 1997.

———. "Volatile Mix in Viper Militia: Hatred Plus a Love for Guns." *New York Times*, July 4, 1996.

Brown, Tina. "Death by Error." *Washington Post,* May 19, 2005.

Brynen, Rex and Neil Caplan. "Israel and Palestine: Implications of the Intifada." In Rex Brynen, ed., *Echoes of the Intifada: Regional Repercussions of the Palestinian-Israeli Conflict.* Boulder, Colo.: Westview, 1992.

Buford, Bill. *Among the Thugs.* London: Mandarin, 1992.

Bullock, Alan. *Hitler: A Study in Tyranny.* New York: Harper, 1958.

Burghardt, Tom. "Leaderless Resistance and the Oklahoma City Bombing." Public Good home page. http://www.nwcitizen.com/publicgood.

Burke, Jason. *Al-Qaeda: Casting a Shadow of Terror.* London: I. B. Tauris, 2003.

——. "Think Again: Al Qaeda." *Foreign Policy* (May/June 2004). http://www.foreign policy.com.

Burns, John F. "Iraq's Ho Chi Minh Trail." *New York Times,* June 5, 2005.

——. "Rebels Kill Egyptian Diplomat, Adding Pressure on Others in Iraq." *New York Times,* July 8, 2005.

——. "Video Appears to Show Insurgents Kill a Downed Pilot." *New York Times,* April 23, 2005.

"But Basques Aren't Irish." *Economist* (London), July 20, 1996.

Butler, Reverend Richard G. "To Our New People." *Aryan Nations* (no place, no date).

Byford-Jones, W. *Grivas and the Story of EOKA.* London: Robert Hale, 1959.

Campbell, Duncan and Rosie Cowan. "Ricin Plot: Terror Trail That Led from Algeria to London." *Guardian* (London), April 14, 2005.

Campbell, James K. "Excerpts from Research Study 'Weapons of Mass Destruction and Terrorism: Proliferation by Non-State Actors.'" Paper presented at International Conference on Aviation Safety and Security in the 21st Century, White House Commission on Aviation Safety and Security and George Washington University, Washington, D.C., January 13–15, 1997.

——. "Excerpts from Research Study 'Weapons of Mass Destruction and Terrorism: Proliferation by Non-State Actors.'" *Terrorism and Political Violence* 9, no. 2 (Summer 1997).

Carlin, John. "DIY Apocalypse." *Independent* (London), April 30, 1995.

——. "'We Need Blood to Cleanse Us.'" *Independent* (London), May 2, 1995.

Carr, Caleb. "Terrorism as Warfare: The Lessons of Military History." *World Policy Journal* 13, no. 4 (Winter 1996–67).

Carruthers, Susan L. *Winning Hearts and Minds: British Governments, the Media, and Colonial Counter-Insurgency, 1944–1960.* London: Leicester University Press, 1995.

Carus, W. Seth. *Bioterrorism and Biocrimes: The Illicit Use of Biological Agents in the Twentieth Century.* Washington, D.C.: Center for Counterproliferation Research, National Defense University, March 1999.

——. "Bioterrorism and Biocrimes: The Illicit Use of Biological Agents Since 1900." Working paper. Washington, D.C.: Center for Counterproliferation Research, National Defense University, February 2001 revision.

———. "The Rajneeshees (1984)." In Jonathan B. Tucker, ed., *Toxic Terror: Assessing Terrorist Use of Chemical and Biological Weapons.* Cambridge, Mass.: MIT Press, 2000.

Carver, Michael. *War Since 1945.* London: Weidenfeld and Nicolson, 1980.

"Caught Red-handed: The Inside Story of an Arms Shipment." *Jane's Foreign Report,* no. 2672, January 17, 2002.

Central Intelligence Agency. *Guide to the Analysis of Insurgency.* Washington, D.C.: U.S. Government Printing Office, no date.

Chaliand, Gerard and Yves Ternon. *The Armenians: From Genocide to Resistance.* Translated by Tony Berrett. London: Zed, 1983.

Chayban, Badih. "Hizbullah Rolls Out New Computer Game: Special Force Lets Players Use Sharon for Target Practice." *Daily Star* (Beirut), March 3, 2003. http://www.specialforce.net/english/news/dailystart.htm.

Chivers, C. J. and Stephen Lee Meyers. "Insurgents Seize School in Russia and Hold Scores." *New York Times,* September 2, 2004.

———. "Terror in Russia: Battle in Beslan." *New York Times,* September 4, 2004.

Churchill, Winston S. *The Second World War.* Vol. 3, *The Grand Alliance.* London: Reprint Society, 1956.

———. *The Second World War.* Vol. 4, *The Hinge of Fate.* London: Reprint Society, 1956.

Clarity, James F. "Obscure Doctor Again Faces Sinn Fein Chief." *International Herald Tribune* (Paris), April 15, 1997.

Clarke, Richard A. *Against All Enemies: Inside America's War on Terrorism.* New York: Free Press, 2004.

Clarke, Thurston. *By Blood and Fire: The Attack on the King David Hotel.* New York: Putnam, 1981.

Clawson, Patrick. "Why We Need More but Better Coverage of Terrorism." *Orbis* 80, no. 4 (Winter 1987).

Cline, Edward. "Terrorists, Period." *Washington Post,* September 11, 2004.

Cline, Ray S. and Yonah Alexander. *Terrorism: The Soviet Connection.* New York: Crane Russak, 1984.

Clutterbuck, Lindsay. "Countering Irish Republican Terrorism in Britain: Its Origin as a Police Function." Unpublished manuscript, 2005.

———. "The Progenitors of Terrorism: Russian Revolutionaries or Extreme Irish Republicans?" *Terrorism and Political Violence* 16, no. 1 (Spring 2004).

CNN. "Alleged bin Laden Tape a Call to Arms." http://cnn.com/2003/WORLD/meast/02/11/sprj.irq.wrap.

CNN.Com. "Live from Afghanistan—Was Al Qaeda Working on a Super Bomb?" January 24, 2004. http://www.isis-online.org/publications/terrorism/transcript.html.

Cohen, Michael J. *Palestine and the Great Powers, 1945–1948.* Princeton, N.J.: Princeton University Press, 1982.

Cohen-Almagor, Raphael. "Vigilant Jewish Fundamentalism: From the JDL to Kach (or 'Shalom Jews, Shalom Dogs')." *Terror and Political Violence* 4, no. 1 (Spring 1992).

Cole, Leonard A. *The Anthrax Letters: A Medical Detective Story.* Washington, D.C.: Joseph Henry Press, 2003.

Cole, Patrick E. "'I'm Just Like Anyone Else.'" *Time*, April 15, 1996.

Collins, Eamon with Mick McGovern. *Killing Rage.* London: Granta, 1997.

Colvin, Marie. "Rabbi Calls for Suicide Bombings." *Sunday Times* (London), April 13, 1997.

Colvin, Marie and Andy Goldberg. "Israel on Alert for Wave of 'Sleeper' Bombers." *Sunday Times* (London), March 10, 1996.

Committee for the Publication of Lehi Writings. *B'Ha'Machterot* [In the underground]. Vols. A, B, and D. Tel Aviv: Yair Press, 1959.

Conquest, Robert. *The Great Terror.* Harmondsworth: Penguin, 1971.

Conway, Flo and Jim Siegelman. "Identity and the Militia." *Arkansas Democrat-Gazette* (Little Rock), December 3, 1995.

Coogan, Tim Pat. *The IRA: A History.* Niwot, Colo.: Roberts Rinehart, 1993.

Cooley, John K. *Green March, Black September: The Story of the Palestinian Arabs.* London: Frank Cass, 1973.

——. "New Arab Unity Hits Palestinian Guerrillas." *Christian Science Monitor* (Boston), September 19, 1973.

Coomaraswamy, Radika. "Women of the LTTE: The Tiger's and Women's Emancipation." *Frontline* (Chennai, India), January 10, 1997.

Corbett, Robert. *Guerrilla Warfare from 1939 to the Present Day.* London: Orbis, 1986.

Corcoran, James. *Bitter Harvest: The Birth of Paramilitary Terrorism in the Heartland.* New York: Penguin, 1995.

Cordes, Bonnie. "When Terrorists Do the Talking: Reflections on Terrorist Literature." In David C. Rapoport, ed., "Special Issue: Inside Terrorist Organizations." *Journal of Strategic Studies* 10, no. 4 (December 1987).

Corr, Ambassador Edwin G. Introduction to Max G. Manwaring, ed., *Gray Area Phenomena: Confronting the New World Disorder.* Boulder, Colo.: Westview, 1993.

Corsun, Andrew. *Research Papers on Terrorism: Armenian Terrorism, 1975–1980.* Washington, D.C.: Office of Security Threat Analysis Group, U.S. Department of State, 1982.

Cottrell, Robert. "French Court Told of Huge Libyan Arms Run by IRA." *Independent* (London), January 8, 1991.

Counter Terrorism Center. *Counter Terrorism 2005.* Washington, D.C.: Central Intelligence Agency, 2004.

Counterterrorism Threat Assessment and Warning Unit. *Terrorism in the United States 1999.* Washington, D.C.: U.S. Department of Justice, FBI Publication #0308, 2000.

——. *Terrorism in the United States 2000/2001.* Washington, D.C.: U.S. Department of Justice, FBI Publication #0308, 2002.

Cowell, Alan. "Berlin Court Says Top Iran Leaders Ordered Killings." *New York Times*, April 11, 1997.

——. "One Conviction in Plot to Spread Deadly Toxins, but 8 Go Free." *New York Times*, April 13, 2005.

——. "Two More Held in Rabin Slaying; Israeli Police See a Conspiracy." *New York Times*, November 10, 1995.

Craig, Gordon. *Germany, 1866–1945*. Oxford: Clarendon, 1978.

Creech-Jones Papers. Rhodes House, Oxford. Boxes 32/3 and 32/6, Letters.

Crenshaw, Martha. *Terrorism and International Cooperation*. Occasional Paper Series 11. New York: Institute for East-West Security Studies, 1989.

Crossette, Barbara. "Sri Lanka's Army Is Hitting Last Guerrilla Group." *New York Times*, May 2, 1991.

——. "Tamil Rebels Said to Recruit Child Soldiers." *New York Times*, July 17, 2000.

Crossette, Barbara, Judith Miller, Steven Lee Myers, and Tim Weiner. "U.S. Says Iraq Aided Production of Chemical Weapons in Sudan." *New York Times*, August 25, 1998.

Crouch, Gregory. "Man on Trial in Dutch Killing Says He'd Do 'Same Again.'" *New York Times*, July 13, 2005.

——. "Suspect in Killing of Dutch Filmmaker Maintains His Silence." *New York Times*, July 12, 2005.

Cullison, Alan. "Inside Al-Qaeda's Hard Drive." *Atlantic Monthly* 294, no. 2 (September 2004).

Davis, Joyce M. *Martyrs: Innocence, Vengeance, and Despair in the Middle East.* New York: Palgrave/Macmillan, 2003.

Davis, Uri, Andrew Mack, and Ira Yuval-Davis. Introduction to Uri Davis, Andrew Mack, and Ira Yuval-Davis, eds., *Israel and the Palestinians*. London: Ithaca Press, 1975.

Declaration of Jihad Against the Country's Tyrants—Military Series. No date.

Dedijer, Vladimir. *The Road to Sarajevo*. London: MacGibbon and Kee, 1967.

Deen, Thailif. "Tigers Try Electronic Terrorism." *Daily News* (Colombo), November 22, 1997.

Dees, Morris with James Corcoran. *Gathering Storm: America's Militia Threat.* New York: HarperCollins, 1996.

deLeon, Peter, Bruce Hoffman, and Konrad Kellen. *The Threat of Nuclear Terrorism: A Reexamination*. Santa Monica, Calif.: RAND Corporation, N-2706, January 1988.

Denning, Dorothy E. "Activism, Hacktivism, and Cyberterrorism: The Internet as a Tool for Influencing Foreign Policy." http://www.nautilus.org/info-policy/workshop/papers/denning.html (April 16, 2002).

Department of Defense Dictionary of Military and Associated Terms. http://www.dtic.mil/doctrine/jel/dodict/data/t/05373.html.

Dettmer, Jamie and Edward Gorman. "Seven Dead in IRA 'Human' Bomb Attacks." *The Times* (London), October 25, 1990.

Dewan, Shalila. "Bomber Offers Guilty Pleas, and Defiance." *New York Times*, April 14, 2005.

Dewar, Michael. *Brush Fire Wars: Minor Campaigns of the British Army Since 1945*. New York: St. Martin's, 1984.

DeYoung, Karen. "U.S. Considering Talks on Hijacking Coverage." *Washington Post*, July 18, 1985.

Diamond, Edwin. "The Coverage Itself: Why It Turned Into 'Terrorvision.'" *TV Guide*, September 21, 1985.

Dillin, John. "NBC News President Defends, but Revises, Terrorism Coverage." *Christian Science Monitor* (Boston), August 5, 1985.

Directorate of Intelligence, Central Intelligence Agency. *Palestinian Organizations: A Reference Aid*. Washington, D.C.: Central Intelligence Agency, LDA 90–11155, March 1990.

"Discussion Paper on Preventing Terrorism: U.S. Government Prevention Capabilities." Unpublished. July 23, 1996.

Dixon, Lloyd and Rachel Kaganoff Stern. *Compensation Losses from the 9/11 Attacks*. Santa Monica, Calif.: RAND Corporation, MG-264-ICJ, 2004.

Dobson, Christopher. *Black September: Its Short, Violent History*. London: Robert Hale, 1974, 1975.

Dobson, Christopher and Ronald Payne. *The Carlos Complex: A Study in Terror*. London: Coronet/Hodder and Stoughton, 1978.

——. *Terror! The West Strikes Back*. London: Macmillan, 1982.

Dolgin, Janet L. *Jewish Identity and the JDL*. Princeton, N.J.: Princeton University Press, 1977.

"Don't Spoil the Party." *Economist* (London), July 13, 1996.

"Do Terrorists Need Television, TV Guide Asks." *United Press International*, February 18, 1985.

Downes-LeGuin, Theo and Bruce Hoffman. *The Impact of Terrorism on Public Opinion, 1988 to 1989*. Santa Monica, Calif.: RAND Corporation, MR-225-FF/RC, 1993.

Doyle, Leonard. "US Militias Show Way for British Fascists." *Independent* (London), April 27, 1995.

Drake, Richard. *The Aldo Moro Murder Case*. Cambridge, Mass.: Harvard University Press, 1995.

Drozdiak, William. "EU Recalls Envoys as Iran Is Found Guilty of Terror." *International Herald Tribune* (Paris), April 11, 1997.

——. "Extremes Squeeze Arafat as Hamas's Power Swells." *International Herald Tribune* (Paris), August 25, 1997.

Dudevitch, Margot. "2003 Terror Report: 50% Decrease in Israeli Casualties." *Jerusalem Post*, January 9, 2004.

Dugger, Celia W. "Rebels Without a Childhood in Sri Lanka War." *New York Times*, September 10, 2000.

Dunn, Ross and Tom Rhodes. "The Stalking Assassin Who Killed Rabin at Third Try." *The Times* (London), November 6, 1995.

Eddy, Paul. "Cover Story: True Detective Stories." *Sunday Times Magazine* (London), August 10, 1997.

Eedle, Paul. "Terrorism.com." *Guardian* (London), July 17, 2002.

Egan, Timothy. "Trying to Explain Contacts with Paramilitary Groups." *New York Times*, May 2, 1995.

Eggen, Dan. "Indictment Cites Plans to Target Financial Hubs: 3 Britons' Extradition to Be Sought." *Washington Post*, April 13, 2005.

Ehrenfeld, Rachel. *Narco-Terrorism*. New York: Basic Books, 1990.

Eickelman, Dale F. "Trans-State Islam and Security." In Susanne Rudolph Hoeber and James Piscatori, eds., *Transnational Religion and Fading States*. Boulder, Colo.: Westview, 1996.

el Deeb, Sarah. "Al-Qaida Reportedly Plans Big New Attack." Associated Press, May 8, 2003.

Electronic newsletter of the Orion Group, April 24, 2003.

Ellul, Jacques. *Propaganda: The Formation of Men's Attitudes*. Translated by Konrad Kellen and Jean Lerner. New York: Knopf, 1965.

El-Nawawy, Mohammed and Adel Iskandar. *Al-Jazeera: The Story of the Network That Is Rattling Governments and Redefining Modern Journalism*. Cambridge, Mass.: Westview,2003.

Engelberg, Stephen. "Contras to Start New Radio Station." *New York Times*, November 5, 1986.

Ensslin, Gudrun. "Statement of 19 January 1976." In Red Army Faction, *Texte der RAF* [RAF texts]. Malmö, Sweden: Verlag Bo Cavefors, 1977.

Eshel, David. "The Al-Aqsa Intifada: Tactics and Strategies." *Jane's Intelligence Review* (May 2001).

Evans, Kathy and Richard Norton-Taylor. "Spain Checks Syrian Link to Lockerbie." *The Times* (London), June 6, 1992.

Evans, Michael. "Iraqis Linked to Sudan Plant." *The Times* (London), August 25, 1998.

"EZLN—¡Ya Basta!" [Enough already]." http://www.ezln.org (June 15, 2005).

Fadl Allah [*sic*], Ayatollah Muhammed Hussein. "Islam and Violence in Political Reality." *Middle East Insight* 4, nos. 4–5 (1986).

Fallaci, Oriana. "Interview with George Habash." *Life Magazine*, June 12, 1970.

Fallows, James. "Who Shot Mohammed Al-Dura?" *Atlantic Monthly* 291, no. 5 (June 2003).

Fanon, Frantz. *The Wretched of the Earth*. London: Penguin, 1990.

Fattah, Hassan M. "Hezbollah Declares Full Support for Syria." *New York Times*, March 6, 2005.

FBIS, Near East/South Asia. "Israel: Palestinian Television Broadcasts Clip Encouraging Martyrdom." *Ma'ariv* (Tel Aviv) (Hebrew), August 11, 2003.

FBI Strategic Plan, 2004–2009. http://www.fbi.gov/publications/strategicplan/strategicplantext.htm.

Feiler, Stuart I. "Terrorism: Is Tourism Really the Target?" *Hotel and Restaurants International*, October 1986.

Ferracuti, Franco and Francesco Bruno. "Psychiatric Aspects of Terrorism in Italy." Unpublished study commissioned by the Italian secret services. No date.

Fetscher, I. and G. Rohrmoser. *Analysen zum Terrorismus* [Analyses on the subject of terrorism]. Vol. 1, *Ideologien und Strategien* [Ideologies and strategies]. Bonn: Westdeutscher Verlag, 1981.

Filkins, Dexter. "Sri Lanka Women at War: Tamil Rebel Group Is Now One-Third Female." *International Herald Tribune* (Paris), March 13, 2000.

Finer, Jonathan and Anthony Faiola. "Insurgents Say They Have Killed Japanese: Video May Show Body of Hostage." *Washington Post*, May 29, 2005.

Finn, Peter and Peter Baker. "Hostages Were Helpless in the Face of Chaos." *Washington Post*, September 5, 2005.

Fiskhoff, Sue. "Gentle, Kind, and Full of Religious Fervor." *Jerusalem Post*, February 27, 1994.

Fitchett, Joseph. "Guerrillas Seeking Leverage." *Christian Science Monitor* (Boston), November 27, 1973.

Foley, Charles. *Island in Revolt*. London: Longmans, 1962.

——, ed. *The Memoirs of General Grivas*. London: Longmans, 1964.

Foley, Charles and W. I. Scobie. *The Struggle for Cyprus*. Stanford, Calif.: Hoover Institution Press, 1975.

Ford, Franklin L. *Political Murder: From Tyrannicde to Terrorism*. Cambridge, Mass.: Harvard University Press, 1985.

"41 Dead, 53 Injured, 52 Missing in Terrorist Attack on Secretariat." *Palestine Post* (Jerusalem), July 23, 1946.

Foster, Anthony. "An Emerging Threat Shapes Up as Terrorists Take to the High Seas." *Jane's Intelligence Review* (July 1998).

Fouda, Yosri and Nick Fielding. *Masterminds of Terror: The Truth Behind the Most Devastating Terrorist Attack the World Has Ever Seen*. New York: Arcade, 2003.

Frank, Gerold. *The Deed*. New York: Simon and Schuster, 1963.

Frankel, Glenn and Craig Whitlock. "London Probe Extends Abroad: Egyptian Arrested, Pakistani Sought." *Washington Post*, July 16, 2005.

Franks, Lucinda. "Annual of Law Enforcement: Don't Shoot—In the New FBI, Patience Comes First." *New Yorker*, July 22, 1996. http://www.threatlink.com/pr/articles/Don't%20Shoot.pdf.

"French Paper Provides Information on ASALA Leader Hagopian." *Mamara* (Istanbul), January 16, 1985.

Friedman, Thomas L. "Jewish Terrorists Freed by Israel." *New York Times*, December 9, 1984.

——. "Strategy of Suicide Bombings." *New York Times*, March 31, 2002.

Fromm, Joseph. "TV: Does It Box in [the] President in a Crisis?" *U.S. News and World Report*, July 5, 1985.

Ganor, Boaz. "Suicide Attacks in Israel." In International Policy Institute for Counter-Terrorism, *Countering Suicide Terrorism: An International Conference*. Jerusalem: Gefen, 2001.

García-Granados, Jorge. *The Birth of Israel: The Drama as I Saw It*. New York: Knopf, 1948.

Gardela, Karen and Bruce Hoffman. *The RAND Chronology of International Terrorism for 1986*. Santa Monica, Calif.: RAND Corporation, R-3890-RC, 1990.

——. *The RAND Chronology of International Terrorism for 1987*. Santa Monica, Calif.: RAND Corporation, R-4006-RC, 1991.

Gaucher, Roland. *Les Terroristes*. Paris: Editions Albin Michel, 1965.

Gearty, Conor. *The Future of Terrorism*. London: Phoenix, 1997.

Geiss, Imanuel, ed. *July 1914: The Outbreak of the First World War*. New York: Norton, 1967.

Gellman, Barton. "Al Qaeda Near Biological, Chemical Arms Production." *Washington Post*, March 23, 2003.

——. "Cyber-Attacks by Al-Qaeda Feared: Terrorists at Threshold of Using Internet as Tool of Bloodshed, Experts Say." *Washington Post*, June 27, 2002.

General Intelligence and Security Service, *Recruitment for the Jihad in the Netherlands: From Incident to Trend*. The Hague: Ministry of the Interior and Kingdom Relations, December 2002.

Genovese, Margaret. "Terrorism: Newspapers Grapple with the Extraordinary Challenges of Covering Worldwide Terrorist Incidents." *Presstime* (New York), August 1986.

German, Mike. "Behind the Lone Terrorists, a Pack Mentality." *Washington Post*, June 5, 2005.

Geyelin, Philip. "NBC: How to Protect a Terrorist." *Washington Post*, May 19, 1986.

Ghattas, Kim and Roula Khalaf. "Shooting Spree in Saudi City Spreads Jitters Among Western Companies." *Financial Times* (London), May 3, 2004.

Ghattas, Sam F. "Syria Foes to Control Lebanon's Parliament." *Washington Post*, June 21, 2005.

Gibb, H. A. R. *Islam*. Oxford: Oxford University Press, 1978.

Glasser, Susan B. "'Martyrs' in Iraq Mostly Saudis: Web Sites Track Suicide Bombings." *Washington Post*, May 15, 2005.

——. "Review May Shift Terror Policies." *Washington Post*, May 29, 2005.

Goldberg, Jeffrey. "The Martyr Strategy: What Does the New Phase of Terrorism Signify?" *New Yorker*, July 9, 2001.

Golden, Tim. "Mexico's New Offensive: Erasing Rebel's Mystique." *New York Times*, February 11, 1995.

Goodwin-Gill, Guy and Ilene Cohn. *Child Soldiers: The Role of Children in Armed Conflict*. Oxford: Clarendon, 1994.

Goren, Roberta. *The Soviet Union and Terrorism*. Edited by Jillian Becker. London: Allen and Unwin, 1984.

Gorman, Edward. "Bomb Disposers Mark 21 Years in Ulster." *The Times* (London), November 7, 1992.

——. "How to Stop the IRA." *The Times* (London), January 11, 1992.

——. "Libyan Arms Shipments Allow IRA to Maintain Campaign of Violence." *The Times* (London), March 7, 1991.

Graham, Ian. "Official: IRA Using 'Bigger, Better' Bombs." *London Press Association*, January 23, 1992.

Greenberg, Joel. "Israeli Police Question Two Rabbis in Rabin Assassination." *New York Times*, November 22, 1995.

——. "Slaying Blended Technology and Guile." *New York Times*, January 10, 1996.

Grivas, General. *Guerrilla Warfare and Eoka's Struggle*. Translated by A.A. Pallis. London: Longmans, 1964.

Grossman, Lawrence K. "Television and Terrorism: A Common Sense Approach." *TVI Report* 6, no. 4 (1986).

Grunwald, Michael. "U.S. Says Bin Laden Sought Nuclear Arms." *Washington Post*, September 26, 1998.

Gunaratna, Rohan. "Case Study: The Liberation Tigers of Tamil Eelam." *Jane's Intelligence Review* (October 2001).

——. "The Conflict in Sri Lanka, 1982–Present." Unpublished paper prepared as part of a project on how terrorism escalates conducted at the Centre for the Study of Terrorism and Political Violence, University of St. Andrews (Scotland), March 1997.

——. *Implications of the Sri Lankan Tamil Insurgency*. Colombo: Alumni Association of the Bandaranaike Centre for International Studies and London: International Foundation of Sri Lankans United Kingdom, 1997.

——. *Inside Al Qaeda: Global Network of Terrorism*. London: Hurst, 2002.

——. *International and Regional Security Implications of the Sri Lankan Tamil Insurgency*. St. Albans, Herts: International Foundation of Sri Lankans, 1997.

——. "Khalid Sheikh Mohammed: The Brain." *Playboy* 52, no. 6 (June 2005).

——. "The LTTE and Suicide Terrorism." *Frontline*, February 2000.

——. "The Rebellion in Sri Lanka: Sparrow Tactics to Guerrilla Warfare (1971–1996)." Unpublished manuscript. No date.

——. "Sea Tiger Success Threatens the Spread of Copycat Tactics." *Jane's Intelligence Review* (March 2001).

——. "Suicide Terrorism: A Global Threat." *Jane's Intelligence Review*, October 20, 2000. http://www.janes.com/security/international_security/news/usscole/jir001020_1_n.shtml.

——. " Suicide Terrorism in Sri Lanka and India: LTTE Suicide Capability, Likely Trends, and Response." Unpublished manuscript. Expanded version of a paper presented at the First International Conference on Countering Suicide Terrorism, Herzilya, Israel, February 20–23, 2000.

——. "Tiger Cubs and Childhood Fall as Casualties in Sri Lanka." *Jane's Intelligence Review* (July 1998).

——. *War and Peace in Sri Lanka*. Sri Lanka: Institute of Fundamental Studies, 1987.

Hacker, Frederick J. *Crusaders, Criminals, Crazies: Terror and Terrorism in Our Time*. New York: Norton, 1976.

Halaby, Jamal. "Zarqawi Among 13 Indicted by Jordan in Plot: Officials Say Militants Planned to Attack Premier's Office, U.S. Embassy in Amman." *Washington Post*, October 18, 2004.

Halsell, Grace. "Why Bobby Brown of Brooklyn Wants to Blow Up Al Aqsa." *Arabia*, August 1984.

"Hamas Issues Statement on Ayyash Killing." Al-Quds Palestinian Radio (in Arabic), 1755 GMT, January 5, 1996.

"Hamas' Mishal: Jihad Palestinians' Sole Option." *Al-Zaman*, November 23, 2000, FBIS-NES, Document ID: GMP 20001123000110.

Hansard. *House of Commons*. 5th series, Parliamentary Debates. London, House of Commons.

Harel, Amos. "Shin Bet: 145 Suicide Bombers Since the Start of the Intifada." *Ha'aretz* (Tel Aviv), September 29, 2002. http://www.haartezdaily.com.

Harik, Judith Palmer. *Hezbollah: The Changing Face of Terrorism*. London: I. B. Tauris, 2004.

Harrison, David. "Jackboot Stamp of the New Right." *Observer* (London), April 23, 1995.

Hart, Alan. *Arafat: A Political Biography. The Definitive Biography Written in Cooperation with Yasser Arafat*. London: Sidgwick and Jackson, 1994.

Hassan, Nasra. "Letter from Gaza: An Arsenal of Believers." *New Yorker*, November 19, 2001.

Hasselbach, Ingo with Tom Reiss. *Führer-Ex: Memoirs of a Former Neo-Nazi*. London: Chatto and Windus, 1996.

Hays, Tom and Larry Neumeister. "Trade Center Bombers Get Life in Prison." Associated Press, May 25, 1994.

Hearst, David. "'Human Bomb' Fails to Explode." *Guardian* (London), November 24, 1990.

——. "IRA Mines Gap in Army Security." *Guardian* (London), April 10, 1990.

——. "Publicity Key Element of Strategy." *Guardian* (London), July 31, 1990.

Hedges, Chris and Joel Greenberg. "West Bank Massacre: Before Killing, a Final Prayer and a Final Taunt." *New York Times*, February 28, 1994.

Heggoy, Alf Andrew. *Insurgency and Counterinsurgency in Algeria*. Bloomington: Indiana University Press, 1972.

Heller, Joseph. *The Stern Gang: Ideology, Politics, and Terror, 1940–1949*. London: Frank Cass, 1995.

Hendawi, Hamza. "Cult Evolves Around Suicide Bombers." Associated Press, April 28, 2002. http://www.news.findlaw.com/ap_stories/i/1107/4–28–2002/2002042 8102000255505.html.

Hendren, John. "Rumsfeld Tells Nations Not to Help Zarqawi." *Los Angeles Times*, June 2, 2005.

Henze, Paul B. *The Plot to Kill the Pope*. New York: Scribner's, 1983.

Herman, Edward and Gerry O'Sullivan. *The "Terrorism" Industry*. New York: Pantheon, 1989.

Herman, Ken. "After the Assault: U.S. Braces for Crusade Against 'Evil.'" *Atlanta Journal-Constitution*, September 17, 2001.

Hermon, Sir John. "The Police, the Media, and the Reporting of Terrorism." In Yonah Alexander and Richard Latter, eds., *Terrorism and the Media*. McLean, Va.: Brassey's, 1990.

Hersh, Seymour M. *Chain of Command: The Road from 9/11 to Abu Ghraib*. New York: HarperCollins, 2004.

Hezbollah. "Open Letter from the Party of God to the Disinherited of Lebanon and the World Revealing the Way and the Intentions which are their Own on the Occasion of the First Anniversary of Ragheb Harb, Symbol of the Islamic Resistance and Exemplary Martyr." Beirut, Lebanon, February 16, 1985.

Hickey, Neil. "Terrorism and Television." *TV Guide*, July 31, 1976.

Hirst, David. *The Gun and the Olive Branch*. London: Futura, 1977.

"Hizbullah's Cyber-Success." *Foreign Report* (London), no. 2527 (January 14, 1999).

Hoagland, Jim. "Palestinian Guerrillas Say They Reject Cease-fire." *Washington Post*, October 23, 1973.

——. "A Shifting Focus on Terrorism." *Washington Post*, April 24, 2005.

Hodson, Peregrine. "Japanese Disband Aum Cult." *The Times* (London), December 15, 1995.

Hoffman, Bruce. "The Bombing of the King David Hotel." *Midstream* 29, no. 7 (August/September 1983).

——. "The Contrasting Ethical Foundations of Terrorism in the 1980s." *Terrorism and Political Violence* 1, no. 3 (July 1989).

——. "Creatures of the Cold War: The JRA." *Jane's Intelligence Review* (February 1997).

——. "'Holy Terror': The Implications of Terrorism Motivated by a Religious Imperative." *Studies in Conflict and Terrorism* 18, no. 4 (Winter 1995).

——. *Insurgency and Counterinsurgency in Iraq*. Santa Monica, Calif.: RAND Corporation, OP-127, 2004.

——. "The Jewish Defense League." *Terrorism, Violence, and Insurgency Journal* 5, no. 1 (Summer 1984).

——. "Jewish Terrorist Activities and the British Government in Palestine 1939 to 1947." D.Phil. thesis, Oxford University, 1986.

——. *Lessons of 9/11: Statement Submitted for the Committee Record to the United States Joint September 11, 2001 Inquiry Staff of the House and Senate Select Committees on Intelligence, 8 October 2002*. Santa Monica, Calif.: RAND Corporation, 2002.

——. "The Logic of Suicide Terrorism: Lessons from Israel that America Must Learn." *Atlantic Monthly* 291, no. 5 (June 2003).

——. "Low-Intensity Conflict: Terrorism and Guerrilla Warfare in the Coming Decades." In Lawrence Howard, ed., *Terrorism: Roots, Impact, Responses.* New York: Praeger, 1992.

——. "Old Madness, New Methods: Revival of Religious Terrorism Begs for Broader U.S. Policy." *RAND Review* 22, no. 2 (Winter 1998).

——. "Recent Trends and Future Prospects of Iranian Sponsored International Terrorism." In Yonah Alexander, ed., *Middle Eastern Terrorism: Current Threats and Future Prospects.* New York: G. K. Hall, 1994.

——. *Recent Trends and Future Prospects of Terrorism in the United States.* Santa Monica, Calif.: RAND Corporation, R-3618, April 1986.

——. "Right-Wing Terrorism in Europe." *Conflict* 5, no. 3 (Fall 1984).

——. "Right-Wing Terrorism in Europe Since 1980." *Orbis* 28, no. 1 (Spring 1984).

——. *Right-Wing Terrorism in Germany.* Research Report no. 13. London: Institute of Jewish Affairs, December 1986.

——. "Right-Wing Terrorism in the United States." *Violence, Aggression, Terrorism Journal*, no. 1 (Winter 1987).

——. *Terrorism in the United States and the Potential Threat to Nuclear Facilities.* Santa Monica, Calif.: RAND Corporation, R-3351-DOE, January 1986.

——. "Why Terrorists Don't Claim Credit." *Terrorism and Political Violence* 9, no. 1 (Spring 1997).

Hoffman, Bruce with David Claridge. "Illicit Trafficking in Nuclear Materials." *Conflict Studies*, nos. 314/315. London: Research Institute for the Study of Conflict and Terrorism, January/February 1999.

Hoffman, Bruce and Donna Kim Hoffman. "Chronology of International Terrorism 1995." *Terrorism and Political Violence* 8, no. 3 (Autumn 1996).

Hoffman, Bruce and Gordon H. McCormick. "Terrorism, Signaling, and Suicide Attack." *Studies in Conflict and Terrorism* 27, no. 4 (July–August 2004).

Hoffman, David. "Reports Renew Suspicions of Iran, Syria Bomb Link." *Washington Post*, April 26, 1992.

Hoge, James W. "The Media and Terrorism." In Abraham Miller, ed., *Terrorism: The Media and the Law.* New York: Transnational, 1982.

Holmes, Steven A. "U.S. Charges 12 in Arizona Plot to Blow Up Government Office." *New York Times*, July 2, 1996.

Horne, Alistair. *A Savage War of Peace: Algeria 1954–1962.* Harmondsworth: Penguin, 1977.

Howard, Michael. "Smoke on the Horizon." *Financial Times* (London), September 7, 2002.

——. "What Friends Are For." *National Interest*, no. 69 (Fall 2002).

Huband, Mark and David Buchan. "Al-Qaeda May Have Access to 18,000 'Potential Operatives,' Says Think-Tank." *Financial Times* (London), May 26, 2004.

Hurwitz, Harry. *Menachem Begin.* Johannesburg: Jewish Herald, 1977.

Hyams, Edward. *Terrorists and Terrorism.* New York: St. Martin's, 1974.

Ibrahim, Youssef M. "Muslim Edicts Take on New Force." *New York Times*, February 12, 1995.

Iglarsh, Harvey J. "Fear of Flying: Its Economic Costs." *Terrorism* 10, no. 1 (Winter 1987).

"In Our Pages: 100, 75, and 50 Years Ago—1947: Zionists' Suicide." *International Herald Tribune* (Paris), April 22, 1997.

"Inside the Red Brigades." *Newsweek*, May 15, 1978.

Institute for Palestine Studies, International Studies Section. *Who Is Menachem Begin? A Documentary Sketch*. Beirut: Institute for Palestine Studies, 1977.

IntelCenter. *Al-Qaeda Targeting Guidance*. Vol. 1.0. Thursday, April 1, 2004. Alexandria, Va.: IntelCenter/Tempest Publishing, 2004.

——. *Evolution of Jihadi Video* (EJV). Vol. 1.0. May 11, 2005. Alexandria, Va.: IntelCenter/Tempest Publishing, 2005.

"Intelligence Battle in Cyberspace." *Intelligence Newsletter*, no. 263 (April 27, 1995).

International Institute for Strategic Studies. *Strategic Survey 2003/4*. Oxford: Oxford University Press, 2004.

"Interview with ASALA." *Panorama Magazine* (Milan), September 1, 1980.

"Introduction. One Year Later: New Yorkers More Troubled, Washingtonians More on Edge." September 5, 2002. http://people-press.org/reports/display.php3?PageID = 160.

"IRA: The Libyan Connection." *Economist* (London), March 31, 1990.

"IRA Bomb-Making Guide on Internet." *Sunday Times* (London), February 9, 1997.

Islamic Group in Egypt. "Statement on U.S. Sentencing of Sheikh Rahman." January 19, 1996.

"Islamic Group Says It Set Off Dagestan Blast." *New York Times*, July 3, 2005.

"Israelis Discover Mass Murder Plot." *Sunday Times* (London), November 26, 1995.

Ivianksi, Zeev. "Fathers and Sons: A Study of Jewish Involvement in the Revolutionary Movement and Terrorism in Tsarist Russia." *Terrorism and Political Violence* 1, no. 2 (April 1989).

——. "Sources of Inspiration for Revolutionary Terrorism: The Bakunin-Nechayev Alliance." *Conflict Quarterly* 8, no. 3 (Summer 1988).

Iwanski, Len. "All 16 Remaining Freemen Surrender Peacefully." Associated Press, June 14, 1996.

Iyad, Abu with Eric Rouleau. *My Home, My Land: A Narrative of the Palestinian Struggle*. Translated by Linda Butler Koseoglu. New York: Times Books, 1981.

Jaber, Hala. *Hezbollah: Born with a Vengeance*. New York: Columbia University Press, 1997.

"Jail Term of Jewish Terrorist Reduced." *Jerusalem Post* (international edition), October 12, 1985.

Jamieson, Alison. *The Heart Attacked: Terrorism and Conflict in the Italian State*. London: Marion Boyars, 1989.

——. *Terrorism*. Hove, East Sussex: Wayland, 1991.

Janke, Peter. *Guerrilla and Terrorist Organisations: A World Directory and Bibliography*. New York: Macmillan, 1983.

Janofsky, Michael. "For Aryan Congress Stridency and Scrutiny." *New York Times*, July 23, 1995.

——. "One Man's Journey from Academia to Extremism." *New York Times*, July 5, 1995.

Jarbawi, Ali and Roger Heacock. "The Deportations and the Palestinian-Israeli Negotiations." *Journal of Palestinian Studies* 22, no. 3 (Spring 1993).

Jehl, Douglas. "Iran Tells the Europeans That It Doesn't Back Terrorism." *New York Times*, March 8, 1996.

——. "Iraq May Be Prime Place for Training of Militants, C.I.A. Report Concludes." *New York Times*, June 22, 2005.

Jenkins, Brian Michael. "International Terrorism: A New Mode of Conflict." In David Carlton and Carlo Schaerf, eds., *International Terrorism and World Security*. London: Croom Helm, 1975.

——. *International Terrorism: The Other World War*. Santa Monica, Calif.: RAND Corporation, R-3302-AF, November 1985.

——. *The Likelihood of Nuclear Terrorism*. Santa Monica, Calif.: RAND Corporation, P-7119, July 1985.

——. *New Modes of Conflict*. Santa Monica, Calif.: RAND Corporation, R-3009-DNA, June 1983.

——. "The Organization Men: Anatomy of a Terrorist Attack." In James F. Hoge Jr. and Gideon Rose, eds., *How Did This Happen? Terrorism and the New War*. New York: Public Affairs, 2001.

——. *The Psychological Implications of Media-Covered Terrorism*. Santa Monica, Calif.: RAND Corporation, P-6627, June 1981.

——. *The Study of Terrorism: Definitional Problems*. Santa Monica, Calif.: RAND Corporation, P-6563, December 1980.

——. *Will Terrorists Go Nuclear?* Santa Monica, Calif.: RAND Corporation, P-5541, November 1975.

Johnson, Keith et al. "British Police Fear More Attacks by Terrorists: Lack of Clues, Hard Leads Suggests Bombers Learned from Madrid-Blast Arrests." *Wall Street Journal*, July 8, 2005.

Johnston, David. "Bomber Is Called Killer Who Is Not on a Political Mission." *New York Times*, November 6, 1995.

——. "Surrender Is a Victory for a Strategy of Patience." *New York Times*, June 13, 1996.

Johnston, David and David E. Sanger. "New Generation of Leaders Is Emerging for Al-Qa'ida." *New York Times*, August 10, 2004.

Joint Inquiry Into Intelligence Community Activities Before and After the Terrorist Attacks of September 11, 2001. *Report of the U.S. Senate Select Committee on Intelligence and U.S. House Permanent Select Committee on Intelligence Together with Additional Views*. December 2002.

Joll, James. *The Anarchists*. Boston: Little, Brown, 1964.

——. *Europe Since 1870: An International History*. New York: Harper and Row, 1973.

Jorisch, Avi. *Beacon of Hatred: Inside Hizballah's Al-Manar Television*. Washington, D.C.: Washington Institute for Near East Policy, 2004.

Joshi, Charu Lata. "Ultimate Sacrifice—Sri Lanka: Suicide Bombers." *Far Eastern Economic Review*, June 1, 2000. http://www.feer.com/006 01/p64current.html.

Joshi, Manoj. "On the Razor's Edge: The Liberation Tigers of Tamil Eelam." *Studies in Conflict and Terrorism* 19, no. 1 (January–March 1996).

Juergensmeyer, Mark. *The New Cold War? Religious Nationalism Confronts the Secular State*. Berkeley: University of California Press, 1993.

——. *Terror in the Mind of God*. Berkeley: University of California Press, 2000.

——. "Terror Mandated by God." *Terrorism and Political Violence* 9, no. 2 (Summer 1997).

——. "The Worldwide Rise of Religious Nationalism." *Journal of International Affairs* 50, no. 1 (Summer 1996).

——, ed. *Violence and the Sacred in the Modern World*. London: Frank Cass, 1992.

Jureidini, Paul A. *Case Studies in Insurgency and Revolutionary Warfare, Algeria 1954–1962*. Washington, D.C.: American University, 1963.

Kahane, Rabbi Meir. *Never Again! A Program for Survival*. Los Angeles: Nash Publishing, 1971.

——. *They Must Go*. New York: Grosset and Dunlap, 1981.

Kamalendran, Chris. "LTTE's Aircraft: Yes, No." *Sunday Times* (Colombo), December 6, 1998.

Kaplan, David E. "National Security Watch: Eurolefties Fund Iraq Insurgency." *U.S. News and World Report*, June 23, 2005. http://www.usnews.com/usnews/news/articles/050623/23euroleft.htm.

Kaplan, David E. and Andrew Marshall. *The Cult at the End of the World: The Incredible Story of Aum*. London: Hutchinson, 1996.

Kaplan, Jeffrey. "Right-Wing Violence in North America." *Terrorism and Political Violence* 7, no. 1 (Spring 1995).

Karouny, Mariam. "Hizbollah Computer Game Recalls Israeli Battles." *Reuters Technology*, March 18, 2003. http://www.specialforce.net/english/news/reuters.htm.

Karpin, Michael and Ina Friedman. *Murder in the Name of God: The Plot to Kill Yitzhak Rabin*. New York: Metropolitan, 1998.

Katz, Samuel M. *The Hunt for the Engineer: How Israeli Agents Tracked the Hamas Master Bomber*. New York: Fromm, 1999.

Kay, Jenny. "Dying for Their Cause." *Eva* (London), June 1998.

Kedward, Roderick. *The Anarchists: The Men Who Shocked an Era*. London: BPC Unit 25, 1971.

Kellen, Konrad. *On Terrorists and Terrorism*. Santa Monica, Calif.: RAND Corporation, N-1942-RC, December 1982.

Kelley, Jack. "Militants Wire Web with Links to Jihad." *USA Today*, July 10, 2002.

——. "Terror Groups Hide Behind Web Encryption: Officials Say Sites Disguise Activities." *USA Today*, February 6, 2001.

Kelly, George Armstrong. *Lost Soldiers: The French Army and Empire in Crisis, 1947–1962*. Cambridge, Mass.: MIT Press, 1965.

Kelsey, Tim. "The Oklahoma Suspect Awaits Day of Reckoning." *Sunday Times* (London), April 21, 1996.

Kempe, Frederick. "Deadly Survivors: The Cold War Is Over but Leftist Terrorists in Germany Fight On." *Wall Street Journal*, December 27, 1991.

Kennedy, Hugh. "Holy Warriors: Telling the Story of the Crusades as History, Not Metaphor." *New York Times Book Review*, April 3, 2005.

Kenworthy, Tom. "Peaceful End Sought to Siege of Montana 'Freemen.'" *Washington Post*, March 30, 1996.

Keppel, Gilles. *The Revenge of God: The Resurgence of Islam, Christianity, and Judaism in the Modern World*. Cambridge, UK: Polity Press, 1995.

Kessler, Glen. "Old Data, New Credibility Issues." *Washington Post*, August 4, 2004.

Khaled, Leila. *My People Shall Live: The Autobiography of a Revolutionary*. London: Hodder and Stoughton, 1973.

"Khaled Tribute." *The Times* (London), September 3, 1997.

Khomeini, Imam. *Islam and Revolution*. Translated by Hamid Algar. London: KPI, 1981.

Kifner, John. "Anti-Syria Alliance Claims Victory in Lebanese Voting." *New York Times*, June 20, 2005.

——. "Antiterrorism Law Used in Poison Smuggling Case." *New York Times*, December 23, 1995.

——. "Israelis Investigate Far Right: May Crack Down on Speech." *New York Times*, November 8, 1995.

——. "Man Arrested in Poison Case Kills Himself in Jail Cell." *New York Times*, December 24, 1995.

——. "A Son of Israel: Rabin's Assassin." *New York Times*, November 19, 1995.

——. "Zeal of Rabin's Assassin Linked to Rabbis of the Religious Right." *New York Times*, November 12, 1995.

King Jr., Neil. "Moving Target: Fighting Terrorism Is Far More Perilous Than It Used to Be." *Wall Street Journal Europe*, August 25, 1998.

King, Peter H. "Guru Revels in Revelation of a 'Paradise' Defiled." *Los Angeles Times*, September 22, 1985.

Kingston, Shane. "Terrorism, the Media, and the Northern Ireland Conflict." *Studies in Conflict and Terrorism* 18, no. 3 (July–September 1995).

Kitfield, James. "The Hezbollah Model." *National Journal* 34, no. 20 (May 18, 2002).

Kitson, Frank. *Low-Intensity Operations*. London: Faber, 1971.

"Klanwatch, a Project of the Southern Poverty Law Center (Montgomery, Alabama)." *Intelligence Report* (Montgomery, Alabama), nos. 84 and 85 (November 1996 and Winter 1997).

Knapp, Wilfrid. *A History of War and Peace, 1939–1965*. London: Royal Institute of International Affairs and Oxford University Press, 1967.

Knickerbocker, Brad. "Patience Is a Virtue in Freeman Standoff." *Christian Science Monitor* (Boston), June 14, 1996.

Koust, Hal, ed. *Cyprus, 1946–1968*. New York: Facts on File, 1970.

Kramer, Martin. "Sacrifice and Fratricide in Shiite Lebanon." In Mark Juergensmeyer, ed., *Violence and the Sacred in the Modern World*. London: Frank Cass, 1992.

Kristof, Nicholas D. "In Shrine of Japan Cult, Police Find Laboratory." *New York Times*, March 11, 1995.

——. "Japanese Cult Planned U.S. Attack." *International Herald Tribune* (Paris), March 24, 1997.

Kristof, Nicholas D. with Sheryl WuDunn. "The Seer Among the Blind: Japanese Sect Leader's Rise." *New York Times*, March 26, 1995.

Krovel, Roy. "www.guerrilla.net." *Internet Today* (London), issue 25 (November 1996).

Kupperman, Robert H. and Darrel Trend. *Terrorism: Threat, Reality, Response*. Stanford, Calif.: Hoover Institution Press, 1979.

Kushner, Harvey W. "Suicide Bombers: Business as Usual." *Studies in Conflict and Terrorism* 19, no. 4 (October–December 1996).

Ladd, Everett Carl. "U.S. Public and Somalia." *Christian Science Monitor* (Boston), October 15, 1993.

Lafore, Lawrence. *The Long Fuse: An Interpretation of the Origins of World War I*. London: Weidenfeld and Nicolson, 1966.

Lapping, Brian. *End of Empire*. New York: St. Martin's, 1985.

Laqueur, Walter. *The Age of Terrorism*. Boston: Little, Brown, 1987.

——. *Guerrilla: A Historical and Critical Study*. Boston: Little, Brown, 1976.

——. *The New Terrorism: Fanaticism and the Arms of Mass Destruction*. Oxford: Oxford University Press, 1999.

——. *No End to War: Terrorism in the Twenty-first Century*. New York: Continuum, 2003.

——. "Postmodern Terrorism." *Foreign Affairs* 75, no. 5 (September–October 1996).

——. "Reflections on Terrorism." *Foreign Affairs* 65, no. 1 (Fall 1986).

——. *Terrorism*. London: Weidenfeld and Nicolson, 1977.

——, ed. *The Israel-Arab Reader: A Documentary History of the Middle East Conflict*. New York: Bantam, 1976.

——, ed. *Voices of Terror: Manifestos, Writings, and Manuals of Al Qaeda, Hamas, and Other Terrorists from Around the World and Throughout the Ages*. New York: Reed Press, 2004.

Laqueur, Walter and Yonah Alexander, eds. *The Terrorism Reader*. New York: Meridian, 1987.

Lawrence, T. E. *Seven Pillars of Wisdom*. Harmondsworth: Penguin Books, 1977.

"Legal Action: Keenan v. Aryan Nations." Southern Poverty Law Center Web site. http://www.splcenter.org/legal/docket/files.jsp?cdrID = 30&sortID = 3.

Lelyveld, Joseph. "All Suicide Bombers Are Not Alike: A Journey to Gaza, Cairo, and Hamburg in Search of What Really Made Sept. 11 Possible." *New York Times Magazine*, October 28, 2001.

Leventhal, Paul and Yonah Alexander, eds. *Nuclear Terrorism: Defining the Threat.* Washington, D.C.: Pergamon-Brassey's, 1986.

Levine, Evyatar and Yaacov Shimoni, eds. *Political Dictionary of the Middle East in the Twentieth Century.* London: Weidenfeld and Nicolson, 1972.

Levitt, Matthew. "Designating the Al-Aqsa Martyrs Brigades." *Peacewatch*, no. 371. Washington, D.C.: Washington Institute for Near East Policy, March 25, 2002.

Lewis, Bernard. *The Assassins: A Radical Sect in Islam.* London: Al Saqi Books, 1985.

Liddell Hart, B. H. *History of the Second World War.* New York: Paragon, 1979.

Lifton, Robert Jay. *Destroying the World to Save It: Aum Shinrikyo, Apocalyptic Violence, and the New Global Terrorism.* New York: Metropolitan Books, 1999.

Linzer, Dafna. "Nuclear Capabilities May Elude Terrorists, Experts Say." *Washington Post*, December 29, 2004.

Lipkin-Shahak, General (Ret.) Amnon. Introduction to International Policy Institute for Counter-Terrorism, *Countering Suicide Terrorism: An International Conference.* Jerusalem: Gefen, 2001.

Lippman, Thomas W. "Capture of Kurd Spurs Rage in Europe." *Washington Post*, February 17, 1999.

Lipton, Eric. "Qaeda Letters Are Said to Show Pre-9/11 Anthrax Plans." *New York Times*, May 21, 2005.

Litwak, Robert S. *Rogue States and U.S. Foreign Policy: Containment After the Cold War.* Washington, D.C.: Woodrow Wilson Center Press, 2000.

Long, David E. *The Anatomy of Terrorism.* New York: Free Press, 1990.

Love, Kennett. *Suez: The Twice-Fought War.* New York: McGraw-Hill, 1969.

"LTTE Declared Total Numbers of Killed During the Last 20 Years." Unpublished manuscript. No date.

Lucas, Edward. "Deadly Image Which Could Give Hezbollah the Edge." *Scotsman* (Edinburgh), April 14, 2000.

Luft, Gal. "The Palestinian H-Bomb: Terror's Winning Strategy." *Foreign Affairs* 81, no. 4 (July/August 2002).

——. "Special Policy Forum Report: The *Karine-A* Affair: A Strategic Watershed in the Middle East?" *Peacewatch*, no. 361. Washington, D.C.: Washington Institute for Near East Policy, January 30, 2002.

Luttwak, Edward and Dan Horowitz. *The Making of the Israeli Army.* New York: Penguin, 1975.

"Luxor Attackers Sought Cleric's Release in U.S.: Tourists Stream Home." *International Herald Tribune* (Paris), November 19, 1997.

MacDonald, Andrew. *The Turner Diaries.* Arlington, Va.: National Alliance/NationalVanguard Books, 1985.

MacDonald, Eileen. *Shoot the Women First.* New York: Random House, 1991.

MacFarquhar, Neal. "After Attack, Company's Staff Plans to Leave Saudi Arabia." *New York Times*, May 3, 2004.

——. "As Terrorists Strike Arab Targets, Escalation Fears Arise." *New York Times*, April 30, 2004.

——. "Firm Pulls 100 from Saudi Arabia After 5 Deaths." *New York Times*, May 2, 2004.

——. "Leader of Hezbollah Discovers a New Fray: Lebanese Politics." *New York Times*, March 13, 2005.

——. "Portrait of a Suicide Bomber: Devout, Apolitical, and Angry." *New York Times*, March 18, 1996.

MacFarquhar, Neal with Jim Rutenberg. "Bin Laden, in a Taped Speech, Says Attacks in Afghanistan Are a War Against Islam." *New York Times*, November 4, 2001.

Macintyre, MD, Anthony G.; Lt COL George W. Christopher, USAF, MC; COL Edward Eitzen, Jr., MC, USA; LTC Robert Gum, MC, USA; Scott Weir, MD; Craig Deatley, PA-C; CDR Kevin Tonat, DrPH, USPHS; and Joseph A. Barbera, MD. "Weapons of Mass Destruction: Events with Contaminated Casualties—Effective Planning for Health Care Facilities." *JAMA (Journal of the American Medical Association)*, no. 263 (January 2000).

Mackenzie Briefing Notes. "Funding Terror: The Liberation Tigers of Tamil Eelam and Their Criminal Activities in Canada and the Western World." Toronto: Mackenzie Centre, December 1995.

MacNeil/Lehrer Productions. *Transcript of "The News Hour with Jim Lehrer."* August 1, 1997.

Maddox, Browne. "Texan Militia at War with US." *The Times* (London), February 22, 1997.

Makovsky, David. "The Seizure of Gaza-Bound Arms: Political Implications." *Peace-watch*, no. 358. Washington, D.C.: Washington Institute for Near East Policy, January 8, 2002.

Mandela, Nelson. *Long Walk to Freedom*. London: Abacus, 1994.

Manwaring. Max G., ed. *Gray Area Phenomena: Confronting the New World Disorder*. Boulder, Colo.: Westview, 1993.

Marcus, Itmar. "PA Music Video Promising 'Maidens of Paradise' to Shahids—2 Days Before Suicide Bombings." *Palestinian Media Watch Multi-media Bulletin*, August 12, 2003. http://www.pmw.org.il.

Marcus, Raine. "Amir: I Wanted to Kill Rabin." *Jerusalem Post*, March 8, 1996.

Marighela, Carlos. *For the Liberation of Brazil*. Translated by John Butt and Rosemary Sheed. Harmondsworth: Penguin, 1971.

Marlowe, Laura. "A Fiery Cleric's Defense of Jihad." *Time*, January 15, 1996.

Martin, David C. and John Walcott. *Best Laid Plans: The Inside Story of America's War Against Terrorism*. New York: Harper and Row, 1988.

"Masked Gunmen Kill Jaffna Mayor." *Daily News* (Colombo), July 28, 1975.

Masker, Roy B. "An All White Nation? Why Not?" *Calling Our Nation*, no. 53 (no date). Aryan Nations.

Maxwell, Bill. "Good Women Help Bring War's End." *Albany Times Union*, June 5, 2000.

McCartney, C. A. *The Habsburg Empire, 1790–1918*. London: Weidenfeld and Nicolson, 1969.

McCullagh, Declan. "Bin Laden: Steganography Master?" Wired News.com, February 7, 2001. http://www.wired.com/news/print/0,1283,41658,00.html.

McDonald, Henry. "How the BBC Dances to an IRA Tune." *Sunday Times* (London), January 19, 1997.

McFadden, Robert D. "Mail Bomber Links an End to Killings to His Manifesto." *New York Times*, June 30, 1995.

Mcgee, Jim and Rachel Stassen-Berger. "5th Suspect Arrested in Bombing." *Washington Post*, March 26, 1993.

McGuire, Maria. *To Take Arms: A Year in the Provisional IRA*. London: Macmillan, 1973.

McKay, Naill. "Do Terrorists Troll the Net?" Wired News.com. http://www.wired.com/news/print/0,1294,15812,00.html.

McKittrick, David. *Despatches from Belfast*. Belfast: Blackstaff Press, 1989.

——. "Voyage Into Business of Terror." *Independent* (London), January 12, 1991.

McKnight, Gerald. *The Mind of the Terrorist*. London: Michael Joseph, 1974.

Melnachak, Joseph M. "A Chronicle of Hate: A Brief History of the Radical Right in America." *Terrorism, Violence, and Insurgency Report* 6, no. 4 (no date).

MEMRI Special Dispatch—Jihad and Terrorism Studies, no. 493 (April 11, 2003), quoting http://www.cubezero.nt/vhsvideo/imagis/?subject = 2&rec = 1043.

Merkl, Peter H. Prologue to Peter H. Merkl, ed., *Political Violence and Terror*. Berkeley: University of California Press, 1986.

Merzer, Martin. "Justice for All in Israel?" *Miami Herald*, May 17, 1985.

Meyer, Christina. *Underground Voices: Insurgent Propaganda in El Salvador, Nicaragua, and Peru*. Santa Monica, Calif.: RAND Corporation, N-3299-USDP, 1991.

Meyer, Josh and Greg Miller. "Fresh Details Back Threats." *Los Angeles Times*, August 3, 2004.

Michel, Lou and Dan Herbeck. *American Terrorist: Timothy McVeigh and the Oklahoma City Bombing*. New York: Regan, 2001.

Michels, Jeffrey. "National Vision and the Negotiation of Narratives: The Oslo Agreement." *Journal of Palestinian Studies* 24 (Autumn 1994).

Mikolus, Edward F. *Transnational Terrorism: A Chronology of Events, 1968–1979*. Westport, Conn.: Greenwood Press, 1980.

Mikolus, Edward F., Todd Sandier, and Jean M. Murdock. *International Terrorism in the 1980s: A Chronology of Events*. Ames: Iowa State University Press, 1989.

"Militant Islamic Political Activism on the Worldwide Web." Seminar by two analysts with the Foreign Broadcast Information Service, presented at the RAND Corporation Washington, D.C., Office, December 19, 2000.

"Militant Islamist: Attack on Cole Cost 10,000 Dollars." *Deutsche Presse-Agentur* (Nicosia), November 12, 2000.

"Militia of Montana: Statement of Purpose." http://www.militiaofmontana.com.

Miller, Abraham H. and Nicholas A. Damask. "The Dual Myths of 'Narco-Terrorism': How Myths Drive Policy." *Terrorism and Political Violence* 8, no. 1 (Spring 1996).

Miller, John. "Interview: Osama Bin Laden (May 1998)." http://www.pbs.org/wgbh/pages/frontline/shows/binladen/who/interview.html.

Miller, Judith. "U.S. Has New Concerns About Anthrax Readiness." *New York Times*, December 28, 2003.

Miller, Judith, Stephen Engelberg, and William Broad. *Germs: Biological Weapons and America's Secret War*. New York: Simon and Schuster, 2001.

Miller, Reuben. "Game Theory and Hostage-Taking Incidents: A Case Study of the Munich Olympics." *Conflict Quarterly* 10, no. 1 (Winter 1990).

Mills, C. Wright. *The Power Elite*. London: Oxford University Press, 1956.

Mishal, Shaul and Reuben Aharoni. *Speaking Stones: Communiqués from the Intifada Underground*. Syracuse, N.Y.: Syracuse University Press, 1994.

Mishal, Shaul and Avraham Sela. *The Palestinian Hamas: Vision, Violence, and Coexistence*. New York: Columbia University Press, 2000.

Mitchell, Alison. "Fingerprint Evidence Grows in World Trade Center Blast." *New York Times*, May 20, 1993.

Monroe, Elizabeth. "Mr. Bevin's 'Arab Policy.'" In Albert Hourani, ed., *St. Antony's Papers no. 11: Middle Eastern Affairs No. 2*. London: Chatto and Windus, 1961.

Mooradian, Moorad. "Terrorists Speak: Interviews with ASALA Members." Unpublished manuscript. No date.

Morris, Benny. *The Birth of the Palestinian Refugee Problem, 1947–1949*. Cambridge: Cambridge University Press, 1987.

——. *Israel's Border Wars, 1949–1956: Arab Infiltration, Israeli Retaliation, and the Countdown to the Suez War*. Oxford: Clarendon, 1993.

Moser, Bob. "Alabama Getaway." Southern Poverty Law Center Web site. http://www.splcenter.org/legal/intel/intelreport/article.jsp?aid = 506.

Mosher, Andy. "Abducted Egyptian Envoy Killed in Iraq." *Washington Post*, July 8, 2005.

Mumcu, Ugur. *Papa-Mafya-Agca* [Pope, Mafia, Agca]. Ankara: Tekin Yayinevi, 1984.

Murakami, Haruki. *Underground*. Tokyo: Kodansha bunko, 1999.

Murdoch, Lindsay. "Reign of Terror by Sri Lanka's Pol Pot." *Sydney Morning Herald* (Australia), June 15, 1995.

Nakashima, Ellen. "Thai Officials Probe Tie to Al-Qa'ida in Attacks." *Washington Post*, January 9, 2004.

National Archives and Record Service. U.S. Office of Strategic Services. RG 226 OSS R&A Report no. 2612, "The Objectives and Activities of the Irgun Zvai Leumi," October 13, 1944; OSS Report XL 18461, "Biographical Information—Menachem Begin," September 11, 1945.

National Commission on Terrorist Attacks Upon the United States. *The 9/11 Commission Report: Authorized Edition*. New York: Norton, 2004.

National Police Agency. "Aum Shinrikyo." *Shoten* (Tokyo), no. 269, chapter 2. http//: www.npa.go.jp/kousi/biki2/seco2/seco2_o9.htm.

——. "Aum Shinrikyo: An Alarming Report on the Terrorist Group's Organization and Activities." *Shoten* (Tokyo), no. 252 (1995).

——. *Keisatsu Hakusyo* (Police White Paper 2000), chapter 5. http://www.pdc.npa. go.jp/hakusyo/h12h120500.html.

——. *Keisatsu Hakusyo 1996* (Police White Paper 1996). http://www.pdc.npa.go.jp/ hakusyo/ho8/ho80101.html.

Naveh, Dani et al. Minister of Parliamentary Affairs. *The Involvement of Arafat, PA Senior Officials, and Apparatuses in Terrorism Against Israel, Corruption, and Crime.* Jerusalem: Ministry of Foreign Affairs, 2002.

Netanyahu, Benjamin, ed. *Terrorism: How the West Can Win.* New York: Avon, 1986.

Neuhauser, Peter. "The Mind of a German Terrorist." *Encounter* 51, no. 3 (September 1978).

New York Times. *A Nation Challenged: A Visual History of 9/11 and Its Aftermath.* New York: Callaway, 2002.

Niv, David. *Ma'archot Ha-Irgun Ha-Zvai Ha-Leumi* [Battle for Freedom: The Irgun Zvai Leumi]. Vol. 3. Tel Aviv: Klausner Institute, 1975.

Niven, Christine, John Noble, Susan Forsyth, and Tony Wheeler. *Sri Lanka: A Lonely Planet Travel Survival Kit.* Victoria, Australia: Lonely Planet, 1996.

"No Flames, No Guns in Montana." *New York Times,* June 15, 1996.

North Atlantic Assembly Papers, Sub-Committee on Terrorism. *Terrorism.* Brussels: International Secretariat, January 1989.

Norton, Graham. "The Terrorist and the Traveller: A Gulf Aftermath Assessment." *World Today* (London), May 1991.

Notes from the International Seminar on Terrorism and the Mass Media, held in Sicily, April 3–5, 1981.

Nunberg, Geoffrey. "Bin Laden's Low-Tech Weapon." *New York Times,* April 18, 2004.

——. "The War of Words: 'Terror' and 'Terrorism.'" *International Herald Tribune* (Paris), July 22, 2004.

Nundy, Julian. "Wounded Jackal Defends Record of Family Values." *Independent* (London), August 31, 1994.

O'Ballance, Edgar. *Arab Guerrilla Power.* London: Faber, 1974.

Okawa, Shoichi. "Aum Shinrikyo." http://www.guardian.co.uk/cults/a-z-cults/a_ cults.html.

Okrent, Daniel. "The War of the Words: A Dispatch from the Front Lines." *New York Times,* March 6, 2005.

Olesen, Thomas. *International Zapatismo: The Construction of Solidarity in the Age of Globalization.* London: Zed, 2005.

One Hundred Seventh Congress of the United States of America. *Homeland Security Act of 2002.* January 23, 2002, o. HR 5005–7. http://www.dhs.gov/dhspublic/ public/display?theme = 46&content = 410.

Onis, Juan de. "Guerrilla Unit Attacks Cairo Proposal." *New York Times*, June 21, 1973.

Oren, Michael B. *Six Days of War: June 1967 and the Making of the Modern Middle East.* Oxford: Oxford University Press, 2002.

"Outrage Not a Reason for Inaction." *Manchester Guardian* (international edition), October 21, 1984.

Oxford English Dictionary, Compact Edition. Oxford: Oxford University Press, 1971.

"The Palestinians of the 1990s." *Foreign Report* (London), no. 2202 (April 2, 1992).

Pallister, David. "Provos Seek to 'Play Havoc with British Nerves and Lifestyle.'" *Guardian* (London), July 31, 1990.

Palmer, A. W. *A Dictionary of Modern History.* Harmondsworth: Penguin, 1962.

Palmer, R. R. *The Age of the Democratic Revolution.* Vol. 2, *The Struggle.* Princeton, N.J.: Princeton University Press, 1970.

——. *Twelve Who Ruled: The Year of the Terror in the French Revolution.* Princeton, N.J.: Princeton University Press, 1973.

——. *The World of the French Revolution.* New York: Harper Torchbooks, 1971.

Pape, Robert A. *Dying to Win: The Strategic Logic of Suicide Terrorism.* New York: Random House, 2005.

——. "The Strategic Logic of Suicide Terrorism." *American Political Science Review* 97, no. 3 (August 2003).

Pappe, Ilan. *The Making of the Arab-Israeli Conflict, 1947–1951.* London: I. B. Tauris, 1994.

Parachini, John. "Putting WMD Terrorism Into Perspective." *Washington Quarterly* 26, no. 4 (Autumn 2003).

——. "The World Trade Center Bombers (1993)." In Jonathan B. Tucker, ed., *Toxic Terror: Assessing Terrorist Use of Chemical and Biological Weapons.* Cambridge, Mass.: MIT Press, 2000.

Parry, Albert. *Terrorism: From Robespierre to Arafat.* New York: Vanguard, 1976.

Parry, Richard Lloyd. "Sect's Poisons 'Could Kill 4.2m.'" *Independent on Sunday* (London), March 26, 1995.

Paz, Reuven. "Arab Volunteers Killed in Iraq: An Analysis." *PRISM Series of Global Jihad* 3, no. 1 (March 2005). http://www.e-prism.org/pages/4/index.htm.

——. "The Islamic Legitimacy of Suicide Terrorism." In International Policy Institute for Counter-Terrorism, *Countering Suicide Terrorism: An International Conference.* Jerusalem: Gefen, 2001.

——. "Sawt al-Jihad: New Indoctrination of Qa'idat al-Jihad." *Occasional Paper, PRISM (Project for the Study of Islamist Movements)* 1, no. 8 (October 2003). http:www.e-prism.org/images/PRISM_no_9.doc.

——. "Who Wants to Email Al-Qaeda?" *Occasional Paper, PRISM (Project for the Study of Islamist Movements)* 1, no. 8 (October 2003); *Occasional Paper, PRISM (Project for the Study of Islamist Movements)* 2, no. 2 (July 2004). http:www.e-prism.org/images/PRISM_vol_2_no_2.doc.

Peci, Patrizio. *Io, l'infame* [I, the scoundrel]. Milan: Arnoldo Mondadori, 1983.

Pedahzur, Ami. *The Israeli Response to Jewish Extremism and Violence: Defending Democracy*. Manchester: Manchester University Press, 2002.

Pew Research Center for People and the Press. "Summary of Findings: A Year After the Iraq War—Mistrust of America in Europe Even Higher, Muslim Anger Persists." March 16, 2004. http:people-press.org/reports/display.php3?ReportID = 206.

Phillips, John and Eve-Ann Prentice. "Tehran Opponent is Shot Dead in Rome." *The Times* (London), March 17, 1994.

"Photoflash Bomb Threat to the Public." *The Scotsman* (Edinburgh), March 16, 1994.

Pillar, Charles. "Terrorists Taking Up Cyberspace: Web Sites Have Become Inexpensive, Easily Accessible Tools for Giving Instructions to Operatives and Raising Funds." *Los Angeles Times*, February 9, 2001.

Pincus, Walter. "Al-Qa'ida Releases Tape Predicting U.S. Defeat." *Washington Post*, September 10, 2004.

——. "British Intelligence Warned Blair of War." *Washington Post*, May 13, 2005.

Pincus, Walter and John Mintz. "Pakistani-U.S. Raid Uncovered Terrorist Cell's Surveillance Data." *Washington Post*, August 2, 2004.

Pipes, Daniel. *Militant Islam Reaches America*. New York: Norton, 2002.

Pisani, Francis. "How to Fight the Terror Network." *Le Monde Diplomatique*, February 6, 2002. http://mondeodiplo.com/2002/06/02network.

Plate, Thomas and William Tuohy. "Los Angeles Times Interview: John Major—Even Under Fire, Britain's Prime Minister Holds His Own." *Los Angeles Times*, June 20, 1993.

Pluchinsky, Dennis. "Al-Qa'ida Identity Crisis." *Washington Times*, April 28, 2003.

——. "Western Europe's Red Terrorists: The Fighting Communist Organizations." In Yonah Alexander and Dennis Pluchinsky, eds., *Europe's Red Terrorists: The Fighting Communist Organizations*. London: Frank Cass, 1992.

Pollack, Andrew. "Earlier Victims' Horrors Revived." *New York Times*, March 22, 1995.

——. "Japanese Police Say They Found Germ-War Material at Cult Site." *New York Times*, March 29, 1995.

——. "Japanese Sect May Struggle to Get By Without Its Leader." *New York Times*, May 17, 1995.

Porath, Y. *The Palestinian Arab National Movement, 1929–1939: From Riots to Rebellion*. London: Frank Cass, 1977.

Potter, William C. "Before the Deluge? Assessing the Threat of Nuclear Leakage from the Post-Soviet States." *Arms Control Today*, October 1995.

Priest, Dana and Walter Pincus. "New Target and Tone: Message Shows Al-Qa'ida's Adaptability." *Washington Post*, April 16, 2004.

Priest, Dana and Susan Schmidt. "Al-Qa'ida's Top Primed to Collapse, U.S. Says." *Washington Post*, March 16, 2003.

"Public Support Adams Talks." *Sunday Times* (London), February 18, 1996.

Purver, Ron. "Chemical Terrorism in Japan." Unpublished manuscript by the Canadian Security Intelligence Service, Ottawa, Canada, June 1995.

Qur'an. http://lexicorient.com/eo/texts/Qur'an/Qur'an004.htm.

Quandt, William B. "Political and Military Dimensions of Contemporary Palestinian Nationalism." In William B. Quandt, Fuad Jabber, and Ann Moseley Lesch, *The Politics of Palestinian Nationalism*. Berkeley: University of California Press, 1974.

Rabbani, Mouin. "Suicide Attacks Fueled by Alienation and Futility." *Philadelphia Inquirer Commentary*, April 3, 2001. http://inq.philly.com/content/inquirer/2001/04/03/opinion/RABBANI03.htm.

"RAF Philosophy." In *The German Guerrilla: Terror, Reaction, and Resistance*. Sanday, Orkney: Cienfuegos Press, no date.

Raines, Howell. "With Latest Bomb, IRA Injures Its Own Cause." *New York Times*, November 15, 1987.

Randal, Jonathan C. "Guerrillas Fear Trade-off of Interests." *Washington Post*, October 12, 1973.

Randolph, Eleanor. "Networks Turn Eye on Themselves." *Washington Post*, June 30, 1985.

Ranstorp, Magnus. *Hizb'allah in Lebanon: The Politics of the Western Hostage Crisis*. Basingstoke: Macmillan, 1997.

Rapoport, David C. "Fear and Trembling: Terrorism in Three Religious Traditions." *American Political Science Review* 78, no. 3 (September 1984).

——. "The International World as Some Terrorists Have Seen It: A Look at a Century of Memoirs." *Journal of Strategic Studies* 10, no. 4 (December 1987).

——. "The Media and Terrorism: Implications of the Unabomber Case." Editorial in *Terrorism and Political Violence* 8, no. 1 (Spring 1996).

——. "The Politics of Atrocity." In Yonah Alexander and Seymour Maxwell Finger, eds., *Terrorism: Interdisciplinary Perspectives*. New York: John Jay Press, 1977.

——. "Terrorism." In Mary Hawkesworth and Maurice Kogan, eds., *Routledge Encyclopedia of Government and Politics*. Vol. 2. London: Routledge, 1992.

——. "Terrorism and Weapons of the Apocalypse." *National Security Studies Quarterly* 5, no. 3 (Summer 1999).

Raufer, Xavier. "Gray Areas: A New Security Threat." *Political Warfare*, no. 19 (Spring 1992).

Ravitch, Norman. "The Armenian Massacre." *Encounter* 57, no. 6 (December 1981).

"Record of Suicide Attacks." *The Times* (London), March 5, 1996.

Reeve, Simon. *One Day in September: The Story of the 1972 Munich Olympics Massacre*. London: Faber and Faber, 2000.

"Remarks by the President [William Jefferson Clinton] to 17th Annual Legislative Conference of the International Association of Fire Fighters," Hyatt Regency Hotel, Washington, D.C., March 15, 1999. http://www.usia.gov/topical/ pol/terror/99031502.html.

The Reporters, Writers, and Editors of *Der Spiegel* Magazine. *Inside 9–11: What Really Happened*. New York: St. Martin's, 2001.

Ressa, Maria A. *Seeds of Terror: An Eyewitness Account of Al-Qaeda's Newest Center of Operations in Southeast Asia.* New York: Free Press, 2003.

Reuters. "Aum Cult Gas Cache." *International Herald Tribune* (Paris), December 13, 1996.

——. "Extremists Post Hidden Messages." Wired News.com, February 6, 2001. http://www.wired.com/news/print/0,1294,41650,00.html.

——. "Propaganda to the People." Wired News.com. http://www.wired.com/news/print/0,1294,11363,00.html (accessed April 11, 2002).

——. "Tokyo Cult Leader Said to Have Made Gas Confession." *The Times* (London), October 5, 1995.

——. "$2 Million Reward for Death of Rushdie Repeated by Iran." *New York Times,* June 18, 1992.

Rhodes, Tom. "Federal US Faces War with 'Army of God.'" *The Times* (London), April 7, 1997.

——. "Sanctions on Iran 'a Failure.'" *The Times* (London), October 13, 1995.

Ridgeway, James. "Arms and the Men: Are Far Right Militia Cells Using Robbery to Fund Their Cause?" *Village Voice* (New York), May 9, 1995.

Risen, James. "New Evidence Ties Sudanese to Bin Laden, U.S. Asserts." *New York Times,* October 4, 1998.

Robberson, Tod. "Loaded Guns and Diskettes: Rebels Win Hearts and Minds on Internet." *International Herald Tribune* (Paris), February 21, 1995.

Roberts, Brad, ed. *Terrorism with Chemical and Biological Weapons: Calibrating Risks and Responses.* Alexandria, Va.: Chemical and Biological Arms Control Institute, 1997.

Romano, Lois. "Domestic Extremist Groups Weaker but Still Worrisome." *Washington Post,* April 19, 2005.

Ronfeldt, David F., John Arquilla, Graham E. Fuller, and Melissa Fuller. *The Zapatista Social Netwar in Mexico.* Santa Monica, Calif.: RAND Corporation, MR-994-A, 1998.

Rose, David. "Devices Reveal IRA Know-how." *Guardian* (London), May 18, 1990.

——. *Guantanamo: America's War on Human Rights.* London: Faber and Faber, 2004.

Ross, Loretta J. "Anti-abortionists and White Supremacists Make Common Cause." *The Progressive* (New York), October 1994.

——. "Using the Bible to Justify Killing." *Baltimore Sun,* August 8, 1994.

Rowan, Roy. "Pan Am 103: Why Did They Die?" *Time,* April 27, 1992.

Rubin, Barry and Judith Colp Rubin, eds. *Anti-American Terrorism and the Middle East: A Documentary Reader.* Oxford: Oxford University Press, 2002.

Rubin, Jeffrey Z. and Nehemia Friedland. "Theater of Terror." *Psychology Today* 20, no. 3 (March 1986).

Ruqaiyah, Brother Abu. "The Islamic Legitimacy of the 'Martrydom Operations,'" originally published in the sixteenth issue of *Nida'ul Islam* (December–January 1996–97). http://www.islam.org.au/articles/16martyrdom.htm.

Ruthven, Malise. *A Fury for God: The Islamist Attack on America.* London: Granta, 2002.

Saad-Horayeb, Amal. *Hizbu'llah: Politics and Religion.* London: Pluto, 2002.

Sanan, Guy R. "Olympic Security, 1972–1996: Threat, Response, and International Cooperation." Ph.D. diss., St. Andrews University, 1997.

Sands, David R. "Al-Qa'ida's Credibility 'on the Line' as War in Iraq Winds Down." *Washington Times,* April 24, 2003.

Sarraj, Eyad. "The Making of a Suicide Bomber." March 10, 1996, e-mail dated March 23, 1997, sent by news@baraka.baraka.org.

"Satanic Verses Publisher Is Shot in Oslo Suburb." *The Times* (London), October 12, 1993.

Satloff, Robert. "*Karine-A*: Strategic Implications of Iranian-Palestinian Collusion." *Policywatch,* no. 539. Washington, D.C.: Washington Institute for Near East Policy, January 15, 2002.

Sayle, Murray. "Martyrdom Complex." *New Yorker,* May 13, 1996.

Schbley, Ayla H. "Religious Terrorists: What They Aren't Going to Tell Us." *Terrorism* 13, no. 3 (Summer 1990).

Scheeres, Julia. "Blacklisted Groups Visible on Web." Wired News.com. http://www. wired.com/news/print/0,1283,47616,00.html (accessed April 19, 2002).

Schere, Peter. "RAF Concentrates on New Target Spectrum." *Die Welt,* December 18, 1991.

Schiff, Zeev and Raphael Rothstein. *Fedayeen: The Story of the Palestinian Guerrillas.* London: Valentine, Mitchell, 1972.

Schiller, David Th. "From a National to an International Response." In H. H. Tucker, ed., *Combating the Terrorists: Democratic Responses to Political Violence.* New York: Facts on File, 1988.

Schmemann, Serge. "Bus Bombing Kills Five in Jerusalem, 100 Are Wounded." *New York Times,* August 22, 1995.

——. "Palestinian Believed to Be Bombing Mastermind Is Killed." *New York Times,* January 6, 1997.

——. "Police Say Rabin Killer Led Sect That Laid Plans to Attack Arabs." *New York Times,* November 11, 1995.

——. "Terror Isn't Alone as a Threat to Middle East Peace." *Jerusalem Post,* March 4, 1996.

Schmid, Alex P. *Political Terrorism: A Research Guide.* New Brunswick, N.J.: Transaction Books, 1984.

——. "Terrorism and the Media: The Ethics of Publicity." *Terrorism and Political Violence* 1, no. 4 (October 1989).

Schmid, Alex P. and Janny de Graaf. *Violence as Communication: Insurgent Terrorism and the Western News Media.* Beverly Hills, Calif.: Sage, 1982.

Schmid, Alex P., Albert J. Jongman, et al. *Political Terrorism: A New Guide to Actors, Authors, Concepts, Data Bases, Theories, and Literature.* New Brunswick, N.J.: Transaction Books, 1988.

Schmidt, William E. "Protestant Gunmen Are Stepping Up the Violence in Northern Ireland." *New York Times*, October 29, 1991.

Schmitt, Eric. "Don't Aid Zarqawi, U.S. Warns Iraqi Neighbors." *New York Times*, June 2, 2005.

Schneider, Howard and Walter Pincus. "Bin Laden Video Includes Sept. 11 Praise." *Washington Post*, April 16, 2002.

Schneider, Keith. "Fearing a Conspiracy, Some Heed a Call to Arms." *New York Times*, November 14, 1994.

Schoenberg, Harris O. *A Mandate for Terror: The United Nations and the PLO.* New York: Shapolsky Books, 1989.

Schorr, Daniel. "The Encouragement of Violence." In Benjamin Netanyahu, ed., *Terrorism: How the West Can Win.* New York: Avon, 1986.

Schuster, Henry. "Lone Wolves: Solitary Threats Harder to Hunt." http://www.cnn.com/2005/US/02/01/schuster.column/index.html.

——. "Studios of Terror: Al Qaeda's Media Strategy." http://www.cnn.com/2005/WORLD/MCAST/02/15/schuster.column/index.html, February 15, 2005.

——. "Why Did Rudolph Do It? Question Lingers After Plea Deal Reached." http://www.cnn.com/2005/US/04/11/schuster.column/index.html.

Schwarz, Benjamin C. *Casualties, Public Opinion, and U.S. Military Intervention: Implications for U.S. Regional Deterrence Strategies.* Santa Monica, Calif.: RAND Corporation, MR-431-A/AF, 1994.

Schweitzer, Yoram. "Suicide Terrorism: Development and Main Characteristics." In International Policy Institute for Counter-Terrorism at the Interdisciplinary Center, Herzilya, *Countering Suicide Terrorism: An International Conference.* Jerusalem: Gefen, 2001.

Seale, Patrick. *Abu Nidal: A Gun for Hire.* New York: Random House, 1992.

Segev, Tom. *1949: The First Israelis.* New York: Free Press, 1986.

September 11 Victims. http://www.september11victims.com/september11victims/COUNTRY_CITIZENSHIP.htm.

Seufert, Michael. "Dissension Among the Terrorists: Killing People Is Wrong." *Encounter* 51, no. 3 (September 1978).

Shahak, Israel. "Hamas and Arafat: The Balance of Power." *Middle East International*, no. 468 (February 4, 1996).

Shales, Tom. "America's Ordeal by Television." *Washington Post*, July 2, 1985.

Shamir, Itzhak. *Summing Up: An Autobiography.* London: Weidenfeld and Nicolson, 1994.

Shannon, Don. "Gromyko Indirectly Supports U.S. in U.N. Drive Against Terrorism." *Los Angeles Times*, September 27, 1972.

Shavit, Ari. "The Enemy Within." *Ha'Aretz, Friday Magazine*, August 20, 2002. http://www.freeman.org/m_online/sept02/shavit.htm.

Sheridan, Michael. "Iranians 'Landing Gulf Infiltrators.'" *Independent* (London), April 8, 1995.

Shirer, William L. *The Rise and Fall of the Third Reich: A History of Nazi Germany.* New York: Simon and Schuster, 1960.

Sick, Gary. "The Political Underpinnings of Terrorism." In Charles W. Kegley Jr., ed., *International Terrorism: Characteristics, Causes, Controls.* New York: St. Martin's, 1990.

Simon, Jeffrey D. *Terrorists and the Potential Use of Biological Weapons: A Discussion of Possibilities.* Santa Monica, Calif.: RAND Corporation, R-3771-AFMIC, December 1989.

Simons, Marlise. "Lockerbie Bomber Loses Appeal and Begins Sentence." *New York Times,* March 15, 2002.

Sipress, Alan. "Key Player in Nuclear Trade Ring Found Hospitable Base in Malaysia." *Washington Post,* February 24, 2004.

Skierka, Volker. "Modern Nazis: A More Devious Version." *Stuttgarter Zeitung,* December 12, 1981.

Slonim, Ori. "The Hamas and Terror: An Alternative Explanation for the Use of Violence." *Strategic Assessment* 2, no. 3. Ramat Aviv: Jaffee Center for Strategic Studies at Tel Aviv University, December 1999.

Smith, Colin. *Carlos: Portrait of a Terrorist.* London: Andre Deutsch, 1976.

Smith, Dan, Kristin Ingstad Sandberg, Pavel Baev, and Wenche Hauge. *The State of War and Peace Atlas.* London: Penguin, 1997.

Smith, Michael. "IRA Use of Radar Guns in Bombings Described." *Daily Telegraph* (London), May 20, 1991.

Smith, M.L.R. *Fighting for Ireland? The Military Strategy of the Irish Republican Movement.* London: Routledge, 1995.

Smith, R. Jeffrey. "Justice Redacted Memo on Detainees: FBI Criticism of Interrogations Was Deleted." *Washington Post,* March 22, 2005.

Sofaer, Abraham D. "Terrorism and the Law." *Foreign Affairs* 64, no. 5 (Summer 1986).

Sofer, Sasson. *Begin: An Anatomy of Leadership.* Oxford: Blackwell, 1988.

Solnick, Aluma. "The Joy of the Mothers of Palestinian 'Martyrs.'" *MEMRI: Inquiry and Analysis Series,* no. 61 (June 25, 2001). http://www.memri.org.

Southern Poverty Law Center. *False Patriots: The Threat of Antigovernment Extremists.* Montgomery, Ala.: Southern Poverty Law Center, 1996.

"Special Edition: The Arrest of Guru Shoko Asahara, and the History of Asahara's Analects." *Yomiuri Shimbun* (Tokyo), May 16, 1995.

"Special Edition: Examination of Aum's Other Crime—Illegal Drug Production." *Yomiuri Shimbun* (Tokyo), February 28, 1996.

"Special Edition: The First Aum Case Will Start on April 24th." *Yomiuri Shimbun* (Tokyo), April 20, 1996.

"Special Edition: 1998 Aum Case—Matsumoto [Asahara] Was a Ringleader." *Yomiuri Shimbun* (Tokyo), December 31, 1998.

"Special Edition: Summary of Aum Case." *Yomiuri Shimbun* (Tokyo), June 14, 1996.

"Special Information Bulletin: Marketing of Terrorism Through the Internet." Intelligence and Terrorism Information Center at the Center for Special Studies (C.S.S.), November 2004. http://www.intelligence.org.il/eng/sib/1_05/n_t.htm (accessed June 16, 2005).

"Spokane Robbery Document." Public Good home page. http://www.nwcitizen. com/publicgood.

Sprinzak, Ehud. *The Ascendance of Israel's Radical Right.* Oxford: Oxford University Press, 1991.

——. *Brother Against Brother: Violence and Extremism in Israeli Politics from Altalena to the Rabin Assassination.* New York: Free Press, 1999.

——. "Fundamentalism, Terrorism, and Democracy. The Case of the Gush Emunim Underground." Wilson Center Occasional Paper no. 4. Washington, D.C.: Smithsonian Institution, 1986.

——. "Outsmarting Suicide Terrorists." *Christian Science Monitor* (Boston), October 24, 2000.

——. "Rational Fanatics." *Foreign Policy*, no. 120 (September/October 2000).

——. "Violence and Catastrophe in the Theology of Rabbi Meir Kahane: The Ideologization of Mimetic Desire." In Mark Juergensmeyer, ed., *Violence and the Sacred in the Modern World.* London: Frank Cass, 1992.

Squiteri, Tom. "U.S.: Return Our Men." *USA Today* (Washington, D.C.), October 6, 1993.

Stafford, David. *From Anarchism to Reformism: A Study of the Political Activities of Paul Brousse Within the First International and the French Socialist Movement, 1870–90.* Toronto: University of Toronto Press, 1971.

Stalinsky, Steven. "Palestinian Authority Sermons, 2000–2003." *MEMRI Special Report*, no. 24 (December 26, 2003). http://www.memri.org.

Stanley, Alessandra. "Russians Shut Down Branch of Japanese Sect." *New York Times*, March 30, 1995.

——. "Top Kurd's Arrest Unleashes Rioting All Across Europe." *New York Times*, February 17, 1999.

Statement for the Record Before the Senate Select Committee on Intelligence, January 28, 1998. http://www.fbi.gov/congress/98archives/threats.htm.

Steinhoff, Patricia G. "Portrait of a Terrorist: An Interview with Kozo Okamoto." *Asian Survey* 16, no. 9 (September 1976).

Sterling, Claire. *The Terror Network: The Secret War of International Terrorism.* New York: Holt, Rinehart, and Winston, 1981.

——. *The Time of the Assassins.* New York: Holt, Rinehart, and Winston, 1983.

Stern, Jessica Eve. "The Covenant, the Sword, and the Arm of the Lord (1985)." In Jonathan B. Tucker, ed., *Toxic Terror: Assessing Terrorist Use of Chemical and Biological Weapons.* Cambridge, Mass.: MIT Press, 2000.

——. "Pakistan's Jihad Culture." *Foreign Affairs* 79, no. 6 (November/December 2000).

Stern, Susan. *With the Weathermen: The Personal Journey of a Revolutionary Woman.* Garden City, N.Y.: Doubleday, 1975.

Stork, Joe. *Erased in a Moment: Suicide Bombing Attacks Against Israeli Civilians.* New York: Human Rights Watch, October 2002.

Straus, Julius. "Serb Attack on British Base." *Daily Telegraph* (London), July 18, 1997.

Strindberg, Anders. "'The Ultimate Sacrifice': The Social and Political Dynamics of Suicide Operations in Palestine." *MIPT Quarterly Bulletin* (Second Quarter, 2002).

Studemann, Frederick et al. "Five Arrested as London Bomb Attack Probe Widens to Egypt and Pakistan." *Financial Times* (London), July 16–17, 2005.

Sullivan, Kevin. "Japan Cult Survives While Guru Is Jailed." *Washington Post*, September 28, 1997.

Sunday Times Insight Team. *Siege! Princes Gate, London, April 30–May 5, 1980.* London: Hamlyn, 1980.

Sunil, K. P. "The Midnight Massacre." *Illustrated Weekly of India*, June 8, 1986.

Suro, Robert. "FBI Walks a Fine Line in Its Pursuit of Militia Extremists." *International Herald Tribune* (Paris), November 12, 1996.

Sverdlik, Alan. "Georgia Militia Members Who Conspired Against ATF Found Guilty." *Washington Post*, November 1, 1996.

Swain, Jon. "Algeria Dies Death of a Thousand Cuts." *Sunday Times* (London), April 6, 1997.

"Syrian Clampdown on Fatah Guerrillas Told." *Los Angeles Times*, September 20, 1973.

"Syria to Remain on US Terrorism List." *The Times* (London), February 17, 1992.

Tabor, James D. "Bible Scholar Claims Branch Davidian Disaster Could Have Been Avoided." *Religious Studies News* (Society of Biblical Literature/American Academy of Religion), September 1995.

Tabor, James D. and Eugene V. Gallagher. *Why Waco? Cults and the Battle for Religious Freedom in America.* Berkeley: University of California Press, 1995.

Taheri, Amir. *Holy Terror: The Inside Story of Islamic Terrorism.* London: Sphere, 1987.

Talbott, John. *The War Without a Name: France in Algeria, 1954–1962.* London: Faber, 1980.

Talmadge, Eric. "Tokyo Police Avert Cyanide Catastrophe." *Sunday Times* (London), May 7, 1995.

Tavin, Eli and Yonah Alexander, eds. *Psychological Warfare and Propaganda: Irgun Documentation.* Wilmington, Del.: Scholarly Resources, 1982.

Taylor, Peter. *Provos: The IRA and Sinn Fein.* London: Bloomsbury, 1997.

——. *States of Terror: Democracy and Political Violence.* London: Penguin, 1993.

Tendler, Stewart. "A Crude and Lethal Weapon to Thwart the Security Forces." *The Times* (London), February 8, 1991.

"Terrorism Update: Understanding the Terrorism Database." In Oklahoma City National Memorial Institute for the Prevention of Terrorism, *MIPT Quarterly Bulletin* (First Quarter 2002).

Terrorist Research and Analytical Center, National Security Division, Federal Bureau of Investigation. *Terrorism in the United States 1995*. Washington, D.C.: U.S. Department of Justice, 1996.

"Terrorists Killed by Their Own Devices." *Independent* (London), February 20, 1996.

"Text of Bin Laden Remarks: 'Hypocrisy Rears Its Ugly Head.'" *Washington Post*, October 8, 2001.

Theodoulu, Michael. "New Attacks Feared After Defiant Vow by Hamas." *The Times* (London), August 22, 1995.

"Three Former TULF MPs Shot Dead in Jaffna." *The Hindu* (Chennai), April 9, 1985.

"30 More Slain by 'Terrorists' near Algiers." *International Herald Tribune* (Paris), April 15, 1997.

"39 Killed in Jerusalem Headquarters." *The Times* (London), July 23, 1946.

This Is Aryan Nations. http://www.stormfront.org/aryan_nations/platform.html. No date.

Thomas, Christopher. "Appeal for Calm as Tamils Deny Train Bombing." *The Times* (London), July 26, 1996.

Thomas, Jo. "Militias Hold a Congress, and Not a Gun Is Seen." *New York Times*, November 1, 1994.

Thomson, David. *Europe Since Napoleon*. Harmondsworth: Penguin, 1978.

Thornton, Mary. "Oregon Guru Disavows Rajneeshism, Vows to Survive Investigations." *Washington Post*, October 20, 1985.

"Threats from Within." *Washington Post*, April 19, 2005.

Toloyan, Kachig. "Martyrdom as Legitimacy: Terrorism, Religion, and Symbolic Appropriation in the Armenian Diaspora." In Paul Wilkinson and A. M. Stewart, eds., *Contemporary Research on Terrorism*. Aberdeen: Aberdeen University Press, 1987.

Townley, Roderick and John Weisman. "The Reporters' Rat Race: Danger, Chaos, and Rumors of Payoffs." *TV Guide*, September 21, 1985.

"Transcript: Full Text from the 18 Minute Tape Released by Al-Jazeera from Osama Bin Laden."

Traynor, Ian. "'Iran Terrorism' Trail Comes to Climax." *Guardian* (London), April 10, 1997.

Trinquier, Roger. *Modern Warfare: A French View of Counterinsurgency*. Translated by Daniel Lee. New York: Praeger, 1964.

Tsfati, Yariv and Gabriel Weimann. "www.terrorism.com: Terror on the Internet." *Studies in Conflict and Terrorism* 25, no. 5 (September–October 2001).

Tucker, Jonathan B. "Chemical/Biological Terrorism: Coping with a New Threat." *Politics and the Life Sciences* 15, no. 2 (1997).

Tucker, Robert C. *Stalin in Power: The Revolution from Above, 1928–1941*. New York: Norton, 1990.

Twersky, David. "The Risks of Cozying Up to Syria." *New York Times*, July 28, 1992.

"Unabomber Manifesto." *Washington Post,* September 19, 1995.

United Nations General Assembly Resolution 52/164. http://www.unodoc.org/uno-doc/terroris_convention_terrorist_bombing.html.

U.S. Department of Defense. *Terrorist Group Profiles.* Washington, D.C.: U.S. Government Printing Office, 1988.

——. *United States Department of Defense Commission on the Beirut International Airport (BIA) Terrorist Act of October 23, 1983* (known as "The Long Commission" in reference to its chairman, retired Admiral Robert L. J. Long, U.S. Navy). No date.

U.S. Department of State. *Libya's Continuing Responsibility for Terrorism.* Washington, D.C.: U.S. Department of State, November 1991.

——. *The Network of Terrorism.* Washington, D.C.: U.S. Department of State, 2001.

——. Bureau of Public Affairs. Office of Public Communication. *Fact Sheet: Additional Information on the Bombing of Pan Am Flight 103.* Washington, D.C.: U.S. Department of State, November 15, 1991.

——. Office of the Coordinator for Counterterrorism. *Country Reports on Terrorism 2004.* April 2005. http://www.state.gov/s/ct/rls/c14813.htm.

——. *Patterns of Global Terrorism 1996.* Washington, D.C.: U.S. Department of State, Publication 10433, April 1997.

——. *Patterns of Global Terrorism 2001.* Washington, D.C.: U.S. Department of State, Publication 10940, May 2002.

——. *Patterns of Global Terrorism 2003.* Washington, D.C.: U.S. Department of State, Publication 11124, April 2004.

U.S. Departments of the Army and the Air Force. *Military Operations in Low Intensity Conflict.* Field Manual 100–20/Air Force Pamphlet 3–20. Washington, D.C.: Headquarters, Departments of the Army and the Air Force, 1990.

U.S. District Court, Southern District of New York, 1734HA01. *United States of America v. Mokhtar Haouri,* S4 00 Cr. 15 (JFK), June 3, 2001.

U.S. District Court for the District of Columbia. *United States of America v. Abdel Basset Ali al-Megrahi and Lamen Khalifa Fhimah.* November 14, 1991.

"U.S.: Al Qaida Is 70 Percent Gone, Their 'Days Are Numbered.'" *WorldTribune. com,* January 23, 2004.

Utley, Garrick. "The Shrinking of Foreign News." *Foreign Affairs* 76, no. 2 (March/April 1997).

Van Biema, David. "Prophet of Poison." *Time,* April 3, 1995.

Venzke, Ben and Aimee Ibrahim. *Al-Qaeda's Advice for Mujahideen in Iraq: Lessons Learned in Afghanistan.* Vol. 1.0. Alexandria, Va.: IntelCenter, April 14, 2003.

——. *The al-Qaeda Threat: An Analytical Guide to al-Qaeda's Tactics and Targets.* Alexandria, Va.: Tempest Publishing, 2003.

Verhovek, Sam Howe. "Showdown at the 'Republic of Texas' Ends in Surrender." *International Herald Tribune* (Paris), May 5, 1997.

Vick, Karl. "Man Gets Hands on Bubonic Plague Germs, but That's No Crime." *Washington Post,* December 30, 1995.

Victor, Barbara. *Army of Roses: Inside the World of Palestinian Woman Suicide Bombers.* New York: Rodale, 2003.

Victor, Peter. "Fascists Take to the Keyboards." *The Independent on Sunday* (London), April 7, 1995.

Vidal-Naquet, P. *Torture: Cancer of Democracy—France and Algeria, 1954–1962.* London: Penguin, 1963.

Viewpoint Kahane: *There Is No More Tal.* No date.

———. *Uncomfortable Questions for Comfortable Jews* (no date).

"Views on National Security." *National Journal* (Washington, D.C.), October 25, 1986.

Vistica, Gregory L. and Daniel Klaidman. "Tracking Terror." *Newsweek*, October 19, 1998.

Wackerngel, Christoph. "Transcript of a Talk by Christoph Wackerngel." September 14, 1995. Unpublished manuscript.

Wakin, Daniel J. "Video Game Mounts Simulated Attacks Against Israeli Targets." *New York Times*, May 18, 2003.

Wald, Matthew L. "Figuring What It Would Take to Take Down a Tower." *New York Times*, March 21, 1993.

Waldman, Amy. "Suicide Bombing Masters: Sri Lankan Rebels." *New York Times*, January 14, 2003.

Walker, Christopher. "Arabs Are Convinced Car Crash Was a Murder Plot." *The Times* (London), September 4, 1997.

———. "Bahrain Arrests 29 in Move to Foil 'Iranian-Backed Coup.'" *The Times* (London), June 4, 1996.

———. "Hamas Calls for Uprising by Muslim Worshippers." *The Times* (London), October 4, 1996.

———. "Hamas Urges Suicide Attack." *The Times* (London), January 11, 1997.

———. "Handing Back of 'Biblical Land' Angers Militants." *The Times* (London), November 6, 1995.

———. "Intelligence Experts See Hand of Tehran in Oslo Shooting." *The Times* (London), October 13, 1993.

———. "£194m 'Missing' as Arafat Seeks Aid from Britain." *The Times* (London), July 14, 1997.

———. "Palestinian 'Was Duped Into Being Suicide Bomber.'" *The Times* (London), March 27, 1997.

———. "Rabin Killer 'Trained by Shin Bet.'" *The Times* (London), November 21, 1995.

———. "Rabin Killing 'Part of Plot Backed by West Bank Rabbis.'" *The Times* (London), November 10, 1995.

Walker, Tom. "British Base Is Attacked as Bosnia Serbs Vow Revenge." *The Times* (London), July 18, 1997.

Wallis, William. "Kenya Terror Attacks 'Planned from Somalia.'" *Financial Times*, November 5, 2003.

Walsh, James. "Shoko Asahara: The Making of a Messiah." *Time*, April 3, 1995.

Walsh, Mary Williams. "German Court Finds Iran's Leaders Ordered Slayings." *Los Angeles Times*, April 11, 1997.

Warraq, Ibn. "Virgins? What Virgins?" *Guardian* (London), January 12, 2002. http://www.guardian.co.uk/saturday_review/story/0%2C3605%2C631332%2C00.html.

Warrick, Joby. "An Al Qaeda 'Chemist' and the Quest for Ricin." *Washington Post*, May 5, 2004.

Warrick, Joby and Joe Stephens. "Before Attack, U.S. Expected Different Hit: Chemical, Germ Agents Focus of Preparations." *Washington Post*, October 2, 2001.

Wardlaw, Grant. "Linkages Between the Illegal Drugs Traffic and Terrorism." *Conflict Quarterly* 8, no. 3 (Summer 1988).

——. *Political Terrorism: Theory, Tactics, and Counter-measures*. Cambridge: Cambridge University Press, 1990.

Watanabe, Manabu. "Religion and Violence in Japan Today: A Chronological and Doctrinal Analysis of Aum Shinrikyo." *Terrorism and Political Violence* 10, no. 4 (Winter 1998).

Watt, Nicholas. "IRA's 'Russian Roulette' Detonator." *The Times* (London), March 16, 1994.

Wazis, Burhan. "Suicide Bombing Is Democratic Right, Says the 'Soul' of Hamas." *Observer* (London), August 19, 2001.

"Wedded to Death in a Blaze of Glory—Profile: The Suicide Bomber." *Sunday Times* (London), March 10, 1996.

Weimann, Gabriel. *Terror on the Internet: The New Arena, the New Challenges*. Washington, D.C.: U.S. Institute of Peace, forthcoming.

Weiser, Benjamin. "U.S. Says Bin Laden Aide Tried to Get Nuclear Material." *New York Times*, September 26, 1998.

Weisman, Steven R. "U.S. Has 'Credible' Word of Syrian Plot to Kill Lebanese." *New York Times*, June 10, 2005.

——. "White House Escalates Its Campaign to Isolate Syria." *New York Times*, June 23, 2005.

Welch, Craig. "Three Guilty in Valley Bombings." *Spokesman-Review* (Spokane, Wash.), July 24, 1997.

"What Is Terrorism?" *Economist* (London), March 2, 1996.

Wheeler-Bennett, John. *Munich: Prologue to Tragedy*. London: Macmillan, 1948.

Whine, Michael. "Islamist Organizations on the Internet." *Terrorism and Political Violence* 11, no. 1 (Spring 1999).

White, Robert W. "The Irish Republican Army: An Assessment of Sectarianism." *Terrorism and Political Violence* 9, no. 1 (Spring 1997).

White House. "Fact Sheet on Combating Terrorism: Presidential Decision Directive 62." May 22, 1998. http://cns.miis.edu/research/cbw/pdd-62.htm.

——. "President Bush Discusses Iraq: Remarks by the President to the Pool Before and After Golf—Crawford, Texas." August 10, 2002. http://www.whitehouse.gov/news/releases/2002/08/20020810-3.html.

——. "The President Delivers State of the Union Address." January 29, 2002. http://www.whitehouse.gov/news/releases/2002/01/20020129-11.html.

——. President George W. Bush, Office of the Press Secretary. "President Declares 'Freedom at War with Fear': Address to a Joint Session of Congress and the American People." September 20, 2001. http://www.whitehouse.gov/news/releases/2001/09/print/20010920-8.html.

Whitlock, Craig. "Islamic Radicals Behead American in Saudi Arabia." *Washington Post*, June 19, 2004.

——. "Terror Probes Find 'the Hands, but Not the Brains.'" *Washington Post*, July 12, 2005.

Whymant, Robert. "Cult Planned Gas Raids on America." *The Times* (London), March 29, 1997.

Wilkinson, Paul. *The New Fascists*. London: Grant Mclntyre, 1981.

——. "Terrorism." In Michael Foley, ed., *Ideas That Shape Politics*. Manchester: Manchester University Press, 1994.

——. "Terrorism and Propaganda." In Yonah Alexander and Richard Latter, eds., *Terrorism and the Media*. McLean, Va.: Brassey's, 1990.

Williams, Phil and Paul N. Woessner. "Nuclear Material Trafficking: An Interim Assessment." *Transnational Organized Crime* 1, no. 2 (Summer 1995).

Willmer, Tanya. "Soldiers' Mothers Pray Their Own Battle Over After Israel Ends Its Vietnam." *Agence France Presse*, May 24, 2000.

Woessner, Paul N. "Recent Developments: Chronology of Nuclear Smuggling Incidents, July 1991–May 1995." *Transnational Organized Crime* 1, no. 2 (Summer 1995).

Wolf, John B. "The Palestine Resistance Movement." *Current History* 60 (1971).

Woodcock, George, ed. *The Anarchist Reader*. Glasgow: Fontana, 1977.

Woodward, Bob. *Bush at War*. New York: Simon and Schuster, 2003.

Worth, Robert F. "Jihadists Take Stand on Web, and Some Say It's Defensive." *New York Times*, March 13, 2005.

Wright, Robin. "Iran Supplies Lebanese Radicals Through Syria, U.S. Aides Say." *International Herald Tribune* (Paris), December 14–15, 1996.

Wright, Robin and Ronald J. Ostrow. "Pan Am 103 Clue Leads to Libyans." *Los Angeles Times*, June 24, 1991.

Wurth-Hough, Sandra. "Network News Coverage of Terrorism: The Early Years." *Terrorism* 6, no. 3 (Summer 1983).

Ya'ari, Ehud. "The Metamorphosis of Hamas." *Jerusalem Report*, January 14, 1993.

Yamazaki, Mayuka. "Aum Shinrikyo." Unpublished manuscript. April 2005.

"Yeltsin Adds to Kremlin Power." *Foreign Report* (London), no. 2365 (August 24, 1995).

Yisra'eli, Rafi. "Islamikaze: Suicide Terrorism Examined." *Nativ* (Tel Aviv), January–April 1997.

"Yogasangari—MP Killed in Madras." *Daily News* (Colombo), June 21, 1990.

Young, Sean. "Online Co. Shuts Down Site with Beheading." *Yahoo! News*, May 14, 2004. http://www.crime-research.org/news/14.05.2004/270.

Zaar, Isaac. *Rescue and Liberation: America's Part in the Birth of Israel*. New York: Bloch, 1954.

Zaman, Amberin. "Swords Into Rabbit Ears." *Washington Post*, February 4, 1999.

Zanini, Michele and Sean J. A. Edwards. "The Networking of Terror in the Information Age." In John Arquilla and David Ronfeldt, eds., *Networks and Netwars: The Future of Terror, Crime, and Militancy*. Santa Monica, Calif.: RAND Corporation, MR-1382-OSD, 2001.

"Zarqawi Statement May 20, 2005, Part 1." English Translation © *Jihad Unspun 2005*, May 26, 2005. http://www.jihadunspun.com/newsarchive/article_internal.php?article = 102833&list = /newsarchive/index.php&.

Zernike, Kate and David Rhode. "Forced Nudity of Iraqi Prisoners Is Seen as a Pervasive Pattern, Not Isolated Incidents." *New York Times*, June 8, 2004.

Zonis, Marvin and Daniel Brumberg. "Behind Beirut Terrorism." *New York Times*, October 8, 1984.

Zuckerman, Mortimer B. "Playing the Terrorists' Game." *U.S. News and World Report*, June 9, 1986.

Briefings and Conference and Seminar Presentations

Boetcher, Mike. "Al-Qa'ida's Nuclear Weapons Program." Presentation at the Centre for the Study of Terrorism and Political Violence Symposium on Islamic Extremism and Terrorism in the Greater Middle East, University of St. Andrews, St. Andrews, Scotland, June 7–8, 2002.

Counter Terrorist Unit. *New Jersey State Police: Kikumura Investigation—A Case Study*. No date.

Denning, Dorothy. "Information Warfare and Cyber-Terrorism." Women in International Security (WIIS) seminar, Washington, D.C., December 15, 1999.

Eedle, Paul. "The Language of Jihad." Presentation at the Centre for the Study of Terrorism and Political Violence Symposium on Islamic Extremism and Terrorism in the Greater Middle East, University of St. Andrews, St. Andrews, Scotland, June 7–8, 2002.

Gunaratna, Rohan. "Maritime Terrorism: Future Threats and Responses." Briefing presented to the International Research Group on Political Violence and Terrorism, Washington, D.C., May 2001.

Israeli Security Agency. "Security Seminar on Combating the Threat of Suicide Bombers." Israeli Embassy, Washington, D.C., September 16, 2003.

Sri Lankan Armed Forces. "Suicide Terrorism in Sri Lanka." No date.

Videos, DVDs, and CD-ROMs

The Destruction of the American Destroyer USS Cole. DVD version, produced by the Assahab (the Cloud) Foundation. No date.

Igniting the Revolution: An Introduction to the Earth Liberation Front. Distributed by the North American Earth Liberation Front Press Office, Portland, Oregon. No date.

IntelCenter. *Hamas Audio/Video Files.* Vol. 1. Alexandria, Va.: www.intelcenter.com, no date.

prohosters.com/pearl/#ogr or the link to the execution clip found at www.ogrish.com.

Special Force Version 1. Registration Card No 336070 and Back Cover. No date.

Video prepared by the Jordanian authorities. No date.

Index